The World Book Student Handbook

# Student Information Finder

# The World Book Student Handbook

## Student Information Finder

Published by

**World Book Encyclopedia, Inc.**

a Scott Fetzer company

Chicago

**The World Book Student Handbook**

1984 Revised Printing
Copyright © 1981, 1978 by
World Book-Childcraft International, Inc.
Merchandise Mart Plaza, Chicago, Illinois 60654
Printed in the United States of America
ISBN 0-7166-3122-9 (Volume 2)
ISBN 0-7166-3120-2 (2-volume set)
Library of Congress Catalog Card No. 81-51365
f/hd

# Using the Student Information Finder

During your years in school, you are asked to read and learn a tremendous amount of information. Sometimes it may seem to you—no matter how much you like school in general or any subject in particular—that you are almost overwhelmed by the many facts that you need to know.

*The World Book Student Handbook: Student Information Finder* has been designed to help you review essential facts in 10 key content areas: language, writing, and spelling; mathematics; physical sciences; earth sciences; life sciences; geography; world history and American history; biography; United States Presidents and Canada's Prime Ministers; and literature. Reviewing the facts in a given area can help you maintain or regain your sense of perspective.

This key concept of *review* was foremost in the minds of the editors of THE WORLD BOOK ENCYCLOPEDIA when they planned and prepared this volume. *The World Book Student Handbook: Student Information Finder* is organized by units. Each unit presents the highlights of a content area in a clear, concise fashion. Naturally, a single volume cannot cover all the information you need to know, but a strong attempt was made to include the crucial highlights of your studies.

Helping you review your schoolwork is but one major purpose of the handbook. Another is to provide you with useful reference material. For example, you can look up the preferred method for using footnotes in a research paper.

You should familiarize yourself with the table of Contents in the front of the book before attempting to use the handbook. To make the best possible use of this volume, you should also consult the Index frequently. Cross-references within the volume will help you find related material.

The handbook is intended as a companion to your textbooks, your encyclopedia, other reference works, and books of other kinds. No one book can take the place of all those others, but this volume—properly used—can aid you in an important way.

You can use Unit 1, for example, to check on the rules of spelling—conveniently summarized in a running table. Or you can look up reference information on footnotes, bibliographies, punctuation, and capitalization. These are topics covered in the unit on writing, language, and spelling.

Unit 2 contains review information on a topic that is troublesome to many students—mathematics. Clear, concise information is presented on selected math topics; this includes the subjects of arithmetic, algebra, geometry, and trigonometry. Also, new math is presented, for students and parents alike.

For the student intent on reviewing topics in the physical sciences, Unit 3 will be of interest. Diagrams are used along with text material to present selected information on astronomy, chemistry, and physics.

The earth sciences are presented for review in Unit 4. Again, diagrams are freely used to present some important facts about the earth, the atmosphere, weather and climate.

A third science unit, Unit 5, deals with the physical sciences. This unit uses diagrams and text to present a selection of key information from cell biology, botany, zoology, human physiology, and human health.

Unit 6 contains maps, population and area statistics, and important facts about the United States government. In addition, this unit presents a brief fact summary for each independent nation in the world—enabling you quickly and easily to look up such information as the population of Canada or the area of Tanzania.

For a chronology of important events in world

history and American history, consult Unit 7. Key facts are arranged by chronological period, then by subject area—politics, social history, the arts, and so on. Thus, you can obtain an overview of major events.

Need reference material on famous people? Check Unit 8, which contains brief biographical entries for about 350 notable men and women from various fields and many countries.

Some famous people whom you have undoubtedly encountered often in your studies are the Presidents of the United States and the Prime Ministers of Canada. Unit 9 features a biography for each of the individuals who has served as President, with information about the individual's life and historical perspective about his place in American history. A reference table of important facts about Canada's Prime Ministers completes the unit.

If you need help selecting a book to read, you should consult Unit 10. This unit contains brief capsule summaries for hundreds of works of literature, many of which are included on school lists of recommended readings.

The editors hope that this brief summary has given you ideas on how *The World Book Student Handbook: Student Information Finder* can help you. Use of this book can give you not only a fund of important facts, but also many hours of interesting and pleasurable reading.

# Staff

**Publisher**
William H. Nault

## Editorial

**Editor in chief**
Robert O. Zeleny

**Senior editor**
Seva Johnson

**Staff editor**
Mike Urban

**Administrative assistant**
Janet T. Peterson

**Writers**
James I. Clark
William D. Leschensky
Mary Alice Molloy
Betty Van Wyk
Joseph A. Zullo

**Cartographic services**
George Stoll, head

## Research services

**Director**
Mary Norton

**Researchers**
Rebecca Chekouras
Frances L. Fu
Robert Hamm
Max R. Kinsey

**Rights and permissions**
Paul E. Rafferty

## Art

**Executive art director**
William Hammond

**Art director**
Roberta Dimmer

**Assistant art director**
Joe Gound

**Design director**
Ronald A. Stachowiak

**Senior designer**
Bernard Arendt

**Designer**
Free Chin

**Production artists**
Hans W. Bobzien
Susan T. Wilson

**Contributing artist**
Robert Keys

## Product production

**Executive director**
Peter Mollman

**Manufacturing**
Joseph C. LaCount, director

**Research and development**
Henry Koval, manager

**Pre-press services**
Jerry Stack, director

**Production control**
Barbara Podczerwinski
George Luehring

**Film separations**
Alfred J. Mozdzen
Barbara J. McDonald

# Contents

# Facts about writing, language, and spelling

Have you ever thought about "words," not about any particular word, but what words are and what they do? Without words, it would be very difficult to communicate your feelings and ideas to other people. And other people would be unable to communicate their feelings and ideas to you. Words are just about the most important "thing" you have.

This unit will show you many interesting things about words. It will give you some rules by which words in English are spelled. It will present some facts about the English language. And it will describe some rules that will help you to become a better writer.

# 1. Rules for spelling

## Facts about spelling

The first rule of spelling is, "When in doubt, consult your dictionary." After you have looked up a word, make it yours by following these simple steps:

1. Copy the word carefully and neatly.
2. Visualize the word and remember how it looks.
3. Say each letter of the word in order.
4. Divide the word into syllables if it has more than one.
5. Study the difficult parts of the word.
6. Pronounce the word out loud.
7. Study the meaning of the word.
8. Make up a meaningful sentence of your own, using the word.
9. Use the word at the first opportunity in writing and conversation.

Once you know how to spell the basic word, most of your spelling difficulties arise when you modify that word in some way, either to form inflections or to change the part of speech.

The following table gives some helpful spelling rules. However, there are some exceptions to almost every rule. You should recognize the problem, learn the rule by learning to apply it, and then learn the exceptions.

## Table of spelling rules

| Problem | Rule | Some exceptions |
|---------|------|-----------------|
| Words with *i*'s and *e*'s: *believe, receive* | Use *i* before *e* except after *c* or when sounded like *a*, as in *neighbor* or *weigh*. | *ancient, financier, counterfeit, either, foreign, seize, weird* |
| Words ending in *cede: precede* | The root *cede* is always spelled this way except in four words and their various forms. | *supersede, exceed, proceed, succeed,* and their other forms (*superseded, exceeding, proceeds, succeeded*) |
| Words ending in *c: panic* | Insert *k* when adding an ending beginning with *e, i,* or *y: panicky.* | *arced, zincic* |
| Words ending in soft *ce* or *ge: trace, courage* | Retain the final *e* before adding *able* or *ous: traceable, courageous.* | |
| Words ending in silent *e: desire* | Drop the final *e* before suffixes beginning with a vowel: *desirable.* | *mileage* |
| Words ending in silent *e: love* | Retain the final *e* before a suffix beginning with a consonant: *lovely.* | *acknowledgment, argument, duly, judgment, ninth, wholly* |
| Words ending in *ie: die* | Change *ie* to *y* when adding *ing: dying.* | |
| Words ending in *oe: toe* | Retain the final *e* before a suffix beginning with any vowel except *e: toeing,* but *toed.* | |

| Problem | Rule | Some exceptions |
|---------|------|-----------------|
| Words ending in *y* preceded by a consonant: *occupy* | Change *y* to *i* before a suffix unless the suffix begins with *i: occupied,* but *occupying.* | |
| Adjectives of one syllable ending in *y: dry* | Retain *y* when adding a suffix: *drying.* | |
| Words of one syllable and words accented on the last syllable, ending in a single consonant preceded by a vowel: *sad, repel, occur* | Double the final consonant before a suffix beginning with a vowel: *sadden, repelled, occurred.* | *crocheting, ricocheted, filleted, transferable* (but *transferred*). Also, if the accent shifts to the first syllable when the suffix is added, the final consonant is not doubled: *deferred,* but *deference.* |
| Words ending in a consonant preceded by more than one vowel: *reveal, boil* | Do not double the consonant before a suffix beginning with a vowel: *revealed, boiling.* | |
| Words ending in more than one consonant: *help, confirm* | Do not double the final consonant: *helped, confirming.* | |
| Words not accented on the last syllable: *benefit, banquet* | Do not double the final consonant: *benefited, banqueted.* | |
| Words ending in *l: accidental* | Retain the *l* before a suffix beginning with *l: accidentally.* | Words ending in double *l* drop one *l* with the suffix *ly: hilly, fully.* |
| Prefixes and suffixes ending in *ll: all-, -full* | Omit one *l* in joining them to other words: *already, thankful.* | |
| Prefixes *dis-, il-, im-, in-, mis-, over-, re-,* and *un-* | Do not change the spelling of the root word: *dissatisfy, illiterate, immortal, innumerable, misspell, overrun, reenter, unnecessary.* | |
| Words ending in a double consonant: *possess, enroll* | Retain both consonants when adding suffixes: *possessor, enrolling.* | |
| Nouns ending in *f, fe, ff: handkerchief* | Form the plural by adding *s: handkerchiefs.* | Some nouns ending in *f* or *fe* form the plural by changing the *f* or *fe* to *ve* and adding *s: knives, elves, halves, calves, leaves, loaves, wives.* |
| Nouns ending in *y* preceded by a consonant: *army* | Form the plural by changing *y* to *i* and adding *es: armies.* | Proper nouns ending in *y* form the plural by adding *s:* "There are four *Marys* in this class." |
| Nouns ending in *ch, sh, j, s, x,* or *z: gas, church, bush, dress, box* | Form the plural by adding *es: gases, churches, bushes, dresses, boxes.* | |
| Nouns ending in *o* preceded by a vowel: *radio* | Form the plural by adding *s: radios.* | |
| Some nouns ending in *o* preceded by a consonant: *tomato* | Form the plural by adding *es: tomatoes.* | *dittos, dynamos* For some nouns, either *s* or *es* is correct: *buffalos* or *buffaloes, volcanos* or *volcanoes.* |
| Compound nouns: *notary public, daughter-in-law, lieutenant general* | Make the modified word plural: *notaries public, daughters-in-law, lieutenant generals.* | |
| Letters, numbers, dates, signs, and words referred to as words | Form the plural by adding *'s:* two *x's,* four *7's,* the *1920's, +'s,* and *'s.* | |

# Spelling sounds

Certain letters or combinations of letters may sound like other letters. Knowing these letters should help you improve your spelling. Look at some letters and their sounds:

## Table of spelling sounds

The letter *a* may sound like short *o* in some words.
The *o* sound in not = the *a* sound in watt.

The letters *o* and *ou* sometimes sound like short *u*.
The *u* sound in up = the *o* sound in done.
The *u* sound in up = the *ou* sound in touch.

Sometimes *y*, *u*, and *o* sound like short *i*.
The *i* sound in him = the *y* sound in hymn.
The *i* sound in him = the *u* sound in busy.
The *i* sound in him = the *o* sound in women.

At other times, *y* may sound like long *i*.
The *i* sound in ice = the *y* sound in rhyme.

*Gh* and *ph* sometimes sound like *f*.
The *f* sound in fur = the *gh* sound in enough.
The *f* sound in fur = the *ph* sound in phonics.

*C*, *ck*, *ch*, and *que* may sound like *k*.
The *k* sound in kill = the *c* sound in catastrophe.
The *k* sound in kill = the *ck* sound in buck.
The *k* sound in kill = the *ch* sound in chorus.
The *k* sound in kill = the *que* sound in antique.

In some words, *qu* sounds like *kw*.
The *kw* sound = the *qu* sound in queen.

The letters *ti* and *ci* may sound like *sh*.
The *sh* sound in shield = the *ti* sound in nation.
The *sh* sound in shield = the *ci* sound in social.

Sometimes *c* sounds like *s*, *ed* like *t*, *s* like *z*, and *n* like *ng*.
The *s* sound in space = the *c* sound in cent.
The *t* sound in sit = the *ed* sound in fixed.
The *z* sound in whiz = the *s* sound in desert.
The *ng* sound in going = the *k* sound in thank.

The letters *ei*, *ey*, *ai*, and *ay* sometimes sound like long *a*.
The *a* sound in snake = the *ei* sound in eight.
The *a* sound in snake = the *ey* sound in they.
The *a* sound in snake = the *ai* sound in gain.
The *a* sound in snake = the *ay* sound in pay.

The letter *i* may sound like long *e*.
The *e* sound in she = the *i* sound in machine.

Sometimes *g* and *dg* sound like *j*.
The *j* sound in jug = the *g* sound in register.
The *j* sound in jug = the *dg* sound in edge.

The letters *a*, *ai*, and *ay* may sound like short *e*.
The *e* sound in set = the *a* sound in many.
The *e* sound in set = the *ai* sound in said.
The *e* sound in set = the *ay* sound in says.

# Review of spelling sounds

This exercise will give you the opportunity to review information on spelling sounds. Please do not write in this book, but place your answers on a separate sheet of paper.

An answer key follows the exercise.

1. Spell the short *o* sound in
   w__nd

2. Spell the short *u* sound in
   tr__ble, c__me, d____ble

3. Spell the short *i* sound in
   bic__cle, b__sy, w__men

4. Spell the long *i* sound in
   n__lon

5. Spell the *f* sound in
   ne____ew, lau____, em____asize,
   tou____, geogra____y, al____abet

6. Spell the *k* sound in
   pla____, an ____or, ro____et, pi__ni__,
   or____estra, uni____, __ancel

7. Spell the *kw* sound in
   e____ator, ____iet

8. Spell the *sh* sound in
   espe____ally, objec____on, pa____ent,
   an____ent, gra____ous

9. Spell the *s* sound in
   practi__e, pronoun__e, exer__ise

## Answers

1. short *o* sound: wand
2. short *u* sound: trouble, come, double
3. short *i* sound: bicycle, busy, women
4. long *i* sound: nylon
5. *f* sound: nephew, laugh, emphasize, tough, geography, alphabet
6. *k* sound: plaque, anchor, rocket, picnic, orchestra, unique, cancel
7. *kw* sound: equator, quiet
8. *sh* sound: especially, objection, patient, ancient, gracious
9. *s* sound: practice, pronounce, exercise

# 2. Facts about parts of speech

Grammar is a type of structure for words. When you study grammar, you study how words are put together to form sentences. Some patterns are correct, and others are not. The *parts of speech* are the basic building blocks for every sentence.

Traditional grammar books indicate eight parts of speech: (1) nouns; (2) verbs; (3) pronouns; (4) adjectives; (5) adverbs; (6) prepositions; (7) conjunctions; and (8) interjections.

Every word in this book belongs to one of those eight parts of speech. In fact, many words belong to more than one part of speech, depending on how they are used. *Cream*, for example, is a noun when you speak of cream for the coffee. *Cream* is an adjective when you use the term to describe something else, like cream pudding. And *cream* is a verb when you *cream* butter and sugar together to make a cake.

Very often, then, you need to know how a word is used in a sentence to label it properly. But that is not as hard as it sounds. Once you practice a little, you can sort words into their special categories with little trouble.

## Nouns

Because they are probably the easiest to recognize, begin with nouns. You are a noun. So is every other person, every place, and every thing. You name it, and it is a noun: *baby, Susan, Mrs. Smith, England, ocean, river, avenue, Michigan, bridge.*

There are two kinds of nouns: common and proper. Proper nouns name particular persons, places, or things; they are capitalized (example: *Ohio*). Common nouns do not tell you which person, which place, or which thing; they are not capitalized (example: *state*).

Common nouns are divided into three groups: abstract, concrete, and collective. Abstract nouns name qualities, actions, and ideas: *courage, help-*

*fulness, loyalty.* Most of the time, you can use *the* before abstract nouns, but not *a*. Ordinarily, you would not say *a helpfulness.*

Concrete nouns name material things that you can see or touch: *door, pencil, car.* Most of the time, you can use either *a* or *the* before a concrete noun, depending on the meaning you want to convey. Also, you can make concrete nouns plural—*doors, pencils, cars*—whereas ordinarily you would not say *courages* or *helpfulnesses.*

Collective nouns are singular in form, but they refer to a group of persons or things: *team, class, herd, set.* Collective nouns are usually followed by singular verbs: "Our *team was* defeated." But often they are followed by a plural verb, especially where they emphasize the individuals more than the groups. "The *people were* discontented."

## Pronouns

Pronouns are substitutes. They take the place of nouns in speech and writing. Imagine how cumbersome language would be without them. We would have to say, "Mrs. Smith asked John to be careful with Mrs. Smith's car when John borrowed the car to take John's date home." However, it is easier to say, "Mrs. Smith asked John to be careful with her car when he borrowed it to take his date home."

Every pronoun must have an antecedent, or *that which goes before.* The antecedent is either stated or understood. In the example above, *Mrs. Smith, John,* and *car* are nouns, and the pronouns *her, he, his,* and *it* relieve you of the necessity of repeating the nouns.

There are five kinds of pronouns: (1) personal; (2) relative; (3) interrogative; (4) demonstrative (definite); and (5) indefinite.

**Personal pronouns.** A pronoun that stands for

the name of a person, a place, or a thing, is called a personal pronoun. There are seven personal pronouns: *I, you, he, she, it, we,* and *they.* All seven are subject form. They "do" things. Any one of them will complete this key sentence: "...saw Mary." Each subject form has an object form: *me, you, him, her, it, us* and *them.* They are receivers of some kind of action. Something happens "to" them. Any one of them will complete this key sentence: "Mary saw...."

Most of the trouble with personal pronouns occurs in sentences using the linking verb *to be* and its many forms (including *is, are, am, was, were*). After linking verbs, the subject form of the personal pronoun should always be used: "It is *I.*"

Choosing the right pronoun to follow a preposition—such as *to, for, at, between*—can be troublesome, too. Prepositions call for the object form of the pronoun. "She talked to Mary and *me.*" (Note: *Mary and I* is wrong here.)

If you add *self* or *selves* to a personal pronoun, it becomes a compound form: *myself, yourself, herself, itself, ourselves, themselves.* This form may be intensive (giving emphasis) or reflexive (expressing action turned back on the subject). Do not use the compound form when you should use a simple personal pronoun. It is wrong to say, "My brother and *myself* are going." You may say, "I *myself* am going" (intensive) and you may also say "He shaves *himself*" (reflexive).

**Relative pronouns.** A relative pronoun serves a double purpose: it connects two clauses, and it relates back to a noun or pronoun in a preceding clause. Words frequently used as relative pronouns are *that, which, what, who, whose, whom.* "She didn't buy the same book *that* he did." In this example, the word *that* refers back to the noun *book.* The compound relative pronouns in common use are *whoever, whichever,* and *whatever.*

**Interrogative pronouns.** The interrogative pronouns, *who, which,* and *what,* are used to ask questions. They ask the identity, the nature, or the possessor of whatever is in question. "*Who* was there?" "*Which* of the books is yours?"

**Demonstrative pronouns.** *This, these, that,* and *those* are pronouns that answer the question "Which?" by pointing out a particular person or thing. They are sometimes called definite pronouns. "*This* is the one I want." "*That* is all wrong." But *this, these, that,* and *those* may also be demonstrative adjectives. "*This* book is mine." "*That* day was a bad one."

**Indefinite pronouns.** These are similar to the demonstrative pronouns in that they answer the question "Which?" But in so doing, they do not refer to definite persons or things. "*Somebody* took my pencil." "*Neither* will do the job." Other indefinite pronouns include *one, each, other, both, many.* Like demonstrative pronouns, many indefinite pronouns may also be used as adjectives. "*Both* boys were absent." "She had *many* dresses."

## Adjectives

An *old* man; a *black* cat; a *long* bill. *Old, black,* and *long* have one thing in common that makes them all adjectives. Each is used to modify, or to give a more exact meaning to, a noun. It is not just any man, it is an *old* man; it is not just any cat, it is a *black* cat; it is not just any bill; it is a *long* bill.

Adjectives may be descriptive or limiting. Descriptive adjectives modify a noun by telling a quality or condition of the object named: a *short* stick, a *sad* girl, a *grassy* slope. Limiting adjectives point out the object talked about or indicate quantity: *this* book, *that* ring, *two* words. Notice that some limiting adjectives are regularly used as pronouns *(this, that, these, those).* *A, an,* and *the,* called articles, are also limiting adjectives.

Word phrases and clauses may also act as adjectives. "The man *with the green hat* saw me." In addition to modifying nouns, adjectives modify a word or a phrase that is acting as a noun: "Going to school *is necessary.*"

## Verbs

The most important word in a sentence is the verb. A verb may express action, or it may express a state of being. In "John the ball." we have a subject, *John;* and we have an object, *ball.* But only after adding a verb, such as *threw,* do we have action, and a sentence. "John threw the ball." *Pull, strike, lift,* and *touch* are typical action verbs. Sometimes the action is mental rather than physical, as in "She *believed* the story."

As mentioned above, not all verbs express action. Those that do not may be either linking verbs or auxiliary verbs. Linking verbs merely link the subject of the sentence to another word, in order to make a statement. "Sara felt ill." The verb *felt* links the subject, *Sara,* with the word *ill,* to make a statement about Sara's health. Some linking verbs regularly used are *appear, be, become, grow, look, remain, seem, smell, sound, stay, taste.*

Auxiliary verbs are used in conjunction with other verbs to help form a verb tense, voice, or mood. "I studied" becomes "I *have* studied," with the addition of the helping, or auxiliary, verb *have.*

Other common auxiliary verbs are *be, may, do, shall, will.*

Verbs may be either transitive or intransitive. A transitive verb takes an object. "He *lifted* the hammer." An intransitive verb does not take an object. "They *ran* fast." Many verbs are transitive in some sentences and intransitive in others. "She *sang* the song" (transitive). "She simply is not able to *sing*" (intransitive).

## Adverbs

Adverbs, like adjectives, give a more exact meaning to other words. But adjectives modify only nouns, and words or phrases acting as nouns. Adverbs modify verbs, adjectives, other adverbs, or entire sentences or clauses. "The boat was *absolutely* waterproof" (adverb modifying adjective). "The radio worked *unusually* well" (adverb modifying adverb). "I didn't go to school *yesterday*" (adverb modifying the rest of the sentence).

An adverb usually answers the question *how? when? where?* or *to what extent?* "He ran quickly down the road" (how). "She went to school *today*" (when). "She dropped the ball *there*" (where). "John sang *interminably*" (to what extent).

Interrogative adverbs ask questions themselves. *"Where* did she go?" *"Why* did she go?" Other common interrogative adverbs are *when* and *how.*

Conjunctive adverbs appear between clauses and serve the double function of connecting the two clauses and modifying one of those clauses. "You signed a contract; *therefore,* we demand payment." Other conjunctive adverbs are *however, moreover, still, otherwise, nevertheless.*

Words commonly used as adverbs are *almost, fast, very,* and most words ending in -*ly: badly, sorely, surely.*

## Prepositions

Prepositions may be small words (*to, for, on, in*), bigger words (*concerning, alongside*), or even groups of words (*in spite of, as far as*), but they all do the same thing—they show the relation of one word (usually a noun or a pronoun) to some other word in the sentence. Some of the relations shown may be:

> In position—"The book is *on* the table."
> In direction—"He walked *toward* the door."
> In time—"She left *before* him."

Words frequently used as prepositions are *between, in, on, toward, at, with, of, up, for, down, over, by.*

## Conjunctions

Conjunctions join together words or word groups. There are three kinds of conjunctions: coordinating, correlative, and subordinating.

Coordinating conjunctions are the simplest, linking two words or word groups that are grammatically equal. "She bought meat *and* potatoes." Other coordinating conjunctions are *but* and *yet.*

When two coordinating conjunctions are used together, they are called correlative conjunctions. *"Both* Henry *and* Bill are gone." Other correlative conjunctions are *either… or, though…yet.*

Subordinating conjunctions connect a subordinate clause to the main clause of a sentence. In this instance, the subordinating conjunction *because* introduces the subordinate clause. "May was happy *because* her mother was home." Other subordinating conjunctions are *when, as, since, if, unless, before.*

## Interjections

Ouch! Oh! Ah! Alas! These are interjections. A unique thing about interjections is that they bear no grammatical relation to the other words in a sentence. They neither affect other words—as do adjectives—nor are they affected by other words—as are nouns. A second thing held in common by interjections is that they all express an emotion. *Ouch!* It hurts. *Alas!* It's a shame.

## Other kinds of grammar

Recently, American linguists have presented new ways of looking at English that depart from traditional grammar. One approach, called "structural linguistics," analyzes English by concentrating on word endings, signal words, and the location of words in sentences.

Nouns, verbs, adjectives, and adverbs have endings that help identify them. Some of the more common endings for nouns include -*ance, -ence, -er, -ion, -ity, -ment, -ness,* and -*or.* Common verb endings are -*ate, -d, -ed, -en, -fy, -ing, -ize,* and -*t.* Common endings for adjectives are -*able, -al, -ant, -ary, -ed, -en, -ent, -ful, -ic, -ish, -less, -ous, -some,* and -*y.* A common adverb ending is -*ly.*

Certain words are called signal words because they announce that certain parts of speech are coming. *A, an, the, both, some,* and similar words signal nouns. Auxiliaries such as *may, have, will, can,* and *should* signal verbs. Prepositions such as *on, in,* and *of* signal nouns or pronouns. Of course, *both* and *some* are sometimes used as nouns, and *have* and other auxiliaries are sometimes verbs.

The position of a word in a sentence is also a good clue to part of speech because the English language contains certain sentence patterns. Consider the sentence "The _____ fumbled the ball." Without knowing the missing word, you can tell that it will be a noun. How? Because of its place in the sentence and its link with the signal word *the*.

Or consider the sentence "The trugy deer gimfeled the grass." Even though you do not know the meaning of *gimfeled*, you can tell that it is a verb. How? Because of its place in the sentence and its *-ed* ending. You also know that *trugy* is an adjective because of its *-y* ending and its place in the sentence.

Another new approach to grammar, called "generative transformational grammar," formulates logical procedures for "generating" new sentences. The basic unit of this grammar is the kernel sentence—an active, positive statement such as "Jim is happy." By applying certain procedures, you can "transform" this kernel sentence into the following sentences:

Jim is not happy. (negative transform)
Is Jim happy? (question transform)

You can also transform two or more kernel sentences into a more complicated sentence. The sentence "Mary smiled and walked away." is a transform of the kernel sentences "Mary smiled" and "Mary walked away." The sentence "The hungry person eats the pie" is a transform of "The person is hungry" and "The person eats the pie." The sentence "I found somebody's ring" is a transform of "somebody had a ring" and "I found the ring."

These two new approaches to grammar use terms not found in traditional grammar. For example, they discuss *morphemes*, which are single units of meaning expressed by a word or a part of a word.

*girl* is one morpheme
*girl's* is two morphemes (girl + possessive)
*girls* is two morphemes (girl + plural)
*girls'* is three morphemes (girl + plural + possessive)

The past tense morpheme is whatever is done to a verb to make it past tense. Usually, *-ed* is added to the end of the word. However, the past tense morpheme is not always shown this way.

*help* is one morpheme
*helped* is two morphemes (help + past)
*teach* is one morpheme
*taught* is two morphemes (teach + past)

The new grammars also classify words in a way slightly different from that of traditional grammar.

All the parts of speech are classified under two main headings—content words and function words.

Content words contain many of the words that are called nouns, verbs, adjectives, and adverbs in traditional grammar. This category of words is constantly expanding because when new words are added to the language, they are almost always content words.

Even though they rarely change, function words are very important. Function words are the little words, like prepositions and conjunctions, that connect content words and hold sentences together. Some other important words are the following:

**Auxiliaries.** The auxiliaries are the familiar verb-helpers like *may, might, have, has, had, can, could, should,* and similar words.

**Determiners.** A determiner is used with a noun and limits the meaning of the noun. A determiner can be an article like *a, an,* or *the;* a demonstrative like *this, that, these,* or *those;* a number like *one, six,* or *thirteen;* a quantifier like *several of* or *many of;* or a possessive like *his* or *hers.* A determiner differs from an adjective in that a determiner usually does not make sense when it is used alone in the predicate. For example, green is an adjective when it is used with a noun. You can say "The green sweater shrank," or "The sweater is green." However, *the* when it is used with a noun is a determiner. You may say "The sweater is green," but you may not say, "Sweater is the."

**Intensifiers.** Intensifiers are words like *very, rather, quite,* and *somewhat.* They intensify or give more specific meaning to adjectives and adverbs.

Structural linguistics and transformational grammar are two new approaches to the study of the English language. No one knows how soon, if ever, either one will replace traditional grammar. However, many teachers of English are incorporating some of the ideas from these new grammars with the traditional approach. For example, consider the sentence "The lion devoured his trainer." In traditional grammar, the third word is called a verb because it expresses action. In structural linguistics, the third word is called a verb because of its position in the sentence and its *-ed* ending. When both the traditional and structural descriptions of a verb are combined into one definition, the advantages of both views are utilized, and the idea of what a verb is becomes clearer.

# 3. Facts about style

Style, as it relates to writing, has two meanings. You use the word style to describe the creative or artistic manner in which an author writes prose or poetry. You can also use *style* to refer to such purely technical matters as capitalization and punctuation.

The creative side has to do with the way in which words are used by a writer to produce a specific effect or to bring out certain reactions from a reader. One writer may use long words and heavy, clumsy phrasing to give what might be considered a scholarly effect. Another writer may use simple, matter-of-fact words to say exactly the same thing.

Style, as explained on the following pages, deals specifically with technical matters. There are many possible variations of the basic styles given here. But the following rules and conventions represent preferred usage as it is taught in most schools in the United States.

## Capitalization

One of the principal uses of capital letters is to distinguish proper nouns and proper adjectives from common nouns and adjectives. A proper noun is the name of a particular person, place, thing, or idea. A proper adjective is a proper noun used as an adjective or an adjective derived from a proper noun. A common noun is the name of any person, place, thing, or idea in a general class.

| Proper nouns | Common nouns |
|---|---|
| Boston | city |
| Mary Smith | girl |
| Hatch Act | law |

Here are some examples of proper adjectives: *Paris* fashions, *Carter* administration, *Farmer-Labor* party, *New York* taxi drivers, *Alfred*

*Hitchcock* film, *Persian* carpet.

Here are some general rules to follow when deciding whether to capitalize a word:

1. Capitalize the first word of a sentence or a word or phrase that has the force of a sentence.

   What are you doing? Nothing. Stop!

2. Capitalize the first word of a direct quotation that is a sentence or has the force of a sentence.

   Bob called, "Hurry up." Joe asked, "Why?"

3. Capitalize the first word of a complete statement following a colon.

   This is our conclusion: The trial was fair.

4. Capitalize the first word in the salutation and the first word of the complimentary close of a letter.

   Dear son:      Gentlemen:
   With love,      Yours sincerely,

5. Capitalize the pronoun *I* whether used alone or in a contraction.

   She said I was right.    Now I've decided.

6. Capitalize the interjection *O*.

   Rejoice, O ye people.

7. Capitalize the names of the days of the week, months, and holidays.

   Saturday    February    Easter

8. Capitalize words showing family relationship when used instead of a name or as part of a name, but not when such words follow a possessive.

I asked Father for a dime. He called
   Uncle Bob.
I asked my father for a dime. He called
   my uncle.

9. Capitalize the first words and all other important words in the titles of books, newspapers, magazines, stories, poems, reports, songs, and other writings.

| | |
|---|---|
| *A Tale of Two Cities* | *Evening News* |
| *Business Week* | "Yesterday" |
| "To a Skylark" | *The Hobbit* |

Note: Capitalize prepositions, conjunctions, and articles only when they come at the beginning or end of a title or when they consist of five or more letters. This exception also applies to the other rules of capitalization.

10. Capitalize nicknames, other identifying names, and special titles and their abbreviations.

| | |
|---|---|
| Old Hickory | Richard the Lion-Hearted |
| Senator Hunt | Mary Grow, Ph.D. |

11. Capitalize the names of all political and geographical subdivisions, the names of all nationalities and tribes, words of direction designating a specific place, and the adjectives derived from such nouns.

Chicago   Sioux Indians   Far East

12. Capitalize the names of streets, highways, plazas, parks, squares, buildings, and other specific locations, including common nouns and abbreviations.

| | |
|---|---|
| Alameda Boulevard | National Bank Building |
| State Street | |

13. Capitalize the names of rivers, oceans, islands, mountains, and other geographical features, including the common nouns that are part of the proper names.

| | |
|---|---|
| Amazon River | Mount Olive |
| Atlantic Ocean | Treasure Island |

14. Capitalize the names of political parties and religious denominations and their members.

| | | |
|---|---|---|
| Labor Party | Republicans | The Baptist Church |

15. Capitalize the names of organizations, business firms, and institutions.

| | |
|---|---|
| Boy Scouts of America | Harvard University |
| Shell Oil Company | Franklin High School |

16. Capitalize the word *Bible* and the names and designations of all sacred writings; also, capitalize all nouns and pronouns that refer to a specific Supreme Being.

The Bible is sometimes called the
   Holy Writ.
the Talmud
The Lord is good.
Great is His mercy.
Buddha
*but:* The Indians believed in many gods.

17. Capitalize the names of historical events, wars, treaties, laws, and documents.

| | |
|---|---|
| Gadsden Purchase | Battle of the Bulge |
| Taft-Hartley Act | Civil War |
| Bill of Rights | Treaty of Ghent |

18. Capitalize the names of divisions, departments, and instrumentalities of government.

Board of Education   Library of Congress

19. Capitalize the names of trains, planes, ships, satellites, and submarines.

| | |
|---|---|
| *Golden State Limited* | *Spirit of St. Louis* |
| *Titanic* | *Nautilus* |
| *Echo I* | |

20. Capitalize the names of stars, planets, constellations, and other astronomical designations.

| | |
|---|---|
| Venus | Big Dipper |
| Sirius | Milky Way |

21. Capitalize personified nouns.

All Nature sang. Let not Evil triumph.

22. Capitalize the names of periods in the history of language, art, and literature.

| | |
|---|---|
| Old French | Age of Reason |
| Renaissance | Dadaist period |

23. Capitalize the names of war decorations.

Purple Heart   Silver Star

24. Capitalize *Preface, Contents, Chapter, Index,* and other parts of a book when referring to a specific part.

# Punctuation

Punctuation is used to make writing clear. The following punctuation rules present the main uses for each punctuation mark.

## Apostrophe

1. Use the apostrophe to form the possessive of a noun.

   the tree's leaves        the boys' bicycles
   Mary's hat               the Johnsons' car
   Charles's book           Tom and Bob's mother

2. Use the apostrophe to show omission of one or more letters, words, or numbers.

   didn't (did not)      '79 (1979)
   o'clock (of the clock)

3. Use the apostrophe to show plurals of numbers, letters, and words discussed as words.

   two 4's      some B's      too many and's

## Brackets

1. Use brackets within quotations to indicate explanations or your own comments.

   He replied, "She [Doris] is going."

2. Use brackets to indicate stage and acting directions in plays.

   CHARLES [waving arms]: Away with you!

3. Use brackets to correct a mistake in a quote.

   "The artist Le[o]nardo painted it."

4. Use brackets for parentheses within parentheses.

   (That was the color [red] he preferred.)

## Colon

1. Use the colon after a complete statement followed by a list.

   Campers must take these items: bedding, linen, and cooking utensils.

2. Use the colon after the salutation of a business letter.

   Dear Sir:     Gentlemen:     Dear Mr. Harris:

3. Use the colon after a statement followed by a clause that extends, explains, or amplifies the preceding statement.

   Judges have a double duty: They must protect the innocent and punish the guilty.

4. Use the colon to separate parts of a citation.

   *Elementary English* XLIV: 114-123
   Exodus 4: 1

5. Use the colon to separate hours from minutes in indicating time.

   3:40 P.M.

## Comma

1. Use the comma to separate the parts of an address.

   He lives at 23 First Avenue, Boise, Idaho.
   167 Park Boulevard, Rolling Acres, El Paso, Texas.

2. Use the comma to separate the day of the month and the month, or a special day, from the year.

   June 1, 1978     Independence Day, 1899

3. Use the comma after the greeting of an informal letter.

   Dear Alice,      My dear Uncle John,

4. Use the comma after the closing of a letter.

   Affectionately,      Sincerely yours,

5. Use the comma between words or phrases in a list or a series and before the *and* or the *or* that precedes the final item in a list.

   Go up the road, across the river, and into the park.
   The paper can be white, yellow, or blue.

6. Use the comma to set off the name of a person spoken to.

   Bill, here is your cap.

Here is your cap, Bill.
Here, Bill, is your cap.

7. Use the comma to set off *yes, no, oh, first, second,* and similar words when these words introduce a sentence.

Yes, the letter came.  Oh, say can you see…
First, who is coming?  Second, why?

8. Use the comma to set off words that explain or define other words (appear in apposition).

Janet Jones, my cousin, won a speech award.
The bullet ricocheted, or bounced, off a brick wall.

9. Use the comma to set off long phrases and dependent clauses preceding the main clause of a sentence.

By the end of the week, most of the work was done.
To be a good jumper, a person needs strong legs.
Although the children were poorly dressed, they looked healthy.

10. Use the comma to separate long coordinate clauses of a compound sentence.

The building collapsed, but no one was hurt.
Snow fell during the night, and the ground was white by morning.

However, two very brief independent clauses that are closely related to each other do not need a comma between them.

He sang and he danced.
The thunder rumbled and the lightning flashed.

11. Use the comma to indicate the omission of one or more words instead of repeating them.

The first game was exciting; the second, dull.
*shortened form of:*
The first game was exciting; the second was dull.

12. Use the comma before any title or its abbreviation that follows a person's name.

H. W. McDowell, M.D.
Sarah Caldwell, Secretary
Byron Phelps, Dean of Students
Patricia Brown, Ph.D.

13. Use the comma to set off words or phrases that suggest a break in thought, such as the connecting words *however, of course,* and *moreover.*

You find, however, that small ones are rare.
Of course, the winner received the medal.

14. Use the comma to set off participles, phrases, or clauses that add to the main thought of a sentence but are not essential to it.

Climbing, Joe skinned his leg.
The girls, busy as they were, found time to help.
The final reports, which were completed today, give all totals.

15. Use the comma to separate identical or closely similar words in a sentence.

Who he was, is a mystery.
When you are eating, talking should stop.

16. Use the comma to separate adjacent words in a sentence that might be mistakenly joined in reading.

To an Asian, Americans are foreigners.
Just as we walked in, the window broke.
Above, the girls made the beds; below, the boys swept the porch.
I had to hurry, for the store was closing.

17. Use the comma to set off thousands, millions, billions, and other high numbers.

4,323   65,001   210,563,270

18. Use the comma to separate unrelated numbers in a sentence.

By 1978, 30,000 people lived in the city.

19. Use the comma to set off coordinate phrases modifying the same noun.

This lake is as deep as, but smaller than, Lake Erie.

20. Use the comma between sentence elements that suggest contrast or comparison.

The more people he met, the lonelier he felt.
The sooner we get started, the sooner we will finish.

# Dash

1. Use the dash (— in handwriting or – – on a typewriter) before a summarizing statement introduced by *all, this,* or similar words.

   > Bob, Bill, Harry—all found summer jobs.
   > To defeat every opponent—this was his ambition.

2. Use the dash before a repeated word or expression in a sentence.

   > He was a gentleman—a gentleman of the old school.

3. Use the dash to emphasize or define a part of a sentence.

   > The Declaration of Independence—that glorious document—was written in 1776.

4. Use the dash to indicate an "aside" or point of view of the speaker.

   > You may—though I doubt it—enjoy this book.

5. Use the dash to suggest halting or hesitant speech.

   > "Well—I—ah—I didn't know," he stammered.

6. Use the dash to indicate a sudden break or interruption in a sentence.

   > "I'm sorry, sir, but—." He was already through the gate.

# Ellipses

1. Use ellipses (three spaced dots) within a quotation to indicate all places where a word or words have been omitted.

   > "The house ... was built in 1935."
   > *for:*
   > "The house on Elm Street was built in 1935."

2. Use ellipses at the end of a quotation to indicate words omitted before the period, but use four dots (the first dot is the period that indicates the end of the sentence).

> "He was a giant of a man...."
> *for:*
> "He was a giant of a man and highly respected."

# Exclamation mark

1. Use the exclamation mark after a word, phrase, or sentence that expresses strong or sudden feelings.

   > Ouch!    That hurts!    Good for you!

2. Use the exclamation mark to emphasize a command or strong point of view.

   > Come here at once!
   > We won't discuss this!

3. Use the exclamation mark to show sarcasm, irony, or amusement.

   > You are a fine one to talk about lazy people!
   > That should be an easy job for you!

# Hyphen

The hyphen is most commonly used to mark the division of a word at the end of a line.

You may divide a word only between syllables, and only in such a way that each part of the hyphenated word contains at least two letters. If you are uncertain about where to break a word into syllables, always consult your dictionary.

In general, avoid dividing a word in a place where division would suggest an incorrect pronunciation—for example, *omni-potent.* Remember that pronunciation is not an accurate guide to syllabication. The word *babble,* for instance, is pronounced BAHB uhl and is syllabified *bab-ble.* Try to avoid dividing a word in a place where either part of the hyphenated word forms a word by itself; for example, *tar-tan.*

You should not divide a word that is a proper name; a number or a figure; a contraction; an abbreviation; a word of one syllable; or a word of five letters or less, regardless of the number of syllables.

The hyphen is also used to join word parts and to separate word parts.

Following are some specific rules about use of the hyphen.

1. You may divide between double consonants unless it is the root that ends in the double consonant.

   run-ning      remit-tance
   col-lection
   *but:*
   roll-ing      bless-edly
   miss-ing

2. You may divide between vowels when one vowel ends a syllable and another vowel begins a syllable.

   fluctu-ate      foli-age
   actu-ary

3. You may divide after a vowel that forms a one-letter syllable.

   presi-dent      deco-rate
   diminu-tive

4. You may divide before a suffix of three or more letters.

   port-able      transi-tion
   argu-ment

5. You may divide after a prefix of three or more letters.

   trans-mission      anti-climax
   pro-logue

6. You may divide a compound word *only* where a hyphen already occurs in the word.

   first-class      vice-president
   self-reliant

7. Use the hyphen in compound numbers between 21 and 99 when spelled out.

   twenty-one      thirty-sixth
   ninety-nine

8. Use the hyphen between the numerator and denominator of fractions that are spelled out and used as modifiers, unless one part of the fraction already contains a hyphen.

   two-thirds vote      one twenty-second piece
   one-fourth part      twenty-one thirtieths part
   *but:*
   Do not use the hyphen between the numerator and the denominator when the fraction is a noun.
   He bought one half.      He took four fifths.

9. Use the hyphen after the prefix *re* when the word being formed might be confused with a similar word.

   re-lay a carpet      re-cover a chair
   *but:*
   a relay race      recover from an illness

10. Use the hyphen after a prefix in these situations: when the prefix ends with the same letter with which the root word begins; when the root word begins with *w* or *y*; or when the root word begins with an initial capital letter. There are some exceptions to this rule; in these cases, your dictionary shows that the preferred spelling is without the hyphen, as in *cooperate*.

    de-emphasize     pre-Columbian     co-worker

11. Use the hyphen between the components of a compound adjective when it appears before the word or phrase it modifies.

    drive-in movie      would-be actor
    foreign-born person
    *but*
    The client was foreign born.

12. Do not hyphenate a compound adjective that includes an adverb ending in *ly* even when it is used before the word or phrase it modifies.

    It was a slowly moving train.
    *but:*
    It was a slow-moving train.

13. Use the hyphen in compounds containing a prepositional phrase, unless the dictionary shows that the preferred spelling is without the hyphen, as in *coat of arms.*

14. Use the hyphen after any prefix that precedes a proper noun or adjective.

    un-American     pre-Revolutionary     pro-Nazi

15. Use the hyphen after each item in a series when the last item requires a hyphen and the earlier items relate to that one.

    first-, second-, and third-grade pupils

16. Use the hyphen after *great* in describing generations or descent.

    great-great-grandfather     great-grandmother

17. Check your dictionary for words beginning with the prefixes *ante, after, pro, pre, super, ultra, non,* and *well.* Some of these words are hyphenated; some are not. Also check com-

pound words beginning or ending with the words *boy, book, shop, store, mill, work, child, maker, payer, like, dealer, girl,* and *man.* Usage varies. Notice these examples:

man-child    man in white    manslaughter

18. Use the hyphen to spell out a word or a name.

s-e-p-a-r-a-t-e    D-i-s-r-a-e-l-i

## Parentheses

1. Use parentheses around explanatory material in a sentence when this material has no essential connection with the rest of the sentence in which it occurs.

    To make holes, use an awl (a sharp, pointed tool).

2. Use parentheses to enclose sources of information within a sentence.

    One chapter in this book (Chapter IV) describes fish hatcheries.
    The population of Iowa is 2,913,387 (1980 census).

3. Use parentheses around numbers or letters that indicate subdivisions of a sentence.

    This committee has three duties: (a) to solicit members, (b) to collect dues, and (c) to send out receipts.

4. Use parentheses around figures that repeat a number written out.

    Enclosed is five dollars ($5.00).
    Please send forty-five (45) copies.

5. Other marks of punctuation are placed inside the parentheses when they belong with the parenthetical matter, rather than with the main body of the sentence.

    Carol's question ("Whom did you take to the dance?") produced a chill in the air.
    *but:*
    John walked to the store in all that snow (even though I asked him to stay home).

## Period

1. Use the period after a statement.

    It is cold outside.

2. Use the period after a command.

    Please hurry.

3. Use the period after an initial.

    J. P. Jones

4. Use the period after an abbreviation or each part of most abbreviations.

    A.M.    lbs.    C.O.D.    yds.    Mr.    Mrs.

5. Use the period after each number or letter that begins a heading in an outline.

    Why I Like to Read
    I. Satisfies my curiosity
      A. About people
        1. In ages past
        2. In the present
      B. About things

## Question mark

1. Use the question mark after a direct question.

    How old is Bill?

2. Use the question mark after a statement followed by a short question.

    It's cold outside, isn't it?

3. Use the question mark after a word that indicates a question.

    What?    How?    Why?

## Quotation marks

1. Use quotation marks to enclose the exact words of a speaker.

    Mary exclaimed, "I refuse to go!"

2. Use quotation marks around each part of a direct quotation when explanatory words come between the parts of the quotation.

> "This material," said the clerk, "washes easily."

3. Use quotation marks to enclose quoted words or quoted phrases that occur within a sentence.

> The leader told us we must "put our shoulders to the wheel."

4. Use quotation marks around the titles of songs or poems.

> We all sang "America."
> The child recited "Little Miss Muffet."

5. Use quotation marks around the titles of lectures, sermons, pamphlets, handbooks, chapters of a book, magazine articles, and any titled material that is less than a whole volume.

> "Rescued" was the most exciting chapter in the book.

6. Use quotation marks around a word or phrase explained or defined by the rest of the sentence.

> The "crib" in cribbage is made up of discards from players' hands.

7. In general writing, use quotation marks around a word to which attention is being called. In formal writing, underline the word to call attention to it.

> You have spelled "parallel" incorrectly.

8. Use quotation marks around a technical or trade name.

> Many people use "Jell-Right" in making jellies.

9. Use quotation marks around a word used in an unusual situation or with a slightly different meaning than usual.

> His "refuge" was a small room in the attic.
> She would not tell anyone her "secret."

10. Use quotation marks before the beginning of each stanza of a quoted poem and after the last stanza. Also use quotation marks before each paragraph of continuous quoted material and after the last paragraph.

11. Use single quotation marks for a quote within a quote.

> She said, "I won't until you say, 'Please.'"

12. Commas and periods are always placed inside the closing quotation marks (in ordinary usage in the United States).

> We all sang "America."

13. Semicolons and colons are always placed outside the closing quotation marks.

> John said, "I'll call you tomorrow"; but I have not heard from him yet.
> Here is what he did when he said, "I'll go": He closed the window, picked up his valise, and walked out of the door.

14. Question marks and exclamation points are placed inside the closing quotation marks if they belong to the quotation.

> "Get out!" she shouted.
> *but:*
> What did you mean when you said, "I didn't know you were here"?

## Semicolon

1. Use the semicolon between the parts of a compound sentence if they are not joined by the conjunctions *and, but, or, for,* or *nor*.

> I must leave you now; you may join me later.

2. Use the semicolon before a conjunction connecting independent clauses when either or both clauses already contain commas.

> During the summer, he accomplished nothing; but finally, during the winter, he finished writing his book.

3. Use the semicolon after each clause in a series of three or more independent clauses.

> Bells rang; whistles shrieked; horns blared; and people screamed.

4. Use the semicolon before words like *therefore, however,* and *nevertheless* when they connect two independent clauses.

> Mr. Black is a busy man; nevertheless, he agreed to help on the committee.

5. Use the semicolon after listings when commas occur within the list.

You will need to call Henrietta Hall, of the First Ward; Warren Holt, of the Second Ward; and Nancy Griffin, of the Third Ward.

6. Use the semicolon to set off lists, enumerations, and explanations introduced by expressions such as *for example*, *for instance*, *that is*, and *namely*.

There are several reasons why this is a good factory site; namely, proximity to fuel, availability of raw materials, and abundance of skilled labor.

## Underscoring

Words underscored in manuscript appear in italics when set in type.

1. Underscore the name of any book or complete volume.

Tom Sawyer is a book about boyhood.

2. Underscore the name of a magazine or periodical.

There are amusing cartoons in The New Yorker.

3. Underscore any foreign word that is not commonly used in English. Such words are labeled Latin, French, Italian, and so on in the dictionary, usually before the definition is given.

The report dealt with de jure segregation.

4. Underscore the names of ships, pictures, and works of art.

Titanic    The Last Supper
Rodin's The Thinker

5. Underscore any word or words considered not for their meaning but as words.

But, for, and or are all conjunctions.

## Virgule

1. Use the virgule, or "slash mark," between two words to indicate that the meaning of

either word pertains.

The man and/or his wife may cash the check.

2. Use the virgule as a dividing line in special constructions like dates, fractions, and abbreviations.

10/7/77    3/4    1/2    c/o    B/W

3. Use the virgule when recording bibliographic matter to indicate where one line ends and another begins; for example, in recounting the position of words on the spine of a book.

The/World Book/Encyclopedia/A/ Volume 1

4. Use the virgule with a run-in passage of poetry to indicate where one line ends and another begins.

He recalled those famous lines by William Shakespeare: "This above all: to thine own self be true,/And it must follow, as the night the day,/Thou canst not then be false to any man."

## Preparing footnotes

Footnotes are important parts of any research paper. When you write a research paper, you will probably use information from many sources, such as books, magazines, encyclopedias, and newspapers. You should give credit in a footnote whenever you quote one of these sources directly, use another author's opinions and ideas, or rely on statements or figures that might be questioned.

Every footnote in a research paper has a number. Footnotes are usually numbered consecutively throughout the paper. If you have 25 footnotes, the first will be numbered 1 and the last 25. Numbers 1 and 2 may be on page 1 of your paper; number 3 may not appear until page 7.

The number of the footnote appears in two places. It first appears after the sentence, fact, or quotation you are crediting. Be certain that you place the number slightly above the line.

Of all the shots in a hockey game, the one goaltenders dread most is the slap shot. Slap shots have been measured at 119 miles per hour.[1] At this speed, the puck becomes a black blur in the air.

Secondly, the footnote number also appears at the bottom of the page. Again, it is slightly raised above the line. The number always appears *before* the citation in this position.

[1] Bobby Hull, <u>Hockey Is My Game</u>, p. 127.

Footnotes can come in other forms. General magazines have few footnotes and may indicate them with an asterisk(*), a dagger(†), or some other symbol. In some books, footnotes appear on the page with the text, and in others the footnotes are grouped at the end of a chapter or the end of the book.

All footnotes follow a certain style. Put commas between the parts of the footnote and a period at the end. Indent the first line of each footnote. Make the second and following lines flush with the left margin of your paper. Single space between lines of a footnote, but double space between separate footnotes on the same page.

Picture the following footnote paired with the one above:

If a slap shot hits a goalie in the face, it can cut like shrapnel. And a goalie is also vulnerable to cuts by skates and sticks. One veteran goaltender, Terry Sawchuk, has more than 400 stitches in his face.[2]

[1]Bobby Hull, <u>Hockey Is My Game</u>, p. 127.
[2]Jim Hunt, <u>The Men in the Nets: Hockey's Tortured Heroes</u>, p. 7.

Put the parts of the footnote in this order: author (first name first), title of the book (underlined), and page number. Here is a typical example of a footnote for a book or pamphlet:

[18]Gene Smith, <u>When the Cheering Stopped: The Last Years of Woodrow Wilson</u>, p. 213.

Here are some variations on the basic footnote form for books and pamphlets:
A work by more than one author:

[7]Frank R. Donovan and Bruce Catton, <u>Ironclads of the Civil War</u>, p. 19.

An edited work:
[15]Frank B. Freidel, ed., <u>Union Pamphlets of the Civil War, 1861-1865</u>, p. 13.

A work whose author is unknown:

[31]<u>Art in South Africa</u>, prepared by the South African Information Service, p. 22.

When the source is a magazine, give the author's name (first name first), the title of the article (in quotation marks), the name of the magazine (underlined), the volume number, the date of the issue, and the page number. If no author's name is given, start out with the title of the article.

[20]Rudolf F. Graf, "Build an Electronic Guard to Foil Car Thieves," <u>Popular Science Monthly</u>, vol. 193, October, 1968, p. 140.

For newspaper articles, use the following style: author if known (first name first), title of the article (in quotation marks), the name of the newspaper (underlined), the date, the section number if there is one, the page number, and the column number:

[6]"Governor Backs Education Bill," <u>Daily Courier</u>, July 30, 1981, sec. 5, p. 2, col. 1.

If the source is an encyclopedia, give the title of the article (in quotation marks), the name of the encyclopedia (underlined), the volume number or letter, and the page number:

[13]"Horse," <u>The World Book Encyclopedia</u>, Vol. 9, p. 314.

For a later reference to the same source, use a shortened form of your first footnote. If the source is the same work and page number as in the preceding footnote, use <u>Ibid</u>. If the page number is different, place a comma after <u>Ibid</u>. and give the new page number.

[30]Oscar Lewis, <u>The Children of Sanchez</u>, p. 200.
[31]<u>Ibid</u>.
[32]<u>Ibid</u>., p. 130.

When you use <u>Ibid</u>., you should underline it and put a period after it, as shown above. <u>Ibid</u>. is an abbreviation for the Latin word ibidem, which means "in the same place."

To refer to a source quoted earlier in your research paper, but not in the footnote immediately preceding, give the last name of the author and the page number:

[1]Bobby Hull, <u>Hockey Is My Game</u>, p. 127.
[2]Jim Hunt, <u>The Men in the Nets: Hockey's Tortured Heroes</u>, p. 7.
[3]Hull, p. 130.

If you use more than one book or article by the same author, give his or her last name, the specific title, and the page number for succeeding references:

[16]Lewis, <u>The Children of Sanchez</u>, p. 200.
[17]Lewis, <u>La Vida</u>, p. 30.

Properly constructed footnotes show not only that you know your subject, but also that you are proud of all the sources that you drew upon to prepare your paper.

# Preparing a bibliography

When you write a research paper, you check many sources, including books, encyclopedias, magazines, and newspapers. Your bibliography lists all the sources that you consulted, whether you quoted from them in your paper or not. The bibliography has two functions. First, it shows how far you went in researching your topic by indicating the complete range of your sources. Second, it shows the reader where to look for additional information if he or she finds your topic interesting.

Bibliographic entries have standard forms. The information included differs somewhat from that in footnotes. Like footnotes, a bibliographic entry contains the author and title, but it also includes facts about the publication of a source. The style of bibliographic entries differs from footnote style in that authors are listed last name first and periods are used to separate the three main parts of the entry (author, title, and facts of publication).

Following are examples of the content and format for various types of entries. Notice the information included and the punctuation used in each type of entry; then follow those formats in your own bibliographies.

*For a book:* author (last name first), title (underlined), place of publication, publisher, and year of publication.

Baumol, William J., and Oates, Wallace E. The Theory of Environmental Policy. Englewood Cliffs, New Jersey: Prentice-Hall, Inc., 1975.

Bookchin, Murray. Our Synthetic Environment. New York: Harper & Row, 1974.

Chanlett, Emil T. Environmental Protection. New York: McGraw-Hill Book Company, 1973.

Mason, William H., and Folkerts, George W. Environmental Problems: Principles, Readings & Comments. Dubuque, Iowa: Wm. C. Brown Company, 1973.

Sauvy, Alfred. Zero Growth. New York: Praeger, Inc., 1976.

Shuttlesworth, Dorothy. Clean Air, Sparkling Water. New York: Doubleday and Company, Inc., 1968.

Victor, Peter. Pollution: Economy and Environment. Toronto: University of Toronto Press, 1972.

*For a magazine article:* author (last name first), title of the article (in quotation marks), name of the magazine (underlined), volume number, date of the issue of the magazine, and page numbers for the entire article.

Cassidy, H.G. "Boundary Conditions in Energy and Ecology." Bulletin of the Atomic Scientists, vol. 33, March, 1977, pp. 31-32.

*For an encyclopedia article:* author (last name first), if known; title of the article (in quotation marks); name of encyclopedia (underlined); date of publication; volume number; and page numbers for the entire article.

"Environmental Pollution." The World Book Encyclopedia (1981), Vol. 6, pp. 260b-260l.

*For a newspaper article:* author if known (last name first), title of the article (in quotation marks), name of the newspaper (underlined), date of the issue, section (if any), and page number.

Romero, Jack. "Panthers Finish First." Prairie Gazette, May 18, 1980, sec. 3, p. 4.

Arrange the entries in your bibliography in alphabetical order according to the last names of the authors—or according to the titles in entries in which authors are not given. When the source has more than one author, put the names of other authors last name first, as well. Connect the authors' names with an "and" if there are two; use semicolons between the authors' names and use the word "and" to conclude the series if there are three or more authors.

Do not number the entries in the bibliography. Start the entry at the left margin. If an entry runs more than one line, indent the additional lines. Use a single space between the lines of an entry, and leave a double space between entries.

If the bibliography includes more than one work by the same author, use a long dash where the name would normally appear, in all listings after the first. For an author with more than one entry, list his or her entries in alphabetical order by the titles of the works.

Falk, Richard A. "Global Populism." The Progressive, vol. 38, June, 1974, p. 37.
————. This Endangered Planet: Prospects and Proposals for Human Survival. New York: Random House, 1972.

# 4. Facts about language

## English words from other languages

Many of the words commonly used in English have been taken from foreign languages, often without change. It is easy to become so accustomed to using these words that they seem to be English, rather than foreign.

The following list gives definitions and source languages of 15 words that have been taken from foreign languages. All 15 of these words are used in the paragraph below. Find a word used in the paragraph to match each definition in the list. Please do not write in this book, but place your answers on a separate sheet of paper. Answers are given on page 43.

1. quarreling, fighting (German)
2. predominant figure in the business world (Japanese-Chinese)
3. having special power (Scottish)
4. self-possession (French)
5. a type of candy (Mexican-Spanish)
6. accomplished (French)
7. station in life (Latin)
8. coming into (French)
9. shining, bright (Scandinavian)
10. a special group of people (French)
11. dabbler in the arts (French)
12. buy (French)
13. sample or illustration of (French)
14. newspaper (French, Italian)
15. lacking color (French)

Arthur Plato, despite a childhood filled with poverty and strife, was now a great industrial tycoon. With uncanny ability and business aplomb, he had devised a method for marketing chocolate that had made him one of the richest men in the world.

Plato had achieved his enviable status through hard work. He had had little time to devote to the finer things in life. Now to make up for this lack and to facilitate his entry into the glittering world of society, he had become a dilettante. He professed an interest in music, literature, and the arts. His great wealth made it possible for him to purchase many rare works of art. His collection of Chinese scrolls was world famous. But it lacked one example from the Ming Dynasty to make it perfect.

As he sat in his comfortable study reading the Evening Gazette, Arthur Plato's face turned pale with anger. Ian Candido, his business rival and arch enemy, had bought the very scroll he coveted.

The exercise that follows will help you to discover 15 more words commonly used in the English language that have been adapted from foreign languages. Each word as it appears in the English language is listed in column A. The original meaning of each word and the language from which each word is derived is listed in column B. Can you match each English word listed in column A with its original meaning and language? Please do not write in this book, but place your answers on a separate sheet of paper. Answers are given on page 43.

**Example**

16. kimono

a. an item of clothing, in Japanese
b. a two-wheeled cart, in Chinese

**Answer:**

16. a. an item of clothing, in Japanese

**A.**

| | |
|---|---|
| 1. scandal | 9. kindergarten |
| 2. ambulance | 10. rapport |
| 3. amuck | 11. shampoo |
| 4. bonanza | 12. azure |
| 5. sloven | 13. tank |
| 6. ketchup | 14. student |
| 7. boom | 15. souvenir |
| 8. alcohol | |

**B**

a. a children's garden, in German
b. be eager, apply oneself to learning, in Latin
c. to smack the lips, in Malay
d. a powdered chemical, in Arabic
e. wash the hair or scalp, in Hindustani
f. a keepsake, remembrance, in French
g. prosperity, fair weather, in Spanish
h. mobile (hospital), in French
i. lapis lazuli, in Persian
j. a tree or pole, in Dutch
k. engaging in battle furiously, attacking with desperate resolution, in Malay
l. offense, to trap with a springing device, in Greek
m. careless, dirty, in Dutch-Flemish
n. relation, connection, in French
o. a cistern, in Gujarati, India

The preceding exercise provides a brief sampling of words from other languages that have been adopted into the English language. What follows is a longer, but still partial, list of such words.

Note the large number of source languages represented in this list. Latin, French, and Italian are encountered most frequently, and more than a dozen other source languages are included—even in this relatively short list.

For each word, a phonetic respelling is given. See page 432 for a key to the respelling system used in this book.

In most cases, the list gives the most common meaning of a word. (Other meanings may be acceptable, but not all have been included.) In a few entries, more than one definition is given; such additional definitions are included to make these entries clearer and more accurate.

# A list of foreign words used in English

**a capella** (AH kuh PEL uh), of choral music or singers: without musical accompaniment. (Italian)

**ad infinitum** (ad IN fuh NY tuhm), without limit; endlessly. (Latin)

**aficionado** (uh FEE syuh NAH doh), 1. a person who takes a very great interest in bullfighting, although not a bullfighter. 2. a person who is very enthusiastic about some sport or hobby or special field. (Spanish)

**aide-de-camp** (AYD duh KAMP), a military officer who acts as an assistant to a superior officer, handling messages and acting as a secretary. (French)

**alter ego** (AL tur EE goh), a very intimate friend or trusted friend or associate. (Latin)

**angina** (an JY nuh), angina pectoris: a condition of the heart that causes sudden and severe pains in the lower part of the chest and a feeling of being suffocated. (Latin)

**aria** (AH ree uh), an air or melody; melody for a single voice with instrumental or vocal accompaniment, in an opera or oratorio. (Italian)

**aurora borealis** (aw RAWR uh BOHR ee AL lihs), the aurora of the northern sky; northern lights. (New Latin)

**balalaika** (BAL uh LY kuh), a Russian musical instrument somewhat like a guitar, with a triangular body. (Russian)

**ballet** (BAL ay, ba LAY), an elaborate dance by a group on a stage. The dance usually tells a story accompanied by music written specially for it. (French)

**bayou** (BY yoo), a marshy inlet or outlet of a lake, river, or gulf in the southern United States. (Louisiana French; Choctaw)

**beret** (buh RAY), a soft, round woolen cap originally worn especially in parts of France and Spain. (French)

**bona fide** (BOH nuh fyd), in good faith; genuine; without make-believe or fraud. (Latin)

**bonbon** (BAHN bahn), a piece of candy with a coating of fondant. (French)

**burro** (BUR oh), a donkey, usually a small one used for carrying loads or packs. (Spanish)

**camaraderie** (KAH muh RAH dur ee), comradeship; friendliness and loyalty among comrades. (French)

**chateau** (sha TOH), a French castle. (French)

**chile con carne** (CHIHL ee kon KAHR nee), a highly seasoned Mexican dish of chopped meat cooked with red peppers and, usually, kidney beans. (American-Spanish)

**chinchilla** (chihn CHIHL uh), a small South American rodent that looks somewhat like a squirrel. (Spanish)

**circa** (SUR kuh), about. (Latin)

**claret** (KLAR uht), the light, dry red wine made in Bordeaux, France. (French)

**cognac** (KOHN yak), a brandy of superior quality distilled from wine at or near Cognac, France. (French)

**collage** (kuh LAHZH), a collection of objects, pieces of paper, and other materials, pasted on a flat surface, sometimes with additions of paint, to make a composition, especially an abstract or surrealistic composition. (French)

**coup d'etat** (KOO day TAH), a sudden and decisive move in politics, especially one effecting a change of government illegally or by force. (French)

**data** (DAY tuh), things known or granted; information from which conclusions can be drawn; facts. (Latin)

**depot** (DEE poh), U.S.: railroad station. (French)

**détente** (day TAHNT), the easing of strained relations, especially in a political situation. (French)

**dirndl** (DIRN duhl), an alpine peasant girl's costume consisting of a blouse, a tight bodice, and a full, brightly colored skirt, gathered at the waist; a skirt of this type. (German)

**dogma** (DAWG muh), a belief taught or held as true, especially by authority of a church; doctrine. (Greek)

**dramatis personae** (DRAM uh tis pur SOH nee), the characters or actors in a play; a list of them. (Latin)

**éclair** (AY klahr), a light, finger-shaped piece of pastry filled with whipped cream or custard and covered with icing. (French)

**emeritus** (ee MEHR uh tuhs), honorably discharged; retired from service, but still holding one's rank and title. (Latin)

**en brochette** (AHN broh SHET), cooked and served on a small pit or skewer. (French)

**en route** (ahn ROOT), on the way. (French)

**entrepreneur** (AHN truh pruh NER), a person who organizes and manages a business or industrial enterprise, taking the risk of not making a profit and getting the profit when there is one. (French)

**exposé** (EKS poh ZAY), a showing up of crime, dishonesty, or fraud. (French)

**facsimile** (fak SIM uh lee), an exact copy or likeness; perfect reproduction. (Latin)

**fakir** (FAY kur), a Moslem holy man who lives by begging. (Arabic)

**falsetto** (fawl SET oh), an unnaturally high-pitched voice, especially in a man. (Italian)

**fiancé** (FEE ahn SAY), a man to whom a woman is engaged to be married. (French)

**fiesta** (fee ES tuh), 1. a religious festival; saint's day. 2. a holiday, festivity. (Spanish)

**fondue** (fon DOO), a dish made of melted cheese, eggs, butter, and other ingredients, into which crackers or small pieces of toast are dipped and eaten. (French)

**gala** (GAY luh), a festive occasion; festival. (French)

**gamin** (GAM uhn), 1. a neglected boy, left to roam about the streets. 2. a small, lively person of either sex. (French)

**geisha** (GAY shuh), a Japanese singing and dancing girl. (Japanese)

**genre** (ZHAHN ruh), kind; sort; style. (French)

**ghetto** (GET oh), the part of a city where Jews were required to live in former times; a part of a city inhabited mainly by a single racial or other minority group. (Italian)

**goulash** (GOO lahsh), a stew made of beef or veal and vegetables, usually highly seasoned. (Hungarian)

**gourmet** (GUR may), a person who is expert at judging and choosing fine foods, wines, and other edibles; epicure. (French)

**guerrilla** (guh RIL uh), a member of a small independent band of fighters who harass the enemy by sudden raids and ambushes. (Germanic)

**haiku** (HY koo), a very brief Japanese poem of three lines and containing only 17 syllables. (Japanese)

**hallelujah** (HAL uh LOO yuh), praise ye the Lord; it occurs in many psalms and anthems. (Hebrew)

**haute couture** (oht kuh TYR), the most notable fashion designers and dressmaking establishments of the world, as those of Paris. (French)

**hoi polloi** (HOY puh LOY), ordinary people; the masses. (Greek)

**hula-hula** (HOO luh HOO luh), a native Hawaiian dance. (Hawaiian)

**hyperbole** (hy PIR buh lee), exaggeration for effect. (Latin)

**ignoramus** (ig nuh RAY muhs), an ignorant person. (Latin)

**incognito** (IN kog NEE toh), with one's name, character, and rank concealed. (Italian)

**influenza** (in flu EN zuh), an acute, contagious disease, caused by a virus, and like a very bad cold in its symptoms, but much more dangerous and exhausting; flu; grippe. (Italian)

**insignia** (in SIG nee uh), the emblems, badges, or other distinguishing marks of a high position, honor, or military order. (Latin)

**item** (EYE tum), a separate thing or article. (Latin)

**jodhpurs** (JAHD puhrz), breeches for horseback riding, loose above the knees and fitting closely below. (Jodhpur, a state in India).

**judo** (JOO doh), jujitsu, a Japanese method of wrestling. (Japanese)

**julienne** (joo lee EN), cut in thin strips or pieces; usually refers to food. (French)

**junta** (HUN tuh), a political or military group holding power after a revolution. (Spanish)

**kaput** (kuh POOT), *Informal.* ruined; defeated; done for. (German)

**kibbutz** (ki BOOTZ), an Israeli communal settlement, especially a farm cooperative. (Hebrew)

**kopek** (KOH pek), a coin of the Soviet Union, worth 1/100 of a ruble. *Informal:* any small coin. (Russian)

**lasagne** (luh ZAHN yuh), an Italian dish consisting of chopped meat, cheese, and tomato sauce, cooked with layers of wide, flat noodles. (Italian)

**lei** (lay), a wreath of flowers, leaves, and other greenery, worn as an ornament around the neck or on the head. (Hawaiian)

**liaison** (lee AY zon), the connection between parts of an army, branches of a service, or offices of a service, to secure proper cooperation; any other system of connection between groups of people to secure cooperation. (French)

**lingerie** (lahn juh RAY), women's underwear. (French)

**liqueur** (li KER), a strong, sweet, highly flavored alcoholic liquor. (French)

**maestro** (MYS troh), a great composer, teacher, or conductor of music. (Italian)

**malaria** (muh LAHR ee uh), a disease characterized by periodic chills and uncontrollable shaking, followed by fever and sweating. (Italian)

**marimba** (muh RIM buh), a musical instrument somewhat like a xylophone, consisting of small bars of hard wood that produce different sounds when they are struck with drumsticks. (Bantu, ultimately)

**marinade** (mar uh NAYD), a spiced vinegar, wine, or oil used to pickle meat or fish. (French)

**memorandum** (mem uh RAN duhm), a short written statement for future use; an informal letter, note, or report. (Latin)

**migraine** (MY grayn), a severe headache, usually recurrent and on one side of the head only. (French)

**moraine** (muh RAYN), a mass of rocks and dirt deposited at the side or end of a glacier, or beneath the ice as the glacier melts. (French)

**mores** (MAWR ays), customs prevailing among a people or a social group that are accepted as right and obligatory; traditional rules; ways; manners. (Latin)

**mufti** (MUF tee), ordinary clothes, not a uniform. (Arabic)

**naive** (nah EEV), simple in nature, like a child; not sophisticated; artless. (French)

**nirvana** (nir VAH nuh), the Buddhist idea of heavenly peace; perfect happiness reached by the complete absorption of oneself into the supreme universal spirit. (Sanskrit)

**noblesse oblige** (noh BLES oh BLEEZH), persons of noble rank should behave nobly. (French)

**nougat** (NOO get), a kind of soft candy made chiefly from sugar and egg whites and containing nuts. (French)

**nuance** (NOO ahns), a shade of expression, meaning, or feeling. (French)

**odium** (OH dee uhm), hatred; dislike. (Latin)

**Olympiad** (oh LIM pee ad), a celebration of the modern Olympic games. (Greek)

**opera** (OP ur ah), a play that is mostly sung, with costumes, scenery, acting, and music to go with the singing. (Italian)

**opus** (OH puhs), a work; composition. (Latin)

**ovum** (OH vuhm), a female gamete; egg. (Latin)

**paella** (pah EH uh), a spicy dish, originally Basque, consisting of seasoned rice, cooked in oil with saffron, and of lobster or shrimp, scraps of chicken, or of beef and pork, and fresh vegetables. (Spanish)

**papier-mâché** (PAY puhr muh SHAY), a paper pulp mixed with some stiffener such as glue and molded when moist. (French)

**pariah** (puh RY uh), any person or animal generally despised; social outcast. (Tamil)

**parole** (puh ROHL), a conditional release from prison or jail before the full term is served. (French)

**pasta** (PAHS tuh), any of various foods, as macaroni, spaghetti, and the like, made of flour, water, salt, and sometimes milk or eggs, shaped in tubular or other forms and dried. (Italian)

**pastel** (pas TEHL), a kind of chalklike crayon used in drawing, made of a dry paste of ground pigments compounded with resin or gum. (French)

**pentathlon** (pen TATH lahn), an athletic contest consisting of five different events. (Greek)

**per capita** (pur KAP uh tuh), for each person. (Latin)

**phobia** (FOH bee uh), a persistent, morbid, or insane fear of a specific thing or group of things. (Greek)

**pilaf** (pih LAHF), an Oriental dish consisting of rice or cracked wheat boiled with mutton, fowl, or fish, and flavored with spices and raisins. (Persian or Turkish)

**polka** (POLE kuh), a kind of lively dance. (Czech)

**post-mortem** (pohst MOWR tuhm), after death. (Latin)

**premiere** (pri MIHR), a first public performance. (Latin)

**propaganda** (PROP uh GAN duh), systematic efforts to spread opinions or beliefs. (Latin)

**protégé** (PROH tuh ZHAY), a person or group under the protection or kindly care of another, especially of a person of superior position or skill. (French)

**pundit** (PUN dit), a very learned person; expert, authority. (Hindi; Sanskrit)

**quisling** (KWIZ ling), any person who treacherously helps to prepare the way for enemy occupation of his own country; traitor. (Norwegian)

**quorum** (KWAR uhm), the number of members of

any society or assembly that must be present if the business done is to be legal or binding. (Latin)

**rabbi** (RAB eye), a teacher of the Jewish religion, leader of a Jewish congregation. (Greek; Aramaic)

**rajah** (RAH juh), a ruler or chief in India, Java, or Borneo. (Hindi)

**rapport** (ra PAWR), relation, location. (French)

**rendezvous** (RAHN day voo), an appointment or engagement to meet at a fixed place or time; meeting by agreement. (French)

**ricochet** (RIK uh SHAY), the skipping or jumping motion of an object as it goes along a flat surface. (French)

**rigor mortis** (RIG uhr MOHR tis), the stiffening of the muscles after death, caused by the accumulation of metabolic products, especially lactic acid, in the muscles. (Latin)

**rodeo** (ROE day oh), a contest or exhibition of skill in roping cattle, riding horses, and similar types of ranch-related activities. (Spanish)

**roulette** (roo LET), a gambling game in which the players bet on the turn of a wheel. (French)

**sarcophagus** (sahr KOF uh guhs), a stone coffin, especially one ornamented with sculptures or bearing inscriptions. (Greek)

**sauerkraut** (SOUR krout), cabbage cut fine, salted, and allowed to ferment. (German)

**schlemiel** (shluh MEEL), a clumsy person; bungler; gullible fool. (Yiddish)

**seance** (SAY ahns), a meeting of people trying to communicate with spirits of the dead by the help of a medium. (French)

**shaman** (SHAH muhn), a priest or medicine man. (Tungusic)

**slalom** (SLAH lum), in skiing, a zigzag race downhill. (Norwegian)

**solo** (SOE loe), a piece of music for one voice or instrument. (Italian)

**studio** (STOO de oh), the workroom of a painter, sculptor, photographer, or other artist. (Italian)

**subpoena** (suh PEE nuh), an official written order commanding a person to appear in court. (Latin)

**tempera** (TEM pur uh), a method of painting in which colors are mixed with white or yolk of egg, the whole egg, or other substances instead of oil. (Italian)

**toreador** (TAWR ee a dawr), a bullfighter, especially one mounted on a horse. (Spanish)

**trauma** (TRAW muh), 1. a physical wound; injury. 2. an unpleasant experience that affects the mind or nerves, inducing hysteria or the like. (Greek)

**trio** (TREE oh), a composition for three voices or instruments. (Italian)

**trivia** (TRIV ee uh), things of little or no importance; trifles. (Latin)

**tympani** (TIM puh nee), a drum, especially a kettledrum. (Latin)

**ukulele** (YOO kuh LAY lee), a small guitar having four strings. (Hawaiian)

**verbatim** (vur BAY tim), word for word; in exactly the same words. (Latin)

**vertigo** (VUR tuh goh), an abnormal condition characterized by a feeling that the person, or the objects around one, are whirling in space, and by a tendency to lose equilibrium and consciousness; dizziness; giddiness. (Latin)

**vignette** (vin YET), a literary sketch; short verbal description. (French)

**vodka** (VOD kuh), an alcoholic liquor, distilled from rye, barley, wheat, potatoes, or other substances. (Russian)

**wanderlust** (WAHN dur lust), a strong desire to wander. (German)

**xenophobia** (ZEN un FOE bee uh), a hatred or fear of foreign persons or things. (Greek)

**yang** (yang), the beneficial element in Chinese dualistic philosophy, representing the male qualities of goodness, light, and the earth. (Chinese)

# Words that have changed with time

Words are the symbols with which you communicate. A common knowledge of these symbols makes it possible for you to tell others what you think and to make yourself understood. But the words themselves are only symbols. The meanings of these symbols may change.

The meaning of words sometimes changes with the passage of time. In some instances, a word takes on a broader meaning than it had originally. *Town*, from the Old English *tun*, once meant any enclosure. It referred to the time in history when a group of people built a wall or fence around their collective buildings to protect themselves from strangers and wild beasts. *Town* now means a large group of houses and other buildings, smaller than a city but larger than a village.

Similarly, the word *demon* is from the Greek word *daimon* and originally meant divinity, or a divine thing. Christian writers changed the meaning to that of a thing of evil, and this is the sense in which the word is used today.

Some words, along with their original meanings, are listed in column A. Column B lists the present meaning of each word. Match the original meaning or meanings of each word to its present meaning or meanings. Please do not write in this book, but place your answers on a separate sheet of paper. Answers are given on page 43.

**Example:**

30. rumor—a great uproar

a. thunderstorm
b. news without proof
c. an assembly hall

**Answer:**

30.   b. news without proof

---

## A

1. rummage—to stow cargo in the hold of a ship
2. senate—a gathering of old men
3. infant—not speaking
4. comrade—roommate
5. pretty—tricky, crafty
6. nice—stupid, ignorant
7. school—leisure
8. companion—one who shares his bread with another
9. carpenter—a carriage maker
10. garble—to sift spices
11. hospital—a place where travelers are entertained and sheltered
12. plunder—household goods
13. measles—wretch
14. umbrage—a shadowy outline
15. rival—one who uses the same stream
16. risk—to skirt the cliffs while sailing
17. silly—rustic, happy, innocent
18. chimney—furnace, oven
19. handsome—easy to handle
20. foyer—fireplace
21. villain—a farm hand
22. cunning—skillful, knowing
23. sarcasm—act of stripping the flesh
24. stomach—throat or gullet
25. explode—to drive out by clapping the hands

## B

a. a very young child
b. agreeable, pleasing
c. to search thoroughly by moving things about
d resentment
e. making fun of a person to hurt his or her feelings
f. to rob by force
g. an entrance hall
h. the legislative assembly of a state or nation
i. danger, chance of harm
j. a friend
k. competitor
l. pleasing in appearance
m. pleasing, dainty
n. a place for teaching and learning
o. a very wicked person, a scoundrel
p. clever in a deceitful way
q. one who goes along with another
r. a virus disease
s. structure connected with fireplace to carry away smoke
t. one who builds or repairs with wood
u. distort meaning by scrambling words
v. a place where the sick are cared for
w. without sense or reason
x. in humans, the saclike dilation of the alimentary canal occupying the upper part of the left side of the abdomen
y. to blow up, burst with a loud noise

# We all use slang

People form groups because they share the same interests or are engaged in the same occupations, trades, or professions. Very often such people invent words and put together phrases that are unfamiliar to those outside the particular group. These special words and phrases are sometimes called jargon and sometimes called slang.

Jargon is language made up of names and expressions referring to a special line of work. For example, journalists speak of "side-bars" (explanatory additions to main stories), "kickers" (eye-catching headlines), and "putting the paper to bed" (getting it to the printing press). Slang is much wider in scope. It usually starts with a special group but may be used by anyone because slang often appeals to many segments of the population.

Teen-agers, soldiers, sailors, and show people are among the groups that contribute to this special language. They invent slang because they feel it expresses their ideas better than the words that already exist in standard language. They also give words in standard language new meanings. Words that are understood and accepted by the majority of people speaking a language and that are used in formal speech and writing are called standard language.

English slang is believed to have begun more than 900 years ago. Many slang words used then have disappeared. But year after year such words appear and disappear, because special groups are always looking for fresh ways to say the same thing. When the general public favors slang words over those already in standard English, the slang words sometimes become a part of informal or even standard usage.

Slang often helps to "break the ice" more easily than standard language can. It creates a sense of belonging among members of a group. It excludes outsiders and brings those in the "in-group" closer together. Slang is like a special pass. When too many people have access to it, another way to say the same thing has to be invented. That is why there are so many slang words for the same thing. For example, an unpopular person is called a *creep, drag, square,* or *turkey.* It is not always the word but the way in which it is used that makes it slang.

There are exceptions, but slang runs the risk of becoming outdated. Certain slang words that were popular among teen-agers a few years ago may be unintelligible to teen-agers now. Other slang words have continued to mean the same thing year after year.

The American poet Carl Sandburg once said that slang is "language that takes off its coat, spits on its hands, and goes to work." G. K. Chesterton, the English author, says, "All slang is metaphor, and all metaphor is poetry."

Whether as working language or poetry, slang always has been a part of language and will probably continue to be as long as people use words and imagination to express their thoughts.

Column A lists slang terms and expressions, some of which were once popular and others of which are still popular. Column B lists a definition for each term or expression. Can you match each slang term or expression in column A with its definition in column B? Please do not write in this book, but place your answers on a separate sheet of paper. Answers are given on page 43.

**Example:**

15. cool

a. reserved, detached
b. a problem to be solved

**Answer:**

15.    a. reserved, detached

| A | B |
|---|---|
| 1. hooligan | a.  snob, snub |
| 2. off the cob | b.  naive, sentimental |
| 3. natty | c.  tell someone the facts |
| 4. Harvest it! | d.  tough guy |
| 5. set straight | e.  retort to a bad joke |
| 6. cooking on the front burner | f.  give unwanted advice |
| 7. jaywalk | g.  stylish, neat |
| 8. Jackson | h.  doing very well |
| 9. high-hat | i.  cross street against traffic rules |
| 10. kibitz | j.  all-around popular boy. |

# What's in a name?

Many of the words that you use every day come from the proper names of persons or places. Do you think you could recognize some of these words that are also proper names? The exercise that follows will help you to discover some often used English words that are also proper names.

Each entry under column A describes a person or place and gives the meaning of the word derived from the name of that person or place. Each entry under column B lists an English word that has been derived from a proper name. Match each entry in column A with the correct word from column B. Please do not write in this book, but place your answers on a separate sheet of paper. Answers are given on page 43.

**Example:**

20. Dame Nellie ————, an opera singer, liked her toast sliced thin and evenly browned. This toast now bears her name.

a. Mrs. Malaprop—malapropism
b. Kameryk—cambric
c. Melba—melba toast

**Answer:**

20.   c. melba—melba toast

---

## A

1. Samuel ————, a Texas cattleman, refused to brand his cattle. Now his name is used to describe anyone who is unconventional.
2. Thomas More gave this name to a novel he wrote about an ideal city with perfect laws. The name is used to describe any ideal state or country.
3. A humorous five-line verse gets its name from this Irish county.
4. This device lifts and moves heavy objects. It gets its name from a hangman of the 1600's.
5. A word meaning to refuse to buy or use a product or a device is named for Captain ————, an English landlord over Irish tenants.
6. A county in England gave its name to this four-wheeled vehicle with two seats facing inward.
7. Nicholas ———— was an old soldier who admired Napoleon. He is responsible for a word that describes any person with a blind enthusiasm for his country's military glory.
8. An early method of photography in which pictures were made on silvered metal plates that were sensitive to light was invented by Louis ————. Certain types of photographs still bear his name.

9. Henry ————, an English army officer, invented an artillery shell that explodes in the air and scatters pellets over a wide area.
10. Jerez, Spain, once called Xeres, was mispronounced and thus gave its name to a wine which varies in color from pale yellow to dark brown.
11. Gabriel D. ————, a physicist, invented a scale for measuring temperature.
12. Mrs. ————, a character in a play, was noted for her ridiculous misuse of words. By adding *ism* to her name, a word meaning the misuse of words became part of the English language.
13. Blue jeans and levis are made from this heavy, coarse cloth named for a town in France.
14. Meaning to follow a winding course, this word comes from the name of a winding river in Caria, Asia Minor.
15. A brave French general, Marquis de ————, helped the Americans during the Revolution. A small, edible fish found on the East Coast is his namesake.

## B

a. Derrick—derrick
b. Xeres—sherry
c. Shrapnel—shrapnel
d. Utopia—utopian
e. Surrey—surrey

f. Lafayette—lafayette
g. Limerick—limerick
h. Maverick—maverick
i. Meander River— meander

j. Mrs. Malaprop— malapropism
k. Daguerre— daguerreotype
l. Boycott—boycott

m. Chauvin—chauvinist
n. Fahrenheit— Fahrenheit
o. Nimes—denim

# Words from special fields

Professions and occupations add new words to the English language. Such words sometimes become part of general usage. And often such words acquire meanings that are far removed from their original meanings.

Each word in column A began as a specialized term in some specific profession or occupation. Each word is listed with the general meaning that it has acquired. Column B contains a list of specialized meanings. Can you match each term and its general meaning in column A with one of the specialized meanings in column B? Please do not write in this book, but place your answers on a separate sheet of paper. Answers are given on page 43.

**Example:**

10. fifth column—traitors within a country

a. fit a particular object
b. Franco sympathizers during the Spanish Civil War

**Answer:**

10.   b. Franco sympathizers during the Spanish Civil War

---

**A**

1. blueprint—a detailed part of any enterprise
2. satellite—a subservient follower
3. face-lift—make superficial improvements
4. backlash—sudden unfavorable reaction
5. stereotype—any fixed form or image
6. gamut—the whole range of anything
7. niche—particular place or position
8. streamline—make more efficient

**B**

a. remove wrinkles by surgery
b. jarring reaction or movement backwards in a machine
c. photographic print of plan or map with either blue lines on white paper or white lines on blue paper
d. a method in which a plate is made from a mold
e. all the notes on a musical scale
f. a heavenly body revolving around a planet
g. motion free from disturbance
h. recess or hollow in wall

---

# Idioms from special fields

Many of the expressions and phrases that you use in everyday conversation are idioms. An idiom is an expression or phrase that has acquired a meaning different from the ordinary meaning of the words that form the idiom.

Idioms usually begin as straightforward descriptions of some phase of a specific occupation or profession. In time, many idioms achieve wider usage.

In many cases, the origin of an idiom is no longer certain. For example, according to some authorities, the idiom "go to pot" is the result of the blacksmiths' practice of keeping a special pot in which unusable pieces of metal were thrown. Other authorities claim that the idiom stems from the cooks' practice of throwing leftover pieces of meat into a soup pot.

The exercise that follows will help you to discover the origin of some commonly used idioms. Each entry in column A is a story that describes the origin of an idiom. Each story also makes some reference to an occupation or a profession. Column B is a list of familiar idioms. Can you match the entries in column A to the idioms in column B? Please do not write in this book, but place your answers on a separate sheet of paper. Answers are given on page 43.

**Example:**

15. In World War I, soldiers used this expression to communicate the fact that the fighting was in a lull. Now it is used generally to describe a situation of peace and calmness.

a. mum's the word
b. all quiet on the Western front

**Answer:**

15.   b. all quiet on the Western front

## A

1. In the days when pirate ships roamed the high seas, they would pretend to be legitimate ships by hoisting the flag of a friendly nation on the masthead. This would lure unsuspecting ships close enough for the pirate ships to attack them. The idiom that comes from this story refers to anyone who gives the impression of being something he or she is not.
2. This device, similar to a hand grenade, was once used by soldiers to make a breach in a wall so that invading armies could enter a city. The device was so poorly constructed that more often than not the soldier hurling the device was blown up with the wall. We now use the idiom to describe anyone caught in his own trap.
3. Over a long period, the mercury used in making felt hats had a poisonous effect on the hatter. He or she would be afflicted with uncontrollable twitching of muscles. People seeing this would think the victim was insane. The idiom describes anyone we think eccentric.
4. Sailors on early sailing vessels used a variety of ropes to manipulate the sails. For the sails to function efficiently, a sailor had to be sure of the use for each rope. Now the idiom means to be familiar with all details.
5. The parallel lines that run the length of the growth of the tree are called the grain. Sawing or planing against these lines causes snags and splinters. The idiom is used to describe something as contrary to our principles.
6. Before the use of street lights, a servant carried a candle to light the master's way along dark streets. The only skill required for the job was to know the way. The idiom is used to compare the abilities of two people.
7. A chip of stone has all the characteristics of the original block. The idiom means a child who is very much like his or her parents.
8. When President Franklin D. Roosevelt surrounded himself with a group of advisers to help him in his election campaign, this idiom came into being. Now the idiom is used to refer to any informal group of experts.
9. A fish that is very hungry will swallow not only the bait, but the line and the hook as well. The idiom now refers to an extremely gullible person.
10. In order to see a parade from a good spot, children would race ahead of the band leading the parade. The idiom is used to express any achievement.

## B

a. hoist with one's own petard
b. know the ropes
c. mad as a hatter
d. sail under false colors
e. beat the band

f. swallow hook, line, and sinker
g. hold a candle to
h. brain trust
i. against the grain
j. chip off the old block

---

# Idioms from animals and foods

Idioms lend color and humor to language. From ancient times and in almost every known language, idioms have been used to say one thing while meaning something entirely different.

At one time or another, idioms have been based on almost every imaginable subject. Two popular categories of idioms are those that have some connection with food or animals.

Each entry under column A is the story of how a particular idiom came into being. Column B contains a list of idioms. Can you match each story from column A with the correct idiom from column B? Please do not write in this book, but

place your answers on a separate sheet of paper. Answers are given on page 43.

**Example:**

15. There is one type of dog that seems to smell food faster than other dogs and, thus, always gets more to eat than others. This term is now used to describe any person who eats a lot.

a. chowhound
b. Chihuahua

**Answer:**

15. a. chowhound

**A**

1. Once in Dunmow, England, any man who could swear that he had not quarreled with his wife for a year and a day or had not wished himself unmarried was awarded a side of bacon. The idiom that comes from this custom means to support your family.
2. It was once a description of an antidote for poison. Later it described something that made food taste better. The idiom is used to warn one against believing everything without question.
3. This animal is an excellent actor. When captured or in danger, it remains motionless, pretending to be dead. The idiom based on the animal's behavior means to pretend ignorance or illness.
4. In Chicago in the late 1800's and early 1900's, a lame horse drew a roller around the White Sox Ball Park. The name that baseball fans gave the horse is now used to describe stiff muscles.
5. Actors once used the fat from the upper part of a pig's hind leg to remove heavy makeup. The idiom that originated in this practice is now used to describe all third-rate performers.
6. The ancient Romans used beans instead of hay as fodder. Horses thrived on this diet. The idiom is used to describe anyone who is lively and healthy.
7. This expression was once used to describe any race horse about which nothing was known. It is now used as a name for a candidate for political office about whom little is known—or whose chances for success seem very limited.
8. One legend says that the great Hindu hero Prithu assumed the form of a cow in order to make his subjects raise edible vegetables. Not knowing which cow he was, the people worshiped all cows. The idiom that grew out of this legend now means anyone or anything that is beyond criticism.
9. For deep-sea fishing, live fish are cut up in chunks and used as bait. The job of cutting the fish is extremely unpleasant. It is usually given to the member of the crew who has not performed other duties satisfactorily. This idiom now means to take action or a political stand or risk the consequences.
10. This idiom comes from the story about a foolish shepherd boy. He was told to cry for help when his flock was in danger. As a joke, the boy cried for help when he was not in danger. He did this so often that when he was in actual danger, he was ignored. Now the idiom means that if you lie too often no one will believe you when you tell the truth.

**B**

a. dark horse
b. to be full of beans
c. play possum
d. charley horse
e. hams
f. fish or cut bait
g. sacred cow
h. bring home the bacon
i. cry wolf
j. take with a grain of salt

# Idioms from old customs

An idiom often remains part of informal language long after the situation that created the idiom has ceased to exist. For example, wealthy people are no longer driven around in private carriages drawn by horses. Yet the idiom "carriage trade" is still used to describe the society elite.

In the list that follows, each entry under column A defines an idiom and describes the old custom that originally gave rise to the idiom. Column B consists of a list of idioms. Can you match the idioms in column B with the customs in column A? Answers are given on page 43.

**Example:**

14. Be discharged for incompetence: This came from the old vaudeville days when bad acts were pulled off the stage with a special instrument.

a. get the hook
b. burn the midnight oil

**Answer:**

14. a. get the hook

## A

1. To be the center of attention: This relates to the stage lighting once used in theaters.
2. A decisive, critical test of something: The idiom came from the days when a substance was tested with nitric acid to see whether it contained gold.
3. To work or study late at night: People did this before electricity was discovered.
4. To accomplish by any means: Tenant farmers were allowed to gather as much firewood as they could reach with these instruments.
5. To be so satisfied with success that we no longer try hard: The ancient Greeks crowned the winners of contests with wreathes of this plant.
6. Excessive concern with petty detail: Documents were tied with this.
7. Another name for rumor or gossip: In the old days, sailors would gather around this lidded cask of water to exchange stories.
8. To lower the pride of: This idiom alludes to the small bolt of wood or metal that was used to raise or lower a ship's flag.
9. To be duped: This originated in the 1600's to describe one easily deceived in a game of snipehunt.
10. Kept from learning about a situation: This idiom is said to come from the old practice of confining the insane to dark rooms.

## B

a. kept in the dark
b. burning the midnight oil
c. scuttlebutt
d. left holding the bag
e. to take down a peg or two
f. by hook or by crook
g. in the limelight
h. acid test
i. to rest on one's laurels
j. red tape

# Acronyms

Scientific discoveries, political parties, and organizations such as charitable institutions and government agencies may have titles that are not only difficult to remember, but also too long and clumsy for daily use. Often the first letter of every word in a title, or parts of words in a title, are combined for easier identification. The new word that results is called an acronym.

The exercise that follows deals with acronyms. The title or definition from which the acronym has been formed is given. Can you identify the acronym?

Please do not write in this book, but place your answers on a separate sheet of paper. Answers are given on page 43.

**Example:**

20. National Association of Stock Car Racing

**Answer:**

20. NASCAR

1. Congress of Racial Equality (_____)
2. gunfire from an anti-aircraft cannon (German: Flieger abwehr kanone) (_____)
3. National Aeronautics and Space Administration (_____)
4. a positive electron (_____)
5. intelligence quotient (___)
6. Federal National Mortgage Association (_____ ____)
7. light amplification by stimulated emission of radiation (_____)
8. absent without leave (_____)
9. radio detecting and ranging (_____)
10. situation normal all fouled up (_____)
11. self-contained underwater breathing apparatus (_____)
12. Strategic Air Command (____)
13. Cooperative for American Remittances to Everywhere (_____)
14. Volunteers in Service to America (_____)
15. a member of the Women's Army Corps (____)
16. microwave amplification by stimulated emission of radiation (_____)

# Unit 1, Section 4 answer key

## English words from other languages
**Page 30**

1. strife (German)
2. tycoon (Japanese, Chinese)
3. uncanny (Scottish)
4. aplomb (French)
5. chocolate (Mexican-Spanish)
6. achieved (French)
7. status (Latin)
8. entry (French)
9. glittering (Scandinavian)
10. society (French)
11. dilettante (French)
12. purchase (French)
13. example (French)
14. gazette (French, Italian)
15. pale (French)

**Page 31**

| | | |
|---|---|---|
| 1. l. | 6. c. | 11. e. |
| 2. h. | 7. j. | 12. i. |
| 3. k. | 8. d. | 13. o. |
| 4. g. | 9. a. | 14. b. |
| 5. m. | 10. n. | 15. f. |

## Words that have changed with time
**Page 36**

| | | |
|---|---|---|
| 1. c. | 10. u. | 19. l. |
| 2. h. | 11. v. | 20. g. |
| 3. a. | 12. f. | 21. o. |
| 4. j. | 13. r. | 22. p. |
| 5. m. | 14. d. | 23. e. |
| 6. b. | 15. k. | 24. x. |
| 7. n. | 16. i. | 25. y. |
| 8. q. | 17. w. | |
| 9. t. | 18. s. | |

## We all use slang
**Page 37**

| | | |
|---|---|---|
| 1. d. | 5. c. | 8. j |
| 2. b. | 6. h. | 9. g. |
| 3. g. | 7. i. | 10. f. |
| 4. e. | | |

## What's in a name
**Page 38**

| | | |
|---|---|---|
| 1. h. | 6. e. | 11. n. |
| 2. d. | 7. m. | 12. j. |
| 3. g. | 8. k. | 13. o. |
| 4. a. | 9. c. | 14. i. |
| 5. l. | 10. b. | 15. f. |

## Words from special fields
**Page 39**

| | | |
|---|---|---|
| 1. c. | 4. b. | 7. h. |
| 2. f. | 5. d. | 8. g. |
| 3. a. | 6. e. | |

## Idioms from special fields
**Page 39**

| | | |
|---|---|---|
| 1. d. | 5. i. | 8. h |
| 2. a. | 6. g. | 9. f. |
| 3. c. | 7. j. | 10. e |
| 4. b. | | |

## Idioms from animals and foods
**Page 40**

| | | |
|---|---|---|
| 1. h. | 5. e. | 8. g. |
| 2. j. | 6. b. | 9. f. |
| 3. c. | 7. a. | 10. i. |
| 4. d. | | |

## Idioms from old customs
**Page 41**

| | | |
|---|---|---|
| 1. g. | 5. i. | 8. e. |
| 2. h. | 6. j. | 9. d. |
| 3. b. | 7. c. | 10. a. |
| 4. f. | | |

## Acronyms
**Page 42**

| | | |
|---|---|---|
| 1. CORE | 7. laser | 12. SAC |
| 2. flak | 8. AWOL | 13. CARE |
| 3. NASA | 9. radar | 14. VISTA |
| 4. positron | 10. snafu | 15. WAC |
| 5. IQ | 11. scuba | 16. maser |
| 6. Fannie Mae | | |

# Basic information about mathematics

2

What is your most difficult school subject to understand? If you are like most students, you will probably answer "math." More students have trouble with math than with any other subject. This is because math is a cumulative subject. Previously learned math skills are the foundation on which new skills are built. If you fail to understand some math skill today, this will keep you from understanding a new math skill tomorrow.

This unit will help you to "firm-up" your foundation of math skills. It will help you to review skills you should already understand. And it will help you to understand additional math skills as you are taught them.

# 1. Reviewing arithmetic

You may want to begin by reviewing four basic arithmetic operations—addition, subtraction, multiplication, and division—and their uses.

## Whole numbers

Addition of whole numbers can be done horizontally or vertically. For example:

$$4 + 19 + 36 = 59$$

$$\begin{array}{r} 2579 \\ 346 \\ + 83 \\ \hline 3008 \end{array}$$

When columns are used, the "ones" digits must be aligned, as must the "tens" digits, the "hundreds" digits, and so on. The individual numbers are called *addends* and the answer is called the *sum*.

Addition is defined for only two numbers at a time. So, to add 5 and 7 and 9 you could

1   add 5 and 7 first
    (5 + 7) + 9
       12 + 9
         21

2   add 7 and 9 first
    5 + (7 + 9)
       5 + 16
         21

3   add 5 and 9 first
    (5 + 9) + 7
       14 + 7
         21

If two whole numbers are added, the sum is always a whole number.

Subtraction of whole numbers is also defined only for pairs of whole numbers. Subtraction can be done horizontally or vertically. For example:

$$16 - 7 = 9$$

$$\begin{array}{r} 16 \\ - 7 \\ \hline 9 \end{array}$$

The number from which an amount is subtracted is called the *minuend,* the number being subtracted is called the *subtrahend,* and the answer is called the *difference.*

Sometimes when subtracting it is necessary to "borrow." Thus to perform the calculation

$$\begin{array}{r} 482 \\ - 153 \\ \hline 329 \end{array}$$

you must borrow 10 from the 8 "tens" in the minuend and add the 10 to 2. Then you can subtract 3 from 12. When you borrowed in the example above, you really were thinking of 482 as

$$400 + 80 + 2 \text{ or } 4(100) + 8(10) + 2$$

and then as

$$4(100) + 7(10) + 12$$

to make the subtraction possible. The following example shows a mechanical way to do this.

**Example:** Subtract 297 from 534.

**Solution:** The minuend is 534 and the subtrahend is 297. Rewrite the problem as shown below.

$$\begin{array}{rl} 534 & \text{minuend} \\ - 297 & \text{subtrahend} \end{array}$$

To subtract, it is necessary to borrow twice. To show the borrowing, you cross out the number from which you borrowed in each case.

$$\begin{array}{r} 42 \\ 5\cancel{3}\cancel{4} \\ - 297 \\ \hline 237 \end{array}$$

The difference is 237.

Subtraction of whole numbers is possible only

when the minuend *is greater than* the subtrahend.

Multiplication of whole numbers can be thought of as "shorthand" addition. For instance,

$$2 + 2 + 2 + 2 + 2 = 5(2) = 10.$$

Numbers can be multiplied horizontally or vertically. For example:

$$7 \cdot 3 = 21 \qquad \begin{array}{r} 7 \\ \times\, 3 \\ \hline 21 \end{array}$$

The numbers being multiplied are called *factors* and the answer is called the *product.* If one of the factors has more than one digit, the multiplication is usually done vertically. In problems of this sort, the factor with the greatest number of digits is written first.

**Example:** Multiply 57 and 6.

**Solution:** Rewrite the problem as shown below.

$$\begin{array}{r} 57 \\ \times\, 6 \\ \hline \end{array}$$

To find the product:

$$\begin{array}{r} 4 \\ 57 \\ \times\, 6 \\ \hline 2 \end{array}$$ 1. Multiply 6 and 7. The result is 42. Write down the 2 below the line under the 6 and "carry" the 4.

$$\begin{array}{r} 57 \\ \times\, 6 \\ \hline 342 \end{array}$$ 2. Multiply 6 and 5. The result is 30. Add 4 and record 34 to the left of 2.

The product is 342.

When one of two factors in a multiplication problem has one digit, the product can usually be found mentally. However, the procedure becomes more involved as the number of digits increases. For example:

$$\begin{array}{r} 38 \\ \times\, 42 \\ \hline 76 \\ 152 \\ \hline 1596 \end{array}$$ first partial product
second partial product
product

In problems of this kind, each partial product is obtained by multiplying a factor with more than one digit and a single digit factor. Each time, the right-most digit of the partial product is recorded in the *same* column as the single-digit multiplier.

Zeros in multiplication may appear troublesome.

**Example:** Multiply 327 and 400.

**Solution:** The factors are 327 and 400. The computation is simplified if you rewrite the problem as

$$\begin{array}{r} 327 \\ \times\, 400 \\ \hline 130800 \end{array} \quad \text{rather than} \quad \begin{array}{r} 400 \\ 327 \\ \hline \end{array} \quad \text{or} \quad \begin{array}{r} 327 \\ 400 \\ \hline \end{array}$$

The product is 130,800.

**Example:** Find the product of 547 and 309.

**Solution:** The factors are 547 and 309. To simplify the computation, rewrite the problem as

$$\begin{array}{r} 547 \\ \times\, 309 \\ \hline 4923 \\ (000) \\ 1641 \\ \hline 169023 \end{array} \quad \text{instead of} \quad \begin{array}{r} 309 \\ \times\, 547 \\ \hline 2163 \\ 1236 \\ 1545 \\ \hline 169023 \end{array}$$

The product is 169,023.

Division is another operation used for pairs of whole numbers. Division may be done horizontally or vertically. For example:

$$20 \div 4 = 5 \qquad 4\overline{)20} \;\; {}^{5}$$

The number being divided is called the *dividend,* the number by which the dividend is divided is called the *divisor,* and the answer is called the *quotient.*

Sometimes when dividing with whole numbers, the quotient is not a whole number. In such cases, there is a remainder.

$$\text{divisor}\;\; 7\overline{)31}\;\;{}^{4} \quad \text{quotient} \atop \text{dividend}$$
$$\underline{28}$$
$$3 \quad \text{remainder}$$

If the divisor has a single digit and the dividend has several digits, we use a procedure called *long division* to find the quotient.

**Example:** Divide 1,579 by 6.

**Solution:** The dividend is 1,579 and the divisor is 6. You can rewrite the problem as $6\overline{)1579}$

You begin by selecting a *trial divisor.* In this case, the trial divisor is some whole number $x$ such that 6 times $x$ is less than or equal to 15. There are three numbers you could use: 0, 1, and 2. If you use 0, you have made no progress at all. If you use 1,

$$\begin{array}{r} 1 \\ 6\overline{)1579} \\ \underline{6} \\ 9 \end{array} \quad \begin{array}{l} 6 \times 1 = 6 \quad \text{product} \\ 15 - 6 = 9 \quad \text{difference} \end{array}$$

the difference is greater than the divisor. This will not

work. Instead, use 2 as the first digit of the quotient.

$$
\begin{array}{r}
2 \\
6{\overline{\smash{\big)}\,1579}} \\
\underline{12} \\
3
\end{array}
$$

$6 \times 2 = 12$   product
$15 - 12 = 3$   difference

Next, you "bring down" the third digit (the "tens" digit) of the dividend. You then consider 37 as the new dividend and repeat the "trial divisor—product—difference" procedure.
Think: $6 \times 6 = 36$ and 36 is less than 37.
Write: 6 as the next digit of the quotient.

$$
\begin{array}{r}
26 \\
6{\overline{\smash{\big)}\,1579}} \\
\underline{12} \\
37 \\
\underline{36} \\
1
\end{array}
$$

$6 \times 6 = 36$   product
$37 - 36 = 1$   difference

Finally, you bring down the last digit (the "ones" digit) of the dividend, consider 19 as the new dividend, and again repeat the procedure.
Think: $6 \times 3 = 18$ and 18 is less than 19.
Write: 3 as the next digit of the quotient.

$$
\begin{array}{r}
263 \\
6{\overline{\smash{\big)}\,1579}} \\
\underline{12} \\
37 \\
\underline{36} \\
19 \\
\underline{18} \\
1
\end{array}
$$

$6 \times 3 = 18$   product
$19 - 18 = 1$   difference

Since there are no other digits in the dividend, the final difference is the remainder. The quotient is 263 and the remainder is 1.

As your skill increases, you will be able to find such quotients without showing products or differences. However, if the divisor has more than one digit and the dividend has several digits, it is always advisable to write the steps.

# Fractions

A fraction is an expression that represents the quotient of two numbers. For example, the fraction $\frac{5}{7}$ is the equivalent of the quotient of $5 \div 7$. In fractions, the dividend is called the *numerator* and the divisor is called the *denominator*. If the numerator is less than the denominator, the fraction is said to be a *proper* fraction. If the numerator is greater than the denominator, the fraction is said to be an *improper* fraction.

| proper fraction | improper fraction |
|---|---|
| $\frac{2}{3}$ numerator denominator | $\frac{5}{4}$ numerator denominator |

The sum of a whole number and a fraction is called a *mixed* number; e.g., $3 + \frac{2}{5}$ or $3\frac{2}{5}$. Mixed numbers are usually written without the plus sign, but it is important to remember that every mixed number can be replaced with a sum. Mixed numbers can be changed to improper fractions as shown below.

mixed number          improper fraction

$$
3\frac{2}{5} = \frac{5 \cdot 3 + 2}{5} = \frac{15 + 2}{5} = \frac{17}{5}
$$

Notice that the "new" numerator is obtained by adding the original numerator to the product of the denominator and the whole number. But the "new" denominator remains the same as the original denominator. To compute with fractions, it is important to be able to change from mixed numbers to improper fractions quickly.

## Simplifying fractions

If the numerator and denominator of a proper fraction have no common factors (other than 1) the fraction is said to be in "lowest" terms or in "simplest" form. The following fractions are in lowest terms:

$$
\frac{2}{3} \qquad \frac{4}{5} \qquad \frac{9}{11}
$$

In mathematics, if two numbers have no common factors other than 1, you describe the numbers as *relatively prime.* In each of the fractions above, the numerator and denominator are relatively prime.

If the numerator and denominator of a proper fraction have common factors, they are not in lowest terms. The following fractions are not in lowest terms:

$$
\frac{6}{8} \qquad \frac{16}{20} \qquad \frac{24}{36}
$$

To rewrite a fraction in lowest terms:
1. find a common factor;
2. divide both the numerator and denominator by the common factor; and
3. continue in this way until the numerator and denominator are relatively prime.

**Example:** Rewrite (**a**) $\frac{6}{8}$ and (**b**) $\frac{18}{30}$ in simplest form.

**Solution:**

(**a**) Since $6 = 3 \cdot 2$ and $8 = 4 \cdot 2$, 2 is a common factor of 6 and 8. To simplify $\frac{6}{8}$, you divide both 6 and 8 by 2.

$$
\frac{6 \div 2}{8 \div 2} = \frac{3}{4}
$$

Notice that 3 and 4 are relatively prime. Therefore, $\frac{6}{8}$ in simplest form is $\frac{3}{4}$.

**(b)** Since $18 = 9 \cdot 2$ and $30 = 15 \cdot 2$, 2 is a common factor of 18 and 30. To simplify $\frac{18}{30}$, you divide both 18 and 30 by 2.

$$\frac{18 \div 2}{30 \div 2} = \frac{9}{15}$$

Since $9 = 3 \cdot 3$ and $15 = 5 \cdot 3$, 3 is a common factor of 9 and 15. To simplify $\frac{9}{15}$, you divide both 9 and 15 by 3.

$$\frac{9 \div 3}{15 \div 3} = \frac{3}{5}$$

The numbers 3 and 5 are relatively prime. Therefore, $\frac{18}{30}$ in simplest form is $\frac{3}{5}$.

You could have rewritten $\frac{18}{30}$ in simplest form in one step if you had divided by the *greatest* common factor. In this case, the greatest common factor is 6.

$$\frac{18 \div 6}{30 \div 6} = \frac{3}{5}$$

Two fractions are equal if they have the same simplest form. For example,

$$\frac{6}{10} = \frac{21}{35} \quad \text{because} \quad \frac{6}{10} = \frac{6 \div 2}{10 \div 2} = \frac{3}{5}$$

$$\frac{21}{35} = \frac{21 \div 7}{35 \div 7} = \frac{3}{5}$$

You can also tell if two fractions are equal by "cross multiplying":

$$10 \cdot 21 = 210 \qquad \frac{6}{10} \diagdown \frac{21}{35}$$

$$6 \cdot 35 = 210$$

If two fractions are not equal, one is greater than (symbol >) the other. If both fractions have the same denominator, the one with the greater numerator is the greater fraction. Hence,

$$\frac{5}{16} > \frac{3}{16}$$

If both fractions have the same numerator, the one with the lesser denominator is the greater fraction. Hence,

$$\frac{7}{4} > \frac{7}{8}$$

If neither the denominators nor the numerators are equal, it is necessary to make the denominators equal to compare the fractions. This can be done by multiplying.

**Example:** Determine which fraction is greater,
$\frac{7}{17}$ or $\frac{11}{34}$.

**Solution:** You can make the denominator of $\frac{7}{17}$ equal to the denominator of $\frac{11}{34}$ if you multiply both the numerator and the denominator of $\frac{7}{17}$ by 2.

$$\frac{7}{17} = \frac{7 \cdot 2}{17 \cdot 2} = \frac{14}{34}$$

Now, $\frac{14}{34} > \frac{11}{34}$ because both denominators are 34 and $14 > 11$.

When using multiplication (or division) to rewrite a fraction, always multiply (or divide) *both* the numerator and the denominator by the *same* number.

## Multiplying fractions and mixed numbers

To multiply two (or more) fractions:
1. multiply the numerators to obtain the numerator of the product;
2. multiply the denominators to obtain the denominator of the product; and
3. rewrite the answer in simplest form.

**Example:** Multiply $\frac{4}{9}$ and $\frac{7}{8}$.

**Solution:** Rewrite the problem using symbols and multiply.

$$\frac{4}{9} \cdot \frac{7}{8} = \frac{4 \cdot 7}{9 \cdot 8} = \frac{28}{72}$$

Write $\frac{28}{72}$ in simplest form.

$$\frac{28 \div 4}{72 \div 4} = \frac{7}{18}$$

Sometimes when multiplying, it is possible to simplify before you obtain the product. To show that you are dividing the numerator and denominator by a number, the numerals are usually "crossed out." This procedure, called *cancellation*, is illustrated below.

$$\frac{4}{9} \cdot \frac{7}{8} = \frac{\overset{1}{\cancel{4}} \cdot 7}{9 \cdot \underset{2}{\cancel{8}}} = \frac{7}{18}$$

The numbers 4 and 8 were both divided by 4.

To multiply when mixed numbers are included:
1. rewrite the mixed numbers as improper fractions; and
2. use the procedure for multiplying fractions to find the product.

**Example:** Multiply $2\frac{1}{4}$ and $4\frac{5}{8}$.

**Solution:** Rewrite the problem using symbols.

$$\left(2\frac{1}{4}\right)\cdot\left(4\frac{5}{6}\right)$$

Replace each mixed number with its corresponding improper fraction and multiply.

$$\frac{9}{4}\cdot\frac{29}{6}=\frac{\overset{3}{\cancel{9}}}{4}\cdot\frac{29}{\underset{2}{\cancel{6}}}=\frac{87}{8}$$

Generally, when the product is an improper fraction, you rewrite the product as a mixed number. To do that, you simply divide the numerator by the denominator and write the remainder as a fraction. In simplest form, the product is $10\frac{7}{8}$.

## Dividing fractions and mixed numbers

Division of fractions is defined in terms of multiplication. To divide two fractions:

1. find the reciprocal of the divisor;
2. multiply the dividend and the reciprocal of the divisor; and
3. write the answer in simplest form.

The reciprocal of a fraction can be found by interchanging the numerator and the denominator of the fraction.

| fraction | reciprocal |
|----------|------------|
| $\frac{2}{5}$ | $\frac{5}{2}$ |

**Example:** Divide $\frac{5}{27}$ by $\frac{2}{3}$.

**Solution:** The dividend is $\frac{5}{27}$ and the divisor is $\frac{2}{3}$. Rewrite the problem using symbols.

$$\frac{5}{27}\div\frac{2}{3}$$

The reciprocal of $\frac{2}{3}$ is $\frac{3}{2}$. Rewrite the problem as a product and multiply.

$$\frac{5}{27}\cdot\frac{3}{2}=\frac{5\cdot\overset{1}{\cancel{3}}}{\underset{9}{\cancel{27}}\cdot 2}=\frac{5}{18}$$

Since 5 and 18 are relatively prime, the quotient in simplest form is $\frac{5}{18}$.

To divide when mixed numbers are included:

1. rewrite the mixed numbers as improper fractions; and
2. multiply the dividend by the reciprocal of the divisor to find the quotient.

**Example:** Divide $7\frac{1}{2}$ by $3\frac{1}{3}$.

**Solution:** The dividend is $7\frac{1}{2}$ and the divisor is $3\frac{1}{3}$. Rewrite the problem using symbols.

$$\left(7\frac{1}{2}\right)\div\left(3\frac{1}{3}\right)$$

Replace the mixed numbers with improper fractions.

$$\frac{15}{2}\div\frac{10}{3}$$

The reciprocal of $\frac{10}{3}$ is $\frac{3}{10}$. Rewrite the problem as a product and multiply.

$$\frac{15}{2}\cdot\frac{3}{10}=\frac{\overset{3}{\cancel{15}}\cdot 3}{2\cdot\underset{2}{\cancel{10}}}=\frac{9}{4}$$

In simplest form, the quotient is $2\frac{1}{4}$.

## Adding fractions and mixed numbers

If two fractions have the same denominator:

1. add the numerators to obtain the numerator of the sum;
2. write the common denominator as the denominator of the sum; and
3. rewrite the answer in simplest form.

**Example:** Add $\frac{5}{16}$ and $\frac{3}{16}$.

**Solution:** The denominators are the same. Rewrite the problem using symbols and add the numerators.

$$\frac{5}{16}+\frac{3}{16}=\frac{5+3}{16}=\frac{8}{16}$$

In simplest form, the sum of $\frac{5}{16}$ and $\frac{3}{16}$ is $\frac{1}{2}$.

If two fractions have different denominators:

1. multiply to make the denominators the same; and
2. apply the rule for adding fractions with the same denominator.

**Example:** Add $\frac{3}{5}$ and $\frac{4}{7}$.

**Solution:** The denominators are different. Rewrite the problem using symbols.

$$\frac{3}{5}+\frac{4}{7}$$

Since 5 and 7 have no common factors (except 1), you can find a common denominator by multiplying the two denominators. The common denominator is 35. Multiply to make both denominators equal to 35 and add.

$$\frac{3\cdot 7}{5\cdot 7}+\frac{4\cdot 5}{7\cdot 5}=\frac{21}{35}+\frac{20}{35}=\frac{21+20}{35}=\frac{41}{35}$$

In simplest form, the sum is $1\frac{6}{35}$.

When the denominators of two addends are not relatively prime, it is not advisable to choose the product of the two denominators as a common denominator. Instead, we look for the *least common denominator*.

**Example:** Add $\frac{5}{6}$ and $\frac{8}{15}$.

**Solution:** First, find the *greatest* common factor of 6 and 15.

$$6 = 2\cdot3 \qquad\qquad 15 = 3\cdot5$$
$$\text{prime factors} \qquad \text{prime factors}$$

The number 3 is in both lists; hence, 3 is the greatest common factor. The least common multiple of 6 and 15 can be found by dividing their product by their greatest common factor.

$$\frac{6\cdot15}{3} = 30$$

Since 30 is the least common multiple of 6 and 15, 30 is the least common denominator. Rewrite the problem using symbols.

$$\frac{5}{6} + \frac{8}{15}$$

Multiply to make both denominators equal to 30 and add.

$$\frac{5\cdot5}{6\cdot5} + \frac{8\cdot2}{15\cdot2} = \frac{25}{30} + \frac{16}{30} = \frac{25+16}{30} = \frac{41}{30}$$

In simplest form, the sum is $1\frac{11}{30}$.

To add when mixed numbers are included:
1. rewrite the mixed numbers as improper fractions; and
2. add the resulting improper fractions.

**Example:** Add $2\frac{1}{2}$ and $3\frac{2}{3}$.

**Solution:** Rewrite the problem using symbols.

$$2\frac{1}{2} + 3\frac{2}{3}$$

Replace the mixed numbers with improper fractions.

$$\frac{5}{2} + \frac{11}{3}$$

Since 2 and 3 are relatively prime, the least common denominator is their product, 6. Multiply to make both denominators equal to 6 and add.

$$\frac{5\cdot3}{2\cdot3} + \frac{11\cdot2}{3\cdot2} = \frac{15}{6} + \frac{22}{6} = \frac{15+22}{6} = \frac{37}{6}$$

In simplest form, the sum is $6\frac{1}{6}$.

## Subtracting fractions and mixed numbers

If two fractions have the same denominator:
1. subtract the numerator of the subtrahend from the numerator of the minuend to obtain the numerator of the difference;
2. write the common denominator as the denominator of the difference; and
3. rewrite the answer in simplest form.

**Example:** Subtract $\frac{3}{10}$ from $\frac{11}{10}$.

**Solution:** The minuend is $\frac{11}{10}$ and the subtrahend is $\frac{3}{10}$. Rewrite the problem using symbols and subtract.

$$\frac{11}{10} - \frac{3}{10} = \frac{11-3}{10} = \frac{8}{10}$$

In simplest form, the difference is $\frac{4}{5}$.

If two fractions have different denominators:
1. multiply to make the denominators the same; and
2. apply the rule for subtracting fractions with the same denominator.

**Example:** Subtract $\frac{3}{8}$ from $\frac{2}{3}$.

**Solution:** The minuend is $\frac{2}{3}$ and the subtrahend is $\frac{3}{8}$. Rewrite the problem using symbols.

$$\frac{2}{3} - \frac{3}{8}$$

Since 3 and 8 are relatively prime, the least common denominator is their product, 24. Multiply to make both denominators equal to 24 and subtract.

$$\frac{2\cdot8}{3\cdot8} - \frac{3\cdot3}{8\cdot3} = \frac{16-9}{24} = \frac{7}{24}$$

Since 7 and 24 are relatively prime, $\frac{7}{24}$ is in simplest form.

To subtract when mixed numbers are included:
1. rewrite the mixed numbers as improper fractions; and
2. subtract the resulting improper fractions.

**Example:** Subtract $2\frac{3}{5}$ from $7\frac{1}{2}$.

**Solution:** The minuend is $7\frac{1}{2}$ and the subtrahend is $2\frac{3}{5}$. Rewrite the problem using symbols.

$$7\frac{1}{2} - 2\frac{3}{5}$$

Replace the mixed numerals with improper fractions.

$$\frac{15}{2} - \frac{13}{5}$$

Since 2 and 5 are relatively prime, the least common denominator is 10. Multiply to make the denominators equal to 10 and subtract.

$$\frac{15\cdot5}{2\cdot5} - \frac{13\cdot2}{5\cdot2} = \frac{75}{10} - \frac{26}{10} = \frac{49}{10}$$

In simplest form, the difference is $4\frac{9}{10}$.

# Decimals

Our number system is a "positional" number system. This means that the position a numeral occupies indicates the "unit" it represents.

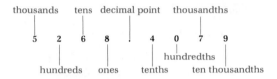

The decimal point always separates the whole-number part from the fractional part in a decimal number. The part of the decimal to the right of the decimal is sometimes called a *decimal fraction*.

The decimal 5,268.407 can be represented as

$$\underset{\text{unit}}{5(1,000)} + \underset{\text{unit}}{2(100)} + \underset{\text{unit}}{6(10)} + \underset{\text{unit}}{8(1)} + \underset{\text{unit}}{4\left(\frac{1}{10}\right)} + \underset{\text{unit}}{0\left(\frac{1}{100}\right)} + \underset{\text{unit}}{7\left(\frac{1}{1000}\right)}.$$

As you move from left to right, each unit is $\frac{1}{10}$ of the preceding unit. None can be omitted; a zero is used to indicate that there are no $\frac{1}{100}$ units in the decimal above.

## Adding decimals

To add decimals:

1. write the problem vertically, aligning the decimal points;
2. place a decimal point for the sum directly below those in the problem; and
3. add as you would for whole numbers.

This procedure assures that only units of the same kind will be added.

**Example:** Add 28.47, 7.062, and 135.9.

**Solution:** Rewrite the problem vertically, aligning the decimal points. Then place the decimal point for the sum and add.

$$\begin{array}{r} 28.47 \\ 7.062 \\ + \ 135.9 \\ \hline 171.432 \end{array}$$

## Subtracting decimals

To subtract decimals:

1. write the problem vertically, aligning the decimal points;
2. place a decimal point for the difference directly below those in the problem; and
3. subtract as you would for whole numbers.

Because subtraction often involves borrowing, zeros are usually filled in so that there is a unit in the minuend for each unit in the subtrahend.

**Example:** Subtract 4.037 from 12.46.

**Solution:** The minuend is 12.46 and the subtrahend is 4.037. Rewrite the problem vertically, aligning the decimal points.

$$\begin{array}{r} 12.46 \\ - \ 4.037 \\ \hline \end{array}$$

Since no digit appears in the thousandths place of the minuend, you fill in a zero for this unit, place the decimal point for the difference, and subtract.

$$\begin{array}{r} 5 \\ 12.4\cancel{6}0 \\ - \ 4.037 \\ \hline 8.423 \end{array}$$

## Multiplying decimals

To multiply decimals:

1. write the problem vertically, aligning the right-hand digits of the two factors;
2. multiply as you would for whole numbers;
3. count the digits in the decimal-fraction part of each factor and place a decimal point that many digits from the right-hand digit of the product.

**Example:** Multiply 2.147 and 36.5.

**Solution:** Rewrite the problem vertically, aligning the right-hand digits of the factors. Since 2.147 has more digits than 36.5, write it first. Multiply.

Note: no decimal points appear in the partial product.

$$\begin{array}{r} 2.147 \\ \times \ 36.5 \\ \hline 10735 \\ 12882 \\ 6441 \\ \hline 783655 \end{array}$$

There are *three* digits in the decimal fraction of the factor 2.147. There is *one* digit in the decimal fraction of the factor 36.5. Altogether there are *four* digits in the decimal fraction of the factors. Thus, you place the decimal point in the product between the 8 and the 3; that is, four digits from the right-hand digit of the product. The product is 78.3655.

## Dividing decimals

To divide decimals:

1. write the problem in long-division form;
2. locate the decimal point for the quotient; and
3. divide as you would for whole numbers.

If the divisor is a whole number (no decimal fraction), the decimal point in the quotient will be directly above the decimal point in the dividend.

**Example:** Divide 45.36 by 21.

**Solution:** The dividend is 45.36 and the divisor is 21. Rewrite the problem in long-division form, place the decimal point, and divide.

```
      2.16
21) 45.36
    42
    ──
    33
    21
    ──
    126
    126
    ───
      0
```

If the divisor possesses a decimal fraction, you eliminate the fraction by multiplying dividend and divisor by a power of ten (*i.e.*, 10, 100, 1,000, etc.). This is usually done mechanically by drawing arrows or using carats. For instance:

┌─── new location of decimal point

3.7) 21.462    Multiply both the divisor
               and dividend by 10.

┌─── new location of decimal point

16.237) 5.71963   Multiply both the divisor
                  and dividend by 1,000.

**Example:** Divide 5.6758 by .037.

**Solution:** The dividend is 5.6758 and the divisor is .037. Rewrite the problem as .037) 5.6758. The divisor has a decimal fraction. To eliminate the decimal fraction, you must multiply by 1,000.

```
       153.4
.037) 5.6758      Locate the decimal point
      3 7          for the quotient and divide.
      ───
      1 97
      1 85
      ────
       125
       111
       ───
       148
       148
       ───
         0
```

When dividing decimals, remainders are usually not left as the final difference in the division process. Instead, zeros are added to the right of the dividend and the division process is continued as long as you wish—most often, however, to a certain specified number of digits (*e.g.*, to the nearest hundredth). This procedure requires rules for rounding numbers.

For instance, if the quotient is to be rounded to the nearest hundredth, the division process is continued until the thousandths digit has been determined; then:

1. If the thousandths digit is 5, 6, 7, 8, or 9, the hundredths digit is increased by 1.
2. If the thousandths digit is 0, 1, 2, 3, or 4, the hundredths digit is kept unchanged.

A similar procedure is followed to round a quotient to the nearest tenth or to the nearest thousandth.

## Changing fractions and mixed numbers to decimals

To change a fraction to a decimal, simply divide the numerator by the denominator. The resulting decimal will be either a repeating decimal or a terminal decimal.

**Example:** Change $\frac{5}{6}$ to a decimal fraction.

**Solution:** Use long division to find the quotient. The decimal point in the dividend is understood to be after the 5.

```
                      .83
Add zeros to     6) 5.000
the dividend.       4 8
                   ───
                    20
                    18
                   ──
                    2
```

If you continue the division process, each additional digit in the quotient will be 3. You can give the answer in either of the following two forms.

$.8\overline{3}$  or  $.83\frac{1}{3}$

The bar over the 3 indicates that it repeats. The decimal is called a *repeating decimal*.

**Example:** Change $\frac{5}{8}$ to a decimal fraction.

**Solution:** Use long division to find the quotient.

```
        .625
8) 5.000
   4 8
   ───
    20
    16
    ──
    40
    40
    ──
     0
```

When the remainder is 0, the resulting decimal is called a *terminal decimal*.

To change a mixed number to a decimal:

1. rewrite the mixed number as an improper fraction; and
2. divide the numerator of the improper fraction by the denominator.

**Example:** Change $4\frac{2}{3}$ to a decimal.

**Solution:** Rewrite $4\frac{2}{3}$ as an improper fraction.

$$4\frac{2}{3} = \frac{14}{3}$$

Then use long division to divide 14 by 3.

```
      4.6
3) 14.0
   12
    2 0
    1 8
      2
```

If the division process is continued, 6 will repeat in the quotient. So, the answer is $4.\overline{6}$ or $4.66\frac{2}{3}$.

## Changing decimals to fractions and mixed numbers

To change a decimal fraction to a proper fraction:
1. multiply the digits of the decimal fraction by the smallest unit named; and
2. write the product in simplest form.

**Example:** Change .125 to a proper fraction.

**Solution:** The smallest unit named in .125 is $\frac{1}{1000}$ (thousandths). So you multiply 125 and $\frac{1}{1000}$ and simplify.

$$125\left(\frac{1}{1000}\right) = \frac{125}{1000} = \frac{1}{8}$$

**Example:** Change $.33\frac{1}{3}$ to a proper fraction.

**Solution:** The smallest unit named in $.33\frac{1}{3}$ is $\frac{1}{100}$ (hundredths). So you multiply $33\frac{1}{3}$ and $\frac{1}{100}$. Then simplify.

$$33\frac{1}{3}\left(\frac{1}{100}\right) = \frac{100}{3} \cdot \frac{1}{100} = \frac{1}{3}$$

To change a decimal to a mixed number:
1. express the decimal as the sum of a whole number and a decimal fraction;
2. change the decimal fraction to a proper fraction in simplest form; and
3. rewrite the sum as a mixed number.

**Example:** Change 5.75 to a mixed number.

**Solution:** Express 5.75 as a sum.

$$5.75 = 5 + .75$$

Change .75 to a proper fraction in simplest form.

$$75\left(\frac{1}{100}\right) = \frac{75}{100} = \frac{3}{4}$$

So $5 + .75$ becomes $5 + \frac{3}{4}$. This sum is $5\frac{3}{4}$.

# Ratio and proportion

A ratio is a comparison of two quantities of the same kind by division. A ratio can be written by using a *fraction bar* or a *colon*. For example, the ratio of 3 to 4 can be written as $\frac{3}{4}$ or 3:4. Both forms are useful.

In the ratio above, 3 is the first term of the ratio and 4 is the second term. If you were to use a fraction to express the ratio of 12 to 16, you would use a fraction in simplest form; namely, $\frac{3}{4}$.

**Example:** Mary's softball team won 16 games out of 24 games played. What is the ratio of games won to games played:

**Solution:** $\dfrac{\text{games won}}{\text{games played}} = \dfrac{16}{24} = \dfrac{2}{3}$

A proportion is an equation whose members are ratios.

For example, $\frac{3}{4} = \frac{15}{20}$ and 3:4 = 15:20 are both proportions. The numerators and denominators of the ratios are called *terms* of the proportion. The terms of a proportion are numbered. In the generalized proportion $\frac{a}{b} = \frac{c}{d}$ or $a{:}b = c{:}d$, $a$ is the first term, $b$ is the second term, $c$ is the third term, and $d$ is the fourth term. The first term and the fourth term of a proportion are called the *extremes* and the second and third terms are called the *means*.

In a proportion, the product of the means is always equal to the product of the extremes; that is, in general, $a \cdot d = b \cdot c$. By using this property of proportions, it is possible to solve a proportion for any one of the terms, given the other three. The letter $x$ is generally used to represent the unknown term of a proportion.

**Example:** Solve for $x$: $\frac{3}{5} = \frac{x}{20}$.

**Solution:** The extremes are 3 and 20. The means are 5 and $x$. To solve the proportion, multiply the means and extremes, set the products equal, and solve for $x$.

$$5 \cdot x = 3 \cdot 20 \qquad \text{Divide both sides by 5.}$$
$$5x = 60$$
$$x = 12$$

**Example:** In a certain school, the ratio of the number of boys to the number of girls is 4 to 3. If there are 600 girls in the school, how many boys are in the school?

**Solution:** Let $x$ represent the number of boys in the school. Write a proportion.

$$\frac{\text{number of boys}}{\text{number of girls}} = \frac{x}{600} = \frac{4}{3}$$

The extremes are $x$ and 3. The means are 600 and 4.

$$3 \cdot x = 4 \cdot 600$$
$$3x = 2,400$$
$$x = 800$$

There are 800 boys in the school.

## Per cent

A per cent is a ratio whose second term is 100. Because the second term is always the same, per cent offers a convenient way to compare two quantities. The symbol %, read "per cent," is used to indicate a per cent. For example:

$$5\% = \frac{5}{100} \qquad \frac{43}{100} = 43\%$$

$$17\% = \frac{17}{100} \qquad \frac{121}{100} = 121\%$$

When solving problems, it is useful to change decimals and fractions to per cents and to change per cents to decimals and fractions.

To change a decimal to a per cent:

1. express the decimal as a fraction whose denominator is 100; and
2. rewrite the fraction as a per cent.

**Example:** Change .37 to a per cent.

**Solution:** Change .37 to $\frac{37}{100}$. Rewrite $\frac{37}{100}$ as a per cent. The answer is 37%.

After becoming familiar with this kind of problem, many people omit the fraction step and simply move the decimal point two places to the right and add a % symbol when changing a decimal to a per cent. Hence:

.17 = 17%     .027 = 2.7%
.01 =  1%     4.67 = 467%

To change a fraction to a per cent:
1. rewrite the fraction so the denominator is 100; and
2. rewrite the resulting fraction as a per cent.

**Example:** Change $\frac{5}{8}$ to a per cent.

**Solution:** Make $x$ the first term of the per cent ratio and write a proportion.

$$\frac{5}{8} = \frac{x}{100}$$

Solve the proportion for $x$.

$$8 \cdot x = 5 \cdot 100$$
$$8x = 500$$
$$x = 62\frac{1}{2}$$

The per cent is $\frac{62\frac{1}{2}}{100}$ or $62\frac{1}{2}\%$.

You can also change a fraction to a per cent by using long division to change the fraction to a decimal and then change the resulting decimal to a per cent.

**Example:** Change $\frac{7}{8}$ to a per cent.

**Solution:** Use long division to change $\frac{7}{8}$ to a decimal.

$$8\overline{)7.000} \quad .875$$

Change .875 to a per cent. The answer is 87.5%.

To change a per cent to a decimal:

1. replace the per cent with a fraction whose denominator is 100; and
2. divide the numerator by 100.

**Example:** Change 36% to a decimal.

**Solution:** Rewrite 36% as $\frac{36}{100}$. Then divide 36 by 100. The answer is .36.

Again, with familiarization, you may omit the fraction step. You simply move the decimal point two places to the left and drop the % symbol when changing from a per cent to a decimal.

To change a per cent to a fraction:

1. replace the per cent with a fraction whose denominator is 100; and
2. rewrite the resulting fraction in simplest form.

**Example:** Change 42% to a fraction.

**Solution:** Rewrite 42% as $\frac{42}{100}$. Write $\frac{42}{100}$ in simplest form.

$$\frac{42 \div 2}{100 \div 2} = \frac{21}{50}$$

The answer is $\frac{21}{50}$.

# Per cent problems

There are three types of basic per cent problems:

1. Finding a per cent of a given number.
2. Finding what per cent one number is of another number.
3. Finding a number, given a per cent of that number.

**Example:** 36% of 75 is a certain number. Find the number.

**Solution:** This problem can be solved in two different ways:

*Method I*
1. Let $x$ = the number sought.
2. Change the per cent to a fraction or a decimal and rewrite the word problem as an equation.

$$x = \frac{36}{100} \cdot 75 \quad \text{or} \quad x = (.36) \cdot 75$$

3. Solve the resulting equation.
$$x = 27$$

*Method II*
1. Let $x$ = the number sought.
2. Change the per cent to a fraction and rewrite the word problem as a proportion.

$$\frac{x}{75} = \frac{36}{100}$$

3. Solve the resulting proportion.
$$\frac{x}{75} = \frac{36}{100}$$
$$100x = 2,700$$
$$x = 27$$

**Example:** 12% of a given number is 48. Find the number.

**Solution:** This problem can be solved two ways:

*Method I*
1. Let $x$ = the number sought.
2. Change the per cent to a fraction or decimal and rewrite the word problem as an equation.

$$\frac{12}{100} \cdot x = 48 \quad \text{or} \quad (.12)x = 48$$

3. Solve the resulting equation.

$$\frac{12}{100} \cdot x = 48 \quad \text{or} \quad (.12)x = 48$$
$$12x = 4,800 \qquad\qquad x = 400$$
$$x = 400$$

*Method II*
1. Let $x$ = the number sought.
2. Change the per cent to a fraction and rewrite the word problem as a proportion.

$$\frac{48}{x} = \frac{12}{100}$$

3. Solve the resulting proportion.

$$\frac{48}{x} = \frac{12}{100}$$
$$12x = 4,800$$
$$x = 400$$

**Example:** 16 is a certain per cent of 80. Find the per cent.

**Solution:** This problem can be solved in two ways:

*Method I*
1. Let $x$ = the per cent sought.
2. Change the per cent to a fraction and rewrite the word problem as an equation.

$$16 = \frac{x}{100} \cdot 80$$

3. Solve the resulting equation.

$$16 = \frac{x}{100} \cdot 80$$
$$1,600 = x \cdot 80$$
$$20 = x$$

*Method II*
1. Let $x$ = the per cent sought.
2. Change the per cent to a fraction and rewrite the word problem as a proportion.

$$\frac{x}{100} = \frac{16}{80}$$

3. Solve the resulting proportion.

$$\frac{x}{100} = \frac{16}{80}$$
$$80x = 1,600$$
$$x = 20$$

# The metric system

The metric system is a sytem of measurement developed about 1792 during the French Revolution. In 1837, France made the metric system compulsory. In 1893, the metric system was adopted as the official system of measurement in the United States and has been used extensively in scientific circles since that time.

## Metric units of length

The basic unit for measuring length in the metric system is the *meter* (abbreviated m). The other units of length are expressed in terms of the meter.

| shorter than a meter | fraction | power of 10 | decimal |
|---|---|---|---|
| 1 millimeter (mm) = | $\frac{1}{1000}$ meter | = $\frac{1}{10^3}$ meter | = .001 meter |
| 1 centimeter (cm) = | $\frac{1}{100}$ meter | = $\frac{1}{10^2}$ meter | = .01 meter |
| 1 decimeter (dm) = | $\frac{1}{10}$ meter | = $\frac{1}{10^1}$ meter | = .1 meter |

**longer**

| than a meter | unit | power of 10 |
|---|---|---|
| 1 decameter (dkm) | = 10 meters | = $10^1$ meters |
| 1 hectometer (hm) | = 100 meters | = $10^2$ meters |
| 1 kilometer (km) | = 1000 meters | = $10^3$ meters |

These units are listed horizontally below from least to greatest.

$$\div 10^1 \quad \div 10^1 \quad \div 10^1 \quad \div 10^1 \quad \div 10^1 \quad \div 10^1$$

mm    cm    dm    m    dkm    hm    km

If you move to the right one unit at a time, you divide by 10. If you move to the right more than one unit at a time, you divide by a *power* of 10.

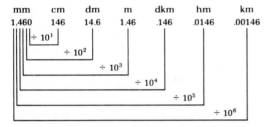

| mm | cm | dm | m | dkm | hm | km |
|---|---|---|---|---|---|---|
| 1,460 | 146 | 14.6 | 1.46 | .146 | .0146 | .00146 |

$\div 10^1$
$\div 10^2$
$\div 10^3$
$\div 10^4$
$\div 10^5$
$\div 10^6$

**Example:** Change 4 mm to centimeters.

**Solution:** On the unit scale, the cm unit is the next unit to the right of the mm unit. So you divide by 10 to find the answer. This can be done by moving the decimal point one place to the left.

4 mm = .4 cm

**Example:** Change 721 dm to hectometers.

**Solution:** On the unit scale, the hm unit is three units to the right of the dm unit. So you divide 721 by $10^3$ to find the answer. This can be done by moving the decimal point three places to the left.

721 dm = .721 hm.

In general, if you are changing from a shorter unit to a longer unit, you must divide by a power of 10.

If you move to the left along the horizontal scale one unit at a time, you multiply by 10. If you move to the left more than one unit at a time, you multiply by a *power* of 10.

$$\times 10^1 \quad \times 10^1 \quad \times 10^1 \quad \times 10^1 \quad \times 10^1 \quad \times 10^1$$

| mm | cm | dm | m | dkm | hm | km |
|---|---|---|---|---|---|---|
| 5,100 | 510 | 51 | 5.1 | .51 | .051 | .0051 |

$\times 10^1$
$\times 10^2$
$\times 10^3$
$\times 10^4$
$\times 10^5$
$\times 10^6$

**Example:** Change 49 dkm to meters.

**Solution:** On the unit scale, the m unit is the next unit to the left of the dkm unit. So you multiply by 10 to find the answer. This can be done by moving the decimal point one place to the right.

49 dkm = 490 m

**Example:** Change 7.46 km to centimeters.

**Solution:** On the unit scale, the cm unit is five units to the left of the km unit. So you multiply by $10^5$ to find the answer. This can be done by moving the decimal point five places to the right.

7.46 km = 746,000 cm

In general, if you are changing from a longer unit to a shorter unit, you must multiply by a power of 10.

## Metric units of area

Area is a number associated with a two-dimensional region, such as a square or a rectangle.

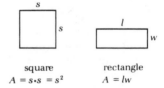

square      rectangle
$A = s \cdot s = s^2$      $A = lw$

The basic unit for measuring area in the metric system is the square meter ($m^2$), the area of a square whose sides are 1 m long. Area units are related as shown below.

$$\div 10^2 \quad \div 10^2 \quad \div 10^2 \quad \div 10^2 \quad \div 10^2 \quad \div 10^2$$

$mm^2$   $cm^2$   $dm^2$   $m^2$   $dkm^2$   $hm^2$   $km^2$

$$\times 10^2 \quad \times 10^2 \quad \times 10^2 \quad \times 10^2 \quad \times 10^2 \quad \times 10^2$$

If you move to the right on the area unit scale, you divide by a power of $10^2$ or 100. If you move to the left on the scale, you multiply by a power of $10^2$ or 100.

**Example:** Change 7 $dm^2$ to square decameters.

**Solution:** On the area unit scale, the $dkm^2$ unit is two units to the right of the $dm^2$ unit. So you divide by $(100)^2$ or 10,000. This can be done by moving the decimal point four places to the left.

7 $dm^2$ = .0007 $dkm^2$

**Example:** Change .05 $m^2$ to square millimeters.

**Solution:** On the area unit scale, the $mm^2$ unit is three units to the left of the m² unit. So you multiply by $(100)^3$ or 1,000,000 to find the answer. This can be done by moving the decimal point six places to the right.

.05 m² = 50,000 mm²

## Metric units of volume

Volume is a number associated with a three-dimensional solid, such as a cube or a rectangular solid.

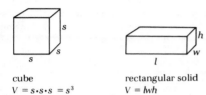

cube
$V = s \cdot s \cdot s = s^3$

rectangular solid
$V = lwh$

The basic unit for measuring volume in the metric system is the cubic meter (m³), the volume of a cube whose sides are 1 m long. The volume units are related as shown below.

| | ÷ 10³ | ÷ 10³ | ÷ 10³ | ÷ 10³ | ÷ 10³ | ÷ 10³ |
|---|---|---|---|---|---|---|
| mm³ | cm³ | dm³ | m³ | dkm³ | hm³ | km³ |
| | × 10³ | × 10³ | × 10³ | × 10³ | × 10³ | × 10³ |

If you move to the right on the volume unit scale, you divide by a power of $10^3$ or 1,000. If you move to the left on the scale, you multiply by a power of $10^3$ or 1,000.

**Example:** Change 49,600 m³ to cubic hectometers.

**Solution:** On the volume unit scale, the hm³ unit is two units to the right of the m³ unit. So you divide by $(1,000)^2$ or 1,000,000 to find the answer. This can be done by moving the decimal point six places to the left.
49,600 m³ = .0496 m³

**Example:** Change .75 cm³ to cubic millimeters.

**Solution:** On the volume unit scale, the mm³ unit is one unit to the left of the cm³ unit. So you multiply by 1,000 to find the answer. This can be done by moving the decimal point three places to the right.

.75 cm³ = 750 cm³

## Converting metric measures of length to English measures of length

To change metric units to English units, you use a conversion table like the one below. The symbol $\doteq$ means "approximately equal to."

| | |
|---|---|
| 1 m $\doteq$ 39.37 in | 1 yd $\doteq$ .91 m |
| 1 m $\doteq$ 1.1 yd | 1 in $\doteq$ 2.54 cm |
| 1 km $\doteq$ .62 mi | 1 mi $\doteq$ 1.61 km |

**Example:** Change 16 m to yards.

**Solution:** Let $x$ = the number of yards and write a proportion.

$$\frac{1}{16} = \frac{1.1}{x}$$

Solve the resulting proportion.

$x = 16(1.1)$
$x = 17.6$
16 m = 17.6 yd

# 2. Reviewing algebra

In algebra you work with the system of *real numbers*. The set of real numbers contains the set of *natural numbers*, the set of *whole numbers*, the set of *integers*, the set of *rational numbers*, and the set of *irrational numbers*. The system of real numbers consists of the set of real numbers, certain basic operations (like addition and multiplication), and properties that apply to these operations. The basic properties are listed below. The variables $a$, $b$, and $c$ represent real numbers.

| | |
|---|---|
| closure property of addition: | $a + b$ is a real number |
| commutative property of addition: | $a + b = b + a$ |
| associative property of addition: | $(a + b) + c = a + (b + c)$ |
| addition property of zero: | $a + 0 = a$ |
| inverse property of addition: | $a + (-a) = 0$ |
| closure property of multiplication: | $a \cdot b$ is a real number |
| commutative property of multiplication: | $a \cdot b = b \cdot a$ |
| associative property of multiplication: | $a \cdot (b \cdot c) = (a \cdot b) \cdot c$ |
| multiplication property of one: | $a \cdot 1 = a$ |
| inverse property of multiplication: | $a \cdot \dfrac{1}{a} = 1$ if $a \neq 0$ |
| distributive property of multiplication over addition: | $a(b + c) = a \cdot b + a \cdot c$ |

## Addition of integers and rational numbers

The set of integers contains the set of whole numbers and all of the "opposites," or negatives, of the whole numbers. A negative sign is used to indicate the opposite of a whole number. Zero is the opposite of zero.

set of integers $= \{ \ldots, -3, -2, -1, 0, 1, 2, 3, \ldots \}$

The set of integers can be associated with the points of a line. If no "operation" sign is written, the number is a positive integer.

The resulting number line can be used to add integers. For example:

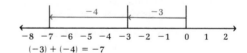

$2 + 3 = 5$

$(-3) + (-4) = -7$

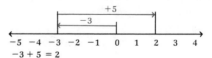

$3 + (-7) = -4$

$-3 + 5 = 2$

It is not always convenient to draw number-line pictures to find sums. So, rules are usually stated. Since every integer is a rational number, and the

59

rules for both sets are the same, you should know all of the rules for rational numbers. A rational number is any number that can be written in the form $\frac{a}{b}$, where $a$ and $b$ are integers and $b \neq 0$.

Before stating the rules, you must consider the idea of "absolute value." In mathematics, the symbol $|\ |$ is used to indicate absolute value. If $x$ is any real number:

$|x| = x$ if $x$ is greater than 0;
$|x| = 0$ if $x = 0$;
$|x| = -x$ if $x$ is less than 0.

**Example:** Find the absolute value of (**a**) $-7$; (**b**) $\frac{2}{3}$.

**Solution:**
(**a**) Since $-7$ is less than 0, the absolute value of $-7$ is the opposite of $-7$.

$$|-7| = -(-7) = 7$$

(**b**) Since $\frac{2}{3}$ is a positive real number, the absolute value of $\frac{2}{3}$ is $\frac{2}{3}$.

## Rules for addition of rational numbers

1. If the direction signs are the same (both positive or both negative), add the absolute values of the addends and use the common sign for the sum.
2. If the direction signs are different (one positive and one negative), subtract the absolute values of the addends and use the sign of the addend with the greater absolute value.

**Example:** Find each sum: (**a**) $-21 + 13$;
(**b**) $-17 + (-29)$; (**c**) $\frac{2}{3} + (-\frac{3}{4})$.

**Solution:**
(**a**) The direction signs are not alike. Subtract the absolute values.

$$|-21| - |13| = 21 - 13 = 8$$

Since $-21$ has the greater absolute value, you use a negative sign for the sum. The sum is $-8$.

(**b**) The direction signs are alike. Add the absolute values.

$$|-17| + |-29| = 17 + 29 = 46$$

Use the common sign for the sum. The sum is $-46$.

(**c**) The direction signs are different. Subtract the absolute values of the addends. To subtract, it is necessary to find a common denominator.

$$\left|-\frac{3}{4}\right| - \left|\frac{2}{3}\right| = \frac{3}{4} - \frac{2}{3} = \frac{9}{12} - \frac{8}{12} = \frac{9-8}{12} = \frac{1}{12}$$

Since $-\frac{3}{4}$ has the greater absolute value, you use a negative sign for the sum. The sum is $-\frac{1}{12}$.

## Rule for subtraction of rational numbers

Subtraction is defined in terms of addition. To subtract two rational numbers, add the opposite of the subtrahend to the minuend. Using symbols, this rule can be restated as follows. If $x$ and $y$ are any two rational numbers, then

$$x - y = x + (-y).$$

**Example:** Find each difference: (**a**) $47 - 29$;
(**b**) $-63 - 14$; (**c**) $\frac{5}{8} - (-\frac{1}{2})$; (**d**) $-56 - (-32)$.

**Solution:**
(**a**) Rewrite $47 - 29$ as a sum and apply the rules for adding rational numbers.

$$47 - 29 = 47 + (-29)$$

The direction signs are different. Subtract the absolute values.

$$|47| - |-29| = 47 - 29 = 18$$

Since $|47| > |-29|$, you use a positive sign for the answer. The difference is 18. (The symbol $>$ represents the phrase "is greater than.")

(**b**) Rewrite $-63 - 14$ as a sum and apply the rules for adding rational numbers.

$$-63 - 14 = -63 + (-14)$$

The addends have the same direction signs so you add the absolute values.

$$|-63| + |-14| = 63 + 14 = 77$$

Use the common sign for the answer. The difference is $-77$.

(**c**) Rewrite $\frac{5}{8} - (-\frac{1}{2})$ as a sum and apply the rules for adding rational numbers. The opposite of the opposite of $\frac{1}{2}$ is $\frac{1}{2}$.

$$\frac{5}{8} - \left(-\frac{1}{2}\right) = \frac{5}{8} + \frac{1}{2} = \frac{5}{8} + \frac{4}{8} = \frac{5+4}{8} = \frac{9}{8}$$

The difference is $\frac{9}{8}$ or $1\frac{1}{8}$.

(**d**) Rewrite $-56 - (-32)$ as a sum and apply the rules for adding rational numbers.

$$-56 - (-32) = -56 + 32$$

The direction signs of the addends are different. Subtract the absolute values.

$$|-56| - |32| = 56 - 32 = 24$$

Since $|-56| > |32|$, you use a negative sign for the answer. The difference is $-24$.

## Rules for multiplication of rational numbers

1. If the direction signs are the same (both positive or both negative), multiply the absolute values of

the factors and use a positive sign for the product.

2. If the direction signs are different (one positive and one negative), multiply the absolute values of the factors and use a negative sign for the product.

**Example:** Find each product: (**a**) $\frac{2}{3} \cdot 6$; (**b**) $(-12)(9)$; (**c**) $(-7)(-9)$.

**Solution:**

(**a**) The direction signs of the factors are alike. Multiply the absolute values of the factors and use a positive sign for the product.

$$\left|\frac{2}{3}\right| \cdot |6| = \frac{2}{3} \cdot 6 = \frac{2}{\overset{1}{\cancel{3}}} \cdot \frac{\overset{2}{\cancel{6}}}{1} = 4$$

The product is 4.

(**b**) The direction signs of the factors are different. Multiply the absolute values of the factors.

$$|-12| \cdot |9| = 12 \cdot 9 = 108$$

Use a negative sign for the product. The product is $-108$.

(**c**) The direction signs of the factors are the same. Multiply the absolute values of the factors and use a positive sign for the product.

$$|-7| \cdot |-9| = 7 \cdot 9 = 63$$

If you are finding the product of more than two factors, count the negative signs. If there is an odd number of negative signs, the product will be negative.

## Rules for division of rational numbers

1. If the direction signs are the same (both positive or both negative), divide the absolute value of the dividend by the absolute value of the divisor. Also, use a positive sign for the quotient.

2. If the direction signs are different (one positive and one negative), divide the absolute value of the dividend by the absolute value of the divisor and use a negative sign for the quotient.

**Example:** Find each quotient: (**a**) $\frac{8}{15} \div \frac{2}{5}$; (**b**) $-28 \div 7$; (**c**) $-42 \div (-3)$.

**Solution:**

(**a**) the direction signs are the same. The quotient will be positive. Divide $\left|\frac{8}{15}\right|$ by $\left|\frac{2}{5}\right|$. To divide fractions, it is necessary to invert the divisor and multiply.

$$\left|\frac{8}{15}\right| \div \left|\frac{2}{5}\right| = \frac{8}{15} \div \frac{2}{5} = \frac{\overset{4}{\cancel{8}}}{\underset{3}{\cancel{15}}} \cdot \frac{\overset{1}{\cancel{5}}}{\underset{1}{\cancel{2}}} = \frac{4}{3}$$

The quotient is $\frac{4}{3}$ or $1\frac{1}{3}$.

(**b**) The direction signs are different. Divide the absolute value of $-28$ by the absolute value of 7.

$$|-28| \div |7| = 28 \div 7 = 4$$

Use a negative sign for the quotient. $-28 \div 7 = -4$.

(**c**) The direction signs are the same. The quotient will be positive. Divide $|-42|$ by $|-3|$.

$$|-42| \div |-3| = 42 \div 3 = 14$$

The quotient is 14.

# Solving open sentences

In mathematics, a *statement* is a sentence that is either true or false but not both. Each of the following is a statement.

| equation | inequality | inequality | equation |
|---|---|---|---|
| $5 + 3 = 10$ | $4 > 0$ | $-7 < -3$ | $2 + 7 = 9$ |
| false | true | true | true |

An *open sentence* contains a variable and is neither true nor false until the variable is replaced with a number. Each of the following is an open sentence.

| equation | inequality | equation |
|---|---|---|
| $x + 2 = 6$ | $x - 3 > 5$ | $2x + 7 = 9$ |

One of the primary objectives of algebra is to develop concepts for solving open sentences. Here you will only consider techniques for solving equations. To solve an equation, it is necessary to determine the number (or numbers) that will make the equation a true statement.

When solving equations, it is necessary to apply one or more of the following properties of equality. The variables represent real numbers.

| addition property of equality: | If $a = b$, then $a + c = b + c$. |
|---|---|
| subtraction property of equality: | If $a = b$, then $a - c = b - c$. |
| multiplication property of equality: | If $a = b$, then $ac = bc$. |
| division property of equality: | If $a = b$, then $\dfrac{a}{c} = \dfrac{b}{c}$ if $c \neq 0$. |

You can tell which property to apply by thinking in terms of "opposite" operations.

**Example:** Solve $x + 5 = 17$ for $x$.

**Solution:** Since 5 is added to $x$ to obtain 17, you apply the subtraction property of equality to solve for $x$. The procedure can be done horizontally or vertically.

$$x + 5 = 17$$
$$x + 5 - 5 = 17 - 5 \quad \text{Subtract 5.}$$
$$x = 12$$

$$x + 5 = 17$$
$$-5 = -5$$
$$\overline{x \qquad = 12}$$

**Example:** Solve $x - 7 = 12$ for $x$.

**Solution:** Since 7 is subtracted from $x$ to obtain 12, you apply the addition property of equality to solve for $x$.

$$x - 7 = 12$$
$$x - 7 + 7 = 12 + 7 \quad \text{Add 7.}$$
$$x = 19$$

$$x - 7 = 12$$
$$+7 = +7$$
$$\overline{x \qquad = 19}$$

Later, as your skills improve, you will be able to solve equations like these without writing the addition or subtraction step. It is always a good idea to identify the reason for each step. For example:

$$x - 3 = 9$$
$$\text{A}_3$$
$$x = 12$$

$$x + 2 = 17$$
$$\text{S}_2$$
$$x = 15$$

$\text{A}_3$ means "add 3 to both sides."

$\text{S}_2$ means "subtract 2 from both sides."

It is important to remember that you must always do the same thing to *both* sides of an equation.

**Example:** Solve $3x = 21$ for $x$.

**Solution:** Since $x$ is multiplied by 3 to obtain 21, you apply the division property of equality to solve for $x$.

$$3x = 21$$
$$\frac{3x}{3} = \frac{21}{3} \quad \text{Divide by 3.}$$
$$x = 7$$

**Example:** Solve $\frac{x}{5} = 12$ for $x$.

**Solution:** Since $x$ is divided by 5 to obtain 12, you apply the multiplication property of equality to solve for $x$.

$$\frac{x}{5} = 12$$
$$5 \cdot \frac{x}{5} = 5 \cdot 12 \quad \text{Multiply by 5.}$$
$$x = 60$$

The multiplication or division step need not be shown. It is a good idea, however, to identify the property of equality that you used to solve the equation.

$$6x = 108$$
$$\text{D}_6$$
$$x = 18$$

$$\frac{x}{9} = 7$$
$$\text{M}_9$$
$$x = 63$$

$\text{D}_6$ means "divide both sides by 6."

$\text{M}_9$ means "multiply both sides by 9."

Each of the preceding equations could be solved in one step by applying a property of equality. It will usually take more than one step to solve an equation.

**Example:** Solve $\frac{2x}{3} + 5 = 17$ for $x$.

**Solution:**

*showing steps*

$$\frac{2x}{3} + 5 = 17$$
$$-5 = -5 \quad \text{Subtract 5.}$$
$$\frac{2x}{3} = 12$$
$$3 \cdot \frac{2x}{3} = 3 \cdot 12 \quad \text{Multiply by 3.}$$
$$2x = 36$$
$$\frac{2x}{2} = \frac{36}{2} \quad \text{Divide by 2.}$$
$$x = 18$$

*short method*

$$\frac{2x}{3} + 5 = 17$$
$$\frac{2x}{3} = 12 \quad \text{S}_5$$
$$2x = 36 \quad \text{M}_3$$
$$x = 18 \quad \text{D}_2$$

When more than one step is involved, it is a good idea to check your solution. This is usually done by rewriting the original equation, substituting the solution for the variable, and doing the arithmetic. To understand this procedure, you can check the solution just obtained.

Check: $\frac{2x}{3} + 5 = 17$ if $x$ is 18

$$\frac{2(18)}{3} + 5 \overset{?}{=} 17$$
$$12 + 5 \overset{?}{=} 17$$
$$17 = 17 \quad \text{The solution checks.}$$

**Example:** Solve $3(2x - 7) + 5 = 14$ for $x$.

**Solution:** This equation contains parentheses. To remove parentheses, it is necessary to apply the distributive property. As a reason, write "RP" for "remove parentheses."

*showing steps*

$$3(2x - 7) + 5 = 14$$
$$6x - 21 + 5 = 14 \quad \text{Remove parentheses.}$$
$$6x - 16 = 14 \quad \text{Add.}$$
$$+16 = +16 \quad \text{Add 16.}$$
$$6x = 30$$
$$\frac{6x}{6} = \frac{30}{6} \quad \text{Divide by 6.}$$
$$x = 5$$

*short method*

$$3(2x - 7) + 5 = 14$$
$$6x - 21 + 5 = 14 \quad \text{RP}$$
$$6x - 16 = 14 \quad \text{Add.}$$
$$6x = 30 \quad \text{A}_{16}$$
$$x = 5 \quad \text{D}_6$$

# Like terms

An expression like $7y$ is called a monomial or a term. In this term, 7 is the *coefficient* of $y$ and $y$ is the *coefficient* of 7. Since 7 is a number, you refer to 7 as the *numerical coefficient.*

Terms like $3x$ and $5x$ are called *like terms* because they have the same variable. You combine like terms by adding or subtracting the numerical coefficients and writing the variable.

**Example:** Combine like terms: (a) $15x - 7x$;
 (b) $21y + 16y - 7y$.

**Solution:**
 (a) $15x - 7x = (15 - 7)x = 8x$
 (b) $21y + 16y - 7y = (21 + 16 - 7)y = 30y$

The ability to combine like terms is useful when solving equations.

**Example:** Solve $8x + 7 - 3x = 42$ for $x$.

**Solution:** Since $8x$ and $-3x$ are like terms on the same side of the equation, they should be combined first. The sign in front of the term remains with that term. Because of the associative and commutative properties, it is possible to rewrite the equation so that like terms are side by side.

$$\left.\begin{array}{l} 8x + 7 - 3x = 42 \\ 8x - 3x + 7 = 42 \\ (8 - 3)x + 7 = 42 \end{array}\right\}$$ As your skills improve, you can easily omit these two steps.

$$5x + 7 = 42$$
$$5x + 7 - 7 = 42 - 7 \quad \text{Subtract 7.}$$

$$5x = 35$$

$$\frac{5x}{5} = \frac{35}{5} \quad \text{Divide by 5.}$$

$$x = 7$$

*short method*
$$8x + 7 - 3x = 42$$
$$5x + 7 = 42$$
$$5x = 35$$
$$x = 7$$

*check*
$$8x + 7 - 3x = 42$$
$$8(7) + 7 - 3(7) \overset{?}{=} 42$$
$$56 + 7 - 21 \overset{?}{=} 42$$
$$42 = 42$$

**Example:** Solve $7x - 4 = 2x + 11$

**Solution:** In this equation, terms containing variables appear on *both* sides of the equation. Our first task is to transfer all of the variables to the same side of the equation. To do this, we subtract $2x$ from both sides of the equation. Then, we solve the resulting equation for $x$.

$$\begin{array}{rcl} 7x - 4 = & 2x + 11 \\ -2x & = -2x & \text{Subtract } 2x. \\ \hline 5x - 4 = & 11 \\ + 4 = & + 4 & \text{Add 4.} \\ \hline 5x & = & 15 \end{array}$$

$$\frac{5x}{5} = \frac{15}{5} \quad \text{Divide by 5.}$$

$$x = 3$$

| *short method* | | *check* |
|---|---|---|
| $7x - 4 = 2x + 11$ | | $7x - 4 = 2x + 11$ |
| $5x - 4 = 11$ | $S_{2x}$ | $7(3) - 4 \overset{?}{=} 2(3) + 11$ |
| $5x = 15$ | $A_4$ | $21 - 4 \overset{?}{=} 6 + 11$ |
| $x = 3$ | $D_5$ | $17 = 17$ |

Formulas are equations that involve more than one variable. The same properties of equality are used to solve equations of this kind for a given variable.

**Example:** Solve $C = \frac{5}{9}(F - 32)$ for $F$.

**Solution:** Since we are solving the equation for $F$, we need to isolate $F$.

$$C = \frac{5}{9}(F - 32)$$

$$9 \cdot C = 9 \cdot \frac{5}{9}(F - 32) \quad \text{Multiply by 9.}$$

$$9C = 5(F - 32)$$

$$\frac{9C}{5} = \frac{5(F - 32)}{5} \quad \text{Divide by 5.}$$

$$\frac{9C}{5} = F - 32$$

$$\frac{9C}{5} + 32 = F - 32 + 32 \quad \text{Add 32.}$$

$$\frac{9C}{5} + 32 = F$$

# Exponents

Exponents are used to indicate products. In the expression $5^3$, 5 is called the base and 3 the exponent. The exponent 3 indicates how many times the base 5 is used as a factor; that is, $5^3 = 5 \cdot 5 \cdot 5$. You write $5 \cdot 5 \cdot 5$ in *exponential form* as $5^3$. If the bases are the same, you can find the product of two numbers written in exponential form by
 1. writing the base; and
 2. adding the exponents.
If $x$ is any rational number and $a$ and $b$ are positive integers, this rule can be written as

$$x^a \cdot x^b = x^{a+b}.$$

**Example:** Multiply $3^2$ and $3^4$.

**Solution:** Rewrite the problem using symbols and apply the rule.

$$3^2 \cdot 3^4 = 3^{2+4} = 3^6$$

If the bases are the same, you can find the quotient of two numbers written in exponential form by

1. writing the base; and
2. subtracting the exponents.

If the exponents are the same, the quotient is 1. When applying the rule for division, you must subtract the lesser exponent from the greater exponent to keep the difference positive. If $x$ is a non-zero rational number and both $x$ and $b$ are positive integers, the rule can be written as follows:

If $a > b$, then $x^a \div x^b = x^{a-b}$

If $b > a$, then $x^a \div x^b = \dfrac{1}{x^{b-a}}$

**Example:** Find each quotient: (a) $7^5 \div 7^2$; (b) $5^4 \div 5^6$.

**Solution:**
(a) The bases are the same, so you can subtract exponents to find the quotient. Because the greater exponent is in the numerator (dividend), you must subtract in the numerator.

$$7^5 \div 7^2 = \frac{7^5}{7^2} = 7^{5-2} = 7^3$$

(b) The bases are the same, so you can subtract exponents to find the quotient. Because the greater exponent is in the denominator, you subtract in the denominator.

$$5^4 \div 5^6 = \frac{5^4}{5^6} = \frac{1}{5^{6-4}} = \frac{1}{5^2}$$

Two other rules involving exponents are stated below. In these rules, $x$ and $y$ are rational numbers and $a$ and $b$ are positive integers.

1. $(x^a)^b = x^{ab}$   2. $(xy)^a = x^a y^a$

**Example:** Find each product: (a) $(3^2)^4$; (b) $(5x)^3$.

**Solution:**
(a) To find this product, you must find a power. Apply Rule 1.

$$(3^2)^4 = 3^{2 \cdot 4} = 3^8$$

(b) In this situation, you have to find a power of a product. Apply Rule 2.

$$(5x)^3 = 5^3 \cdot x^3 = 5 \cdot 5 \cdot 5 \cdot x^3 = 125x^3$$

# Systems of linear equations

A linear equation is any equation whose graph is a straight line. Any linear equation can be written in the form $ax + by = c$, in which $x$ and $y$ are variables and $a$, $b$, and $c$ are real numbers. You are assuming that $a$ and $b$ are not both zero. To graph a linear equation:

1. find three ordered pairs of numbers that make the equation a true statement;
2. graph the three ordered pairs of numbers in the coordinate plane; and
3. draw the line that contains the three points.

**Example:** Graph $2x + y = 4$.

**Solution:** Make a table for the equation. The table should contain at least three entries. These entries can be found by:

1. choosing a number replacement for $x$ (or $y$);
2. substituting that number for $x$ (or $y$) in the equation; and
3. solving the resulting equation for the other variable.

This procedure can usually be done mentally if you choose the replacements for $x$ and $y$ carefully. For example, the computations are easy if you let $x$ equal zero or $y$ equal zero.

$$2x + y = 4$$
Let $x = 0$.   $2(0) + y = 4$
$$y = 4$$

$$2x + y = 4$$
Let $y = 0$.   $2x + 0 = 4$
$$x = 2$$

$$2x + y = 4$$
Let $x = 3$.   $2(3) + y = 4$
$$6 + y = 4$$
$$y = -2$$

table

| x | y |
|---|---|
| 0 | 4 |
| 2 | 0 |
| 3 | -2 |

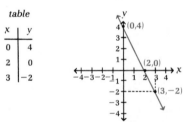

The simplest system of linear equations contain two linear equations in two variables. To solve a system of linear equations in two variables, you must find an ordered pair of numbers that will make both equations true simultaneously. There are three basic methods for solving a system of two linear equations in two variables. The first one to be considered here is called the "graphing method."

**Example:** Use the graphing method to solve the following system of linear equations.

  **1**  $2x + y = 5$
  **2**  $x - y = 4$

**Solution:** Graph both equations on the same coordinate axes.

  $2x + y = 5$    $x - y = 4$

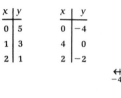

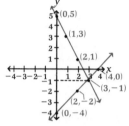

The two graphs intersect at $(3, -1)$. So, the solution set is $\{(3, -1)\}$; that is, $x = 3$ and $y = -1$.

If the two graphs were parallel (did not intersect), there would be no solution. And if both equations described the same line, there would be infinitely many solutions; every solution of one equation would automatically be a solution of the other equation.

Because it is not always convenient to develop the solution from a graph, algebraic methods have been devised for solving systems of linear equations. The first of these that you should keep in mind is called the "substitution method."

**Example:** Use the substitution method to solve the following system of linear equations.
  **1**  $x - y = 2$
  **2**  $x + 2y = 5$

**Solution:** Solve equation **1** for $x$.
  **1**  $x - y = 2$
       $x = 2 + y$
Substitute $2 + y$ for $x$ in equation **2** and solve the resulting equation for $y$.
  **2**     $x + 2y = 5$
     $(2 + y) + 2y = 5$
     $2 + y + 2y = 5$
       $2 + 3y = 5$
          $y = 1$
To find $x$, substitute 1 for $y$ in equation **1** and solve for $x$.
  **1**  $x - y = 2$
     $x - 1 = 2$
        $x = 3$
The solution set is $\{(3, 1)\}$.

The second algebraic method is called the "addition/subtraction method."

**Example:** Use the addition/subtraction method to solve the following system of linear equations.
  **1**  $3x - y = 7$
  **2**  $2x + y = 8$

**Solution:** Look at the coefficients of the variables. If the coefficients of the $x$'s (or $y$'s) are the same, that variable can be eliminated by subtraction. If the coefficients of the $x$'s (or $y$'s) are "opposites," that variable can be eliminated by addition. In the system above, the coefficients of the $y$'s are opposites. You can eliminate the $y$'s by addition.

  **1**  $3x - y = 7$  $\Big\}$ Add.
  **2**  $2x + y = 8$
      $5x\quad\ \ = 15$
        $x = 3$
To find $y$, substitute 3 for $x$ in one of the original equations and solve for $y$.
  **2**    $2x + y = 8$
     $2(3) + y = 8$
       $6 + y = 8$
          $y = 2$
The solution set is $\{(3, 2)\}$.

If no pairs of coefficients are the same (or opposites), they can be made the same (or opposites) by multiplication.

**Example:** Solve the following system of linear equations.
  **1**  $2x - 3y = 5$
  **2**  $x - 2y = 3$

**Solution:** If equation **2** is multiplied by 2, the coefficients of the $x$'s would be the same. Then the $x$'s could be eliminated by subtraction. Or, if equation **2** is multiplied by $-2$, the coefficients of the $x$'s would be opposites and the $x$'s could be eliminated by addition. Similar thinking could be used to eliminate the $y$'s. Eliminate the $x$'s by addition, as follows:
  **1**    $2x - 3y = \ \ \ 5$  $\Big\}$ Add.
  **2**  $-2x + 4y = -6$
          $y = -1$
To find $x$, substitute $-1$ for $y$ in one of the equations and solve for $x$.
  **1**    $2x - 3y = 5$
    $2x - 3(-1) = 5$
     $2x + 3 = 5$
         $x = 1$
The solution set is $\{(1, -1)\}$.

# Polynomials

The simplest polynomial is a monomial. A monomial is the same as a term; that is, a monomial may be a number, a variable, or a product of numbers and variables. For example, $5$, $\frac{1}{2}$, $x$, $w$, $9y$, $10x^2$, $6x^6y$, and $x^2y^3z$ are all monomials. The degree of a monomial can be found by *adding* the exponents of the variables.

The degree of 4 is 0 (no variable).

The degree of $3x^2$ is 2 (exponent of $x$).

The degree of $5x^2y$ is 3 (exponent of $x$ + exponent of $y$).

The degree of $\frac{1}{2}xy^2z^3$ is 6 (exponent of $x$ + exponent of $y$ + exponent of $z$).

You learned to add and subtract monomials when you combined like terms. To multiply monomials, you multiply the numerical coefficients and then apply rules for exponents to multiply the variables.

**Example:** Find each product: (**a**) $(-2x)(3x^2)$; (**b**) $4(5y^2)(6y^3)$; (**c**) $(3xy)(5x^2y^3)$.

**Solution:**

(**a**) The commutative and associative properties of multiplication make it possible to rewrite $(-2x)(3x^2)$ as shown below.

$(-2 \cdot 3)(x \cdot x^2)$
multiply ⌋    ⌊write the base; add the exponents.

The product is $-6x^3$. As your skills increase, you can find the product directly without rewriting the factors.

(**b**) $4(5y^2)(6y^3) = (4 \cdot 5 \cdot 6)(y^2 \cdot y^3) = 120(y^{2+3}) = 120y^5$

(**c**) $(3xy)(5x^2y^3) = (3 \cdot 5)(x \cdot x^2)(y \cdot y^3) = 15x^3y^4$.

To divide monomials, you divide the numerical coefficients and then apply rules for exponents to divide the variables.

**Example:** Find each quotient: (**a**) $\frac{20x^2}{4x^2}$; (**b**) $40x^3y^5 \div 8xy^3$; (**c**) $\frac{6x^2y^3}{12x^5y^2}$.

**Solution:**

(**a**) $\frac{20x^2}{4x^2} = \left(\frac{20}{4}\right)\left(\frac{x^2}{x^2}\right)$ Since $x^2 \div x^2 = 1$, the quotient is $\frac{20}{4} \cdot 1 = 5$, if $x \neq 0$.

(**b**) Rewrite $40x^3y^5 \div 8xy^3$ as a fraction; then divide. Assume that $x \neq 0$.

$\frac{40x^3y^5}{8xy^3} = \left(\frac{40}{8}\right)\left(\frac{x^3}{x}\right)\left(\frac{y^5}{y^3}\right) = 5\,(x^{3-1})(y^{5-3}) = 5x^2y^2$

(**c**) $\frac{6x^2y^3}{12x^5y^2} = \left(\frac{6}{12}\right)\left(\frac{x^2}{x^5}\right)\left(\frac{y^3}{y^2}\right) = \frac{1}{2} \cdot \frac{1}{x^{5-2}} \cdot \frac{y^{3-2}}{1} = \frac{1}{2} \cdot \frac{1}{x^3} \cdot \frac{y}{1} = \frac{y}{2x^3}$

Remember, when the greater exponent is in the denominator, you must write the base in the denominator and subtract exponents in the denominator.

A polynomial is a monomial, a sum of monomials, or a difference of monomials. A polynomial with *two* terms is called a *binomial,* and a

polynomial with *three* terms is called a *trinomial.* For simplicity, this discussion will concentrate on polynomials with one variable.

## Adding and subtracting polynomials

You can add polynomials vertically or horizontally.

**Example:** Add $3x^2 + 4x - 6$, $x^2 - 2x + 4$, and $2x^2 + 5x - 1$.

**Solution:** To add vertically, align like terms and add the monomials in each column.

$$\begin{aligned}
3x^2 + 4x - 6 \\
x^2 - 2x + 4 \\
\underline{2x^2 + 5x - 1} \\
6x^2 + 7x - 3 \quad \text{sum}
\end{aligned}$$

To add horizontally, rewrite the problem using symbols, remove parentheses, and combine like terms.

$(3x^2 + 4x - 6) + (x^2 - 2x + 4) + (2x^2 + 5x - 1) =$
$3x^2 + 4x - 6 + x^2 - 2x + 4 + 2x^2 + 5x - 1 =$
$6x^2 + 7x - 3$

You can subtract polynomials horizontally or vertically.

**Example:** Subtract $2x^2 - 3x + 5$ from $5x^2 + 4x - 7$.

**Solution:** To subtract horizontally, rewrite the problem using symbols, remove parentheses, and combine like terms.

$(5x^2 + 4x - 7) - (2x^2 - 3x + 5) =$
$5x^2 + 4x - 7 - 2x^2 + 3x - 5 =$
$3x^2 + 7x - 12$

To subtract vertically, align the like terms and subtract the monomials in each column. Remember when subtracting to add the opposite of the subtrahend to the minuend.

$$\begin{aligned}
5x^2 + 4x - 7 \quad &\text{Think: change the sign of} \\
\underline{2x^2 - 3x + 5} \quad &\text{the subtrahend and add.} \\
3x^2 + 7x - 12
\end{aligned}$$

## Multiplying Polynomials

To multiply a monomial and a polynomial, multiply each term of the polynomial by the monomial.

**Example:** Multiply $2x^2 - 3x + 5$ and $7x$.

**Solution:** $7x(2x^2 - 3x + 5) = 7x(2x^2) - (7x)(3x) + (7x)(5) = 14x^3 - 21x^2 + 35x$

To multiply two binomials, multiply each term of one binomial by each term of the other. This can be done horizontally or vertically.

**Example:** Multiply $(x + 3)$ and $(x + 2)$.

**Solution:** To multiply horizontally, rewrite the problem using symbols. Think of one binomial as a monomial and multiply, Then remove parentheses and combine like terms.

$$(x + 3)(x + 2) = (x + 3)x + (x + 3)2 \quad \text{Think of } (x + 3)$$
$$= x^2 + 3x + 2x + 6 \quad \text{as a monomial.}$$
$$= x^2 + 5x + 6$$

To multiply vertically, rewrite the problem. Align the right-hand digits of the factors and multiply.

$$
\begin{array}{r}
x + 3 \\
x + 2 \\
\hline
\end{array}
$$

| | |
|---|---|
| partial product | $2x + 6 \longleftarrow 2(x + 3)$ |
| partial product | $x^2 + 3x \longleftarrow x(x + 3)$ |
| product | $\overline{x^2 + 5x + 6}$ |

Products of trinomials and binomials are usually done vertically.

There is a technique, called the *FOIL* method, for multiplying binomials mentally.

1. Multiply the *first* terms of each binomial.
2. Multiply the two *outer* terms.
3. Multiply the two *inner* terms.
4. Multiply the *last* terms of each binomial.
5. Add the products.

$$
\begin{array}{c}
\overset{F \quad\quad L}{(x + 7)(x + 5)} \\
\underset{O}{\overset{I}{}}
\end{array}
$$

| first | outer | inner | last |
|-------|-------|-------|------|
| F | O | I | L |
| $x^2$ | $5x$ | $7x$ | $35$ |

$$x^2 + 12x + 35$$

The *FOIL* method will be very useful later when factoring polynomials.

## Dividing polynomials

To divide a polynomial by a monomial, divide each term of the polynomial by the monomial.

**Example:** Divide $6x^3 + 4x^2 - 18x$ by $2x$.

**Solution:** Rewrite the problem as a fraction. Then divide each term of the dividend by the divisor.

$$\frac{6x^3 + 4x^2 - 18x}{2x} = \frac{6x^3}{2x} + \frac{4x^2}{2x} - \frac{18x}{2x} =$$

$$\left(\frac{6}{2}\right)\left(\frac{x^3}{x}\right) + \left(\frac{4}{2}\right)\left(\frac{x^2}{x}\right) - \left(\frac{18}{2}\right)\left(\frac{x}{x}\right)$$

$$= 3(x^{3-1}) + 2(x^{2-1}) - 9 \cdot 1$$

$$= 3x^2 + 2x - 9$$

When dividing a polynomial of more than two terms by a binomial, the long-division form is usually best.

**Example:** Divide $x^2 + 2x - 35$ by $x + 7$.

**Solution:** Rewrite the problem in long-division form.

$$
\begin{array}{r}
x \phantom{xxxxxxx} \\
x + 7 \overline{) x^2 + 2x - 35}
\end{array}
$$

1. Divide the first term of the dividend by the first term of the divisor to find the first term of the quotient.

$$
\begin{array}{r}
x - 5 \phantom{xxx} \\
x + 7 \overline{) x^2 + 2x - 35} \\
\underline{x^2 + 7x} \phantom{xxxx} \\
- 5x - 35
\end{array}
$$

2. Multiply the divisor and the first term of the quotient.

3. Subtract the product in step 2 from the dividend and bring down the next term of the dividend.

$$
\begin{array}{r}
- 5x - 35 \\
\hline
0
\end{array}
$$

4. Repeat the procedure until the remainder is 0 or is a degree less than the degree of the divisor.

If there is a remainder, it may be left as the final difference or rewritten as a fraction in the form

$$\frac{\text{remainder}}{\text{divisor}} .$$

Sometimes not all of the powers are included in the dividend. When this occurs, zeros are used to represent missing powers.

**Example:** Divide $x^3 - 7x + 5$ by $x - 2$.

**Solution:** Rewrite the problem in long-division form. Since the $x^2$ term is missing in the dividend, you use $0x^2$ to represent that term.

$$
\begin{array}{r}
x^2 + 2x - 3 \phantom{xxx} \\
x - 2 \overline{) x^3 + 0x^2 - 7x + 5} \\
\underline{x^3 - 2x^2} \phantom{xxxxxxxx} \\
2x^2 - 7x \phantom{xxx} \\
\underline{2x^2 - 4x} \phantom{xxx} \\
- 3x + 5 \\
\underline{- 3x + 6} \\
- 1
\end{array}
$$

1. $\dfrac{x^3}{x} = x^2$

2. $x^2(x - 2) = x^3 - 2x^2$

3. Subtract and bring down the next term of the dividend.

4. $\dfrac{2x^2}{x} = 2x$

5. $2x (x - 2) = 2x^2 - 4x$

6. Subtract and bring down the last term of the dividend.

7. $\dfrac{-3x}{x} = -3$

8. $-3(x - 2) = -3x + 6$

9. Subtract.
The remainder may be left as is or rewritten as the fraction $\frac{-1}{x-2}$.

# Square roots

The symbol $\sqrt{\phantom{x}}$, called a *radical sign,* is used to indicate "square root." The number inside a radical sign is called the *radicand.* A radicand *cannot* be a negative number. In the example $\sqrt{16}$, the number 16 is the radicand. One square root of 16 is 4 because $4^2 = 16$. Another square root of 16 is $-4$ because $(-4)^2 = 16$. In symbols,

$$\sqrt{16} = 4 \text{ and } -\sqrt{16} = -4.$$

The symbol $\sqrt{\phantom{x}}$ without the negative sign indicates the *principal square root or positive square root. A perfect square,* such as 16, is a square of an integer or a rational number. The following are perfect squares.

integer perfect squares: 1, 4, 9, 16, 25, 49, 64, 81, 100

rational perfect squares: $1, \frac{1}{4}, \frac{1}{9}, \frac{4}{9}, \frac{9}{16}$

The square root of zero is zero.

## Simplifying radicals

Radicals are in simplest form if
  1. the radicand does not contain a whole-number factor (other than 1) that is a perfect square;
  2. no radicand is a fraction; and
  3. no denominator contains a radical sign.
To simplify radicals, you apply one (or both) of the following properties of radicals.
*Property 1:* If $a$ and $b$ are nonnegative real numbers, then $\sqrt{ab} = \sqrt{a} \cdot \sqrt{b}$.
*Property 2:* If $a$ is a nonnegative real number and $b$ is a positive real number,

$$\sqrt{\frac{a}{b}} = \frac{\sqrt{a}}{\sqrt{b}}$$

**Example:** Simplify each radical: (a) $\sqrt{50}$; (b) $\sqrt{\frac{4}{9}}$; (c) $\sqrt{\frac{3}{4}}$; (d) $\sqrt{\frac{1}{5}}$.

**Solution:**
(a) Rewrite the radicand as a product so that one of the factors is a perfect square. Then apply Property 1 and simplify.

$$\underset{\text{perfect square}}{\sqrt{50} = \sqrt{25 \cdot 2}} = \sqrt{25} \cdot \sqrt{2} = 5\sqrt{2}$$

(b) The radicand is a perfect square. So $\sqrt{\frac{4}{9}} = \frac{2}{3}$.

(c) The radicand is a fraction. The denominator is a

perfect square. Apply Property 2 and simplify.

$$\sqrt{\frac{3}{4}} = \frac{\sqrt{3}}{\sqrt{4}} = \frac{\sqrt{3}}{2}$$

(d) The radicand is a fraction. Multiply to make the denominator a perfect square. Apply Property 2 and simplify.

$$\sqrt{\frac{1}{5}} = \sqrt{\frac{1 \cdot 5}{5 \cdot 5}} = \sqrt{\frac{5}{25}} = \frac{\sqrt{5}}{\sqrt{25}} = \frac{\sqrt{5}}{5}$$

## Multiplying and dividing radicals

To multiply and divide radicals, apply Property 1 and Property 2 in reverse.

**Example:** Multiply: (a) $\sqrt{2} \cdot \sqrt{3}$; (b) $\sqrt{2x} \cdot \sqrt{5x}$.

**Solution:**
(a) Apply Property 1. $\sqrt{2} \cdot \sqrt{3} = \sqrt{2 \cdot 3} = \sqrt{6}$.
Since 6 does not contain a perfect square other than 1, $\sqrt{6}$ is in simplest form.

(b) When variables are in the radicand, you assume that they represent nonnegative real numbers.

$$\sqrt{2x} \cdot \sqrt{5x} = \sqrt{(2x)(5x)} = \sqrt{10x^2} = \sqrt{x^2} \cdot \sqrt{10} = x\sqrt{10}$$

**Example:** Divide: (a) $\sqrt{10} \div \sqrt{2}$; (b) $\sqrt{5} \div \sqrt{3}$.

**Solution:**
(a) Rewrite the problem as a fraction and apply Property 2.

$$\sqrt{10} \div \sqrt{2} = \frac{\sqrt{10}}{\sqrt{2}} = \sqrt{\frac{10}{2}} = \sqrt{5}$$

(b) Rewrite the problem as a fraction and apply Property 2. Then multiply to make the denominator a perfect square and simplify.

$$\sqrt{5} \div \sqrt{3} = \frac{\sqrt{5}}{\sqrt{3}} = \sqrt{\frac{5}{3}} = \sqrt{\frac{5 \cdot 3}{3 \cdot 3}} = \sqrt{\frac{15}{9}} = \frac{\sqrt{15}}{\sqrt{9}} = \frac{\sqrt{15}}{3}$$

## Adding and subtracting radicals

To add and subtract radicals, the radicands must be the same.

**Example:** Add $3\sqrt{2}$ and $7\sqrt{2}$.

**Solution:** Rewrite the problem using symbols and add.

$$3\sqrt{2} + 7\sqrt{2} = (3 + 7)\sqrt{2} = 10\sqrt{2}$$

**Example:** Subtract $5\sqrt{6}$ from $16\sqrt{6}$.

**Solution:** Rewrite the problem using symbols and subtract.

$$16\sqrt{6} - 5\sqrt{6} = (16 - 5)\sqrt{6} = 11\sqrt{6}$$

Sometimes it is necessary to simplify radicals before you can add or subtract.

**Example:** Add $\sqrt{18}$ and $\sqrt{50}$.

**Solution:** Simplify $\sqrt{18}$ and $\sqrt{50}$.

$$\sqrt{18} = \sqrt{9 \cdot 2} = \sqrt{9} \cdot \sqrt{2} = 3\sqrt{2}$$
$$\sqrt{50} = \sqrt{25 \cdot 2} = \sqrt{25} \cdot \sqrt{2} = 5\sqrt{2}$$

Since the radicands are now the same, you can now add.

$$\sqrt{18} + \sqrt{50} = 3\sqrt{2} + 5\sqrt{2} = (3 + 5)\sqrt{2} = 8\sqrt{2}$$

# Factoring polynomials

Factoring polynomials is the reverse of multiplying polynomials. *To factor* a polynomial means to re-write the polynomial as an indicated product of polynomials. The simplest kind of factoring is common monomial factoring. You already considered common monomial factoring when you applied the distributive property to express sums and differences as products.

**Example:** Factor each polynomial: (**a**) $5x + 20$;
(**b**) $5x^3 + 35x^2 - 10x$.

**Solution:**
(**a**) You can express $5x + 20$ as $5 \cdot x + 5 \cdot 4$. By applying the distributive property, $5x + 20 = 5 \cdot x + 5 \cdot 4 = 5(x + 4)$. The common monomial factor is 5. The other factor is a binomial factor.

(**b**) To find the common monomial factor, you can think of $5x^3 + 35x^2 - 10x$ as $5x \cdot x^2 + 5x \cdot 7x - 5x \cdot 2$. Since $5x$ is a factor of each term, it is a common monomial factor. In factored form, $5x^3 + 35x^2 - 10x = 5x (x^2 + 7x - 2)$. Since $x^2 + 7x - 2$ has no common factor other than 1, you say that $5x$ is the *greatest common factor*. You can check the factors by multiplication.

A binomial that can be written in the form

minus sign
$$a^2 \overset{|}{-} b^2$$
perfect square   perfect square

is called a difference of two squares. The difference of two squares can be factored as follows.

$$a^2 - b^2 = (a + b)(a - b)$$

**Example:** Factor $x^2 - 16$.

**Solution:** The polynomial is a difference of two squares. The factors are $x + 4$ and $x - 4$.

$$x^2 - 16 = (x + 4)(x - 4)$$

You can check the factors by using the *FOIL* method for multiplying binomials.

Sometimes it is necessary to remove a common monomial factor before you can recognize the difference of two squares.

**Example:** Factor $28x^2 - 7$.

**Solution:** As written, neither the first term nor the second term is a perfect square. However, there is a common monomial factor.

$$28x^2 - 7 = 7(4x^2 - 1)$$

The resulting binomial factor is a difference of two squares and can be factored.

$$28x^2 - 7 = 7(4x^2 - 1) = 7(2x + 1)(2x - 1)$$

# Solving quadratic equations in one variable

A quadratic equation in one variable is any equation that can be written as $ax^2 + bx + c = 0$; in which $a, b,$ and $c$ are real numbers and $a \neq 0$. Simple quadratic equations like $x^2 = 16$ can be solved for $x$ by finding the square root of both sides of the equation. $x = \sqrt{16} = \pm 4$.

Certain polynomial equations can also be solved by factoring.

**Example:** Solve $x^2 + 4x - 21 = 0$ for $x$.

**Solution:** $x^2 + 4x - 21 = 0$
$(x + 7)(x - 3) = 0$ Factor the left member of the equation.

When a product is equal to 0, one of the factors must be equal to 0.

| either | or |
|---|---|
| $x + 7 = 0$ | $x - 3 = 0$ |
| $x = -7$ | $x = 3$ |

The solution set is $\{-7, 3\}$. Sometimes, $-7$ and 3 are called solutions (or roots) of $x^2 + 4x - 21 = 0$.

Not all quadratic equations in one variable can be solved by factoring. However, every quadratic equation that has real-number solutions can be solved by using the quadratic formula. If $a, b,$ and $c$ are real numbers and $a \neq 0$, then the solutions for $ax^2 + bx + c = 0$ can be found by applying the following formula.

$$x = \frac{-b \pm \sqrt{b^2 - 4ac}}{2a}$$

If $b^2 - 4ac$ is less than 0, $\sqrt{b^2 - 4ac}$ is not a real number, and there are no real-number solutions of the equation.

# 3. Reviewing geometry

Geometry is one of the first chances students usually receive to study a mathematical system. A mathematical system contains

1. undefined terms;
2. definitions;
3. properties that are accepted as true without proof;
4. a system of logic for making decisions; and
5. statements that are proved.

The undefined terms of geometry are *point*, *line*, *plane*, and *space*.

| point | line | plane |
|---|---|---|
| Identified by a capital letter, for example, point A. | $\overleftrightarrow{AB}$ or $\ell$. | Identified by a capital script letter, for example, plane M. |

To understand geometry, you must first understand the undefined terms. A *point* has *no* dimensions. A *line* (straight line) is a set of points and has *one* dimension—length. A *plane* is a set of points that has *two* dimensions—length and width. *Space* is the set of all points. The undefined terms are used to define other geometric terms like line segment, ray, angle, triangle, circle, and solid, as will be shown below.

The study of logic for geometry could comprise an entire unit. However, most geometric statements are "if, then" statements or "conditionals." For example:

$$\underbrace{\text{if } 2x = 6}_{\text{hypothesis}} \quad \underbrace{\text{then } x = 3.}_{\text{conclusion}}$$

The "if" part of an "if, then" statement is assumed to be true, whereas the "then" part of the statement must be proved. The most common logical reasoning pattern used in geometric proof is called the law of detachment, or modus ponens. (Three dots ∴ represent the word "therefore.")

law of detachment
If *p*, then q.  (general statement)
   *p* is true.  (specific statement)
∴ q is true.  (conclusion)

In a geometric proof, the form is somewhat different:

| statements | reasons |
|---|---|
| *p* (specific statement) ∴ *q* (conclusion) | Given. If *p*, then *q* (general statement). |

**Example:** Prove: If $2x = 6$, then $x = 3$.

**Solution:**

| statements | reasons |
|---|---|
| 1. $2x = 6$ | 1. Given. |
| 2. $x = 3$ | 2. If equals are divided by equals, the quotients are equal. |

The properties that function as general statements in geometric proofs are definitions, assumed statements (called axioms, postulates, or simply assumptions), or previously proved statements (called theorems). Some of the more common introductory axioms of geometry are listed below.

AXIOMS:

1. A line contains at least two distinct points.
2. Given two distinct points, there is exactly one line that contains them.
3. A plane contains at least three points that are not collinear (in line).
4. Given three distinct points not on the same line, there is exactly one plane that contains them.
5. Space contains at least four points that are not coplanar (on the same plane).

6. If a plane contains two points of a line, the plane contains the line.
7. If two distinct planes intersect, the intersection is a line.

In addition to these axioms, all of the properties of real numbers (from Section 2) are assumed. Other axioms are necessary as you progress through geometry and will be stated as you proceed through this section.

## Distance

In geometry, distance is a *positive* real number.

AXIOM: Given any two distinct points, there is a positive real number that represents the distance from one to the other.

The distance from A to B (AB) can be found by counting or by subtracting the coordinates of the points ($-3$ is the coordinate of point A and 5 is the coordinate of point B). Since distance is a positive number, you must always subtract the lesser coordinate from the greater or use absolute value symbols. The distance from A to B is 8.

## Betweenness

The concept of "between" for points is included in most modern geometry textbooks. This concept was introduced to eliminate dependence on figures in geometric proof.

DEFINITION: Point Q is between points P and R whenever (1) points P, Q, and R are collinear; and (2) the distance from P to Q plus the distance from Q to R is equal to the distance from P to R; that is, $PQ + QR = PR$.

Q is *not* between P and R.     Q is *not* between P and R.
(P, Q, and R are not collinear.)   ($PQ + QR \neq PR$)

The idea of "betweenness" lends itself to rather easy geometric proofs. There are two types of geometric proof—direct and indirect. Direct proof is the most common. A direct proof consists of

1. a figure;
2. given information (in terms of the figure);
3. a statement of what to prove (in terms of the figure):

4. a plan; and
5. statements and reasons.

A direct proof is usually organized as follows. Mathematical symbols are often used to abbreviate key words in the reasons in a proof.

Given:
Prove:
Proof:

| statements | reasons |
| --- | --- |
|  |  |

**Example:** Write statements and reasons to complete the following proof.
Given: P, Q, and R are points of line $\ell$ and Q is between P and R.
Prove: $QR = PR - PQ$.

**Solution:** Plan: We can use the fact that Q is between P and R (given) and the definition of "between" for points to prove that $PQ + QR = PR$. Then, by applying the subtraction property of equality, we can subtract PQ from both sides of the equation to obtain $QR = PR - PQ$. The proof can be written as follows:

Proof:

| statements | reasons |
| --- | --- |
| 1. P, Q, and R are points of line $\ell$. | 1. Given. |
| 2. Q is between P and R. | 2. Given. |
| 3. $PQ + QR = PR$ | 3. Definition of "between" for points. |
| 4. $QR = PR - PQ$ | 4. Subtraction property of equality. |

When writing a proof, it is a good idea to list one statement per step. All of the given information must be included in the proof. The first step contains information about the figure. Statement 2 and statement 3 comprise a basic reasoning pattern (law of detachment).

| | |
| --- | --- |
| 2. Q is between P and R (specific statement). | 2. Given. |
| 3. $PQ + QR = PR$ (conclusion). | 3. If Q is between P and R, then $PQ + QR = PR$ (general statement). |

The conclusion of this reasoning pattern becomes the specific statement in the next reasoning pattern.

| | |
| --- | --- |
| 3. $PQ + QR = PR$ | |
| 4. $QR = PR - PQ$ | 4. If equals are subtracted from equals, then the differences are equal. |

## Line segments and rays

A *line segment* is a set of points in a plane—a subset of a line.

DEFINITION: If P and Q are distinct points, line segment PQ is the set whose elements are P, Q, and all points of line PQ between P and Q.

line segment PQ
symbol: $\overline{PQ}$

P and Q are the endpoints of $\overline{PQ}$.

The measure of a line segment is the distance from one endpoint to the other. Each line segment has exactly *one* measure.

**Example:** Find the measure (symbol m) of each line segment: (**a**) $\overline{AB}$: (**b**) $\overline{CD}$.

**Solution:**
(**a**) The distance from A to B is 6. So, m($\overline{AB}$) = 6.

(**b**) The distance from C to D is 7. So, m($\overline{CD}$) = 7.

If two line segments have the same measure, we say that the line segments are *congruent*. The symbol $\cong$ *is used to indicate congruence.*

**Example:** Tell which two segments are congruent.

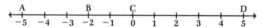

**Solution:** Find the measures of the segments
m($\overline{AB}$) = 3; m($\overline{AC}$) = 5; m($\overline{AD}$) = 10;
m($\overline{BC}$) = 2; m($\overline{CD}$) = 5; m($\overline{BD}$) = 7. Since
m($\overline{CD}$) = m($\overline{AC}$) = 5, you can conclude that
$\overline{CD} \cong \overline{AC}$.

A *ray* is also a subset of a line.

DEFINITION: If P and Q are distinct points, ray PQ is the union of $\overline{PQ}$ and the set of all points R such that Q is between P and R.

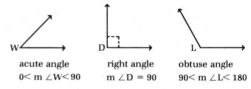

ray PQ
symbol: $\overrightarrow{PQ}$

P is the endpoint of $\overrightarrow{PQ}$.

The endpoint of a ray is always named first. If two collinear rays have the same endpoint and extend in opposite directions, they are called "opposite" rays.

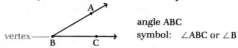

$\overrightarrow{PR}$ and $\overrightarrow{PQ}$ are opposite rays.

# Angles

An *angle* is a set of points in a plane.

DEFINITION: An angle is the union of two noncollinear rays that have a common endpoint.

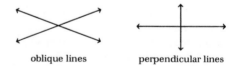

angle ABC
symbol: $\angle ABC$ or $\angle B$

$\overrightarrow{BA}$ and $\overrightarrow{BC}$ are called *sides*. When three letters are used to name an angle, the vertex letter of the angle is always given in the center.

AXIOM: To every angle there corresponds a unique real number greater than 0 and less than 180. The angle measures most commonly used are degree measures. Angles are classified according to "size."

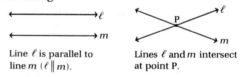

acute angle
0< m $\angle W$< 90

right angle
m $\angle D$ = 90

obtuse angle
90< m $\angle L$< 180

**Example:** Classify each angle, given that
(**a**) m $\angle A$ = 37; (**b**) m $\angle X$ = 126; (**c**) m $\angle B$ = 90.

**Solution:**
(**a**) Since 37 is greater than 0 and less than 90, $\angle A$ is an acute angle.

(**b**) Since 126 is greater than 90 and less than 180, $\angle X$ is an obtuse angle.

(**c**) Since m $\angle B$ = 90, $\angle B$ is a right angle.

If two angles have the same measure, the angles are congruent.

# Lines and planes

Two lines in the same plane are either *parallel* or *intersecting*.

Line $\ell$ is parallel to line $m$ ($\ell \| m$).

Lines $\ell$ and $m$ intersect at point P.

If two lines intersect, they are either *oblique* or *perpendicular*.

oblique lines

perpendicular lines

Angles formed by perpendicular lines are right angles. Angles formed by oblique lines are either acute or obtuse angles.

If two lines intersect, there is exactly one plane that contains both lines.

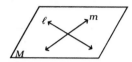

If two planes intersect, the intersection is a line.

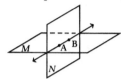

The intersection of plane M and plane N is AB.

A line can be parallel to a plane or can intersect the plane.

Line ℓ ∥ plane M.      Line ℓ intersects plane M at P.

Remember from the list of axioms that if a plane contains two points of a line, it contains the line.

If two planes do not intersect, they are parallel.

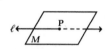

Plane M ∥ plane N.

# Circles, line segments, and lines

A *circle* is a set of points in a plane.

DEFINITION: A circle is the set of all points in a plane that are a given distance from a given point of the plane.

circle O
symbol:  ⊙O

Three line segments are associated with every circle.

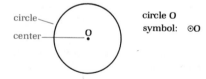

$\overline{OA}$ is a radius.
$\overline{EF}$ is a chord.
$\overline{BC}$ is a diameter.

One endpoint of a *radius* is the center of the circle and the other endpoint is a point of the circle. Both endpoints of a *chord* are points of the circle. A *diameter* is a chord that contains the center of the circle.

There are two lines associated with a circle.

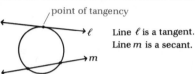

point of tangency

Line ℓ is a tangent.
Line m is a secant.

A *tangent* intersects a circle in exactly one point. The radius drawn to the point of tangency is perpendicular to the tangent. A *secant* contains a chord of the circle. As a result, it intersects the circle in two points.

# Pairs of angles

If the measures of two angles are added and

1. the sum is 90, the angles are *complementary angles*.
2. the sum is 180, the angles are *supplementary angles*.

**Example:** Two complementary angles have measures of $x + 40$ and $2x - 10$. Find the measure of each angle.

**Solution:** Since the angles are complementary, the sum of their measures is 90. You can use this fact to write an equation and then solve it for $x$.

$$(x + 40) + (2x - 10) = 90$$
$$3x + 30 = 90$$
$$3x = 60$$
$$x = 20$$

Now, by substituting 20 for $x$, you can find the measure of each angle.

$$x + 40 = 20 + 40 = 60 \quad 2x - 10 = 2(20) - 10 = 30$$

**Example:** Angles A and B are supplementary angles. If the measure of ∠B is 20 more than 3 times the measure of ∠A, find the measure of each angle.

**Solution:** You begin by representing the measures of both angles.

Let: $x$ = the measure of ∠A.
$3x + 20$ = the measure of ∠B.

Because the two angles are supplementary, the sum of their measures is 180.

$$x + (3x + 20) = 180$$
$$4x + 20 = 180$$
$$4x = 160$$
$$x = 40$$
$$3x + 20 = 140$$

Adjacent angles are *two* angles that (1) are co-planar; (2) have the same vertex; (3) have a common side; and (4) have no common interior points.

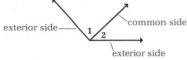

exterior side

common side

exterior side

∠1 and ∠2 are adjacent angles.

If the exterior sides of two adjacent angles are opposite rays, the angles are supplementary.

**Example:** Refer to the figure below. Find the measure of ∠1 given that m ∠2 = 72.

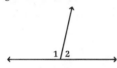

**Solution:** The two angles are adjacent and the exterior sides are opposite rays. So, the angles are supplementary.

m ∠1 + m ∠2 = 180

Now if you substitute 72 for m ∠2, you can solve for m ∠1.

m ∠1 + 72 = 180
m ∠1 = 108

The nonadjacent angles formed by two intersecting lines are called *vertical angles.*

∠1 and ∠3 are vertical angles.
∠2 and ∠4 are vertical angles.

If two angles are vertical angles, they are congruent.

## Triangles

A triangle is a set of points in a plane.

DEFINITION: If A, B, and C are three distinct noncollinear points, triangle ABC is the union of $\overline{AB}$, $\overline{BC}$, and $\overline{AC}$.

triangle ABC
symbol: △ABC
angles: ∠A, ∠B, ∠C
sides: $\overline{AB}$, $\overline{AC}$, $\overline{BC}$

Triangles can be classified by side.

scalene:
no congruent
sides

isosceles:
two congruent
sides

equilateral:
three congruent
sides

Or they can be classified by angle.

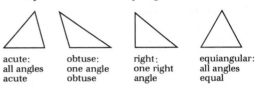

acute:
all angles
acute

obtuse:
one angle
obtuse

right:
one right
angle

equiangular:
all angles
equal

The sides of a right triangle are given special names.

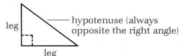

leg

hypotenuse (always opposite the right angle)

leg

The sum of the measures of the angles of a triangle is always 180.

## Triangles and congruence

Congruence of triangles is an important geometric concept. In general terms, two triangles are congruent if they have the same *size* and *shape.* In modern geometry courses, however, congruence of triangles is developed by using the idea of one-to-one correspondence.

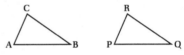

There are six different ways to match the vertices of △ABC with those of △PQR. One of them is given below.

A↔P, B↔Q, C↔R

This correspondence automatically pairs angles and sides of the two triangles.

| corresponding angles | corresponding sides |
|---|---|
| ∠A↔∠P | $\overline{AB}$↔$\overline{PQ}$ |
| ∠B↔∠Q | $\overline{BC}$↔$\overline{QR}$ |
| ∠C↔∠R | $\overline{AC}$↔$\overline{PR}$ |

Now, if corresponding angles *and* corresponding sides are congruent, that is, if

∠A ≅ ∠P          $\overline{AB}$ ≅ $\overline{PQ}$
∠B ≅ ∠Q   and   $\overline{BC}$ ≅ $\overline{QR}$
∠C ≅ ∠R          $\overline{AC}$ ≅ $\overline{PR}$

the correspondence is a congruence of triangles. You can indicate that the triangles are congruent by writing △ABC ≅ △PQR.

The order in which the vertices are named indicates the corresponding parts of congruent triangles.

**Example:** Given that $\triangle WDL \cong \triangle SRO$, identify the congruent corresponding parts.

**Solution:** Because of the order in which the letters are written:

$\angle W \cong \angle S$      $\overline{WD} \cong \overline{SR}$

$\angle D \cong \angle R$      $\overline{DL} \cong \overline{RO}$

$\angle L \cong \angle O$      $\overline{WL} \cong \overline{SO}$

Once you know that two triangles are congruent, you know automatically that all six corresponding parts are congruent. To prove that two triangles are congruent, it is necessary to accept new axioms.

AXIOM: Two triangles are congruent if three sides of one triangle are congruent to three sides of the other triangle (abbreviated SSS).

AXIOM: Two triangles are congruent if two sides and the included angle of one triangle are congruent to two sides and the included angle of the other triangle (abbreviated SAS).

AXIOM: Two triangles are congruent if two angles and the included side of one triangle are congruent to two angles and the included side of the other triangle (abbreviated ASA).

AXIOM: Two right triangles are congruent if the hypotenuse and leg of one right triangle are congruent to the hypotenuse and leg of the other right triangle (abbreviated HL).

**Example:** Given: $\triangle PQS$ and $\triangle RSQ$ with common side $\overline{SQ}$; $\overline{PQ} \cong \overline{RS}$; $\overline{PS} \cong \overline{RQ}$.
Prove: $\angle P \cong \angle R$.

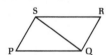

**Solution:** Plan: We will prove that $\triangle PQS$ is congruent to $\triangle RSQ$. Then $\angle P$ will be congruent to $\angle R$ because they are corresponding parts of congruent triangles. To help yourself decide which congruence axiom to use, mark the congruent segments on the figure. Since $\overline{SQ}$ is in both triangles, three sides of one triangle are congruent to three sides of the other triangle.

Proof:

| statements | reasons |
|---|---|
| 1. $\triangle PQS$ and $\triangle RSQ$ with common side $\overline{SQ}$. | 1. Given. |
| 2. $\overline{PQ} \cong \overline{RS}$ | 2. Given. |
| 3. $\overline{PS} \cong \overline{RQ}$ | 3. Given. |
| 4. $\overline{SQ} \cong \overline{SQ}$ | 4. A line segment is congruent to itself. |
| 5. $\triangle PSQ \cong \triangle RSQ$ | 5. SSS congruence axiom. |
| 6. $\therefore \angle P \cong \angle R$ | 6. Corresponding parts of congruent triangles are congruent. |

## Parallel lines

Two lines in the same plane that do not intersect are *parallel*. A line that intersects two coplanar lines at distinct points is called a *transversal*. Line $t$ in the following diagrams is a transversal.

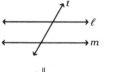

$\ell \parallel m$            $\ell$ not parallel to $m$

A transversal and two coplanar lines form eight angles.

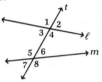

The four angles outside the given lines are called *exterior* angles. The four angles inside the given lines are called *interior* angles.

exterior angles: $\angle 1$, $\angle 2$, $\angle 7$, $\angle 8$
interior angles: $\angle 3$, $\angle 4$, $\angle 5$, $\angle 6$

Certain pairs of these angles have special names. *Alternate interior angles* are two interior angles, like $\angle 3$ and $\angle 6$, that

1. have different vertices; and
2. are on opposite sides of the transversal.

*Alternate exterior angles* are two exterior angles, like $\angle 1$ and $\angle 8$, that

1. have different vertices; and
2. are on opposite sides of the transversal.

*Corresponding angles* are two angles, like $\angle 1$ and $\angle 5$, that

1. have different vertices;
2. are on the same side of the transversal; and
3. comprise one interior angle and one exterior angle.

*alternate interior angles*
     $\angle 3$ and $\angle 6$
     $\angle 4$ and $\angle 5$

*alternate exterior angles*
   ∠1 and ∠8
   ∠2 and ∠7
*corresponding angles*
   ∠1 and ∠5; ∠3 and ∠7
   ∠2 and ∠6; ∠4 and ∠8

To develop ideas concerning these angles and parallel lines, you accept two axioms.

AXIOM 1: If two parallel lines are cut by a transversal, each pair of corresponding angles is congruent.

Once this axiom has been accepted, it is possible to prove two useful theorems.

THEOREM 1: If two parallel lines are cut by a transversal, each pair of alternate interior angles is congruent.

THEOREM 2: If two parallel lines are cut by a transversal, each pair of alternate exterior angles is congruent.

**Example:** Prove Theorem 1 for one pair of alternate angles.

**Solution:** Draw a figure that accurately depicts the conditions described in the theorem. Write the "given" and "prove" in terms of the figure. Given: Lines ℓ and *m* cut by transversal *t*; ℓ∥*m*.
*Prove:* ∠1 ≅ ∠2.

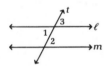

Plan: We will use the axiom to prove that ∠2 ≅ ∠3 and the fact that ∠1 and ∠3 are vertical angles to prove that ∠1 ≅ ∠3. Then, the transitive property guarantees that ∠1 ≅ ∠2.

Proof:

| statements | reasons |
|---|---|
| 1. Lines ℓ and *m* cut by transversal *t*. | 1. Given. |
| 2. ∠2 and ∠3 are corresponding angles. | 2. Definition of corresponding angles. |
| 3. ℓ ∥ *m* | 3. Given. |
| 4. ∠2 ≅ ∠3 | 4. If two parallel lines are cut by a transversal, each pair of corresponding angles are congruent. |
| 5. ∠1 and ∠3 are vertical angles. | 5. Definition of vertical angles. |

| | |
|---|---|
| 6. ∠1 ≅ ∠3 | 6. If two angles are vertical angles, they are congruent. |
| 7. ∴ ∠1 ≅ ∠2 | 7. Steps 4 and 6 and the transitive property of equality (if ∠1 ≅ ∠3 and ∠3 ≅ ∠2, then ∠1 ≅ ∠2). |

AXIOM 2: If two lines are cut by a transversal so that a pair of corresponding angles is congruent, the lines are parallel.

This axiom makes it possible to prove the following theorems.

THEOREM: If two lines are cut by a transversal so that a pair of alternate interior angles is congruent, the lines are parallel.

THEOREM: If two lines are cut by a transversal so that a pair of alternate exterior angles is congruent, the lines are parallel.

# Indirect proof

An indirect proof uses the following type of reasoning:
1. assume the opposite of the statement you are trying to prove;
2. show that this assumption leads to a statement that contradicts a known fact; and
3. so the assumption must be false and its opposite (the statement you wanted to prove) is true.

**Example:** Given: Lines ℓ and *m* cut by transversal *t*; ∠1 ≇ ∠2.
Prove: ℓ is not parallel to *m*.

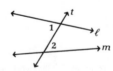

**Solution:** Plan: Assume that ℓ is parallel to *m*. Then show that ∠1 ≅ ∠2, which contradicts the given statement.

Indirect Proof: Assume ℓ ∥ *m*. Since ∠1 and ∠2 are alternate interior angles (definition of alternate interior angles), they are congruent. If two parallel lines are cut by a transversal, each pair of alternate interior angles is congruent, so ∠1 ≅ ∠2. But this contradicts the fact that ∠1 ≇ ∠2 (given). Therefore, the assumption must be false, and ℓ is not parallel to *m*.

# Polygons

The simplest polygon is a triangle. The sum of the measures of the angles of a triangle is 180.

Polygons are named by the number of sides.

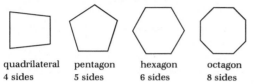

| quadrilateral | pentagon | hexagon | octagon |
|---|---|---|---|
| 4 sides | 5 sides | 6 sides | 8 sides |

Each polygon has interior angles and exterior angles.

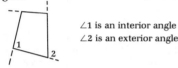

$\angle 1$ is an interior angle
$\angle 2$ is an exterior angle

The number of interior angles of a polygon is equal to the number of its sides. To find the sum of the measures of the *interior* angles of a polygon, you apply the formula $I = 180\,(n - 2)$, in which the variable $n$ represents the number of sides. The sum of the measures of the *exterior* angles of a polygon is always 360.

**Example:** Find the sum of the measures of the interior angles of a pentagon.

**Solution:** A pentagon has 5 sides. Write the formula, substitute 5 for $n$, and solve the resulting equation for $I$. $I = 180\,(n - 2) = 180\,(5 - 2) = 540$. The sum of the measures of the interior angles of a pentagon is 540.

You can also use this formula to find the number of sides (or interior angles) a polygon has, given the sum of the measures of the interior angles. Write the formula, substitute the sum of the measures of the interior angles for $I$, and solve for $n$.

A regular polygon is a polygon that has all of its interior angles congruent and all of its sides congruent. Since the angles of a regular polygon are congruent, it is possible to find the measure of one interior angle (or one exterior angle) by dividing the sum of the measures of the interior angles (or exterior angles) by the number of sides in the polygon.

The measure of one exterior angle of a regular polygon with $n$
sides $= E_1 = \dfrac{360}{n}$

The measure of one interior angle of a regular polygon with $n$
sides $= I_1 = \dfrac{180(n - 2)}{n}$

**Example:** Find the number of degrees in (**a**) one exterior angle of a regular hexagon; (**b**) one interior angle of a regular pentagon.

**Solution:**

(**a**) A regular hexagon has 6 sides. To find the number of degrees in each exterior angle, we divide 360 by 6.

$$E_1 = \frac{360}{n} = \frac{360}{6} = 60$$

(**b**) A regular pentagon has 5 sides. To find the number of degrees in each interior angle, you write the formula, substitute 5 for $n$ and solve for $I_1$.

$$I_1 = \frac{180(n - 2)}{n} = \frac{180(5 - 2)}{5} = 108.$$

These formulas can also be used to determine the number of sides a regular polygon has, given the measure of one interior (or exterior) angle. Write the appropriate formula, substitute the measure of one interior (or exterior) angle for $E_1$, and solve the resulting equation for $n$.

# Quadrilaterals

A *quadrilateral* is a polygon with four sides. If both pairs of opposite sides are parallel, the quadrilateral is a *parallelogram*.

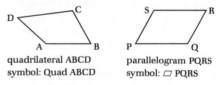

quadrilateral ABCD
symbol: Quad ABCD

parallelogram PQRS
symbol: ▱ PQRS

A line segment that joins two nonadjacent vertices of a quadrilateral is called a *diagonal* of the quadrilateral.

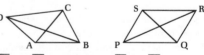

$\overline{BD}$ and $\overline{AC}$ are diagonals of Quad ABCD.

$\overline{PR}$ and $\overline{SQ}$ are diagonals of ▱ PQRS.

By using diagonals and ideas from parallel lines, you can prove four important theorems about parallelograms.

THEOREM 1: Either diagonal of a parallelogram separates the parallelogram into two congruent triangles.

THEOREM 2: The opposite angles of a parallelogram are congruent.

THEOREM 3: The opposite sides of a parallelogram are congruent.

THEOREM 4: The diagonals of a parallelogram bisect each other.

The definition of parallelogram or one of the following theorems can be used to prove that a quadrilateral is a parallelogram.

THEOREM 5: A quadrilateral is a parallelogram if one pair of opposite sides is both congruent and parallel.

THEOREM 6: A quadrilateral is a parallelogram if both pairs of opposite sides are congruent.

THEOREM 7: A quadrilateral is a parallelogram if the diagonals bisect each other.

The following quadrilaterals are special parallelograms.

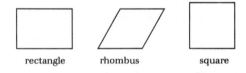

rectangle          rhombus          square

A *rectangle* is a parallelogram that has four right angles. A *rhombus* is a parallelogram that has four congruent sides. A *square* is a rectangle that has four congruent sides and four right angles.

Since rectangles, rhombuses, and squares are parallelograms, all of the theorems proved for parallelograms apply to these figures. There are some special theorems, however, that apply only to rectangles, rhombuses, and squares.

THEOREM 8: The diagonals of a rectangle (square) are congruent line segments.

THEOREM 9: The diagonals of a rhombus (square) are perpendicular to each other.

If only two sides of a quadrilateral are parallel, the quadrilateral is a *trapezoid*.

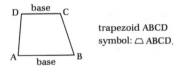

trapezoid ABCD
symbol: ▱ ABCD.

The two parallel sides of a trapezoid are called its bases. A trapezoid has three important line segments associated with it—two diagonals and the line segment joining the midpoints of the nonparallel sides, called the *median*.

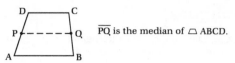

$\overline{PQ}$ is the median of ▱ ABCD.

The median of any trapezoid is a line segment that
1. is parallel to both bases $(\overline{PQ} \parallel \overline{AB}$ and $\overline{PQ} \parallel \overline{CD})$; and
2. has a measure that is one-half the sum of the measures of the two bases $[PQ = \frac{1}{2}(AB + CD)]$.

**Example :** Find the measure of the median of a trapezoid if one base is 9 inches long and the other base is 15 inches long.

**Solution:** The measure of the median is one-half the sum of the measures of the bases. In symbols, the median $= \frac{1}{2}(9 + 15) = \frac{1}{2}(24) = 12$. The median is 12 inches long.

In an isosceles trapezoid, the nonparallel sides are congruent.

## Similarity

Two polygons are similar if they have the same shape. By definition, two polygons are similar if

1. the corresponding angles are congruent; and
2. the lengths of corresponding sides are proportional.

To prove that two triangles are similar (symbol~), we use the following axiom.

AXIOM: Two triangles are similar if two angles of one triangle are congruent to two angles of the other triangle (abbreviated AA).

**Example:** Given: △ABC with $\overline{BD} \perp \overline{AC}$; ∠ABC is a right angle.
Prove: △ADB ~ △ABC.

**Solution:** Plan: Prove that two angles of △ABC are congruent to two angles of △ADB.

Proof:

| statements | reasons |
| --- | --- |
| 1. △ ABC; $\overline{BD} \perp \overline{AC}$ | 1. Given. |
| 2. ∠ BDA is a right angle. | 2. If two lines are perpendicular, they intersect to form right angles. |
| 3. ∠ ABC is a right angle. | 3. Given. |
| 4. ∠ BDA ≅ ∠ ABC | 4. All right angles are congruent. |
| 5. ∠ A ≅ ∠ A | 5. An angle is congruent to itself. |
| 6. ∴ △ ADB ~ △ ABC | 6. AA axiom. |

By using the same procedure, it is possible to prove that $\triangle BDC \sim \triangle ABC$ and that $\triangle ADB \sim \triangle BDC$. Hence, it becomes possible to prove the following theorem.

THEOREM: The altitude to the hypotenuse of a right triangle forms two other right triangles that are similar to the given right triangle and to each other.

Once this theorem has been proved, three algebraic relationships can easily be established.

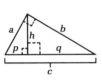

a = length of a leg
b = length of other leg
c = length of the hypotenuse
h = length of the altitude to the hypotenuse
p = length of one segment of the hypotenuse
q = length of other segment of the hypotenuse

| Property 1 | Property 2 | Property 3 |
|---|---|---|
| $\dfrac{p}{h} = \dfrac{h}{q}$ | $\dfrac{c}{a} = \dfrac{a}{p}$ | $\dfrac{c}{b} = \dfrac{b}{q}$ |

In Property 1, the length of the altitude to the hypotenuse is the *mean proportional* between the lengths of the segments of the hypotenuse. In Property 2 and Property 3, the length of a leg is the *mean proportional* between the length of the hypotenuse and the length of one segment of the hypotenuse (the one that shares an endpoint with that leg).

**Example:** The altitude to the hypotenuse of a right triangle separates the hypotenuse into two segments whose lengths are 4 and 9. Find the length of the altitude.

**Solution:** You know the lengths of the segments of the hypotenuse and you want to find the length of the altitude. Apply Property 1.

$$\frac{p}{h} = \frac{h}{q}$$

$$\frac{4}{h} = \frac{h}{9}$$

$$h^2 = 36$$

$$h = \pm 6$$

$$h = 6 \quad \text{Measures are always positive.}$$

# Pythagorean theorem

The Pythagorean theorem is probably the best known theorem of high school geometry. More than one hundred "proofs" are known for this theorem, including one submitted by U.S. President James A. Garfield.

PYTHAGOREAN THEOREM: If $c$ is the measure of the hypotenuse of a right triangle and $a$ and $b$ are the measures of the legs, then $a^2 + b^2 = c^2$.

**Example:** Refer to the figure below. Find $y$

**Solution:** Apply the Pythagorean theorem.

$$a^2 + b^2 = c^2$$
$$5^2 + 12^2 = x^2$$
$$25 + 144 = x^2$$
$$169 = x^2$$
$$\pm 13 = x$$
$$13 = x \quad \text{Measures are always positive.}$$

If the answer is not a perfect square, it should be left in simplest radical form.

**Example:** Refer to the figure below. Find $x$.

**Solution:** Apply the Pythagorean theorem.

$$a^2 + b^2 = c^2$$
$$x^2 + 4^2 = 10^2$$
$$x^2 + 16 = 100$$
$$x^2 = 84$$
$$x = \pm \sqrt{84}$$
$$x = \sqrt{84}$$

Since 84 is not a perfect square, you express $\sqrt{84}$ in simplest radical form.

$$\sqrt{84} = \sqrt{4 \cdot 21} = \sqrt{4} \cdot \sqrt{21} = 2\sqrt{21}$$

# Special right triangles

There are two special right triangles. One is a 30-60-90 triangle.

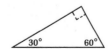

The side opposite the 60° angle is the longer leg.
The side opposite the 30° angle is the shorter leg.

The lengths of the sides of a 30-60-90 triangle are related algebraically.

1. The length of the shorter leg is one-half the length of the hypotenuse.
2. The length of the longer leg is $\sqrt{3}$ times the length of the shorter leg.

These relationships are summarized in the following reference triangle.

Hence, if you know the length of one side of a 30-60-90 triangle, you can readily find the length of the other two sides.

The other special right triangle is a 45-45-90 triangle, shown below. In such a triangle, both legs are the same length.

The lengths of the sides of a 45-45-90 triangle are related as follows:

1. The length of either leg can be found by dividing the length of the hypotenuse by $\sqrt{2}$.
2. The length of the hypotenuse can be found by multiplying the length of either leg by $\sqrt{2}$.

The reference triangle for a 45-45-90 triangle is shown below.

**Example:** Find the length of the diagonal of a square if the length of one side of the square is 4.

**Solution:** The diagonal of a square bisects two right angles of the square, forming a 45-45-90 triangle. If the length of one side of the square is 4, then the length of the diagonal is $4\sqrt{2}$.

# 4. Reviewing trigonometry

The word "trigonometry" comes from the Greek words for "triangle measurement." The ancient Greeks invented trigonometry to help them in their study of astronomy. Since ancient times, the study of trigonometry has broadened until now trigonometry is essential in such fields as engineering, physics, and navigation. It is one high school mathematics course that has a great number of practical applications.

## Angles

An angle is the union of two rays that have the same endpoint.

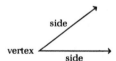

A number called the *measure* is associated with each angle. The number depends on the choice of unit. Angles are usually measured in *degrees* or *radians*.

| degrees | radians |
|---|---|

$\angle A \cong \angle B$

⊙A    ⊙B

There are 360 degrees in a circle. One degree is $\frac{1}{360}$ of a circle.

There are $2\pi$ radians in a circle. One radian is $\frac{1}{2\pi}$ of a circle.

one degree

one radian

An angle of 1° has the same measure as an angle of $\frac{\pi}{180}$ radians.

An angle of 1 radian has the same measure as an angle of $\frac{180}{\pi}$ degrees.

To change from radian measure to degree measure, you multiply the radian measure by $\frac{180}{\pi}$.

$$m_{\text{degree}} \angle A = \frac{180}{\pi} m_{\text{radian}} \angle A$$

**Example:** Change $\frac{5\pi}{6}$ radians to degree measure.

**Solution:** To change radian measure to degree measure, you multiply by $\frac{180}{\pi}$.

$$m_{\text{degree}} \angle A = \frac{180}{\pi} m_{\text{radian}} \angle A = \frac{180}{\pi}\left(\frac{5\pi}{6}\right) = 150$$

To change from degree measure to radian measure, you multiply by $\frac{\pi}{180}$.

$$m_{\text{radian}} \angle A = \frac{\pi}{180} m_{\text{degree}} \angle A$$

**Example:** Change 120° to radian measure.

**Solution:** To change from degree measure to radian measure, you must multiply the degree measure by $\frac{\pi}{180}$.

$$m_{\text{radian}} \angle A = \frac{\pi}{180} m_{\text{degree}} \angle A = \frac{\pi}{180}(120) = \frac{2\pi}{3}$$

A table of common degree/radian equivalences is given below.

| degree measure: | 360° | 180° | 150° | 120° | 90° | 60° | 45° | 30° |
|---|---|---|---|---|---|---|---|---|
| radian measure: | $2\pi$ | $\pi$ | $\frac{5\pi}{6}$ | $\frac{2\pi}{3}$ | $\frac{\pi}{2}$ | $\frac{\pi}{3}$ | $\frac{\pi}{4}$ | $\frac{\pi}{6}$ |

## Right triangles

A *right triangle* is any triangle that has a right angle. Triangle ACB is a right triangle.

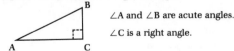

$\angle A$ and $\angle B$ are acute angles.

$\angle C$ is a right angle.

The sum of the measures of the angles of any triangle is 180°. In a right triangle, the sum of the measures of the acute angles is 90°. Whenever the sum of the measures of two angles is 90°, you can say that the angles are *complementary*. Thus, the acute angles of a right triangle are complementary. The sides of a right triangle have special names.

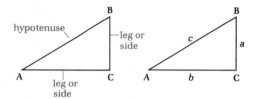

Lower-case letters are used to represent the measures of the sides of a triangle. If the vertices are A, B, and C, then a, b, and c would be used to represent the measures of the sides opposite A, B, and C respectively. It is customary to let C represent the right angle.

The Pythagorean theorem relates the measures of the sides of a right triangle.

**Pythagorean theorem:** If c is the measure of the hypotenuse of a right triangle and a and b are the measures of the legs, then $a^2 + b^2 = c^2$.

If the measures of any two sides of a right triangle are given, the measure of the third side can be found easily by substituting the known values in the Pythagorean theorem and then solving the resulting equation for the unknown quantity.

# Trigonometric ratios

Six trigonometric ratios can be defined for each acute angle of a right triangle. These definitions are made in terms of the measures of the sides of the right triangle. The names of the trigonometric ratios and their abbreviations are given below.

| sine | cosine | tangent | cotangent | cosecant | secant |
|------|--------|---------|-----------|----------|--------|
| sin | cos | tan | cot | csc | sec |

To define the trigonometric ratios, the following right triangle will be used as an example:

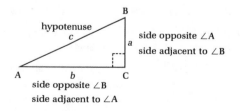

The sine ratio and the cosine ratio are usually defined first.

$$\sin A = \frac{\text{length of the side opposite } \angle A}{\text{length of the hypotenuse}} = \frac{a}{c}$$

$$\cos A = \frac{\text{length of the side adjacent to } \angle A}{\text{length of the hypotenuse}} = \frac{b}{c}$$

The other four trigonometric ratios are defined in terms of sin and cos.

$$\tan A = \frac{\sin A}{\cos A} = \frac{\text{length of the side opposite } \angle A}{\text{length of the side adjacent to } \angle A} = \frac{a}{b}$$

$$\cot A = \frac{\cos A}{\sin A} = \frac{\text{length of the side adjacent to } \angle A}{\text{length of the side opposite } \angle A} = \frac{b}{a}$$

$$\csc A = \frac{1}{\sin A} = \frac{\text{length of the hypotenuse}}{\text{length of the side opposite } \angle A} = \frac{c}{a}$$

$$\sec A = \frac{1}{\cos A} = \frac{\text{length of the hypotenuse}}{\text{length of the side adjacent to } \angle A} = \frac{c}{b}$$

If the product of two numbers is 1, the numbers are reciprocals. Notice that sin A and csc A are reciprocals; cos A and sec A are reciprocals; and tan A and cot A are reciprocals.

The trigonometric ratios for ∠B of right triangle ACB are similar to those stated for ∠A.

$$\sin B = \frac{\text{length of the side opposite } \angle B}{\text{length of the hypotenuse}} = \frac{b}{c}$$

$$\cos B = \frac{\text{length of the side adjacent to } \angle B}{\text{length of the hypotenuse}} = \frac{a}{c}$$

$$\tan B = \frac{\text{length of the side opposite } \angle B}{\text{length of the side adjacent to } \angle B} = \frac{b}{a}$$

$$\cot B = \frac{\text{length of the side adjacent to } \angle B}{\text{length of the side opposite } \angle B} = \frac{a}{b}$$

$$\csc A = \frac{\text{length of the hypotenuse}}{\text{length of the side opposite } \angle B} = \frac{c}{b}$$

$$\sec B = \frac{\text{length of the hypotenuse}}{\text{length of the side adjacent to } \angle B} = \frac{c}{a}$$

**Example:** Refer to the 30-60-90 triangle below. Find the trigonometric ratio for each acute angle.

**Solution:** To find the trigonometric ratios for the acute angles, you simply apply the definitions stated for ∠A and ∠B of right triangle ACB.

$$\sin 30° = \frac{1}{2} \qquad \cot 30° = \frac{\sqrt{3}}{1} = \sqrt{3}$$

$$\cos 30° = \frac{\sqrt{3}}{2} \qquad \csc 30° = \frac{2}{1} = 2$$

$$\tan 30° = \frac{1}{\sqrt{3}} = \frac{\sqrt{3}}{3} \qquad \sec 30° = \frac{2}{\sqrt{3}} = \frac{2\sqrt{3}}{3}$$

$$\sin 60° = \frac{\sqrt{3}}{2}$$

$$\cot 60° = \frac{1}{\sqrt{3}} = \frac{\sqrt{3}}{3}$$

$$\cos 60° = \frac{1}{2}$$

$$\csc 60° = \frac{2}{\sqrt{3}} = \frac{2\sqrt{3}}{3}$$

$$\tan 60° = \frac{\sqrt{3}}{1} = \sqrt{3}$$

$$\sec 60° = \frac{2}{1} = 2$$

In the example above, it is interesting to notice that

$$\left(\frac{1}{2}\right)^2 + \left(\frac{\sqrt{3}}{2}\right)^2 = \frac{1}{4} + \frac{3}{4} = \frac{4}{4} = 1.$$

Since $\sin 30° = \frac{1}{2}$ and $\cos 30° = \frac{\sqrt{3}}{2}$, it follows that $\sin^2 30° + \cos^2 30° = 1$. It is also true that $\sin^2 60° + \cos^2 60° = 1$. In fact, it can be shown that this relationship holds for any angle A.

$$\sin^2 A + \cos^2 A = 1$$

A relationship of this kind, one that holds for any replacement of a variable, is called an *identity*. This particular trigonometric identity is called a *Pythagorean Identity*. Although there are several trigonometric identities, the one stated above is one of the most useful.

Special right triangles (30-60-90 and 45-45-90) occur quite often in mathematics. In the following table, you will find the trigonometric ratios associated with these triangles.

| angle | sin | cos | tan | cot | csc | sec |
|---|---|---|---|---|---|---|
| $\frac{\pi}{6}$ or 30° | $\frac{1}{2}$ | $\frac{\sqrt{3}}{2}$ | $\frac{1}{\sqrt{3}}$ or $\frac{\sqrt{3}}{3}$ | $\sqrt{3}$ | 2 | $\frac{2}{\sqrt{3}}$ or $\frac{2\sqrt{3}}{3}$ |
| $\frac{\pi}{4}$ or 45° | $\frac{1}{\sqrt{2}}$ or $\frac{\sqrt{2}}{2}$ | $\frac{1}{\sqrt{2}}$ or $\frac{\sqrt{2}}{2}$ | 1 | 1 | $\sqrt{2}$ | $\sqrt{2}$ |
| $\frac{\pi}{3}$ or 60° | $\frac{\sqrt{3}}{2}$ | $\frac{1}{2}$ | $\sqrt{3}$ | $\frac{1}{\sqrt{3}}$ or $\frac{\sqrt{3}}{3}$ | $\frac{2}{\sqrt{3}}$ or $\frac{2\sqrt{3}}{3}$ | 2 |

# Solving right triangles

Trigonometry is used to "solve" right triangles. To solve a right triangle, it is necessary to find the lengths of the three sides and the measures of the three angles.

**Example:** Solve right triangle ACB if m $\angle$B = 30° and $c = 4$.

**Solution:** First draw a sketch and label the resulting triangle. To solve the triangle, you must find m $\angle$A, $a$, and $b$. First, you will use the definition of sine to find $b$.

$$\sin 30° = \frac{b}{c} = \frac{b}{4}$$

From the table, $\sin 30° = \frac{1}{2}$. So, you can substitute $\frac{1}{2}$ for $\sin 30°$ and solve the resulting equation for $b$.

$$\frac{1}{2} = \frac{b}{4}$$

$$b = 2$$

You can now find $a$ by using either the Pythagorean theorem or a trigonometric ratio.

| Pythagorean theorem | trigonometry |
|---|---|
| $a^2 + b^2 = c^2$ | $\cos 30° = \frac{a}{c} = \frac{a}{4}$ |
| $a^2 + 2^2 = 4^2$ | |
| $a^2 + 4 = 16$ | $\frac{\sqrt{3}}{2} = \frac{a}{4}$ |
| $a^2 = 12$ | $2\sqrt{3} = a$ |
| $a = \pm\sqrt{12}$ | |
| $a = \sqrt{12}$ | |
| $a = 2\sqrt{3}$ | |

You can use the fact that the acute angles of a right triangle are complementary to find m $\angle$A.

$$m \angle A + m \angle B = 90°$$
$$m \angle A + 30° = 90°$$
$$m \angle A = 60°$$

Not all right triangles are special right triangles. To solve most right triangles, it is necessary to use a trigonometric table. A portion of a trigonometric table has been reproduced below.

| angle | sin | cos | tan | cot | sec | csc | |
|---|---|---|---|---|---|---|---|
| 38° 00′ | .6157 | .7880 | .7813 | 1.280 | 1.269 | 1.624 | 52° 00′ |
| 10′ | .6180 | .7862 | .7860 | 1.272 | 1.272 | 1.618 | 50′ |
| 20′ | .6202 | .7844 | .7907 | 1.265 | 1.275 | 1.612 | 40′ |
| 30′ | .6225 | .7826 | .7954 | 1.257 | 1.278 | 1.606 | 30′ |
| 40′ | .6248 | .7808 | .8002 | 1.250 | 1.281 | 1.601 | 20′ |
| 50′ | .6271 | .7790 | .8050 | 1.242 | 1.284 | 1.595 | 10′ |
| 39° 00′ | .6293 | .7771 | .8098 | 1.235 | 1.287 | 1.589 | 51° 00′ |
| 10′ | .6316 | .7753 | .8146 | 1.228 | 1.290 | 1.583 | 50′ |
| 20′ | .6338 | .7735 | .8195 | 1.220 | 1.293 | 1.578 | 40′ |
| 30′ | .6361 | .7716 | .8243 | 1.213 | 1.296 | 1.572 | 30′ |
| 40′ | .6383 | .7698 | .8292 | 1.206 | 1.299 | 1.567 | 20′ |
| 50′ | .6406 | .7679 | .8342 | 1.199 | 1.302 | 1.561 | 10′ |
| 40° 00′ | .6428 | .7660 | .8391 | 1.192 | 1.305 | 1.556 | 50° 00′ |
| 10′ | .6450 | .7642 | .8441 | 1.185 | 1.309 | 1.550 | 50′ |
| 20′ | .6472 | .7623 | .8491 | 1.178 | 1.312 | 1.545 | 40′ |
| 30′ | .6494 | .7604 | .8541 | 1.171 | 1.315 | 1.540 | 30′ |
| 40′ | .6517 | .7585 | .8591 | 1.164 | 1.318 | 1.535 | 20′ |
| 50′ | .6539 | .7566 | .8642 | 1.157 | 1.322 | 1.529 | 10′ |
| | cos | sin | cot | tan | csc | sec | angle |

The values of the trigonometric ratios in this table are approximate. The symbol $\approx$ is used to indicate that an approximate number is being used.

To find the trigonometric ratios associated with acute angles whose measures are less than or equal to 45°,

1. read *down* the angle column on the left-hand side of the table to the correct angle; and
2. read *across* the row to the desired trigonometric-ratio column (labeled at the top).

**Example:** Find sin 39° 20'.

**Solution:** Since 39° 20' is less than 45°, we can find sin 39° 20' by

1. reading down the angle column of the left-hand side of the table to 39° 20'; and
2. reading across the 39° 20' row to the sin column (labeled at the top).

The resulting number is .6338. Therefore, sin 39° 20' $\approx$ .6338.

Similarly, to find the trigonometric ratios associated with acute angles whose measures are greater than 45°,

1. read *up* the angle column on the right-hand side of the table to the correct angle; and
2. read *across* the row to the desired trigonometric-ratio column (labeled at the bottom).

**Example:** Find tan 51° 30'.

**Solution:** Since 51° 30' is greater than 45°, you can find tan 51° 30' by

1. reading up the angle column on the right-hand side of the table to 51° 30' (you must read above 51°); and
2. reading across the 51° 30' row to the tan column (labeled at the bottom).

The resulting number is 1.257. Therefore, tan 51° 30' $\approx$ 1.257.

When using the table to solve right triangles, it is important to remember that the answers you obtain will only be approximate.

**Example:** Solve △ACB if m ∠A = 50° 40', m ∠C = 90°, and b = 20.

**Solution:** First draw a sketch and label the resulting triangle. To solve this triangle, you must find m ∠B, a, and c.
First, use the definition of tangent to find a.

$$\tan A = \frac{a}{b}$$

$$\tan 50° 40' = \frac{a}{20}$$

From the table, tan 50° 40' $\approx$ 1.220. To find a, you can substitute 1.220 for tan 50° 40' and solve the resulting equation.

$$1.220 \approx \frac{a}{20}$$

$$24.40 \approx a$$

To find c, you could use the Pythagorean theorem, the cosine ratio, or the secant ratio. The Pythagorean theorem would be quite involved and the cosine ratio involves division. So, you should use the secant ratio.

$$\sec 50° 40' = \frac{c}{b} = \frac{c}{20}$$

$$1.578 \approx \frac{c}{20}$$

$$31.56 \approx c$$

You can use the fact that ∠A and ∠B are complementary to find m ∠B.

$$m \angle A + m \angle B = 90°$$
$$50° 40' + m \angle B = 90°$$

To subtract 50° 40' from 90°, it is necessary to think of 90° as 89° 60'.

$$89° 60'$$
$$\underline{50° 40'}$$
$$39° 20'$$

The measure of ∠B is 39° 20'.

# Solving oblique triangles

Trigonometry can also be used to solve *oblique triangles; i.e.,* triangles that are not right triangles. There are two kinds of oblique triangles, acute and obtuse. An *acute triangle* is a triangle with three acute angles. An *obtuse triangle* is a triangle with one obtuse angle and two acute angles.

To solve an oblique triangle, we use the *law of sines* or the *law of cosines.* In any triangle ABC, in which a, b, and c are the measures of the sides opposite ∠A, ∠B, and ∠C respectively:

*law of sines*                  *law of cosines*

$$a^2 = b^2 + c^2 - 2bc \cos A$$

$$\frac{\sin A}{a} = \frac{\sin B}{b} = \frac{\sin C}{c} \qquad b^2 = a^2 + c^2 - 2ac \cos B$$

$$c^2 = a^2 + b^2 - 2ab \cos C$$

The law of sines can be applied whenever you are given

1. the measures of two angles and the measure of a side opposite one of them; or
2. the measures of two sides and the measure of an angle opposite one of them.

The second set of conditions may determine *two* triangles. For this reason, it is often called the ambiguous case.

**Example:** Refer to the triangle below. Find $b$.

**Solution:** You are given m $\angle A$, m $\angle B$, and the length of the side opposite $\angle A$. You can find $b$ by applying the law of sines.

$$\frac{\sin A}{a} = \frac{\sin B}{b}$$

$$\frac{\sin 45°}{10} = \frac{\sin 60°}{b}$$

$$\frac{\left(\frac{\sqrt{2}}{2}\right)}{10} = \frac{\left(\frac{\sqrt{3}}{2}\right)}{b}$$

$$\frac{\sqrt{2}}{2}b = 5\sqrt{3}$$

$$b = \frac{10\sqrt{3}}{\sqrt{2}} = 5\sqrt{6}$$

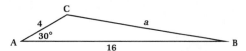

The law of cosines can be applied whenever you are given

1. the measure of three sides of a triangle; or
2. the measures of two sides of a triangle and the measure of the angle included by those sides.

**Example:** Refer to the triangle below. Find $b$.

**Solution:** You are given the measures of two sides of the triangle and the measure of the included angle. You can find $b$ by applying the law of cosines.

$$b^2 = a^2 + c^2 - 2ac \cos B$$
$$b^2 = 2^2 + 3^2 - 2(2)(3) \cos 60°$$
$$b^2 = 2^2 + 3^2 - 2(2)(3)\tfrac{1}{2} = 4 + 9 - 6 = 7$$
$$b = \pm\sqrt{7}$$
$$b = \sqrt{7}$$

**Example:** Refer to the triangle below. Find m $\angle A$.

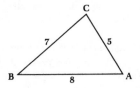

**Solution:** You are given the measures of three sides of $\triangle ABC$. You can find m $\angle A$ by applying the law of cosines.

$$a^2 = b^2 + c^2 - 2bc \cos A$$
$$7^2 = 5^2 + 8^2 - 2(5)(8) \cos A$$
$$49 = 25 + 64 - 80 \cos A$$
$$49 = 89 - 80 \cos A$$
$$-40 = -80 \cos A$$
$$\tfrac{1}{2} = \cos A$$

The angle whose cosine is $\tfrac{1}{2}$ has a measure of 60°. Therefore, m $\angle A = 60°$.

# Areas of triangles

Trigonometry can be used to find the area of a triangle if you are given the measures of two sides of the triangle and the measure of the angle included by those sides.

*Area formulas*

$$A = \tfrac{1}{2}bc \sin A$$
$$A = \tfrac{1}{2}ab \sin C$$
$$A = \tfrac{1}{2}ac \sin B$$

**Example:** Refer to the triangle below. Find the area of $\triangle ABC$.

**Solution:** Since you are given m $\angle A$, $b$, and $c$, you can find the area of $\triangle ABC$ by applying the formula $A = \tfrac{1}{2}bc \sin A$. $A = \tfrac{1}{2}bc \sin A = \tfrac{1}{2}(4)(16) \sin 30° = \tfrac{1}{2}(4)(16)\tfrac{1}{2} = 16$.

# 5. Reviewing "new math"

"Modern mathematics" or "new math" is an approach to mathematics that is designed to

1. clarify mathematical concepts by using careful language; and
2. broaden your understanding by incorporating unifying ideas.

In this unit, some of these fundamental ideas will be illustrated and discussed. Anyone who studies a "new math" course will need to be familiar with four basic concepts—sets, relations, functions, and logic.

## Sets

A *set* is a collection of things. Each of the things that belong to a set is an *element,* or *member,* of the set. Braces {} are used to indicate a set. For example:

$A = \{a, b, c\}$    A is the name of the set. The letters $a$, $b$, and $c$ are the elements of the set.
read: "The set whose elements are $a$, $b$, and $c$."

When each element of a set is listed, the set has been described using *roster notation.* Set $A$ was described using roster notation. Each of the following sets is also described using roster notation. The order in which the elements of a set are listed is *not* important.

$B = \{\square, \bigcirc, \triangle, \square\}$    $C = \{3, w, \triangle, \bigcirc, 7, \pi\}$

When using roster notation, it is easy to determine which things belong to a set and which things do not. The symbol $\in$ means "is an element of" and the symbol $\notin$ means "is not an element of." For example:

$\square \in B$    $\square \notin C$
$\square$ is an element of set $B$    $\square$ is not an element of set $C$

A set described using roster notation is always a *finite* set because it is possible to count all of the elements. There are two other notations for describing sets—partial roster and rule. Instances of each are illustrated below.

*partial roster:*
example of a finite set: $\{1, 2, 3, \cdots, 100\}$
read: "The set whose elements are 1, 2, 3, *and so on until* 100."

*rule:*
example of a finite set: $\{x \mid x$ is a whole number less than 7$\}$
read: "The set of all $x$ *such that* $x$ is a whole number less than 7."

These two notations can also be used to describe *infinite* sets. An infinite set is any set that is not finite. Examples are given below.

*partial roster:*
example of an infinite set: $\{1, 2, 3, \ldots\}$
read: "The set whose elements are 1, 2, 3, *and so on.*"

*rule*
example of an infinite set: $\{x \mid x$ is a whole number$\}$
read: "The set of all $x$ *such that* $x$ is a whole number."

When using partial roster notation or a rule, you must be certain that the set is *well defined;* that is, you must be certain that you can tell exactly which elements belong to the set and which do not.

The *empty set* (or *null set*) has no elements. The symbol for the empty set is $\phi$. By agreement, the empty set is a finite set.

**Example:** Use roster notation to describe each set:
(a) $\{x \mid x \text{ is a whole number less than 7}\}$ ;
(b) $\{1, 2, 3, \cdots, 10\}$ ; (c) $\phi$.

**Solution:** (a) $\{0, 1, 2, 3, 4, 5, 6\}$
(b) $\{1, 2, 3, 4, 5, 6, 7, 8, 9, 10\}$
(c) $\{\ \ \}$

## Set relationships

Two sets are equal if they have exactly the same elements.

**Example:** Suppose that $A = \{1, 3, 5\}$ and $B = \{5, 1, 3\}$. Is set $A$ equal to set $B$?

**Solution:** Since $1 \in A$ and $1 \in B$, $3 \in A$ and $3 \in B$, $5 \in A$ and $5 \in B$, and there are no other elements in either set, you can conclude that $A = B$.

Another set relationship is the subset relationship. Set $A$ is a *subset* of set $B$ if every element of $A$ is an element of $B$. You use the symbol $\subseteq$ to mean "is a subset of." If set $B$ contains elements that are not in set $A$, then $A$ is a *proper subset* of set $B$. You use the symbol $\subset$ to mean "is a proper subset of." The empty set is a subset of every set.

**Example:** Suppose that $A = \{1, 2, 3\}$ and $B = \{1, \triangle, 2, \square, 3, \bigcirc, \pi\}$. Is set $A$ a subset of set $B$? A proper subset of set $B$?

**Solution:** Since $1 \in A$ and $1 \in B$, $2 \in A$ and $2 \in B$, and $3 \in A$ and $3 \in B$, you can conclude that $A \subseteq B$. And, because $B$ contains elements other than 1, 2, and 3, $A \subset B$.

In any discussion, the *universal set* is the set of all things being considered. For example, if you designate the set of integers as the universal set, you have restricted your considerations to integers. The letter $U$ is generally used for the universal set.

The *complement* of a given set is the set of all elements in the universal set that do not belong to the given set. For example, if the universal set is the set of integers and set $A$ is the set of odd integers, then the complement of set $A$, denoted by $A'$ (read $A$ prime) is the set of all integers that are *not* odd. Thus,

$A' = \{x \mid x \text{ is an even integer}\}$.

**Example:** If $U = \{2, 4, 7, 8, 11, 16\}$ and $A = \{4, 11, 16\}$, find $A'$.

**Solution:** The complement of set $A$ contains all elements of $U$ that are not in $A$.

$A' = \{2, 7, 8\}$

Pictures are often used to represent set ideas. Pictures that show a universal set and depict set relationships are called *Venn diagrams*. The following Venn diagram shows the relationship between set $A$, its complement $A'$ and the universal set $U$ to which both belong.

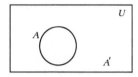

## Set operations

There are three set operations—union, intersection, and Cartesian product.

DEFINITION: The *union* of set $A$ and set $B$ is the set whose elements belong to set $A$, set $B$, or both.

The symbol $A \cup B$ is used to represent the union of set $A$ and set $B$. The shaded portion of the Venn diagram below identifies the union of $A$ and $B$.

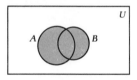

**Example:** If $A = \{a, b, c\}$ and $B = \{1, a, 2\}$, find $A \cup B$.

**Solution:** You must find all elements that are in set $A$ or set $B$ or both. It is not necessary to name an element more than once.

$A \cup B = \{a, b, c, 1, 2\}$

DEFINITION: The *intersection* of set $A$ and set $B$ is the set whose elements are in both $A$ and $B$.

The symbol $A \cap B$ is used to represent the intersection of set $A$ and set $B$. The shaded portions of the following Venn diagrams represent the intersection of $A$ and $B$.

| I | II | III |
|---|---|---|
|  |  |  |
| $A \cap B = \phi$ | $A \cap B$ | $A \cap B = A$ |

If the intersection of two sets is the empty set (diagram I), you say that the two sets are *disjoint*. In diagram III, set $A$ is a subset of set $B$.

**Example:** Suppose that $A = \{2, 4, 6\}$; $B = \{2, a, 3, b, 4, c\}$; and $C = \{1, 3\}$. Find (a) $A \cap B$; (b) $A \cap C$.

**Solution:**

(a) To find $A \cap B$, you must find all the elements that are in both sets. $2 \in A$ and $2 \in B$; $4 \in A$ and $4 \in B$. $A \cap B = \{2, 4\}$

(b) Set $A$ and set $C$ have *no* common elements. Set $A$ and set $C$ are disjoint.

$A \cap C = \phi$

DEFINITION: The *Cartesian product* of set $A$ and set $B$ is the set whose elements are ordered pairs of the form $(x, y)$, in which $x \in A$ and $y \in B$.

You use the symbol $A \times B$ to represent the Cartesian product of set $A$ and set $B$. In an ordered pair, the first term is called the *first component* and the second term is called the *second component*.

```
                    ┌─ second component
              (x, y)
first component ─┘
```

**Example:** Suppose that $A = \{1, 2\}$ and $B = \{a, b\}$. Find $A \times B$.

**Solution:** You must find all possible ordered pairs of the form $(x, y)$ where $x \in A$ and $y \in B$.

$A \times B = \{(1,a), (1,b), (2,a), (2,b)\}$

## Relations

A *relation* is a subset of a Cartesian product of two sets. As a result, a relation is always a set of ordered pairs. For example:

$R = \{(1,a), (2,b), (3,c)\}$.

$R$ is the name of the relation and the elements enclosed in braces comprise the set of ordered pairs.

The set of all first components of the ordered pairs of a relation is called the *domain* of the relation and the set of all second components is called the *range* of the relation. For instance, in the relation $R = \{(1,a), (2,b), (3,c)\}$, the domain is $\{1, 2, 3\}$ and the range is $\{a, b, c\}$.

**Example:** If $R = \{2,3), (1,0), (4,5)\}$ determine: (a) the domain; (b) the range.

**Solution:**

(a) The domain is the set of all first components of the ordered pairs of $R$.

$D_R = \{2, 1, 4\}$

(b) The range is the set of all second components of the ordered pairs of $R$.

$R_R = \{3, 0, 5\}$

## Function

A *function* is a special kind of relation. In a function, no two ordered pairs have the same first component.

**Example:** Determine which relations are functions:
(a) $R = \{(2,3), (3,4), (2,5)\}$; (b) $S = \{(1,2), (2,2), (3,2), (4,2)\}$;
(c) $T = \{1, 2, 3\}$.

**Solution:**

(a) Both (2,3) and (2,5) have the same first component. So relation $R$ is not a function.

(b) Set $S$ is a relation because it is a set of ordered pairs. No two ordered pairs have the same first component. Therefore, $S$ is a function.

(c) Set $T$ is not a set of ordered pairs. Therefore set $T$ cannot be a function.

A lower-case letter (like $f$) is usually used to represent a function. Since a function is a relation, a function has a domain and a range. If $x$ is an element of the domain, $f(x)$ is the element of the range that corresponds to it.

**Example:** If $f = \{(1,3), (2,5), (3,7)\}$, find $f(1)$.

**Solution:** $f(1)$ is the range element of function $f$ that corresponds to domain element 1. Since $(1,3) \in f$, 3 corresponds to domain element 1. Therefore, $f(1) = 3$. Similarly, $f(2) = 5$ and $f(3) = 7$.

In many functions, each domain element is related to its corresponding range element by a rule. For example, assume that the universal set is the set of integers (each variable represents an integer), and

$f = \{(x,y) \mid y = x + 3\}$.

A rule for this function is $y = x + 3$. You can use the rule to find ordered pairs of function $f$.

If $x = 0$, then $y = 0 + 3 = 3$.

If $x = 1$, then $y = 1 + 3 = 4$.

If $x = 2$, then $y = 2 + 3 = 5$.

$f = \{\cdots, (0,3), (1,4), (2,5), \cdots\}$

**Example:** If $f(x) = 2x - 1$ is a rule for a function, find the range element that corresponds to each domain element: (a) $-3$; (b) 5.

**Solution:**

(a) To find the range element that corresponds to $-3$, you substitute $-3$ for $x$ in the rule $f(x) = 2x - 1$.

$$f(x) = 2x - 1$$
$$f(-3) = 2(-3) - 1 = -7$$

The required range element is $-7$. The ordered pair $(-3,-7)$ is an element of the function.

(**b**) Substitute 5 for $x$ in $f(x) = 2x - 1$.

$$f(x) = 2x - 1$$
$$f(5) = 2(5) - 1 = 9$$

The required range element is 9. The ordered pair $(5,9)$ is an element of the function.

# Logic

"Modern mathematics" emphasizes proof. Before a statement can be proved, it is necessary to develop a system of logic so that the "truth value" of a statement can be determined.

DEFINITION: A *statement* is a sentence that is either true or false but not both.

There are two kinds of statements—simple statements and compound statements. A *simple statement* expresses a single complete thought. A *compound statement* is formed by joining at least two simple statements with a "connective." The connectives that are generally considered in mathematics are listed below with their symbols.

| name | connective | symbol |
|------|-----------|--------|
| negation | not | $\sim$ |
| conjunction | and | $\wedge$ |
| disjunction | or | $\vee$ |
| conditional | if, then | $\rightarrow$ |
| biconditional | if and only if | $\leftrightarrow$ |

## Negation

The *negation* of a simple statement is formed by using the word "not" or the phrase "it is not true that." For example:

*simple statement:* Sara is a beautiful girl.

*negation:* Sara is not a beautiful girl.
It is not true that Sara is a beautiful girl.

Negation is often defined by using a *truth table.* In the following truth table, $p$ represents a simple statement; $\sim p$ represents its negation.

| $p$ | $\sim p$ |
|-----|----------|
| T | F |
| F | T |

This table indicates the truth value of the negation of any simple statement represented by $p$. The negation of a true statement is a false statement and the negation of a false statement is a true statement.

**Example:** Form the negation of the statement "Tim has red hair."

**Solution:** "Tim does *not* have red hair."
"*It is not true that* Tim has red hair."

# Conjunction

A *conjunction* is a compound statement formed by joining two simple statements with the connective "and."

**Example:** Form the conjunction of the following two simple statements: "John is tall." "Martha is short."

**Solution:** "John is tall *and* Martha is short."

The conjunction of any two statements $p$ and $q$ is represented symbolically as $p \wedge q$. The truth table for conjunction is given below. This table indicates the truth value of the conjunction of any pair of simple statements represented by $p$ and $q$.

| $p$ | $q$ | $p \wedge q$ |
|-----|-----|--------------|
| T | T | T |
| T | F | F |
| F | T | F |
| F | F | F |

The conjunction of two simple statements is true if both simple statements are true; it is false in all other cases.

**Example:** Determine the truth value of the statement "$3 \neq 2$ and $5 > 4$."

**Solution:** The simple statement "$3 \neq 2$" is true and the simple statement "$5 > 4$" is true. The first row of the truth table for conjunction tells you that when both simple statements are true, the conjunction of the two simple statements is true. Therefore, "$3 \neq 2$ and $5 > 4$" is true.

# Disjunction

A *disjunction* is a compound statement formed by joining two simple statements with the connective "or." The "or" you are using is the "inclusive or," which means *one or the other or both.*

**Example:** Form the disjunction of the following two simple statements:
"Carl plays chess." "Carl plays football."

**Solution:** To form the disjunction, you join the two simple statements with "or."
"Carl plays chess *or* Carl plays football."

The disjunction of any two simple statements $p$ and $q$ is represented symbolically as $p \vee q$. The truth table for disjunction is given below. This table indicates the truth value of the disjunction of any pair of simple statements represented by $p$ and $q$.

| $p$ | $q$ | $p \vee q$ |
|-----|-----|-----|
| T | T | T |
| T | F | T |
| F | T | T |
| F | F | F |

The disjunction of two simple statements is false if both simple statements are false; it is true in all other cases.

**Example:** Determine the truth value of the statement "$3 > 1$ or $5 = 2$."

**Solution:** The simple statement "$3 > 1$" is true and the simple statement "$5 = 2$" is false. The second row of the truth table for disjunction tells us that a disjunction is true under these conditions. Therefore, "$3 > 1$ or $5 = 2$" is true.

## Conditional

A *conditional* is a compound statement formed by joining two simple statements with the connective "if, then."

**Example:** Form the conditional of the following two simple statements.
"It is windy today." "The fishing is good."

**Solution:** To form the conditional, you join the two simple statements with "if, then."
"*If* it is windy today, *then* the fishing is good."

The conditional of any two simple statements $p$ and $q$ is represented symbolically as p→q. The "if" part of a conditional is often called the *hypothesis* and the "then" part is called the *conclusion*. If the hypothesis and conclusion of a true conditional are interchanged, the resulting conditional *need not be true*. The truth table for conditional statements is given below. This table indicates the truth value of the conditional of any two simple statements represented by $p$ and $q$.

| $p$ | $q$ | $p \to q$ |
|-----|-----|-----|
| T | T | T |
| T | F | F |
| F | T | T |
| F | F | T |

The conditional of two simple statements is false if the hypothesis is true and the conclusion is false; it is true in all other cases.

**Example:** Determine the truth value of the statement "If $3 = 5$, then $7 > 2$."

**Solution:** The simple statement "$3 = 5$" is false and the simple statement "$7 > 2$" is true. The third row of the truth table for conditional tells you that the conditional is true under these conditions. Therefore, "If $3 = 5$, then $7 > 2$" is true.

## Biconditional

A *biconditional* is a compound statement formed by joining two simple statements with the connective "if and only if."

**Example:** Form the biconditional of the following two simple statements.
"Jane can win the race." "It is snowing."

**Solution:** To form the biconditional, you join the two simple statements with "if and only if."
"Jane can win the race *if and only if* it is snowing."

The biconditional of any two simple statements $p$ and $q$ can be represented symbolically as p↔q. A biconditional has two parts—the "if" part ($p$ if $q$) and the "only if" part ($p$ only if $q$). The "if" part of a biconditional can be replaced by $q{\to}p$ and the "only if" part can be replaced by $p{\to}q$. So, it is possible to rewrite a biconditional as a *conjunction of two conditionals*.

p↔q means $(p{\to}q)$ and $(q{\to}p)$.

The truth table for biconditional statements is given below. This table indicates the truth value of the biconditional of any two simple statements represented by $p$ and $q$.

| $p$ | $q$ | p⟷q |
|-----|-----|-----|
| T | T | T |
| T | F | F |
| F | T | F |
| F | F | T |

The biconditional of two simple statements is true whenever both simple statements are true or both simple statements are false; it is false in all other cases.

**Example:** Determine the truth value of the statement "$5 < 3$ if and only if $7 = 2$."

**Solution:** The simple statement "$5 < 3$" is false and the simple statement "$7 = 2$" is false. The fourth row of the truth table for biconditional tells you that the biconditional is true under these conditions. Therefore, "$5 < 3$ if and only if $7 = 2$" is true.

# Glossary: Unit 2

**acute angle** An angle whose degree measure is greater than 0 and less than 90.

**addends** The numbers you add to obtain a sum.

**adjacent angles** Two angles that are coplanar, have the same vertex, share a common side, and have interiors that are disjoint sets.

**alternate angles** Angles formed by a transversal and two parallel lines. The angles are on opposite sides of the transversal and have different vertices.

**angle** The union of two noncollinear rays that have the same end point.

**area** A number associated with a region of a plane determined by a polygon or a circle.

**average** The sum of several numbers divided by the number of addends.

**axiom** A statement in mathematics that is accepted as true without proof.

**biconditional** A compound statement formed by joining two simple statements with the connective "if and only if."

**binomial** A polynomial with two terms.

**centimeter** A unit of length in the metric system of measurement equal to one-hundredth of a meter.

**chord** A line segment whose end points are points of a circle.

**circle** A set of points in a plane that are a given distance from a given point of the plane called the center.

**circumference** The length of any given circle.

**complement** The set of all elements of a universal set that are not elements of a given set.

**complementary angles** Two angles whose degree measures add up to 90.

**composite number** Any number that is not a prime number.

**conditional** A compound statement that is formed by joining two simple statements with the connective "if, then."

**congruent angles** Two angles that have the same measure.

**congruent segments** Two segments that have the same measure.

**conjunction** A compound statement that is formed by joining two simple statements with the connective "and."

**constant function** A function that has a single range element.

**convergent sequence** A sequence that has a limit.

**coordinate system** A one-to-one correspondence between the set of real numbers and the set of points of a line or plane.

**coplanar points** Points of the same plane.

**corresponding angles** A pair of angles formed by a transversal and two parallel lines. Both angles are on the same side of the transversal, they have different vertices, and one is an interior angle while the other is an exterior angle.

**cosine** A trigonometric ratio defined for an acute angle of a right triangle.

**degree** A unit of angle measure.

**denominator** The number or term below the division bar in a fraction.

**diameter of a circle** A chord that contains the center of a circle.

**disjoint sets** Two sets whose intersection is an empty set.

**disjunction** A compound statement formed by joining two simple statements with the connective "or."

**distance** The length of the line segment that joins two points.

**divergent sequence** A sequence that does not converge, that is, an infinite sequence that does not have a limit.

**domain** The set of all first components of the ordered pairs of a relation or function.

**element** A member of a set.

**empty set** A set that has no elements.

**equal sets** Two sets that have exactly the same elements.

**equation** A statement in mathematics that two expressions are equal.

**exponent** A number that indicates how many times another number, called the base, is used as a factor.

**extremes** The first and fourth terms of a proportion.

**factor** One of the numbers you multiply to obtain a product.

**finite set** A set that has a countable number of elements.

**formula** An open sentence that expresses a general rule in mathematics.

**function** A set of ordered pairs no two of which have the same first component.

**hypotenuse** The side of a right triangle that is opposite the right angle.

**improper fraction** A fraction in which the numerator is greater than the denominator.

**inequality** A statement that two mathematical expressions are not equal.

**infinite set** A set that is not finite.

**inverse** A conditional formed by negating the hypothesis and conclusion of a given conditional.

**inverse operation** An operation that undoes a given operation.

**isosceles triangle** A triangle with at least two sides congruent.

**least common denominator** The least common multiple of the denominators of two or more fractions.

**least common multiple** Given two or more numbers, the least positive integer that is divisible by these given numbers.

**linear function** A function whose graph is a line.

**means** The second and third terms of a proportion.

**measure of an angle** A real number greater than zero and less than 180, associated with an angle.

**meter** The standard unit of length in the metric system. A meter is about 39.37 inches.

**millimeter** A unit of length in the metric system equal to one-thousandth of a meter.

**monomial** A polynomial with one term.

**negation of a statement** A statement formed by inserting the phrase "it is not true that" before a given simple statement.

**number line** A line to which a coordinate system has been assigned.

**numeral** A symbol for a number.

**numerator** The number or term above the division bar in a fraction.

**obtuse angle** An angle whose degree measure is greater than 90 and less than 180.

**octagon** A polygon with eight sides.

**parallel lines** Two or more lines in the same plane that do not intersect.

**parallelogram** A quadrilateral that has both pairs of opposite sides parallel.

**pentagon** A polygon with five sides.

**per cent** A ratio of some number to 100.

**perpendicular lines** Any two lines that intersect to form right angles.

**pi** The ratio of the circumference of a circle to the measure of a diameter of that circle.

**postulate** A mathematical statement that is accepted as true without proof.

**prime number** A positive integer greater than 1 whose only factors are 1 and the number itself.

**proportion** An equation in which both numbers of the equation are ratios.

**quadrilateral** A polygon with four sides.

**radian** A unit of measure for angles.

**radius of a circle** A line segment that joins the center of a circle to any point of the circle.

**range** The set of all second components of the ordered pairs of a relation or function.

**ratio** An indicated quotient of two numbers.

**ray** The subset of a line.

**real number** Any rational or irrational number.

**rectangle** A parallelogram that has four right angles.

**relation** Any set of ordered pairs.

**right angle** An angle whose degree measure is 90.

**secant** A line that intersects a given circle in two points.

**semicircle** An arc of a circle determined by the end points of a diameter of the circle.

**set** A collection of things.

**similar triangles** Two triangles whose corresponding angles are congruent and the measures of whose corresponding sides are in proportion. Similar triangles have the same shape but not necessarily the same size.

**sine** A trigonometric ratio defined for an acute angle of a right triangle.

**skew lines** Lines in space that are not coplanar and do not intersect.

**slope** The measure of the steepness of a line.

**solution set** The set that contains all of the numbers which make a given open sentence, or system of open sentences, true.

**square** A rectangle that has four congruent sides.

**square root** One of two equal factors of any given number.

**supplementary angles** Two angles whose degree measures add up to 180.

**tangent** A trigonometric ratio defined for an acute angle of a right triangle.

**theorem** A statement in mathematics that must be proved.

**transversal** A line that intersects two or more lines at distinct points.

**triangle** A polygon with three sides.

**trinomial** A polynomial with three terms.

**universal set** The set whose elements are under consideration in a given situation.

**value of a function** The range element of the function that is associated with a given domain element.

**Venn diagram** A diagram in which regions are used to represent set ideas.

**vertex of an angle** The common end point of the rays that determine an angle.

**vertical angles** Two nonadjacent angles formed by two intersecting lines.

**$x$-axis** The horizontal axis in a coordinate plane; the abscissa.

**$y$-axis** The vertical axis in a coordinate plane; the ordinate.

# Basic information from the physical sciences

**3**

What is the distance between the Earth and the Sun? What is the atomic weight of copper? How does a laser work? Physical science classes are concerned with this kind of information every day.

This unit provides you with the answers to these and many similar physical science questions. And the unit presents you with a review of some basic information from the physical sciences.

# 1. Facts about astronomy

Astronomy is the study of the universe. The universe consists of numerous *galaxies*—star clusters of up to a trillion stars revolving around the core of the galaxy. Gases and tiny dust particles make up the galaxies and the universe. The size and temperature of a star determine how much energy it gives off. However, the star's apparent brightness, or *magnitude,* depends not only on its size and temperature but also on its distance from the viewer. In this section, you can review important facts about astronomy, including facts about the *solar system* in which you live.

**Table: the planets at a glance***

|  | Mercury | Venus | Earth | Mars |
|---|---|---|---|---|
| Distance from the sun: |  |  |  |  |
|   Mean | 36,000,000 mi. (57,900,000 km) | 67,230,000 mi. (108,200,000 km) | 92,960,000 mi. (149,600,000 km) | 141,700,000 mi. (228,000,000 km) |
|   Shortest | 28,600,000 mi. (46,000,000 km) | 66,800,000 mi. (107,500,000 km) | 91,400,000 mi. (147,100,000 km) | 128,500,000 mi. (206,800,000 km) |
|   Greatest | 43,000,000 mi. (69,200,000 km) | 67,700,000 mi. (108,900,000 km) | 94,500,000 mi. (152,100,000 km) | 154,900,000 mi. (249,200,000 km) |
| Closest approach to Earth | 57,000,000 mi. (91,700,000 km) | 25,700,000 mi. (41,400,000 km) | ——————— | 48,700,000 mi. (78,390,000 km) |
| Length of year (earth-days) | 88 | 225 | 365 | 687 |
| Average orbital speed | 30 mi. per sec. (48 km per sec.) | 22 mi. per sec. (35 km per sec.) | 19 mi. per sec. (31 km per sec.) | 15 mi. per sec. (24 km per sec.) |
| Diameter at equator | 3,031 mi. (4,878 km) | 7,520 mi. (12,100 km) | 7,926 mi. (12,756 km) | 4,200 mi. (6,790 km) |
| Rotation period | 59 earth-days | 243 earth-days | 23 hrs. 56 min. | 24 hrs. 37 min. |
| Tilt of axis (degrees) | about 0 | 177 | 23½ | 25 |
| Temperature | −315° to 648° F. (−193° to 342° C) | 850° F. (455° C) | −126.9° to 136° F. (−88.29° to 58° C) | −191° to −24° F. (−124° to −31° C) |
| Atmosphere: |  |  |  |  |
|   Pressure | 0.00000000003 lb. per sq. in. (0.000000000002 kg per cm²) | 1.5 to 1,323 lbs. per sq. in. (0.1 to 93 kg per cm²) | 14.7 lbs. per sq. in. (1.03 kg per cm²) | 0.1 lbs. per sq. in. (0.007 kg per cm²) |
|   Gases | Helium, hydrogen, oxygen | Carbon dioxide, nitrogen, helium, neon, argon, water vapor, sulfur, hydrogen, carbon, oxygen | Nitrogen, oxygen, carbon dioxide, water vapor | Carbon dioxide, nitrogen, argon, oxygen, carbon monoxide, neon, krypton, xenon, water vapor |
| Mass (Earth = 1) | 0.06 | 0.82 | 1 | 0.11 |
| Density (g/cm³) | 5.44 | 5.27 | 5.52 | 3.95 |
| Gravity (Earth = 1) | 0.38 | 0.9 | 1 | 0.38 |
| Number of satellites | 0 | 0 | 1 | 2 |

*All figures are approximate.

## The solar system

Our solar system consists of the sun, nine planets, and a ring of minor planets called *asteroids*. Most scientists believe the sun formed more than 4.5 billion years ago from a disk of hot, swirling gases. As the sun was forming, dense regions on its edges spun off and condensed as planets, moons, and asteroids. Jupiter is the largest of the planets, with a diameter 11 times greater than the Earth's. Pluto is the smallest, about a fourth of the Earth's diameter. The planets and asteroids revolve around the sun in paths called orbits. The orbits vary in their distances from the sun—Mercury is closest to the sun, with a mean distance of 36 million miles (57.9 million kilometers); Pluto is farthest from the sun, as you will note.

### The solar system

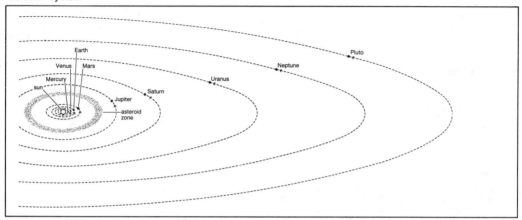

| Jupiter | Saturn | Uranus | Neptune | Pluto |
|---|---|---|---|---|
| 483,700,000 mi. (778,400,000 km) | 885,200,000 mi. (1,424,600,000 km) | 1,781,000,000 mi. (2,866,900,000 km) | 2,788,000,000 mi. (4,486,100,000 km) | 3,660,000,000 mi. (5,890,000,000 km) |
| 460,000,000 mi. (740,000,000 km) | 838,000,000 mi. (1,349,000,000 km) | 1,700,000,000 mi. (2,740,000,000 km) | 2,754,000,000 mi. (4,432,500,000 km) | 2,748,000,000 mi. (4,423,200,000 km) |
| 507,000,000 mi. (816,000,000 km) | 932,000,000 mi. (1,500,000,000 km) | 1,860,000,000 mi. (2,999,000,000 km) | 2,821,000,000 mi. (4,539,800,000 km) | 4,571,200,000 mi. (7,356,000,000 km) |
| 390,700,000 mi. (628,760,000 km) | 762,700,000 mi. (1,277,400,000 km) | 1,700,000,000 mi. (2,720,000,000 km) | 2,700,000,000 mi. (4,350,000,000 km) | 3,583,000,000 mi. (5,765,500,000 km) |
| 4,333 | 10,759 | 30,685 | 60,188 | 90,700 |
| 8 mi. per sec. (13 km per sec.) | 6 mi. per sec. (10 km per sec.) | 4 mi. per sec. (6 km per sec.) | 3 mi. per sec. (5 km per sec.) | 3 mi. per sec. (5 km per sec.) |
| 88,700 mi. (142,700 km) | 74,600 mi. (120,000 km) | 31,570 mi. (50,800 km) | 30,200 mi. (48,600 km) | 1,900 mi. (3,000 km) |
| 9 hrs. 55 min. | 10 hrs. 39 min. | 16 to 28 hrs. | 18 to 20 hrs. | 6 earth-days |
| 3 | 27 | 98 | 29 | 90 |
| −236° F. (−149° C) | −285° F. (−176° C) | −357° F. (−216° C) | −360° F. (−218° C) | About −300° F. (−184° C) |
| 2.35 to 1,470 lbs. per sq. in. (0.17 to 103 kg per cm²) | 1.5 to 15 lbs. per sq. in. (0.1 to 1 kg per cm² or higher) | ? | ? | ? |
| Hydrogen, helium, methane, ammonia, ethane, acetylene, phosphine, water vapor, carbon monoxide | Hydrogen, helium, methane, ammonia, ethane, phosphine (?) | Hydrogen, helium, methane | Hydrogen, helium, methane, ethane | Methane, ammonia (?), water (?) |
| 318 | 95 | 14.6 | 17.2 | 0.0017 (?) |
| 1.31 | 0.704 | 1.21 | 1.66 | 1.0 (?) |
| 2.87 | 1.32 | 0.93 | 1.23 | 0.03 (?) |
| 16 | 23 | 5 | 2 | 1 |

## Planetary orbits

The planets and asteroids of the solar system revolve around the sun in elliptical orbits, as shown. The sun's gravity keeps the planets and asteroids in their orbital paths. Though orbits are generally the same shape, they of course occur in different sizes.

In the table (right), note that the mean distance of the planet Pluto from the sun is 3,660,000,000 mi. (5,890,000,000 km). This means that Pluto has a much larger orbit around the sun than does Venus, for example. The planet Venus, as you will note, has a mean distance from the sun of "only" 67,230,000 mi. (108,200,000 km).

The speed at which a particular planet or astral body moves is affected by its distance from the sun in that part of its orbit. It moves faster when closer to the sun, slower when farther away.

## Features of orbits

The closest point to the sun during an orbital swing is called the *perihelion*. The farthest point in the orbital swing is called the *aphelion*. As each planet revolves around the sun, the planet also rotates around its own imaginary axis. On earth, this results in day and night. Man-made objects can be placed into orbit, too; spacecraft have been put into orbit around the Earth and other planets.

## The sun's composition

The sun has three outer layers—*corona, chromosphere,* and *photosphere.* Usually invisible, the corona is the extremely hot outer atmosphere of the sun. The average temperature there is about 4,000,000° F. (2,200,000° C). The chromosphere is the reddish layer above the sun's surface. At its outer edge, temperatures can rise to 50,000° F. (27,800° C). The photosphere, the sun's surface, is a textured area with an average temperature of 10,000° F. (5,500° C). The interior of the sun is a violent furnace fueled by thermonuclear reactions. As the nuclei of atoms in the sun's core fuse, they release huge amounts of high-energy radiation. The radiation passes through the radiative zone and triggers hot gas currents in the convection zone, which rise to the photosphere. The sun's energy then shoots into space. The sun has a diameter of about 865,000 mi. (1,392,000 km).

## Table: distances in the universe

| Planet | Mean distance from the sun* In miles | In kilometers |
|---|---|---|
| Mercury | 36,000,000 | 57,900,000 |
| Venus | 67,230,000 | 108,200,000 |
| Earth | 92,960,000 | 149,600,000 |
| Mars | 141,700,000 | 228,000,000 |
| Jupiter | 483,700,000 | 778,400,000 |
| Saturn | 885,200,000 | 1,424,600,000 |
| Uranus | 1,781,000,000 | 2,866,900,000 |
| Neptune | 2,788,000,000 | 4,486,100,000 |
| Pluto | 3,660,000,000 | 5,890,000,000 |

*The mean between the farthest distance from the sun and the closest.

## Planetary orbits

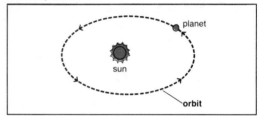

## Features of orbits

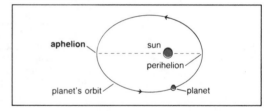

## The sun's composition

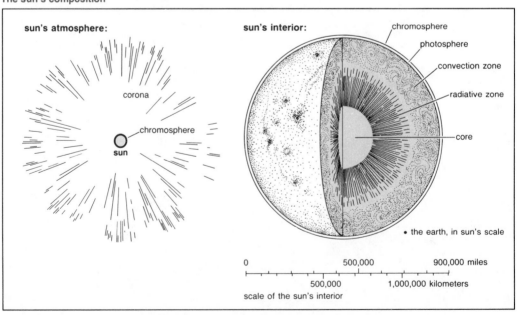

## The moon—earth's natural satellite

Though bright in the sky at varying times of the month, the moon does not produce its own light; it merely reflects sunlight. The moon travels around the earth once every 27⅓ days. It is about 222,000 miles (357,000 kilometers) from the earth at the closest part of its elliptical orbit—the *perigee.* At the farthest, the *apogee,* the moon is about 253,000 miles (407,153 kilometers) away. Half of the moon's surface is always exposed to sunlight. However, you cannot always see the illuminated side fully because the moon's orbit places it in different viewing positions during the month, thus creating the eight phases of the moon. The amount of moonlight visible on the earth ranges from very little during a new moon (when the moon lies almost between the sun and earth) to a full moon (when the moon rises in the east as the sun sets).

## Eclipses of the sun and moon

Fairly rare, eclipses can be seen from only a limited number of places on earth. Lunar eclipses take place when the moon's slightly tilted orbit takes it to a point where the earth lies directly between the sun and moon. The earth then shadows the moon's surface. The darkest part of the shadow, called the *umbra,* causes a total lunar eclipse. As the moon's orbit swings out of the umbra, the moon becomes only partially shadowed as it enters a cone-shaped area, called the *penumbra.* In a solar eclipse, the moon's shadow is cast on the earth when it passes directly between the sun and earth. The umbra causes the sky to blacken during a total eclipse. Only the sun's corona can be seen to protrude beyond the moon's edges. (Never look directly at a total solar eclipse because of possible eye damage.) The penumbra, the area of partial solar eclipse, extends over a larger area than the umbra and can often be seen by many more people.

## Table: the 20 brightest stars

| Star | Distance (Light-Years) |
| --- | --- |
| 1. Sirius | 8.8 |
| 2. Canopus | 98 |
| 3. Alpha Centauri | 4.3 |
| 4. Arcturus | 36 |
| 5. Vega | 26 |
| 6. Capella | 46 |
| 7. Rigel | 900 |
| 8. Procyon | 11 |
| 9. Betelgeuse | 490 |
| 10. Achernar | 114 |
| 11. Beta Centauri | 290 |
| 12. Altair | 16 |
| 13. Alpha Crucis | 390 |
| 14. Aldebaran | 68 |
| 15. Spica | 300 |
| 16. Antares | 250 |
| 17. Pollux | 35 |
| 18. Fomalhaut | 23 |
| 19. Deneb | 1,630 |
| 20. Beta Crucis | 490 |

## Constellations in the sky

Constellations are imaginary figures traced in the sky by ancient observers. By assigning shapes of familiar objects to star patterns, they mapped the stars in the year-round skies. Ursa Major and Ursa Minor were especially important constellations because Ursa Minor contains the North Star—an ancient guide for travelers—and the North Star can be found by its relation to the easily seen Big Dipper portion of Ursa Major. Other important constellations included Leo the Lion (in the southern spring sky), Cygnus the Swan (part of the Northern Cross), Scorpius (The Scorpion), and Orion the Hunter.

## The moon—earth's natural satellite

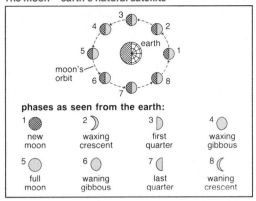

**phases as seen from the earth:**

1 new moon
2 waxing crescent
3 first quarter
4 waxing gibbous
5 full moon
6 waning gibbous
7 last quarter
8 waning crescent

## Eclipses of the sun and moon

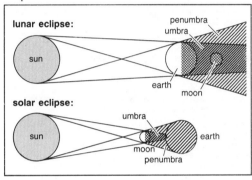

lunar eclipse:

solar eclipse:

## Constellations in the sky

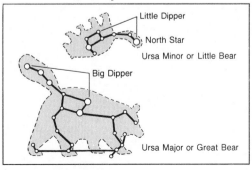

# Characteristics of the planet earth

Third closest planet to the sun, the earth is the only planet on which life is known to exist. Densest of all the planets, it has a density about 5.5 times greater than water. In its yearly revolution around the sun, the earth travels at an average speed of 19 miles (31 kilometers) a second. As it revolves, it also rotates on an imaginary axis through the North and South poles. This axis tilts slightly, positioning the Northern Hemisphere away from the sun in winter and toward it in summer. The opposite happens to the Southern Hemisphere. The earth is essentially a rocky ball with a hot interior, as hot as 9,000°F. (5,000°C). But the earth is not perfectly round; it has a slight bulge at the equator. Water covers much of its surface. The earth's land areas are in the form of seven continents.

## Table: the earth at a glance

**Age:** 4,500,000,000 (4½ billion) years.

**Weight:** 6,600,000,000,000,000,000,000,000 (6.6 sextillion) short tons (6.0 sextillion metric tons).

**Motion:** *Rotation* (spinning motion around an imaginary line connecting the North and South poles)—once every 23 hours, 56 minutes, 4.09 seconds. *Revolution* (motion around the sun)—once every 365 days, 6 hours, 9 minutes, 9.54 seconds.

**Size:** *Polar Diameter* (distance through the earth from North Pole to South Pole)—7,899.83 miles (12,713.54 kilometers). *Equatorial Diameter* (distance through the earth at the equator)—7,926.41 miles (12,756.32 kilometers). *Polar Circumference* (distance around the earth through the poles)—24,859.82 miles (40,008.00 kilometers). *Equatorial Circumference* (distance around the earth along the equator)—24,901.55 miles (40,075.16 kilometers).

**Area:** *Total Surface Area*—196,951,000 square miles (510,100,000 square kilometers). *Land Area*—approximately 57,259,000 square miles (148,300,000 square kilometers), about 30 per cent of total surface area. *Water Area*—approximately 139,692,000 square miles (361,800,000 square kilometers), about 70 per cent of total surface area.

**Surface features:** *Highest Land*—Mount Everest, 29,028 feet (8,848 meters) above sea level. *Lowest Land*—shore of Dead Sea, 1,299 feet (396 meters) below sea level.

**Ocean depths:** *Deepest Part of Ocean*—Challenger Deep in Pacific Ocean southwest of Guam, 36,198 feet (11,033 meters) below surface. *Average Ocean Depth*—12,450 feet (3,795 meters).

**Temperature:** *Highest,* 136° F. (58° C) at Al 'Aziziyah, Libya, *Lowest,* −126.9° F. (−88.29° C) at Vostok in Antarctica. *Average Surface Temperature,* 57° F. (14° C).

**Atmosphere:** *Height*—99 per cent of the atmosphere is less than 100 miles (160 kilometers) above the earth's surface, but particles of the atmosphere are 1,000 miles (1,600 kilometers) above the surface. *Chemical Makeup of Atmosphere*—78 per cent nitrogen, 21 per cent oxygen, 1 per cent argon with small amounts of other gases.

**Chemical makeup of the earth's crust (in per cent of the crust's weight):** oxygen 46.6, silicon 27.7, aluminum 8.1, iron 5.0, calcium 3.6, sodium 2.8, potassium 2.6, magnesium 2.0, and other elements totaling 1.6.

## Characteristics of the planet earth

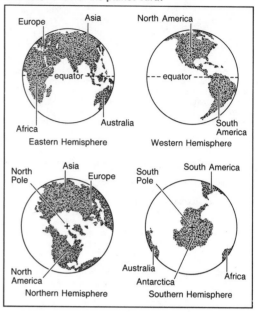

Eastern Hemisphere

Western Hemisphere

Northern Hemisphere

Southern Hemisphere

## The earth's radiation belts

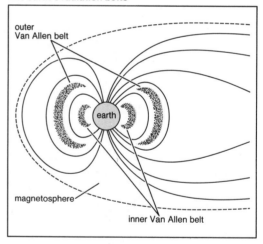

## The earth's radiation belts

Two doughnut-shaped bands of charged particles, called the *Van Allen belts* after their discoverer, ring the earth at the equator—trapped by the earth's magnetic field. The belts consist mainly of protons and electrons, supplied by cosmic rays, sun radiation, and high-altitude nuclear explosions. The Van Allen belts are part of the magnetic region surrounding the earth called the *magnetosphere.* The magnetosphere has a tearlike shape because the force of the *solar wind,* a stream of high-energy particles from the sun, pushes the earth's magnetic field away from the sun. Fluctuations in the Van Allen belts cause protons and electrons from them to rain the earth, producing such vivid nightly displays as the aurora borealis and aurora australis.

**Distances and contents of space**

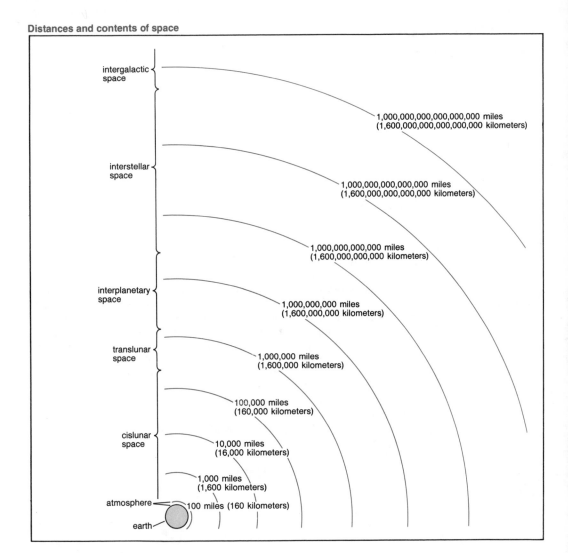

intergalactic space

1,000,000,000,000,000,000 miles
(1,600,000,000,000,000,000 kilometers)

interstellar space

1,000,000,000,000,000 miles
(1,600,000,000,000,000 kilometers)

1,000,000,000,000 miles
(1,600,000,000,000 kilometers)

interplanetary space

1,000,000,000 miles
(1,600,000,000 kilometers)

translunar space

1,000,000 miles
(1,600,000 kilometers)

100,000 miles
(160,000 kilometers)

cislunar space

10,000 miles
(16,000 kilometers)

1,000 miles
(1,600 kilometers)

atmosphere — 100 miles (160 kilometers)

earth

## Distances and contents of space

The light-year is a unit of astronomical measurement. Light spans 5,880,000,000,000 miles (9,460,000,000,000 kilometers) in a calendar year. Light from the sun, the nearest star, takes about 8 minutes 20 seconds to reach earth; from Alpha Centauri, a nearby star cluster, 4.3 years; from the center of our galaxy, the Milky Way, many thousands of years. Measurement of the earth's atmosphere and the makeup of cis- and translunar space have been made through instrument-bearing space probes. Spectrum analysis, using the imprint from the wavelengths of energy emitted or absorbed by chemical elements and compounds, is used to detect space matter. Radiation instruments also enable astronomers to uncover the X rays, gamma rays, and other radiation in space.

Interplanetary space consists of solar wind radiation, large rocks called meteoroids, and dust called micrometeorites, tons of which fall to earth each day. Comets—masses of metal, rock, and vapors of icy gases—also circle the sun in interplanetary space. Interstellar space consists of such cosmic rays as protons and some atomic nuclei, as well as hydrogen, helium, and other gases.

# 2. Facts about chemistry

Chemistry is the study of matter and its changes. Matter consists of chemical elements, their mixtures, or their compounds. Chemists have accepted 103 elements so far; 3 others have been claimed but not verified.

Elements share some characteristics. They have measurable physical properties, such as boiling point, melting point, hardness, mass, and density. Their chemical properties are determined by their electron configuration. An element's chemical properties enable a reaction with other elements to form compounds. Reactivity depends on the stability of an element's outer shell of electrons. Neon, xenon, and others have their outer electrons stably locked. Lithium, sodium, and others have their outer electrons bound so unstably that they can fly away and leave a gap in the shell. When an atom loses an electron and becomes a positively charged ion while another gains that electron and becomes a negatively charged ion, the two are attracted into an *ionic bond.* A more stable linkage occurs in a *covalent bond,* when the outer shells of two or more atoms merge and the combined electrons become "thick" enough to prevent the positively charged nuclei of the atoms from repelling the electrons.

Certain elements share chemical properties. They are grouped in the *periodic table of the elements* (see pages 110–111). The vertical groups relate to common physical traits.

## The atom

The atom is the basic unit of an element. The atom consists of a nucleus and one or more electrons orbiting the nucleus. The nucleus contains protons with positive (+) charges and neutrons with no charges. Electrons have negative (−) charges. The force of electron motion around the nucleus keeps them from being attracted by the oppositely charged protons. An atom's *atomic number* is determined by the number of protons in its nucleus. Its mass, or *atomic weight*, is the sum of its protons and neutrons. Nitrogen, for example, has an atomic number of 7 and an atomic weight of 14.0067, or $_7N^{14}$. The proton, electron, and neutron are types of particles.

## Atoms form molecules

Molecules are combinations of atoms. They can be of the same element, such as the molecules of hydrogen gas, $H_2$, or they can form from atoms of different elements, as when hydrogen and oxygen combine to form a molecule of water, $H_2O$.

Each atom has a *valence* number that shows its ability to combine with others to form molecules. Hydrogen has a valence of 1, and oxygen has a valence of 2. The outer shell of an oxygen atom can share space with the electrons of two hydrogen atoms. In a complex molecule like benzene, six carbon atoms link together in ringlike covalent bonds, while each carbon atom also forms a covalent bond with a hydrogen atom.

Carbon is a unique atom; it can bond with many other elements. Molecules containing carbon are found in living things and are thus called *organic compounds.* Organic chemistry is the study of these carbon compounds.

## The atom

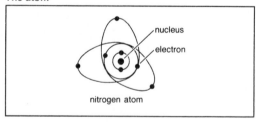

nucleus

electron

nitrogen atom

## Atoms form molecules

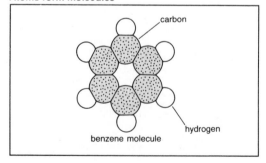

carbon

hydrogen

benzene molecule

### Ionic bonding

When atoms lose or gain electrons, they become electrically charged *ions*. Each electron shell, or layer, accommodates a maximum number of electrons.

A filled shell is stable; it does not readily give up or attract other electrons. Sodium (atomic number 11) has 11 protons to hold 11 electrons. Those electrons orbit in three shells—the first has two electrons (stable), the second has eight electrons (stable), and the third has one electron (unstable).

Sodium can gain stability by losing an electron, leaving the stable eight-electron shell as the outer one. When it does this, sodium becomes a positively charged *cation*. In contrast, chlorine (atomic number 17) can achieve a stable eight-electron outer shell by gaining an electron. When it does so, it becomes a negatively charged chloride *anion*. Ionically bound sodium and chloride ions form $Na^+Cl^-$, or common table salt. However, an ionic bond is broken easily; sodium and chloride ions constantly *dissociate* in solution and seek others to bond with.

### Radioactive decay

Some elements are *radioactive*. This term describes the process by which certain nuclei that are unstably bound together will spontaneously release particles of mass and radiation. When this happens, the nucleus loses some mass and may even become a different element. Radioactive decay is measured by half-life—the time it takes for one-half of a radioactive element to decay. One common radioactive substance is radium isotope 226. When the nucleus of this isotope breaks up, an alpha particle made of two protons and two neutrons is set free, and an atom of radon-222 is then formed. It takes approximately 1,660 years for one half of a given amount of radium 226 to decay to radon-222.

# Chemical reactions

Chemical elements can combine to form compounds when they share electrons or when their ions or ionlike groups, called *radicals*, electrically attract each other. Water is an example of electron sharing or *covalence*. Two atoms of hydrogen share one atom of oxygen in a water molecule. This can be written as H–O–H, where each – represents two electrons shared by each atom in the molecule. Sodium chloride, common table salt, is an example of the electrical combining power of ions. The sodium ion has an electrical charge, or *electrovalence*, of +1; the chloride ion has an electrovalence of −1. The two ions are attracted and combined as $Na^+Cl^-$

## Oxidation and reduction

An atom is said to be *oxidized* when it loses electrons. Once, oxidation meant merely that oxygen combined with a substance during combustion. Now, it means any chemical reaction in which an atom increases its positive charge by losing electrons. By contrast, an atom is *reduced* when it gains electrons and thus increases its negative charge. Oxidation-reduction activity, or a *redox* reaction, features substance A losing electrons (being oxidized) while substance B picks them up (becomes reduced). The degree to which a sub-

### Ionic bonding

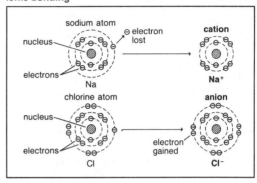

### Radioactive decay

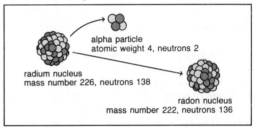

alpha particle
atomic weight 4, neutrons 2

radium nucleus
mass number 226, neutrons 138

radon nucleus
mass number 222, neutrons 136

stance can be oxidized is indicated by its *oxidation number*. Electrovalent elements have identical oxidation and electrovalence numbers. For example, the oxidation number of sodium is +1, as is its electrovalence number. However, covalent elements do not always have identical oxidation and covalence numbers. Sometimes, they combine in molecular groups called *radicals*. The hydroxyl radical, OH, is an example. The charge on each atom of the radical accounts for the oxidation number of a radical ($O^{-2} H^{+1} = OH^{-1}$). A free element (uncombined with others) has an oxidation number of 0.

Oxidation-reduction reactions always involve a change in the oxidation numbers of the chemical participants. For example, the formation of zinc chloride and hydrogen gas from free zinc and hydrochloric acid is an oxidation-reduction reaction:
$$Z^0n + 2H^{+1}Cl^{-1} \longrightarrow Zn^{+2}Cl^{-1}_2 + H^0_2.$$
Zinc is oxidized (loses electrons) and hydrogen is reduced (gains electrons).

## Catalysts

Chemical reactions can be sped or slowed by *catalysis*. Catalysts are chemicals that affect the reaction rate without being changed in the reaction. Chemical compound formation needs *activation energy* to loosen the chemical bonds of the reactants. Catalysts function by altering the amount of activation energy needed.

# States of matter

Matter ordinarily exists in one of three inter-changeable forms—solid, liquid, or gas. The rate of molecular vibration and movement determines the physical state of a substance. It is a solid if its molecules are arranged in an orderly, closely bound sequence. Some molecular vibration occurs but only in a tight area. As more energy acts on a solid, its molecules move more easily around each other until they assume a liquid flow. Liquids can take the shape of their containers. As still more energy acts on a liquid, its molecules begin to fly apart in all directions as a gas. Gases fill up their containers.

## Effects of temperature and pressure

Each element or compound needs a certain amount of heat energy at a given amount of pres-sure to enter the next physical state. For example, at sea level where the atmosphere pressure is 14.7 pounds per square inch (1.03 kilograms per square centimeter), water boils at 212°F. (100°C); that is, it changes from the liquid to the gaseous state at that temperature and pressure. However, as the elevation above sea level increases, the pressure decreases, so that at mountainous altitudes, water boils at lower temperatures.

## Boyle's law and Charles's (Gay-Lussac's) law

Temperature and pressure affect gases considera-bly. According to *Boyle's law*, a change in the vol-ume occupied by a gas produces an opposite change in the pressure exerted by the gas as long as the temperature remains the same. When pres-sure decreases, the gas volume increases, and vice versa. According to *Charles's law* or *Gay-Lussac's law* (two pre-19th century scientists observed the same principle), a gas increases by 1/273 of its original volume for each degree of temperature rise above 0°C as long as the pressure remains the same. The Kelvin temperature scale starts at a point where molecular motion ceases—*absolute zero* (0°K or −273.15°C). Kelvin temperatures are found by adding 273 to the Celsius reading (10°C = 283°K). A *general gas law* has been formulated to account for all the natural forces that affect the behavior of gases—$pv=RT$. Pressure $(p)$ multiplied by volume $(v)$ equals Kelvin temperature $(T)$ mul-tiplied by a constant number $(R)$.

## Avogadro's law

Early in the 19th century, the Italian chemist Amedeo Avogadro proposed that the atoms of gases join in pairs to form molecules, such as $H_2$ (hydrogen), $O_2$ (oxygen), and $N_2$ (nitrogen). He also suggested all gases behaved alike and that equal amounts of gases (having the same pressure and temperature) would contain the same number of molecules. The number of molecules in a gram-molecular weight of a gas is called *Avogadro's number*—$6.02 \times 10.^{23}$

# Determining molecular weight

The molecular weight of a substance is the sum of its weights. Because of the extreme tininess of atoms, any expression of their weight must be a relative measure. The atomic weight of an atom is its heaviness or lightness compared with the weight of a standard isotope of carbon—car-bon–12. Atomic weights, or *mass numbers*, for each element are listed in the periodic table. When using the table's atomic weights, round off the figures. For example, the atomic weight of chlorine is 35.453. When determining the molecu-lar weight of a chlorine-containing molecule, use 35.5 for chlorine's atomic weight. As an example, the molecular weight of calcium chloride, $CaCl_2$, is 111. The molecule contains one atom of calcium (atomic weight = 40) and two atoms of chlorine (atomic weight = 35.5). Adding them up, we get $40 + 35.5 + 35.5 = 111$. Unit weights of molecular substances are expressed in *gram-moles*. A mole of calcium chloride contains 111 grams. Using Avogadro's number, a mole of $CaCl_2$ (111 grams) contains $6.02 \times 10^{23}$ calcium chloride molecules.

## Strengths of solutions

Solutions consist of substances dissolved in other substances. The chemical mixing of the two sub-stances in solution is so complete that they can-not be separated by filtration or through settling. A solution is comprised of a *solute* and a *solvent*. The solute is the chemical that dissolves in the solvent. Solutes can be solids, liquids, or gases. *Solubility* is the measure of how much solute can dissolve in a given amount of solvent. A solid usu-ally becomes more soluble when the solvent is heated. By contrast, the solubility of a gas lessens when the solvent is heated.

Percentages sometimes indicate the concentra-tion of a solute in a solvent. A 10% sugar solution, for instance, has 10 parts of sugar (by weight) to 90 parts of water (by weight).

## Electrolytic action

When an electric current passes through an ionic substance, a chemical reaction can occur. The process is called *electrolysis*. Acids, bases, and salts largely dissociate into ions in water solution and permit large electric currents to pass through the solution. They are called *strong electrolytes*. *Weak electrolytes* can carry little current because they dissociate only slightly. When the electric current is supplied by some outside source, electrons are supplied to the electrolyte at the cathode and accepted from the electrolyte at the anode. Positively charged hydrogen ions ($H^+$) are attracted electrically to the cathode, where they pick up electrons to form molecules of hydrogen gas. Oxygen-containing ($OH^-$) ions are drawn to the anode, and they release electrons and form oxygen gas. Electrolysis results in separating the hydrogen and oxygen of water and combining them into two molecules of hydrogen gas and one molecule of oxygen gas. The chemical shorthand way of describing this is:

$$2 H_2O \xrightarrow{\text{electric current}} 4 H^+ + 2 O \quad 2 H_2^\uparrow + O_2^\uparrow$$

When the electrolyte is water-free, other reactions occur.

### Electrolytic action

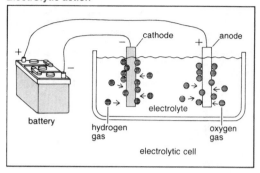

electrolytic cell

## Electrolytic action of a dry cell

A dry cell is one means of generating an electric current by electrolysis. The cell consists of a positive anode of carbon, a pasty mixture of manganese dioxide and carbon grains, cardboard soaked with ammonium chloride (the electrolyte), and a negative cathode of zinc.

The top is sealed to keep the cell dry. When the electrodes of the dry cell are connected, an electric current flows between the cathode and the anode; this is because carbon attracts electrons better than zinc. The electrons come from the zinc, which breaks down into positively charged zinc ions. They then combine with the negatively charged ions of the ammonium chloride electrolyte to form zinc chloride. Meanwhile, electrons flow back to the carbon anode. There, they combine with hydrogen ions from the ammonium component of the electrolyte and form hydrogen gas.

Ordinarily, hydrogen gas would act as an insulator, *polarize* the cell, and stop the current (electron flow). However, the hydrogen gas is absorbed by the pasty mix of manganese dioxide and carbon grains.

### Electrolytic action of a dry cell

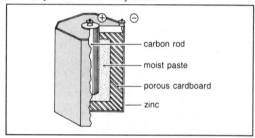

- carbon rod
- moist paste
- porous cardboard
- zinc

## Acids and bases

Acids and bases are two important groups of compounds that react easily with each other. An *acid* is a compound containing hydrogen that gives up hydrogen ions ($H^+$) when it dissociates in water. An acid is also a compound that can replace its hydrogen ions with a metal. Sulfuric acid, hydrochloric acid, and nitric acid are strong acids. This means that they tend to give up their hydrogen ions easily.

A *base* is a compound containing either a hydroxyl ion ($OH^-$) or a hydroxyl group (OH) that will give up hydroxyl ions when it dissociates in water. Many metals have hydroxyl compounds. Sodium hydroxide and potassium hydroxide are strong bases. The reactiveness between acids and bases is evident—acids want to replace their hydrogen ions with metals, and bases have metals to exchange for hydrogen ions. The hydrogen ion concentration of a substance in solution determines its pH (the logarithm of the reciprocal of the hydrogen ion concentration).

Pure water has an $H^+$ concentration of 0.0000001; it has a "neutral" pH of 7. Substances at the low end of the pH scale are strong acids, like lemons.

### Acids and bases

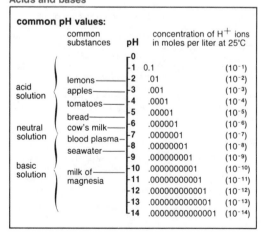

**common pH values:**

| common substances | pH | concentration of $H^+$ ions in moles per liter at 25°C | |
|---|---|---|---|
| | 0 | | |
| | 1 | 0.1 | ($10^{-1}$) |
| lemons | 2 | .01 | ($10^{-2}$) |
| apples | 3 | .001 | ($10^{-3}$) |
| tomatoes | 4 | .0001 | ($10^{-4}$) |
| bread | 5 | .00001 | ($10^{-5}$) |
| cow's milk | 6 | .000001 | ($10^{-6}$) |
| blood plasma | 7 | .0000001 | ($10^{-7}$) |
| seawater | 8 | .00000001 | ($10^{-8}$) |
| | 9 | .000000001 | ($10^{-9}$) |
| milk of magnesia | 10 | .0000000001 | ($10^{-10}$) |
| | 11 | .00000000001 | ($10^{-11}$) |
| | 12 | .000000000001 | ($10^{-12}$) |
| | 13 | .0000000000001 | ($10^{-13}$) |
| | 14 | .00000000000001 | ($10^{-14}$) |

acid solution / neutral solution / basic solution

## The Petri dish

The Petri dish is used in biochemical research. The unique design of the dish allows scientists to grow microorganisms on nutrients in the dish without fear of outside contamination. A typical biochemical experiment might study the effects of a drug on the chemical life activities of pathogenic (harmful) bacteria. The biochemist would first grow the pathogens in a Petri dish and then introduce an experimental drug into areas of the bacterial culture. Afterward, the dish would be checked to see if the drug used in the experiment altered the bacterial growth patterns in any way.

## The compound microscope

The compound microscope is used in both biochemical and chemical research. Chemists sometimes study the crystal patterns of compounds through a microscope. The magnifying power of a microscope is the power of each objective multiplied by the power of the eyepiece. For example, if the eyepiece is 10X and the objective is 10X, then the magnifying power is 100X, or 100 diameters. A viewing object is placed on a glass slide on the stage, and light is reflected off the mirror and through the object. The object is brought into focus by the eyepiece adjuster. To avoid breaking the slide when viewing something under high magnification, move the objective downward carefully until it barely touches the slide, then adjust upward while looking through the eyepiece.

## The Bunsen burner

Many chemical experiments call for heating a solution or finding its boiling point, which is a physical property of a compound. The high heat needed to bring a substance to its boiling point quickly is usually furnished by a *Bunsen burner*. Ports in the base of the burner tube allow air to mix with the fuel gas for maximum combustion. The spark of a flint lighter is used to ignite the flame. The temperature at the tip of the hottest part of the flame—the middle, *reducing* cone—is some 2,700°F. (1,480°C). Flasks containing solutions for heating are supported on wire meshes over the flame. The mesh spreads the flame evenly over the base of the flask. Obviously, a Bunsen burner should be handled with the utmost concern for safety.

## Use of the burette in titration

In chemical analysis by *titration*, drop-by-drop amounts of a measured amount of reagent are released from a calibrated burette until an *end point* is reached—usually a color change. For example, a known amount of silver nitrate is slowly added to an unknown amount of a chloride solution mixed with potassium chromate to find the chloride concentration. When the last chloride ions combine with silver ions, the solution turns reddish brown. This is because silver ions now combine with chromate ions from the potassium chromate to form reddish-brown silver chromate. Calculations using the amount of silver nitrate titrated can then be used to determine the amount of chloride in the test solution.

## Distillation

Distillation separates liquid compounds with different boiling points from each other in solution. The compounds having the lowest boiling points will separate first; those with the highest, last. To separate compound A having a boiling point of 150°F. (65°C) and compound B having a boiling point of 250°F. (121°C), heat the solution in the distillation flask to compound A's boiling point and maintain the heat. (Distillation apparatuses ordinarily have a thermometer in the stopper of the distillation flask.) Compound A will vaporize and flow as a gas out of the flask outlet and into the condenser tube. Cool water circulating in a jacket around the condenser will lower the vapor temperature of compound A until it liquefies and collects as distillate in a flask under the condenser outlet. After distillate no longer accumulates, raise the flame under the distillation flask until the boiling point of compound B is reached.

**The Petri dish**

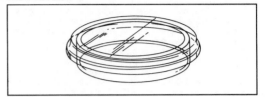

**The compound microscope**

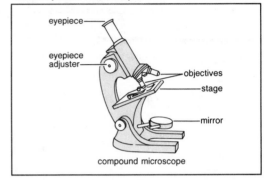

eyepiece
eyepiece adjuster
objectives
stage
mirror

compound microscope

**The Bunsen burner**

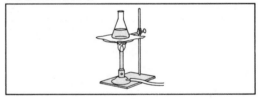

**Use of the burette in titration**

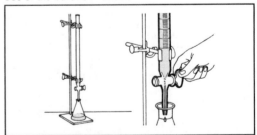

**Process of distillation**

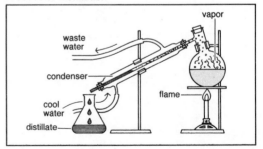

vapor
waste water
condenser
flame
cool water
distillate

# Simple chemical procedures

Certain simple experiments show chemical reactions or illustrate the chemical characteristics of some common substances. Most can be performed with the materials available in a school science laboratory. All should be performed cautiously and carefully.

## Testing for acids and bases

Mix the following solutions in five test tubes: sugar dissolved in water; sodium bicarbonate (baking soda) in water; acetic acid (vinegar) in water; lemon juice in water; and corn starch in water. Place five strips of red litmus paper in a row, then five strips of blue litmus paper in another row. Using a clean medicine dropper, put one drop of the first solution on one of the red and the blue litmus papers. Rinse the dropper and repeat the process with the remaining solutions. Acids turn blue litmus paper red; bases turn red litmus paper blue; neutral substances do not affect the color of the test papers. Judging from the color changes, which of the test solutions was acidic, basic, neutral?

## Neutralizing an acid with a base

Place 30 ml of an acetic acid solution in a 100-ml beaker, and place 10 ml of an ammonium hydroxide solution in a 50-ml. beaker. Put a piece of blue litmus paper into the beaker of acetic acid. What color does the litmus paper turn? Using a clean medicine dropper, add the ammonium hydroxide drop by drop to the acetic acid, stirring after each drop. Continue adding the ammonium hydroxide until the litmus is no longer red. This is the neutralization point. How many drops of base were needed to neutralize the acid? If you continue to add ammonium hydroxide after the neutralization point, the solution will become basic and the litmus will turn blue.

## Finding starch in foods

Starch is a chemical called a carbohydrate. Iodine turns starch bluish-black. Moisten a small piece of each of the following foods separately and test for starch: an apple; a potato; flour; bread; crumbled cornflakes; and cheese. Drop the moistened food sample into a test tube and add a few drops of iodine solution from a medicine dropper. If the food turns bluish-black, it contains starch; if it turns rusty brown, it does not. Foods with large concentrations of starch turn the darkest; those with small amounts turn light blue.

## Precipitation

In certain chemical reactions that take place in solution, insoluble solids called *precipitates* form and fall out of solution to the bottom of the container. Using three test tubes, place 1 ml of silver nitrate ($AgNO_3$) solution into each. Add 1 ml of sodium bromide (NaBr) to the first test tube, 1 ml of sodium iodide (NaI) to the second, and 1 ml of sodium chloride (NaCl) to the third. Note the precipitation that occurs in each case. The precipitates are silver bromide (AgBr), silver iodide (AgI), and silver chloride (AgCl), respectively.

## Forming a gas

Formation of gas can be evidence that a chemical reaction has taken place. To a large beaker half filled with dilute acetic acid (vinegar), add a teaspoon of sodium bicarbonate (baking soda). Note the bubbles forming in the solution. Carbon dioxide is the gas escaping from it. Light a match and hold it over the beaker while the gas continues to bubble. What happens to the flame? What can you say about the ability of carbon dioxide to support combustion?

## Heat of solution

Heat energy is released in many chemical reactions or when the state of a substance (solid, liquid, or gas) changes. The following experiment, which illustrates heat of solution, should take place in a supervised school laboratory because a strong base is used.

Place 10 ml of water in three test tubes and put them in a rack. Fill a 200-ml beaker with 100 ml of water and place it in a box containing insulation. Record its temperature and keep the thermometer in the beaker of water. Into the first test tube, *carefully* put two pellets of sodium hydroxide (NaOH). Place the test tube into the beaker of water, gently swirl it in the water, and record the water temperature. Carefully put four NaOH pellets in the second test tube containing 10 ml of water and place it in the beaker containing a new batch of water, again recording the temperature rise. Repeat the procedure a third time, using six pellets of NaOH in the 10 ml of water. How much heat was released in each case? This can be determined by computing the before-and-after temperatures and knowing that 1 calorie of heat energy is needed to raise 1 ml of water 1°C.

## Table: the elements and their discoverers

| Name | Symbol | Atomic weight* | Atomic number | Specific gravity | Discoverer | Country of discovery | Date of discovery |
|------|--------|----------------|---------------|------------------|------------|----------------------|-------------------|
| Actinium | Ac | [227] | 89 | _____ | André Debierne | France | 1899 |
| Aluminum | Al | 26.9815 | 13 | 2.70 | Hans Christian Oersted | Denmark | 1825 |
| Americium | Am | [243] | 95 | _____ | G. T. Seaborg; R. A. James; L. O. Morgan; A. Ghiorso | United States | 1945 |
| Antimony | Sb | 121.75 | 51 | 6.684 | | Known to ancients | |
| Argon | Ar | 39.948 | 18 | .00178 | Sir William Ramsay; Baron Rayleigh | Scotland | 1894 |
| Arsenic | As | 74.9216 | 33 | 5.7 | | Known to ancients | |
| Astatine | At | [210] | 85 | _____ | D. R. Corson; K.R. MacKenzie; E. Segrè | United States | 1940 |
| Barium | Ba | 137.33 | 56 | 3.5 | Sir Humphry Davy | England | 1808 |
| Berkelium | Bk | [247] | 97 | _____ | G. T. Seaborg; S. G. Thompson; A. Ghiorso | United States | 1949 |
| Beryllium | Be | 9.0122 | 4 | 1.85 | Friedrich Wöhler; A. A. Bussy | Germany; Fr. | 1828 |
| Bismuth | Bi | 208.980 | 83 | 9.80 | | Known to ancients | |
| Boron | B | 10.811 | 5 | 2.45 | H. Davy; J. L. Gay-Lussac; L. J. Thenard | England; Fr. | 1808 |
| Bromine | Br | 79.909 | 35 | 3.12 | Antoine J. Balard | France | 1826 |
| Cadmium | Cd | 112.41 | 48 | 8.65 | Friedrich Stromeyer | Germany | 1817 |
| Calcium | Ca | 40.08 | 20 | 1.55 | Sir Humphry Davy | England | 1808 |
| Californium | Cf | [251] | 98 | _____ | G. T. Seaborg; S. G. Thompson; A. Ghiorso; K. Street, Jr. | United States | 1950 |
| Carbon | C | 12.01115 | 6 | 3.52 | | Known to ancients | |
| Cerium | Ce | 140.12 | 58 | 6.90 | W. von Hisinger; J. Berzelius; M. Klaproth | Sweden; Germany | 1803 |
| Cesium | Cs | 132.905 | 55 | 1.90 | Gustav Kirchhoff, Robert Bunsen | Germany | 1860 |
| Chlorine | Cl | 35.453 | 17 | 0.0032 | Carl Wilhelm Scheele | Sweden | 1774 |
| Chromium | Cr | 51.996 | 24 | 7.1 | Louis Vauquelin | France | 1797 |
| Cobalt | Co | 58.9332 | 27 | 8.9 | Georg Brandt | Sweden | 1737 |
| Copper | Cu | 63.54 | 29 | 8.92 | | Known to ancients | |
| Curium | Cm | [247] | 96 | _____ | G. T. Seaborg; R. A. James; A. Ghiorso | United States | 1944 |
| Dysprosium | Dy | 162.50 | 66 | _____ | Paul Émile Lecoq de Boisbaudran | France | 1886 |
| Einsteinium | Es | [254] | 99 | _____ | Argonne; Los Alamos; U. of Calif. | United States | 1952 |
| Element 104 | _____ | _____ | 104 | _____ | Claimed by G. Flerov and others | Russia | 1964 |
| | | | | | Claimed by A. Ghiorso and others | United States | 1969 |
| Element 105 | _____ | _____ | 105 | _____ | Claimed by G. Flerov and others | Russia | 1968 |
| Element 106 | _____ | _____ | 106 | _____ | Claimed by G. Flerov and others | Russia | 1974 |
| | | | | | Claimed by A. Ghiorso and others | United States | 1974 |
| Erbium | Er | 167.26 | 68 | 4.77 | Carl Mosander | Sweden | 1843 |
| Europium | Eu | 151.96 | 63 | _____ | Eugène Demarçay | France | 1901 |
| Fermium | Fm | [257] | 100 | _____ | Argonne; Los Alamos; U. of Calif. | United States | 1953 |
| Fluorine | F | 18.998403 | 9 | 0.0017 | Henri Moissan | France | 1886 |
| Francium | Fr | [223] | 87 | _____ | Marguerite Perey | France | 1939 |
| Gadolinium | Gd | 157.25 | 64 | _____ | Jean de Marignac | Switzerland | 1880 |
| Gallium | Ga | 69.72 | 31 | 5.9 | Paul Émile Lecoq de Boisbaudran | France | 1875 |
| Germanium | Ge | 72.59 | 32 | 5.36 | Clemens Winkler | Germany | 1886 |
| Gold | Au | 196.967 | 79 | 19.3 | | Known to ancients | |
| Hafnium | Hf | 178.49 | 72 | _____ | Dirk Coster; Georg von Hevesy | Denmark | 1923 |
| Helium | He | 4.0026 | 2 | 0.00018 | Sir William Ramsay; Nils Langlet; P. T. Cleve | Scotland; Sweden | 1895 |
| Holmium | Ho | 164.930 | 67 | _____ | J. L. Soret | Switzerland | 1878 |
| Hydrogen | H | 1.00797 | 1 | 0.00009 | Henry Cavendish | England | 1766 |
| Indium | In | 114.82 | 49 | 7.3 | Ferdinand Reich; H. Richter | Germany | 1863 |
| Iodine | I | 126.9044 | 53 | 4.93 | Bernard Courtois | France | 1811 |
| Iridium | Ir | 192.2 | 77 | 22.4 | Smithson Tennant; A. F. Fourcroy; L. N. Vauquelin; H. V. Collet-Descotils | England; France | 1804 |
| Iron | Fe | 55.847 | 26 | 7.87 | | Known to ancients | |
| Krypton | Kr | 83.80 | 36 | 0.0037 | Sir William Ramsay; M. W. Travers | Great Britain | 1898 |
| Lanthanum | La | 138.91 | 57 | 6.15 | Carl Mosander | Sweden | 1839 |
| Lawrencium | Lr | [256] | 103 | _____ | A. Ghiorso; T. Sikkeland; A. E. Larsh; R. M. Latimer | United States | 1961 |
| Lead | Pb | 207.19 | 82 | 11.34 | | Known to ancients | |
| Lithium | Li | 6.939 | 3 | 0.534 | Johann Arfvedson | Sweden | 1817 |

*A number in brackets indicates the mass number of the most stable isotope.

| Name | Symbol | Atomic weight* | Atomic number | Specific gravity | Discoverer | Country of discovery | Date of discovery |
|---|---|---|---|---|---|---|---|
| Lutetium | Lu | 174.97 | 71 | _____ | Georges Urbain | France | 1907 |
| Magnesium | Mg | 24.312 | 12 | 1.74 | Sir Humphry Davy | England | 1808 |
| Manganese | Mn | 54.9380 | 25 | 7.2 | Johann Gahn | Sweden | 1774 |
| Mendelevium | Md | [258] | 101 | _____ | G. T. Seaborg; A. Ghiorso; B. Harvey; G. R. Choppin; S. G. Thompson | United States | 1955 |
| Mercury | Hg | 200.59 | 80 | 13.55 | | Known to ancients | |
| Molybdenum | Mo | 95.94 | 42 | 10.2 | Carl Wilhelm Scheele | Sweden | 1778 |
| Neodymium | Nd | 144.24 | 60 | 6.9 | C. F. Auer von Welsbach | Austria | 1885 |
| Neon | Ne | 20.183 | 10 | 0.0009 | Sir William Ramsay; M. W. Travers | England | 1898 |
| Neptunium | Np | [237] | 93 | _____ | E. M. McMillan; P. H. Abelson | United States | 1940 |
| Nickel | Ni | 58.71 | 28 | 8.90 | Axel Cronstedt | Sweden | 1751 |
| Niobium | Nb | 92.906 | 41 | 8.4 | Charles Hatchett | England | 1801 |
| Nitrogen | N | 14.0067 | 7 | 0.00125 | Daniel Rutherford | Scotland | 1772 |
| Nobelium | No | [255] | 102 | _____ | Nobel Institute for Physics | Sweden | 1957 |
| Osmium | Os | 190.2 | 76 | 22.57 | Smithson Tennant | England | 1804 |
| Oxygen | O | 15.9994 | 8 | 0.001429 | Joseph Priestley; Carl Wilhelm Scheele | England; Sweden | 1774 |
| Palladium | Pd | 106.4 | 46 | 12.16 | William Wollaston | England | 1803 |
| Phosphorus | P | 30.9738 | 15 | 1.83 | Hennig Brand | Germany | 1669 |
| Platinum | Pt | 195.09 | 78 | 21.37 | Julius Scaliger | Italy | 1557 |
| Plutonium | Pu | [244] | 94 | _____ | G. T. Seaborg; J. W. Kennedy; E. M. McMillan; A. C. Wahl | United States | 1940 |
| Polonium | Po | [210] | 84 | _____ | Pierre and Marie Curie | France | 1898 |
| Potassium | K | 39.0983 | 19 | 0.86 | Sir Humphry Davy | England | 1807 |
| Praseodymium | Pr | 140.907 | 59 | 6.5 | C. F. Auer von Welsbach | Austria | 1885 |
| Promethium | Pm | [145] | 61 | _____ | J. A. Marinsky; Lawrence E. Glendenin; Charles D. Coryell | United States | 1945 |
| Protactinium | Pa | [231] | 91 | _____ | Otto Hahn; Lise Meitner; Frederick Soddy; John Cranston | Germany England | 1917 |
| Radium | Ra | [226] | 88 | 5.0 | Pierre and Marie Curie | France | 1898 |
| Radon | Rn | [222] | 86 | 0.00973 | Friedrich Ernst Dorn | Germany | 1900 |
| Rhenium | Re | 186.2 | 75 | 20.53 | Walter Noddack; Ida Tacke; Otto Berg | Germany | 1925 |
| Rhodium | Rh | 102.905 | 45 | 12.5 | William Wollaston | England | 1803 |
| Rubidium | Rb | 85.47 | 37 | 1.53 | R. Bunsen; G. Kirchhoff | Germany | 1861 |
| Ruthenium | Ru | 101.07 | 44 | 12.2 | Karl Klaus | Russia | 1844 |
| Samarium | Sm | 150.35 | 62 | 7.7 | Paul Émile Lecoq de Boisbaudran | France | 1879 |
| Scandium | Sc | 44.956 | 21 | 2.5 | Lars Nilson | Sweden | 1879 |
| Selenium | Se | 78.96 | 34 | 4.8 | Jöns Berzelius | Sweden | 1817 |
| Silicon | Si | 28.0855 | 14 | 2.4 | Jöns Berzelius | Sweden | 1823 |
| Silver | Ag | 107.870 | 47 | 10.5 | | Known to ancients | |
| Sodium | Na | 22.9898 | 11 | 0.97 | Sir Humphry Davy | England | 1807 |
| Strontium | Sr | 87.62 | 38 | 2.6 | A. Crawford | Scotland | 1790 |
| Sulfur | S | 32.064 | 16 | 2.0 | | Known to ancients | |
| Tantalum | Ta | 180.948 | 73 | 16.6 | Anders Ekeberg | Sweden | 1802 |
| Technetium | Tc | [97] | 43 | _____ | Carlo Perrier; Émilio Segrè | Italy | 1937 |
| Tellurium | Te | 127.60 | 52 | 6.24 | Franz Müller von Reichenstein | Romania | 1782 |
| Terbium | Tb | 158.924 | 65 | _____ | Carl Mosander | Sweden | 1843 |
| Thallium | Tl | 204.37 | 81 | 11.85 | Sir William Crookes | England | 1861 |
| Thorium | Th | 232.038 | 90 | 11.2 | Jöns Berzelius | Sweden | 1828 |
| Thulium | Tm | 168.934 | 69 | _____ | Per Theodor Cleve | Sweden | 1879 |
| Tin | Sn | 118.69 | 50 | 7.3 | | Known to ancients | |
| Titanium | Ti | 47.90 | 22 | 4.5 | William Gregor | England | 1791 |
| Tungsten | W | 183.85 | 74 | 19.3 | Fausto and Juan José de Elhuyar | Spain | 1783 |
| Uranium | U | 238.03 | 92 | 18.7 | Martin Klaproth | Germany | 1789 |
| Vanadium | V | 50.942 | 23 | 5.96 | Nils Sefström | Sweden | 1830 |
| Xenon | Xe | 131.30 | 54 | 0.0058 | Sir William Ramsay; M. W. Travers | England | 1898 |
| Ytterbium | Yb | 173.04 | 70 | 5.51 | Jean de Marignac | Switzerland | 1878 |
| Yttrium | Y | 88.905 | 39 | 3.80 | Johann Gadolin | Finland | 1794 |
| Zinc | Zn | 65.37 | 30 | 7.14 | Andreas Marggraf | Germany | 1746 |
| Zirconium | Zr | 91.22 | 40 | 6.4 | Martin Klaproth | Germany | 1789 |

*A number in brackets indicates the mass number of the most stable isotope.

# Periodic table of the elements

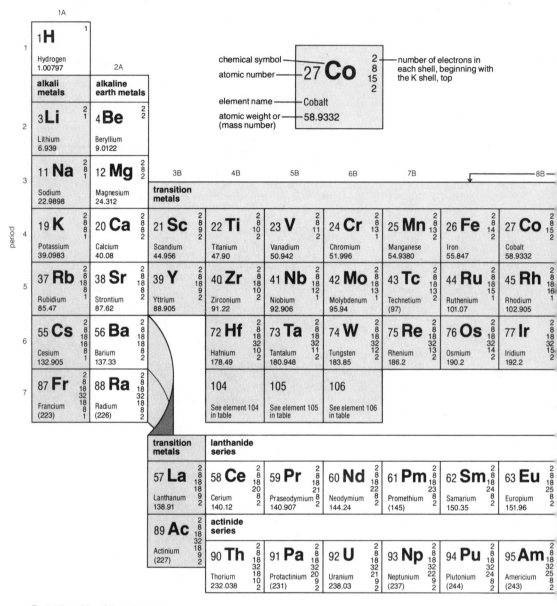

## Periodic table of the elements

This table gives basic information about the known chemical elements. Eight major classes of elements are shown, differentiated by color. Hydrogen stands alone, in that it does not clearly belong to any one class.

A key to understanding the information about each element is found in the enlarged sample square for Cobalt at the top of this page. This key will help you identify the chemical symbol, the atomic number, atomic weight, and other important information about each element.

An alphabetical table of the elements, with information about their discovery, is found on pages 108-109.

8A

| | | | | | | noble gases |
|---|---|---|---|---|---|---|

3A      4A      5A      6A      7A

2 **He** $\begin{smallmatrix}2\end{smallmatrix}$

Helium
4.0026

**nonmetals**

| 5 **B** $\begin{smallmatrix}2\\3\end{smallmatrix}$ | 6 **C** $\begin{smallmatrix}2\\4\end{smallmatrix}$ | 7 **N** $\begin{smallmatrix}2\\5\end{smallmatrix}$ | 8 **O** $\begin{smallmatrix}2\\6\end{smallmatrix}$ | 9 **F** $\begin{smallmatrix}2\\7\end{smallmatrix}$ | 10 **Ne** $\begin{smallmatrix}2\\8\end{smallmatrix}$ |
|---|---|---|---|---|---|
| Boron 10.811 | Carbon 12.01115 | Nitrogen 14.0067 | Oxygen 15.9994 | Fluorine 18.998403 | Neon 20.183 |

1B      2B

**other metals**

| 13 **Al** $\begin{smallmatrix}2\\8\\3\end{smallmatrix}$ | 14 **Si** $\begin{smallmatrix}2\\8\\4\end{smallmatrix}$ | 15 **P** $\begin{smallmatrix}2\\8\\5\end{smallmatrix}$ | 16 **S** $\begin{smallmatrix}2\\8\\6\end{smallmatrix}$ | 17 **Cl** $\begin{smallmatrix}2\\8\\7\end{smallmatrix}$ | 18 **Ar** $\begin{smallmatrix}2\\8\\8\end{smallmatrix}$ |
|---|---|---|---|---|---|
| Aluminum 26.9815 | Silicon 28.0855 | Phosphorus 30.9738 | Sulfur 32.064 | Chlorine 35.453 | Argon 39.948 |

| 28 **Ni** $\begin{smallmatrix}2\\8\\16\\2\end{smallmatrix}$ | 29 **Cu** $\begin{smallmatrix}2\\8\\18\\1\end{smallmatrix}$ | 30 **Zn** $\begin{smallmatrix}2\\8\\18\\2\end{smallmatrix}$ | 31 **Ga** $\begin{smallmatrix}2\\8\\18\\3\end{smallmatrix}$ | 32 **Ge** $\begin{smallmatrix}2\\8\\18\\4\end{smallmatrix}$ | 33 **As** $\begin{smallmatrix}2\\8\\18\\5\end{smallmatrix}$ | 34 **Se** $\begin{smallmatrix}2\\8\\18\\6\end{smallmatrix}$ | 35 **Br** $\begin{smallmatrix}2\\8\\18\\7\end{smallmatrix}$ | 36 **Kr** $\begin{smallmatrix}2\\8\\18\\8\end{smallmatrix}$ |
|---|---|---|---|---|---|---|---|---|
| Nickel 58.71 | Copper 63.54 | Zinc 65.37 | Gallium 69.72 | Germanium 72.59 | Arsenic 74.9216 | Selenium 78.96 | Bromine 79.909 | Krypton 83.80 |
| 46 **Pd** $\begin{smallmatrix}2\\8\\18\\18\\0\end{smallmatrix}$ | 47 **Ag** $\begin{smallmatrix}2\\8\\18\\18\\1\end{smallmatrix}$ | 48 **Cd** $\begin{smallmatrix}2\\8\\18\\18\\2\end{smallmatrix}$ | 49 **In** $\begin{smallmatrix}2\\8\\18\\3\end{smallmatrix}$ | 50 **Sn** $\begin{smallmatrix}2\\8\\18\\4\end{smallmatrix}$ | 51 **Sb** $\begin{smallmatrix}2\\8\\18\\5\end{smallmatrix}$ | 52 **Te** $\begin{smallmatrix}2\\8\\18\\6\end{smallmatrix}$ | 53 **I** $\begin{smallmatrix}2\\8\\18\\7\end{smallmatrix}$ | 54 **Xe** $\begin{smallmatrix}2\\8\\18\\8\end{smallmatrix}$ |
| Palladium 106.4 | Silver 107.870 | Cadmium 112.41 | Indium 114.82 | Tin 118.69 | Antimony 121.75 | Tellurium 127.60 | Iodine 126.9044 | Xenon 131.30 |
| 78 **Pt** $\begin{smallmatrix}2\\8\\18\\32\\17\\1\end{smallmatrix}$ | 79 **Au** $\begin{smallmatrix}2\\8\\18\\32\\18\\1\end{smallmatrix}$ | 80 **Hg** $\begin{smallmatrix}2\\8\\18\\32\\18\\2\end{smallmatrix}$ | 81 **Tl** $\begin{smallmatrix}2\\8\\18\\32\\18\\3\end{smallmatrix}$ | 82 **Pb** $\begin{smallmatrix}2\\8\\18\\32\\18\\4\end{smallmatrix}$ | 83 **Bi** $\begin{smallmatrix}2\\8\\18\\32\\18\\5\end{smallmatrix}$ | 84 **Po** $\begin{smallmatrix}2\\8\\18\\32\\18\\6\end{smallmatrix}$ | 85 **At** $\begin{smallmatrix}2\\8\\18\\32\\18\\7\end{smallmatrix}$ | 86 **Rn** $\begin{smallmatrix}2\\8\\18\\32\\18\\8\end{smallmatrix}$ |
| Platinum 195.09 | Gold 196.967 | Mercury 200.59 | Thallium 204.37 | Lead 207.19 | Bismuth 208.980 | Polonium (210) | Astatine (210) | Radon (222) |

| 64 **Gd** $\begin{smallmatrix}2\\8\\18\\25\\9\\2\end{smallmatrix}$ | 65 **Tb** $\begin{smallmatrix}2\\8\\18\\27\\8\\2\end{smallmatrix}$ | 66 **Dy** $\begin{smallmatrix}2\\8\\18\\28\\8\\2\end{smallmatrix}$ | 67 **Ho** $\begin{smallmatrix}2\\8\\18\\29\\8\\2\end{smallmatrix}$ | 68 **Er** $\begin{smallmatrix}2\\8\\18\\30\\8\\2\end{smallmatrix}$ | 69 **Tm** $\begin{smallmatrix}2\\8\\18\\31\\8\\2\end{smallmatrix}$ | 70 **Yb** $\begin{smallmatrix}2\\8\\18\\32\\8\\2\end{smallmatrix}$ | 71 **Lu** $\begin{smallmatrix}2\\8\\18\\32\\9\\2\end{smallmatrix}$ |
|---|---|---|---|---|---|---|---|
| Gadolinium 157.25 | Terbium 158.924 | Dysprosium 162.50 | Holmium 164.930 | Erbium 167.26 | Thulium 168.934 | Ytterbium 173.04 | Lutetium 174.97 |

| 96 **Cm** $\begin{smallmatrix}2\\8\\18\\32\\25\\9\\2\end{smallmatrix}$ | 97 **Bk** $\begin{smallmatrix}2\\8\\18\\32\\26\\9\\2\end{smallmatrix}$ | 98 **Cf** $\begin{smallmatrix}2\\8\\18\\32\\28\\8\\2\end{smallmatrix}$ | 99 **Es** $\begin{smallmatrix}2\\8\\18\\32\\29\\8\\2\end{smallmatrix}$ | 100 **Fm** $\begin{smallmatrix}2\\8\\18\\32\\30\\8\\2\end{smallmatrix}$ | 101 **Md** $\begin{smallmatrix}2\\8\\18\\32\\31\\8\\2\end{smallmatrix}$ | 102 **No** $\begin{smallmatrix}2\\8\\18\\32\\32\\8\\2\end{smallmatrix}$ | 103 **Lr** $\begin{smallmatrix}2\\8\\18\\32\\32\\9\\2\end{smallmatrix}$ |
|---|---|---|---|---|---|---|---|
| Curium (247) | Berkelium (247) | Californium (251) | Einsteinium (254) | Fermium (257) | Mendelevium (258) | Nobelium (255) | Lawrencium (256) |

# 3. Facts about physics

Physics deals with matter and energy, and how they interact. Energy forms include light, heat, sound, magnetism, and electricity. Gravitation, a pervasive force in the universe, influences the orbits of planets around the sun, as well as a gymnast's movements. One part of physics called *mechanics* is concerned with forces and motion. Another deals with the electromagnetic spectrum of radiation. Nuclear physics studies the particles and energy exchanges in atoms of matter.

Physics begins by examining the information that people sense about the world around them. Objects are seen to move from place to place, and when completely free of contact with other objects, they move in straight lines at a steady speed. Being at rest is moving at a steady zero speed. Whenever objects do not behave this way, they are said to be accelerated, and a *force* is said to act on them.

Different objects may accelerate differently with the same force, and their relative sluggishness is related to the internal quality of the object called mass. When forces act on objects, the accelerations produce changes in such things as position, size, shape, and chemical nature. The kind and size of any change is judged by use of a quantity called *energy*. Energy is generally subdivided into types by the form of the change that is seen. Thus, an increase in speed is linked to an increase in *kinetic* (motion) energy.

Energy can change from one type to another. But any total batch of energy cannot be changed in amount—though it may be spread around, changed in form, or moved from one place to another. This "savings" plan is called the *law of conservation of mass-energy*, to allow for some of a system's energy being converted into matter and some of the matter being converted into energy.

## Center of gravity

The science of *mechanics* studies the forces dormant in bodies at rest and the working forces in bodies in motion. Civil engineers use information from *statics*—how bodies behave at rest—to prevent disastrous movement in stable structures, such as bridges and buildings. Aeronautical engineers use the principles of *dynamics*—how bodies behave in motion—to design flyable airplanes and rockets.

One of the mechanical principles important to both those studies is *center of gravity*. Solid objects have one of many configurations, such as the hexagon, cylinder, or pyramid shown at the right. All of the weight of a solid body is considered to be centered at one point (represented by the dot in each solid). At this point, the downward pull of gravity is counteracted by equal forces pushing upward to keep the center at rest.
However, if the upward or supporting forces are overcome by gravity at the object's center, the object becomes unstable and can topple in some cases. In other cases, the forces rotate the object when the force acts along a line that does not pass through the object's gravitational center.

Turning forces are called *torques*. They make an object rotate around an axis that supports the center of gravity. All torques acting on an object's center of gravity must be balanced for the object to remain in *equilibrium*.

Center of gravity

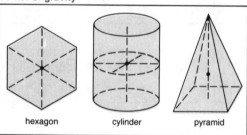

hexagon          cylinder          pyramid

112

## Swing of a pendulum

The swing of a pendulum is simple *harmonic motion*. It is the circular counterpart of the back-and-forth *oscillating* motions of a spring when stretched and released. The bob (mass) of a pendulum is suspended from the center of an imaginary circle and held at rest by the downward pull of gravity (0°). When the bob is moved 45 degrees to the right along the arc of the circle and then released, it will swing past the 0° centerline and to a point 45 degrees to the left of centerline. The *amplitude* of the swing is 45°. During the swing, *potential* and *kinetic* energies are continually exchanged. Potential energy is stored energy, or energy that is ready for work. Kinetic energy is the energy of motion. Eventually, the pendulum will stop swinging because its energy has been expended working to overcome the friction of air resistance.

## Centripetal and centrifugal forces

Centripetal and centrifugal forces are counteracting forces. *Centripetal force* keeps an object accelerating in a circular path while it tries to pull the object toward the center of the circle. *Acceleration* occurs when an object's direction continually and uniformly changes, as it does in a circular path. Centripetal acceleration can be found from the formula *a* equals $v^2$ over *r*, where *a* is the centripetal acceleration, *v* is the velocity (speed) in meters per second, and *r* is the radius of the circle in meters.

An equal but opposite force called *centrifugal force* keeps the object from being pulled to the circle's center. For example, a ball being swung in a circle by a string exhibits centripetal acceleration. The string supplies centripetal force; it pulls in on the ball. However, the ball itself reacts to the pull and exerts an outward pull on the string—the centrifugal force.

If the string should break, both forces would be canceled out and the ball would fly away at a tangent to its circular path. Centripetal force accelerates the planets as they revolve around the sun.

## Dimensions of forces

A *force* is anything of the same nature as a human push or pull. It has both size and direction, and is expressed as *newtons* in the metric system or *pounds* in the English system. Force is a *vector* quantity because it is always associated with direction. Different, or *concurrent*, forces will act as a single force with a single magnitude on an object if they act in the same direction. For instance, a 40 newton force and a 30 newton force pushing an object 45 degrees northeast have the effect of a 70 newton force. However, if they act in opposite directions, the total force on the object would be only 10 newtons. When the concurrent forces act on an object from different directions (as in the illustration), the magnitude and direction of the *resultant* force can be found by drawing a parallelogram using the two concurrent forces as sides of the parallelogram.

## Types of fluid flow

When a fluid flows through a pipe or channel or over some other kind of surface, it maintains either *laminar flow* or *turbulent flow*. Ordinarily, fluid begins to flow in a laminar, or evenly layered, manner, but the flow becomes turbulent later in the course of the flow. This occurs because fluids encounter *shearing forces* at the boundaries of their flow.

These boundaries might be the inside surface of metal pipes in the case of water flow, or the boundaries might be the surfaces of airplane wings in the case of air flow (air is considered a viscous fluid). The rougher the surface, the greater is the amount of shear, and thus the greatest resistance, or *drag*, to the fluid flow. Shear causes the even, laminar flow to begin churning.

Streamlining the surfaces over which a fluid flows encourages laminar flow. Aeronautical engineers design aircraft wings (technically called *airfoils*) that allow a smooth, laminar flow of air over the wing surfaces and discourage turbulence. The familiar "swept-wing" design thus is crucial scientifically.

### Swing of a pendulum

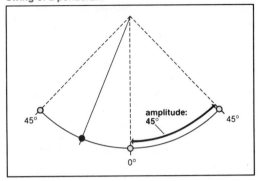

amplitude: 45°

45°      45°

0°

### Centripetal and centrifugal forces

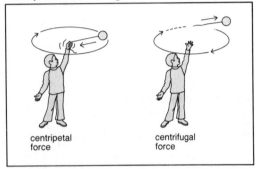

centripetal force      centrifugal force

### Dimensions of forces

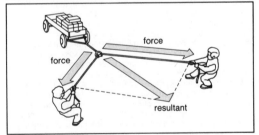

force

force

resultant

### Types of fluid flow

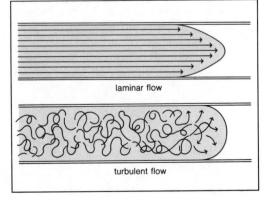

laminar flow

turbulent flow

## Table: the laws of thermodynamics

| Law | Formal statement | What it means | Example |
|---|---|---|---|
| First law of thermodynamics | The change in a system's internal energy equals the heat absorbed by the system minus the work done by the system. | All the universe's energy is constant. Even when energy forms are inter-changed, energy is not destroyed. Heat is a form of energy, and it can do work. | In a heat engine, 5 units of heat energy are converted into 5 units of mechanical energy. |
| Second law of thermodynamics | A reversible, isothermal change occurs when the entropy increase in a system absorbing a given amount of heat at a given temperature equals the ratio of heat absorbed by the system to its absolute temperature. | Outside energy must be applied to lessen the amount of natural disorder, or entropy, in a system. This law explains why heat flows from hotter substances (losing entropy, gaining order) to colder substances (gaining entropy, losing order), and not vice versa. | A beaker of water over a Bunsen burner flame does not freeze while the flame gets increasingly hotter. Instead, the water temperature rises. |
| Third law of thermodynamics | The entropy of ordered solids is nil at the absolute zero of temperature. | No disorder exists in a system where there is no molecular movement (absolute zero). Though substances can get near absolute zero, they can never reach it. | There is hardly any electrical resistance in a metal conductor cooled almost to absolute zero ($-273.16°C$) because its molecules scarcely move. |

## A gasoline engine in operation

A two-stroke cycle *internal combustion engine* performs work through the conversion of the chemical energy in gasoline into the mechanical energy needed to spin the engine's crankshaft. The engine has a hard metal cylinder capable of withstanding great heat and pressure, a spark plug, a piston, a connecting rod, and a crankshaft in the engine crankcase. During the intake-compression stroke, a mixture of vaporized gasoline and air is compressed as the piston head pushes it toward the top of the combustion chamber in the cylinder. A series of rings seal the piston with the wall of the cylinder during the stroke to prevent gas from escaping into the crankcase. At maximum compression, the spark plug electrically ignites the fuel-air mixture, causing the mixture to burn. The combustion temperature is between 3,000°–4,000°F (1,500°–2,200°C). The explosive expansion of the heated gases produces pressure large enough to force the piston downward. This starts the power-exhaust stroke, in which the expanding gases do mechanical work. The downward motion of the piston also forces the connecting rod downward. As it does, the connecting rod turns the crankshaft, which then transmits torque to anything attached to it. The base of the connecting rod makes a circular swing around the bottom of the crankcase, and the rod's upward motion forces the piston upward too. This starts another intake-compression stroke. A fuel-air mixture drawn into the crankcase during the preceding stroke is now admitted into the combustion chamber through an intake port, while the burned gases exit through an exhaust port. The fresh charge of fuel and air undergoes compression and will be ignited by another spark. The cycle continues until the fuel is used up.

A gasoline engine in operation

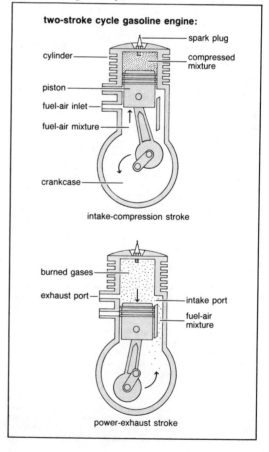

**two-stroke cycle gasoline engine:**

spark plug
cylinder
compressed mixture
piston
fuel-air inlet
fuel-air mixture

intake-compression stroke

burned gases
exhaust port
intake port
fuel-air mixture

power-exhaust stroke

## Measuring light intensity

The *candela* (also called *candle*) is the measuring unit of light, the visible part of the electromagnetic spectrum. One candela equals the light intensity given off by a 0.0167-square-centimeter piece of platinum while melting (or 1/60 of the light intensity of a nonreflecting surface heated to the solidification temperature of platinum).

The amount of light emitted from a luminous source in a given period of time is measured in *lumens*. If a point of light emitting one candela (candle) is located in the center of a sphere having a one-foot radius, the intensity of light on a one-square-foot section of the sphere's surface has an *illuminance* of one foot-candle. The intensity of illumination at any distance from a light source can be determined from the *inverse-square law*.

This law states that a surface's illumination intensity is inversely proportional to the square of its distance from the light source. The formula is: $E = I/d^2$, where E is the illuminance in lumen/feet² or lumen/meter², I is the light intensity in lumens, and d is the distance in feet or meters.

## Effects of lenses on light rays

Rays of light travel in a vacuum at the speed of 186,000 miles per second (300,000 kilometers per second). However, when light rays strike an *optically dense* medium, such as glass, they slow down. The speed of light through glass is 124,000 miles per second (200,000 kilometers per second). As a light ray passes through glass, it is *refracted,* or bent. Whether the light rays converge or not at a point in back of the lens after being refracted depends on the shape of the glass surface. Converging lenses are *convex.* They are thicker in the center than at the edges. An imaginary line called the *principal axis* passes through the centers of the lens's curved surfaces. As light rays are refracted through a convex lens, they cross at a common point along the principal axis called the *principal focus.* The distance between the lens center and the principal focus is called the *focal length* by scientists.

When an object is more than one focal length away, a convex lens forms a *real image* of it; that is, an image that can be formed on a screen on the eye's retina. The real image is always *inverted* (upside down). It is enlarged when the object is between one and two focal lengths away and reduced when more than two focal lengths distant. A *virtual image* is formed when the object is less than one focal length away from a convex lens; we see the image as though it was formed in front of the lens. This is always the case of images formed by *diverging lenses. Concave* lenses are diverging lenses. They are thinner at the center than at the edges. Light rays passing through a concave lens do not cross, but when they enter the eye, they seem to come from a point in front of the lens.

A virtual image is right side up. It is the result of the brain's interpretation of where it "thinks" the light rays meet in front of the lens.

## Prisms refract light rays

Prisms can *refract,* or bend, light rays. Viewed from all around, an *oblique prism* has no equal sides. A *right prism* viewed from all around has three equal sides. Prisms have different abilities to bend light.

The bending ability of any refracting substance is its *index of refraction*—the ratio of the speed of light in a vacuum and the speed of light in the refracting substance. For example, water has an index of refraction of 1.33; ice, 1.5; and flint glass, 1.61. When a light ray strikes the surface of a refracting substance, it is bent at a certain angle, the *angle of refraction.*

At the border where air (the incident medium) and a prism's glass (the refracting medium) meet, there is a perpendicular line called the *normal.* The *angle of incidence* exists between the path of the incident light ray and the normal. The angle of refraction, on the other hand, exists between the path of the refracted light ray and the normal. Its size depends on the prism's index of refraction. Two right prisms on top of each other refract light like a convex lens.

**Measuring light intensity**

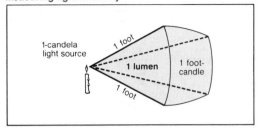

1-candela light source
1 lumen
1 foot
1 foot
1 foot-candle

**Effects of lenses on light rays**

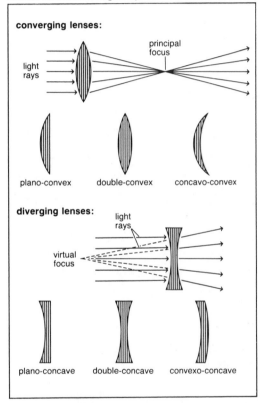

**converging lenses:**

light rays
principal focus

plano-convex     double-convex     concavo-convex

**diverging lenses:**

light rays
virtual focus

plano-concave     double-concave     convexo-concave

**Prisms refract light rays**

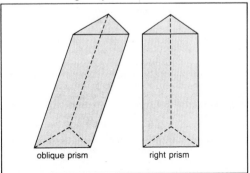

oblique prism          right prism

## The spectrum of visible light

Light is considered to have the properties of a wave. Every wave has *wavelength,* the distance between one crest of the wave and the next. Sunlight is *polychromatic*—it is a mixture of light waves having different wavelengths. It is also considered *white light* because it contains different wavelengths of colored light mixed in right proportions. An incandescent light bulb emits white light.

The rays in a beam of white light travel through the air at about the same speed. However, when a beam of white light strikes the face of a glass prism, the beam is bent and dispersed into its seven component colors through refraction. Dispersion occurs because the varying wavelengths of white light are refracted differently. Red light, having the longest wavelength, is slowed the least by the prism and thus is bent the least. Violet light, having the shortest wavelength, is slowed the most and therefore bent the most.

The *angle of deviation* is between the path of refraction and the path the beam of white light would have traveled unrefracted. The *angle of dispersion* is the amount of spread of the different colors as they disperse into the *color spectrum.* Another prism can refract the dispersed colors back into a beam of white light.

## Measuring the angle of light rays

Light can *reflect,* or bounce off a surface. Light rays travel in a straight line, and when they encounter a reflecting surface, they bounce off in straight lines. Before they strike the surface, the light rays are called *incident rays;* after they bounce off, they are called *reflected rays.*

The amount of reflection is measured from a *normal* line that is perpendicular to the reflecting surface. The angle between the incident rays and the normal line is the *angle of incidence.* The angle between the normal line and the reflected rays is the *angle of reflection.* The angle of incidence always equals the angle of reflection. For example, if the angle of incidence is 45°, the angle of reflection will be 45°.

A beam of light actually contains a number of parallel incident rays. If the beam strikes a very shiny surface, the normal lines will all be parallel and all the incident rays will be reflected at equal angles, allowing the reflected rays to keep the same spatial pattern. This is why a mirror produces a true image of what the eye sees. However, when the incident rays strike a rough surface, the normal lines will not be parallel, and the reflected rays will be scattered.

## Optical telescopes

Telescopes enlarge the image of far-off objects. Two telescopes in common use are *refracting* telescopes and *reflecting* telescopes. Refracting telescopes are often used as terrestrial (land-use) viewers. They consist of an objective lens, a long tube, and an eyepiece lens. Light rays from an object are refracted through a convex objective lens and form a real image in the tube of the telescope. However, the real image is *less* than one focal length of the convex eyepiece lens. As a result, the eye of the viewer sees the image of the object as a virtual image, inverted and enlarged. The magnification (m) of a refracting telescope is found by dividing the focal length of the objective lens ($f_o$) by the focal length of the eyepiece lens ($f_e$): $m = f_o/f_e$. The refractor described here is a Galilean type, like the telescope designed by the Italian scientist Galileo Galilei in 1602.

A reflecting telescope works in much the same way, but it uses mirrors instead of objective lenses to collect the light rays from an object. The incident light rays enter the telescope's tube and strike a concave mirror at the base of the tube. As the rays reflect off the base mirror, they strike a slanted mirror in the tube. The newly reflected light rays then converge at a focus in front of the eyepiece and the viewer sees an enlarged image.

The reflector shown here is modeled after one designed by the English scientist Isaac Newton in 1668. Reflecting telescopes can be more powerful than refractors because large mirrors can collect more light than can lenses.

The spectrum of visible light

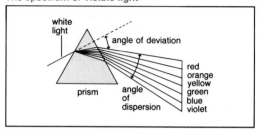

Measuring the angle of light rays

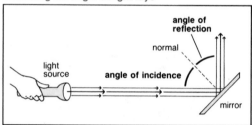

Optical telescopes

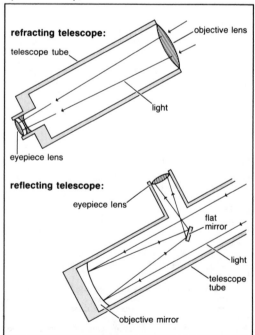

### Generating a laser beam

A laser is a device that generates a light wave. Its wave flow is *coherent*—steadily rippling—instead of being interrupted and patchy like that of incandescent light, and *monochromatic*—having a single wavelength. The ruby laser's beam is red. The laser has an artificial ruby rod with chromium impurities, a heavily silvered mirror end, a lightly silvered mirror end, and a flash tube. As the energy of the flash tube pumps the chromium atoms to a high level of excitation, energy packets called photons bounce back and forth between the mirrors until they finally emerge as a unified red wave.

### Holograms—laser photographs

Holography is a way of producing a three-dimensional image. A *hologram* is a pattern of interference lines cast on a reflective surface. The pattern is formed from the interference caused when reflected laser light strikes a *reference beam* of nonreflected laser light. The two beams are out of *phase* (step) and thus interfere with each other. The portion of the laser beam reflected off a mirror strikes an object and is reflected off varying parts of the object. When these varying reflections of the laser beam react with the reference beam, they form a number of interference lines in the hologram. The hologram is only a middle step in holography. It holds an information pattern but does not bear a visual image of the object. When the hologram is lighted by another laser beam, the hologram is "translated" into a three-dimensional image of the object.

## Laser beams

A laser produces an intense beam of light. It produces its light energy by "pumping" atoms to high energy levels. As they are pumped, or stimulated, the atoms give off light waves. The name "laser" is an acronym of the technical description of its action—*L*ight *a*mplification from *s*timulated *e*mission of *r*adiation.

## How light waves are made

Scientists explain light production by first assuming certain events take place in an atom. The electrons of an atom spin around the nucleus in a variety of paths, or levels. Each level exists at a certain distance from the nucleus. Inner electrons are close to the nucleus, outer electrons are far. A fixed amount of energy is required for each electron to keep in its orbital level. Whenever an atom is jostled hard enough, one of its electrons may receive enough energy through heating to jump to a higher level; that is, spin farther from the nucleus. But it does not stay there long and will fall back to its original orbital level. As it falls back into position, it releases energy in the form of an electromagnetic radiation. The energy is released because the electron no longer needs it to stay in the original orbit. If the wavelength of the released radiation is in the visible range of the electromagnetic spectrum, light waves are produced.

Light seems to have a dual nature. It is believed to be a wave and a particle at the same time. It flows like a wave but comes in definite short

Generating a laser beam

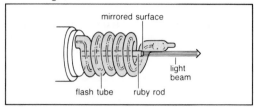

mirrored surface

light beam

flash tube    ruby rod

Holograms—laser photographs

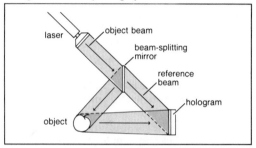

laser    object beam

beam-splitting mirror

reference beam

hologram

object

bursts of energy, called *photons*. Photons of light are produced from an atom as long as its electrons continue to rise and to drop between energy levels.

Waves of radiation in the visible range have somewhat different wavelengths and frequencies. Because of this, white light contains a mixture of the colors of the visible spectrum. When white light is bent through a prism, seven distinct colors can be seen. Red has the longest wavelength and the lowest frequency in the visible light range; violet has the shortest wavelength and the highest frequency.

A source of white light radiates in all directions, scattering the light. As an object's distance from a source of white light increases, less and less light strikes the surface of the object because of scattering. However, this is not the case with a laser light beam. It is coherent. All its waves travel in step with each other. Because laser light only contains a single wavelength, it only has a single color (is *monochromatic*).

## How laser light is made

A laser *amplifies* (builds up) light rays by shooting energy into atoms and causing their electrons to change energy levels. Light waves are emitted in the process. The light wave emitted by each excited atom stimulates another excited atom to produce a light wave that is in phase with the first one. That is, the crests and troughs of all the waves travel parallel to each other. This goes on and on until the emitted light waves are absorbed by enough unexcited atoms to stop the amplification.

A ruby laser produces a red laser beam. This type of laser consists of an artificial ruby rod containing chromium atoms. Chromium atoms can become excited by blue light. This wavelength of light is furnished by a flash tube surrounding the ruby rod. A mirror is at either end of the ruby rod to reflect and help amplify the stimulated emission of light. One mirror has a heavy coating of silver, which acts as a barrier to the light waves. The other mirror has a lighter coating of silver.

Blue light from the flash tube excites most of the chromium atoms in the ruby, causing their electrons to jump to a higher energy level. As they fall back to their original level (called the *ground state*), they release waves of red light. The energy of the light waves stimulates other excited chromium atoms to give off more light waves. During the process, the growing number of red light waves reflect back and forth in phase between the mirrored ends of the ruby rod. When the waves acquire enough energy, they break through the partially silvered end as a beam of laser light.

Gas lasers produce beams of green light or other colors. These lasers maintain a steady lasing action by adding new atoms in the upper level continually as the old ones drop to a lower level after stimulation. As a result, the laser light does not become absorbed and the beam continues.

## Laser uses

Eye surgeons can use laser beams to "weld" detached retinas back onto the eyeball without cutting into the eye. The laser beam is directed onto the retina through the pupil of the eye. Scar tissue forms at the impact site of the laser beam and at that point fastens the retina to the inner surface of the eye.

Laser beams have been used for industrial purposes. The diamond dies through which extremely thin wire filaments are drawn can be drilled with a laser beam. The already narrow beam of light can be further reduced to a diameter of less than 0.001 inch. The energy concentrated in this tiny beam is known to be sufficient to cut through diamond.

Laser beams are sometimes used as reference points in building construction. They accurately mark straight lines along the course of large buildings. A laser beam is used by scientists to detect whether portions of a two-mile-long particle accelerator in Stanford, California, move out of alignment.

Three-dimensional images can be produced by laser beams. Holography, or laser photography, relies on the coherent beam of laser light to produce a *hologram*, a three-dimensional information record of an object on photographic film. A portion of a laser beam is reflected off the object and into the path of a reference beam of unreflected laser light. The interaction of the two beams produces a unique interference pattern in the film. When another laser beam is aimed through the hologram's interference "picture," a three-dimensional image of the original object is reconstructed. The image looks like a picture or a slide.

The distance between the earth and the moon has been measured accurately by means of a laser beam. Scientists recorded the time taken for a laser beam to bounce off a reflector placed by astronauts on the moon. Knowing the speed of light in a given period of time, scientists were able to compute the distance with accuracy.

### Magnetic fields

Magnetism is a force. A *magnetic field* is a region in which a magnet will experience a magnetic force. Every magnet contains a north pole and a south pole. The rule is: opposite poles attract; like poles repel. For example, a magnet's north pole attracts a south pole but repels another north pole. The directions in the field along which the magnetic force acts are called "lines of force." A line of force can be followed in the region outside of a magnetic field from the north to the south pole. There are many such paths; they all come very close together near the poles but never cross each other. The greater the strength of the magnetic field, called the *flux density*, the closer are these imaginary lines of force. The flux density of a horseshoe magnet is greater than a bar magnet's, permitting the horseshoe magnet to attract more magnetic substances. The permanent magnetism of a bar magnet derives from spinning atomic electrons in the magnet. Any moving electric charge creates a magnetic field (*electromagnetism*), and electrons are thought to spin so that they have a north pole–south pole axis. Two electrons with paired opposite spins would cancel each other's magnetic effects; unpaired electrons make "atomic electro-magnets" out of their atoms.

### Magnetic fields

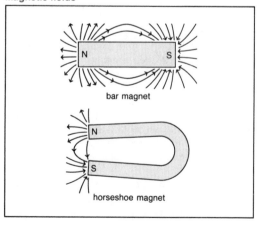

bar magnet

horseshoe magnet

## The electromagnetic spectrum

Different forms of energy spread across a range called the *electromagnetic spectrum*. Energy forms in this spectrum have both electrical and magnetic characteristics. They travel as electromagnetic *waves*. All waves have *wavelength* and *frequency*. A wave has an uppermost crest and a bottommost trough. Wavelength is the distance between the crest of one wave and the next (or between the trough of one wave and the next). Wavelength may be expressed in millimicrons. Frequency is the number of waves that pass a given point in a given time. Frequency is expressed in *hertz,* or cycles per second. An inverse relationship exists in the electromagnetic spectrum. As the wavelengths of energy forms grow longer, their frequencies diminish. Gamma rays have the shortest wavelengths and the highest frequencies; long radio waves have the longest wavelengths and the lowest frequencies. We can directly sense only a small portion of the electromagnetic spectrum. We can see visible light and feel the heat of infrared rays. Other forms require instruments that convert the energy into perceptible forms, such as gamma ray counters or radio receivers.

## Generating X rays

X rays are forms of radiation higher on the electromagnetic spectrum than closely related ultraviolet waves. X rays have great penetrating power because their short wavelength and high frequency lets them travel easily between the atoms of a substance. X rays are emitted from many sources in the universe. They can also be generated for medical and industrial uses. When photographic film is placed behind an object being X-rayed, the developed *roentgenogram* reveals a shadow picture of the object. For instance, when a hand is X-rayed, the roentgenogram shows the bones of the hand as white shapes against a black background. This is because X rays do not penetrate the dense, *radiopaque* bones as easily as the less dense flesh and thus do not expose (darken) the areas of the film covered by the bones. X rays can be generated in a *Coolidge tube*. This type of X ray tube consists of a cathode and an anode in a vacuum. A high-voltage current applied between the anode and the cathode releases electrons from heated tungsten cathode. The electrons stream across a gap to an anode made of tungsten or molybdenum. There, the electrons collide with and "excite" the target atoms, causing them to release electrons from the inner orbits of the atoms. The release causes electrons in outer orbits of the atoms to drop back into the inner orbits as replacements. When they do, the electrons give up some of their energy as X rays. The reaction also generates considerable heat. The heat is channeled off through a radiator attached to the Coolidge tube.

## Television tube operation

A television tube is one type of *cathode-ray tube.* A cathode ray tube has a cathode and heater at the base, a high-voltage focusing anode in the neck, horizontal and vertical deflecting plates ahead of the focusing anode, and a screen coated with a fluorescent material.

Electrons from the hot cathode speed toward the anode, where they form a thin electron beam. The beam then passes through plates having magnetic fields capable of deflecting the beam horizontally or vertically. By varying the voltages of the deflecting plates, the electron beam can be made to sweep in a specific path across the fluorescent screen. At each point where the beam hits, light energy is emitted. The point will glow for a short time after the beam moves to another point. Someone looking at the screen will "see" a continuous line because of the persistence of human vision. Electron beams can sweep quickly across the screen because the extremely small mass and inertia of electrons allow them to react instantaneously to changes in the magnetic fields of the deflecting plates.

The electron beam of a television receiver tube sweeps 525 alternating lines of the screen from left to right and from top to bottom in 1/30 of a second. The eye retains what it sees for only 1/16 of a second, so the image "blends" while it is forming twice on the screen, making it appear to be continuous.

## The electromagnetic spectrum

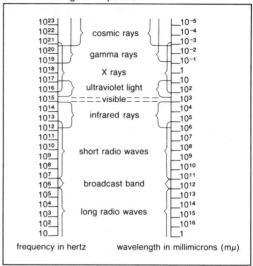

| frequency in hertz | | wavelength in millimicrons (m$\mu$) |
|---|---|---|

## Generating X rays

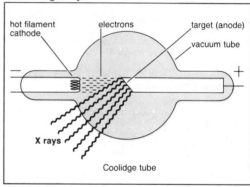

Coolidge tube

## Television tube operation

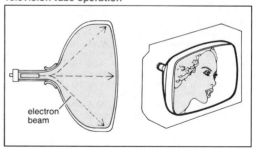

## Electrical circuits

An electric current is a flow of charged particles in the direction of the positive charges. Current flows whenever there is a potential difference in the amount of charged particles between one point of an electrolyte or conductor and another. Potential difference is measured in *volts*. The current's rate of flow is measured in *amperes* (amps). The resistance encountered in a metal conductor is measured in *ohms*. If any two of these three facts about a circuit are known, the other can be found by Ohm's law. It uses the formula: $R=\frac{V}{I}$, where R is the resistance, V is the voltage, and I is the amperage. An electric circuit can be structured in parallel or in series. All bulbs in a parallel circuit operate independently; if one bulb burns out, the others continue to burn. In series, however, if any of the bulbs burn out, the charge stops flowing.

## Detecting electrical charges

Static electricity is electrical energy at rest. Electrical charges can be placed on or removed from objects according to the *conservation of charge* principle. This holds that when objects are electrified by friction or by contact, two charges are produced that are equal in size but opposite in sign. In addition, unlike charges attract and like charges repel each other. Electrical charges can be detected and studied by use of an *electroscope*. When the electroscope has a neutral charge, its metallic components have equal numbers of positive and negative charges. It becomes positively charged on contact with a positively charged object. Afterward, when a positively charged rod comes close to the metal ball, electrons are attracted to the ball from the aluminum leaves. The leaves now have an excess of positive charges, and they spread apart by repulsion. However, when a negatively charged rod comes close to the positively charged electroscope, electrons in the metal ball are repelled downward into the leaves, which now become less positive and come together.

## Releasing nuclear energy

The nucleus of an atom contains tremendous energy. This energy is needed to hold together, or bind, all the particles in the nucleus. Scientists estimate that the nuclear binding energy of one helium atom could light a 100-watt electric bulb for 220 years. Some atoms can release part of their nuclear energy during *radioactive decay*. In the process, radioactive elements transform into lighter elements, while emitting particles and radiation. Heavy radioactive elements, such as uranium-235 (a uranium isotope), can split when struck by high-speed neutrons. The *chain reaction* resulting from *fission*, or splitting, releases considerable energy. After a high-speed neutron splits an atom of uranium-235, two smaller atoms are produced and neutrons are released. The two smaller atoms, which may be barium, strontium, krypton, or xenon, among others, are also radioactive for a while, emitting gamma waves and beta particles until they acquire nonradioactive, stable forms. Meanwhile, the neutrons released by fission strike other atoms of uranium-235 and cause similar reactions. Each atom of uranium-235 releases some 200-million-electron-volts of energy during fission. When fission takes place in a controlled setting, such as a *nuclear reactor,* the energy released can be used to generate electrical power. The heat produced by nuclear fission boils water, which in turn produces steam to drive the power turbines.

**Electrical circuits**

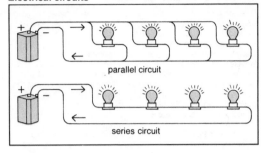

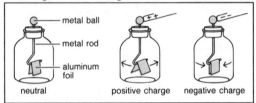

parallel circuit

series circuit

**Detecting electrical charges**

metal ball

metal rod

aluminum foil

neutral          positive charge          negative charge

**Releasing nuclear energy**

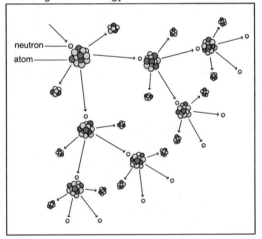

neutron
atom

# Glossary: Unit 3

**absolute zero** Temperature at which an ideal gas has no volume—zero degrees Kelvin.

**acid** A chemical compound that forms a salt by exchanging its hydrogen with a metal or a positively electrovalent radical; usually tastes sour; can neutralize a base.

**alpha particle** A helium nucleus; a positively charged, low-speed particle with two protons and two neutrons, caused by some nuclear reactions.

**angstrom** Unit of electromagnetic wavelength measurement; one A = 0.00000001 centimeter.

**angular acceleration** Rate of increase of a body moving in a curve; directly proportional to the square of the linear velocity and inversely proportional to the curve's radius: $a = \frac{v^2}{r}$.

**atom** Smallest part of an element retaining the characteristics of the element.

**atomic number** Number of protons in an atom's nucleus; indicates place in the periodic table.

**atomic weight** Weight of an atom compared with the weight of a carbon-12 atom.

**base** A chemical compound that forms a salt when reacting with an acid.

**Bernoulli's principle** Pressure by a fluid on a surface decreases as the fluid's speed increases, and vice versa.

**bond** Chemical combining unit that equals the combining power of one hydrogen atom.

**Boyle's law** Gas volume varies inversely with pressure at a constant temperature.

**burette** A calibrated tube used in chemical analysis; its precise calibrations indicate how much of a reagent is dripped into a test solution.

**British thermal unit (BTU)** The amount of energy needed to increase the temperature of one pound of water one degree Fahrenheit.

**calorie** The amount of energy needed to increase the temperature of one gram of water one degree Celsius.

**candela** The amount of brightness of a 1/60-square-centimeter piece of platinum at its melting point.

**catalyst** Chemical substance that helps other chemicals react with each other without itself being affected by the reaction.

**cathode** The negative electrode of an electrolytic cell or an electronic tube.

**cell** A device that generates electricity.

**Celsius** Unit of temperature on the Celsius scale, which has 100 units between the freezing point of water (0°C) and its boiling point (100°C).

**center of gravity** Point where the weight of a body is concentrated.

**Charles's law** When pressure is constant, the volume of a gas is directly proportional to its absolute temperature, measured in degrees K.

**chemical reaction** Process in which chemical substances react with others, resulting in new chemical substances and the release of energy.

**compound** Two or more chemical elements combined to form a new substance having different properties than the precursor elements.

**cosmic rays** High-energy charged particles from interstellar space having great penetrating power.

**covalent bond** A strong bond created between chemical elements by sharing electron pairs.

**cycle** An entire oscillation, or vibration, of an alternating wave.

**decibel** Unit of sound intensity, or power per area unit, measured against a standard intensity of $10^{-16}$ watts per square centimeter.

**density** Mass of a unit volume of a substance; for example, aluminum's density is 2.7 grams per cubic centimeter.

**dew point** Temperature at which the atmosphere is filled with water vapor, causing condensation.

**diffraction** Scattering of waves in back of a solid object after they strike it; diffraction is greatest when the solid object is much smaller than the length of the diffracted waves.

**direct current** Single-direction movement of electrons through an electrical conductor.

**dyne** The metric unit of force needed to accelerate a mass of one gram at the rate of one centimeter per second each second the force is applied.

**electrolysis** Chemical breakdown of a substance in solution by an electric current.

**electromagnetic spectrum** Range of radiations having electrical and magnetic properties.

**electromotive force** The voltage, or potential difference, between poles of an electrical source.

**electron** A negatively charged atomic particle.

**electron volt** Energy acquired by an electron as it speeds through a potential difference of one volt.

**energy** The capacity to do work possessed by all matter; exists in many interchangeable forms, such as heat, light, electricity.

**erg** A metric unit of the work done when one dyne of force moves an object one centimeter.

**Fahrenheit** Unit of temperature on the Fahrenheit scale, which has 180 units between the freezing point of water ($32°F$) and its boiling point ($212°F$).

**foot-candle** The amount of illumination on a surface one foot away from a source emitting one candle of light.

**foot-pound** An English unit of work done when one pound of force moves an object one foot.

**friction** A force counteracting a body's movement on or through another substance.

**fulcrum** Point around which a lever turns.

**fusion** Release of energy from the combination of two light nuclei, such as hydrogen nuclei, into a heavier nucleus, such as a helium nucleus; source of solar energy.

**gram** A metric unit of mass equal to that of one cubic centimeter of water at $4°C$.

**gravitation** The force of attraction exerted between all matter in the universe.

**half-life** Time required for half the atoms of a radioactive element to decay.

**heat** Energy released by molecular motion.

**hertz** Unit of wave frequency; one hertz equals one cycle per second.

**hypothesis** A scientific "guess" about why an observed event takes place.

**inertia** Resistance of matter to any change while it is either in motion or at rest.

**ion** An electrically charged particle made when an atom loses or gains electrons.

**isotope** An atom that differs from others of the same element by having fewer or more neutrons but the same number of protons.

**Joule's law** Heat developed in an electrical conductor is directly proportional to the square of the current, the conductor's resistance, and the rate of current flow; one joule equals 0.239 calorie.

**Kelvin** Unit of temperature on the absolute Kelvin scale; $0 \text{ K} = -273.16°C \ (-459.69°F)$.

**kinetic energy** Energy of motion.

**lambert** One lumen of light reflected or given off from a one-square-centimeter surface.

**law** A scientific statement that a specific, observable event will take place every time it is tested.

**lever** A simple machine consisting of a bar that can rotate around a fulcrum.

**light-year** Distance that light traveling at 186,000 miles per second (300,000 kilometers per second) spans in one year.

**line of force** Imaginary line traceable to a north pole in a magnetic field or by a positive charge in an electric field.

**lumen** Amount of light on a one-square-foot area

that is one foot from a light source of one candle.

**magnetic field** Space where a magnet experiences a force; present near a magnetic or an electric current.

**magnetic force** Attraction or repulsion experienced by magnets and electrical currents.

**mass** Amount of matter in a substance; permits substances to have inertia and react to gravitation.

**matter** Anything having weight and inertia.

**mechanical equivalent of heat** Work and mechanical energy expressed as heat; 1 calorie = 4.19 joules, 1 BTU = 778 foot-pounds.

**meter** Unit of length; expressed as equal to 1,650,763.73 times the orange-red color of krypton-86 in certain circumstances.

**molecule** Smallest amount of a substance that can exist freely and still keep all the chemical characteristics of the substance.

**neutron** Uncharged particle in an atom's nucleus; has a mass of $1.67 \times 10^{-27}$ kilograms.

**nucleus** Central core of an atom; has a positive charge and contains most of the atom's mass.

**Ohm's law** The ratio between an electrical conductor's voltage and current flow through the conductor is constant at a given temperature.

**orbit** Path taken by a body moving around another, such as an electron around an atom's nucleus.

**period** Length of time for a complete vibration or revolution.

**periodic table** Orderly arrangement of chemical elements according to atomic number.

**pH** Number of free hydrogen ions in a solution; measures acidity.

**pipette** Thin, calibrated glass tube used for collecting, measuring, and transferring liquids.

**proton** Positively charged particle in an atom's nucleus with the same mass as a neutron.

**quantum theory** Idea that electromagnetic energy is given off in small parcels called *quanta*, also called photons.

**radiant energy** Energy that spreads in all directions from its source.

**radioactivity** Ability of the nucleus of a radioactive element's atoms to break down into lighter atoms, releasing small subatomic particles and energy in the process.

**satellite** A smaller body that circles around a larger one, such as the moon orbiting the earth.

**shock wave** Flow discontinuity when pressure and velocity change suddenly.

**sound** Energy level of vibrating matter sensed by the human ear.

**superconductivity** Zero resistance to electric current shown by metals at low temperature.

**temperature** Hotness or coldness of a substance in terms of its average molecular kinetic energy.

**theory** Explanation of observed events as supported by experimental evidence.

**thermodynamics** Study of how heat and other energy forms are related, and how conversions between the energy forms take place.

**torque** Force producing rotation; found by multiplying the force times the length of the arm it acts on.

**velocity** Speed and direction of a moving body.

**volt** Unit of potential difference between two sites in an electric field.

**watt** Unit of electric power from a one-amp current driven through a one-volt potential difference.

**weightlessness** Zero gravity; absence of gravity's pull.

**work** Force multiplied by the distance a body is moved by the force.

**X ray** Highly penetrating electromagnetic radiation having a wavelength shorter than an ultraviolet ray's.

# Basic information from the earth sciences

How much do you know about the planet on which you live? Could you tell someone what per cent of the Earth is covered by land and what per cent is covered by water? What is the Earth's atmosphere made of? Why does it rain? To understand the world around you, you must study the earth sciences.

This unit presents you with many interesting facts about the earth, its atmosphere, and its climates. The unit will help you to review some of the basic information you must know from the earth sciences.

# 1. Land and water on the earth

People have always been interested in finding out as much as they can about the place where they live, the planet earth. Their curiosity about what they see every day has created many sciences. Each of these separate sciences studies a different aspect of the earth.

*Geology* studies the solid parts of the earth, or the rocks, while *geochemistry* looks at the composition and chemical changes that occur on earth's crust. *Geophysics* studies the arrangements and interactions of the forces found there.

Other branches of the earth sciences study very specific things. *Seismology,* for example, studies earthquakes and attempts to predict them. *Mineralogy* studies the minerals found in the rocks. *Geodesy* measures shapes and sizes found on earth and the effects of gravity.

Still other sciences study other aspects of earth. Two sciences study earth's water. *Oceanography* explores the oceans, studying the water itself, the ocean floors, and the ocean's plant and animal life. *Hydrology* looks at the distribution of water on land, especially underground.

The air above the earth is studied by the *atmospheric sciences. Meteorology* examines the changes in temperature, moisture, and winds in the air to determine what the weather will be.

*Climatology* studies the patterns of these conditions over a period of time.

Each of these sciences has branches that look at parts of the total picture. Things learned in one area often affect studies in another. And you benefit by getting a constantly better idea of what your home is like.

### Earth's surface

Less than 30 per cent of the earth's surface is actually land. Land is the rock of the earth's crust exposed to view in the form of continents and islands. This solid portion of the earth's crust is called the *lithosphere*.

More than 70 per cent of the earth's surface is covered by water. The oceans, rivers, lakes, and other bodies of water on earth are called the *hydrosphere*.

Of course, the land and the water are closely related. The rocky crust that lies under the surface of the land also extends under all of the ocean. The part of the earth's crust that lies under the ocean is called the *ocean basins*. The earth's crust varies in size or thickness, from about 5 miles (8 kilometers) under the oceans to about 20 miles (32 kilometers) under the continents.

The waters of the hydrosphere are important in many ways. Plants and animals need water to live. The waters of the oceans are important in their effect on weather and climate. Also, water wears away rock over long periods of time; some of this *erosion* may be harmful, but erosion is necessary in general to create new soil for the lithosphere.

A dramatic example of the power of water erosion can be seen in the Grand Canyon, in the southwestern United States. The Colorado River created the canyon by cutting more than 1 mile (1.6 kilometers) into solid rock.

### Earth's surface

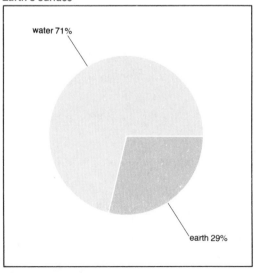

water 71%

earth 29%

## Drifting continents

In 1912, German scientist Alfred Wegener suggested that the earth once consisted of only one supercontinent and that today's continents were the result of blocks of the great continent breaking off and drifting slowly away from each other. He gave these early land masses strange-sounding names like Panagaea, Laurasia, and Gondwanaland.

Scientists now think that Wegener was right when he observed that the continental coastlines seemed to fit together. The eastern shore of North and South America matches almost like a puzzle piece with the western coast of Europe and Africa. Oceanographers have proved that the floor of the Atlantic Ocean is spreading at a rate of a few inches or centimeters each year, and that these continents are moving further and further apart.

It is also known that India drifted away from Africa and bumped into Asia, causing the Himalaya Mountains to rise up, and that Australia and Antarctica drifted off to the east and south in the same way that the Americas have drifted to the west.

## Moving plates

The study of the forces within the earth that form the earth's mountains and ocean basins is called *tectonics*. The *plate tectonic theory* involves the idea that the earth's crust is divided into a number of very large, rigid plates. Scientists differ on the details of just how many plates there are and what their boundaries are. Some plates follow continental boundaries, and others do not. Some plates include continental landforms and ocean basins, too.

Tectonic activity, thought to be powered by heat energy, takes place when the edges of the plates push against each other. As mentioned in connection with the "drifting continents" diagram above, scientists now think that mountains were formed when the edge of one tectonic plate was pushed upward by another plate sliding beneath the first.

Two of the giant plates can slide toward each other, but "miss" and pass each other. This movement is experienced as an *earthquake*. A *fault* is a line between two plates where the plates did not meet exactly. A volcano is another feature of the earth's surface that stems from tectonic activity.

### Drifting continents

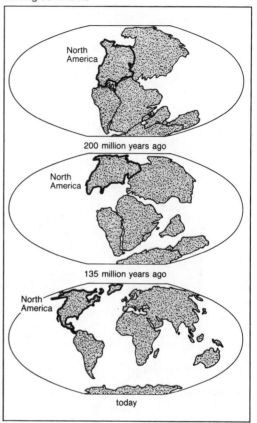

200 million years ago

135 million years ago

today

## Moving plates

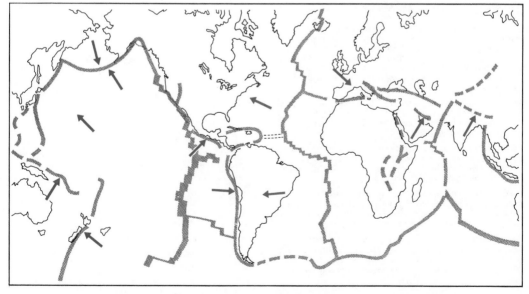

## The earth in profile

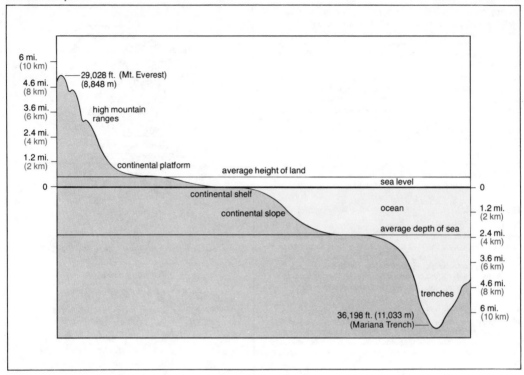

The earth in profile — diagram. Elevations marked on left axis: 6 mi. (10 km), 4.6 mi. (8 km), 3.6 mi. (6 km), 2.4 mi. (4 km), 1.2 mi. (2 km), 0. Labels: 29,028 ft. (Mt. Everest) (8,848 m), high mountain ranges, continental platform, average height of land, sea level, continental shelf, continental slope, ocean, average depth of sea, trenches, 36,198 ft. (11,033 m) (Mariana Trench). Right axis: 0, 1.2 mi. (2 km), 2.4 mi. (4 km), 3.6 mi. (6 km), 4.6 mi. (8 km), 6 mi. (10 km).

## The earth in profile

It has been relatively easy for scientists to study the land portions of the earth. It has been known for a long time that land is usually the lowest along the coastlines of the oceans. As you move inland, the land slopes upward gradually toward various points where high mountains have been pushed up.

Only recently, during the 1900's, have scientists learned a very basic fact about the floors of the oceans: they are actually mirror images of the land forms that you can observe yourself. On page 126, you noted that the solid portion of the earth, also called the lithosphere, extends under the oceans, too. Modern exploring techniques have verified that the continental land mass—another name for a portion of the lithosphere—actually extends under the oceans, in the form of a continental shelf and a continental slope. The slope drops off to various depressions, or low points, called *trenches*.

All research to date indicates that the deepest trench, or the lowest point in the earth's crust, is the Mariana Trench in the Pacific Ocean near the Philippine Islands. The Mariana Trench is 36,198 feet (11,033 meters) deep.

The highest mountain, or the most elevated point on the earth's crust, is Mount Everest, a mountain in the Himalaya range, on the borders of Nepal and Tibet. Mount Everest has been measured at 29,028 feet (8,848 meters) in height.

The diagram portrays a theoretical continental land mass and some of its features. The markings for the Mariana Trench and Mount Everest are included simply to give you an idea of the perspective involved, "the high" in contrast to "the low."

In any case, the high points and the low points in the earth's crust are unusual. The average height of land, including the land under the water on the continental shelf, is only about 2,700 feet (875 meters) above sea level. The average depth of the ocean floor is 12,400 feet (3,730 meters).

**Earth's land: high lands**

## Earth's land: high lands

About one-fifth of the land portion of the earth is mountain land. Most frequently, mountains are formed by either folding or faulting. If the crust pushes up into rolling, wavelike shapes, *folded mountains* are formed as a result. The low part of each fold is called the trough or syncline. The highest part of each fold is called the anticline. If the crust breaks so that some huge blocks move up while others move down, fault blocks, or block mountains, are formed.

A ridge formed by the tilted rock is called a *hogback,* and the steep side of a high ridge is known as an *escarpment.* Very often, folding and faulting occur together, with narrow openings called gorges, gaps, and passes between the steep heights.

Sometimes a single section of the earth's crust rises above the land around it to form a *dome mountain.* Or, magma (molten material from deep inside the earth) may work its way up through the crust, causing an eruption of lava and ash that produces a *volcano.*

Whenever fault, folded, or volcanic mountains are connected to each other, they form a *mountain range.* A group of related mountain ranges form a *mountain chain,* or cordillera. Many striking high lands are found in the great cordilleras along the western coasts of North America and South America and across Europe and Asia. Africa and Australia do not have cordilleras.

Other features of elevated areas are the result of various forces at work on the earth's crust. Glaciers have carved away vast areas of mountains, leaving behind high, irregularly-edged ridges called *arêtes* and broad, sloping areas called *cirques*— the latter indicating where wide parts of the glacier once settled. A *tarn* is a small lake formed in a cirque. When the soft rocks around an old volcano are eroded away, the harder lava core may be left standing alone. This feature is called a *volcanic neck.* *Foothills,* or piedmonts, are slightly elevated areas that essentially serve as borders between mountain zones and the surrounding lower plains. Elevation is, of course, relative, because the plains may be many feet (or kilometers) above sea level.

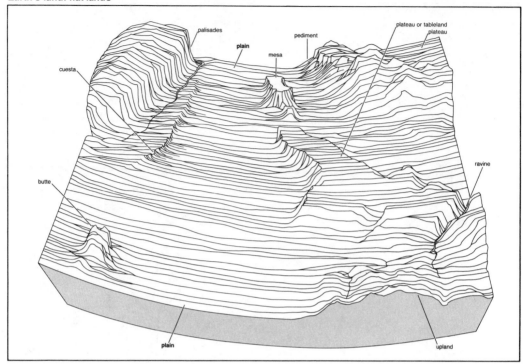

## Earth's lands: flat lands

Vast areas of lands along the seacoasts and far into the interior of the continents are flat lands, with only an occasional low raised area or shallow river valley. These vast areas are called the *plains*. By definition, plains are never very high above sea level, even when they are located great distances from the ocean. Large areas of level land found at high elevations are called *plateaus* or *tablelands*. Plateaus or tablelands often occur between mountain ranges.

Many features of plains and plateaus are the same, as you can see on this idealized composite of a plain and a plateau. Some very distinctive features may be more clearly defined, however, on a plateau. For example, rivers cut deep, narrow passages called *ravines* through the flat land of a plateau.

Ground raised above the surrounding region has the general name of *upland*. A high plateau or tableland with steep sides is designated a *mesa*. A small mesa is a *butte*. But in either case, with a mesa or a butte, the plateau rises sharply above the surrounding plain. A *pediment* is the sloping area at the base of a mountainous region in the desert or in a semiarid area. The pediment consists of bedrock covered by a thin layer of gravel eroded from the mountain.

A raised area that features a steep drop on one side but a long, gentle slope on the other side is called a *cuesta*. Very steep slopes that rise abruptly above the surrounding flat land are called *palisades*. Palisades reveal a cross-section of the rock of the region, often basalt rock.

Depending upon the amount of moisture in the atmosphere and the altitude of the plain or plateau, flat lands can be deserts, forests, or grasslands. Grasslands on the plains of North America are called *prairies*. In your own section of the country, or elsewhere when you are on vacation, you may be able to spot some of these land formations. For example, there are many beautiful and scenic palisades in California, and there are abundant grasslands in Nebraska and Kansas.

Earth's land: shore lands

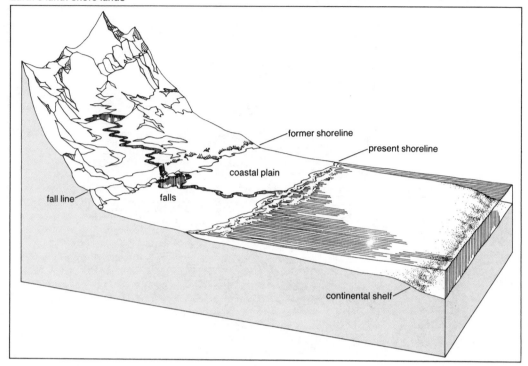

## Earth's lands: shore lands

*Coastal plains* are areas of low land located along the shore of the ocean. A coastal plain may be formed when rock from a mountain is slowly eroded away by running waters. The mountain need not be nearby, as long as there is a mountain stream running down to the shoreline to carry the rock. Naturally, it takes a very long time for a plain to be formed in this manner.

Sometimes the coastal plain merges with the part of the ocean basin known as the *continental shelf*. Or, the continental shelf may push up toward the shore to form a coastal plain. This, again, is a process that will take place over centuries. In such cases, scientists are usually able to detect where the former shoreline was, as shown on the diagram. Depending upon the size of the coastal plain, there can be a great distance between the former shoreline and the present shoreline.

On the land side, there is usually a distinct boundary marking the inland edge of a coastal plain. This boundary is called the *fall line* because the rivers that flow over it drop down this edge from the harder, rocky land above to the softer ground below—that is, the "new" coastal plain.

A coastal plain often consists of rich, fertile land that attracts a considerable population. Such is the case with the Atlantic Coastal Plain. This plain is located along the eastern shore of North America, from New England to Florida. Many coastal plains have poor harbors or few harbors, but this does not happen to be the case with the Atlantic Coastal Plain.

A *flood plain* (not shown) is similar to a coastal plain, but it is formed near a river—rather than on the shoreline of an ocean. The mud and sand carried along by the river are deposited nearby, in small quantities normally and in great quantities during a flood (hence the name). Some rivers around the world with notable flood plains are the Mississippi in the United States, the Nile in Egypt, the Ganges in India, and the Po in Italy. The Nile flood plain contains some of the richest land in the world.

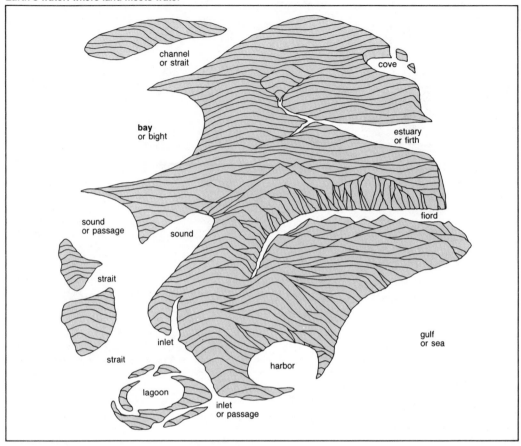

## Earth's water: where land meets water

As mentioned earlier in this section, seas, rivers, and lakes can have powerful effects on nearby landforms. The waters will erode away portions of land to make passages of various sizes and shapes, as shown on this idealized composite diagram. Note that the diagram portrays these passages in and around some small islands, but they also do appear on the great continents.

A *bay* is a portion of a sea or a lake that extends into the land. By common agreement, scientists define a *cove* as a smaller version of bay and a *gulf* (not shown) as considerably larger than a bay.

A *harbor* is an area of fairly deep water protected from the currents and the winds. The definition of a harbor includes a practical element; it must be a place that has proven to be a shelter for ships that anchor there. Large population centers often spring up around a good harbor because of the shipping business that is generated.

Two larger bodies of water may be connected by a *strait* or *straits* through or between pieces of land. A *sound* is similar to a strait but is generally defined as a very long, narrow strip of water connecting two larger bodies of water. The Long Island Sound is a notable example of its type.

An *estuary* or *firth* is a small inlet of the sea into the land. A *lagoon* is a pond or small lake connected to some larger body of water. A lagoon at first glance may appear to be self-contained, but it will have one or more outlets.

## Earth's water: the ocean floor

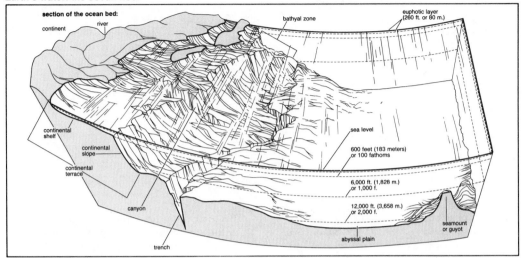

**section of the ocean bed:**

continent

river

euphotic layer
(260 ft. or 80 m.)

bathyal zone

continental
shelf

continental
slope

continental
terrace

canyon

trench

sea level

600 feet (183 meters)
or 100 fathoms

6,000 ft. (1,828 m.)
or 1,000 f.

12,000 ft. (3,658 m.)
or 2,000 f.

abyssal plain

seamount
or guyot

## Earth's water: the ocean floor

The edge of each continent extends under the ocean for a comparatively small distance; the area so encompassed is known as the *continental shelf*. The shelf slopes down gradually, as you can see in this idealized diagram, to a depth of about 600 feet (183 meters). Just before the shelf ends, it drops off to form an area known as the *continental* slope. Both of these features together may be referred to as the *continental terrace*.

A sharp cut or depression in the continental shelf is called a *canyon,* as on land. Sometimes the canyons are gigantic features that extend from the shelf, down to the slope, and down to the ocean basin itself. (The Hudson River Canyon off the Atlantic Coast of North America is a large canyon that has been studied in detail.)

The vast ocean basins begin where the continental slope leaves off. Taken together, the ocean basins cover almost three fourths of the earth's surface. The most common feature of the ocean floor is a very broad, very flat area that resembles a plain on land and is, therefore, called an *abyssal plain*. The word *abyssal* is derived from the Greek words meaning "without bottom" and has been applied to the oceans since ancient times, when the seas were thought to be endless and literally bottomless. This was long before scientific means of measuring the oceans were available.

Of course, the ocean floor is not totally flat or featureless. In some spots, hills or mountains rise up from the ocean basin. The generalized name for these features is *seamount*. A seamount with a flattened top is called a *guyot* and is thought to be volcanic in origin.

As mentioned above, a canyon may extend into the ocean basin from the continental shelf. In addition, the basin features large and deep cuts called *trenches*. The lowest recorded point in the earth's crust is a trench in the Pacific Ocean, the Mariana Trench (see also "The earth in profile," page 128). Not only is the Mariana located in the Pacific, but the greatest number of trenches in the ocean basin taken as a whole are located in that ocean. Trenches occur more frequently near edges of the ocean basin that are relatively near groups of islands or mountainous coastlines.

The *euphotic zone* or layer is that area of the water that receives sunlight. Thus, photosynthesis takes place in this zone, down to about 260 feet, or 80 meters, and new life is created there. The *bathyal zone* extends from about 600 feet (183 meters) to 6,000 feet (1,828 meters) below sea level.

# 2. Air around the earth

Surrounding the land and water on the earth is another vital ingredient, the air. You cannot see, smell, or taste clean air, yet it is a very real and very vital substance. What is this vital substance made of? Air is a mixture of several gases (see the diagram at the left on page 135, "Chemicals in the atmosphere").

Though air is a gas and not a solid, it still has weight. Also, air shows resistance to motion, so that you have to exert some force simply to walk along the ground. But the air itself, like any gas, flows easily and moves easily. Air expands under heat and compresses under pressure.

The "air ocean" surrounding the earth is referred to as the atmosphere. The atmosphere is much greater in size even than the vast oceans.

This section discusses the characteristics of the air or the atmosphere, including the layers of the atmosphere, chemical composition of the atmosphere, and atmospheric pressure.

Understanding the atmosphere is necessary to understanding all life on earth. Oxygen and nitrogen, two key elements in the air, must be present in order for plants and animals to live. Humans can survive for some time without food or water, but only for brief minutes without air. (See also Unit 5: "Basic Information from the Life Sciences," sections 2, 3, and 4.)

As you know, the "health" of the air has become a major concern in recent years. Air pollution has been on the increase, especially in large cities, as smoke and soot are poured into the air.

## Layers of the atmosphere

There are four layers in the atmosphere: the *troposphere*, the *stratosphere*, the *mesosphere*, and the *thermosphere*.

The *troposphere* is the layer in which humans live and in which weather occurs. When you think of "the air" or "the atmosphere," chances are that you are thinking of the troposphere—but this is only one layer. Note that the troposphere begins at the earth's surface and continues to about 10 miles (16 kilometers) up. At the earth's surface, the temperature averages 60°F. At the top of the troposphere, in the area called the tropopause, the temperature drops to −67°F. (−56°C). Changes in the weather are made possible by this occurrence of cold air on top of warm air in the troposphere.

The *stratosphere* extends from about 10 miles (16 kilometers) from the earth to about 20 miles (32 kilometers) out. At the base of the stratosphere, the temperature averages −67°F. (−56°C). But in this layer, the temperature rises—rather than falls—as you go up toward the top, reaching 28°F. (−3°C) in the upper area of this layer.

In the *mesosphere*, or the third layer from the earth's surface, scientists have regularly recorded the lowest temperatures in the earth's atmosphere. Near the top of that layer, the average temperature is −135°F. (−93°C). The mesosphere ranges from 20 miles (32 kilometers) to 50 miles (80 kilometers) above the earth's surface. At the top of the *thermosphere* (50 miles, or 80 kilometers, up), temperatures soar to 2700°F. (1500°C).

## Layers of the atmosphere

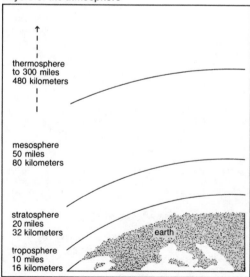

thermosphere
to 300 miles
480 kilometers

mesosphere
50 miles
80 kilometers

stratosphere
20 miles
32 kilometers

earth

troposphere
10 miles
16 kilometers

## Chemicals in the atmosphere

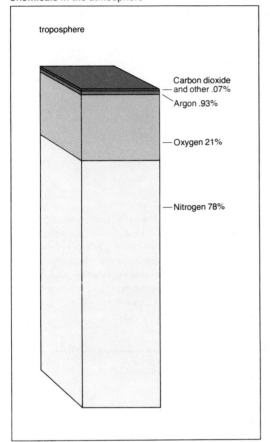

troposphere

Carbon dioxide and other .07%

Argon .93%

Oxygen 21%

Nitrogen 78%

## Pressure in the atmosphere

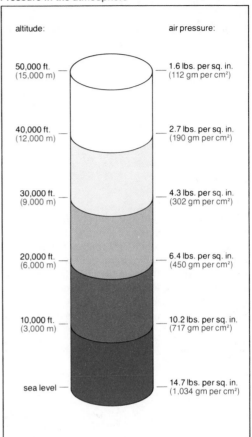

| altitude: | | air pressure: |
|---|---|---|
| 50,000 ft. (15,000 m) | | 1.6 lbs. per sq. in. (112 gm per cm²) |
| 40,000 ft. (12,000 m) | | 2.7 lbs. per sq. in. (190 gm per cm²) |
| 30,000 ft. (9,000 m) | | 4.3 lbs. per sq. in. (302 gm per cm²) |
| 20,000 ft. (6,000 m) | | 6.4 lbs. per sq. in. (450 gm per cm²) |
| 10,000 ft. (3,000 m) | | 10.2 lbs. per sq. in. (717 gm per cm²) |
| sea level | | 14.7 lbs. per sq. in. (1,034 gm per cm²) |

### Chemicals in the atmosphere

The diagram above shows the breakdown of chemical elements in the troposphere layer of the atmosphere. The gas of the atmosphere in this layer is broken down as follows: nitrogen, 78 per cent; oxygen, 21 per cent; argon, .93 per cent; and other (including carbon dioxide), .07 per cent.

Actually, these percentages are generally valid for the other areas of the lower atmosphere, up to 50 miles (80 kilometers) from the earth's surface. However, beginning in the stratosphere and continuing upward to the outer atmosphere, the percentage of ozone increases steadily. Ozone is vital to life on earth because it prevents harmful rays from the sun from reaching this planet. As you probably know, the percentage of oxygen in the atmosphere steadily decreases as you enter the outer atmosphere. This, and the thinness of the air, is why astronauts have to be equipped with special oxygen equipment for their space walks.

The lower atmosphere also contains, in addition to the chemicals mentioned above and depicted in the diagram, quantities of water vapor and solid particles called dust. The percentage of water vapor in the area varies from place to place on the earth's surface; there may be almost none or there may be as much as 4 per cent. Water vapor serves an important function; when the vapor condenses, precipitation forms and falls on the earth. The dust particles in the atmosphere are also thought to be crucial for weather patterns, as the concentration of atmospheric dust will determine cloud formation, including cloud type and cloud size.

### Pressure in the atmosphere

This graph illustrates how air pressure decreases, or goes down, as you go up in altitude. At sea level, the average air pressure is 14.7 pounds per square inch (1,034 grams per square centimeter). By 10,000 feet from the earth's surface, air pressure has dropped to 10.2 pounds per square inch (717 grams per square centimeter).

At 30,000 feet (9,000 meters) above sea level—or the height at which many jet planes are flown—air pressure has dropped to 4.3 pounds per square inch (302 grams per square centimeter). By 50,000 feet (15,000 meters) above sea level, air pressure is a scant 1.6 pounds per square inch (112 grams per square centimeter).

The figures on this graph cover only the troposphere, or the layer of the atmosphere closest to the earth's surface. But as you continue to go up in altitude, pressure continues to drop.

What exactly is air pressure? It is the weight of the air, or atmosphere, pressing from all sides on any object. Because the weight of the air is a key factor in air pressure, it is easy to see why air pressure falls as you go up in the atmosphere—there is less and less air to press down on that below.

A barometer is an instrument used to measure air pressure. On the weather report, you may hear the "barometric pressure" expressed as a single figure in millibars.

# 3. Climate and weather on the earth

Weather consists of all the changes that occur each day in temperature, humidity, precipitation, and air pressure. Sometimes the words *weather* and *climate* are used interchangeably, but they actually have very different meanings. *Climate* is the correct term for a long-term pattern of weather changes in an area.

Facts about the earth's surface, the oceans, and the atmosphere are crucial to understanding weather and climate. The air uses moisture from the earth's waters to bring life-giving precipitation to the earth. The contours of the earth are an important factor in determining weather and climate. A mountainous region may have one type of weather pattern, and a valley nearby may have a very different weather pattern.

The four seasons

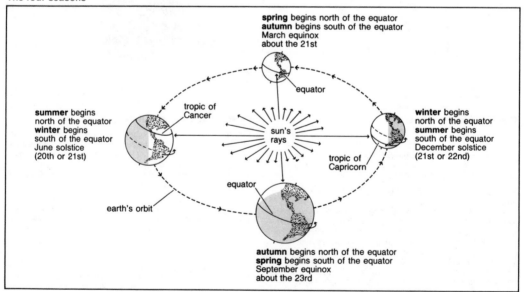

**spring** begins north of the equator
**autumn** begins south of the equator
March equinox
about the 21st

equator

tropic of Cancer

sun's rays

**summer** begins north of the equator
**winter** begins south of the equator
June solstice (20th or 21st)

**winter** begins north of the equator
**summer** begins south of the equator
December solstice (21st or 22nd)

tropic of Capricorn

equator

earth's orbit

**autumn** begins north of the equator
**spring** begins south of the equator
September equinox
about the 23rd

## The four seasons

The four seasons—spring, summer, autumn (or fall), and winter—are crucial to both weather and climate. The sun supplies light and heat to all points on the earth. In this diagram, you can see how the seasons change as the earth travels in its elliptical orbit around the sun. (For more information on orbits, see "Features of orbits" and "Planetary orbits" on page 98.) As you will note, the seasons are reversed north and south of the equator. When it is winter in Montana and Wyoming, it is summer in Brazil and Kenya. The length of the day, and thus the amount of sunlight to be received in a given place at a given time, depends on two factors. One is the season of the year, and the other is the fact that the earth is tilted on its axis. These two factors are closely related in making the days short in the winter and long in the summer, in both hemispheres. Other factors enter into climate, however, and a "winter" day in a tropical country is quite warm when compared to one in the northern latitudes.

## Clouds and the weather

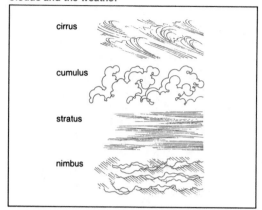

cirrus

cumulus

stratus

nimbus

### Clouds and the weather

A cloud is a mass of very small water drops or ice crystals. Clouds are the vehicle for bringing precipitation to the earth's surface. There are many varieties of clouds, but some basic types are shown in this diagram. *Stratus* clouds are low-level clouds, or closer to the ground than the others. Another wispy-looking cloud is the *nimbus,* or nimbostratus, that usually occurs at middle altitudes. *Cirrus* clouds are very high in the sky and are always made of ice crystals. *Cumulus* clouds appear to be billowy and large and can appear at any altitude; they are the clouds that bring thunderstorms and heavy rains.

### Fronts and the weather

A *front* is the boundary of an air mass touching a second air mass that differs in temperature. When a front moves in, that means that the temperature is changing in the affected area. In the case of a *cold front* (top), cold air moves in, forcing the warm air that was there to move up and away. This makes sense when you recall from physics that heat tends to rise. If you happen to be outdoors when a cold front moves in, you can actually feel the temperature dropping rapidly. Cold fronts come very quickly, but this means that they may go quickly, too. Note the pointed symbol used to show the cold front on a weather map.

A *warm front* (center) precedes a mass of warm air moving into a particular area. A warm front moves more slowly than a cold front, and thus it may stay around longer, also. If you are outdoors when a warm front moves in, you might not notice it as the fronts are changing—because the warming trend is so slow and gradual. Note that as the warm front moves in, the warm air moves up (again, the principle of heat rising). The cold air is thus forced back in the direction it was coming from. The semicircular symbol is used to mark a warm front.

In the case of an *occluded front* (bottom), the cold front basically wins the "battle" between the two air masses, but the warm air is dispelled more gradually. Thus, the resulting temperature will be "cool" rather than "cold," because the warm air has some influence. Note that the symbol for an occluded front combines the cold front and the warm front symbols.

There are other types of fronts, but these are the three basic types to be familiar with. When any kind of front moves in, there are more changes than simply the change in temperature. Air pressure changes, too. A different type of cloud may appear in the sky, or the number of clouds in the sky may simply multiply. Precipitation generally results, either rain or snow, depending on the type of front and other factors. Note that precipitation is indicated with each of the fronts shown on the diagram.

## Fronts and the weather

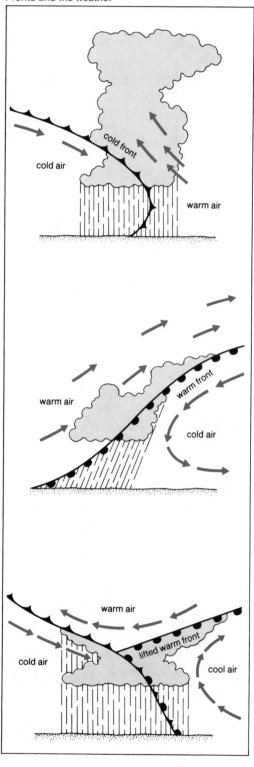

# Precipitation

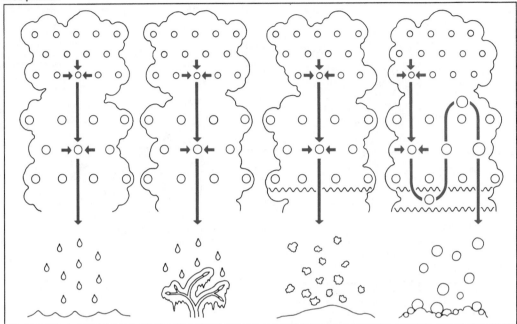

## Precipitation

Water vapor is taken up into the atmosphere by means of evaporation. Water condenses to form clouds and eventually returns to earth as precipitation. To return to earth, water in the atmosphere must be made heavy enough to fall. It must be converted from a gas or a vapor into either a liquid or a solid. The only way to do this is to cool the air to below the point where it can hold water vapor. This temperature is called the *dew point*. It can vary, depending on the amount of cooling and the amount of water present.

Salt evaporated from sea spray, acids from pollution, and dust in the atmosphere all attract water vapor. They are the nuclei around which water vapor is converted into the four forms of precipitation.

*Rain* (far left) occurs when water-soaked nuclei attract other water drops until they become so large they can no longer be held up by air currents. Rain that is frozen by cold air near the ground turns to *sleet* (not shown).

Rain sometimes becomes very cold before it falls. Then it will fall as rain but freezes and becomes ice when it lands. This form of precipitation is called *glaze* (second from left).

*Snow* (second from right) is formed when water vapor is converted into its solid ice form directly, without first becoming a liquid. This process is called *sublimation*. Tiny six-pointed ice crystals form and collect into flakes.

*Hail* (right) is formed when raindrops become ice as they fall through freezing areas and then are carried up above the freezing point by strong air currents. (Note how the arrow in the diagram changes direction before the precipitation emerges.) Each time this frozen water tries to fall through the freezing point each particle picks up a new layer of ice until finally it is so heavy that the air currents can no longer hold it.

## Recording temperature

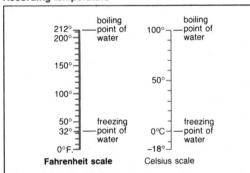

| Fahrenheit scale | | Celsius scale | |
|---|---|---|---|
| 212° | boiling point of water | 100° | boiling point of water |
| 200° | | | |
| 150° | | | |
| | | 50° | |
| 100° | | | |
| 50° | freezing point of water | 0°C | freezing point of water |
| 32° | | | |
| 0°F. | | –18° | |

**Fahrenheit scale**      Celsius scale

## Recording temperatures

One of the most basic and most important aspects of weather is temperature. Everyone depends on a reliable method for measuring how hot it is or how cold it is and a common system for expressing those temperatures.

In the 1700's, Gabriel Daniel Fahrenheit, a German instrument maker, perfected the thermometer by using mercury in a glass tube instead of alcohol. Fahrenheit designated 0° as the freezing point for a mixture of water, ice, and salt (written as 0° F.). The freezing point for water on his scale then became 32°; the boiling point for water, 212°.

Later in the 1700's, the Swedish astronomer Anders Celsius set up a different temperature scale, using an even 100 points between the freezing (0°C) and boiling points of water. The Celsius or centigrade scale is part of the international metric system. If you know a temperature in Fahrenheit, subtract 32 from that and multiply the number by 5/9 to get the Celsius reading. If you are starting with a Celsius reading, multiply by 9/5 and then add 32 to get the Fahrenheit equivalent.

## Reading a weather map

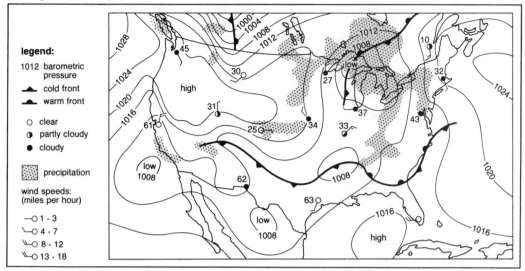

legend:

1012 barometric pressure

▲▲ cold front

◢◣ warm front

○ clear

◐ partly cloudy

● cloudy

▨ precipitation

wind speeds:
(miles per hour)

—○ 1 - 3

╰○ 4 - 7

╲○ 8 - 12

╲╲○ 13 - 18

### Reading a weather map

Much of the science of weather forecasting, called *meteorology*, has been developed since 1900. Until about 1920, forecasts were based primarily upon reports of barometric pressure. Forecasters knew that areas of low pressure, called *cyclones* because the winds in them swirl around, bring wet weather and usually move to the north and east. High pressure areas, called *anticyclones*, with winds moving out from their centers, tend to move to the south and east and usually signal fair weather.

Today millibars of *barometric pressure* adjusted to sea level are noted on weather maps. Lines called isobars connect all the places with the same pressure reading.

After 1920, a group of Norwegian meteorologists began careful studies of weather patterns and found that the low pressure cyclones are formed by the meeting of cold and warm air masses. As a result, weather maps began to show the location of the cold, warm, occluded, and stationary fronts, and weather forecasting for longer time spans improved tremendously.

Meteorologists began establishing weather recording and re-porting stations all over the world. This network was essentially complete by the late 1950's. It now consists of land observing stations, sounding stations that report events throughout the troposphere, radar stations, and specially equipped ships, air-craft, and weather satellites.

Also in the 1950's, a series of standard procedures and codes was adopted on a worldwide basis. Numbers are used on maps to record instrument readings such as temperature and press-ure, and symbols represent visual observations of precipitation and clouds.

On a weather map, a circle indicates a reporting station. The amount of the circle that is filled in corresponds to the amount of cloud cover. Numbers and symbols around the circle supply the details. The map above shows temperature in numbers and wind direction in the form of an arrow-like line. The line is placed to show the wind's direction, and the flags on it indicate the wind's speed in miles per hour.

To indicate larger weather features, shaded areas show precipi-tation and long heavy lines mark fronts. Cold fronts have triang-ular markings and warm fronts, half circles (see also page 137). These symbols are placed on the side of the line in which the front is moving. An occluded front shows warm and cold symbols on the same side of the line, while a stationary front shows warm symbols on one side and cold ones on the other.

### Climate zones

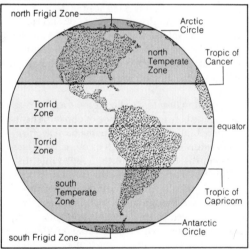

### Climate zones

Weather, especially temperature, depends a great deal on the position of the sun overhead. Traditionally, the earth has been di-vided into five climate zones whose boundaries are the same latitudes that mark the changes of the seasons. The winterless Torrid Zone extends from the equator to the 23½° north and south latitudes, called the Tropic of Cancer and the Tropic of Capricorn respectively. Between 23½° and 66½° are the north and south Temperate Zones, which have warm summers and cold winters. Above the 66½° north and south latitudes, which mark the Arctic and Antarctic Circles, are the summerless Frigid Zones.

This classification accounts for the roles of the sun's light and heat on climate. But precipitation is another important factor in climate. Wet and dry variations occur at different times of the year throughout the torrid and temperate zones. These variations have convinced scientists that it is necessary to establish many regional climate types and subtypes. There are a number of systems for classifying climates.

# Types of climates

These are the major climatic groups, according to the system devised by geographer Glenn T. Trewartha.

**Tropical climates.** The tropical climates form a band around the equator. Temperatures are always warm, and heavy rainfall is common. There are two types of these climates. The *tropical wet climate*, where the tropical rain forests are found, has rain for at least 10 months a year. The *tropical wet-and-dry climate*, with its tall grasses or savanna, has less annual rainfall, a shorter wet season, and a longer dry season than the tropical wet climate.

**Subtropical climates.** Here the seasons begin to become noticeable. There is some freezing, but at least eight months of the year have average temperatures of 50° F. (10° C) or more. There are two types of subtropical climates. The *subtropical dry-summer climate* is usually found on the western sides of continents. This sunny Mediterranean climate has warm dry summers and mild rainy winters. The *subtropical humid climate* is typically found on eastern sides of continents. It has more precipitation than the Mediterranean climate, and summer is usually the wet season.

**Temperate climates.** Called temperate because they occur between the zones of constant heat and constant cold, these climates have average temperatures of 50° F. (10° C) or more for at least four months, but not more than seven months, each year. Of the two types, the *temperate oceanic climate* is usually found on the western sides of continents. Although in the high latitudes, this type is warmed by mild oceanic currents. Precipitation is common all year around. Found only in the Northern Hemisphere, the *temperate continental climate* has sharp weather contrasts, from cold winters to warm summers. Temperature ranges of over 50° F. or 30° C are common, and precipitation is generally lighter, with more than half the area experiencing subhumid conditions.

**Boreal climate.** Winters are long and very cold and summers last no more than one to three months in these northern taiga regions dominated by coniferous forests. The impact of long days in summer and long nights in winter becomes significant on the *boreal climate*. Precipitation is limited, permafrost is common, and the growing season is short.

**Polar climates.** Because low humidity accompanies low temperatures, precipitation is extremely low in the polar climates. For half the year, there is constant darkness; for the other half, constant light, with little warmth because of the steep angles of the sun's rays. There are two types of polar climates. The *polar tundra climate* has a few months with temperatures above freezing but none with temperatures above 50° F. (10° C). Permafrost prevents surface drainage, and swamps abound. Most tundra areas are found around the edges of the northern icecaps. In the *polar icecap climate*, long sunless periods and the ability of the snow surface to reflect back 80 per cent of the solar radiation it receives keep average temperatures below freezing.

**Highland climates.** Altitude becomes an important factor in the *highland climates*. Above 6,000 feet (1,800 meters), the air grows thin, precipitation increases, and solar radiation becomes intense. There are large swings in temperature between day and night. The wet highlands are the sources of the major waterways.

**Dry climates.** The rate of precipitation is always lower than the rate of evaporation in a dry climate. Arid deserts and semiarid steppes, transition belts around deserts, are found in the dry climate areas. Three main types are distinguished by their temperature conditions. Hot *tropical-subtropical dry climates* occur where dry, stable air masses form near the equator. *Cool coastal deserts* are refreshed by ocean currents. *Middle-latitude dry climates* occur deep inside continents when mountains block the arrival of water vapor from the oceans.

## Cities and their climates

| City or reporting station | Average temperature, °F. (°C) | | | Annual precipitation, in. (mm) |
|---|---|---|---|---|
| | Annual | Jan. | July | |
| **Tropical wet climate:** | | | | |
| Belém, Brazil | 78 (26) | 77 (25) | 78 (26) | 108 (2743) |
| Kisangani, Zaire | 76 (24) | 77 (25) | 74 (23) | 69.4 (1763) |
| Singapore | 80 (27) | 79 (26) | 81 (27) | 95 (2413) |
| **Tropical wet-and-dry climate:** | | | | |
| Calcutta, India | 78 (26) | 65 (18) | 83 (28) | 58.8 (1494) |
| Normanton, Australia | 81 (27) | 86 (30) | 72 (22) | 37.5 (952) |
| **Subtropical dry-summer climate:** | | | | |
| Santa Monica, California | 59 (15) | 53 (12) | 66 (19) | 14.8 (376) |
| Perth, Australia | 64 (18) | 74 (23) | 55 (13) | 33.9 (861) |
| Naples, Italy | 62 (17) | 48 (9) | 77 (25) | 34.3 (811) |
| **Subtropical humid climate:** | | | | |
| Charleston, South Carolina | 66 (19) | 50 (10) | 82 (28) | 47.3 (1202) |
| Sydney, Australia | 63 (17) | 72 (22) | 52 (11) | 47.7 (1212) |
| Buenos Aires, Argentina | 61 (16) | 74 (23) | 51 (11) | 39.1 (993) |
| **Temperate oceanic climate:** | | | | |
| Paris, France | 50 (10) | 37 (3) | 66 (19) | 22.6 (574) |
| Hokitika, New Zealand | 53 (12) | 60 (16) | 45 (7) | 116.1 (2949) |
| Valentia, Ireland | 50.8 (11) | 44 (7) | 59 (15) | 55.6 (1413) |
| **Temperate continental climate:** | | | | |
| New York City, New York | 52 (11) | 31 (−1) | 74 (23) | 42 (1067) |
| Montreal, Quebec, Canada | 42 (6) | 13 (−10) | 69 (21) | 40.7 (1017) |
| Moscow, U.S.S.R. | 39 (4) | 12 (−11) | 66 (19) | 21.1 (536) |
| **Boreal climate:** | | | | |
| Yakutsk, Siberia, U.S.S.R. | 12 (−11) | −46 (−43) | 66 (19) | 13.7 (348) |
| Fort Vermilion, Alberta, Canada | 27 (−3) | −14 (−26) | 60 (16) | 12.3 (313) |
| **Polar tundra climate:** | | | | |
| Sagastyr, Siberia, U.S.S.R. | 1 (−17) | −34 (−37) | 41 (5) | 3.3 (84) |
| Upernivik, Western Greenland | 16 (−9) | − 7 (−22) | 41 (5) | 9.2 (234) |
| **Polar icecap climate:** | | | | |
| South Pole, Antarctica | −57 (−49) | −20 (−29) | −74 (−59) | — |
| Eismitte, Greenland | −22 (−30) | −42 (−41) | 12 (−11) | — |
| **Highland climates:** | | | | |
| Quito, Ecuador | 54.7 (13) | 54.5 (13) | 54.9 (13) | 42.2 (1072) |
| Longs Peak, Colorado | 37 (3) | 23 (−5) | 55 (13) | 21.6 (548) |
| **Tropical-subtropical dry climates:** | | | | |
| Phoenix, Arizona | 70 (21) | 51 (11) | 91 (33) | 7.2 (185) |
| Benghazi, Libya | 69 (21) | 55 (13) | 78 (26) | 11.9 (302) |
| Kayes, Mali | 85 (29) | 77 (25) | 84 (29) | 29.1 (739) |
| **Cool coastal deserts climate:** | | | | |
| Lima, Peru | 66 (19) | 71 (22) | 61 (16) | 1.8 (45) |
| **Middle-latitude dry climates:** | | | | |
| Santa Cruz, Argentina | 47 (9) | 59 (15) | 35 (2) | 6.1 (155) |
| Williston, North Dakota | 39 (4) | 6 (−14) | 69 (21) | 14.4 (366) |
| Ulan Bator, Mongolia | 28 (−2) | −16 (−27) | 63 (17) | 7.6 (193) |

# Glossary: Unit 4

**absolute zero** The temperature at which all molecular action stops; zero degrees on the Kelvin scale, or−273.15°C.

**altitude** Height above a base line. Altitude is usually measured from sea level.

**anticline** The high point of a fold in the earth's crust.

**anticyclone** An air mass that moves around a center of high pressure, also called a high pressure system, or high.

**atmosphere** The air around the earth.

**bar** A unit of measure of air pressure. Air pressure at sea level at 45° north latitude is 1.0132 bars.

**climate** The weather pattern of an area as it occurs over a long period of time.

**cold front** The forward edge of a cold air mass that is replacing a warm air mass.

**continental drift** The movement of the continents away from each other, caused by tectonic forces (see *plate tectonics*).

**continental shelf** The edge of each continent that extends under the ocean.

**continental slope** The area of steep dropping off of the continental shelf under the oceans.

**cordillera** A series of mountain ranges that forms a single system.

**cyclone** An air mass that moves around a center of low pressure, also called a low pressure system or low.

**dew point** The temperature at which air begins to condense as it cools.

**diastrophism** The process causing changes in the earth's crust that lead to movements on the surface, such as faulting and folding.

**earthquake** Movement of the earth's crust, usually caused by slippage along the sides of a fault or by volcanic activity.

**epicenter** The point on the earth's surface closest to the underground origin of an earthquake.

**equinox** A time occurring twice each year when the sun passes directly over the equator. Day and night are of about equal lengths all over the earth.

**erosion** The slow wearing away, or weathering, of soil and rocks by wind, rain, waves, and other weather forces.

**faulting** The breaking of the earth's crust into huge blocks, some of which move upward while others move downward, to form fault block or block mountains.

**folding** The upward and downward movement of the earth's crust into wavelike folds that form folded mountains. The high point of such folding is the anticline and the low point is the syncline.

**gravity** The attraction between the earth and other objects.

**horizon** The curved line where the earth and sky appear to meet.

**humidity** The water vapor present in the air.

**hydrologic cycle** The sequence in which the earth uses and reuses its water supply.

**isobar** A line on a weather map that connects areas having the same barometric pressure.

**isotherm** A line on a weather map that connects areas having the same temperature.

**latitudes** Distances north or south of the equator shown as parallel lines around the earth. The equator is 0° latitude.

**lithosphere** The solid portion of the earth's surface, often called the crust.

**longitude** Distance as measured east or west of a prime meridian, a line running north and south on the earth's surface. The meridian usually selected as 0° longitude runs through Greenwich, England.

**mantle** A thick layer of solid rock that begins below the earth's crust and extends 1,800 miles (2,900 kilometers) toward the earth's core.

**mountain** An area that lies at least 2,000 feet (610 meters) above the area around it. Most mountains are formed by the faulting or folding of the earth's crust.

**occluded front** The forward edge of a cold air mass that is overtaking a warm front and meeting the cool air ahead of it.

**ocean** The massive body of water that covers two-thirds of the earth's surface. There are five principal divisions of the ocean: The Atlantic, Pacific, Indian, Arctic, and Antarctic oceans.

**ozone** A form of oxygen that has three atoms of oxygen in each molecule ($O_3$). Ozone in the stratosphere absorbs the harmful untraviolet rays of the sun.

**permafrost** Permanently frozen subsoil. In the tundra, permafrost prevents proper drainage of the land, causing bogs and swamps to form in summer.

**plate tectonics** The theory that says that forces beginning below earth's crust cause the plates on which the continents are based to move about on earth's surface.

**precipitation** The removal of water vapor from the atmosphere and the form the water vapor takes as it falls to earth.

**sial** The rocky layer of the earth's crust that forms the continents.

**sima** The rocky layer of the earth's crust that lies under the continents and forms the ocean floor.

**solstice** A time occurring twice each year when the sun is farthest from the equator. The longest or shortest days of the year occur on the solstice.

**stationary front** The edge formed by a cold air mass and a warm air mass when neither is able to replace the other.

**taiga** The name in Russian for subarctic areas covered with coniferous forests. The name is also used for similar areas in North America.

**talus** The rocks and gravel piled up at the base of the cliff or slope from which they fell.

**temperature inversion** The condition that oc-curs when the air mass nearest the earth's surface is cooler than the mass above it. This is the opposite of the normal condition.

**thrust** The horizontal movement of the earth's surface in the process of diastrophism.

**turbulence** Irregular conditions in the atmosphere that cause violent winds.

**uplift** The upward movement of the earth's surface in the process of diastrophism.

**volcano** An opening in the earth's surface through which lava, hot gases, and rock fragments erupt. Volcanoes are also the mountains formed by the build-up of the material thrown out during eruptions.

**warm front** The forward edge of a warm air mass that is replacing a cold air mass.

**water table** The level in the ground below which the rock is saturated with water.

**weather** The effect of all conditions occurring in the atmosphere in one place during a short period of time.

**weathering** Changes in the earth's surface brought about by the forces of weather.

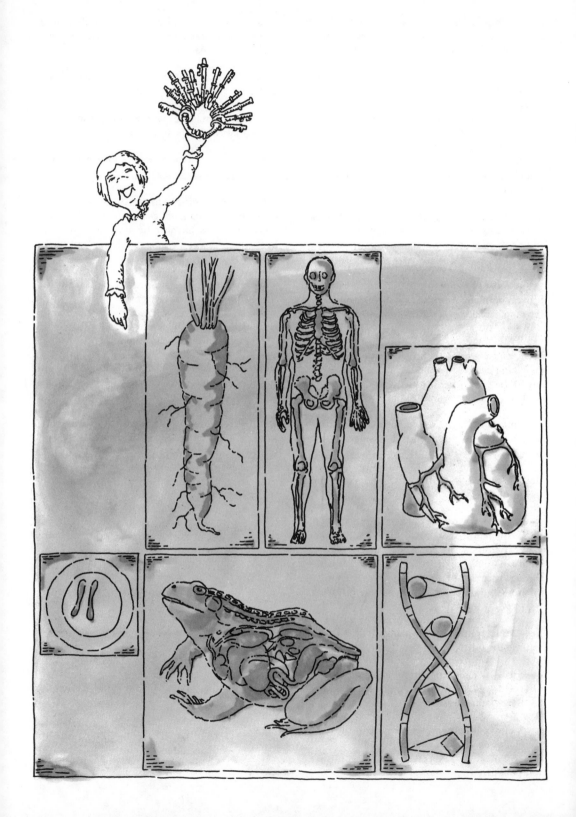

# Basic information from the life sciences

5

Life, both plant and animal, is very complex. What are the basic parts of a cell? How do plants reproduce? How do animals breathe? Which bones make up the human skeleton? What foods should you eat to keep your body healthy?

This unit answers these and many other questions about living organisms. The unit is a handy, easy-to-use review of basic information from the life sciences.

# 1. A look at the cell

All living things consist of cells. The simplest forms of independent life are single cells. Each captures or makes its own food, uses the food for growth and cell repair, and divides into other cells like itself. Cells in more advanced living things are specialized into tissues and organs. Some types of special cells may form a food-manufacturing leaf in plants or a leg muscle in animals. The rule is: as the forms of life in the plant and animal kingdoms become more complex, their cells become more and more specialized into systems.

An ameba is an example of a one-celled animal. It has the attributes of a typical cell. And on a simpler level, it does many of the things done by many-celled creatures. The ameba's cell has *organization.* It is an orderly array of chemicals and cell parts organized in an efficient package to sustain life. The ameba's cell undergoes *metabolism* to get energy from food, grow, and repair worn out parts. The energy needed to power the cell comes from food, which is chemically broken down through *respiration* to extract its energy. The ameba *excretes,* or gets rid of, harmful waste products after the food is metabolized. It is capable of purposeful *movement,* one of life's attributes. It also shows *responsiveness;* that is, it can react to changes in its immediate surroundings. For example, an ameba will try to move away from a harsh chemical added to water around it. The ameba *reproduces* by cell division and splits into two daughter cells, each containing the ingredients and instructions needed for independent life. In more advanced organisms, reproduction is carried out by special sex cells.

The science of *biology* delves into the activities of all living things in their environment. *Botany* concentrates on plant activities, and *zoology* deals with the lives of animals. The general principles of life and the specialized adaptations made by plants and animals will be discussed in the first part of the following unit. Later in the unit, the human body and how it works will be explained. The discussion will include the importance of good eating habits for a healthy life, as well as other ways of keeping your body sound and healthy. First aid measures that anyone can use for emergency care will also be shown.

## Table of conditions for life

Certain conditions are necessary for life. All the requirements are found in a thin region called the *biosphere* near the surface of the earth.

| | |
|---|---|
| Temperature range | Most living things exist within a narrow temperature range between 0°C (32°F) and 80°C (176°F). As a rule, life processes stop near 0°C—the freezing point of water—and at about 80°C. Very few plants or animals can live at temperatures that exceed 80°C. |
| Altitude range | Some birds live as high as 27,000 ft. (8,230 m) above sea level. No animals are known to live at a depth greater than 35,800 ft. (10,910 m) below sea level. |
| Sunlight | Most plants require sunlight for the energy to make their own food by photosynthesis. |
| Water | Living things need water, which is a main component of protoplasm—the living substance of a cell. |
| Carbon dioxide | Green plants need carbon dioxide from the air plus water for photosynthesis. |
| Oxygen | Most plant and animal cells require oxygen from the air or dissolved in water for cell energy processes. |
| Food | Green plants make their own food; animals acquire energy by eating green plants or other animals. |
| Carbon | Needed for carbohydrate fuel. |
| Nitrogen | Needed for making proteins for body growth. |

## A look at typical cells

A typical animal or plant cell contains three essential parts—the cell membrane, the cytoplasm, and the nucleus. The *cell membrane* separates the cell from its watery surroundings. It is a semipermeable membrane, allowing only select substances to pass through. Tiny molecules easily get through the membrane by simple diffusion. Larger molecules must be actively transported across the cell membrane, a process that requires cell energy. Still larger substances can be engulfed by portions of the membrane and brought into the cell, a process called pinocytosis. The *cytoplasm* is a watery-to-sirupy mix of nutrients and pigments in liquid suspension. Activities in the cytoplasm keep the cell alive. The *nucleus* is the control center of the cell. It contains coded information used by the cell for growth, repair, and reproduction.

The cytoplasm contains organelles, minute specialized parts, involved in producing energy for the cell. Other structures are concerned with making proteins to repair damaged cell parts. Food molecules are oxidized, or "burned" for energy, in each *mitochondrion*—one of the cell's many such "powerhouses." *Ribosomes,* located along membraned passageways in the cell called endoplasmic reticulum, manufacture the proteins needed for growth and repair. The *Golgi apparatus* is a saclike storehouse where proteins made in the ribosomes are kept for future distribution.

A plant cell differs somewhat from an animal cell by having a rigid, cellulose *cell wall* around the cell membrane. The stiff cell

## A look at typical cells

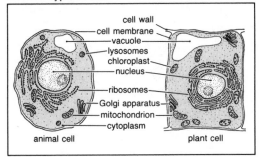

walls give support to plant stalks and stems. The cellulose required for the cell wall is made in the cytoplasm of a plant cell. An organelle called a *chloroplast* is also found in a plant cell. Chloroplasts contain chlorophyll, the respiratory pigment used by green plants to manufacture food. *Vacuoles* are scattered through the cytoplasm of plant and animal cells, carrying dissolved food molecules for use by the mitochondria. Some cells have contractile vacuoles that help get rid of excess water by forcing it out of the cell. *Lysosomes* are similar to vacuoles but appear to digest food particles.

## How cells divide

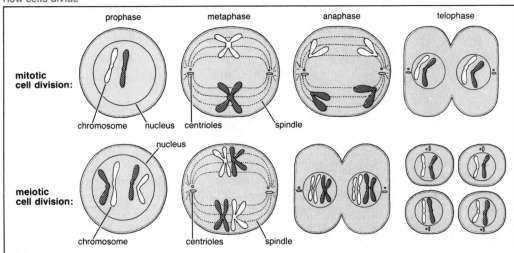

## How cells divide

Body cells reproduce by *mitosis.* At the start of mitosis, strands of deoxyribonucleic acid (DNA)—the carrier of hereditary information—form into chromosomes. By *prophase,* the first stage of mitosis, each chromosome in the cell nucleus has duplicated. In the next stage, *metaphase,* the membrane around the nucleus disappears, *centrioles* are in place at opposite ends of the cell, *spindle* fibers appear between the centrioles, and homologous, or like, chromosomes line up at the cell midline. During *anaphase,* the third mitotic stage, one set of homologous chromosomes moves along the spindles toward each of the centrioles. In the final stage of mitosis, called the *telophase,* the centrioles and spindles disappear, a nuclear membrane forms around each set of chromosomes, and the cell membrane pinches in two. Two new body cells become formed, each with the same type and number of chromosomes as the parent cell (46 in a human body cell).

Sex cells, or gametes, reproduce by a two-step method called *meiosis.* During the first meiotic prophase, homologous chromosomes pair and duplicate into tetrads. The tetrads line up at the midline in the first meiotic metaphase, and separate and move toward a centriole during the first meiotic anaphase. By the end of the first meiotic telophase, two daughter cells form with the same number of chromosomes as the parent. However, meiosis keeps going on. During the second step, chromosomes *do not* duplicate. Four stages occur again, and four gametes are eventually produced from the original parent cell. But each new gamete contains only half the number of chromosomes in a body cell (23 in a human sex cell). Fertilization of a female gamete by a male gamete restores the original chromosome number.

## Mendel's law of segregation

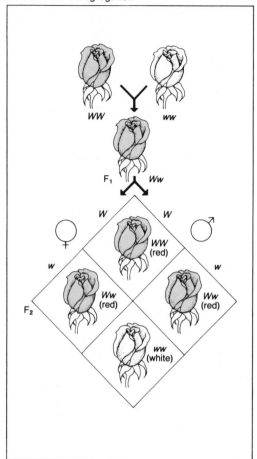

## Mendel's law of independent assortment

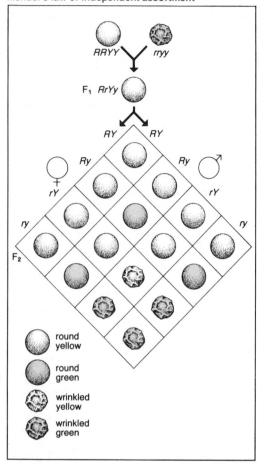

### Mendel's law of segregation

Gregor Mendel, a 19th century Austrian monk, experimented with pea plants and discovered principles of inheritance that apply to all living things. Physical traits, or *phenotypes,* are controlled by gene pairs called *alleles* that reside on *homologous,* or like, chromosomes. Alleles for traits pass from generation to generation in the gametes. Certain traits dominate others. For example, red flowers are dominant over white flowers, whether you are considering pea plants, roses, or other varieties. The *genotype,* or genetic makeup, of each allele remains independent, however, even when masked by a dominant one. For example, the phenotype of red-flowerness is caused by two *homozygous* alleles with the genotype WW or by two *heterozygous* alleles with the genotype Ww. The phenotype of white-flowerness results only from two homozygous alleles with the genotype ww. The alleles of any given trait remain independent and will be segregated when new gametes form during meiosis.

Crossing a homozygous dominant rose plant with red flowers (WW) with a homozygous recessive rose plant with white flowers (ww) illustrates the law. First generation offspring (F₁) are all heterozygous plants with red flowers (Ww) because all received one of each allele from the parents' gametes. However, if two F₁ plants are crossed and have four offspring (F₂), segregated alleles can combine in a way that three offspring probably will have red flowers and one will have white flowers, in the 3:1 ratio shown above.

### Mendel's law of independent assortment

Mendel discovered another law of inheritance while working with pea plants: different traits exist independently of each other. If a trait such as green seed color is not expressed in one generation, it may be in another as long as the allele for the trait exists.

Alleles for different traits are independently assorted during meiosis and parceled out to the new gametes. A gene for greenness of seed coat may or may not be in a gamete with a gene for roundness of a pea. However, a gene for greenness would never be in a gamete with a gene for yellowness. A Plunkett square, named after a British geneticist who pioneered its use, shows the possible combinations that result from the independent assortment of particular alleles. If a homozygous dominant plant having round, yellow peas (RRYY) is crossed with a homozygous recessive plant having wrinkled, green peas (rryy), the first generation (F₁) offspring all will be heterozygotes and will show the dominant phenotypes because of their RrYy genotypes. But combinations of the different traits will appear in the F₂ generation. Of 16 possible offspring from crossing two F₁ heterozygotes, 9 could have round, yellow peas (1 RYRY, 2 RYrY, 2 RYRy, 2 RyrY, 2 RYry); 3 could have round, green peas (1 RyRy, 2 Ryry); 3 could have wrinkled, yellow peas (1 rYrY, 2 rYry); and 1 would have wrinkled, green peas (rryy). The 9:3:3:1 ratio of predicted phenotypes is shown in the illustration above.

## DNA—the "ladder" of heredity

The genes in chromosomes are strands of DNA. The genetic code that carries traits lies in the sequence of chemical groups in the DNA gene. The DNA molecule looks like a twisted ladder or a spiral staircase, which scientists call a *double helix.*

Each side of the molecule consists of an alternating chain of *deoxyribose* sugar and *phosphate* groups; that is, these chemical groups repeat themselves along the DNA molecule. Attached to each deoxyribose sugar molecule is a nitrogenous base molecule.

DNA contains four nitrogenous bases—*thymine* (T), *adenine* (A), *guanine* (G), and *cytosine* (C). The two chains of a DNA molecule are linked by complementary base pairs, the "steps" of the ladder. Complementary objects are connected together like a key in a lock. Adenine and guanine are chemically called purines; thymine and cytosine are pyrimidines. Purines complement pyrimidines. This means that adenine always pairs with thymine and guanine always pairs with cytosine in a DNA molecule. The A-T and G-C linkages are hydrogen bonds, fairly weak but still strong enough to hold together both chains of the DNA molecule. However, the ends can become "unzipped" and nearby bases can pair with complementary partners on the separated strand of DNA.

## How DNA duplicates itself

The DNA molecule is able to *replicate,* or make an exact copy of itself, because of its unique pairing of complementary bases. This important attribute enables it to pass on its genetic information to other DNA molecules.

Each new DNA contains the same sequence of deoxyribose sugar-phosphate group-nitrogenous base units, or *nucleotides,* as the parent molecule. As an example, assume that a DNA molecule has the following sequence of nine nucleotide pairs: A-T T-A C-G G-C C-G T-A A-T C-G C-G. The nucleotide sequence on one side of the molecule would be: TAGCGATGG. The sequence on the other side would be: ATCGCTACC. Each nitrogenous base is linked with its complementary partner by hydrogen bonds. When those bonds break, the molecule becomes separated and "unzips." However, the bonding sites on the separated bases are now free to accept other complementary nucleotides to restore the molecule to its unbroken form. Thus, both sides can form new molecules. As the TAGCGATGG side of the old molecule is free, nearby nucleotides attach to their complementary partners until the entire molecule is re-formed: A-T T-A C-G G-C C-G T-A A-T C-G C-G. This also happens with the other side of the old molecule, where ATCGCTACC becomes A-T T-A C-G G-C C-G T-A A-T C-G C-G also.

An original DNA molecule can be replicated with the same sequence of nucleotides for generation after generation, unless a *mutation* occurs to break the sequence of nucleotides. Groups of three nucleotides are called *codons.* The codon sequence in the DNA molecules of any particular living thing makes up its *genetic code.* From our prior example, the codons of the DNA molecule are: ATC GCT ACC. These codons are a *template,* or pattern, on which a nucleic acid called *ribonucleic acid* (RNA) is formed.

RNA transcribes the genetic code and carries it to special sites in the cell—ribosomes—where proteins are manufactured. Protein synthesis, or manufacture, is an extremely important cell activity. Proteins give form to many living things and are used in cell, tissue, and organ repair. Proteins are also important in the energy transactions of a cell. The catalysts that help chemical reactions in a cell are proteins. All proteins are made from basic building blocks called *amino acids.* The amino acids must be in a certain sequence for the making of any given protein. The amino-acid sequence is in an "order form" determined by the sequence of codons in the genetic code of an organism. A codon usually contains the instructions for the assembly of a specific amino acid in a protein molecule. However, some codons can call a halt to the assembly process.

DNA—the "ladder" of heredity

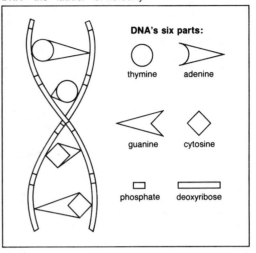

**DNA's six parts:**

thymine          adenine

guanine          cytosine

phosphate        deoxyribose

How DNA duplicates itself

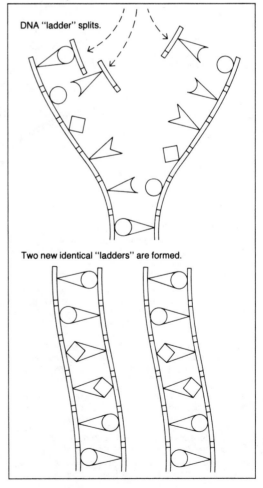

DNA "ladder" splits.

Two new identical "ladders" are formed.

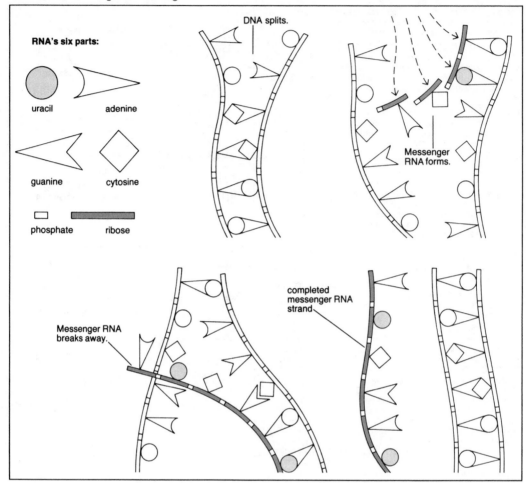

RNA's six parts:

uracil  adenine

guanine  cytosine

phosphate  ribose

DNA splits.

Messenger RNA forms.

Messenger RNA breaks away.

completed messenger RNA strand

## How RNA carries the genetic message

Ribonucleic acid (RNA) is similar to DNA. The RNA "backbone" has alternating sugar and phosphate groups like DNA. However, the RNA sugar is *ribose* instead of deoxyribose. Also, RNA contains a pyrimidine called *uracil* (U), in addition to adenine, guanine, and cytosine. Uracil is closely related to DNA's thymine, and the adenine nucleotide of DNA can combine with uracil as well as with thymine. This important ability allows RNA to be the "translator" of genetic information in the DNA molecule. RNA is usually a single-stranded molecule, but it can pair complementary bases like DNA and thus assume a double-helix shape.

A typical cell contains two kinds of RNA—*messenger* RNA (mRNA) and *transfer* RNA (tRNA). The mRNA is made from a template, or pattern, of separated DNA strands. Free RNA nucleotides in the cell nucleus combine with complementary nucleotides on the "unzipped" DNA molecule and form strands of mRNA. These new molecules contain an altered transcription of the genetic code that will revert back into the original genetic message during protein manufacture. For example, if the nucleotide sequence of a separated DNA strand is TAGCGATGG, the nucleotide sequence of the mRNA strand will be AUCGC-UACC (the adenine of DNA links with uracil of RNA).

After completion of the code transcription, the mRNA strand breaks free from the DNA template, leaves the cell nucleus, and travels to *binding sites* on ribosomes in the cytoplasm. There, the mRNA strand acts as a template for the assembly of amino acids into "beginner" proteins called *peptides*. The tRNA molecules are extremely small. They consist of triplet nucleotides, like the codons of DNA.

Each tRNA triplet has an amino acid attached to it. As tRNA and its amino acid arrives at the ribosome's binding site, it temporarily links with its nucleotide complement on the mRNA strand located there. If the nucleotide sequence of the mRNA molecule contains the message AUCGCUACC, then three tRNAs with the nucleotides TAG, CGA, and TGG would link one after the other with the mRNA and drop off their amino acids for assembly into a peptide. Thus, the original DNA message TAGCGATGG is restored and the peptide ordered by the DNA is made.

One of the nucleotide sequences of the mRNA strand calls a stop to the synthesis, and the newly made peptide or polypeptide (if long enough) breaks free and travels to wherever it is needed. The rule is as follows: one gene (DNA codon) orders the synthesis of only one kind of peptide. However, a given mRNA strand may contain many thousands of A, U, C, or G nucleotides, resulting in the synthesis of heavy, long-chained polypeptide molecules (proteins).

## The Krebs cycle—a cell energy provider

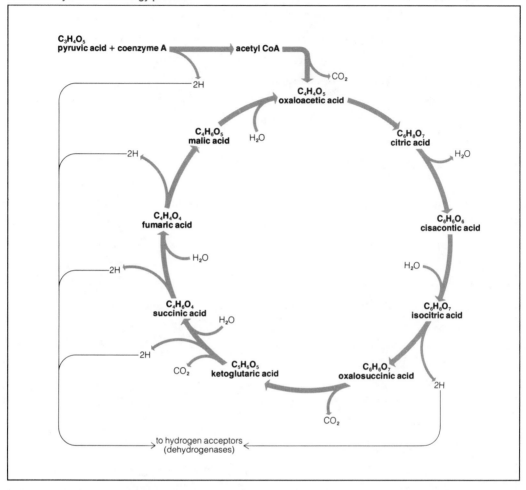

### The Krebs cycle—a cell energy provider

All living things need energy. The essential source of all energy on earth is the sun's radiant energy. However, this energy must be in a form usable by the cell. Usable energy is provided by the chemical bonds of certain molecules in the cell. Energy is generated when such organic compounds as glucose sugar are oxidized. In oxidation, hydrogen atoms are removed from one compound and transferred to another. The compound that accepts the hydrogen atoms is reduced.

Glucose is an important food substance that provides some energy. In the 1800's, the first studies of the chemical transformations in cells dealt with the chemical breakdown of glucose into ethyl alcohol. Later studies revealed the oxidation-reduction reactions of *glycolysis,* when glycogen breaks down into pyruvic acid. In glycolysis, energy is released from the chemical bonds of inorganic *phosphate groups.*

The key energy molecule is *adenosine triphosphate* (ATP). It contains three high-energy phosphate bonds. Energy is released when ATP loses one of its high-energy bonds and becomes adenosine diphosphate (ADP). The reaction is reversible, however, and energy can be stored when ADP gains a high-energy bond and converts back to ATP. But scientists have noted that glycolysis cannot provide all the energy generated in a cell. It was later found that the *Krebs cycle* produces most of the cell's

energy. Also called the citric acid cycle, The Krebs cycle is shown above. It is so packed with energy that it generates about 20 times more energy than glycolysis.

The Krebs cycle begins with pyruvic acid and coenzyme A reacting to produce acetyl coA. In turn, acetyl coA acts on oxaloacetic acid to form citric acid. The cycle continues until its completion, when oxaloacetic acid is formed again and acetyl coA restarts the cycle. In short, what happens is that pyruvic acid is broken down into carbon dioxide molecules. Also, pairs of hydrogen atoms are transferred to a group of hydrogen-accepting coenzymes that are part of the *respiratory cycle.* ATP and water molecules are produced during the respiratory cycle. The coenzymes NAD (nicotinamide adenine dinucleotide) and FAD (flavin adenine dinucleotide) are oxidized in the process. Involved also are dehydrogenase and a chemical group called the cytochromes.

The oxidation-reduction reactions that result in ATP formation take place in the cell's "powerhouses"—the mitochondria. The process is called *oxidative phosphorylation.* Oxidative phosphorylation is responsible for energizing a host of cell activities, including the active transport of large molecules across the cell membrane. It also provides the energy needed for carbohydrate, fat, and protein synthesis.

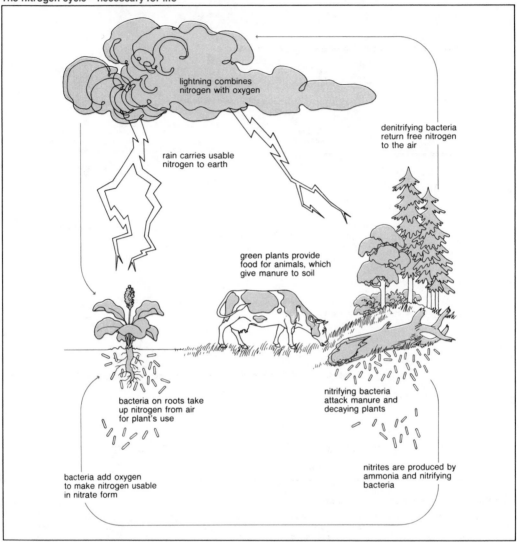

lightning combines nitrogen with oxygen

denitrifying bacteria return free nitrogen to the air

rain carries usable nitrogen to earth

green plants provide food for animals, which give manure to soil

bacteria on roots take up nitrogen from air for plant's use

nitrifying bacteria attack manure and decaying plants

bacteria add oxygen to make nitrogen usable in nitrate form

nitrites are produced by ammonia and nitrifying bacteria

## The nitrogen cycle—necessary for life

Nitrogen is one of the most important chemicals of life. All living things need nitrogen for protein construction. Nearly 80 per cent of the atmosphere is made of free nitrogen in gas form. But most living things cannot use nitrogen gas for protein synthesis. It must be combined with oxygen and other chemicals into nitrate compounds. Animals cannot use nitrogen compounds directly to manufacture proteins and must eat plants or other animals to get the necessary nitrogen.

In nature, free nitrogen is converted into usable nitrogen compounds by a cycle containing two processes—one requiring lightning energy and the other using a chemical conversion by certain bacteria. Lightning flashes combine nitrogen and oxygen gases into nitrogen dioxide, which then joins with the water in rainfall to form nitric acid. Soil chemicals react with the nitric acid to form nitrate compounds, which green plants take up through their roots and use for making proteins. Later, some animals eat the plants and use the plant protein for making animal protein.

But the lightning method of making nitrates does not provide enough usable nitrogen to fulfill the needs of all living things. The conversion action of *nitrogen-fixing* bacteria provides the rest.

Some bacteria are able to *fix* nitrogen, or transform nitrogen gas in the air directly into the nitrates needed by the bacterial cells for their own protein manufacture. These bacteria live on the roots of legume plants, such as peas, clover, and alfalfa. The extra amounts of nitrates made by the nitrogen-fixing bacteria go into the soil, where they can be taken up by plant roots. When plants and animals die, decay bacteria break down body proteins and release ammonia, a gas that contains nitrogen and hydrogen. The ammonia that remains in the soil is changed into nitrite by *nitrifying* bacteria. Oxygen is then added to the nitrites by bacteria to form usable nitrates again. However, some of the body proteins during plant and animal decay are converted to nitrogen gas by *denitrifying* bacteria and released into the air for another turn of the nitrogen cycle.

# 2. Facts about botany

Botany is a study of plant life. The plant kingdom is a very large part of the living world. More than 350,000 different kinds of plants exist. They range from tiny, one-celled plants, such as bacteria, to giant redwood trees. At the lowest level of the plant world, plants and animals are sometimes indistinguishable because some "plants" behave more like "animals." However, at more advanced levels, plants are clearly distinguished from animals.

A key characteristic of plants is the way that most plants get food. They make it directly from carbon dioxide and water by *photosynthesis*. The action of sun energy on plant chlorophyll makes possible the conversion of carbon dioxide and water into glucose, a food sugar. One of the by-products of plant photosynthesis is free oxygen, which helps maintain oxygen levels in the air. This is important for animals, too, because they also need oxygen for their life processes. However, not all plants are able to photosynthesize their food. Some are parasites, drawing their food directly from other organisms. Fungi are examples of parasites. They sometimes can be seen growing on decaying tree trunks. These fungi perform a valuable service by preventing the accumulation of dead matter. Bacteria are other examples of plant parasites. However, they can cause harmful diseases in animals and humans.

The plant kingdom is broken down into two major categories—*nonvascular* plants and *vascular* plants. Nonvascular plants lack the roots, stems, and leaves that characterize the vascular plants. Examples of nonvascular plants are algae, fungi, and mosses. Blue-green algae are the simplest plants and have been on earth the longest. Their fossils were found on 2-billion-year-old rocks. They can live in many places and even have been found in hot springs where temp-eratures reach 80°C (176°F). The simplest nonvascular plants reproduce by simple cell division. The more complex ones have a two-stage life cycle. A gametophyte, or egg, stage is produced first, followed by a sporophyte stage, in which a stalk grows from the fertilized egg. Eventually, spores develop from the stalk tip and become the first steps in the next gametophyte stages. In the vascular plants, which are more advanced, the sporophyte stage is the main plant you commonly see—the leaves, stem, and roots. A vascular network of nutrient-carrying tubes allows food and liquids to spread throughout the plant. The roots can penetrate deep in soil to find moisture and soil chemicals needed for the plant's life processes. The stem can support many leaves, the "food factories" in which photosynthesis takes place, and thus helps increase the plant's likelihood for survival. Though important, the reproductive (gametophyte) parts of vascular plants are smaller than the main plant (sporophyte).

Vascular plants are divided into two major divisions—spore-bearers and seed plants. Ferns and other related plants reproduce by spores, which have life cycles that result in new plants. Seed plants have male (pollen) and female (egg) sex cells that produce fertilized seeds, which will grow into new plants. Seed plants are further divided into *gymnosperms* and *angiosperms*. Pines, spruces, and many other evergreen trees produce their pollen and seeds in cones. They rely on the wind to spread fertilized seeds through their range. Maples, elms, and other angiosperms produce their pollen and seeds in flowers. Although some angiosperms can fertilize themselves to produce seeds, those with flowers rely on insects to cross-pollinate flowers and produce seeds.

## Seeds—future plants

Botanists classify angiosperms according to whether the plants produce *monocot* seeds or *dicot* seeds. All angiosperms produce seeds in the ovaries of their flowers. After the fertilization of an ovule, each seed develops a tiny embryo that will grow into a new plant. The seed leaves of plant embryos are called *cotyledons* (*cots,* for short). Some angiosperms produce seeds with a single cot (monocots) and others produce seeds with two cots (dicots). The corn kernel is an example of a monocot seed. The corn embryo is protected by a *seed coat,* or testa, that completely surrounds the seed contents. A *silk scar* on the coat marks the point where the pollen tube of the corn plant, or *silk,* penetrated the ovule to fertilize it with pollen.

The cotyledon will furnish the growing corn embryo with food from the starchy *endosperm* until it develops leaves and can produce its own food. The cotyledon also protects the *plumule,* the baby plant's first bud. The plumule will develop into the stem of the new plant. The *hypocotyl* is the future root of the new plant. Its tip, the radicle, is the first part of the baby plant to break out of the seed coat. The bean is an example of a dicot seed. It has two cotyledons, but is very similar to a monocot seed. The *hilum,* also part of the monocot seed, is a scar at the point where the ovule was attached to the parent plant's ovary. The *micropyle* is a tiny hole where the pollen tube entered the ovule and fertilized it. However, unlike the grassy monocots, the bean embryo will use up all its endosperm by the time the seed germinates.

Both monocot and dicot seedlings are further classified according to the positions of their cotyledons after germination. Those seedlings that show *epigeal* germination keep their cotyledons above the ground while developing. They are usually green and can perform photosynthesis right away. Those seedlings with *hypogeal* germination, such as corn, keep their cotyledons in the soil.

## Flowers form seeds

A typical flower is held to a plant stem by the *receptacle.* The colorful *sepals* help the petals attract insects to pollinate the flower. The flower's male reproductive part is the *stamen.* It consists of an *anther* and a stalklike *filament.* Pollen grains are made and held in the anther. A number of stamens usually circle the flower's female reproductive part, the *pistil.* The pistil consists of a topmost *stigma* connected by the *style* to the vase-shaped *ovary.* When pollen grains are ripe, they are released from the anthers and caught by the sticky stigma.

Insects attracted to the flower help move pollen to the stigma. Each pollen grain then sends a pollen tube through the style and into an ovule in the ovary. Plant sperm cells in the pollen tubes fertilize the ovules, and seeds begin to develop.

## Leaf—a plant food factory

Leaves have the important job of making plant food. Each leaf is divided into two main parts—the *petiole* and the *blade.* The base of the petiole is wider than the rest of the leaf stem and holds the leaf firmly to the plant stem. Some petioles have *stipules,* tiny leaflike structures that help provide food for the plant. The blade consists of an epidermis, or outer cover, that encloses a network of veins and a spongy inner area that contains chlorophyll cells. Water needed for photosynthesis is carried through the plant and into a leaf through the petiole. The water then moves through the veins to the "factory" areas of chlorophyll cells.

When light strikes a leaf, it filters through the upper epidermis and floods the cells below. A number of pores, called *stomata,* pierce the epidermis of the leaf's underside. Stomata are valves. They let in air containing the carbon dioxide needed for photosynthesis, and they let out oxygen waste and water vapor. Stomata usually open during the day and close at night, when the plant rests and requires less carbon dioxide.

Seeds—future plants

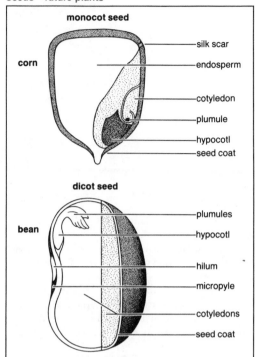

monocot seed

corn

- silk scar
- endosperm
- cotyledon
- plumule
- hypocotl
- seed coat

dicot seed

bean

- plumules
- hypocotl
- hilum
- micropyle
- cotyledons
- seed coat

Flowers form seeds

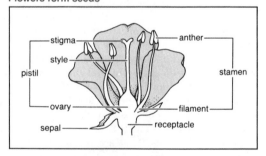

pistil — stigma, style, ovary, sepal
stamen — anther, filament, receptacle

Leaf—a plant food factory

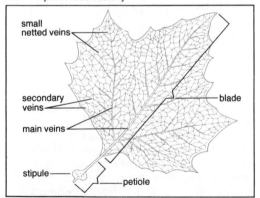

small netted veins
secondary veins
main veins
stipule
blade
petiole

## Stems support plants

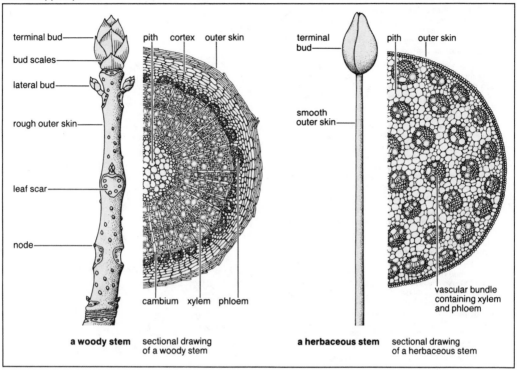

terminal bud

bud scales

lateral bud

rough outer skin

leaf scar

node

pith   cortex   outer skin

cambium   xylem   phloem

**a woody stem**   sectional drawing of a woody stem

terminal bud

smooth outer skin

pith   outer skin

vascular bundle containing xylem and phloem

**a herbaceous stem**   sectional drawing of a herbaceous stem

### Stems support plants

The stems of plants support the flowers and leaves. Stems hold these parts up to the air and sunlight for photosynthesis. Stems also conduct water and minerals from the roots to the leaves, where they are used for food manufacture. After food is made, the stem carries the sugary *sap* throughout the plant. Cells that carry water upward make up the stem's *xylem* tissue. Cells that carry sap make up the *phloem* tissue.

Depending on the species of plant, a stem may be large or small. The stem of an oak tree, for example, consists of the trunk, branches, and twigs. By contrast, the stems of a cabbage or lettuce plant are so short that the plants seem stemless. The stems of still other plants, such as the potato, are not apparent because they grow underground. Stems that grow underground are called *subterranean* stems; those that grow above ground are *aerial* stems. Aerial stems are either *woody* or *herbaceous*.

Dicots produce woody stems, and monocots produce herbaceous stems. Woody stems have a rough, brown skin. A *terminal bud* is at the topmost portion. When this bud grows, the plant grows taller. Leaflike *bud scales* protect the terminal bud and the *lateral buds* that grow from *nodes* on the stem. Lateral buds will grow either into branches or into flowers or leaves. The *leaf scar* is where a leaf petiole has separated from the stem.

A microscopic view of a cross section of a woody stem would reveal many vascular bundles of cells contained in the *cortex* under the outer skin. The cortex is comprised of woody xylem and phloem. The *cambium* is the narrow layer where xylem and phloem cells are made. New cells grow from the cambium each year. These annual rings can be seen in crosscut stems. Pith cells store food. They are in the center of woody stems. A herbaceous stem has a different arrangement. It has a smooth, green skin and has very little xylem. A crosscut view reveals many vascular bundles occurring randomly through the stem. The bundles consist of xylem and phloem. They are separated by pith.

### Kinds of roots

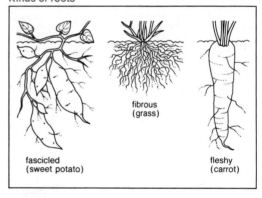

fibrous (grass)

fascicled (sweet potato)

fleshy (carrot)

### Kinds of roots

Roots draw in water and dissolved minerals from the soil. These materials are transported to the leaves by the stem's vascular system to provide the raw materials of plant growth. The root contains many *root hairs* in back of the *root tip*. Water absorbed by the root hairs is conducted upward by osmosis. Osmotic pressure pushes the water molecules in the soil upward through the plant, in order to replace the water vapor lost from the leaves by transpiration.

Three kinds of roots are illustrated—*fascicled, fibrous,* and *fleshy*. Fascicled roots are made of bundles and can grow large and deep. Fibrous roots are stringy and pierce the upper soil in many directions to extract a maximum amount of water. Fleshy roots store food in addition to providing anchorage.

## Makeup of a flowering plant

Flowering plants are the most common members of the plant world. Each flowering plant contains four main parts—the roots, stems, leaves, and flowers. Roots, stems, and leaves are called the *vegetative* parts of the plant. Flowers and their fruits and seeds are the *reproductive* parts.

The flowers develop the seeds that will allow the plant to reproduce and continue its line in the plant kingdom. The seeds are enclosed in *fruits* that develop after the female parts of the flower have been fertilized by pollen, the male sex cells of plants. Each part of a flowering plant is the result of adaptation over millions of years. The first plants were tiny, one-celled organisms capable of making their own food by photosynthesis. Eventually, communities of cells arose that were better able to cope with changing conditions of the environment by banding together into many-celled organisms. The functions of these cells in the organism became increasingly specialized—some cells becoming solely involved in reproduction activities, others developing into tissues concerned with transporting food raw materials and with food storage, and still others concentrating on the important job of food making.

Plant propagation is the responsibility of the plant's reproductive parts. When pollen is wind-blown or carried by insects from the flower's anthers to its stigma, the sticky, sugary surface of the stigma causes the pollen to germinate. A pollen tube develops and grows through the stigma and style to the ovary. In the ovary, the pollen tube penetrates an ovule, and one of the sperm cells in the tube fertilizes the egg in the ovule's *embryonic sac*. This fertilized cell will eventually develop into a new plant through a series of mitotic cell divisions that will result in different plant tissues. Another sperm cell in the pollen tube fuses with *polar nuclei* given off during meiotic cell division in the ovary and produces endosperm tissue. The endosperm will nourish the embryonic plant until it can produce food on its own.

After the ovules of a flowering plant are fertilized, they develop into seeds and the ovary becomes a fruit that encloses the seeds. Having fruit is a way the plant can scatter its seeds over a wide area. When an animal eats the fruit, the seeds are deposited in the animal's solid wastes wherever the animal flies or roams. Some seeds rely so heavily on animals that the seeds cannot germinate unless softened during animal digestion.

The time of the year during which a plant flowers is determined by its biological clock that ticks off the hours of darkness. Some plants are short-day types. They flower at the time of year when the nights are longer than the days. Long-day types flower when the nights become shorter. This *photoperiodism* also affects seed germination, the length of plant stems, and plant pigments.

## Makeup of a flowering plant

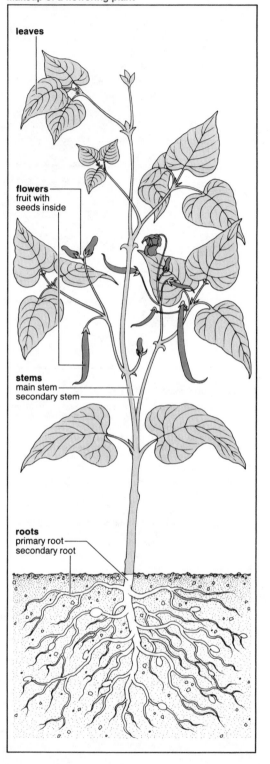

leaves

flowers
fruit with
seeds inside

stems
main stem
secondary stem

roots
primary root
secondary root

## Photosynthesis—how a green plant makes food

Green plants produce their own food by photosynthesis. Because of this, they are *autotrophs*. Plants that lack chlorophyll must get their food by parasitizing other plants; they are *heterotrophs* or *saprophytes*. Photosynthesis usually takes place in the leaves of autotrophs, but herbaceous (nonwoody) plants can also photosynthesize food in their stems.

The term *photosynthesis* comes from Greek words meaning "light" *(photo)* and "put together" *(synthesis)*. Light energy puts together carbon dioxide and water into glucose—a sugar used by the plant for food. Carbon dioxide in the air enters the leaves through the stomata on their undersides. Water is absorbed by the plant roots from the soil and conducted to the leaves through the stem's vascular system. After glucose is made, it is transported to all the plant cells, where it is *oxidized,* or burned, for the energy needed for their life processes.

The oxidative process, called *respiration,* requires oxygen. So, a plant both gives off and takes in oxygen. The atmospheric amount of carbon dioxide and oxygen is kept in balance because more carbon dioxide is used by plants during the day when they photosynthesize food, and more oxygen is used during the night for the ongoing task of cell respiration. Animals also contribute to the balance because they use oxygen in their respiratory processes and give off carbon dioxide as a waste product into the air.

Photosynthesis always requires a chlorophyll pigment, chlorophyll *a* or chlorophyll *b* being the most common. Chlorophyll *a* has a blue-green color; chlorophyll *b* is yellow-green. The chlorophyll molecule absorbs wavelengths of light and transfers the light energy into chemical energy. The chlorophyll molecules are contained in chloroplasts in the leaf or stem. A large number of chloroplasts are located near the upper surface of the leaf, where their chlorophyll molecules can be stimulated by sunlight. For example, a 1-millimeter-square section of leaf contains some 400,000 chloroplasts. Chlorophyll and sunlight will break down six molecules of carbon dioxide ($CO_2$) and six molecules of water ($H_2O$) into one molecule of glucose ($C_6H_{12}O_6$) and six molecules of oxygen gas ($O_2$). This is chemically written as: $6\ CO_2 + 6\ H_2O \xrightarrow{\text{sunlight}} C_6H_{12}O_6 + 6\ O_2 \uparrow$. Respiration in the plant cells is the reverse of photosynthesis. Glucose combines with oxygen to form carbon dioxide and water. The chemical equation for respiration is: $C_6H_{12}O_6 + 6\ O_2 \rightarrow 6\ H_2O \uparrow + 6\ CO_2 \uparrow$.

Although a green plant constantly undergoes photosynthesis during the day, not all the glucose is used for instant food. Some is changed into other sugars, or converted into starch and fats for storage, or changed into cellulose—the stiffening material for plant cell walls. Plant cells also make proteins by joining carbohydrates with nitrogen and other elements in minerals. Green plants also contain growth-regulating *auxins,* made in the tips of roots and stems.

## Photosynthesis—how a green plant makes food

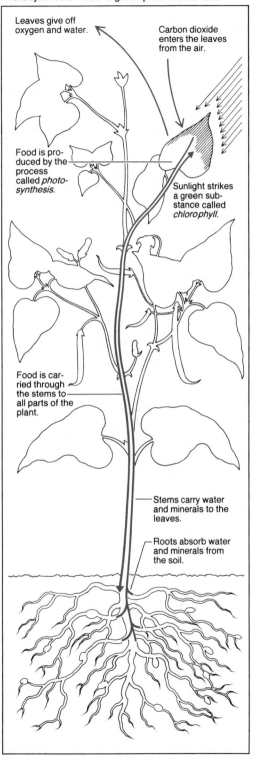

Leaves give off oxygen and water.

Carbon dioxide enters the leaves from the air.

Food is produced by the process called *photosynthesis.*

Sunlight strikes a green substance called *chlorophyll.*

Food is carried through the stems to all parts of the plant.

Stems carry water and minerals to the leaves.

Roots absorb water and minerals from the soil.

## Where photosynthesis takes place

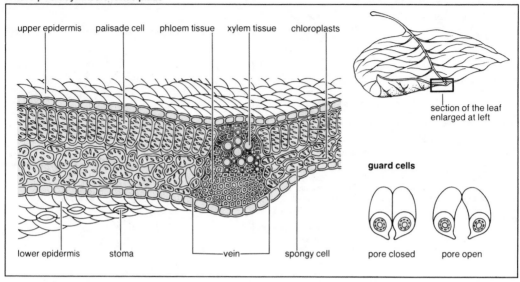

upper epidermis · palisade cell · phloem tissue · xylem tissue · chloroplasts

section of the leaf enlarged at left

guard cells

lower epidermis · stoma · vein · spongy cell · pore closed · pore open

## Where photosynthesis takes place

Under a microscope, a section of a leaf reveals the structures involved in photosynthesis and food transportation. Two kinds of cells contain chlorophyll—the green pigment of photosynthesis. They are column-shaped *palisade cells* located under the upper epidermis and the irregular *spongy cells* between the palisade cells and the lower epidermis. Water and minerals are carried to the food-making cells by the xylem tissue of the leaf veins.

The palisade and spongy cells contain chloroplasts, structures bearing the light-energy-absorbing chlorophyll. The glucose made in the chloroplasts is carried away to other parts of the plant through the phloem tissue.

Stomata are scattered throughout the lower epidermis. Each stoma contains *guard cells* that circle the stoma pore. They regulate the amount of carbon dioxide taken in and the amount of oxygen and water vapor released through the pores. The guard cells regulate the amount of gases and moisture passing through the pores.

## From seed to grown plant

The seed of a green plant *germinates,* or sprouts into a new plant, when it gets the proper amount of moisture, oxygen, and warmth. Moisture softens the seed coat and allows the embryonic plant parts to break through. Oxygen is needed for cell respiration and growth during germination. In most places, seeds lay dormant over the winter and sprout in spring. Scientists have determined that the best temperature range for germination is between 18°C (65°F) and 29°C (85°F).

Prior to germination, all the embryonic plant parts are held in by the seed coat. As the seed coat softens and splits, the *hypocotyl* emerges and forms the primary root. The *epicotyl* grows upward and begins to form the plant stem. After the stem breaks through the soil, the *cotyledons* open and free the *plumule.*

Cotyledons provide food for the seedling until it can make its own. As the stem grows upward toward the sunlight, the plumule develops into the first leaves, which begin to make plant food by photosynthesis.

## From seed to grown plant

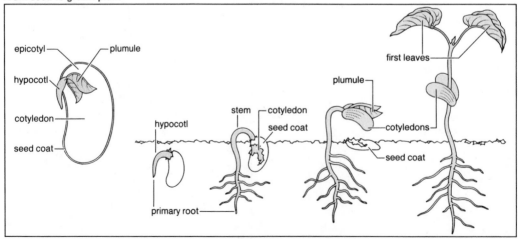

epicotyl · plumule · hypocotl · cotyledon · seed coat · hypocotl · primary root · stem · cotyledon · seed coat · plumule · first leaves · cotyledons · seed coat

# How a plant grows larger

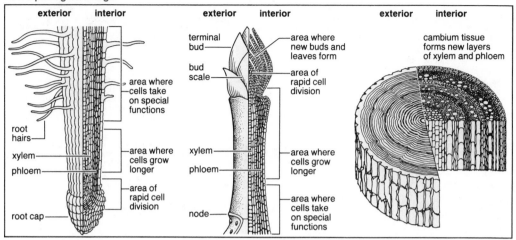

exterior | interior

terminal bud

bud scale

—area where new buds and leaves form

—area of rapid cell division

area where cells take on special functions

root hairs

xylem

phloem

root cap

—area where cells grow longer

—area of rapid cell division

xylem—

phloem—

node—

—area where cells grow longer

—area where cells take on special functions

cambium tissue forms new layers of xylem and phloem

## How a plant grows larger

Plants grow rapidly at the tips of their roots and stems. There, the cells undergo rapid mitotic divisions and push deeper into the soil or higher into the air. Cells behind the rapidly dividing ones grow longer because of auxin growth hormones.

Farther back within the plant, cells develop into specialized tissues and structures. Trees and many other plants grow wider because of a ringlike area of cell division below the bark called cambium. Each year, cambium cells lay down new xylem and phloem tissues in the roots and stems.

The root tip is protected by a tough root cap. When encountering a hard object, the root cap "tells" cells behind it to move in another direction.

## How flowering plants reproduce

The flower is the reproductive structure of angiosperm plants. A flower is a short branch of a stem containing specialized sex parts. The anthers of the flower break open and release pollen, the male sex cells. Pollen grains contain high-energy fats and are surrounded by a tough covering, permitting pollen to survive even after being blown many miles from a plant. When pollen falls on the sticky stigma of a flower, it sends a pollen tube through the style. The tube carries sperm cells, one of which will fertilize an egg in the ovary and produce a seed. The other sperm cell will fertilize the polar nuclei, and the result will be nutrient endosperm for the seed. This double fertilization is unique to angiosperms. After germination, the seed will develop into a new plant.

## How flowering plants reproduce

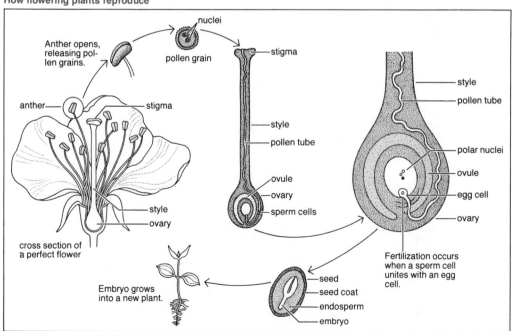

nuclei

Anther opens, releasing pollen grains.

pollen grain

—stigma

anther—

—stigma

—style

—pollen tube

—ovule

—ovary

—sperm cells

style—

—style

—pollen tube

—polar nuclei

—ovule

—egg cell

—ovary

Fertilization occurs when a sperm cell unites with an egg cell.

cross section of a perfect flower

—style

—ovary

Embryo grows into a new plant.

—seed

—seed coat

—endosperm

—embryo

## The plant kingdom

| | | |
|---|---|---|
| **Kingdom**<br>*Plantae* | 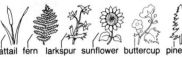  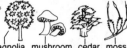 cattail fern larkspur sunflower buttercup pine alga crowfoot magnolia mushroom cedar moss | Plants |
| **Phylum**<br>*Tracheophyta* |  | Plants that have (1) xylem and phloem tissues, which carry materials from one part of the plant to another. |
| **Class**<br>*Angiospermae* |  | Plants that have (1) xylem and phloem tissues and (2) flowers that have *ovaries,* structures that protect the fertilized sex cells as they develop into seeds. |
| **Order**<br>*Ranales* |  | Plants that have (1) xylem and phloem tissues, (2) flowers that have ovaries, and (3) floral parts (petals, sepals, stamens) that grow from beneath the ovary. |
| **Family**<br>*Ranunculaceae* |   | Plants that have (1) xylem and phloem tissues, (2) flowers that have ovaries, (3) floral parts growing from beneath the ovary, and (4) many spirally arranged stamens. |
| **Genus**<br>*Ranunculus* | | Plants that have (1) xylem and phloem tissues, (2) flowers that have ovaries, (3) floral parts growing from beneath the ovary, (4) many spirally arranged stamens, and (5) all petals exactly alike. |
| **Species**<br>*Ranunculus acris* |  | Plants that have (1) xylem and phloem tissues, (2) flowers that have ovaries, (3) floral parts growing from beneath the ovary, (4) many spirally arranged stamens, (5) all petals exactly alike, and (6) yellow flowers. |

## The plant kingdom

Most plants and animals have common names in all languages of the world. But if scientists did not have a working knowledge of all these languages, they would have a difficult time discussing or writing about living things by common names. As a result, an international committee of scientists has formulated a Latin scientific name for every living thing. For example, the scientific name of a tea rose is *Rosa odorata. Rosa* is the name of the *genus,* or group, to which the plant belongs; *odorata* is the *species,* or individual name.

The generic and specific names are always given together. This is called the binomial (two-name) nomenclature system of classifying living things. It was devised by Carolus Linnaeus, an 18th century Swedish botanist.

All living things are ordinarily classified in seven major groups. Each descending rank narrows the classification of the plant or animal. The groups are: (1) kingdom, (2) phylum (plural: phyla), (3) class, (4) order, (5) family, (6) genus, and (7) species.

The plant kingdom *Plantae* is divided into 10 phyla. All plants with vascular tissues belong to the phylum *Tracheophyta.* All tracheophytes with flowers are in the class *Angiospermae.* Angiosperms with floral parts beneath the plant ovary belong to the order *Ranales.* If the stamens of these plants occur in spirals, they belong to the family *Ranunculaceae.* If members of this family have petals that are exactly alike, they belong to the genus *Ranunculus.* Any member of this genus having yellow flower petals is *Ranunculus acris,* a flower that you commonly call a "buttercup."

# 3. Facts about zoology

Zoology is the study of animals. There is an enormous number of animals on earth, about a million species. Unlike most plants, animals are *heterotrophs;* they must get food energy from plants or from other animals that they eat. Animals live nearly everywhere on earth—in the oceans, on land, in trees. Some attach themselves to underwater rocks and never budge from the site; others run or fly great distances. Animals have a wide variety of body forms and structures. A paramecium consists only of a single, specialized cell. A whale, the largest kind of animal, contains millions of cells.

Basically, animals are divided into *invertebrates,* or animals without backbones, and *vertebrates,* or animals with backbones. Ninety-five per cent of all animals are invertebrates. Some of them are sim-

ple animals, such as sponges. Jellyfish and sea anemones are more advanced than sponges because they contain two kinds of basic tissue, an inner *endoderm* that lines the digestive cavity and an outer *ectoderm* that covers the body. Planarians are still more advanced, having a third, bulky tissue called *mesoderm.*

The largest phylum of animals consists of the arthropods, a group that includes insects, shellfish, and spiders. Three out of four animal species are arthropods. Vertebrate animals have protected spinal cords. The great classes of vertebrates are fish, amphibians, reptiles, birds, and mammals. The first three are cold-blooded; birds and mammals are warm-blooded and have heat regulators to help them survive drastic temperature changes.

## How invertebrates and vertebrates differ

The nerve network in the bodies of many kinds of animals helps them respond to changes in the *environment,* or surroundings. Nerves with incoming messages about conditions in the environment are called *sensory* nerves. Nerves with outgoing messages telling the body how to react to environmental changes are called *motor* nerves. Sensory and motor nerves in some kinds of animals are contained in a main nerve called the *spinal cord.*

Invertebrate animals, such as the centipede, lack a protective backbone around the main nerve. The invertebrate's main nerve usually lies unprotected near the *ventral,* or belly, part of the body, as shown in the diagram (the simplest invertebrates do not have a main nerve). Invertebrates include amebas, sponges, starfish, mollusks, and insects. Invertebrates are commonly known as *lower animals.*

Vertebrates, animals with backbones, are *higher animals.* The main nerve of a vertebrate is located near the *dorsal,* or back, part of the body. The main nerve of vertebrates is protected by a bony enclosure, as illustrated. Vertebrates include fishes, amphibians, reptiles, birds, and mammals. A small marine animal called amphioxus has a *notochord,* a rod of cartilage that serves as a backbone and partly protects the main nerve. The amphioxus (not illustrated) is regarded as the link between the lower and higher animals. A notochord is present in the embryos of all vertebrates. However, as the embryos of the higher vertebrates develop, the notochord cartilage is replaced by bone, and *vertebra,* or bony segments, develop around the spinal cord.

## How invertebrates and vertebrates differ

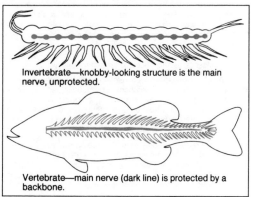

Invertebrate—knobby-looking structure is the main nerve, unprotected.

Vertebrate—main nerve (dark line) is protected by a backbone.

## How animals reproduce

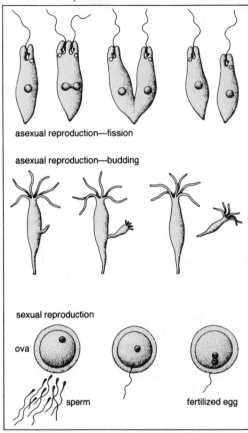

asexual reproduction—fission

asexual reproduction—budding

sexual reproduction

ova

sperm

fertilized egg

## How different animals breathe

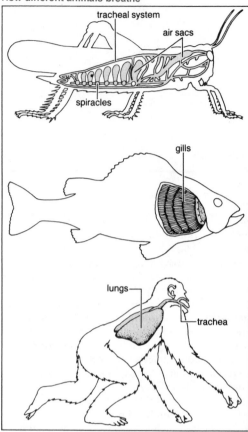

tracheal system

air sacs

spiracles

gills

lungs

trachea

## How animals reproduce

All species of animals *reproduce,* or make more of their kind. Offspring are formed by one of two ways—asexual reproduction or sexual reproduction. *Asexual reproduction* requires only one parent to produce offspring. *Sexual reproduction* requires a male and a female parent. Many of the simplest animals usually reproduce asexually. These include protozoans, sponges, jellyfish, flatworms, and sea squirts. But they sometimes reproduce sexually, too. Most other animals reproduce only sexually.

One kind of asexual reproduction involves division of the parent into two new organisms. Planarians reproduce in this way. Some sponges and hydra reproduce asexually by budding. Small projections, or buds, grow from the side of the parent's body. Some of the buds develop their own feeding organs, and then break off from the parent as individuals.

Animals that reproduce only sexually have special sex cells to produce their young. Female sex cells are called *eggs,* or *ova.* Male sex cells are called *sperm.* In the process of fertilization, a sperm unites with an egg, and the resulting *zygote* develops into a new individual. Some animals that reproduce sexually never meet their mates. For example, sea urchins release millions of eggs or sperm in the ocean for random fertilization. Some sperm cells eventually drift to the egg cells and fertilize them.

Most kinds of animals that reproduce sexually require mating. By a variety of attracting methods, male and female animals come together in order to allow the sperm cells to fertilize the egg cells. For example, female moths release a perfume to attract males. Male grasshoppers and cicadas use sounds to attract females.

## How different animals breathe

Oxygen is essential for animal life. Land animals take in oxygen from the air. Water animals get their oxygen from dissolved gases in the water. Each type of animal has special respiratory organs used for oxygen intake. A few animal species live where oxygen is not freely available. These animals, which include tapeworms and other parasites, live in intestinal organs and take in oxygen from the host's food.

Insects, the most common invertebrates, take in oxygen through air tubes called *tracheae. Spiracles,* or pores, on the outside of the insect body are connected to a tracheal air system. Body muscles pump in oxygen through the pores. The tracheal system distributes oxygen throughout the insect body. Carbon dioxide, the waste product of animal respiration, is pumped out through the spiracles.

Vertebrate animals ordinarily breathe with gills if they live in water or with lungs if they live on land. A fish gulps water and passes it over the thin tissues of its gills. The oxygen dissolved in water becomes absorbed by gill tissue (the oxygen concentration in water is *higher* than in the gills), and carbon dioxide in the gills passes into the water (the carbon dioxide concentration in water is *lower* than in the gills). The gulped water is forced out through the gill openings.

The bodies of land vertebrates develop pressure changes to bring oxygen into the lungs. Warm-blooded animals—birds and mammals—need much oxygen because their bodies use considerable energy to control temperature. Air with oxygen is inhaled into the lungs through the *trachea* and then exhaled.

162

## Earthworm and frog anatomy

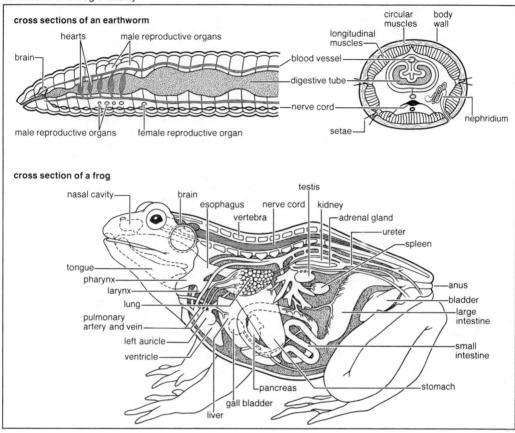

cross sections of an earthworm

hearts — male reproductive organs — circular muscles — body wall — longitudinal muscles — brain — blood vessel — digestive tube — nerve cord — nephridium — male reproductive organs — female reproductive organ — setae

cross section of a frog

nasal cavity — brain — testis — esophagus — nerve cord — kidney — vertebra — adrenal gland — ureter — spleen — tongue — pharynx — larynx — lung — anus — bladder — large intestine — pulmonary artery and vein — left auricle — ventricle — small intestine — pancreas — stomach — gall bladder — liver

## Earthworm and frog anatomy

The internal anatomy, or structure, of an animal is studied by dissection, or cutting into its preserved tissues and organs. The earthworm, an annelid worm, and the frog, an amphibian, are commonly dissected in classrooms.

The earthworm body is divided into a number of segments. A lengthwise cut of the body wall reveals the internal organs in the segments. In the forward part of the body are the earthworm's five hearts, which pump blood between the dorsal (top) and ventral (bottom) blood vessels. The digestive tube spans the entire body. The nerve cord, an extension of the brain, runs along the ventral part of the body cavity. A cross-cut of a segment reveals the longitudinal and circular muscles used by the worm to crawl. In addition to digestive tube, blood vessels, and nerve cord, *setae* and *nephridia* are exposed. Setae are bristles that prevent the worm from slipping. A nephridium removes waste products from the bloodstream and excretes them through one of many excretory tubules.

The internal anatomy of the more complex frog is best studied system by system. The *circulatory system* includes the heart, arteries, and veins. The *respiratory system* includes the skin, nose, pharynx, and lungs. The *digestive system* includes the mouth, stomach, intestines, and liver. The *excretory system* includes the skin, kidneys, and bladder. The *nervous system* includes the brain, spinal cord, nerves, and sense organs. The *endocrine system* includes the pituitary, thyroid, and adrenal glands, and the pancreas and sex organs. The *reproductive system* includes the sex organs and their ducts, or outlet tubes.

# The animal kingdom

The following abbreviated classification of the animal kingdom is one of several taxonomic rankings that zoologists have devised. Only the more common classes are listed and only one order—that of placental animals—is shown.

**Subkingdom Protozoa**—all one-celled animals.
Phylum Protozoa—protozoans.
  Subphylum Sarcomastigophora—some with flagella; some with false feet.
        Class Mastigophora—have flagella; *Euglena, Volvox.*
        Class Sarcodina—have false feet; *Ameba.*
  Subphylum Sporozoa—parasites without locomotion.
  Subphylum Cnidospora—spore-forming parasites.
  Subphylum Ciliophora—have cilia; *Paramecium.*

**Subkingdom Metazoa**—animals with many-celled tissues and organs.
Phylum Porifera—sponges.
  Class Calcarea—chalky sponges.
  Class Hexactinellida—glass sponges; *Venus's flower basket.*
  Class Demospongiae—horny sponges; *bath sponge.*
  Class Sclerospongiae—coralline sponges.
Phylum Coelenterata—coelenterates.
  Class Hydrozoa—hydroids; *Obelia, Hydra, Portuguese man-of-war.*
  Class Scyphozoa—jellyfishes.
  Class Anthozoa—corals with sea anemones.
Phylum Ctenophora—comb jellies.
Phylum Platyhelminthes—flatworms.
  Class Turbellaria—planarians; *Dugesia.*
  Class Trematoda—parasitic flukes.
  Class Cestoidea—parasitic tapeworms.
Phylum Gnathostomulida—jawed marine worms.
Phylum Nemertinea—ribbon worms.
Phylum Entoprocta—entoprocts.
Phylum Aschelminthes—cylindrical worms.
  Class Rotifera—rotifers.
  Class Gastrotricha—gastrotrichs.
  Class Kinorhyncha—have retractile proboscises.
  Class Nematoda—roundworms; *Ascaris.*
  Class Nematomorpha—horsehair worms.
Phylum Acanthocephala—spiny-headed worms.
Phylum Bryozoa—moss animals.
Phylum Phoronidea—phoronids.
Phylum Brachiopoda—lamp shells.
Phylum Mollusca—mollusks.
  Class Monoplacophora—monoplacophors.
  Class Aplacophora—solenogasters.
  Class Polyplacophora—chitons.
  Class Scaphopoda—tooth shells.
  Class Gastropoda—univalves; *limpet, abalone.*
  Class Bivalvia—bivalves; *clams, oysters.*
  Class Cephalopoda—cephalopods; *octopuses, squids.*
Phylum Annelida—segmented worms.
  Class Polychaeta—sandworms and tubeworms.
  Class Oligochaeta—earthworms.
  Class Hirudinea—leeches.
Phylum Sipunculoidea—"peanut " marine worms.
Phylum Echiuroidea—echiuroid marine worms.
Phylum Priapuloidea—"sausage" marine worms.
Phylum Arthropoda—animals with jointed feet.
  Class Merostomata—horseshoe crab.
  Class Pycnogonida—sea spiders.
  Class Arachnida—scorpions, spiders, and other arachnids.
  Class Crustacea—crabs, lobsters, and other crustaceans.

Class Insecta—insects.
Class Chilopoda—centipedes.
Class Diplopoda—millipedes.
Class Pauropoda—pauropods.
Class Symphyla—garden centipede.
Phylum Pentastomida—parasitic tongue worms.
Phylum Tardigrada—water bears.
Phylum Chaetognatha—arrow worms.
Phylum Echinodermata—echinoderms.
  Class Crinoidea—sea lillies and feather stars.
  Class Asteroidea—starfishes.
  Class Ophiuroidea—brittle stars.
  Class Echinoidea—sea urchins and sand dollars.
  Class Holothuroidea—sea cucumbers.
Phylum Pogonophora—beard worms.
Phylum Hemichordata—hemichordates.
Phylum Chordata—chordates.
  Subphylum Tunicata—tunicates.
    Class Larvacea—larvaceans.
    Class Ascidiacea—ascidians.
    Class Thaliacea—chain tunicates.
  Subphylum Caephalochordata—lancelets.
  Subphylum Agnatha—jawless vertebrates.
    Class Cyclostomata—hagfishes and lampreys.
  Subphylum Gnathostomata—jawed vertebrates.
    Class Chondrichthyes—cartilaginous fishes; *sharks, rays.*
    Class Osteichthyes—bony fishes.
    Class Amphibia—amphibians.
    Class Reptilia—reptiles.
    Class Aves—birds.
    Class Mammalia—mammals.
      Subclass Protheria—egg-laying mammals; *duckbilled platypus.*
      Subclass Theria—marsupials and placental mammals.
        Order Marsupialia—pouched mammals; *kangaroo, opossum.*
        Order Insectivora—moles and shrews.
        Order Dermoptera—flying lemurs.
        Order Chiroptera—bats.
        Order Primates—lemurs, monkeys, apes, and humans.
        Order Edentata—anteaters, sloths, armadillos.
        Order Pholidota—scaly anteater.
        Order Lagomorpha—conies, hares, and rabbits.
        Order Rodentia—rodents; *mouse, rat.*
        Order Cetacea—porpoises and whales.
        Order Carnivora—carnivores; *lion, dog.*
        Order Pinnipedia—sea lions and seals.
        Order Tubulidentata—aardvark.
        Order Proboscidea—elephants.
        Order Hydracoidea—conies.
        Order Sirenia—sea cows.
        Order Perissodactyla—odd-toed hoofed mammals; *horse, zebra.*
        Order Artiodactyla—even-toed hoofed mammals; *deer, bison.*

# 4. Facts about the human body

Human physiology deals with the manner in which the various systems of the human body work to maintain life. Some body activities go on unnoticed by us because they are not controlled on a conscious, or aware, level. Food digestion is an example. But we are quite aware of other body events, such as a toothache or the hunger pains resulting from an empty stomach.

All the body structures play some role in either getting energy from food, using that energy for cell respiration, nerve impulse energy, or muscle contraction energy, or for the generation of offspring. The skeletal and muscle systems support the body and make it move. The respiratory system maintains normal breathing so that vital oxygen is continually inhaled and carbon dioxide is exhaled. The digestive system breaks down food into its basic chemical parts, which then can be carried by the circulatory system to all body cells for energy uses. An endocrine system of hormones— chemical messengers—starts and stops many body activities at the correct time. The urinary system removes poisonous wastes from the bloodstream and excretes them from the body. The reproductive system, which is closely related to the urinary system in the body, and which is primarily under the control of hormones, prepares the stage for producing human offspring. All of these systems are under the control of the nervous system and its chief organ—the brain.

When the body systems are not operating in tune, illness results. Malfunction of the body can result from bacterial or viral invasion, lack of proper food or other nutrients, or inherited body errors. However, medical and nutritional steps can correct most of these situations. Preventive medicine is a field that attempts to maintain healthy bodies by teaching persons about how the body operates and what it needs for health.

## Table of facts about the body

Your body is an amazing complex of parts coordinated in a way that allows it to function as a healthy unit. The facts in this table are only a few of the facets of the human body. All weights and volumes are average figures for adults. Some figures are slightly lower for females because the data is based on body weight and females ordinarily weigh less than males.

Total number of bones—206.
Number of vertebrae—26 in all (7 cervical, 12 thoracic, 5 lumbar, 1 sacral [made of 5 fused bones], and 1 coccygeal [made of 4 fused bones]).
Total volume of blood—about 5 qts. (about 5 l) in a 155-lb. (70-kg) person.
Number of cells in one cubic millimeter of blood:
  Red blood cells (erythrocytes)—4.5 million–5.5 million.
  White blood cells (leucocytes)—6,000–10,000.
  Platelets (thrombocytes)—200,000–800,000.
Total volume of body water—65% of male body weight; 55% of female body weight.
Normal body temperature—98.6° F. (37° C).
Weight of the human heart—about 11 oz. (310 g) in males; about 9 oz. (255 g) in females.
Average number of heartbeats per minute—72 (the heart will beat about 3 billion times in a 70-year period).
Weight of the human brain—about 50 oz. (1,400 g) in males; about 45 oz. (1,260 g) in females.
Length of the small and large intestines—28 ft. (8.5 m)
Daily weight of sweat secreted from the skin—24.5-31.5 oz. (700-900 g).

## The human skeleton gives support

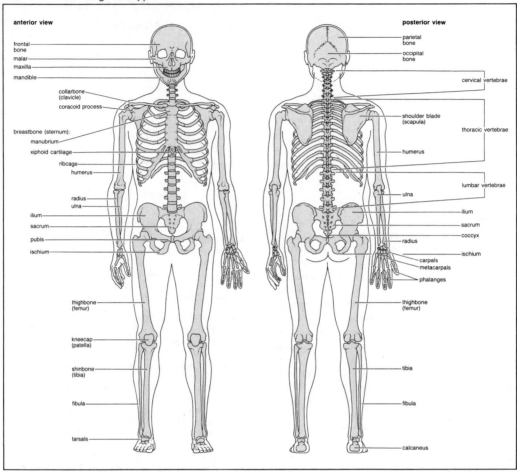

**anterior view**

frontal bone
malar
maxilla
mandible
collarbone (clavicle)
coracoid process
breastbone (sternum):
manubrium
xiphoid cartilage
ribcage
humerus
radius
ulna
ilium
sacrum
pubis
ischium
thighbone (femur)
kneecap (patella)
shinbone (tibia)
fibula
tarsals

**posterior view**

parietal bone
occipital bone
cervical vertebrae
shoulder blade (scapula)
thoracic vertebrae
humerus
lumbar vertebrae
ulna
ilium
sacrum
coccyx
radius
ischium
carpals
metacarpals
phalanges
thighbone (femur)
tibia
fibula
calcaneus

## The human skeleton gives support

The skeleton is the framework of the human body. Its hard, strong, calcium-containing bones are connected by tough cords called *ligaments.* The bony framework is divided into two components—the *axial* skeleton and the *appendicular* skeleton. The *axial skeleton* includes the skull, rib cage, and the vertebral column. The *appendicular skeleton* comprises the body limbs.

Enclosing the brain, the skull consists of close-fitting bones. It has two main parts—the *cranium* and the *face.* The cranium has eight bones—*frontal,* two *temporals,* two *parietals, occipital, sphenoid,* and *ethmoid.* The 14 bones of the face include the two *maxillae* (upper jaw) and the hinged *mandible* (lower jaw), the largest bones of the face. The other facial bones include the *palatine* (forming the back of the mouth roof), the *nasal* (nose bone), and the *zygomatics* (cheekbones).

The *vertebral column,* or backbone, contains 26 bones (33 in the embryo but 9 bones fuse into 2 bones in development). The seven *cervical* vertebrae form the neck. The first cervical vertebra is the *atlas;* it supports the skull and pivots with the second cervical vertebra, the *axis.* The 12 *thoracic* vertebrae have ribs attached to them. The first seven pairs of ribs connect directly to the *sternum,* or breastbone. The next three pairs are joined to the ribs directly above them by cartilage. The last two pairs of ribs, called *floating ribs,* are unattached to any other. Five *lumbar* vertebrae connect the upper body with the lower body. Linking

the two bony portions of the hips is the *sacrum,* made of 5 fused bones. The *coccyx,* or tailbone, is made of 4 fused bones.

The upper appendicular skeleton consists of the *pectoral girdle,* or shoulder, and the arm and hand bones suspended from it. The pectoral girdle consists of two *scapulae,* or shoulder blades, and two *clavicles,* or collarbones. The head of the *humerus,* or upper arm bone, fits into a socket under the *coracoid process* of the scapula. This ball-and-socket hinge allows the arm to have a wide range of motion. The *radius* and *ulna* are the two forearm bones. Their overlapping ends give the forearm its distinctive rotation. The eight carpal bones constitute the wrist. The five *metacarpals* form the hand and lower thumb. Fourteen *phalanges* make up the fingers and the thumb.

The lower appendicular skeleton consists of the *pelvic girdle* and the lower limb bones attached to it. The pelvic girdle consists of two hipbones formed from three fused bones (in adults)—the *ilium, ischium,* and *pubis.* The head of the *femur,* or thighbone, fits into a socket in the hipbone. The *tibia* and *fibula* are two bones that make up the lower leg. The tibia, or shinbone, is linked with the femur by a swinging joint, capped by a kneebone called the *patella.* Seven *tarsal* bones make up the ankle. The *calcaneus,* largest of the tarsals, forms the heel of the foot. Five *metatarsal* bones make up the foot itself, and 14 *phalanges* form the toes.

## Muscles make the body move

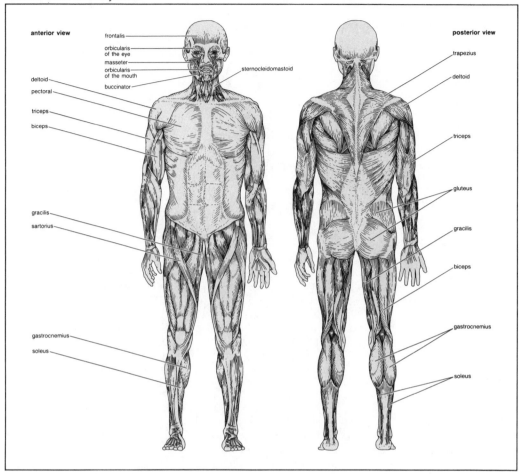

anterior view

frontalis
orbicularis of the eye
masseter
orbicularis of the mouth
buccinator
sternocleidomastoid
deltoid
pectoral
triceps
biceps
gracilis
sartorius
gastrocnemius
soleus

posterior view

trapezius
deltoid
triceps
gluteus
gracilis
biceps
gastrocnemius
soleus

## Muscles make the body move

The human body contains more than 500 muscles. They make up some 45 per cent of the total body weight. Each muscle is made of long cells called muscle fibers. These, in turn, consist of many, very thin fibers that can slide on each other. When the nerves attached to muscles trigger muscle contraction, the muscle fibers shorten as their component fibers slide over each other. During contraction, the muscle fibers shorten to about half their normal length. When a muscle is not in a state of contraction, it relaxes. The body contains three kinds of muscles—*voluntary, involuntary,* and *cardiac.*

Voluntary muscles are so called because we can control their contractions. Many of them are attached to the body's bony framework and are thus called *skeletal* muscles. They are responsible for body movement and posture. Involuntary, or smooth, muscles are part of the various digestive and endocrine organs, and also line the blood vessels. Their contractions are controlled by portions of the brain that operate at below-conscious levels, making us unaware, for instance, of every contraction of blood-vessel muscles. Cardiac, or heart, muscle fibers are interconnected in a way that allows a uniform spread of the electrical signals that trigger a heartbeat.

A skeletal muscle consists of three sections—*origin, body,* and *insertion.* The origin is one end of the muscle ordinarily fixed to an anchoring bone. The body is the bulk of the muscle. The insertion is the other end, fixed to the bone it will move. Some skeletal muscles are grouped in *antagonistic* pairs. When one contracts, the other relaxes.

Some of the major skeletal muscles are illustrated above. However, it is important to remember that individual body movements are usually the result of many muscles acting together as mechanical units. The facial muscles, such as the *frontalis,* the *orbicularis* of the eye, and the *orbicularis* of the mouth, give rise to the facial expressions so characteristic of humans and other primates. The *buccinator,* another facial muscle, controls cheek movements. The *masseter* is the powerful muscle that closes the jaw. The *sternocleidomastoid* is a neck muscle that draws the head downward toward the shoulder. The *deltoid* is a large, triangular shoulder muscle that *abducts* the arm—pulls it away from the side of the body. The *biceps* flexes the arm and forearm. Its antagonist, the *triceps,* pulls the arm downward and parallel to the body. The *pectoral* muscle *adducts* the arm—pulls it in toward the side of the body. The *gluteus* muscles in the lower back move and rotate the thigh. The *gracilis,* a thin muscle on the inner edge of the thigh, pulls the thigh in toward the center of the body and flexes the leg. The *sartorius,* which is the longest muscle in the body, flexes the thigh and leg, and also rotates the thigh. The *biceps* of the leg flexes and rotates that limb. The *gastrocnemius* makes up most of the leg calf. It and the *soleus* flex the foot.

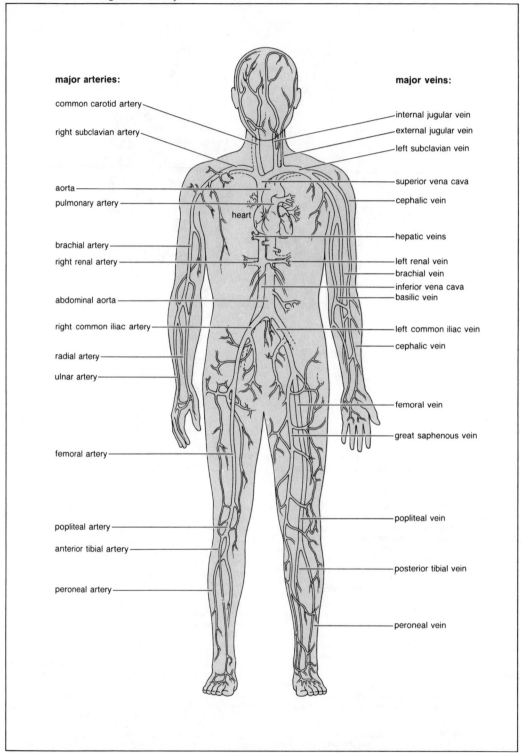

**major arteries:**

common carotid artery

right subclavian artery

aorta

pulmonary artery

heart

brachial artery

right renal artery

abdominal aorta

right common iliac artery

radial artery

ulnar artery

femoral artery

popliteal artery

anterior tibial artery

peroneal artery

**major veins:**

internal jugular vein

external jugular vein

left subclavian vein

superior vena cava

cephalic vein

hepatic veins

left renal vein

brachial vein

inferior vena cava

basilic vein

left common iliac vein

cephalic vein

femoral vein

great saphenous vein

popliteal vein

posterior tibial vein

peroneal vein

## Blood circulates throughout the body

The more than 5 quarts (4.75 liters) of blood in the body circulate once every minute. Blood carries vital food and oxygen to all cells and removes the waste products of metabolism. With cells able to destroy harmful bacteria and viruses, blood is important in the body's fight against disease. Blood consists of a solid part and a liquid, or *plasma*, part of carbohydrates, fats, and proteins in a watery solution.

Blood has three kinds of cells—*red blood cells* (erythrocytes), *white blood cells* (leukocytes), and *platelets* (thrombocytes). Red blood cells are disks with flattened centers where nuclei once existed. They contain a red protein called *hemoglobin*. Oxygen combines with hemoglobin and is carried by the erythrocytes to other cells for respiration. Every minute, the body needs 250 cubic cm of oxygen. Red blood cells wear out quickly and are replaced constantly. The body makes about 21 billion erythrocytes each day. White blood cells mobilize and attack foreign substances that invade the bloodstream. These defense cells have chemical sensors that detect bacteria, viruses, or other harmful intruders. Some white blood cells are *phagocytes*; they eat the intruders. Others coat the intruders in a way that makes them "tasty" to phagocytes. Still others maintain a memory system to help the body defend against similar intruders in the future. The platelets plug small leaks in the blood vessels. They work in combination with fibery proteins in plasma to seal small holes and cuts with *blood clots*.

The circulatory system is a closed network of *arteries, veins,* and *capillaries*. Arteries carry oxygenated blood from the lungs to the rest of the body. Arteries are linked with veins, which bring blood back to the lungs for more oxygen. Tiny, thin-walled capillaries are the links. All body tissues have capillaries. Oxygen and food molecules pass from the capillaries into surrounding tissue cells. In turn, carbon dioxide and nitrogenous wastes pass into the capillaries for removal. Carbon dioxide is transported to the lungs for exhalation; nitrogenous wastes are carried to the kidneys for excretion.

Arteries and veins have slightly different structures. The walls of arteries are circled by involuntary (smooth) muscles and elastic tissue. The elastic nature of the arterial wall maintains the wave, or *pulse,* of high-pressure blood flow when blood is pumped from the *heart*. The walls of veins have less elastic tissue and have longer openings than arteries to accommodate the low-pressure blood flow back to the heart. Most arteries have namesake veins; and most blood vessels occur in pairs, one for each side of the body.

The *aorta* is the major artery. Oxygenated blood returned from the lungs through the *pulmonary* veins (the only case of a vein carrying oxygenated blood) is pumped to the body through the aorta. The *common carotid* and *subclavian* arteries are offshoots of the aorta. Blood is pumped to the head through the common carotid and to the upper limbs through the right and left subclavians. The *brachial* artery feeds the upper arm; the *radial* and *ulnar* arteries, the forearm and hand. The *internal* and *external jugular* veins drain the head. The *pulmonary* artery carries deoxygenated blood to the lungs for oxygenation (the only case of an artery carrying deoxygenated blood). The *abdominal aorta* brings arterial blood to the trunk and lower limbs. Offshoots of the abdominal aorta transport blood to the digestive glands and organs. The *renal* arteries feed the kidneys and carry waste products there for excretion. The abdominal aorta splits into the *common iliac* arteries, which continue into the legs as the *femoral* arteries. The *popliteal* artery threads in back of the knee joint, the *anterior tibial* artery runs the course of the shinbone, and the *peroneal* artery ends near the heel. Deoxygenated blood from the lower limbs first flows through the *great saphenous* veins, into the *common iliac* veins, and then into the *inferior vena cava,* which drains the lower limbs and trunk. The *hepatic* vein stems from the liver to the inferior vena cava. The *basilic, brachial,* and *cephalic* veins drain the arm. The *subclavian* veins connect with the *superior vena cava.* Through the two venae cavae, all venous blood flows back into the heart, where the blood will again be pumped to the lungs for more oxygen and again throughout the body.

## The heart pumps blood

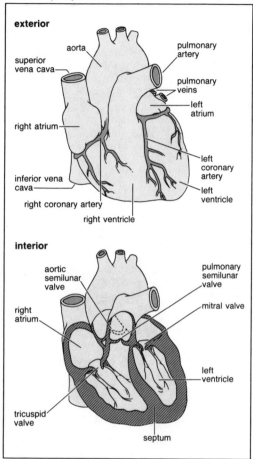

**exterior**

aorta

pulmonary artery

superior vena cava

pulmonary veins

left atrium

right atrium

left coronary artery

inferior vena cava

left ventricle

right coronary artery

right ventricle

**interior**

aortic semilunar valve

pulmonary semilunar valve

mitral valve

right atrium

left ventricle

tricuspid valve

septum

### The heart pumps blood

The heart is a fist-sized muscular pump. It beats about 72 times every minute. The heart contains four chambers—*right atrium, left atrium, right ventricle,* and *left ventricle.* The two ventricles are separated by a thick *septum.* The atria are separated from the ventricles by valves. Once blood moves from the atria to the ventricles, the valves prevent it from backing into the atria. This is also true of the valves in the pulmonary artery and the aorta.

Each heartbeat has two stages—a relaxation stage (diastole) and a contraction (systole). During the first part of the relaxation stage, deoxygenated blood from the body enters the right atrium from the inferior and superior venae cavae. At the same time, oxygenated blood from the lungs enters the left atrium from the pulmonary veins. As the atria fill, the *tricuspid* and *mitral valves* open, allowing blood into both ventricles. An electrical wave from the heart's pacemaker in the right atrium causes the ventricles to contract. Blood in the right ventricle pushes open the *pulmonary semilunar valve* and moves through the pulmonary artery to the lungs for oxygenation. At the same time, blood in the left ventricle pushes open the *aortic semilunar valve* and moves into the aorta for distribution throughout the body.

Like other muscles, the heart needs blood with food and oxygen, and it requires removal of waste products. The *coronary* arteries and veins provide for this crucial blood circulation to the heart.

**The digestive system**

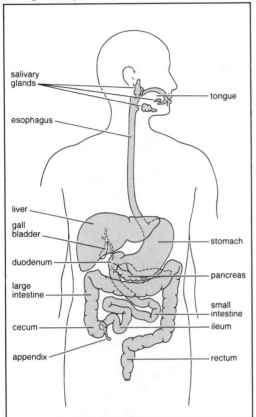

**How you breathe**

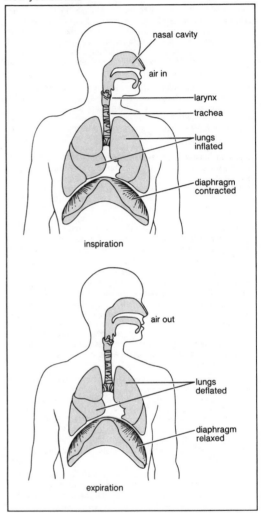

nasal cavity
air in
larynx
trachea
lungs inflated
diaphragm contracted

inspiration

air out
lungs deflated
diaphragm relaxed

expiration

## The digestive system

The digestion of food begins in the mouth. Enzymes from the *salivary glands* begin to reduce starches into sugars, and the *tongue* starts the swallowing process. Chewed food is swallowed down the 10-inch-long (250 millimeters) *esophagus* into the *stomach*. Stomach enzymes and acids continue to reduce starches to sugars and break down proteins to peptides and amino acids. The stomach churns and stores the digested food, now called *chyme*, and releases small amounts of it into the 12-inch-long (300 millimeters) *duodenum*, the first part of the small intestine.

Blood vessels in the many wall projections of the small intestine absorb the digested food molecules for distribution throughout the body. Muscles in the walls of the 22-foot-long (660 centimeters) small intestine contract in a rhythmic wave called peristalsis that moves the chyme to the *ileum* of the small intestine and into the *cecum*, the start of the *large intestine*. The cecum has a functionless *appendix*, which sometimes becomes seriously inflamed. When chyme gets to the 5-foot-long (150 centimeters) large intestine, most of the food has been absorbed into the bloodstream. Water is removed from the liquidlike remains in the large intestine until a hard feces is formed and eliminated.

Some accessory organs aid food digestion and distribution. The *liver*, the largest internal organ, receives food from the digestive system and determines if it will be used or stored. The liver also removes poisons from the blood and reduces them to bile. The *gall bladder* stores and concentrates bile, and empties it into the digestive tract. The *pancreas* produces insulin, an important hormone in carbohydrate metabolism, and the pancreas also makes digestive enzymes.

## How you breathe

Breathing is a rhythmic activity that brings oxygen-rich air into the lungs and removes carbon-dioxide-filled air from them. The *diaphragm*, a large, dome-shaped muscle that separates the chest cavity from the abdominal cavity, plays a key part in breathing. Rib and belly muscles also help. When the diaphragm contracts, the chest cavity becomes larger and gains volume. Because of this, a suction develops as pressure in the chest drops. Outside air rushes in through the nasal cavity and/or mouth and then down the *trachea*, or windpipe, to inflate the lungs. This process is called *inspiration*. During *expiration*, the diaphragm relaxes and reduces the chest volume. As a result, pressure builds in the chest cavity, deflating the lungs or forcing air out of them.

At the ends of the long air passages are spongy air sacs called *alveoli*, surrounded by many capillaries. Oxygen enters the bloodstream and carbon dioxide leaves it at the alveoli, which eventually link with the trachea.

Voice sounds are controlled by vocal cords in the *larynx*, or voice box, located above the trachea. Sounds are made when air passes across the vocal cords and vibrates them.

## The female reproductive system

Inside the female body, *ovaries*—the primary female reproductive organs—produce *ova*, or eggs. Accessory reproductive organs in a female help move an egg to a place where it can be fertilized by a male sperm or harbor the developing human embryo when fertilization occurs and pregnancy begins.

The monthly cycle of egg release, pregnancy preparation, and uterine tissue breakdown if pregnancy does not occur is called the *menstrual cycle*. It usually lasts 28 days. Hormones from the brain start the menstrual cycle by triggering development of a *follicle* in an ovary. The ripening follicle releases its own hormones, called *estrogens,* which thicken the lining of the uterus and develop a rich blood supply in readiness for harboring a fertilized egg. At about the 14th day of the menstrual cycle, *ovulation* occurs. An egg is released from an ovary, captured by the fingery end of a *Fallopian tube*, and transported through the tube to the uterus. If sperm are in the tube, one of them will probably fertilize the egg. But if the egg is not fertilized, it dies within 12 hours and passes out of the body. The uterine lining will then be sloughed off at the end of the cycle, and discharged from the body through the *vagina* and past the *vulva*. However, if fertilization takes place, the developing embryo will implant or attach itself to the uterine lining, and a baby will grow in the uterus until it is born nine months later.

Girls mature usually between 12 and 16 years of age, but it is perfectly normal to mature earlier or later than those years. Sex hormones released from the brain and developing follicles cause the body changes of adolescence.

**The female reproductive system**

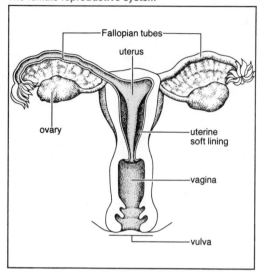

## The male reproductive system

The male reproductive system shares many of its parts with the urinary system that removes liquid wastes from the body. The primary male reproductive organ is the *testicle,* or testis. Each of the two testes contains many tiny tubes in which sperm cells develop.

The testicles are suspended from the body in a saclike *scrotum.* Suspension in the scrotum keeps the sperm in the testicles away from the destructive heat of the abdominal cavity. Accessory reproductive structures transport the sperm cells out of storage sites on top of the testicles during the process of *ejaculation,* when they are forced through an erect *penis.*

The penis consists of spongy tissue around the *urethra,* a tube between the *urinary bladder* and the end of the penis. When the bladder becomes filled, voluntary muscles in the penis can relax and permit a flow of urine. Each *vas deferens,* one of a pair of tubes from the testicles, connects with the urethra. An involved process of stimulation allows blood to engorge the spongy tissue of the penis, causing it to become erect. Before ejaculation, sperm cells are mixed with lubricating secretions of the *seminal vesicles, prostate,* and other glands, resulting in a fluid called *semen.* During ejaculation, the semen is discharged from the penis.

Boys usually begin to produce sperm between the ages of 11 and 15. Hormones from the brain start the production of sperm and the development of secondary sex characteristics. In males, these include voice deepening and the growth of pubic, underarm, and facial hair.

**The male reproductive system**

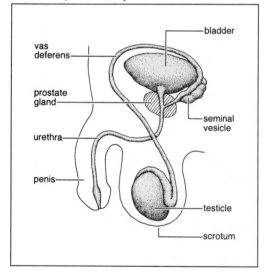

# The nervous system—a communications network

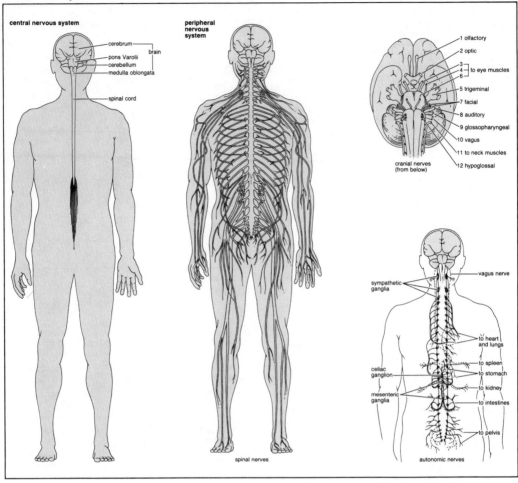

**central nervous system**

cerebrum
brain
pons Varolii
cerebellum
medulla oblongata

spinal cord

**peripheral nervous system**

spinal nerves

1 olfactory
2 optic
3
4 — to eye muscles
6
5 trigeminal
7 facial
8 auditory
9 glossopharyngeal
10 vagus
11 to neck muscles
12 hypoglossal

cranial nerves (from below)

vagus nerve

sympathetic ganglia

to heart and lungs
to spleen
to stomach

celiac ganglion

to kidney

mesenteric ganglia

to intestines

to pelvis

autonomic nerves

## The nervous system—a communications network

The *central, peripheral,* and *autonomic* nervous systems make up the body's communications network. The central nervous system consists of the *brain* and *spinal cord.* The peripheral nervous system contains *cranial* and *spinal* nerves. The autonomic nervous system has cranial nerves and nerves from bundles called *ganglia* near the spinal cord. Most nerve information is sent to the brain for interpretation and then to the muscles for action. Nerve impulses can only travel in one direction. Incoming signals are passed along *sensory* nerves, while outgoing signals are passed along *motor* nerves.

The brain is the key part of the nervous system. The *cerebrum* controls memory, awareness, motivation, and other "higher" mental activities. The *pons, cerebellum,* and *medulla* control "lower" activities, such as balancing or breathing.

The 12 cranial nerves have sensory, motor, or combined fibers. Some of the major sensory nerves are: the *olfactory* (smell), *optic* (sight), and *auditory* (hearing). The *vagus* has motor fibers that control many internal activities, including heartbeat.

In the autonomic system (over which you have no conscious control), the *sympathetic* ganglia serve autonomic nerves in the upper body; the *celiac* and *mesenteric* ganglia send off fibers to the stomach, intestines, and other abdominal organs.

## The lymphatic system—drainage and defense

The lymphatic system has two functions—it helps the veins drain body tissues, and it plays a major part in body defense against infection. Like the circulatory system, the lymphatic system is a network of tubular vessels. They carry tissue fluid called *lymph* and range from capillary size to large-diameter vessels. However, the lymphatic system is not a closed system and eventually drains into the large veins below the neck. The *thoracic duct,* the main collector of lymph fluid, empties into the left subclavian vein. The lymphatic vessels also serve to drain fat particles from the body's tissues after fatty foods are absorbed by the intestine.

The work of body defense goes on in *lymph glands,* filters scattered throughout the lymph pathways. Bacteria and other harmful substances easily get into the lymphatic system through the many lymph capillaries in the skin and elsewhere. Once in the lymph flow, bacteria can infect the entire body. However, as lymph fluid filters through the lymph glands, special cells in them attack and destroy the bacteria.

The *spleen,* a lymphoid organ near the left kidney, also fights infection. Both the spleen and the lymph glands manufacture *lymphocytes,* which are special cells that can destroy foreign substances in the body.

**The lymphatic system—drainage and defense**

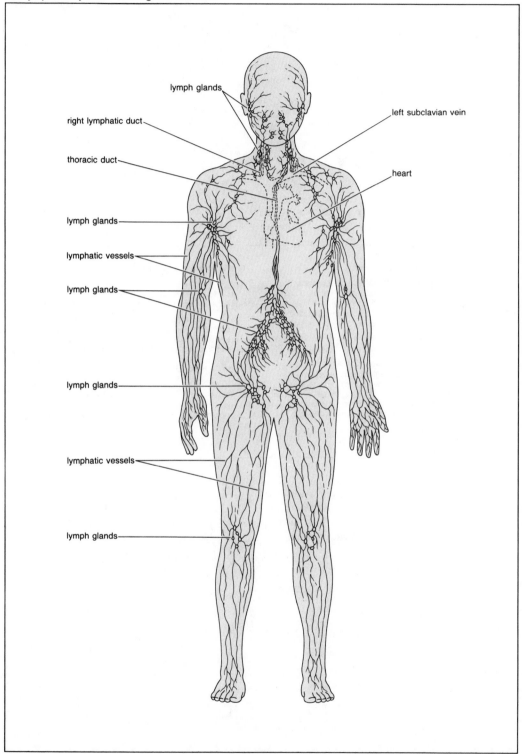

lymph glands

right lymphatic duct

thoracic duct

lymph glands

lymphatic vessels

lymph glands

lymph glands

lymphatic vessels

lymph glands

left subclavian vein

heart

## The eye—your window to the world

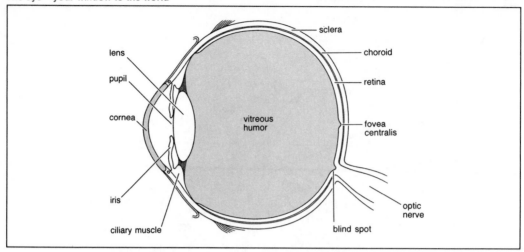

---

## The eye—your window to the world

Incoming light rays enter the eye through the clear *cornea*. Then they pass through the *pupil,* an adjustable hole controlled by the *iris* muscles. The light rays are focused by the *lens*—made thicker or thinner by the *ciliary muscle* to accommodate near and far objects—as a reduced and inverted image on the *retina.*

The watery *aqueous humor* behind the lens maintains the eyeball shape. The *sclera* is the tough, white outer coat of the eyeball.

The *choroid* layer contains blood vessels. The retina has rods, cones, and nerve cells that transmit information about the inverted retinal image along the optic nerve to a visual center in the brain. There, the image is reverted to its rightside-up position. The *fovea centralis* is the center point of the retina. The *blind spot* is a small area where the retinal blood vessels emerge; it is insensitive to light.

## The ear enables you to hear

The ear is a complex hearing and balance organ. In the outer ear, sound waves are caught by the *auricle* and channeled through the *auditory canal* to the *tympanum,* or eardrum.

As sound vibrates the eardrum, the vibrations are transmitted through three delicate bones of the middle ear—*the malleus, incus,* and *stapes*—to the *oval window.* There, the vibrations are passed to fluid in the *cochlea* of the middle ear. Hair cells in the cochlea pick up the vibrations and send them along the *cochlear nerve* to the brain for translation as sounds.

Three *semicircular canals* in the inner ear contain fluid and tiny "pebbles" that shift position whenever the body tilts out of line. This information is sent to the brain very rapidly over the *vestibular nerve* for corrective muscle action to restore body equilibrium.

## The ear enables you to hear

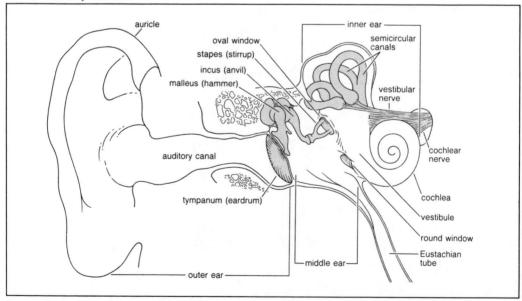

## The nose—organ of smell

The sense of smell is a chemical sense closely linked with the process of breathing. Currents of air brought in each *nostril* during an inspiration, or breath intake, swirl up to the top of the nasal cavity. Air circulates over outcropping called *conchae* in the nasal sinuses, or passages, to be warmed or cooled to body temperature before going to the lungs. At the top of the nasal cavity are free nerve endings of the *olfactory nerves.* They project through openings in cranial bone from the *olfactory bulb,* the terminal of the first cranial nerve. The olfactory nerve cells are very sensitive to odors. Odors result from the volatile, or vaporous, components of various substances breathed in. Much of the "taste" of food is the result of odors intercepted by the olfactory nerves and transmitted to the brain. For example, you have probably observed that when you have a head cold and your nasal passages become filled with fluid, almost everything you eat tastes the same.

The nasal cavity is the beginning of the pharynx, the part of the body where the breathing and eating processes cross each other. The *epiglottis* is a "valve" that keeps food out of the windpipe. When food is swallowed, it forces the epiglottis over the windpipe as it passes into the *esophagus.* The *Eustachian tube,* a "pressure valve," connects the pharynx with the middle ear.

The pharynx also has lymphoid tissues, such as the *adenoids* and the *tonsils.* The tonsils are located in the throat near the point where the *uvula* hangs from the roof of the mouth.

## Taste buds in the tongue

Taste, like smell, is a chemical sense. *Taste buds* capable of sensing chemicals in the mouth are located on the top and side surface of the tongue.

The surface covering of the tongue senses the texture and the temperature of food. The taste buds are housed in bumpy projections called *papillae.* The *vallate* papillae, which range in number between 8 and 12, are in a V-shaped row on the rear surface of the tongue. The mushroom-shaped *fungiform* papillae, more numerous than the vallate, are scattered over the sides and the tip of the tongue. The taste buds attach to sensory nerves that carry taste messages to the brain.

In varying degrees, the taste buds can distinguish four tastes: sweetness, bitterness (alkalinity), sourness, and saltiness. The sweet taste is usually detected by taste buds in the forward edges of the tongue. Bitterness is registered mainly at the back surface. Sourness can be discerned at the middle edges. And saltiness can be distinguished over a wide area of the tongue. However, few tastes can be clearly distinguished at the center surface of the tongue.

## Nerve endings in the skin

Sensation receptors are located in the skin and other body sites. The receptors range from bare nerve endings to highly specialized organs involved in sight and hearing. Some receptors respond to touch, some to chemicals, and some to light.

The skin has many nerve endings. Four sensations can be detected by skin receptors: cold, warmth, touch, and pain. Cold and warmth are detected by nerve endings deep in the skin. Tactile sensation, or light touch, is sensed by cup-shaped nerve endings just below the *epidermis,* the top layer of the skin. Pressure, or very heavy touch, is detected by bulb-shaped nerve endings deep in the *dermis* of the skin and in tendons and other deep body tissues. Pain is detected by bare nerve endings in the upper portions of the dermis, as well as within the linings of certain body cavities.

Nerve fiber stimulation is basically an electrical event. The exchange of sodium and potassium ions in the nerve fiber changes the polarity of the fiber and starts a wave of depolarization—an *action potential,* or nerve impulse—along the fiber. The nerve impulses move at an incredible speed from fiber to fiber across links called *synapses.*

### The nose—organ of smell

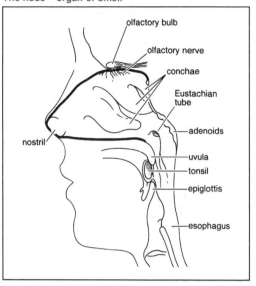

### Taste buds in the tongue

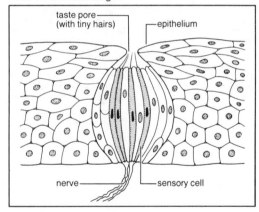

### Nerve endings in the skin

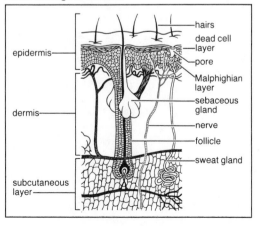

## Teeth and the dental system

Teeth are the hardest tissues of the human body. A tooth consists of a *crown,* an underlying *dentin,* and a soft *pulp.* The crown is the hard, white part of the tooth that appears above the gum line. The *neck* of the tooth is at the gum line, and the *root* is anchored in the bony jaws. These parts of the tooth are shown and labeled in the diagram at the right.

The crown is made of carbonate apatite crystals filled in with calcium phosphate. It is nonliving material; holes or cracks in the enamel cannot be repaired by the body. Most of the tooth consists of living dentin. Similar to bone in its composition, dentin is about 50 per cent calcium phosphate. Blood vessels and nerves from the pulp infiltrate the dentin and make it alive. If the enamel becomes decayed or cracked, the exposed dentin can convey the sensations of warmth, cold, and pain. The tooth root is covered by bonelike *cementum.* Tiny fibers extend from the cementum and anchor the root into the bony tooth socket.

The adult mouth contains 32 teeth. The maxilla, or upper jaw, contains four *incisors,* two *canines,* four *bicuspids,* and six *molars.* The mandible, or lower jaw, contains the same kind and number of teeth. The incisors and canines bite and tear food. The premolars crush and the molars grind food.

Humans develop two sets of teeth—primary, or deciduous, teeth and permanent teeth. The central incisors are the first primary teeth to erupt through the gums.They appear when a baby is about 6 months old. The lateral incisors appear next, at about 8 months old, followed by the bicuspids, at about 14 months of age. The first and second molars erupt between 14 and 36 months after a baby is born.

The permanent teeth start to replace the baby teeth at 6 years of age and end the process about 6 years later. However, the third molars, or "wisdom" teeth, do not usually erupt until a person is between 18 and 22 years old—or, in some cases, even older.

Preventive care is considered especially important by dentists and dental hygienists. Most dentists advise that young people have their teeth checked by a dentist every six months. And, as you know, many school systems require a dental checkup at least once a year—that is, before the student starts school in the late summer or early fall.

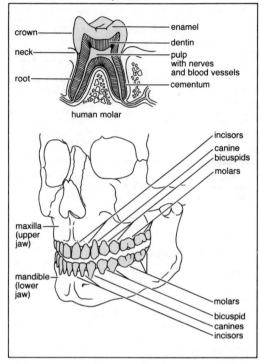

human molar

# 5. Your good health

Maintaining body health is one of the most important tasks in life. A healthy body requires nutritional foods and liquids for growth, development, and defense against disease. A healthy body also requires cleanliness, fresh air, exercise, and rest.

Maintaining body health requires conscious effort. You choose the foods you eat. You choose whether you get fresh air and exercise. You choose how much rest you get.

Nutrition is one of the most important components of body health. When people do not eat enough food or do not take in certain essential nutrients, they can suffer from *primary malnutrition*. Sometimes, disease robs the body of essential nutrients in the diet. This condition is called *secondary malnutrition*. Sometimes a diet contains too many otherwise necessary nutrients, such as too many calories or too many fatty foods. Excess calories can lead to overweight. Excess fatty foods can eventually lead to heart and blood vessel disease. The key is to maintain the proper diet.

Three essential foods are carbohydrates, fats, and proteins. Carbohydrates provide body fuel. Fats are stored in the body for future energy uses. Proteins are required for repairing body tissues and other growth needs, and for defending against disease. Certain vitamins are needed for metabolic processes in the body cells. Without them, deficiency diseases can occur. Certain minerals are also needed in the diet. These include calcium for bone and tooth development, and sodium and potassium for muscle action and a healthy nervous system. Essential amino acids for certain proteins must be in the diet because they cannot be made by the body.

A healthy body usually can ward off disease. However, vaccines have been developed to help the body in its fight against disease. These vaccines should be administered regularly to infants and schoolchildren to protect against such possibly harmful diseases as measles and chicken pox. In particular, polio vaccine should be given to children at required intervals to prevent recurrences of the dread, crippling disease.

Regular visits to the physician and dentist are essential. The physician checks to make certain that all the body systems work well. If not, corrective measures can be prescribed. The physical examination includes an eyesight checkup. When a student cannot read the chalkboard or textbooks because of failing vision, learning can be impaired. Corrective glasses often improve this situation. Dental health is very important. Once cavities form in the teeth, the body cannot repair them. A dentist must then fill the cavity. Also, permanent teeth cannot be replaced by the body once lost, so it is very important for children to develop dental hygiene habits to keep their permanent teeth healthy. These habits include toothbrushing regularly to prevent mouth bacteria from causing tooth cavities. Fluorides have also proved beneficial in maintaining healthy teeth. A checkup by a dentist twice a year will, as noted, determine the condition of a person's teeth.

Mental health is as important as bodily health. Stimulating activities should be part of everyone's everyday life. Depression can sap a person's desire to accomplish realistic goals and result in loss of self-esteem. When this happens, the body can also suffer because the person loses concern over good nutrition, proper exercise, and sufficient rest. Social workers and other behavioral scientists can help a person recognize and side-step blocks in the way of sound mental health.

The following section will outline some of the requirements for maintaining good body health. It will also describe first-aid steps anyone can use during some emergencies that threaten health.

## Table of nutrition essentials

| Food group or food element | Food sources | Recommended daily intake (single servings or combinations for food groups) | What it provides to the body |
|---|---|---|---|
| Dairy foods | Milk, cheese, ice cream, yogurt | 4 or more glasses (milk) | Carbohydrate (lactose), fats, essential amino acids, vitamins A and D |
| Meats | Red meat, eggs, poultry, fish, cheese, dry beans, nuts, peanut butter | 3–6 ounces (85–170 grams) of lean meat, or 2 eggs, or 4 tablespoons of peanut butter, or 1 cup of dry beans | Proteins for body growth and development |
| Vegetables and fruits | Green vegetables: broccoli, Brussels sprouts, kale, cabbage; Yellow vegetables: carrot, corn, squash; Fruits: apple, orange, pear, peach, banana, grapefruit | 2 or more cups; an equivalent serving is 1 cup of vegetable and 2 servings of fruit, such as a medium-sized apple and a medium-sized grapefruit | Green and yellow vegetables provide vitamin A; citrus fruits and green vegetables provide vitamin C; all provide various amounts of carbohydrates and minerals |
| Breads and cereals | Enriched or whole-grained breads, selected breakfast cereals | 4 slices of bread, or 4 ounces (113 grams) of dry breakfast cereal, or 3 cups of cooked cereal, or any combination totaling 4 servings | Starches for energy; enriched breads also contain vitamins and minerals, as do fortified breakfast cereals |
| Protein | Milk, meat, dry beans, fish, poultry | 54 grams (2 ounces) for boys, 15–18; 48 grams (1⅔ ounces) for girls, 15–18 | Nitrogen for protein-building in body cells |
| Calcium | Milk, leafy green vegetables | 1,200 milligrams (0.04 ounce) for boys and girls, 11–18 | Builds and maintains bones and teeth; also used for healthy muscles and nerves |
| Iron | Liver, bread, egg yolks, peas, cereals | 18 milligrams for boys and girls, 11–18 | Component of red blood cells, used for carrying vital oxygen to all body cells for respiration |

## Table of nutritional values of common food items

| Food | Portion | Calo-ries | Pro-tein (gm) | Cal-cium (mg) | Iron (mg) | A (I.U.) | C (mg) | D (I.U.) | Thia-mine (mcg) | Ribo-flavin (mcg) | Nia-cin (mg) |
|---|---|---|---|---|---|---|---|---|---|---|---|
| Apple, raw | 1 large | 117 | 0.6 | 12 | 0.6 | 180 | 9 | 0 | 80 | 60 | 0.4 |
| Banana, raw | 1 large | 176 | 2.4 | 16 | 1.2 | 860 | 20 | 0 | 80 | 100 | 1.4 |
| Beans, green, cooked | 1 cup | 27 | 1.8 | 45 | 0.9 | 830 | 18 | 0 | 90 | 120 | 0.6 |
| Beef, round, cooked | 1 serving | 214 | 24.7 | 10 | 3.1 | 0 | 0 | 0 | 74 | 202 | 5.1 |
| Bread, white, enriched | 1 slice | 63 | 2.0 | 18 | 0.4 | 0 | 0 | 0 | 60 | 40 | 0.5 |
| Broccoli, cooked | ⅔ cup | 29 | 3.3 | 130 | 1.3 | 3,400 | 74 | 0 | 70 | 150 | 0.8 |
| Butter | 1 tablespoon | 100 | 0.1 | 33 | 0.0 | 460 | 0 | 5 | tr. | tr. | tr. |
| Cabbage, cooked | ½ cup | 20 | 1.2 | 39 | 0.4 | 75 | 27 | 0 | 40 | 40 | 0.3 |
| Carrots, raw | 1 cup, shredded | 42 | 1.2 | 39 | 0.8 | 12,000 | 6 | 0 | 60 | 60 | 0.5 |
| Cheese, cheddar, American | 1 slice | 113 | 7.1 | 206 | 0.3 | 400 | 0 | 0 | 10 | 120 | tr. |
| Chicken, fried | ½ breast | 232 | 26.8 | 19 | 1.3 | 460 | 0 | 0 | 67 | 101 | 10.2 |
| Egg, boiled | 1 medium | 77 | 6.1 | 26 | 1.3 | 550 | 0 | 27 | 40 | 130 | tr. |
| Liver, beef, fried | 1 slice | 86 | 8.8 | 4 | 2.9 | 18,658 | 10 | 19 | 90 | 1,283 | 5.1 |
| Margarine, fortified | 1 tablespoon | 101 | 0.1 | 3 | 0.0 | 460 | 0 | 0 | 0 | 0 | 0.0 |
| Milk, whole, cow's | 1 glass | 124 | 6.4 | 216 | 0.2 | 293 | 2 | 4 | 73 | 311 | 0.2 |
| Orange, whole | 1 medium | 68 | 1.4 | 50 | 0.6 | 285 | 74 | 0 | 120 | 45 | 0.3 |
| Pork, shoulder, roasted | 2 slices | 320 | 19.2 | 9 | 2.0 | 0 | 0 | 0 | 592 | 144 | 3.2 |
| Tomatoes, raw | 1 large | 40 | 2.0 | 22 | 1.2 | 2,200 | 46 | 0 | 120 | 80 | 1.0 |
| Potatoes, white, baked | 1 medium | 98 | 2.4 | 13 | 0.8 | 20 | 17 | 0 | 110 | 50 | 1.4 |
| Rice, white, cooked | 1 cup | 201 | 4.2 | 13 | 0.5 | 0 | 0 | 0 | 20 | 10 | 0.7 |
| Sugar, white, granulated | 1 tablespoon | 48 | 0.0 | 0 | 0.0 | 0 | 0 | 0 | 0 | 0 | 0.0 |

gm = grams; mg = milligrams; mcg = micrograms; I.U. = International Units; tr. = trace.

## Table of major diseases and their treatment

| Disease | Type | Cause | Symptoms | Prevention |
|---|---|---|---|---|
| Atherosclerosis | Noninfectious | Fatty deposits in blood vessel linings | Activity slowdown from oxygen loss in muscles and tissues | Diet low in saturated fats, regular exercise, no smoking |
| Cancer | Noninfectious | Uncontrolled and excessive growth of body cells | Usually pain and rampant growth of tumors in affected body organs | Eradication of environmental causes; regular checkups to detect |
| Chicken pox | Infectious | Virus in air | Fever, headache, skin eruptions | |
| Coryza (common cold) | Infectious | Viruses in air | Headache, runny nose, cough, sore throat | No effective method |
| Emphysema | Noninfectious | Degeneration of lung alveoli | Shortness of breath, painful breathing during exercise or climbing stairs | Refraining from smoking |
| Gonorrhea | Infectious | Bacteria from infected victim | Discharge of pus from sex organs | Avoid sexual contact with infected individuals |
| Hepatitis | Sometimes infectious | Virus, mainly in contaminated blood transfusions or injection devices | Weakness, tender liver, occasional jaundice (skin yellowing), tiredness | Blood screening; sterilized hypodermic needles |
| Hypertension (high blood pressure) | Noninfectious | Aging; other causes unknown | Higher than normal blood pressure readings, headache and dizziness | Early detection through routine blood pressure checks |
| Influenza (flu) | Infectious | Viruses in air | Headache, chills, nausea, fever, weakness | Vaccines against some flu viruses |
| Mononucleosis | Infectious | Virus from contact with "mono" victim | Swollen lymph glands and spleen, fever, sore throat, considerable tiredness | No effective method |
| Mumps | Infectious | Virus, mainly in air | Swollen salivary glands, fever, headache | Vaccine |
| Poliomyelitis | Infectious | Virus, from contact with polio victim | Headache, neck and back stiffness, paralysis | Vaccine |
| Rabies | Infectious | Virus from infected animal bite | Listlessness, fever, throat pain and spasms | Vaccine |
| Rheumatic fever | Infectious | Bacteria, from contact with strep throat or scarlatina victim | Inflamed joints and heart valves, fever | Eradication of strep bacteria by antibiotics |
| Rubella (German measles) | Infectious | Virus in air | Itchy rash on face, chest, and arms, stiff joints, headache | Vaccine |
| Rubeola (measles) | Infectious | Virus in air | Spots in mouth, itchy rash on skin, fever, cough | Vaccine |
| Scarlatina (scarlet fever) | Infectious | Bacteria, from contact with scarlet fever victim | Inflamed and bumpy tongue, skin rash | Antibiotic treatments, usually |
| Sickle cell anemia | Noninfectious | Inherited disorder of red blood cells, mainly affecting blacks | Achy muscles, slow-down of activity from reduced tissue oxygen | Tests and genetic counseling to determine carriers |
| Syphilis | Infectious | Parasite, from infected victim during sexual activity | Skin sore, followed by sore throat and tiredness, later followed by rubbery sores and tissues | Avoid sexual contact with infected individuals |
| Tetanus (lockjaw) | Infectious | Bacteria, from contaminated wounds | Chills, fever, stiff jaw muscles | Vaccine |
| Tuberculosis (TB) | Infectious | Bacteria in air and on contaminated objects | Bloody cough, chest pain, loss of weight | Periodic X-ray detection; sometimes a vaccine |

## Table of drugs, their use and misuse

| Drug category | Examples | Medical uses | Dangers of misuse |
|---|---|---|---|
| Narcotic analgesics | Morphine, opium, heroin, codeine, paregoric, methadone | Heroin is illegal; other opiates are prescription drugs for short-term use to relieve pain; codeine, to control coughing; paregoric, to control diarrhea | Physiological and psychological dependence and severe withdrawal symptoms; drowsiness and stupor; sometimes death |
| Central nervous system depressants | Barbiturates (sleeping pills): pentobarbital (Nembutal), secobarbital (Seconal) | Prescription drugs: for calming purposes; high blood pressure; epilepsy | Physiological and psychological dependence, and severe withdrawal symptoms; slurred speech; drowsiness; possible death |
| | Volatile hydrocarbons: glue, paint thinner, lighter fluid | None | Hallucinations; blurred vision; nausea; breathing failure and possible death |
| | Belladonna alkaloids: belladonna, scopolamine, atropine | Prescription drugs: for relaxing overactive smooth muscles, as those of the lungs and intestines | Thirst; restlessness; delirium |
| | Other sedatives and tranquilizers: meprobamate (Miltown), chlordiazepoxide (Librium), diazepam (Valium) | Prescription drugs: to relieve anxiety; sometimes for epilepsy | Physical dependence: withdrawal symptoms include hallucinations and muscle tremors |
| Central nervous system stimulants | Amphetamines (pep pills): amphetamine (Benzedrine), methamphetamine (Methedrine), dextroamphetamine (Dexedrine) | Prescription drugs: for weight reduction; to control mild depression; to quell excessive sleepiness | Psychological dependence; sleeplessness; hallucinations; diarrhea; muscle tremors |
| | Cocaine | Prescription drug: for local anesthesia in dental work | Psychological dependence; violent headache; nausea and vomiting; anxiety |
| Hallucinogens | Peyote, lysergic acid diethylamide (LSD), mescaline, psilocybin | Scientific studies of brain behavior | Hallucinations; anxiety; confusion; increased blood pressure and pulse rate; psychological depression |
| Cannabis | Marijuana, hashish, or any product of *Cannabis sativa,* the hemp plant | No common therapeutic use | Hallucinations; increased pulse rate; dizziness; nausea |
| Legal and Socially Acceptable Drugs That May Cause Dependency | Alcohol | Bactericide for sterilizing uses | Disorientation; blurred vision; slurred speech; hallucinations; psychological depression; organ damage |
| | Caffeine | Treating poisoning by barbiturates and other depressants | Psychological dependence; sometimes sleeplessness |
| | Aspirin | Headache relief; fever reduction | Stomach bleeding; death from large doses |

## Table of smoking and health

| | | | |
|---|---|---|---|
| Cigarette smoking and health | Cigarette smoke contains more than a thousand potentially harmful chemicals. Carbon monoxide in it is a poison. The tar part of cigarette smoke contains cancer-causing substances. Nicotine in cigarette smoke affects the nervous system. Cigarette smoking in confined areas is an air pollutant that harms nonsmokers as well as smokers. Since 1966, cigarette packages and advertising must warn that cigarette smoking may be a health hazard. | Cigarette smoking and pregnancy | The chance of a pregnant woman delivering a stillborn baby doubles when she smokes more than two packs of cigarettes a day. Pregnant women who smoke between one and two packs of cigarettes a day usually deliver babies who are a quarter- to a half-pound lighter than babies born to nonsmoking mothers. |
| Cigarette smoking and appearance | Cigarette smoke leaves a yellow stain on teeth. It also results in an unpleasant mouth and breath odor. | Cigarette smoking and cancer | Lung cancer is the chief type of fatal cancer among males, and male smokers have a 10 times greater chance of dying from lung cancer than male nonsmokers. The lung cancer death rate of female smokers has risen, too. Other types of cancer have also been linked to cigarette smoking. |

## Mouth-to-mouth resuscitation

Suffocation, electric shock, drowning, and asphyxiation from poison gases can stop a person's breathing and result in death in just a few minutes by depriving brain cells of vital oxygen. However, mouth-to-mouth breathing and other forms of artificial respiration can force enough oxygen into the lungs to save the victim until normal breathing can be restored.

Act quickly. First, clear the victim's air passage by prying the tongue forward with your finger. Tilt the prone victim's head backward by lifting the victim's neck and holding the forehead down with one of your hands. Then, pull back the victim's chin with your other hand to prevent the tongue from falling back over the air passage. Take a deep breath, place your mouth tightly over the victim's mouth, pinch the victim's nose, and blow into the mouth until you see the victim's chest rise. Then, break off contact and let the victim exhale. When you hear the end of the exhalation, repeat the procedure—15 times a minute.

Artificial respiration can also be performed by mouth-to-nose breathing. Take the same steps that are outlined above, but breathe into the victim's nose while sealing his or her mouth with your thumb.

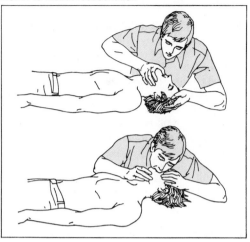

**Mouth-to-mouth resuscitation**

## Applying splints

Falls or other accidents can result in fractures—bone breakages. As a result of an accident, if a body limb appears misshapen or does not move normally, suspect a fracture. Apply a splint to the limb as a first-aid measure only if you must move the victim before emergency help arrives. However, it is better to wait for expert assistance. If a fractured limb is not immobilized by splinting, a *closed* fracture—one that does not break the skin—can develop into an *open* fracture—one that pierces the skin and invites infection.

Unless the person is in imminent danger, do not move him or her. Find the fracture and use any long, stiff object—a pole, board, metal rod, even a rolled newspaper—as a splint. The splint must be long enough; it has to extend beyond the joints above and below the bone break. Secure the splint with a bandage or cloth at least in three places—at the joints above and below the fracture, and at a point by the fracture. If an open fracture, also try to control the bleeding by pressing a clean cloth firmly over the wound. Keep the victim lying down.

Fractures of the foot and hand can be immobilized by wrapping a pillow or blanket around the extremity. Keep in mind that these are *emergency* procedures. Professional care must be sought for all fractures.

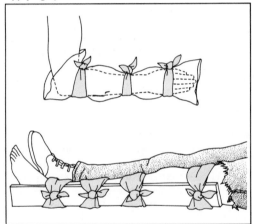

**Applying splints**

## Performing the Heimlich maneuver

The Heimlich maneuver is one of the methods used to rescue a choking victim. When food lodges in a person's windpipe, the victim can choke to death in four minutes if the food is not dislodged. Three signs of food choking are: (1) the victim cannot speak or breathe; (2) the victim's hand clutches the throat and the victim turns blue; (3) the victim collapses.

Stand behind an erect or seated victim, make a fist, and put the thumb side of your fist into the victim's belly between the navel and ribcage. Grab the fist with your other hand and make a quick upward thrust. Do this as many times as needed to dislodge the food. If the victim is lying down, place your hands on top of each other on the person's belly and push with a quick upward thrust.

**Performing the Heimlich maneuver**

# Glossary: Unit 5

**adrenal (uh DREE nuhl) gland** The endocrine gland on each kidney. These glands secrete hormones that include epinephrine (adrenaline), a substance that causes a rise in heartbeat, increased blood sugar, and other body responses to emergencies.

**alveoli (al VEE uh ly)** Spongy air sacs in the lungs, where oxygen and carbon dioxide exchange occurs.

**amino (uh MEE noh) acids** Nitrogen-containing compounds that form proteins when strung together.

**anaerobic (AN air OH bihk) respiration** The process of breaking down carbohydrates in the absence of free oxygen. Tetanus bacteria get energy in this way.

**angiosperms (AN jee uh spurmz)** The flowering plants. They form the largest subphylum of the plant kingdom.

**artery** A vessel that carries blood away from the heart.

**axon** A nerve cell part that conducts impulses away from the cell body toward another nerve cell.

**bacteria (bak TIHR ee uh)** Microscopically small organisms divided into three groups: bacilli (rod-shaped), cocci (round-shaped), and spirilli (spiral-shaped).

**biology** The study of all living things.

**blood** The vital fluid in higher animals that carries food, gases, and disease-fighting substances.

**bone marrow** A substance inside the body's long bones where blood cells are made and fat is stored.

**botany** The study of plants.

**bronchi (BRAHNG ky)** Branching tubes connecting the lung's alveoli with the trachea.

**cell** The basic unit of life. The cell consists of a nucleus, cytoplasm, and enclosing membrane.

**chromosomes (KROH muh sohmz)** Combinations of nucleic acid and proteins in body and sex cells engaged in transmitting hereditary information.

**dendrite (DEHN dryt)** A nerve cell part that conducts an impulse toward the cell body from another nerve cell.

**DNA** Deoxyribonucleic acid; a chemical in the cell nucleus that stores genetic information.

**drug** A nonfood substance that changes body makeup or activity. Drugs are used to control or cure disease; addiction can occur when the body tolerates increasing dosages of certain drugs.

**ecology (ee KAHL uh jee)** The study of how living things interact with their surroundings.

**endocrine (EHN doh krihn) system** A body system of ductless glands that secrete chemical hormones into the blood. Target organs are influenced by the hormones.

**enzyme** A protein serving as a catalyst to speed up or slow down chemical processes in the body.

**fetus (FEE tuhs)** In higher animals, a developing embryo. The human embryo is referred to as a fetus between three months of age and birth.

**flagella (fluh JEHL luh)** Threadlike projections in some microorganisms, used for locomotion.

**gametes (GAM eets)** Sex cells produced during meiosis.

**gene (JEEN)** The unit of biological inheritance; a specific sequence of nucleotides in a DNA molecule in a chromosome.

**gymnosperms (JIHM nuh spurmz)** Evergreen plants, or conifers. These plants bear naked seeds in cones.

**heterozygous (HEHT uhr uh ZY guhs)** Type of gene pairing where each of the two genes is different.

**homozygous (HOH muh ZY guhs)** A type of gene pairing where the two genes are similar.

**kidney** A structure in animals that filters liquid waste products from the blood but retains the water.

**meiosis (my OH sihs)** A type of cell division that produces gametes, which contain a haploid number of chromosomes.

**metabolism** The chemical processes that occur in living things; a combination of the *anabolic* build-up of cell materials and the *catabolic* breakdown of them.

**mitochondrion (MIHT uh KAHN dree uhn)** A cell organelle where energy transformations occur; a cell "powerhouse."

**mitosis (mih TOH sihs)** A type of cell division that produces body cells containing the diploid number of chromosomes.

**neuron (NUR ahn)** A nerve cell. The cell conducts nerve impulses from other neurons through its dendrites and transmits them to still other neurons through its axons.

**nucleolus (noo KLEE oh luhs)** A round mass in a cell nucleus where RNA is located. This mass disappears during mitosis.

**nucleotide (NOO klee uh tyd)** A chemical combination of a sugar, phosphate group, and nitrogenous base that forms the basis of the nucleic acids.

**nucleus** The "master control" of the cell. The nucleus controls life processes in all living cells except bacteria.

**organelle** A cell structure having a special task.

**osmosis (ahz MOH suhs)** Diffusion of small molecules through a *semipermeable*, or selective, membrane.

**ovulation (oh vyuh LAY shuhn)** The release of an egg cell during the midpoint of the menstrual cycle.

**parasite** An organism that lives in or on a host organism and gets its food from the host. The parasite is often harmful to the host.

**peristalsis (peh ruh STAL sihs)** Waves of muscular contractions and relaxations of the gastrointestinal tube that move food through the human digestive system.

**phenotype (FEE nuh typ)** How genetic makeup appears as body traits; examples are tallness, shortness, skin coloration.

**pituitary (pih TOO uh tehr ee) gland** The endocrine gland beneath the brain; the source of important hormones that trigger hormone secretions from other endocrine glands.

**radial symmetry** A wheel-like body structure. Two equal parts result, with similar structures in each part, no matter how the body is divided.

**regeneration** The ability of some organisms to grow new body parts when injured or severed.

**respiration (REHS puh RAY shuhn)** An energy process requiring oxygen and giving off carbon dioxide.

**ribosomes (RY buh sohmz)** Cell structures where proteins are made.

**RNA** Ribonucleic acid; carries genetic information from DNA in the cell nucleus to the ribosomes.

**saprophyte (SAP ruh FYT)** An organism that lives off dead organic substances.

**synapse (sih NAPS)** The junction between axons of one neuron and dendrites of another.

**thorax** A body part between the head and abdomen. This part is enclosed by ribs in humans.

**tissue** A group of cells in the body having the same makeup and function.

**trachea (TRAY kee uh)** An air tube.

**vein (VAYN)** A vessel that carries blood back to the heart.

**X chromosome** The chromosome determining "femaleness."

**Y chromosome** The chromosome determining "maleness."

**yolk** The food stored to feed a growing embryo.

**zygote (ZY goht)** A fertilized egg resulting from the union of male and female sex cells.

# Places around the world

**6**

Have you ever had to find the location of one of the nations of the world? Did you ever have to explain the structure and function of the federal government of the United States? Have you ever had to find the area or size of Canada or of Argentina? If so, then this unit contains useful information for you.

This unit is an overall review of geographic, political, and economic facts about the nations of the world. Use of this unit will help you to develop greater understanding of many of the places and events that fill today's news.

# 1. A political atlas

This section presents information on the contemporary world that you might wish to consult and review for your social science or geography work. Included are nine political maps: the world, North America, the United States, South America, Europe, Asia, Africa, the Middle East, and Australia. Also included, to supplement the information on those maps, are tables of comparative population and comparative area (pages 202 and 203).

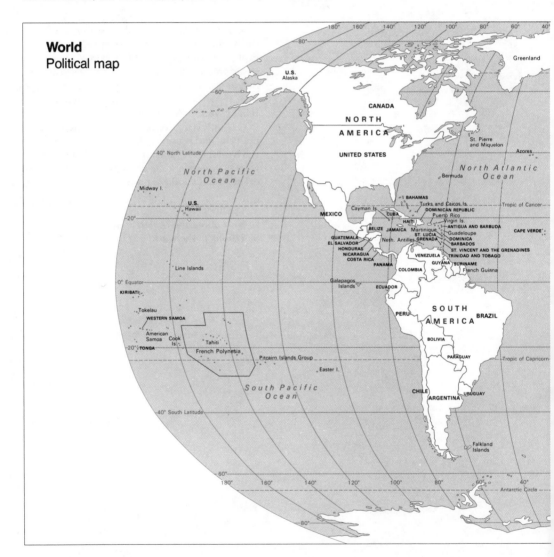

**World**
Political map

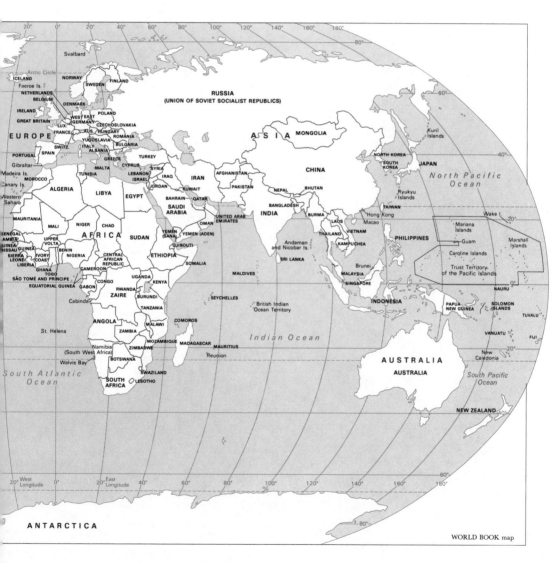

WORLD BOOK map

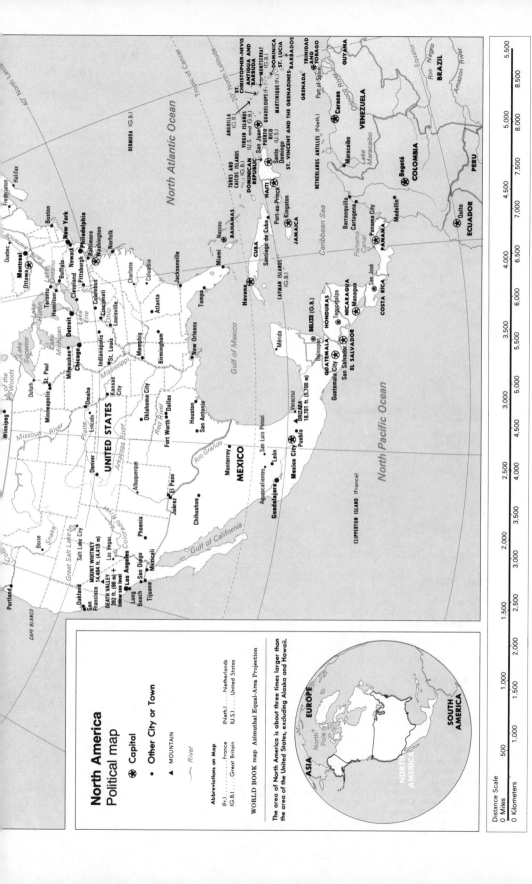

# North America
## Political map

⊛ Capital

• Other City or Town

▲ MOUNTAIN

〜 River

**Abbreviations on Map**

(Fr.) ........... France     (Neth.) ..... Netherlands
(G.B.) ..... Great Britain     (U.S.) ..... United States

WORLD BOOK map   Azimuthal Equal-Area Projection

The area of North America is about three times larger than
the area of the United States, excluding Alaska and Hawaii.

North Atlantic Ocean

North Pacific Ocean

Gulf of Mexico

Caribbean Sea

Tropic of Cancer

40° North Latitude

20° North Latitude

**Distance Scale**

| 0 Miles | 500 | 1,000 | 1,500 | 2,000 | 2,500 | 3,000 | 3,500 | 4,000 | 4,500 | 5,000 | 5,500 |

| 0 Kilometers | 1,000 | 1,500 | 2,000 | 2,500 | 3,000 | 3,500 | 4,000 | 4,500 | 5,000 | 5,500 | 6,000 | 6,500 | 7,000 | 7,500 | 8,000 | 8,500 |

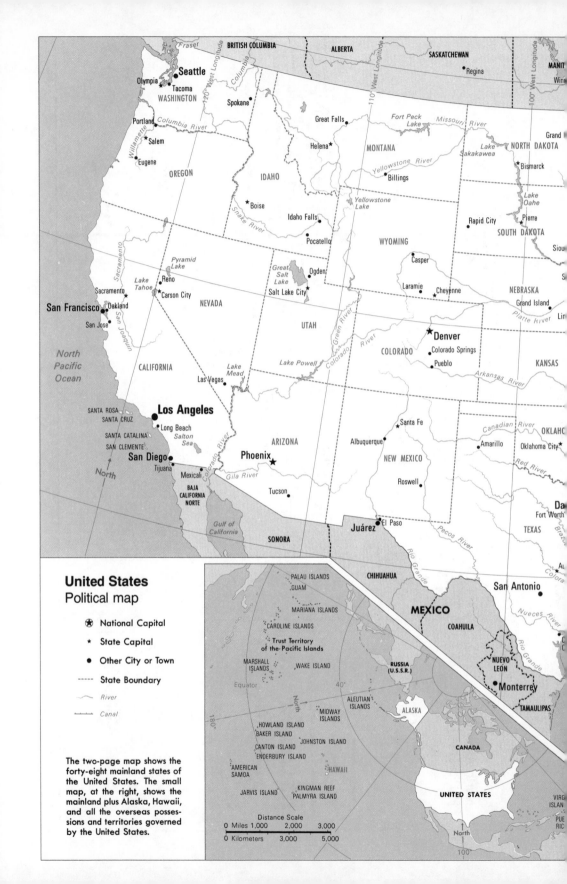

**United States**
Political map

⊛ National Capital

★ State Capital

● Other City or Town

----- State Boundary

～ River

⊶⊶ Canal

The two-page map shows the forty-eight mainland states of the United States. The small map, at the right, shows the mainland plus Alaska, Hawaii, and all the overseas possessions and territories governed by the United States.

Distance Scale

0 Miles 1,000    2,000    3,000

0 Kilometers    3,000    5,000

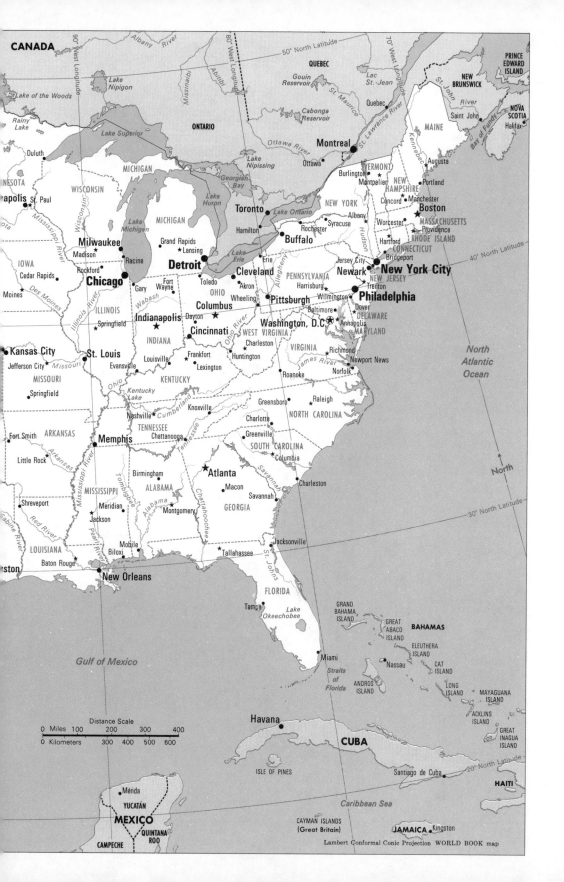

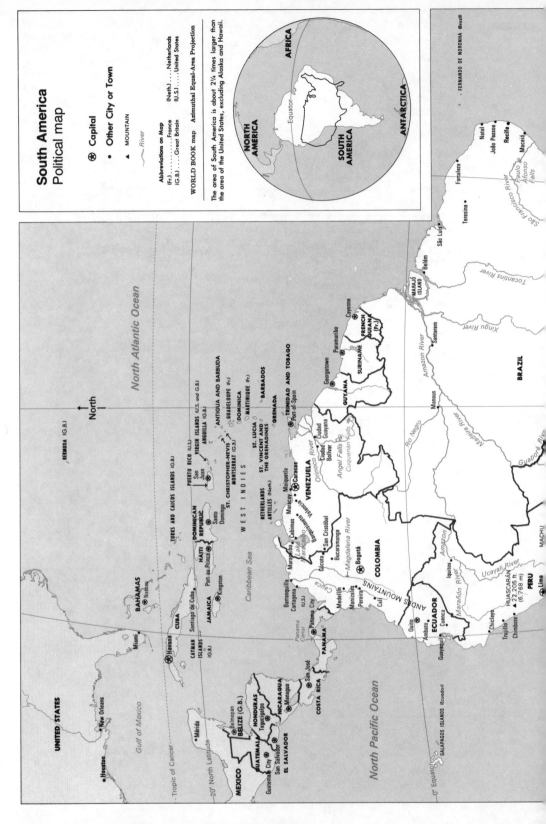

# South America
## Political map

⊛ Capital
• Other City or Town
▲ MOUNTAIN
〜 River

**Abbreviations on Map**
(Fr.) . . . . . . . . . . France  (Neth.) . . . . . Netherlands
(G.B.) . . . . . Great Britain  (U.S.) . . . . . United States

WORLD BOOK map   Azimuthal Equal-Area Projection

The area of South America is about 2¼ times larger than the area of the United States, excluding Alaska and Hawaii.

192

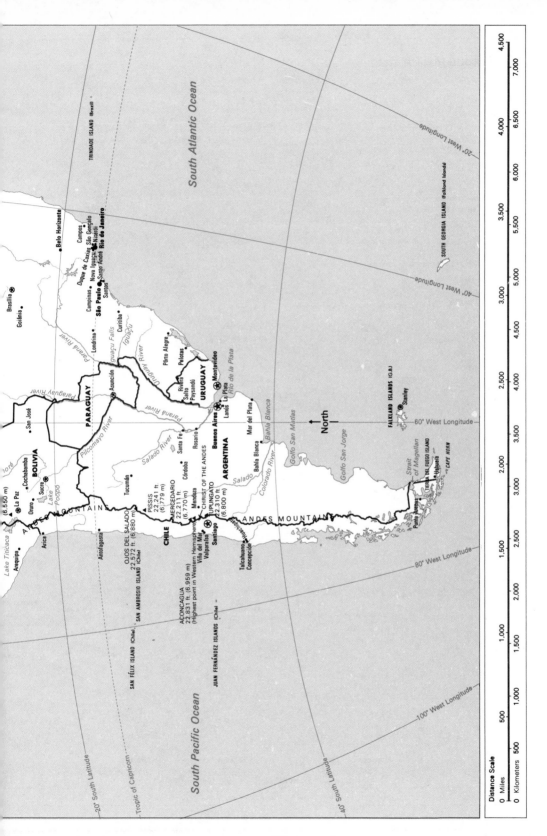

South Atlantic Ocean

TRINDADE ISLAND (Brazil)

SOUTH GEORGIA ISLAND (Falkland Islands)

20° West Longitude

40° West Longitude

Belo Horizonte

Campos
Duque de Caxias São Gonçalo
Nova Iguaçu Niterói
Santo André Rio de Janeiro
Santos

Campinas
São Paulo

Curitiba

Paranaguá

Londrina

Iguaçu Falls

Uruguay River

Pôrto Alegre

Pelotas

Rivera
Salto
Paysandú

URUGUAY

Montevideo

Río de la Plata

FALKLAND ISLANDS (G.B.)

Stanley

60° West Longitude

North

Brasília

Goiânia

Paraná River

PARAGUAY

Asunción

Paraguay River

Pilcomayo River

Paraná River

Salado River

Santa Fe

Rosario

La Plata
Lanús
Buenos Aires

Mar del Plata

Bahía Blanca

Golfo San Matías

Golfo San Jorge

San José

BOLIVIA

Cochabamba
Sucre
Oruro

La Paz
(6,650 m)

Lake
Poopó

Lake Titicaca

Arequipa

Arica

Antofagasta

SAN AMBROSIO ISLAND (Chile)

SAN FÉLIX ISLAND (Chile)

JUAN FERNÁNDEZ ISLANDS (Chile)

South Pacific Ocean

ANDES MOUNTAINS

Córdoba

Tucumán

PISSIS
22,241 ft
(6,779 m)

MERCEDARIO
22,211 ft
(6,770 m)

OJOS DEL SALADO
22,572 ft (6,880 m)

CHILE

ACONCAGUA
22,831 ft (6,959 m)
(Highest point in Western Hemisphere)

CHRIST OF THE ANDES

TUPUNGATO
22,310 ft
(6,800 m)

Mendoza

Viña del Mar
Valparaíso

Santiago

Talcahuano
Concepción

ARGENTINA

Salado

Colorado River

ANDES MOUNTAINS

Bahía Blanca

Strait
of Magellan

TIERRA DEL FUEGO ISLAND

Punta Arenas
Ushuaia

CAPE HORN

20° South Latitude

Tropic of Capricorn

40° South Latitude

80° West Longitude

100° West Longitude

Distance Scale

0 Miles          500        1,000        1,500        2,000        2,500        3,000        3,500        4,000        4,500

0 Kilometers  500    1,000    1,500    2,000    2,500    3,000    3,500    4,000    4,500    5,000    5,500    6,000    6,500    7,000

# Europe Political map

❊ Capital

• Other City or Town

▲ MOUNTAIN

⌒ River

Azimuthal Equal-Area Projection
WORLD BOOK map

The area of Europe is about one third larger than the area of the United States, excluding Alaska and Hawaii.

NORTH AMERICA  + North Pole

ASIA

EUROPE

AFRICA

Arctic Circle
20° West Longitude
0° Prime Meridian

North Atlantic Ocean

Norwegian Sea

North

60° North Latitude

FAEROE ISLANDS (Denmark)

Trondheim

SHETLAND ISLANDS

NORWAY      SWEDEN

Bergen

Oslo          Lake Vänern

HEBRIDES      ORKNEY ISLANDS

Stockholm

NORTHERN IRELAND    SCOTLAND

Skaggerak

Göteborg

Glasgow  Edinburgh

North Sea

Belfast

Newcastle upon Tyne

DENMARK

Dublin    ISLE OF MAN   ENGLAND

Copenhagen   Malmö

IRELAND   Liverpool  Leeds  GREAT BRITAIN

Baltic S

Cork

Manchester

Birmingham

Gdańsk

WALES

Cardiff

Amsterdam     Hamburg

The Hague

West  East Berlin Berlin

London

NETHERLANDS

EAST GERMANY    POLA

English Channel

Antwerp  Essen

CHANNEL ISLANDS

Brussels  Düsseldorf  Cologne

Lille          Bonn

Leipzig   Dresden

Ł

Wrocła

BELGIUM

Frankfurt

Elbe   Oder River

LUXEMBOURG

Prague

Kr

Paris

WEST GERMANY

CZECHOSLOVAKIA

Nantes

Stuttgart

Brno

Loire River

Seine

Rhine  Danube  Munich

Bratisla

Bay of Biscay

FRANCE

Basel  Zürich

Vienna

Bern    SWITZERLAND  LIECHTENSTEIN  AUSTRIA  Budapest

Bordeaux

Lyon  Geneva

Graz

HUNGA

North Atlantic Ocean

Rhône

Turin   Milan  Venice

Zagreb

Po River

40° North Latitude

Porto

Genoa  Bologna

YUGOSLAV

Douro River

Ebro River

ANDORRA

Marseille  MONACO

San Marino  Sarajevo

PORTUGAL   SPAIN   Saragossa

Florence

Lisbon    Madrid

Barcelona

ITALY

Adriatic Sea

Tagus River

CORSICA

Valencia

VATICAN CITY   Rome

ALBA

Seville

BALEARIC ISLANDS

SARDINIA

Tyrrhenian Sea

Naples

Tir

Tangier   GIBRALTAR (Great Britain)

Mediterranean Sea

Ior S

Rabat

Algiers

Palermo  ▲ MOUNT ETNA

Casablanca

Tunis

SICILY  Catania

MOROCCO       ALGERIA       TUNISIA

MALTA

AFRICA

| Distance Scale | | | | | |
|---|---|---|---|---|---|
| 0 Miles | 500 | | 1,000 | | 1,500 |
| 0 Kilometers | 500 | 1,000 | 1,500 | 2,000 | 2,500 | 3,000 |

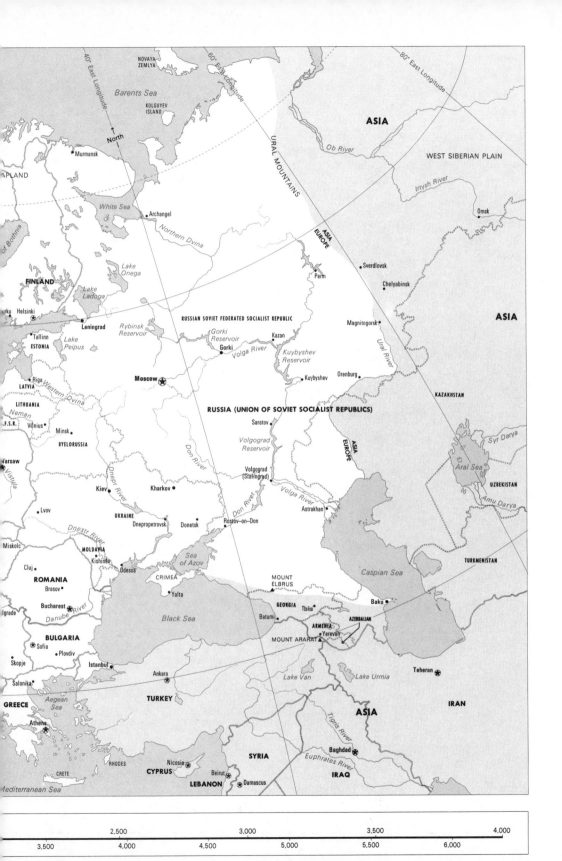

NOVAYA
ZEMLYA

*Barents Sea*

KOLGUYEV
ISLAND

*40° East Longitude*

*60° East Longitude*

*80° East Longitude*

**ASIA**

*Ob River*

**WEST SIBERIAN PLAIN**

• Murmansk

North

*White Sea*

• Archangel

*Northern Dvina*

URAL MOUNTAINS

ASIA
EUROPE

*Irtysh River*

• Omsk

LAPLAND

Gulf of Bothnia

*Lake Onega*

*Lake Ladoga*

**FINLAND**

• Sverdlovsk

• Perm

• Chelyabinsk

urku • Helsinki

• Leningrad

*Rybinsk Reservoir*

**RUSSIAN SOVIET FEDERATED SOCIALIST REPUBLIC**

*Gorki Reservoir*

• Kazan

• Gorki

*Volga River*

*Kuybyshev Reservoir*

Magnitogorsk •

**ASIA**

• Tallinn

**ESTONIA**

*Lake Peipus*

• Moscow ✪

• Kuybyshev

Orenburg •

*Ural River*

**KAZAKHSTAN**

• Riga

**LATVIA**

*Western Dvina*

**RUSSIA (UNION OF SOVIET SOCIALIST REPUBLICS)**

Saratov •

*Syr Darya*

**LITHUANIA**

*Neman*

.F.S.R.

• Vilnius

• Minsk

**BYELORUSSIA**

*Volgograd Reservoir*

ASIA
EUROPE

*Aral Sea*

Warsaw

*Vistula*

*Dnepr River*

*Don River*

Volgograd
(Stalingrad) •

*Volga River*

**UZBEKISTAN**

*Amu Darya*

• Kiev

• Kharkov

*Don River*

• Lvov

**UKRAINE**

• Dnepropetrovsk

• Donetsk

• Rostov-on-Don

Astrakhan•

• Miskolc

*Dnestr River*

**MOLDAVIA**

• Kishinev

**TURKMENISTAN**

• Cluj

**ROMANIA**

• Odessa

*Sea of Azov*

*Caspian Sea*

Brasov •

**CRIMEA**

MOUNT
ELBRUS

• Bucharest

*Danube River*

• Yalta

**GEORGIA**

Tbilisi •

Baku •

lgrade

*Black Sea*

Batumi •

**AZERBAIJAN**

**BULGARIA**

**ARMENIA**

• Yerevan

✪ Sofia

• Plovdiv

MOUNT ARARAT ▲

• Skopje

• Istanbul

Ankara •

*Lake Van*

*Lake Urmia*

• Teheran ✪

• Salonika

**GREECE**

*Aegean Sea*

**TURKEY**

**ASIA**

**IRAN**

Athens ✪

**CRETE**

**RHODES**

Nicosia •

**CYPRUS**

• Beirut

**SYRIA**

*Tigris River*

Baghdad ✪

*Euphrates River*

**LEBANON**

✪ Damascus

**IRAQ**

*Mediterranean Sea*

| 2,500 | | 3,000 | | 3,500 | | 4,000 |
|---|---|---|---|---|---|---|
| 3,500 | 4,000 | 4,500 | 5,000 | 5,500 | 6,000 | |

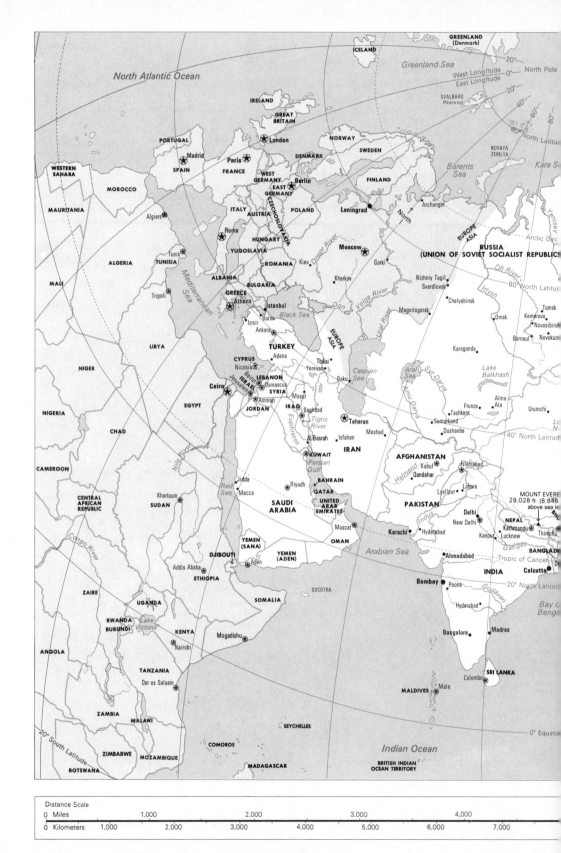

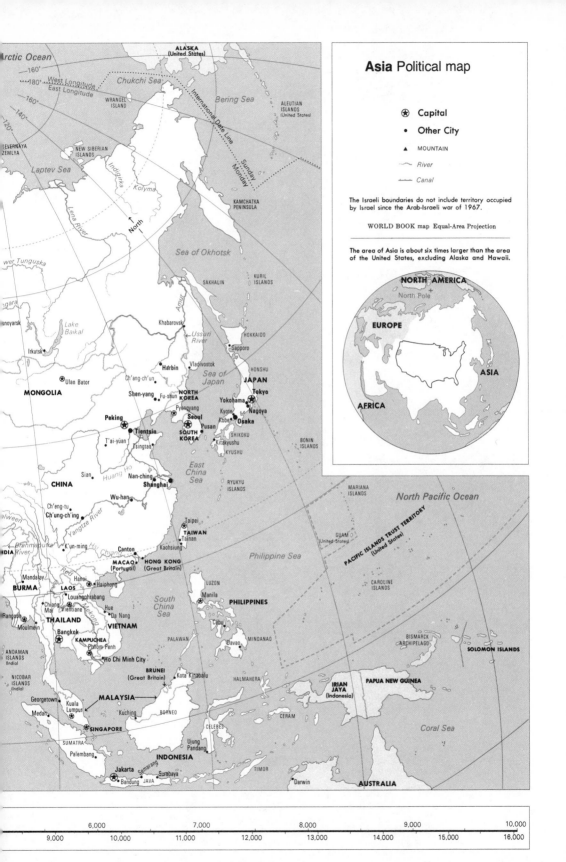

Arctic Ocean

ALASKA
(United States)

160°
180° West Longitude
East Longitude
Chukchi Sea
160°
140°
120°
WRANGEL
ISLAND

Bering Sea

International Date Line

ALEUTIAN
ISLANDS
(United States)

SEVERNAYA
ZEMLYA

NEW SIBERIAN
ISLANDS

Sunday
Monday

KAMCHATKA
PENINSULA

Laptev Sea

Indigirka

Kolyma

Lena River

North

Sea of Okhotsk

wer Tunguska

Khabarovsk

SAKHALIN

KURIL
ISLANDS

Amur

ngara

Lake
Baikal

Ussuri
River

HOKKAIDO

snoyarsk

Irkutsk

Sapporo

Harbin

Vladivostok

HONSHU

Sea of
Japan

JAPAN

Tokyo

Ch'ang-ch'un

Ulan Bator

Shen-yang Fu-shun

NORTH
KOREA

Yokohama
Kyoto Nagoya

MONGOLIA

Peking

Pyongyang

Seoul

Kobe Osaka

Tientsin

SOUTH
KOREA

Pusan

SHIKOKU

Kitakyushu

BONIN
ISLANDS

T'ai-yüan

Tsingtao

KYUSHU

Sian

Huang Ho

Nan-ching

CHINA

Wu-han

Shanghai

East
China
Sea

RYUKYU
ISLANDS

MARIANA
ISLANDS

North Pacific Ocean

Ch'eng-tu
Ch'ung-ch'ing

Yangtze River

Taipei

TAIWAN

Tainan

GUAM
(United States)

PACIFIC ISLANDS TRUST TERRITORY
(United States)

alween

K'un-ming

Hsi Chiang

Kaohsiung

Philippine Sea

Brahmaputra
River

Canton

NDIA

MACAO
(Portugal)

HONG KONG
(Great Britain)

CAROLINE
ISLANDS

Mandalay

Red River

Hanoi

BURMA

LAOS

Haiphong

LUZON

Manila

Louangphrabang

Chiang
Mai

Vientiane

Hue
Da Nang

PHILIPPINES

South
China
Sea

Rangoon
Moulmein

THAILAND

VIETNAM

Cebu

BISMARCK
ARCHIPELAGO

Bangkok

Mekong

SOLOMON ISLANDS

ANDAMAN
ISLANDS
(India)

KAMPUCHEA

Phnom Penh

PALAWAN

MINDANAO

Davao

Ho Chi Minh City

NICOBAR
ISLANDS
(India)

BRUNEI
(Great Britain)

Kota Kinabalu

HALMAHERA

IRIAN
JAYA
(Indonesia)

PAPUA NEW GUINEA

Georgetown

MALAYSIA

Medan

Kuala
Lumpur

Kuching

BORNEO

CERAM

Coral Sea

SINGAPORE

CELEBES

SUMATRA

Ujung
Pandang

Palembang

INDONESIA

Jakarta
Bandung

Samarang

JAVA

Surabaya

TIMOR

Darwin

AUSTRALIA

| | 6,000 | 7,000 | 8,000 | 9,000 | 10,000 |
|---|---|---|---|---|---|
| 9,000 | 10,000 | 11,000 | 12,000 | 13,000 | 14,000 | 15,000 | 16,000 |

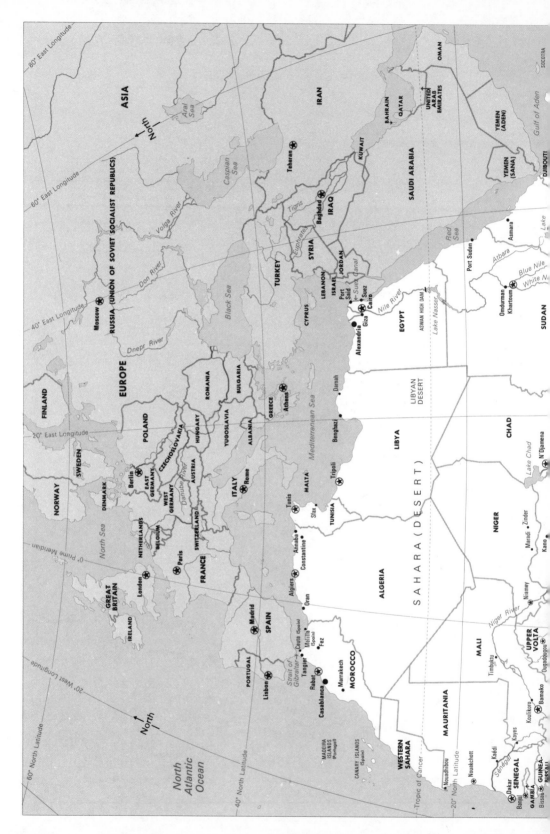

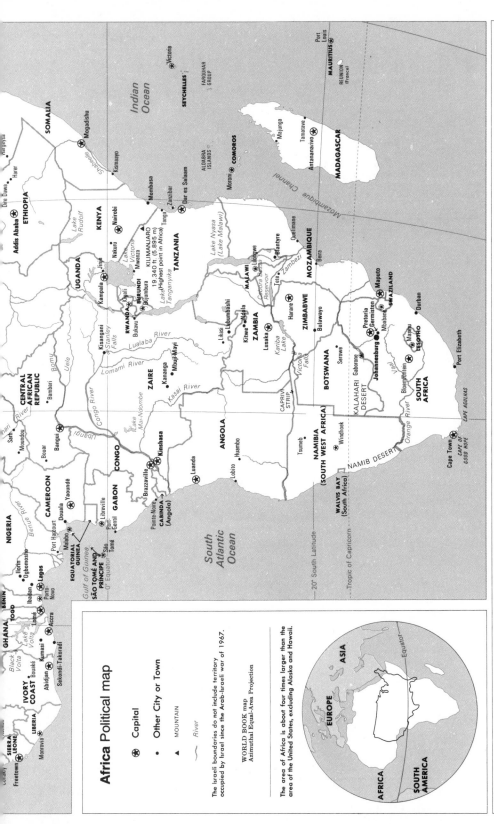

# Africa Political map

⊛ Capital

● Other City or Town

▲ MOUNTAIN

〜 River

The Israeli boundaries do not include territory
occupied by Israel since the Arab-Israeli war of 1967.

WORLD BOOK map
Azimuthal Equal-Area Projection

The area of Africa is about four times larger than the
area of the United States, excluding Alaska and Hawaii.

Distance Scale

| 0 Miles | 500 | 1,000 | 1,500 | 2,000 | 2,500 | 3,000 | 3,500 | 4,000 | 4,500 | 5,000 |
|---|---|---|---|---|---|---|---|---|---|---|
| 0 Kilometers 500 | 1,000 | 1,500 | 2,000 | 2,500 | 3,000 | 3,500 | 4,000 | 4,500 | 5,000 | 5,500 | 6,000 | 6,500 | 7,000 | 7,500 | 8,000 |

199

# Middle East Political map

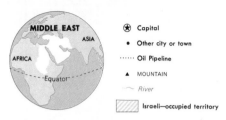

★ Capital
● Other city or town
⋯⋯ Oil Pipeline
▲ MOUNTAIN
〜 River
▨ Israeli—occupied territory

The map below shows the Middle East countries in white.
Asia, Africa, and Europe come together in this region.
The smaller map, *right*, shows Arab territory that Israel
has occupied since the Arab-Israeli war of 1967.

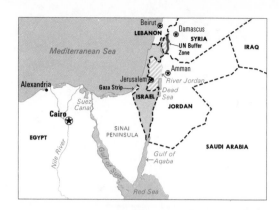

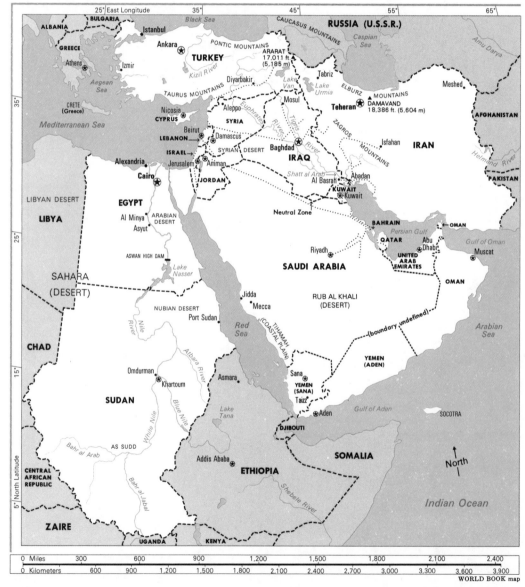

WORLD BOOK map

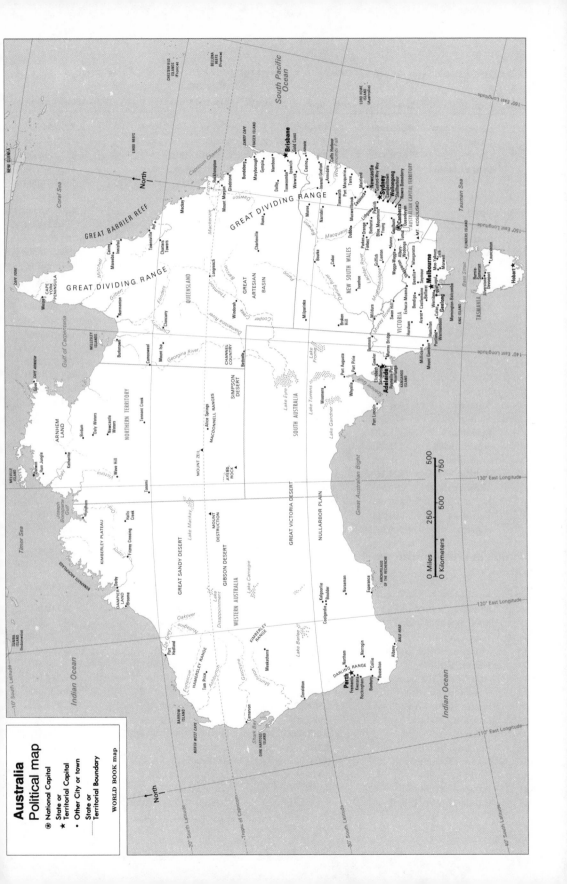

## 30 largest countries of the world by area

| Rank | Country | In sq. mi. | In km² |
|------|---------|-----------|--------|
| 1. | Soviet Union | 8,649,500 | 22,402,000 |
| 2. | Canada | 3,831,033 | 9,922,330 |
| 3. | China | 3,678,470 | 9,527,200 |
| 4. | United States | 3,618,465 | 9,371,781 |
| 5. | Brazil | 3,286,487 | 8,511,965 |
| 6. | Australia | 2,966,150 | 7,682,300 |
| 7. | India | 1,269,346 | 3,287,590 |
| 8. | Argentina | 1,072,163 | 2,776,889 |
| 9. | Sudan | 967,500 | 2,505,813 |
| 10. | Algeria | 919,595 | 2,381,741 |
| 11. | Zaire | 905,568 | 2,345,409 |
| 12. | Saudi Arabia | 830,000 | 2,149,690 |
| 13. | Indonesia | 788,425 | 2,042,012 |
| 14. | Mexico | 758,136 | 1,972,552 |
| 15. | Libya | 679,362 | 1,759,540 |
| 16. | Iran | 636,296 | 1,648,000 |
| 17. | Mongolia | 604,250 | 1,565,000 |
| 18. | Peru | 496,225 | 1,285,216 |
| 19. | Chad | 495,755 | 1,284,000 |
| 20. | Niger | 489,191 | 1,267,000 |
| 21. | Angola | 481,354 | 1,246,700 |
| 22. | Mali | 478,767 | 1,240,000 |
| 23. | Ethiopia | 471,778 | 1,221,900 |
| 24. | South Africa | 471,445 | 1,221,037 |
| 25. | Colombia | 439,737 | 1,138,914 |
| 26. | Bolivia | 424,164 | 1,098,581 |
| 27. | Mauritania | 397,956 | 1,030,700 |
| 28. | Egypt | 386,662 | 1,001,449 |
| 29. | Tanzania | 364,900 | 945,087 |
| 30. | Nigeria | 356,669 | 923,768 |

## 30 largest countries of the world by population

| Rank | Country | Population |
|------|---------|-----------|
| 1. | China | 1,025,844,000 |
| 2. | India | 726,154,000 |
| 3. | Soviet Union | 272,775,000 |
| 4. | United States | 233,450,000 |
| 5. | Indonesia | 156,864,000 |
| 6. | Brazil | 127,427,000 |
| 7. | Japan | 120,246,000 |
| 8. | Bangladesh | 91,281,000 |
| 9. | Pakistan | 89,230,000 |
| 10. | Nigeria | 84,721,000 |
| 11. | Mexico | 74,507,000 |
| 12. | West Germany | 61,412,000 |
| 13. | Philippines | 58,378,000 |
| 14. | Vietnam | 57,990,000 |
| 15. | Italy | 57,902,000 |
| 16. | Great Britain | 55,705,000 |
| 17. | France | 54,360,000 |
| 18. | Thailand | 50,027,000 |
| 19. | Turkey | 48,410,000 |
| 20. | Egypt | 44,697,000 |
| 21. | Iran | 40,919,000 |
| 22. | South Korea | 39,275,000 |
| 23. | Spain | 38,679,000 |
| 24. | Burma | 37,670,000 |
| 25. | Poland | 36,463,000 |
| 26. | Ethiopia | 33,552,000 |
| 27. | South Africa | 31,444,000 |
| 28. | Zaire | 30,824,000 |
| 29. | Colombia | 29,810,000 |
| 30. | Argentina | 28,964,000 |

## 30 largest cities of the world by population

| Rank | City | Population* | Rank | City | Population* |
|------|------|-----------|------|------|-----------|
| 1. | Shanghai, China | 10,820,000 | 16. | Teheran, Iran | 4,716,000 |
| 2. | Mexico City, Mexico | 9,373,353 | 17. | Tientsin, China | 4,280,000 |
| 3. | Tokyo, Japan | 8,349,209 | 18. | Leningrad, Soviet Union | 4,073,000 |
| 4. | Moscow, Soviet Union | 7,831,000 | 19. | Santiago, Chile | 3,899,495 |
| 5. | Peking, China | 7,570,000 | 20. | Karachi, Pakistan | 3,515,402 |
| 6. | New York City, U.S. | 7,071,030 | 21. | Ho Chi Minh City, Vietnam | 3,460,500 |
| 7. | São Paulo, Brazil | 7,033,529 | 22. | Dehli, India | 3,287,883 |
| 8. | Seoul, South Korea | 6,889,502 | 23. | Madrid, Spain | 3,201,234 |
| 9. | London, England | 6,696,008 | 24. | Calcutta, India | 3,148,746 |
| 10. | Cairo, Egypt | 6,133,000 | 25. | Berlin (East and West) | 3,038,689 |
| 11. | Bombay, India | 5,970,575 | 26. | Chicago, U.S. | 3,005,072 |
| 12. | Jakarta, Indonesia | 5,490,000 | 27. | Baghdad, Iraq | 2,969,000 |
| 13. | Hong Kong | 5,315,000 | 28. | Los Angeles, U.S. | 2,966,763 |
| 14. | Bangkok, Thailand | 5,153,902 | 29. | Lima, Peru | 2,941,473 |
| 15. | Rio de Janeiro, Brazil | 5,093,232 | 30. | Buenos Aires, Argentina | 2,908,001 |

*Latest census or government estimate.

## Continents of the world

| Continent | Area in sq. mi. | in km² | Rank by area | Population | Rank by pop. | Density Persons per sq. mi. | Persons per km² | Rank by density |
|-----------|-----------------|--------|--------------|------------|--------------|-----------------------------|-----------------|-----------------|
| Africa | 11,714,000 | 30,339,000 | 2 | 514,000,000 | 3 | 44 | 17 | 3 |
| Antarctica | 5,100,000 | 13,209,000 | 5 | 0 | 7 | 0 | 0 | 7 |
| Asia | 17,011,000 | 44,059,000 | 1 | 2,810,000,000 | 1 | 166 | 64 | 2 |
| Australia | 2,966,000 | 7,682,000 | 7 | 15,000,000 | 6 | 5 | 2 | 6 |
| Europe | 4,063,000 | 10,524,000 | 6 | 674,000,000 | 2 | 166 | 64 | 1 |
| North America | 9,400,000 | 24,345,000 | 3 | 387,000,000 | 4 | 41 | 16 | 4 |
| South America | 6,883,000 | 17,828,000 | 4 | 255,000,000 | 5 | 36 | 14 | 5 |

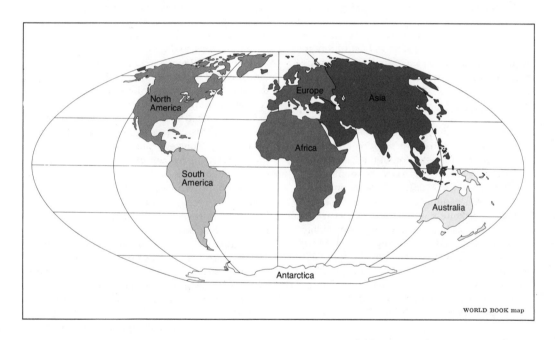

WORLD BOOK map

# 2. Facts about the United States

In this section, you will find a summary of useful information about the United States government and how it works. The section starts with a brief discussion of the United States Constitution, the document that serves as a basis for the government and its operations.

## The Constitution

The federal government of the United States is based upon one of history's most remarkable documents, the Constitution of the United States. Drafted in 1787, and ratified by the required number of states in 1788, the Constitution is the oldest written national constitution in use today.

One of the major reasons for the success of the Constitution has been its flexibility—the ability to adjust to meet needs and changing times. Another reason for the long life of the Constitution has been the acceptance of its basic principles by the American people. These basic principles are (1) the idea of a limited government, (2) the concept of popular sovereignty, and (3) the idea of rule by law.

The principle of a limited government is achieved by granting certain powers to the federal government and by granting other powers to the various state governments. A few powers are shared. In this way, the Constitution ensures that the power of the federal government will remain limited because it can exercise only those powers granted by the Constitution. This system of dividing power between the federal government and the state government is called *federalism*. It is a system of government that was originated by the Founding Fathers when they wrote the Constitution.

The second basic principle of the Constitution is that of popular sovereignty. Simply stated, popular sovereignty is rule by the people. It is a basic principle found in all truly democratic societies—that is, societies in which the people have the power to determine and to control the policies of their government. The Constitution has provided for popular sovereignty by ensuring that the American people have the power to change the Constitution and to select officials.

Closely related to the idea of popular sovereignty is the idea of rule by law. Rule by law means that all citizens, regardless of their position, power, or prestige, are bound by the laws of the United States and are to be treated equally before the law. No one, from the President to the average citizen, is above the law. Instead, all citizens and all government officials must obey the laws and the Constitution of the United States.

In addition to establishing the basic principles of the government, the Constitution also establishes the structure of the federal government. In essence, this is done in the first three articles of the Constitution. These articles establish the powers and the structure of the executive, the legislative, and the judicial branches of our government.

## Structure and function of the government

**The executive branch.** Every four years—on the first Tuesday after the first Monday in November in even-numbered years—the American voters cast their ballots and choose a President. The President is elected indirectly. The voters choose electors who are pledged to a particular presidential candidate. These electors then cast their ballots in December and the President is officially elected. The following month the President is inaugurated for a four-year term.

The oath that the President takes at the inauguration binds him to "preserve, protect, and defend the Constitution of the United States." The President also is bound by the Constitution to "take care that the laws be faithfully executed." The inaugural oath and the Constitution establish two basic functions of the presidency. These two functions are to follow the Constitution and to carry out and enforce the laws of the United States as the nation's chief executive.

As the nation's chief executive, the President is in charge of the executive branch of the federal government. This branch is made up of three parts. The first part is the President's Executive Office. This office has 10 branches that deal with a variety of concerns—from the federal budget to international trade negotiations. The second part of the executive branch consists of 13 executive departments: (1) State, (2) Treasury, (3) Defense, (4) Justice, (5) Interior, (6) Agriculture, (7) Commerce, (8) Labor, (9) Health and Human Services, (10) Housing and Urban Development, (11) Transportation, (12) Energy, and (13) Education. The heads of these departments form the President's *Cabinet*—a group that advises the President. The third part of the executive branch consists of the various independent government agencies that are directed by the President.

In addition to his duties as chief executive, the President also functions in other roles. The Constitution, in Article II, Sections 2 and 3, specifies the additional responsibilities of the President. For example, the President is the commander in chief of the nation's armed forces and thus controls the military forces of the United States. The President also is given the power (with the advice and consent of the Senate) to make treaties and to appoint ambassadors. Therefore, the President is responsible for the nation's relations with other countries. Thus, he is also the nation's chief diplomat. The President functions as the nation's chief legislator when he exercises the legislative powers granted by the Constitution. These powers include recommending legislation to Congress, calling special sessions of Congress (when necessary), and signing or vetoing bills passed by Congress.

Over the years, some strong Presidents have used their power to influence the other two branches of government. But the principle of a *separation of power* and the system of *checks and balances* established by the Constitution (see page 206) have worked to maintain a balance of power among the three branches of the federal government.

**The legislative branch.** Congress and several administrative agencies make up the legislative branch of the federal government. Congress consists of two houses, the *Senate* and the *House of Representatives*. The two houses of Congress meet separately in the Capitol in Washington, D.C. The administrative agencies (for example, the Architect of the Capitol, the Congressional Budget Office, the General Accounting Office, the Library of Congress, the Government Printing Office, and the United States Botanic Garden) operate under the direction of Congress.

Article I, Section 8 of the Constitution establishes the powers and duties of Congress. Some of these powers are (1) to levy and collect taxes, (2) to coin and to regulate the value of money, (3) to borrow money, (4) to regulate commerce, and so on. To carry out these powers, Congress meets in annual sessions to pass needed legislation. This legislation, unless vetoed by the President or overruled by the federal courts, becomes part of the body of law that governs the nation.

Each house of Congress shares the powers granted by the Constitution, with a few exceptions. For example, only the Senate has the power to confirm treaties and to approve certain presidential appointments. The House of Representatives, on the other hand, has the sole power to initiate tax legislation. And only the House of Representatives can bring charges of impeachment against a federal official. The Senate then has the sole power to try the individual.

Today, Congress has 535 members. There are 100 senators—two from each state as specified by the Constitution. This number changes only when a new state enters the union and its senators enter Congress. The number of representatives is determined by Congress and it can be changed if Congress desires.

The 435 representatives in the House of Representatives are apportioned among the states based upon their population. Each state must have at least one representative. Thus, the largest state in population, California, has forty-five representatives plus two senators. In contrast, Alaska, Delaware, North Dakota, Vermont, and Wyoming—the smallest states in terms of population—each have only one representative and two senators. The number of representatives is reapportioned every ten years when a new census is taken.

The members of Congress are chosen by the voters. Congressional elections are held every two years in November of even-numbered years. Senators are elected for six-year terms, and representatives are elected for two-year terms. Thus, all representatives come up for election every two years. But since the terms for senators are staggered, only about one-third of the Senate is chosen in each election.

Normally, Congress begins its annual session in January of each year. During a typical session, it is not unusual to have nearly 10,000 bills introduced for consideration. But for a bill to become a law it must pass both houses of Congress and be signed, or at least not vetoed, by the President. To handle this enormous workload, Congress has developed a process that enables members of Congress to consider only those bills that reflect the needs of at least a part of the American society (see page 207).

**The judicial branch.** The federal courts—the judicial branch of the federal government—derive their jurisdiction and powers from Article III of the Constitution. Today, this branch consists of the Supreme Court, about 90 district courts, 11 courts of appeal, and a number of special courts. These special courts deal with such matters as taxes, patents, and customs duties.

All federal judges are appointed by the President and approved by the Senate. These judges serve for life (or during good behavior) and can only be removed from office through impeachment and conviction.

The highest court of the land is the Supreme Court of the United States. It is the only federal court that is specifically mentioned in the Constitution. It has a chief justice and eight associate justices. The Supreme Court's jurisdiction and its powers are covered in Article III, Section 2 of the Constitution. However, the Constitution also gives Congress the power to decide what type of cases the Supreme Court can hear on appeal from lower federal courts and, in some cases, from state courts.

The Constitution also provides that the other federal courts are to be established by Congress. Of these courts, the district courts handle most of the cases involving federal laws or the Constitution. Decisions from the district courts can be appealed to the courts of appeal and, from there, to the Supreme Court if the Supreme Court decides to accept them. Cases involving the Constitution may also be appealed from state courts to the federal courts.

An important power of the federal courts—the power of *judicial review*—is not mentioned in the Constitution. Judicial review is the power of a federal court to overrule an act of a government official or a law that is in violation of the Constitution. This power applies to acts of government officials at all levels, and to laws passed by local, state, and federal legislatures.

The federal courts' power of judicial review grew out of actions by the federal courts early in the nation's history. It was firmly established in 1803 in the case of *Marbury v. Madison* when the Supreme Court declared part of a law passed by Congress as unconstitutional. From that time on, judicial review has become an accepted power of the judicial branch of the federal government.

# Features of the federal government

**The separation of power and the system of checks and balances.** The Constitution divides the powers of the federal government among the three branches. Congress has the power to pass laws, the President has the power to enforce the laws, and the courts have the power to interpret and apply the laws as cases arise. By and large, each of the three branches is independent and does not share its power with the other branches. For example, Congress does not enforce the laws it passes. And the President does not pass laws he enforces. Similarly, the federal courts cannot interpret or apply a law until a case involving a law or the Constitution comes before a federal court.

This separation of power among the three branches of government is maintained by a built-in system of *checks and balances.* In this system of checks and balances, each branch of government has some means of checking or limiting the actions of the other branches. Congress, for example, can check the actions of the President through its exclusive power to appropriate—make available —money. Thus, while the President may order a program to begin, it cannot be started until Congress makes the needed money available. Congress also has the power to maintain a check upon the courts through its power to remove judges through impeachment and conviction. However, Congress also can be checked by the other branches as well. The President has the power to veto bills passed by Congress. And the federal courts have the power to declare laws passed by Congress unconstitutional. In the final analysis, the Constitution has established a federal government composed of three branches, each with powers that check and balance the powers of the other branches.

**How a bill becomes a law.** The process through which a bill becomes a law differs slightly in the Senate and in the House of Representatives. But the basic steps are the same. By following a bill as it progresses through the House of Representatives and then through the Senate, you can understand the logic and the sequence of the legislative process.

Normally, a bill originates in one of three ways. First it may be proposed by individual citizens or by an interest group that represents a specific group within American society. Second, a bill may originate with a member of Congress. Third, a bill may be proposed by the executive branch or by an agency of the federal government. Today, most major bills begin in the executive branch.

Once a bill is proposed, the next step is to get it introduced. Every bill must be introduced by a member of Congress. It must be "sponsored" by a senator or a representative. In this example, it will be sponsored by a member of the House of Representatives.

When the proposed bill is written in its proper legal form it is placed in a basket (called a "hopper") on the floor of the House of Representatives. The Clerk of the House reads the bill (by title only). This is called the first reading. The bill is then assigned a number and sent to the Government Printing Office to be printed.

After the bill is printed, it is sent to the Speaker of the House (the presiding officer) and assigned to an appropriate committee. After the committee or a subcommittee studies the bill, the committee can take several actions. It can release, or *report out*, the bill with a recommendation to pass it; revise the bill and release it; or lay it aside so that the House cannot vote on it. Laying the bill aside is called *tabling*. If the committee approves the bill, it is sent to the House floor for consideration. At this point, the bill is put on a House Calendar. The bill then must wait its turn for consideration. However, if the bill is an important one, it can be pushed ahead of other bills by the House Rules Committee.

When the bill comes up for consideration, it receives a second reading, in full, and copies are distributed to the members of the House. The bill is then debated. At this point, it may be amended and/or approved, or it may be sent back to the committee for further consideration and adjustment. If a majority of the House approves the bill, it then receives its third reading (by title only) and is voted on again. If the bill passes—receives a majority vote—it is signed by the Speaker of the House and sent to the Senate for its consideration.

Upon reaching the Senate, the bill begins to go through the same steps again. The bill receives a first reading and is assigned to a Senate committee for study. Once again, the bill may die in committee, or it may be amended, rewritten, and/or approved. If the bill survives the committee, it is sent to the floor of the Senate. The bill is then placed on the Senate Calendar, and it must wait its turn unless pushed ahead by unanimous consent—without objection.

When its turn arrives, the bill receives a second reading, in full, and it is debated. The bill may be returned to the committee, or it may be amended, rejected, or approved. If approved, the bill receives its third reading (by title only) and is voted on again. If the bill receives a majority vote, it is passed. It is then signed and sent to the White House for the President's signature. However, before a bill can be sent to the President, any differences in the version passed by the House and the version passed by the Senate must be resolved. Therefore, if changes have been made in the Senate, the bill must be returned to the House for its approval. If the House of Representatives does not agree to the changes, a conference committee—made up of members from both houses—is appointed to resolve the differences. When an agreement is finally reached, the bill is sent back to both houses for their approval. If the bill is approved by both houses, it is then sent to the President.

The President, when he receives the bill, can do one of four things. First, he can sign the bill and it becomes a law. Second, he can refuse to sign the bill, and in ten days (excluding Sunday) it becomes a law without his signature. Third, he can veto the bill and send it back to Congress with the reasons for the veto. Congress then can override the President's veto, but it takes a two-thirds vote of both houses to do so. If Congress fails to override the veto, the bill is dead. Fourth, the President can "pocket veto" the bill. This can be done if after the bill arrives at the White House, Congress adjourns within ten days. The President then can decline to take action and the bill dies.

Obviously, the process that a bill must go through to become a law is complicated and time-consuming. Of the more than 20,000 bills usually introduced during a term of Congress (two annual sessions), only a few survive beyond the committee stage. And of those that do survive, only a very few actually become laws. The process effectively screens out most of the less important bills that are introduced each year. It also ensures that the bills passed are widely supported.

**Amending the Constitution.** Not all changes in the nation's laws must take the form of a bill. The basic law of the United States is the Constitution, and it can be changed to meet new needs or the wishes of the people. The Constitution is changed with an amendment.

Over the years, more than 7,000 amendments to the Constitution have been considered. But to date, only 33 of these have been approved by Congress. And of these, only 26 have been ratified by the states.

Ten of the 26 amendments were ratified in 1791, and they form what is known as the *Bill of Rights.* Freedom of speech, freedom of religion, the right to assemble or meet publicly, and freedom from unreasonable searches by the government—these are some of the basic rights guaranteed to all American citizens in the Bill of Rights.

Amendments can originate in two ways. They can begin in Congress, receive the approval of two-thirds of both houses, and be sent to the states for ratification. They also can originate in a national convention called by Congress on the request of two-thirds of the state legislatures. However, as yet, none of the amendments has begun in a national convention.

Ratification of a proposed amendment can be done in one of two ways. The first method is by the approval of the amendment by the legislatures of three-fourths of the states. The second method is through approval by state ratification conventions in three-fourths of the states. This second method has been used only once.

Unlike most state constitutions, the Constitution of the United States has had relatively few amendments. One reason for this is that over the years the Constitution has proved flexible enough to meet most new conditions. Another reason is the acceptance by the American people of the basic principles of government contained in the Constitution.

## Table of the states

| State | Date of entry into Union | Capital city | Largest city** | Area in square miles | Area in square kilometers | Population* | Rank by popu- lation* | Popular name |
|-------|--------------------------|--------------|----------------|----------------------|---------------------------|-------------|-----------------------|--------------|
| Alabama | 1819 | Montgomery | Birmingham | 51,609 | 133,667 | 3,890,061 | 22 | Yellowhammer State |
| Alaska | 1959 | Juneau | Anchorage | 589,757 | 1,527,464 | 400,481 | 50 | Last Frontier |
| Arizona | 1912 | Phoenix | Phoenix | 113,909 | 295,023 | 2,717,866 | 29 | Grand Canyon State |
| Arkansas | 1836 | Little Rock | Little Rock | 53,104 | 137,539 | 2,285,513 | 33 | Land of Opportunity |
| California | 1850 | Sacramento | Los Angeles | 158,693 | 411,013 | 23,668,562 | 1 | Golden State |
| Colorado | 1876 | Denver | Denver | 104,247 | 269,998 | 2,888,834 | 28 | Centennial State |
| Connecticut | 1788 | Hartford | Bridgeport | 5,009 | 12,973 | 3,107,576 | 25 | Constitution State |
| Delaware | 1787 | Dover | Wilmington | 2,057 | 5,328 | 595,225 | 47 | First State |
| Florida | 1845 | Tallahassee | Jacksonville | 58,560 | 151,670 | 9,739,992 | 7 | Sunshine State |
| Georgia | 1788 | Atlanta | Atlanta | 58,876 | 152,488 | 5,464,265 | 13 | Empire State of the South |
| Hawaii | 1959 | Honolulu | Honolulu | 6,450 | 16,705 | 965,000 | 39 | Aloha State |
| Idaho | 1890 | Boise | Boise | 83,557 | 216,412 | 943,935 | 41 | Gem State |
| Illinois | 1818 | Springfield | Chicago | 56,400 | 146,075 | 11,418,461 | 5 | Land of Lincoln |
| Indiana | 1816 | Indianapolis | Indianapolis | 36,291 | 93,993 | 5,490,179 | 12 | Hoosier State |
| Iowa | 1846 | Des Moines | Des Moines | 56,290 | 145,790 | 2,913,387 | 27 | Hawkeye State |
| Kansas | 1861 | Topeka | Wichita | 82,264 | 213,063 | 2,363,208 | 32 | Sunflower State |
| Kentucky | 1792 | Frankfort | Louisville | 40,395 | 104,623 | 3,661,433 | 23 | Bluegrass State |
| Louisiana | 1812 | Baton Rouge | New Orleans | 48,523 | 125,674 | 4,203,972 | 19 | Pelican State |
| Maine | 1820 | Augusta | Portland | 33,215 | 86,026 | 1,124,660 | 38 | Pine Tree State |
| Maryland | 1788 | Annapolis | Baltimore | 10,577 | 27,394 | 4,216,446 | 18 | Old Line State |

*1980 census.
**Latest available data.

## Table of the states

| State | Date of entry into Union | Capital city | Largest city** | Area in square miles | Area in square kilometers | Population* | Rank by population* | Popular name |
|---|---|---|---|---|---|---|---|---|
| Massachusetts | 1788 | Boston | Boston | 8,257 | 21,386 | 5,737,037 | 11 | Bay State |
| Michigan | 1837 | Lansing | Detroit | 58,216 | 150,779 | 9,258,344 | 8 | Wolverine State |
| Minnesota | 1858 | St. Paul | Minneapolis | 84,068 | 217,735 | 4,077,148 | 21 | Gopher State |
| Mississippi | 1817 | Jackson | Jackson | 47,716 | 123,584 | 2,520,638 | 31 | Magnolia State |
| Missouri | 1821 | Jefferson City | St. Louis | 69,686 | 180,486 | 4,917,444 | 15 | Show Me State |
| Montana | 1889 | Helena | Billings | 147,138 | 381,086 | 786,690 | 44 | Treasure State |
| Nebraska | 1867 | Lincoln | Omaha | 77,227 | 200,017 | 1,570,006 | 35 | Cornhusker State |
| Nevada | 1864 | Carson City | Las Vegas | 110,540 | 286,297 | 799,184 | 43 | Silver State |
| New Hampshire | 1788 | Concord | Manchester | 9,304 | 24,097 | 920,610 | 42 | Granite State |
| New Jersey | 1787 | Trenton | Newark | 7,836 | 20,295 | 7,364,158 | 9 | Garden State |
| New Mexico | 1912 | Santa Fe | Albuquerque | 121,666 | 315,113 | 1,299,968 | 37 | Land of Enchantment |
| New York | 1788 | Albany | New York City | 49,576 | 128,401 | 17,557,288 | 2 | Empire State |
| North Carolina | 1789 | Raleigh | Charlotte | 52,586 | 136,197 | 5,874,429 | 10 | Tar Heel State |
| North Dakota | 1889 | Bismarck | Fargo | 70,665 | 183,022 | 652,695 | 46 | Flickertail State |
| Ohio | 1803 | Columbus | Cleveland | 41,222 | 106,764 | 10,797,419 | 6 | Buckeye State |
| Oklahoma | 1907 | Oklahoma City | Oklahoma City | 69,919 | 181,089 | 3,025,266 | 26 | Sooner State |
| Oregon | 1859 | Salem | Portland | 96,981 | 251,180 | 2,632,663 | 30 | Beaver State |
| Pennsylvania | 1787 | Harrisburg | Philadelphia | 45,333 | 117,412 | 11,866,728 | 4 | Keystone State |
| Rhode Island | 1790 | Providence | Providence | 1,214 | 3,144 | 947,154 | 40 | Ocean State |
| South Carolina | 1788 | Columbia | Columbia | 31,055 | 80,432 | 3,119,208 | 24 | Palmetto State |
| South Dakota | 1889 | Pierre | Sioux Falls | 77,047 | 199,551 | 690,178 | 45 | Sunshine State |
| Tennessee | 1796 | Nashville | Memphis | 42,244 | 109,411 | 4,590,750 | 17 | Volunteer State |
| Texas | 1845 | Austin | Houston | 267,336 | 692,397 | 14,228,383 | 3 | Lone Star State |
| Utah | 1896 | Salt Lake City | Salt Lake City | 84,916 | 219,931 | 1,461,037 | 36 | Beehive State |
| Vermont | 1791 | Montpelier | Burlington | 9,609 | 24,887 | 511,456 | 48 | Green Mountain State |
| Virginia | 1788 | Richmond | Norfolk | 40,817 | 105,716 | 5,346,279 | 14 | Old Dominion |
| Washington | 1889 | Olympia | Seattle | 68,192 | 176,616 | 4,130,163 | 20 | Evergreen State |
| West Virginia | 1863 | Charleston | Huntington | 24,181 | 62,628 | 1,949,644 | 34 | Mountain State |
| Wisconsin | 1848 | Madison | Milwaukee | 56,154 | 145,438 | 4,705,335 | 16 | Badger State |
| Wyoming | 1890 | Cheyenne | Cheyenne | 97,914 | 253,596 | 470,816 | 49 | Equality State |

*1980 census.
**Latest available data.

## Table of principal territories and dependencies of the United States

| Territory | Location | Date acquired | Capital | Area in sq. mi. | Area in km² | Population** |
|---|---|---|---|---|---|---|
| American Samoa | In the South Pacific | 1900–25 | Pago Pago | 76 | 197 | 34,000 |
| District of Columbia | East coast of the U.S. | 1791 | * | 68 | 176 | 637,651 |
| Guam | In the Mariana Island group in the Pacific Ocean | 1898 | Agana | 212 | 549 | 111,000 |
| Puerto Rico | Southeast of Florida in the Caribbean Sea | 1898 | San Juan | 3,435 | 8,897 | 3,187,570 |
| Trust Territory of the Pacific Islands | In the Pacific Ocean near the equator | 1947 | N/A | 717 | 1,857 | 134,000 |
| Virgin Islands | Between the Caribbean Sea and the Atlantic Ocean, east of Puerto Rico | 1917 | Charlotte Amalie | 133 | 344 | 95,591 |

*The district is the capital of the United States.
**Latest available estimate.

# Suggested reading on American government

This reading list will help you further explore topics from American history and government reviewed in this section. The suggested books are frequently recommended in high school classrooms.

The books probably can be found in your school or public library. If not, your librarian may arrange to get them for you from other sources.

If you ask, your librarian can also suggest additional resources on American history and government that will help expand your knowledge and enjoyment of the subject.

Alden, John Richard. *The American Revolution, 1775-1783.* New York: Harper & Row, 1954.

Bailey, Thomas A., and Kennedy, David M. *The American Pageant: A History of the Republic.* 2 vols. 6th ed. Boston: D.C. Heath & Co., 1979.

Beard, Charles A., and Beard, Mary R. *The Beards' New Basic History of the United States.* New York: Doubleday & Co., 1968.

Bedford, Henry F., and Colbourn, Trevor. *The Americans: A Brief History.* 2 vols. 2nd ed. New York: Harcourt Brace Jovanovich, 1976.

Burns, James M., and others. *Government by the People: The Dynamics of American National Government.* 10th ed. Englewood Cliffs, N.J.: Prentice-Hall, Inc., 1978.

Chambers, William N., and Burnham, Walter D., eds. *The American Party System: Stages of Political Development.* 2nd ed. New York: Oxford University Press, 1975.

Commager, Henry Steele, ed. *Documents of American History.* 9th ed. New York: Appleton-Century-Crofts, 1974.

Curti, Merle E. *The Growth of American Thought.* 3rd ed. New York: Harper & Row, 1964.

*Dictionary of American History.* 8 vols. rev. ed. New York: Charles Scribner's Sons, 1976.

Ferguson, John H. *The American Federal Government.* 13th ed. New York: McGraw-Hill, 1977.

Graff, Henry F. *The Free and the Brave.* 4th ed. Chicago: Rand McNally, 1980.

Hofstadter, Richard. *The American Political Tradition and the Men Who Made It.* 2nd ed. New York: Alfred A. Knopf, 1973.

Magruder, Frank. *Magruder's American Government.* rev. ed. Edited by William A. McClenaghan. Boston: Allyn & Bacon, 1980.

Morison, Samuel Eliot, and others. *The Growth of the American Republic.* 2 vols. 7th ed. New York: Oxford University Press, 1980.

Nevins, Allan, and Commager, Henry Steele. *A Short History of the United States.* 6th ed. New York: Alfred A. Knopf, 1976.

Todd, Lewis Paul, and Curti, Merle E. *Rise of the American Nation.* New York: Harcourt Brace Jovanovich, 1977.

# 3. Nations of the world

This section contains "facts in brief" for all the independent nations of the world. Countries appear according to their commonly known names. In parentheses, you will also find a formal or official name for each country. Other useful facts then follow, including the name of the capital, the area of the country, its type of government, its largest cities, population figures, and brief information about its economy.

For more detailed information about the U.S. government, see Section 2 of this Unit. A world map and regional maps can be found in Section 1 of the Unit, along with tables of comparative information about the world's countries.

## Afghanistan
(Democratic Republic of Afghanistan)
Afghanistan is located in southwestern Asia. It is bordered by the Soviet Union, China, Pakistan, and Iran. About 90 per cent of the labor force works in agriculture.
*Capital:* Kabul.
*Area:* 250,000 sq. mi. (647,497 km²).
*Government:* Republic.
*Largest cities (1975 est.):* Kabul (749,000) and Quandahar (209,000).
*Population:* 1983 estimate—14,238,000; density—57 persons per sq. mi (22 per km²).
*Economy:* Mainly agricultural, with some mining and limited manufacturing.

## Albania
(People's Socialist Republic of Albania)
Albania is located on the eastern coast of the Adriatic Sea. It is bordered by Yugoslavia and Greece. Most of its workers are farmers.
*Capital:* Tiranë.
*Area:* 11,100 sq. mi. (28,748 km²).
*Government:* Communist dictatorship.
*Largest cities (1976 est.):* Tiranë (192,300), Shkodër (62,500), and Durrës (61,000).
*Population:* 1983 estimate—2,944,000; density—264 persons per sq. mi. (102 km²).
*Economy:* Mainly agricultural, with some mining and forestry, but very limited manufacturing and fishing.

## Algeria
(Democratic and Popular Republic of Algeria)
Algeria is located in northern Africa. It is bordered by Morocco, Western Sahara, Mauritania, Mali, Niger, Tunisia, and Libya. Most of its workers are farmers or herders.
*Capital:* Algiers.
*Area:* 919,595 sq. mi. (2,381,741 km²).
*Government:* Republic.
*Largest cities (1974 est.):* Algiers (1,503,720) and Oran (485,139).
*Population:* 1983 estimate—20,377,000; density—23 persons per sq. mi. (9 per km²).
*Economy:* Mainly agricultural, with some mining and limited manufacturing.

## Andorra
(Valleys of Andorra)
Andorra is located in the Pyrenees mountains in western Europe. It is bordered by Spain and France. Most of its workers are involved in the tourist trade.
*Capital:* Andorra.
*Area:* 175 sq. mi. (453 km²).
*Government:* Principality.
*Largest cities (1975 census):* Andorra (10,932) and Escaldes (7,372).
*Population:* 1983 estimate—39,000; density—223 persons per sq. mi. (86 per km²).
*Economy:* Based mainly on tourism, with some farming and limited mining.

## Angola
(People's Republic of Angola)
Angola is located on the southwestern coast of Africa. It is bordered by Zaire, Zambia, Congo, and Namibia. Most of Angola's workers are engaged in agriculture.
*Capital:* Luanda.
*Area:* 481,354 sq. mi. (1,246,700 km²).
*Government:* Socialist dictatorship.
*Largest cities (1972 est.):* Luanda (600,000) and Huambo (61,885)
*Population:* 1983 estimate—7,622,000; density—16 persons per sq. mi. (6 per km²).
*Economy:* Mainly agricultural, with limited mining and developing industries.

## Antigua and Barbuda
(Antigua and Barbuda)
Antigua and Barbuda is a country composed of three islands, Antigua, Barbuda, and Redonda. It is located in the Caribbean Sea about 430 miles (692 kilometers) north of Venezuela. Most workers are engaged in the tourist industry.
*Capital:* St. John's.
*Area:* 171 sq. mi. (442 km²).
*Government:* Constitutional monarchy.
*Largest city (1975 est.):* St. John's (24,000).
*Population:* 1983 estimate—79,000; density—482 persons per sq. mi. (186 per km²).
*Economy:* Mainly tourism, with some farming and manufacturing.

## Argentina
(Republic of Argentina)
Argentina is located in southeastern South America. It is bordered by Chile, Bolivia, Paraguay, Brazil, and Uruguay. Most of Argentina's workers are engaged in manufacturing, farming, ranching, meat packing, and the processing of farm products.
*Capital:* Buenos Aires.
*Area:* 1,072,163 sq. mi. (2,776,889 km²).
*Government:* Republic (military rule).
*Largest cities (1980 census):* Buenos Aires (2,908,001), Córdoba (968,664), and Rosario (875,623).
*Population:* 1983 estimate—28,964,000; density—26 persons per sq. mi. (10 per km²).
*Economy:* Mainly industrial production, service industries, agriculture, and trade, with some mining.

## Australia
(Commonwealth of Australia)
Australia is both a continent and a country. It lies between the Indian Ocean and the Pacific Ocean. Most of the workers in Australia are engaged in manufacturing, service industries, and trade.
*Capital:* Canberra.
*Area:* 2,966,150 sq. mi. (7,682,300 km²).
*Government:* Constitutional monarchy.
*Largest cities (1981 census):* Sydney (2,874,415), Melbourne (2,578,527), and Brisbane (942,636).
*Population:* 1983 estimate—15,150,000; density—5 persons per sq. mi. (2 per km²).
*Economy:* Based mainly on agriculture and mining, with increasing manufacturing.

## Austria
(Republic of Austria)
Austria is located in central Europe. It is bordered by Switzerland, Liechtenstein, West Germany, Czechoslovakia, Hungary, Italy, and Yugoslavia. Most of Austria's workers are employed in manufacturing, services, and trade.
*Capital:* Vienna.
*Area:* 32,374 sq. mi. (83,849 km²).
*Government:* Federal republic.
*Largest cities (1971 census):* Vienna (1,614,841), Graz (248,500), Linz (202,874), Salzburg (128,845), and Innsbruck (115,197).
*Population:* 1983 estimate—7,530,000; density—233 persons per sq. mi. (90 per km²).
*Economy:* Mainly manufacturing and trade, with some agriculture and forestry, but limited mining.

## Bahamas
(Commonwealth of the Bahamas)
Bahamas is a country composed of about 3,000 islands in the northern part of the West Indies. Most workers are engaged in the tourist industry.
*Capital:* Nassau.
*Area:* 5,380 sq. mi. (13,935 km²).
*Government:* Constitutional monarchy.
*Largest cities (1970 census):* Nassau (100,000) and Freeport (15,277).
*Population:* 1982 estimate—240,000; density—44 persons per sq. mi. (17 per km²).
*Economy:* Based mainly on tourism and related activities.

## Bahrain
(The State of Bahrain)
Bahrain is an island country in the Persian Gulf in Southwest Asia. Most of the land is desert, and most of the workers in Bahrain are employed in the oil industry or by the government.
*Capital:* Manama.
*Area:* 240 sq. mi. (622 km²).
*Government:* Emirate.
*Largest cities (1975 est.):* Manama (94,697) and Al Muharraq (44,567).
*Population:* 1983 estimate—414,000; density—1,725 persons per sq. mi. (666 per km²).
*Economy:* Based mainly on the production and refining of oil, with limited construction, fishing, and manufacturing.

## Bangladesh
(People's Republic of Bangladesh)
Bangladesh is a nation in South Asia. It is bor-

dered by India and Burma. About 80 per cent of the workers are engaged in agriculture.
*Capital:* Dacca.
*Area:* 55,598 sq. mi. (143,998 km²).
*Government:* Republic (military rule).
*Largest cities (1974 census):* Dacca (1,679,572) and Chittagong (889,760).
*Population:* 1983 estimate—91,281,000; density— 1,642 persons per sq. mi. (634 per km²).
*Economy:* Mainly agricultural, with some limited industry.

## Barbados
(Barbados)
Barbados is an island country in the West Indies. It lies about 250 miles (402 km) northeast of the South American mainland. About 50 per cent of its workers are engaged in agriculture, the tourist trade, and other service industries.
*Capital:* Bridgetown.
*Area:* 166 sq. mi. (431 km²).
*Government:* Constitutional monarchy.
*Largest city (1976 est.):* Bridgetown (8,789).
*Population:* 1983 estimate—253,000; density— 1,520 persons per sq. mi. (587 per km²).
*Economy:* Based mainly on tourism, trade, and agriculture.

## Belgium
(Kingdom of Belgium)
Belgium is located in northwestern Europe. It is bordered by the Netherlands, West Germany, Luxembourg, and France. Most workers in Belgium are found in manufacturing or service industries.
*Capital:* Brussels.
*Area:* 11,781 sq. mi. (30,513 km²).
*Government:* Constitutional monarchy.
*Largest cities (1975 est.):* Antwerp (209,200), Brussels (153,409), and Ghent (142,551).
*Population:* 1983 estimate—9,877,000; density— 839 persons per sq. mi. (324 per km²).
*Economy:* Mainly industrial and commercial, with limited agriculture.

## Belize
(Belize)
Belize is located in Central America. It is bordered by Mexico and Guatemala. Most of its workers are in agriculture, forestry, and fishing.
*Capital:* Belmopan.
*Area:* 8,867 sq. mi. (22,965 km²).
*Government:* Constitutional monarchy.

*Largest city (1972 est.):* Belize City (41,500).
*Population:* 1983 estimate—158,000; density—18 persons per sq. mi. (7 per km²).
*Economy:* Based mainly on agriculture, with limited fishing and industry.

## Benin
(People's Republic of Benin)
Benin is located in West Africa. It is bordered by Upper Volta, Niger, Nigeria, and Togo. More than 50 per cent of the nation's workers are engaged in agriculture.
*Capital:* Porto-Novo.
*Area:* 43,484 sq. mi. (112,622 km²).
*Government:* Republic.
*Largest cities (1975 est.):* Contonou (178,000) and Porto-Novo (104,000).
*Population:* 1983 estimate—3,875,000; density—88 persons per sq. mi. (34 per km²).
*Economy:* Based mainly on agriculture.

## Bhutan
(Kingdom of Bhutan)
Bhutan is located in south-central Asia. It is bordered by China and India. Almost all the people in Bhutan are engaged in farming or the raising of livestock.
*Capital:* Thimphu.
*Area:* 18,147 sq. mi. (47,000 km²).
*Government:* Monarchy.
*Largest city (1977 est.):* Thimphu (8,922).
*Population:* 1983 estimate—1,390,000; density—77 persons per sq. mi. (30 per km²).
*Economy:* Almost entirely agricultural and pastoral, but with very limited mining.

## Bolivia
(Republic of Bolivia)
Bolivia is located in South America. It is bordered by Brazil, Paraguay, Argentina, Chile, and Peru. About 65 per cent of the labor force is engaged in agriculture.
*Capital:* Sucre (official); La Paz (actual).
*Area:* 424,164 sq. mi. (1,098,581 km²).
*Government:* Republic.
*Largest cities (1976 census):* La Paz (654,713), Santa Cruz (256,946), Cochabama (205,002), and Oruro (124,121).
*Population:* 1983 estimate—6,048,000; density—16 persons per sq. mi. (6 per km²).
*Economy:* Mainly agricultural, with manufacturing and mining growing in importance.

## Botswana

(Republic of Botswana)
Botswana is located in southern Africa. It is bordered by Namibia, Zimbabwe, and South Africa. Most of the workers are engaged in agriculture and mining.
*Capital:* Gaborone.
*Area:* 231,805 sq. mi. (600,372 km²).
*Government:* Republic.
*Largest cities (1976 est.):* Gaborone (37,300), Francistown (25,000).
*Population:* 1983 estimate—885,000; density—3 persons per sq. mi. (1 per km²).
*Economy:* Based mainly on agriculture and herding, but with a growing mining industry.

## Brazil

(Federative Republic of Brazil)
Brazil is located in South America. It is bordered by every country in South America except Chile and Ecuador. About 32 per cent of the workers are engaged in agriculture, and most of the rest are employed in the nation's growing industries or in service occupations.
*Capital:* Brasília.
*Area:* 3,286,487 sq. mi. (8,511,965 km²).
*Government:* Federal republic.
*Largest cities (1980 census):* São Paulo (7,003,529), Rio de Janeiro (5,093,232), and Belo Horizonte (1,442,483).
*Population:* 1983 estimate—127,427,000; density—39 persons per sq. mi. (15 per km²).
*Economy:* Based mainly on industry and services.

## Bulgaria

(People's Republic of Bulgaria)
Bulgaria is located in southeastern Europe on the Balkan Peninsula. It is bordered by Romania, Turkey, Greece, and Yugoslavia. Many of the nation's workers are farmers, while others are employed in industry.
*Capital:* Sofia.
*Area:* 42,823 sq. mi. (110,912 km²).
*Government:* Communist dictatorship.
*Largest cities (1975 census):* Sofia (965,729) and Plovdiv (300,242).
*Population:* 1983 estimate—9,049,000; density—212 persons per sq. mi. (82 per km²).
*Economy:* Primarily industrial, with some agriculture.

## Burma

(Socialist Republic of the Union of Burma)
Burma is located in Southeast Asia. It is bordered by China, Laos, Thailand, Bangladesh, and India. About 70 per cent of the workers are engaged in agriculture and forestry, and most of the rest are factory workers, craftspeople, or merchants.
*Capital:* Rangoon.
*Area:* 261,218 sq. mi. (676,552 km²).
*Government:* Republic.
*Largest cities (1979 est.):* Rangoon (1,315,964) and Mandalay (472,512).
*Population:* 1983 estimate—37,670,000; density—145 persons per sq. mi. (56 per km²).
*Economy:* Mainly agriculture and forestry, with some limited mining.

## Burundi

(Republic of Burundi)
Burundi is located in central Africa. It is bordered by Rwanda, Tanzania, and Zaire. Almost all of its people are engaged in agriculture.
*Capital:* Bujumbura.
*Area:* 10,747 sq. mi. (27,834 km²).
*Government:* Republic.
*Largest city (1979 est.):* Bujumbura (151,000).
*Population:* 1983 estimate—4,355,000; density—404 persons per sq. mi. (156 per km²).
*Economy:* Mainly agricultural, with very limited industry.

## Cameroon

(United Republic of Cameroon)
Cameroon is located in west-central Africa. It is bordered by Chad, the Central African Republic, Congo, Gabon, Equatorial Guinea, and Nigeria. Most of the workers are engaged in agriculture.
*Capital:* Yaoundé.
*Area:* 183,569 sq. mi. (475,442 km²).
*Government:* Republic.
*Largest cities (1976 census):* Douala (458,246) and Yaoundé (313,706).
*Population:* 1983 estimate—9,103,000; density—49 persons per sq. mi. (19 per km²).
*Economy:* Based mainly on agriculture.

## Canada

(Canada)
Canada is the second largest nation in area in the world. It is located in North America, and it is bordered by the United States. A large majority of workers in Canada are employed in manufacturing, service occupations, or in wholesale and retail trade.

*Capital:* Ottawa.
*Area:* 3,831,033 sq. mi. (9,922,330 km²).
*Government:* Constitutional monarchy.
*Largest cities (1976 census):* Montreal (1,080,546), Toronto (633,318), Winnipeg (560,874), Calgary (469,917), Edmonton (461,361), and Vancouver (410,188).
*Population:* 1983 estimate—24,541,000; density—5 persons per sq. mi. (2 per km²).
*Economy:* Mainly manufacturing, with trade and services contributing significantly.

## Cape Verde
(Republic of Cape Verde)
Cape Verde is an island country composed of 10 islands and 5 islets in the Atlantic Ocean. It lies north of the equator, off the west coast of Africa. Many of the people are engaged in agriculture and fishing.
*Capital:* Praia.
*Area:* 1,557 sq. mi. (4,033 km²).
*Government:* Republic.
*Largest cities (1970 census):* Mindelo (28,797) and Praia (21,494).
*Population:* 1983 estimate—342,000; density—220 persons per sq. mi. (85 per km²).
*Economy:* Based largely upon agriculture and fishing, with limited mining.

## Central African Republic
(Central African Republic)
The Central African Republic is located in the center of Africa. It is bordered by Chad, Sudan, Zaire, Congo, and Cameroon. About three-fifths of its workers live in country areas.
*Capital:* Bangui.
*Area:* 240,535 sq. mi. (622,984 km²).
*Government:* Republic.
*Largest cities (1974 est.):* Bangui (301,000) and Berbérati (93,000).
*Population:* 1983 estimate—2,385,000; density—10 persons per sq. mi. (4 per km²).
*Economy:* Based mainly on farming, with some mining and very limited manufacturing.

## Chad
(Republic of Chad)
Chad is located in north-central Africa. It is bordered by Libya, Sudan, the Central African Republic, Niger, Nigeria, and Cameroon. Most of the workers are engaged in agriculture, hunting, fishing, and food gathering.
*Capital:* N'Djamena.
*Area:* 495,755 sq. mi. (1,284,000 km²).

*Government:* Republic.
*Largest cities (1975 est.):* N'Djamena (224,000) and Sarh (50,000).
*Population:* 1983 estimate—4,843,000; density—10 persons per sq. mi. (4 per km²).
*Economy:* Based almost entirely on agriculture.

## Chile
(Republic of Chile)
Chile is located on the southwest coast of South America. It is bordered by Peru, Argentina, and Bolivia. Only about 33⅓ per cent of its work force is engaged in agriculture. Most of the other workers are employed in manufacturing, mining, and service occupations.
*Capital:* Santiago.
*Area:* 292,258 sq. mi. (756,945 km²).
*Government:* Military rule.
*Largest cities (1980 est.):* Santiago (3,899,495), Viña del Mar (277,068), and Valparaíso (266,354).
*Population:* 1983 estimate—11,675,000; density—39 persons per sq. mi. (15 per km²).
*Economy:* Based mainly on mining and manufacturing.

## China
(People's Republic of China)
China is located in eastern and central Asia. It is bordered by Russia, Afghanistan, India, Nepal, Pakistan, Bhutan, and a number of other Asian nations. More than three-fourths of China's workers are engaged in agriculture and fishing.
*Capital:* Peking.
*Area:* 3,678,470 sq. mi. (9,527,200 km²).
*Government:* Communist dictatorship.
*Largest cities (1970 est.):* Shanghai (10,820,000), Peking (7,570,000), Tientsin (4,280,000), and Shenyang (2,411,000)*.
*Population:* 1983 estimate—1,025,874,000 (based on UN data); density—280 persons per sq. mi. (108 per km²).
*Economy:* Based primarily on agriculture, though industries are developing.
*1957 government estimate.

## Colombia
(Republic of Colombia)
Colombia is located in northwestern South America. It is bordered by Venezuela, Brazil, Peru, Ecuador, and Panama. A large portion of the labor force is engaged in agriculture.
*Capital:* Bogotá.
*Area:* 439,737 sq. mi. (1,138,914 km²).

*Government:* Republic.
*Largest cities (1973 census):* Bogotá (2,850,000) and Medellín (1,064,741).
*Population:* 1983 estimate—29,810,000; density—67 persons per sq. mi. (26 per km²).
*Economy:* Mainly agricultural, with some mining and manufacturing.

## Comoros
(Federal and Islamic Republic of the Comoros)
Comoros is an island nation of Africa. It is composed of several islands located in the Indian Ocean. Most workers are engaged in agriculture.
*Capital:* Moroni.
*Area:* 838 sq. mi. (2,171 km²).
*Government:* Republic.
*Largest city (1976 est.):* Moroni (19,778).
*Population:* 1983 estimate—358,000; density—427 persons per sq. mi. (165 per km²).
*Economy:* Almost entirely agricultural.

## Congo
(People's Republic of the Congo)
Congo is located in west-central Africa. It is bordered by Cameroon, the Central African Republic, Zaire, Angola, and Gabon. Most of the workers are engaged in agriculture.
*Capital:* Brazzaville.
*Area:* 132,047 sq. mi. (342,000 km²).
*Government:* Republic.
*Largest cities:* Brazzaville (250,000)*, Pointe-Noire (135,000)**, and Dolisie (25,000)**.
*Population:* 1983 estimate—1,660,000; density—13 persons per sq. mi. (5 per km²).
*Economy:* Based mainly on agriculture and forestry, with some mining.
*1972 estimate.
**1970 preliminary census.

## Costa Rica
(Republic of Costa Rica)
Costa Rica is located in Central America. It is bordered by Nicaragua and Panama. Almost 50 per cent of its workers are engaged in agriculture, and about 10 per cent are in manufacturing. Most of the others work in service occupations.
*Capital:* San José.
*Area:* 19,575 sq. mi. (50,700 km²).
*Government:* Republic.
*Largest cities (1973 census):* San José (215,441), Alajuela (30,190), and Limón (29,621).

*Population:* 1983 estimate—2,411,000; density—124 persons per sq. mi. (48 per km²).
*Economy:* Mainly agricultural, but there is growing industry.

## Cuba
(Republic of Cuba)
Cuba is an island nation in the Caribbean Sea. It lies in the West Indies, about 90 miles (140 kilometers) south of Florida. About 24 per cent of the Cuban workers are engaged in forestry, fishing, and agriculture; 21 per cent in services; and 20 per cent in manufacturing.
*Capital:* Havana
*Area:* 44,218 sq. mi. (114,524 km²).
*Government:* Socialist republic (Communist dictatorship).
*Largest cities:* Havana (1,900,240)*, Santiago de Cuba (275,970)**, and Camagüey (196,854)**.
*Population:* 1983 estimate—10,252,000; density—231 persons per sq. mi. (89 per km²).
*Economy:* Based on services, agriculture and manufacturing.
*1975 government estimate.
**1970 census.

## Cyprus
(Republic of Cyprus)
Cyprus is an island nation located in Southwest Asia at the eastern end of the Mediterranean Sea. About 40 per cent of the workers are engaged in manufacturing.
*Capital:* Nicosia.
*Area:* 3.572 sq. mi. (9,251 km²).
*Government:* Republic.
*Largest cities (1975 est.):* Nicosia (147,100) and Limassol (80,600).
*Population:* 1982 estimate—623,000; density—147 persons per sq. mi. (67 per km²).
*Economy:* Based on agriculture, manufacturing, mining, and tourism.

## Czechoslovakia
(Czechoslovak Socialist Republic)
Czechoslovakia is located in central Europe. It is bordered by Poland, Russia, Hungary, Austria, and East and West Germany. About 35 per cent of its workers are engaged in industry and almost 20 per cent in government and other services.
*Capital:* Prague.
*Area:* 49,370 sq. mi. (127,869 km²).
*Government:* Socialist republic (Communist dictatorship).

Largest cities (1978 est.): Prague (1,188,573), Brno (369,028), Bratislava (367,743), and Ostrava (322,358).
Population: 1983 estimate—15,682,000; density—319 persons per sq. mi. (123 per km²).
Economy: Mainly manufacturing, with some agriculture.

## Denmark

(Kingdom of Denmark)
Denmark is located in northern Europe. It is bordered by West Germany. Most of the workers in Denmark are employed in manufacturing or service occupations. Only about 8 per cent of the workers are engaged in agriculture, forestry, and fishing.
Capital: Copenhagen.
Area: 16,629 sq. mi. (43,069 km²).
Government: Constitutional monarchy.
Largest cities (1978 est.): Copenhagen (515,594), Århus (245,386), Odense (167,768), and Ålborg (154,226).
Population: 1983 estimate—5,169,000; density—311 persons per sq. mi. (120 per km²).
Economy: Mainly manufacturing.

## Djibouti

(Republic of Djibouti)
Djibouti is a small nation located in eastern Africa. It lies on the western shore of the Gulf of Aden, and it is bordered by Ethiopia and Somalia. Djibouti is an extremely poor and underdeveloped country with a high unemployment rate. Most of the workers are involved in livestock herding.
Capital: Djibouti.
Area: 8,494 sq. mi. (22,000 km²).
Government: Republic.
Largest city (1973 est.): Djibouti (100,000).
Population: 1983 estimate—355,000; density—41 persons per sq. mi. (16 per km²).
Economy: Based almost entirely on shipping and railway transportation.

## Dominica

(Commonwealth of Dominica)
Dominica is a small island country in the Caribbean Sea. It lies north of the Venezuelan coast. About 60 per cent of the nation's workers are engaged in agriculture.
Capital: Roseau.
Area: 290 sq. mi. (751 km²).
Government: Republic.
Largest city (1976 est.): Roseau (10,157).

Population: 1983 estimate—80,000; density—277 persons per sq. mi. (107 per km²).
Economy: Based on the export of agricultural goods, with some food processing, tourism, and mining.

## Dominican Republic

(Dominican Republic)
The Dominican Republic is located on the island of Hispaniola between the Atlantic Ocean and the Caribbean Sea. About 65 per cent of the nation's workers are engaged in agriculture.
Capital: Santo Domingo
Area: 18,816 sq. mi. (48,734 km²).
Government: Republic.
Largest cities (1976 est.): Santo Domingo (979,608) and Santiago (219,846).
Population: 1983 estimate—5,935,000; density—316 persons per sq. mi. (122 per km²).
Economy: Based mainly on agriculture, with some manufacturing.

## Ecuador

(Republic of Ecuador)
Ecuador is located in South America. It is bordered by Colombia and Peru. About 43 per cent of Ecuador's workers are engaged in agriculture, forestry, and fishing. About 37 per cent are employed in manufacturing and services.
Capital: Quito.
Area: 109,484 sq. mi. (283,561 km²).
Government: Republic.
Largest cities (1974 census): Guayaquil (814,064) and Quito (597,133).
Population: 1983 estimate—9,235,000; density—85 persons per sq. mi. (33 per km²).
Economy: The mainstay of the economy is agriculture, with limited mining, manufacturing, and trade.

## Egypt

(Arab Republic of Egypt)
Egypt is a nation that lies in northeastern Africa and southwestern Asia. It is bordered by Israel, Sudan, and Libya. About 42 per cent of the workers in Egypt are engaged in agriculture, and about 35 per cent are engaged in manufacturing, mining, and service occupations.
Capital: Cairo.
Area: 386,662 sq. mi. (1,001,449 km²).
Government: Republic.
Largest cities (1976 est.): Cairo (6,133,000), Alexandria (2,320,000)*, and Giza (933,900).

*Population:* 1983 estimate—44,697,000; density—
117 persons per sq. mi. (45 per km²).

*Economy:* Largely agricultural, but with growing
industries.

*1975 estimate.

## El Salvador
(Republic of El Salvador)

El Salvador is a nation in Central America. It is
bordered by Honduras and Guatemala. Almost 60
per cent of its workers are engaged in agriculture, and about 20 per cent are employed in
various industries.

*Capital:* San Salvador.

*Area:* 8,124 sq. mi. (21,041 km²).

*Government:* Republic.

*Largest cities (1977 est.):* San Salvador (397,126),
Santa Ana (112,830), and San Miguel (72,874).

*Population:* 1983 estimate—5,229,000; density—
645 persons per sq. mi. (249 per km²).

*Economy:* Based mainly on farming and the export of agricultural products.

## Equatorial Guinea
(Republic of Equatorial Guinea)

Equatorial Guinea is a nation in western Africa. It
is bordered by Cameroon and Gabon. Many
workers are engaged in agriculture.

*Capital:* Malabo.

*Area:* 10,830 sq. mi. (28,051 km²).

*Government:* Military rule.

*Largest cities (1973 est.):* Malabo (60,000) and Bata
(30,000).

*Population:* 1983 estimate—389,000; density—36
persons per sq. mi. (14 per km²).

*Economy:* Based on agriculture, forestry, and
fishing.

## Ethiopia
(Ethiopia)

Ethiopia is a nation located in eastern Africa. It is
bordered by Sudan, Djibouti, Somalia, and Kenya.
Most of the workers in Ethiopia are engaged in
agriculture.

*Capital:* Addis Ababa.

*Area:* 471,778 sq. mi. (1,221,900 km²).

*Government:* Military rule.

*Largest cities (1980 est.):* Addis Ababa (1,277,159)
and Asmara (443,060).

*Population:* 1983 estimate—33,552,000; density—
70 persons per sq. mi. (27 per km²).

*Economy:* Largely dependent upon agriculture,
with some mining but very limited industry.

## Fiji
(Fiji)

Fiji is an island nation in the southwest Pacific
Ocean. It is composed of more than 800 islands.
Most of the workers are engaged in agriculture.

*Capital:* Suva.

*Area:* 7,056 sq. mi. (18,274 km²).

*Government:* Constitutional monarchy.

*Largest cities (1976 census):* Suva (63,628) and
Lautoka (22,672).

*Population:* 1983 estimate—664,000; density—93
persons per sq. mi. (36 per km²).

*Economy:* Based upon agriculture and the export
of agricultural products, with some tourism
and manufacturing.

## Finland
(Republic of Finland)

Finland is a nation located in northern Europe.
It is bordered by Norway, Russia, and Sweden.
Almost 60 per cent of Finland's workers are em-
ployed in manufacturing or in service industries.
Only 13 per cent of the nation's workers are
engaged in agriculture, forestry, and fishing.

*Capital:* Helsinki.

*Area:* 130,120 sq. mi. (337,009 km²).

*Government:* Republic.

*Largest cities (1977 est.):* Helsinki (499,205) and
Tampere (165,418).

*Population:* 1983 estimate—4,821,000; density—36
persons per sq. mi. (14 per km²).

*Economy:* Mainly based upon industry, with agriculture, commerce, forestry, and trade also important.

## France
(French Republic)

France is a nation located in western Europe. It
is bordered by Belgium, Luxembourg, West Germany, Switzerland, Italy, Monaco, Andorra, and
Spain. Almost 75 per cent of France's workers are
engaged in manufacturing, trade, or service occupations. Only about 9 per cent of the French
workers are engaged in agriculture, forestry, and
fishing.

*Capital:* Paris.

*Area:* 211,208 sq. mi. (547,026 km²).

*Government:* Republic.

*Largest cities (1975 census):* Paris (2,299,830), Marseille (908,600), Lyon (456,716), Toulouse
(373,796), and Nice (344,481).

*Population:* 1983 estimate—54,360,000; density—
256 persons per sq. mi. (99 per km²).

*Economy:* Mainly industrial, with some agriculture.

## Gabon

(Gabon Republic)

Gabon is a nation located in west-central Africa. It is bordered by Equatorial Guinea, Cameroon, and the Congo. About 65 per cent of Gabon's workers are engaged in agriculture.

*Capital:* Libreville.

*Area:* 103,347 sq. mi. (267,667 km²).

*Government:* Republic.

*Largest cities (1976 est.):* Libreville (251,000) and Port-Gentil (85,000).

*Population:* 1983 estimate—569,000; density—5 persons per sq. mi. (2 per km²).

*Economy:* Based largely upon agriculture and forestry.

## Gambia

(The Gambia)

Gambia is a nation located in western Africa. It is bordered by Senegal. Most of the workers in Gambia are engaged in agriculture.

*Capital:* Banjul.

*Area:* 4,361 sq. mi. (11,295 km²).

*Government:* Republic.

*Largest city (1978 est.):* Banjul (45,600).

*Population:* 1983 estimate—653,000; density—150 persons per sq. mi. (58 per km²).

*Economy:* Mainly agricultural.

## East Germany

(German Democratic Republic)

East Germany is a nation located in north-central Europe. It is bordered by Poland, Czechoslovakia, and West Germany. More than half of East Germany's workers are employed in manufacturing and trade. Only about 11 per cent of its workers are engaged in agriculture and forestry.

*Capital:* East Berlin.

*Area:* 41,768 sq. mi. (108,178 km²).

*Government:* Communist dictatorship.

*Largest cities (1978 est.):* East Berlin (1,128,983), Leipzig (563,980), and Dresden (514,508).

*Population:* 1983 estimate—16,637,000, including East Berlin; density—399 persons per sq. mi. (154 per km²).

*Economy:* Based largely on industry and services.

## West Germany

(Federal Republic of Germany)

West Germany is a nation located in north-central Europe. It is bordered by Denmark, the Netherlands, East Germany, Czechoslovakia, Austria, Switzerland, France, Belgium, and Luxembourg. About 70 per cent of the workers are engaged in manufacturing, trade, or service occupations.

*Capital:* Bonn.

*Area:* 96,005 sq. mi. (248,651 km²).

*Government:* Federal republic.

*Largest cities (1978 est.):* West Berlin (1,909,706), Hamburg (1,664,305), and Munich (1,296,970).

*Population:* 1983 estimate—61,412,000, including West Berlin; density—640 persons per sq. mi. (247 per km²).

*Economy:* Mainly industrial, with trade, finance, and agriculture as important segments.

## Ghana

(Republic of Ghana)

Ghana is a nation located in western Africa. It is bordered by Upper Volta, Togo, and Ivory Coast. Over two-thirds of the workers in Ghana are engaged in agriculture, and most of the other workers are employed in mining or service occupations.

*Capital:* Accra.

*Area:* 92,100 sq. mi. (238,537 km²).

*Government:* Military rule.

*Largest cities (1970 census):* Accra (564,194) and Kumasi (260,286).

*Population:* 1983 estimate—12,585,000; density—137 persons per sq. mi. (53 per km²).

*Economy:* Mainly agriculture, with some mining.

## Great Britain

(United Kingdom of Great Britain and Northern Ireland)

Great Britain is a nation composed of two large islands (Great Britain and part of Ireland) and many small islands that lie off the northwest coast of Europe. It is bordered by the Republic of Ireland. Most of the nation's workers are employed in industry and service occupations.

*Capital:* London.

*Area:* 94,249 sq. mi. (244,104 km²).

*Government:* Constitutional monarchy.

*Largest cities (1981 census):* Greater London (6,696,008), Birmingham (1,006,908), and Glasgow (762,288).

*Population:* 1982 estimate—56,019,000; density—591 persons per sq. mi. (228 per km²).

*Economy:* Based mainly upon manufacturing and services.

## Greece

(Hellenic Republic)

Greece is a nation located in southeastern Europe. It is bordered by Bulgaria, Yugoslavia, Albania, and Turkey. About 30 per cent of the workers in Greece are employed in manufacturing or service occupations; about 40 per cent, in farming, fishing, and forestry.

*Capital:* Athens.

*Area:* 50,944 sq. mi. (131,944 km²).

*Government:* Republic.

*Largest cities (1971 census):* Athens (867,023), Salonika (345,799), and Piraeus (187,362).

*Population:* 1983 estimate—9,919,000; density— 194 persons per sq. mi. (75 per km²).

*Economy:* Based mainly on industry and services, with agriculture also contributing.

## Grenada

(State of Grenada)

Grenada is an island nation that is located in the Windward Islands of the West Indies. Most of Grenada's workers are engaged in agriculture, forestry, or fishing.

*Capital:* St. George's.

*Area:* 133 sq. mi. (344 km²).

*Government:* Constitutional monarchy.

*Largest city (1976 est.):* St. George's (10,000).

*Population:* 1983 estimate—115,000; density—865 persons per sq. mi. (334 per km²).

*Economy:* Mainly agriculture, fishing, and tourism.

## Guatemala

(Republic of Guatemala)

Guatemala is a nation located in Central America. It is bordered by Mexico, Honduras, Belize, and El Salvador. About 54 per cent of its workers are engaged in agriculture, fishing, and forestry.

*Capital:* Guatemala City.

*Area:* 42,042 sq. mi. (108,889 km²).

*Government:* Military rule.

*Largest cities (1973 census):* Guatemala City (700,504) and Quezaltenango (53,021).

*Population:* 1983 estimate—7,935,000; density— 189 persons per sq. mi. (73 per km²).

*Economy:* Mainly agricultural, with trade and industry also significant.

## Guinea

(Republic of Guinea)

Guinea is a nation in western Africa. It is bordered by Guinea-Bissau, Senegal, Mali, Ivory Coast, Liberia, and Sierra Leone. Most of its workers are engaged in agriculture.

*Capital:* Conakry.

*Area:* 94,926 sq. mi. (245,857 km²).

*Government:* Republic.

*Largest cities:* Conakry (45,304)* and Kankan (50,000)**.

*Population:* 1983 estimate—5,415,000; density—57 persons per sq. mi. (23 per km²).

*Economy:* Based mainly upon agriculture and mining, with some commerce.

*1972 estimate for metropolitan area.

**1967 estimate.

## Guinea-Bissau

(Republic of Guinea-Bissau)

Guinea-Bissau is a nation located on the west coast of Africa. It is bordered by Senegal and Guinea. More than half its workers are engaged in agriculture.

*Capital:* Bissau.

*Area:* 13,948 sq. mi. (36,125 km²).

*Government:* Military rule.

*Largest city: (1971 est.):* Bissau (65,000).

*Population:* 1983 estimate—834,000; density—60 persons per sq. mi. (23 per km²).

*Economy:* Based largely upon agriculture.

## Guyana

(Cooperative Republic of Guyana)

Guyana is a nation located on the northeast coast of South America. It is bordered by Suriname, Brazil, and Venezuela. Most of its workers are engaged in agriculture or mining.

*Capital:* Georgetown.

*Area:* 83,000 sq. mi. (214, 969 km²).

*Government:* Republic.

*Largest cities (1976 est.):* Georgetown (72,049) and New Amsterdam (17,782).

*Population:* 1983 estimate—919,000; density—10 persons per sq. mi. (4 per km²).

*Economy:* Based on agriculture and mining.

## Haiti

(Republic of Haiti)

Haiti is a nation located on the western part of the island of Hispaniola in the Caribbean Sea. Most of its workers are engaged in agriculture.

*Capital:* Port-au-Prince.

*Area:* 10,714 sq. mi. (27,750 km²).

*Government:* Dictatorship.

*Largest city (1978 est.):* Port-au-Prince (745,700).

*Population:* 1983 estimate—5,284,000; density— 492 persons per sq. mi. (190 per km²).

*Economy:* Based on agriculture and tourism.

## Honduras
(Republic of Honduras)
Honduras is a nation located in Central America. It is bordered by Nicaragua, El Salvador, and Guatemala. About 57 per cent of the workers in Honduras are engaged in agriculture, fishing, and forestry.
*Capital:* Tegucigalpa.
*Area:* 43,277 sq. mi. (112,088 km²).
*Government:* Republic.
*Largest cities (1974 census):* Tegucigalpa (267,754) and San Pedro Sula (146,842).
*Population:* 1983 estimate—4,104,000; density—96 persons per sq. mi. (37 per km²).
*Economy:* Mainly agriculture, with some mining and limited manufacturing.

## Hungary
(Hungarian People's Republic)
Hungary is a nation located in central Europe. It is bordered by Czechoslovakia, Russia, Romania, Yugoslavia, and Austria. More than 50 per cent of Hungary's workers are employed in manufacturing and service occupations. About 22 per cent of its workers are engaged in agriculture and forestry.
*Capital:* Budapest.
*Area:* 35,919 sq. mi. (93,030 km²).
*Government:* Communist dictatorship.
*Largest cities (1979 est.):* Budapest (2,093,187), Miskolc (210,948), Debrecen (199,742), and Szeged (177,677).
*Population:* 1983 estimate—10,818,000; density—300 persons per sq. mi. (116 per km²).
*Economy:* Mainly industrial, with some contribution from agriculture.

## Iceland
(Republic of Iceland)
Iceland is an island nation located in the North Atlantic Ocean. About 20 per cent of the workers are engaged in fishing or in the fish-processing industry. Only about 15 per cent of the workers are farmers.
*Capital:* Reykjavík.
*Area:* 39,769 sq. mi. (103,000 km²).
*Government:* Republic.
*Largest cities (1979 est.):* Reykjavík (83,536) and Kopavogur (13,533).
*Population:* 1983 estimate—236,000; density—5 persons per sq. mi. (2 per km²).
*Economy:* Mainly fishing and fish processing, with some agriculture and manufacturing.

## India
(Union of India)
India is a large nation located in southern Asia. It is bordered by China, Nepal, Bhutan, Bangladesh, Burma, and Pakistan. About 72 per cent of India's workers are engaged in agriculture, forestry, and fishing.
*Capital:* New Delhi.
*Area:* 1,269,346 sq. mi. (3,287,590 km²).
*Government:* Federal republic.
*Largest cities (1971 census):* Bombay (5,970,575), Delhi (3,287,883), Calcutta (3,148,746), Madras (2,469,449), and Hyderabad (1,607,396).
*Population:* 1983 estimate—726,154,000; density—572 persons per sq. mi. (221 per km²).
*Economy:* Based mainly on agriculture, with some mining and manufacturing.

## Indonesia
(Republic of Indonesia)
Indonesia is an island nation in Southeast Asia. It is bordered by Malaysia and Papua New Guinea. About 60 per cent of Indonesia's workers are engaged in agriculture, fishing, and forestry; about 20 per cent are in manufacturing and trade.
*Capital:* Jakarta.
*Area:* 788,425 sq. mi. (2,042,012 km²).
*Government:* Republic.
*Largest cities (1974 est.):* Jakarta (5,490,000), Surabaya (1,660,355), Bandung (1,282,121), and Medan (700,363).
*Population:* 1983 estimate—156,864,000; density—199 persons per sq. mi. (77 per km²).
*Economy:* Mainly agriculture, with some manufacturing.

## Iran
(Islamic Republic of Iran)
Iran is a nation located in southwestern Asia. It is bordered by Russia, Afghanistan, Pakistan, Iraq, and Turkey. About 45 per cent of Iran's workers are engaged in agriculture. Most of the other workers are employed in the petroleum industry or other industries.
*Capital:* Teheran (Tehran).
*Area:* 636,296 sq. mi. (1,648,000 km²).
*Government:* Islamic republic.
*Largest cities (1976 est.):* Teheran (4,716,000), Isfahan (618,000), Meshed (584,000), and Tabriz (571,000).

*Population:* 1983 estimate—40,919,000; density—
65 persons per sq. mi. (25 per km²).

*Economy:* Based mainly on agriculture and oil
production.

## Iraq
(Republic of Iraq)

Iraq is a nation located in southwestern Asia. It is
bordered by Turkey, Iran, Kuwait, Saudi Arabia,
Jordan, and Syria. About 50 per cent of Iraq's
workers are engaged in agriculture, and about 20
per cent are employed in the petroleum industry
or service occupations.

*Capital:* Baghdad.

*Area:* 167,925 sq. mi. (434,924 km²).

*Government:* Republic.

*Largest city (1976 est.):* Baghdad (2,969,000).

*Population:* 1983 estimate—14,506,000, density—
85 persons per sq. mi. (33 per km²).

*Economy:* Based mainly on the oil industry and
agriculture.

## Ireland
(Repubic of Ireland)

Ireland is a nation located in northwestern Europe. It is bordered by Great Britain and Northern Ireland. About 50 per cent of Ireland's workers are employed in manufacturing, trade, or
service occupations.

*Capital:* Dublin.

*Area:* 27,136 sq. mi. (70,283 km²).

*Government:* Republic.

*Largest cities (1979 census):* Dublin (544,586) and
Cork (138,267).

*Population:* 1983 estimate—3,575,000; density—
132 persons per sq. mi. (51 per km²).

*Economy:* Mainly industrial, with some agriculture.

## Israel
(State of Israel)

Israel is a nation located in southwestern Asia. It
is bordered by Lebanon, Syria, Jordan, and Egypt.
About 70 per cent of the workers in Israel are
employed in manufacturing and mining, in government service, and in other service occupations.

*Capital:* Jerusalem.

*Area:* 8,019 sq. mi. (20,770 km²)*.

*Government:* Republic.

*Largest cities (1973 est.):* Tel Aviv-Yafo (367,600),
Jerusalem (326,400), and Haifa (225,800).

*Population:* 1983 estimate—4,152,000; density—
518 persons per sq. mi. (200 per km²)**.

*Economy:* Based largely upon manufacturing and
commerce, with some agriculture.

*Does not include Arab territory occupied by Israel.
Total including Arab territory is 34,501 sq. mi.
(89,357 km²).

**Excluding population of Arab territory occupied by
Israel.

## Italy
(Italian Republic)

Italy is a nation located in southern Europe. It is
bordered by Switzerland, Austria, Yugoslavia, and
France. More than 50 per cent of Italy's workers
are engaged in manufacturing, trade, or service
occupations. Only about 14 per cent of Italy's
workers are engaged in agriculture, forestry, and
fishing.

*Capital:* Rome.

*Area:* 116,314 sq. mi. (301,252 km²).

*Government:* Republic.

*Largest cities (1972 est.):* Rome (2,868,248)*, Milan
(1,738,487), Naples (1,223,659), Turin (1,172,476),
and Genoa (815,708).

*Population:* 1983 estimate—57,902,000; density—
497 persons per sq. mi. (192 per km²).

*Economy:* Based mainly on manufacturing, with
commerce and agriculture also contributing.

*1975 government estimate.

## Ivory Coast
(Republic of the Ivory Coast)

Ivory Coast is a nation located in western Africa.
It is bordered by Mali, Upper Volta, Ghana, Liberia, and Guinea. Most of the workers are engaged
in agriculture.

*Capital:* Abidjan.

*Area:* 124,504 sq. mi. (322,463 km²).

*Government:* Republic.

*Largest cities: (1978 est.):* Abidjan (1,100,000) and
Bouaké (230,000).

*Population:* 1983 estimate—9,018,000; density—73
persons per sq. mi. (28 per km²).

*Economy:* Mainly based upon agriculture, forestry, and fishing.

## Jamaica
(Jamaica)

Jamaica is an island nation in the West Indies,
about 90 miles (140 kilometers) south of Cuba in
the Caribbean Sea. More than a third of Jamaica's workers are engaged in agriculture. Others
are employed in manufacturing and service occupations.

*Capital:* Kingston.
*Area:* 4,244 sq. mi. (10,991 km²).
*Government:* Constitutional monarchy.
*Largest cities (1978 est.):* Kingston (665,050), Montego Bay (43,754)*, and Spanish Town (40,731)*.
*Population:* 1982 estimate—2,273,000; density—536 persons per sq. mi. (207 per km²).
*Economy:* Manufacturing, mining, agriculture, and tourism.
*1970 census.

## Japan

(Japan)
Japan is an island nation located in the Pacific Ocean, off the east coast of Asia. Over 60 per cent of the Japanese workers are employed in industry or service occupations; only about 10 per cent are engaged in agriculture and forestry.
*Capital:* Tokyo.
*Area:* 145,834 sq. mi. (377,708 km²).
*Government:* Constitutional monarchy.
*Largest cities (1980 census):* Tokyo (8,349,209), Yokohama (2,773,822), Osaka (2,648,158), and Nagoya (2,087,884).
*Population:* 1983 estimate—120,246,000; density—824 persons per sq. mi. (318 per km²).
*Economy:* Mainly based upon manufacturing and trade.

## Jordan

(Hashemite Kingdom of Jordan)
Jordan is a nation located in southwestern Asia. It is bordered by Syria, Iraq, Saudi Arabia, and Israel. Most of its workers are engaged in agriculture.
*Capital:* Amman.
*Area:* 37,738 sq. mi. (97,740 km²).
*Government:* Constitutional monarchy.
*Largest cities (1979 census):* Amman (648,587) and Az Zarqa (215,687).
*Population:* 1983 estimate—2,460,000; density—65 persons per sq. mi. (25 per km²).
*Economy:* Mainly agricultural, with some developing industry.

## Kampuchea

(Democratic Kampuchea)
Kampuchea is located in Southeast Asia. It is bordered by Thailand, Laos, and Vietnam. Almost all of its people are engaged in agriculture.
*Capital:* Phnom Penh.
*Area:* 69,898 sq. mi. (181,035 km²).
*Government:* Communist dictatorship.
*Largest cities:* Data unavailable.

*Population:* 1983 estimate—9,360,000, based on a United Nations estimate; but many experts estimate the population at 5,000,000; density—135 persons per sq. mi. (52 per km²).
*Economy:* Based mainly on agriculture.

## Kenya

(Republic of Kenya)
Kenya is a nation located in eastern Africa. It is bordered by Sudan, Ethiopia, Somalia, Tanzania, and Uganda. More workers in Kenya are engaged in agriculture than in any other activity.
*Capital:* Nairobi.
*Area:* 224,961 sq. mi. (582,646 km²).
*Government:* Republic.
*Largest cities (1979 census):* Nairobi (835,000) and Mombasa (342,000).
*Population:* 1983 estimate—18,185,000; density—88 persons per sq. mi. (34 per km²).
*Economy:* Mainly agricultural, with growing manufacturing.

## Kiribati

(Republic of Kiribati)
Kiribati is a small island country in the southwest Pacific Ocean. It consists of 33 islands scattered over about 2 million square miles (5 million square kilometers) of ocean. Most of its people are engaged in agriculture and fishing.
*Capital:* Tarawa.
*Area:* 278 sq. mi. (719 km²).
*Government:* Republic.
*Largest city (1978 census):* Tarawa (17,921).
*Population:* 1983 estimate—56,000; density—184 persons per sq. mi. (71 per km²).
*Economy:* Based mainly on agriculture, with some trade and limited mining.

## North Korea

(Democratic People's Republic of Korea)
North Korea is a nation located in the northern portion of a peninsula in northeastern Asia that projects southeastward from China. It is bordered by China, Russia, and South Korea. About 50 per cent of its workers are engaged in agriculture.
*Capital:* Pyongyang.
*Area:* 46,540 sq. mi. (120,538 km²).
*Government:* Communist dictatorship.
*Largest cities (1971 est.):* Pyongyang (2,500,000), Hamhung (525,000), Sinuiju (500,000), Chongjin (400,000), and Kaesong (400,000).
*Population:* 1983 estimate—19,291,000; density—414 persons per sq. mi. (160 per km²).

*Economy:* Mainly based upon manufacturing and mining, with limited agriculture.

## South Korea
(Republic of Korea)
South Korea is a nation located in the southern portion of a peninsula in northeastern Asia that projects southeastward from China. It is bordered by North Korea. About 50 per cent of South Korea's workers are engaged in agriculture, and about 20 per cent are in industry.
*Capital:* Seoul.
*Area:* 38,025 sq. mi. (98,484 km²).
*Government:* Republic.
*Largest cities (1975 census):* Seoul (6,879,464), Pusan (2,450,125), Taegu (1,310,768), and Inchon (800,007).
*Population:* 1983 estimate—39,275,000; density— 1,033 persons per sq. mi. (399 per km²).
*Economy:* Based mainly on manufacturing and agriculture.

## Kuwait
(State of Kuwait)
Kuwait is a nation located in the northeastern portion of the Arabian Peninsula in southwestern Asia. It is bordered by Iraq, Iran, and Saudi Arabia. Most workers in Kuwait are employed by the government or work in business or the oil industry.
*Capital:* Kuwait.
*Area:* 7,780 sq. mi. (20,150 km²)*.
*Government:* Emirate.
*Largest cities (1975 census):* Hawalli (130,565), As Salimiyah (113,943), and Kuwait (78,116).
*Population:* 1983 estimate—1,610,000; density— 207 persons per sq. mi. (80 per km²).
*Economy:* Based almost entirely upon oil.
*Includes offshore islands.

## Laos
(Lao People's Democratic Republic)
Laos is a nation located in Southeast Asia. It is bordered by China, Vietnam, Kampuchea, Thailand, and Burma. Almost all of the workers in Laos are engaged in agriculture.
*Capital:* Vientiane.
*Area:* 91,429 sq. mi. (236,800 km²).
*Government:* Socialist republic (Communist dictatorship).
*Largest cities (1973 est.):* Vientiane (174,229), Savannakhet (50,691), and Pakxe (44,860).
*Population:* 1983 estimate—3,995,000; density—44 persons per sq. mi. (17 per km²).
*Economy:* Based almost entirely on agriculture.

## Lebanon
(Republic of Lebanon)
Lebanon is a nation located in southwestern Asia at the eastern end of the Mediterranean Sea. It is bordered by Syria and Israel. Most of Lebanon's workers are engaged in agriculture, service occupations, or industry.
*Capital:* Beirut.
*Area:* 4,015 sq. mi. (10,400 km²).
*Government:* Republic.
*Largest cities (1974 est.):* Beirut (702,000) and Tarabulus (Tripoli) (175,000).
*Population:* 1983 estimate—3,404,000; density— 847 persons per sq. mi. (327 per km²).
*Economy:* Based mainly on trade and commerce, with agriculture and industry also important.

## Lesotho
(Kingdom of Lesotho)
Lesotho is a nation surrounded by the Republic of South Africa. Most of its workers are engaged in raising livestock and food crops.
*Capital:* Maseru.
*Area:* 11,720 sq. mi. (30,355 km²).
*Government:* Constitutional monarchy.
*Largest city (1976 census):* Maseru (38,440).
*Population:* 1983 estimate—1,442,000; density— 124 persons per sq. mi. (48 per km²).
*Economy:* Based mainly on agriculture.

## Liberia
(Republic of Liberia)
Liberia is a nation located on the west coast of Africa. It is bordered by Guinea, Ivory Coast, and Sierra Leone. Most of the workers are engaged in agriculture.
*Capital:* Monrovia.
*Area:* 43,000 sq. mi. (111,369 km²).
*Government:* Military rule.
*Largest city (1978 est.):* Monrovia (208,629).
*Population:* 1983 estimate—2,071,000; density—49 persons per sq. mi. (19 per km²).
*Economy:* Based mainly on mining, with agriculture and trade also important.

## Libya
(People's Socialist Libyan Arab Jamahiriya)
Libya is a nation located on the northern coast of Africa. It is bordered by Egypt, Sudan, Chad, Niger, Algeria, and Tunisia. About four-fifths of Libya's workers are engaged in agriculture.
*Capital:* Tripoli.
*Area:* 679,362 sq. mi. (1,759,540 km²).
*Government:* Jamahiriya*.

*Largest cities (1973 census):* Tripoli (735,083) and Benghazi (337,423).
*Population:* 1983 estimate—3,226,000; density—5 persons per sq. mi. (2 per km²).
*Economy:* Based mainly on production of oil.
*The Libyan government's name for a kind of republic.

### Liechtenstein
(Principality of Liechtenstein)
Liechtenstein is a small nation located in south-central Europe. It is bordered by Austria and Switzerland. More than half of Liechtenstein's workers are employed in manufacturing or trade.
*Capital:* Vaduz.
*Area:* 61 sq. mi. (157 km²).
*Government:* Principality.
*Largest city (1977 census):* Vaduz (4,704).
*Population:* 1983 estimate—28,000; density—461 persons per sq. mi. (178 per km²).
*Economy:* Based mainly on industry, trade, and agriculture.

### Luxembourg
(Grand Duchy of Luxembourg)
Luxembourg is a small nation located in north-western Europe. It is bordered by Belgium, West Germany, and France. About 33 per cent of the workers in Luxembourg are employed in the nation's steel mills, and about 33 per cent of its workers are engaged in agriculture.
*Capital:* Luxembourg.
*Area:* 998 sq. mi. (2,586 km²).
*Government:* Constitutional monarchy.
*Largest city (1979 est.):* Luxembourg (79,600).
*Population:* 1983 estimate—368,000; density—368 persons per sq. mi. (142 per km²).
*Economy:* Largely based upon mining and industry.

### Madagascar
(Democratic Republic of Madagascar)
Madagascar is an island nation located in the Indian Ocean about 240 miles (386 kilometers) from the east coast of Africa. About 80 per cent of its workers are engaged in agriculture.
*Capital:* Antananarivo.
*Area:* 226,658 sq. mi. (587,041 km²).
*Government:* Republic (military rule).
*Largest cities (1977 est.):* Antananarivo (484,000) and Fianarantsoa (73,000).
*Population:* 1983 estimate—9,387,000; density—41 persons per sq. mi. (16 per km²).
*Economy:* Mainly agricultural, with some mining and very limited industry.

### Malawi
(Republic of Malawi)
Malawi is a small nation located in southeastern Africa. It is bordered by Tanzania, Mozambique, and Zambia. Most of Malawi's workers are engaged in agriculture.
*Capital:* Lilongwe.
*Area:* 45,747 sq. mi. (118,484 km²).
*Government:* Republic.
*Largest cities (1977 census):* Blantyre (229,000), Lilongwe (102,924), and Zomba (16,000).
*Population:* 1983 estimate—6,427,000; density—140 persons per sq. mi. (54 per km²).
*Economy:* Almost entirely agricultural.

### Malaysia
(Malaysia)
Malaysia is a nation located in Southeast Asia. It covers the southern portion of the Malay Peninsula and most of the northern portion of the island of Borneo. It is bordered by Thailand and Indonesia. About half of the workers in Malaysia are engaged in agriculture.
*Capital:* Kuala Lumpur.
*Area:* 127,317 sq. mi. (329,749 km²).
*Government:* Constitutional monarchy.
*Largest cities:* Kuala Lumpur (1,072,000)* and Georgetown (270,019)**.
*Population:* 1983 estimate—14,554,000; density—114 persons per sq. mi. (44 per km²).
*Economy:* Mainly agricultural, with some manufacturing and mining.
*1980 estimate.
**1970 census.

### Maldives
(Republic of Maldives)
Maldives is a small nation composed of about 2,000 islands located in the Indian Ocean. Most of the nation's workers are engaged in the fishing industry.
*Capital:* Male.
*Area:* 115 sq. mi. (298 km²).
*Government:* Republic.
*Largest city (1978 census):* Male (29,555).
*Population:* 1983 estimate—159,000; density—1,383 persons per sq. mi. (534 per km²).
*Economy:* Based on the fishing industry, which is government controlled.

### Mali
(Republic of Mali)
Mali is a nation located in western Africa. It is bordered by Algeria, Niger, Upper Volta, Ivory

Coast, Guinea, Senegal, and Mauritania. Most of its workers are engaged in agriculture, raising livestock, and farming.
*Capital:* Bamako.
*Area:* 478,767 sq. mi. (1,240,000 km²).
*Government:* Republic (military rule).
*Largest cities (1976 census):* Bamako (404,022) and Mopti (35,000).
*Population:* 1983 estimate—7,481,000; density—16 persons per sq. mi. (6 per km²).
*Economy:* Based mainly upon farming and livestock raising.

## Malta
(Republic of Malta)
Malta is an island nation in the Mediterranean Sea. It is composed of two main islands and several smaller islands. The large majority of Malta's workers are employed in industry, primarily shipbuilding and repairing.
*Capital:* Valletta.
*Area:* 122 sq. mi. (316 km²).
*Government:* Republic.
*Largest cities (1979 est.):* Sliema (20,095), Birkirkara (16,832), Qormi (15,784), and Valletta (14,042).
*Population:* 1983 estimate—377,000; density—3,090 persons per sq. mi. (1,193 per km²).
*Economy:* Based mainly on shipbuilding and ship repairing, with very limited agriculture and tourism.

## Mauritania
(Islamic Republic of Mauritania)
Mauritania is a nation located in western Africa. It is bordered by Western Sahara, Algeria, Mali, and Senegal. About 90 per cent of the workers are engaged in farming and livestock herding.
*Capital:* Nouakchott.
*Area:* 397,956 sq. mi. (1,030,700 km²).
*Government:* Republic (military rule).
*Largest cities (1976 census):* Nouakchott (134,986)* and Nouadhibou (21,961).
*Population:* 1983 estimate—1,775,000; density—5 persons per sq. mi. (2 per km²).
*Economy:* Based mainly on agriculture, with some small industry and mining.
*Metropolitan area.

## Mauritius
(Mauritius)
Mauritius is an island nation located in the Indian Ocean, about 500 miles (800 kilometers) east

of Madagascar. About two-thirds of the nation's workers raise or process sugar.
*Capital:* Port Louis.
*Area:* 790 sq. mi. (2,045 km²).
*Government:* Constitutional monarchy.
*Largest cities (1979 est.):* Port Louis (144,412), Beau Bassin (83,714)*, and Curepipe (54,356)*.
*Population:* 1983 estimate—1,003,000; density—1,269 persons per sq. mi. (490 per km²).
*Economy:* Based mainly upon the raising and processing of sugar and sugar by-products.
*1978 estimate.

## Mexico
(United Mexican States)
Mexico is a nation located in North America. It is bordered by the United States, Belize, and Guatemala. About 41 per cent of Mexico's workers are engaged in agriculture, fishing, and forestry; another 40 per cent are employed in services and manufacturing.
*Capital:* Mexico City.
*Area:* 758,136 sq. mi. (1,963,564 km²).
*Government:* Republic.
*Largest cities (1980 census):* Mexico City (9,373,353) and Guadalajara (1,725,000).
*Population:* 1983 estimate—74,507,000; density—98 persons per sq. mi. (38 per km²).
*Economy:* Based mainly on agriculture, with increasing manufacturing, trade, and petroleum.

## Monaco
(Principality of Monaco)
Monaco is one of the smaller nations in the world. It is located on the Mediterranean Sea and is bordered on three sides by southeastern France. Most workers are employed in tourist and service occupations, controlled by the government.
*Capital:* Monaco.
*Area:* 0.58 sq. mi. (1.49 km²).
*Government:* Principality.
*Largest cities (1968 census):* La Condamine (11,438) and Monte Carlo (9,948).
*Population:* 1983 estimate—27,000; density—46,993 persons per sq. mi. (18,121 per km²).
*Economy:* Based mainly on tourism, with some small, local industries.

## Mongolia
(Mongolian People's Republic)
Mongolia is a nation located in east-central Asia. It is bordered by Russia and China. Most of the

nation's workers are engaged in livestock herding, and they live and work on cooperatively owned livestock farms.

*Capital:* Ulan Bator.

*Area:* 604,250 sq. mi. (1,565,000 km²).

*Government:* Communist dictatorship.

*Largest city (1980 census):* Ulan Bator (418,700).

*Population:* 1983 estimate—1,795,000; density—3 persons per sq. mi. (1 per km²).

*Economy:* Based mainly on livestock raising and related industries, with some developing industry.

## Morocco

(Kingdom of Morocco)

Morocco is a nation located in northwest Africa. It is bordered by Algeria and Western Sahara. About 70 per cent of its workers are engaged in farming and raising livestock.

*Capital:* Rabat.

*Area:* 172,414 sq. mi. (446,550 km²).

*Government:* Constitutional monarchy.

*Largest cities (1971 census):* Casablanca (1,506,373), Rabat (367,620), Marrakech (332,741), and Fez (325,327).

*Population:* 1983 estimate—22,119,000; density—129 persons per sq. mi. (50 per km²).

*Economy:* Based mainly on agriculture and commerce.

## Mozambique

(People's Republic of Mozambique)

Mozambique is a nation located on the eastern coast of Africa. It is bordered by Swaziland, South Africa, Zimbabwe, Malawi, and Tanzania. Almost all of its workers are engaged in agriculture.

*Capital:* Maputo.

*Area:* 309,496 sq. mi. (801,590 km²).

*Government:* Communist dictatorship.

*Largest cities (1970 census):* Maputo (341,922), Nampula (120,188), and Beira (110,752).

*Population:* 1983 estimate—12,910,000; density—41 persons per sq. mi. (16 per km²).

*Economy:* Based on agriculture and trade, with some limited industry.

## Nauru

(Republic of Nauru)

Nauru is an island nation located in the Pacific Ocean, just south of the equator. Most workers in Nauru are employed in the phosphate industry.

*Capital:* None.

*Area:* 8 sq. mi. (21 km²).

*Government:* Republic.

*Largest city:* None; population concentrated in coastal settlements and villages.

*Population:* 1983 estimate—8,000; density—987 persons per sq. mi. (381 per km²).

*Economy:* Based almost entirely on the production of phosphate for export, with an attempt at building a shipping industry.

## Nepal

(Kingdom of Nepal)

Nepal is a nation located in south-central Asia. It is bordered by China and India. About 90 per cent of the workers in Nepal are engaged in agriculture.

*Capital:* Kathmandu.

*Area:* 54,362 sq. mi. (140,797 km²).

*Government:* Constitutional monarchy.

*Largest city (1971 census):* Kathmandu (150,402).

*Population:* 1983 estimate—14,955,000; density—275 persons per sq. mi. (106 per km²).

*Economy:* Based mainly on agriculture, with some limited local industry.

## The Netherlands

(Kingdom of the Netherlands)

The Netherlands is a nation located in northwestern Europe. It is bordered by West Germany and Belgium. Most of the workers are in manufacturing, mining, commerce, and service occupations.

*Capital:* Amsterdam.

*Area:* 15,892 sq. mi. (41,160 km²).

*Government:* Constitutional monarchy.

*Largest cities (1975 est.):* Amsterdam (757,958), Rotterdam (620,867), and The Hague (482,879).

*Population:* 1983 estimate—14,427,000; density—909 persons per sq. mi. (351 per km²).

*Economy:* Based mainly on manufacturing and commerce.

## New Zealand

(New Zealand)

New Zealand is an island nation located in the southwest Pacific Ocean. It is composed of two principal islands and many smaller islands. More than half of New Zealand's workers are engaged in industry or in service occupations, and about 12 per cent are in agriculture, forestry, and fishing.

*Capital:* Wellington.

*Area:* 103,883 sq. mi. (269,057 km²).

*Government:* Constitutional monarchy.

*Largest cities (1981 census):* Auckland (766,183), Wellington (319,615), and Christchurch (289,392).

*Population:* 1983 estimate—3,180,000; density—31 persons per sq. mi. (12 per km²).

*Economy:* Based mainly on manufacturing, farming, and trade.

## Nicaragua
(Republic of Nicaragua)

Nicaragua is a nation located in Central America. It is bordered by Honduras and Costa Rica. Almost half of Nicaragua's workers are engaged in agriculture, fishing, and forestry; and most of the rest are employed in industry and in service occupations.

*Capital:* Managua.

*Area:* 50,193 sq. mi. (130,000 km²).

*Government:* Republic (Junta).

*Largest cities:* Managua (677,680)* and León (83,693)**.

*Population:* 1983 estimate—2,980,000; density—60 persons per sq. mi. (23 per km²).

*Economy:* Based mainly on agriculture, with industry and commerce growing in importance.
*1980 estimate.
**1979 estimate.

## Niger
(Republic of Niger)

Niger is a nation located in west-central Africa. It is bordered by Algeria, Libya, Chad, Nigeria, Benin, Upper Volta, and Mali. Most of the workers farm or herd livestock.

*Capital:* Niamey.

*Area:* 489,191 sq. mi. (1,267,000 km²).

*Government:* Republic (military rule).

*Largest cities (1977 est.):* Niamey (225,300) and Zinder (58,400).

*Population:* 1983 estimate—5,780,000; density—13 persons per sq. mi. (5 per km²).

*Economy:* Based almost entirely on agriculture.

## Nigeria
(Federal Republic of Nigeria)

Nigeria is a nation located on the west coast of Africa. It is bordered by Niger, Chad, Cameroon, and Benin. About 75 per cent of the workers in Nigeria are engaged in agriculture.

*Capital:* Lagos.

*Area:* 356,669 sq. mi. (923,768 km²).

*Government:* Republic.

*Largest cities (1977 est.):* Lagos (1,149,200) and Ibadan (855,300).

*Population:* 1983 estimate—84,721,000; density—238 persons per sq. mi. (92 per km²).

*Economy:* Based mainly upon agriculture and the production of oil.

## Norway
(Kingdom of Norway)

Norway is a nation located in northern Europe. It is bordered by Sweden, Finland, and Russia. Most of Norway's workers are employed in the nation's industries or in service occupations.

*Capital:* Oslo.

*Area:* 125,182 sq. mi. (324,219 km²).

*Government:* Constitutional monarchy.

*Largest cities (1978 est.):* Oslo (460,377) and Bergen (211,861).

*Population:* 1983 estimate—4,128,000; density—34 persons per sq. mi. (13 per km²).

*Economy:* Based largely upon manufacturing and trade.

## Oman
(Sultanate of Oman)

Oman is a small nation located on the southern tip of the Arabian Peninsula. It is bordered by the United Arab Emirates, Yemen (Aden), and Saudi Arabia. Most of Oman's workers are engaged in agriculture or work in the oil industry.

*Capital:* Muscat.

*Area:* 82,030 sq. mi. (212,457 km²).

*Government:* Sultanate.

*Largest cities (1974 est.):* Matrah (20,000), Salalah (10,000), and Nazwa (10,000).

*Population:* 1983 estimate—976,000; density—13 persons per sq. mi. (5 per km²).

*Economy:* Based mainly on agriculture and the oil industry.

## Pakistan
(Islamic Republic of Pakistan)

Pakistan is a nation located in southern Asia. It is bordered by Iran, Afghanistan, China, and India. About 65 per cent of Pakistan's workers are engaged in agriculture.

*Capital:* Islamabad.

*Area:* 310,404 sq. mi. (803,943 km²).

*Government:* Military rule.

*Largest cities (1972 census):* Karachi (3,515,402), Lahore (2,169,742), Lyallpur (823,343), Hyderabad (628,631), and Rawalpindi (614,809).

*Population:* 1983 estimate—89,230,000; density—287 persons per sq. mi. (111 per km²).

*Economy:* Based mainly on agriculture, with some limited manufacturing.

## Panama

(Republic of Panama)

Panama is a nation located in Central America. It is bordered by Colombia and Costa Rica. About half of the workers in Panama are engaged in agriculture; many others are employed in commerce, trade, manufacturing, and transportation.

*Capital:* Panama City.

*Area:* 29,856 sq. mi. (77,326 km²).

*Government:* Republic.

*Largest cities (1980 est.):* Panama City (465,160) and San Miguelito (169,870).

*Population:* 1983 estimate—2,013,000; density—67 persons per sq. mi. (26 per km²).

*Economy:* Based mainly on agriculture and transportation.

## Papua New Guinea

(Papua New Guinea)

Papua New Guinea is a nation that occupies the eastern half of the island of New Guinea and a chain of smaller islands. It is bordered by Indonesia. Most of the people in Papua New Guinea are engaged in subsistence agriculture.

*Capital:* Port Moresby.

*Area:* 178,260 sq. mi. (461,691 km²).

*Government:* Constitutional monarchy.

*Largest cities (1977 est.):* Port Moresby (106,600) and Lae (45, 100).

*Population:* 1983 estimate—3,348,000; density—18 persons per sq. mi. (7 per km²).

*Economy:* Based almost entirely upon agriculture, with some limited manufacturing and mining.

## Paraguay

(Republic of Paraguay)

Paraguay is a nation located in South America. It is bordered by Brazil, Argentina, and Bolivia. About 70 per cent of the workers in Paraguay are engaged in agriculture.

*Capital:* Asunción.

*Area:* 157,048 sq. mi. (406,752 km²).

*Government:* Republic.

*Largest cities (1972 census):* Asunción (392,753) and Fernando de la Mora (36,834).

*Population:* 1983 estimate—3,361,000; density—21 persons per sq. mi. (8 per km²).

*Economy:* Based mainly on agriculture, with some manufacturing.

## Peru

(Republic of Peru)

Peru is a nation located on the west coast of South America. It is bordered by Ecuador, Colombia, Brazil, Bolivia, and Chile. Most of the workers in Peru are engaged in agriculture; but fishing, mining, and manufacturing also employ many workers.

*Capital:* Lima.

*Area:* 496,225 sq. mi. (1,285,216 km²).

*Government:* Republic.

*Largest cities (1972 census):* Lima (2,941,473), Callao (313,316), and Arequipa (302,316).

*Population:* 1983 estimate—19,317,000; density—39 persons per sq. mi. (15 per km²).

*Economy:* Based largely on manufacturing, mining, agriculture, and fishing.

## Philippines

(Republic of Philippines)

The Philippines is an island nation composed of more than 7,000 islands. It is located off the coast of Southeast Asia. About 50 per cent of the workers are engaged in agriculture.

*Capital:* Manila.

*Area:* 115,831 sq. mi. (300,000 km²).

*Government:* Parliamentary republic.

*Largest cities (1975 census):* Manila (1,479,116), Quezon City (956,864), Davao (484,678), and Cebu (413,025).

*Population:* 1983 estimate—51,598,000; density—445 persons per sq. mi. (172 per km²).

*Economy:* Mainly agricultural, with some mining and growing manufacturing.

## Poland

(Polish People's Republic)

Poland is a nation located in central Europe. It is bordered by Russia, Czechoslovakia, and East Germany. About 30 per cent of the Polish workers are occupied in agriculture and forestry; 26 per cent in manufacturing and 16 per cent in service industries.

*Capital:* Warsaw.

*Area:* 120,725 sq. mi. (312,677 km²).

*Government:* People's republic (Communist dictatorship).

*Largest cities (1978 est.):* Warsaw (1,552,400), Łódź (825,200), and Kraków (693,200).

*Population:* 1983 estimate—36,463,000; density—303 persons per sq. mi. (117 per km²).

*Economy:* Based mainly upon manufacturing and heavy industries.

## Portugal

(Portuguese Republic)

Portugal is a nation located in western Europe. It is bordered by Spain. Most of the Portuguese workers are engaged in agriculture, forestry, or fishing.

*Capital:* Lisbon.

*Area:* 35,553 sq. mi. (92,082 km²).

*Government:* Republic.

*Largest cities (1973 est.):* Lisbon (757,700) and Porto (304,000).

*Population:* 1983 estimate—10,264,000; density—287 persons per sq. mi. (111 per km²).

*Economy:* Based mainly upon mining and manufacturing, with agriculture and fishing also important.

## Qatar
(State of Qatar)

Qatar is a nation located in southwestern Asia, on a peninsula that reaches into the Persian Gulf. It is bordered by Saudi Arabia and the United Arab Emirates. The greatest number of Qatar's workers are engaged in the oil industry.

*Capital:* Doha.

*Area:* 4,247 sq. mi. (11,000 km²).

*Government:* Emirate.

*Largest city (1975 est.):* Doha (140,000).

*Population:* 1983 estimate—242,000, density—57 persons per sq. mi. (22 per km²).

*Economy:* Based mainly upon the oil industry, with very limited agriculture.

## Romania
(Socialist Republic of Romania)

Romania is a nation located in southeastern Europe. It is bordered by Russia, Bulgaria, Yugoslavia, and Hungary. About 36 per cent of Romania's workers are engaged in agriculture and forestry.

*Capital:* Bucharest.

*Area:* 91,699 sq. mi. (237,500 km²).

*Government:* Socialist republic (Communist dictatorship).

*Largest cities (1977 census):* Bucharest (1,807,044), Timişoara (268,785), Iaşi (264,947), and Cluj (262,421).

*Population:* 1983 estimate—22,874,000; density—249 persons per sq. mi. (96 per km²).

*Economy:* Based mainly upon manufacturing, mining, and agriculture.

## Russia
(Union of Soviet Socialist Republics)

Russia, also commonly known as the Soviet Union or the U.S.S.R., is a large nation located in northern Eurasia. Russia stretches from the Baltic Sea to the Pacific Ocean. It is the largest nation in area in the world. It is bordered by

Norway, Finland, Poland, Czechoslovakia, Hungary, Romania, Turkey, Iran, Afghanistan, China, Mongolia, and North Korea. Twenty-six per cent of the workers in the U.S.S.R. are employed in manufacturing, mining, and utilities.

*Capital:* Moscow.

*Area:* 8,649,500 sq. mi. (22,402,000 km²).

*Government:* Communist dictatorship.

*Largest cities (1979 census):* Moscow (7,831,000), Leningrad (4,073,000), Kiev (2,144,000), Tashkent (1,779,000), and Kharkov (1,444,000).

*Population:* 1983 estimate—272,775,000; density—31 persons per sq. mi. (12 per km²).

*Economy:* Based mainly upon industry and agriculture.

## Rwanda
(Republic of Rwanda)

Rwanda is a nation located in central Africa. It is bordered by Uganda, Tanzania, Burundi, and Zaire. Almost all the workers in Rwanda are engaged in agriculture.

*Capital:* Kigali.

*Area:* 10,169 sq. mi. (26,338 km²).

*Government:* Republic.

*Largest cities (1978 census):* Kigali (117,700) and Butare (21,700).

*Population:* 1983 estimate—5,450,000; density—536 persons per sq. mi. (207 per km²).

*Economy:* Based mainly upon agriculture, with some limited mining.

## St. Christopher-Nevis
(St. Christopher-Nevis)

St. Christopher-Nevis is an island nation in the Caribbean Sea. It is composed of two islands, St. Christopher (commonly called St. Kitts) and Nevis. Most workers are engaged in agriculture.

*Capital:* Basseterre.

*Area:* 101 sq. mi. (259 km²).

*Government:* Republic.

*Largest city (1975 est.):* Basseterre (15,930).

*Population:* 1980 estimate—44,400; density—440 persons per sq. mi. (171 per km²).

*Economy:* Agriculture and some tourism.

## Saint Lucia
(Saint Lucia)

St. Lucia is a small island country composed of a single island in the Caribbean Sea. It lies about 240 miles (386 kilometers) north of Venezuela. Most of its workers are engaged in agriculture.

*Capital:* Castries.

*Area:* 238 sq. mi. (616 km²).

*Government:* Constitutional monarchy.
*Largest city (1979 est.):* Castries (45,000).
*Population:* 1983 estimate—121,000; density—508
  persons per sq. mi. (196 per km²).
*Economy:* Based mainly on agriculture.

### Saint Vincent and the Grenadines
(Saint Vincent and the Grenadines)
St. Vincent and the Grenadines is an island coun-
try composed of about 100 islands in the Carib-
bean Sea. It lies about 200 miles (320 kilometers)
north of Venezuela. Most of its people work on
farms.
*Capital:* Kingstown.
*Area:* 150 sq. mi. (388 km²).
*Government:* Constitutional monarchy.
*Largest city (1977 est.):* Kingstown (29,831).
*Population:* 1983 estimate—126,000; density—842
  persons per sq. mi. (325 per km²).
*Economy:* Based mainly on agriculture, with
  some fishing, manufacturing, and tourism.

### San Marino
(The Most Serene Republic of San Marino)
San Marino is the smallest republic in Europe. It
is located in the Apennine Mountains, and it is
entirely surrounded by Italy. Most of the workers
in San Marino are engaged in agriculture, manu-
facturing, or in service occupations related to
tourism.
*Capital:* San Marino.
*Area:* 24 sq. mi. (61 km²).
*Government:* Republic.
*Largest city (1977 est.):* San Marino (4,628).
*Population:* 1983 estimate—22,000; density—935
  persons per sq. mi. (360 per km²).
*Economy:* Based upon agriculture, tourism, and
  limited local manufacturing.

### São Tomé and Príncipe
(Democratic Republic of São Tomé and Príncipe)
São Tomé and Príncipe is an island nation com-
posed of two large islands and several smaller
ones that lie about 180 miles (290 kilometers) off
the west coast of Africa. Most of its workers are
engaged in agriculture.
*Capital:* São Tomé.
*Area:* 372 sq. mi. (964 km²).
*Government:* Republic.
*Largest city (1970 census):* São Tomé (17,380).
*Population:* 1983 estimate—88,000; density—236
  persons per sq. mi. (91 per km²).
*Economy:* Based almost entirely on agriculture
  and fishing.

### Saudi Arabia
(Kingdom of Saudi Arabia)
Saudi Arabia is a nation located on the Arabian
Peninsula in southwestern Asia. It is bordered by
Jordan, Iraq, Kuwait, Qatar, the United Arab
Emirates, Oman, Yemen (Sana), and Yemen
(Aden). About 33 per cent of the nation's workers
are engaged in agriculture, forestry, and fishing,
and about 30 per cent work in construction and
trade jobs. Only about 1 per cent of all Saudi
workers are employed by the oil industry.
*Capital:* Riyadh.
*Area:* 831,313 sq. mi. (2,153,090 km²).
*Government:* Monarchy.
*Largest cities (1974 census):* Riyadh (666,840),
  Jidda (561,104), and Mecca (366,801).
*Population:* 1983 estimate—9,169,000; density—10
  persons per sq. mi. (4 per km²).
*Economy:* Based mainly upon the oil industry
  and agriculture.

### Senegal
(Republic of Senegal)
Senegal is a nation located in west Africa. It is
bordered by Mauritania, Mali, Gambia, Guinea,
and Guinea-Bissau. Most of Senegal's workers are
engaged in agriculture, fishing, mining, and serv-
ice occupations.
*Capital:* Dakar.
*Area:* 75,750 sq. mi. (196,192 km²).
*Government:* Republic.
*Largest cities (1976 census):* Dakar (798,792), Thiès
  (117,333), and Kaolack (106,899).
*Population:* 1983 estimate—6,114,000; density—80
  persons per sq. mi. (31 per km²).
*Economy:* Based mainly upon agriculture with
  commerce and mining also important.

### Seychelles
(Republic of Seychelles)
Seychelles is an island nation composed of ap-
proximately 90 islands in the Indian Ocean.
About 35 per cent of the nation's workers are
employed by the government. Only about 15 per
cent are farmers.
*Capital:* Victoria.
*Area:* 171 sq. mi. (443 km²).
*Government:* Republic.
*Largest city (1971 census):* Victoria (13,736).
*Population:* 1983 estimate—69,000; density—404
  persons per sq. mi. (156 per km²).
*Economy:* Based mainly on tourism with a grow-
  ing fishing industry.

## Sierra Leone
(Republic of Sierra Leone)
Sierra Leone is a nation located in western Africa. It is bordered by Guinea and Liberia. Most of the nation's workers are engaged in agriculture.
*Capital:* Freetown.
*Area:* 27,699 sq. mi. (71,740 km²).
*Government:* Republic.
*Largest city (1974 census):* Freetown (274,000).
*Population:* 1983 estimate—4,071,000; density— 148 persons per sq. mi. (57 per km²).
*Economy:* Based mainly on agriculture and mining.

## Singapore
(Republic of Singapore)
Singapore is an island nation that lies south of the Malay Peninsula in Southeast Asia. Most of the workers in Singapore are employed in industry or service occupations.
*Capital:* Singapore.
*Area:* 238 sq. mi. (616 km²).
*Government:* Republic.
*Largest city (1980 est.):* Singapore (2,390,800).
*Population:* 1983 estimate—2,577,000; density— 10,834 persons per sq. mi. (4,183 per km²).
*Economy:* Based primarily upon trade and commerce, with manufacturing also important.

## Solomon Islands
(Solomon Islands)
Solomon Islands is an island country in the South Pacific Ocean. It lies about 1,000 miles (1,610 kilometers) northeast of Australia. Most of the workers are engaged either in agriculture, including fishing, or in administration and social services.
*Capital:* Honiara.
*Area:* 11,500 sq. mi. (29,785 km²).
*Government:* Constitutional monarchy.
*Largest city (1976 census):* Honiara (14,942).
*Population:* 1983 estimate—241,000; density—21 persons per sq. mi. (8 per km²).
*Economy:* Based upon agriculture, fishing, and forestry.

## Somalia
(Somali Democratic Republic)
Somalia is a nation located in eastern Africa. It is bordered by Djibouti, Kenya, and Ethiopia. About 70 per cent of its workers are nomads.
*Capital:* Mogadiscio.
*Area:* 246,201 sq. mi. (637,657 km²).
*Government:* Republic (military rule).

*Largest city (1977 est.):* Mogadiscio (444,882).
*Population:* 1983 estimate—3,914,000; density—16 persons per sq. mi. (6 per km²).
*Economy:* Based mainly upon agriculture, including the raising of livestock.

## South Africa
(Republic of South Africa)
South Africa is a nation located on the southern tip of Africa. It is bordered by Namibia, Botswana, Zimbabwe, Lesotho, Swaziland, and Mozambique. Most of South Africa's workers are employed in agriculture, mining, manufacturing, or in service occupations.
*Capitals:* Cape Town (legislative); Pretoria (administrative); Bloemfontein (judicial).
*Government:* Republic.
*Area:* 471,445 sq. mi. (1,221,037 km²).
*Largest cities (1970 census):* Cape Town (691,296), Johannesburg (654,682), and Pretoria (543,950).
*Population:* 1983 estimate—31,444,000; density— 67 persons per sq. mi. (26 per km²).
*Economy:* Based mainly upon mining and manufacturing, with some agriculture.

## Spain
(Spanish State)
Spain is a nation located in western Europe. It occupies most of the Iberian Peninsula. It is bordered by France, Andorra, and Portugal. About 30 per cent of its workers are employed in the nation's industries.
*Capital:* Madrid.
*Area:* 194,885 sq. mi. (504,750 km²).
*Government:* Parliamentary monarchy.
*Largest cities (1975 est.):* Madrid (3,201,234), Barcelona (1,754,714), Valencia (714,086), and Seville (590,235).
*Population:* 1983 estimate—38,679,000; density— 199 persons per sq. mi. (77 per km²).
*Economy:* Based mainly upon agriculture, services, and manufacturing.

## Sri Lanka
(Democratic Socialist Republic of Sri Lanka)
Sri Lanka is an island nation located in the Indian Ocean off the southeastern tip of India. Most of its workers are engaged in agriculture.
*Capital:* Colombo.
*Area:* 25,332 sq. mi. (65,610 km²).
*Government:* Republic.
*Largest cities (1977 est.):* Colombo (616,000) and Dehiwala-Mount Lavinia (169,000).

*Population:* 1983 estimate—15,640,000; density—
616 persons per sq. mi. (238 per km²).
*Economy:* Based mainly upon agriculture and
mining.

## Sudan
(Democratic Republic of the Sudan)
Sudan is the largest nation in Africa. It is located
in northeastern Africa. It is bordered by Egypt,
Ethiopia, Kenya, Uganda, Zaire, the Central Afri-
can Republic, Chad, and Libya. Most of its work-
ers are engaged in agriculture.
*Capital:* Khartoum.
*Area:* 967,500 sq. mi. (2,505,813 km²).
*Government:* Republic.
*Largest cities (1973 census):* Khartoum (333,921)
and Omdurman (299,401).
*Population:* 1983 estimate—20,246,000; density—
21 persons per sq. mi. (8 per km²).
*Economy:* Based mainly upon agriculture.

## Suriname
(Republic of Suriname)
Suriname is a nation located on the northeastern
coast of South America. It is bordered by French
Guiana, Brazil, and Guyana. Most of its workers
are employed in the mining industry or in agri-
culture.
*Capital:* Paramaribo.
*Area:* 63,037 sq. mi. (163,265 km²).
*Government:* Republic.
*Largest city (1971 census):* Paramaribo (102,300).
*Population:* 1983 estimate—361,000; density—5
persons per sq. mi. (2 per km²).
*Economy:* Based mainly upon mining and metal
processing, with some agriculture.

## Swaziland
(Kingdom of Swaziland)
Swaziland is a nation located in southern Africa.
It is almost entirely surrounded by South Africa,
except for a small area that borders Mozam-
bique. Most of its workers are engaged in agricul-
ture and livestock herding.
*Capitals:* Mbabane (administrative) and Lobamba
(traditional).
*Area:* 6,704 sq. mi. (17,363 km²).
*Government:* Monarchy.
*Largest city (1979 est.):* Mbabane (22,262).
*Population:* 1983 estimate—603,000; density—91
persons per sq. mi. (35 per km²).
*Economy:* Based mainly upon agriculture and
mining.

## Sweden
(Kingdom of Sweden)
Sweden is a nation located in northern Europe
on the Scandinavian Peninsula. It is bordered by
Finland and Norway. Most workers are employed
in manufacturing, government, and business.
*Capital:* Stockholm.
*Area:* 173,732 sq. mi. (449,964 km²).
*Government:* Constitutional monarchy.
*Largest cities (1977 est.):* Stockholm (658,435) and
Göteborg (440,082).
*Population:* 1983 estimate—8,370,000; density—49
persons per sq. mi. (19 per km²).
*Economy:* Based mainly upon manufacturing and
various service industries.

## Switzerland
(Swiss Confederation)
Switzerland is a nation located in central Europe.
It is bordered by West Germany, Austria, Liech-
tenstein, Italy, and France. About 32 per cent of
its workers are employed in manufacturing;
about 40 per cent, in commerce or service occu-
pations.
*Capital:* Bern.
*Area:* 15,941 sq. mi. (41,288 km²).
*Government:* Federal republic.
*Largest cities (1978 est.):* Zurich (379,600), Basel
(185,300), and Geneva (150,100).
*Population:* 1983 estimate—6,348,000; density—
399 persons per sq. mi. (154 per km²).
*Economy:* Based mainly upon manufacturing and
agriculture, with tourism and other services
also important.

## Syria
(Syrian Arab Republic)
Syria is a nation located in southwestern Asia. It
is bordered by Turkey, Iraq, Jordan, Israel, and
Lebanon. About 50 per cent of the Syrian workers
are engaged in agriculture, and about 15 per cent
work in the nation's industries.
*Capital:* Damascus.
*Area:* 71,498 sq. mi. (185,180 km²).
*Government:* Republic.
*Largest cities (1980 est.):* Damascus (1,200,000)
and Aleppo (961,000).
*Population:* 1983 estimate—9,869,000; density—
137 persons per sq. mi. (53 per km²).
*Economy:* Based mainly upon agriculture, com-
merce, and industry.

## Taiwan
(Republic of China)
Taiwan is an island nation composed of one major island and several small islands located off the coast of mainland China. About 50 per cent of its workers are employed in the nation's industries or in service occupations.
*Capital:* Taipei.
*Area:* 13,885 sq. mi. (35,961 km²)*.
*Government:* Republic.
*Largest cities (1977 est.):* Taipei (2,196,237) and Kaohsiung (1,172,977).
*Population:* 1983 estimate—18,783,000; density—1,352 persons per sq. mi. (522 per km²).
*Economy:* Based mainly upon manufacturing.
*Area does not include the islands of Quemoy and Matsu.

## Tanzania
(United Republic of Tanzania)
Tanzania is a nation located in East Africa. It is bordered by Kenya, Uganda, Mozambique, Malawi, Zambia, Rwanda, Burundi, and Zaire. Most of its workers are engaged in agriculture.
*Capital:* Dar es Salaam.
*Area:* 364,900 sq. mi. (945,087 km²).
*Government:* Republic.
*Largest cities (1978 census):* Dar es Salaam (870,000), Mwanza (171,000), and Tanga (144,000).
*Population:* 1983 estimate—20,629,000; density—57 persons per sq. mi. (22 per km²).
*Economy:* Based mainly on agriculture, with some mining.

## Thailand
(Land of the Free)
Thailand is a nation located in Southeast Asia. It is bordered by Laos, Kampuchea, Malaysia, and Burma. More than 75 per cent of the workers in Thailand are engaged in agriculture.
*Capital:* Bangkok.
*Area:* 198,457 sq. mi. (514,000 km²).
*Government:* Constitutional monarchy.
*Largest cities (1980 census):* Bangkok (5,153,902), Chiang Mai (100,146), and Hat Yai (98,091).
*Population:* 1983 estimate—50,027,000; density—251 persons per sq. mi. (97 per km²).
*Economy:* Based mainly upon agriculture and manufacturing, with some mining.

## Togo
(Republic of Togo)
Togo is a nation located in western Africa. It is bordered by Upper Volta, Benin, and Ghana.

About 80 per cent of its workers are engaged in agriculture, and a small percentage work in the nation's mining industry.
*Capital:* Lomé.
*Area:* 21,622 sq. mi. (56,000 km²).
*Government:* Presidential regime.
*Largest city (1977 est.):* Lomé (229,400).
*Population:* 1983 estimate—2,793,000; density—129 persons per sq. mi. (50 per km²).
*Economy:* Based largely upon agriculture, with mining also important.

## Tonga
(Kingdom of Tonga)
Tonga is an island nation located in the South Pacific Ocean. It is composed of about 150 islands located 400 miles (640 kilometers) west of Fiji. Almost all of Tonga's workers are engaged in agriculture or in fishing.
*Capital:* Nukualofa.
*Area:* 270 sq. mi. (699 km²).
*Government:* Constitutional monarchy.
*Largest city (1977 est.):* Nukualofa (18,200).
*Population:* 1983 estimate—98,000; density—363 persons per sq. mi. (140 per km²).
*Economy:* Based almost entirely upon agriculture.

## Trinidad and Tobago
(Republic of Trinidad and Tobago)
Trinidad and Tobago is an island nation composed of two islands located in the West Indies. Most of the nation's workers are employed in the oil industry, manufacturing, or construction.
*Capital:* Port-of-Spain.
*Area:* 1,980 sq. mi. (5,128 km²).
*Government:* Republic.
*Largest cities (1977 est.):* Port-of-Spain (42,950) and San Fernando (36,650).
*Population:* 1983 estimate—1,232,000; density—622 persons per sq. mi. (240 per km²).
*Economy:* Based mainly upon the production and the refining of oil.

## Tunisia
(Republic of Tunisia)
Tunisia is a nation located in northern Africa. It is bordered by Libya and Algeria. About 70 per cent of Tunisia's workers are engaged in farming or the raising of livestock.
*Capital:* Tunis.
*Area:* 63,170 sq. mi. (163,610 km²).
*Government:* Republic.

*Largest cities (1975 census):* Tunis (540,404) and
Sfax (171,297).
*Population:* 1983 estimate—7,083,000; density—
111 persons per sq. mi. (46 per km²).
*Economy:* Based mainly upon agriculture, with
very limited mining.

## Turkey
(Republic of Turkey)
Turkey is a nation in southwestern Asia and
southeastern Europe. It is bordered by Russia,
Iran, Iraq, Syria, Greece, and Bulgaria. About 64
per cent of Turkey's workers are engaged in agri-
culture, forestry, and fishing; and about 8 per
cent are employed in the nation's manufacturing.
*Capital:* Ankara.
*Area:* 301,382 sq. mi. (780,576 km²).
*Government:* Republic (military rule).
*Largest cities (1975 census):* Istanbul (2,547,364)
and Ankara (1,701,004).
*Population:* 1983 estimate—48,410,000; density—
161 persons per sq. mi. (62 per km²).
*Economy:* Based mainly upon agriculture, but the
nation's industries are expanding rapidly.

## Tuvalu
(Tuvalu)
Tuvalu is a small country consisting of nine is-
lands in the South Pacific Ocean. It lies about
2,000 miles (3,200 kilometers) northeast of Aus-
tralia. Tuvalu has poor soil, few natural re-
sources, and almost no manufacturing or min-
ing. The people produce copra (dried coconut
meat) and weave baskets and mats for export.
Many young islanders also work on ocean ships.
*Capital:* Funafuti.
*Area:* 10 sq. mi. (26 km²).
*Government:* Constitutional monarchy.
*Largest city (1973 census):* Funafuti (871).
*Population:* 1983 estimate—7,000; density—697
persons per sq. mi. (269 per km²).
*Economy:* Based mainly on the export of copra
and handicrafts.

## Uganda
(Republic of Uganda)
Uganda is a nation located in east-central Africa.
It is bordered by Zaire, Sudan, Kenya, Tanzania,
and Rwanda. Most of the workers in Uganda are
engaged in farming or in herding.
*Capital:* Kampala.
*Area:* 91,134 sq. mi. (236,036 km²).
*Government:* Republic.

*Largest cities (1976 est.):* Kampala (531,022) and
Jinja (189,540).
*Population:* 1983 estimate—15,117,000; density—
164 persons per sq. mi. (64 per km²).
*Economy:* Mainly based on agriculture, with very
limited mining.

## United Arab Emirates
(United Arab Emirates)
The United Arab Emirates is a federation of seven
independent Arab states located in southwestern
Asia. It is bordered by Qatar, Oman, and Saudi
Arabia. Most of its workers are employed in the
nation's oil industry.
*Capital:* Abu Dhabi.
*Area:* 32,278 sq. mi. (83,600 km²).
*Government:* Federation.
*Largest cities (1975 est.):* Abu Dhabi (150,000) and
Dubayy (76,000).
*Population:* 1983 estimate—1,256,000; density—39
persons per sq. mi. (15 per km²).
*Economy:* Based mainly upon the production
and refining of oil.

## United States
(United States of America)
The United States is a large nation located in
North America. It is bordered by Canada and
Mexico. A large majority of its workers are em-
ployed in nonagricultural industries or services.
*Capital:* Washington, D.C.
*Area:* 3,618,465 sq. mi. (9,371,781 km²).
*Government:* Republic.
*Largest cities (1980 census):* New York (7,071,030),
Chicago (3,005,072), Los Angeles (2,966,763),
Philadelphia (1,688,210), Houston (1,594,086),
and Detroit (1,203,399).
*Population:* 1983 estimate—233,450,000; density—
65 persons per sq. mi. (25 per km²).
*Economy:* Based mainly upon manufacturing,
commerce, and trade.

## Upper Volta
(Republic of Upper Volta)
Upper Volta is a nation located in western Africa.
It is bordered by Mali, Niger, Benin, Togo, Ghana,
and the Ivory Coast. Most of Upper Volta's work-
ers are engaged in farming or raising livestock.
*Capital:* Ouagadougou.
*Area:* 105,869 sq. mi. (274,200 km²).
*Government:* Republic (military rule).
*Largest city (1977 est.):* Ouagadougou (180,000).

*Population:* 1983 estimate—7,439,000; density—70 persons per sq. mi. (27 per km²).

*Economy:* Based mainly upon farming and the raising of livestock.

## Uruguay
(The Eastern Republic of Uruguay)
Uruguay is a small country in South America. It is located on the southeastern coast of South America, and it is bordered by Brazil and Argentina. About 50 per cent of its workers are engaged in farming or the raising of livestock.
*Capital:* Montevideo.
*Area:* 68,037 sq. mi. (176,215 km²).
*Government:* Republic (military rule).
*Largest cities (1975 census):* Montevideo (1,229,750), Salto (71,880), and Paysandú (62,410).
*Population:* 1983 estimate—2,952,000; density—44 persons per sq. mi. (17 per km²).
*Economy:* Based mainly upon agriculture.

## Vanuatu
(Republic of Vanuatu)
Vanuatu is an island country in the South Pacific Ocean. It consists of a group of 12 principal islands and many smaller ones which lie about 1,000 miles (1,600 kilometers) northeast of the Queensland coast of Australia. Most of its people are engaged in agriculture and raising livestock.
*Capital:* Port-Vila.
*Area:* 5,700 sq. mi. (14,763 km²).
*Government:* Republic
*Largest city (1979 census):* Port-Vila (10,158).
*Population:* 1983 estimate—125,000; density—21 persons per sq. mi. (8 per km²).
*Economy:* Based mainly on agriculture, with tourism also important.

## Vatican City
(State of the Vatican City)
Vatican City is the smallest independent state in the world. It lies entirely within the city of Rome, Italy. Vatican City is the spiritual and administrative center of the Roman Catholic Church. Vatican City is under the direction of the pope.
*Area:* 0.17 sq. mi. (0.44 km²).
*Population:* 1983 estimate—1,000; density—5,884 persons per sq. mi. (2,272 per km²).
*Economy:* All residents are connected with the activities of the Roman Catholic Church.

## Venezuela
(Republic of Venezuela)
Venezuela is a nation located on the northern coast of South America. It is bordered by Colombia, Brazil, and Guyana. About 20 per cent of its workers are engaged in agriculture, and about 20 per cent are employed in the oil industry.
*Capital:* Caracas.
*Area:* 352,145 sq. mi. (912,050 km²).
*Government:* Federal republic.
*Largest cities (1978 est.):* Caracas (1,279,600), Maracaibo (845,000), Valencia (471,000), and Barquisimeto (459,000).
*Population:* 1983 estimate—15,203,000; density—44 persons per sq. mi. (17 per km²).
*Economy:* Based mainly upon the production of oil and on agriculture.

## Vietnam
(Socialist Republic of Vietnam)
Vietnam is a nation located in the eastern part of the Indochinese Peninsula in Southeast Asia. It is bordered by China, Laos, and Kampuchea. About 65 per cent of the workers in Vietnam are engaged in agriculture.
*Capital:* Hanoi.
*Area:* 127,242 sq. mi. (329,556 km²).
*Government:* Communist dictatorship.
*Largest cities (1976 census):* Ho Chi Minh City (3,460,500), Hanoi (1,443,500), Haiphong (1,190,900), and Da Nang (492,194)*.
*Population:* 1983 estimate—57,990,000; density—456 persons per sq. mi. (176 per km²).
*Economy:* Based mainly upon agriculture.
*1973 estimate.

## Western Samoa
(Independent State of Western Samoa)
Western Samoa is an island nation in the South Pacific Ocean. It lies about 1,700 miles (2,740 kilometers) northeast of New Zealand. It is composed of two main islands and several smaller islands. About 70 per cent of its workers are engaged in agriculture and fishing.
*Capital:* Apia.
*Area:* 1,097 sq. mi. (2,842 km²).
*Government:* Parliamentary.
*Largest city (1976 census):* Apia (32,099).
*Population:* 1983 estimate—160,000; density—145 persons per sq. mi. (56 per km²).
*Economy:* Mainly based on agriculture.

## Yemen (Aden)

(People's Democratic Republic of Yemen)
Yemen (Aden) is a nation located in the southern part of the Arabian Peninsula in southwestern Asia. It is bordered by Saudi Arabia, Oman, and Yemen (Sana). About 80 per cent of its workers are in farming, fishing, and raising livestock.
*Capital:* Aden.
*Area:* 128,560 sq. mi. (332,968 km²).
*Government:* Republic.
*Largest city (1977 est.):* Aden (271,600).
*Population:* 1983 estimate—2,083,000; density—16 persons per sq. mi. (6 per km²).
*Economy:* Largely undeveloped except for oil refining and port facilities.

## Yemen (Sana)

(The Yemen Arab Republic)
Yemen (Sana) is located on the southwestern edge of the Arabian Peninsula in southwestern Asia. It is bordered by Saudi Arabia and Yemen (Aden). About 75 per cent of its workers are engaged in farming and the raising of livestock.
*Capital:* Sana.
*Area:* 75,290 sq. mi. (195,000 km²).
*Government:* Military rule.
*Largest cities:* Sana (192,045)* and Hodeida (106,080)**.
*Population:* 1983 estimate—6,270,000; density—83 persons per sq. mi. (32 per km²).
*Economy:* Based mainly upon agriculture and very limited light industry.
*1979 estimate
**1978 estimate

## Yugoslavia

(Socialist Federal Republic of Yugoslavia)
Yugoslavia is a nation in the Balkan Peninsula in south-central Europe. It is bordered by Italy, Austria, Hungary, Romania, Bulgaria, Greece, and Albania. About 52 per cent of the nation's workers are engaged in industry and manufacturing.
*Capital:* Belgrade.
*Area:* 98,766 sq. mi. (255,804 km²).
*Government:* Socialist republic.
*Largest cities (1971 census):* Belgrade (746,105), Zagreb (566,224), and Skopje (312,980).
*Population:* 1983 estimate—23,129,000; density—233 persons per sq. mi. (90 per km²).
*Economy:* Based mainly upon manufacturing and the mining industry, with some agriculture.

## Zaire

(Republic of Zaire)
Zaire is a nation located in south-central Africa. It is bordered by the Congo, the Central African Republic, Sudan, Uganda, Rwanda, Burundi, Tanzania, Angola, and Zambia. Most of its workers are engaged in agriculture.
*Capital:* Kinshasa.
*Area:* 905,568 sq. mi. (2,345,000 km²).
*Government:* Presidential regime.
*Largest cities (1974 est.):* Kinshasa (2,008,352) and Kananga (601,239).
*Population:* 1983 estimate—30,824,000; density—34 persons per sq. mi. (13 per km²).
*Economy:* Based mainly upon the mining industry, with very limited manufacturing.

## Zambia

(Republic of Zambia)
Zambia is a nation located in south-central Africa. It is bordered by Zaire, Tanzania, Malawi, Mozambique, Zimbabwe, Botswana, Namibia and Angola. Many of its workers are employed in construction and mining.
*Capital:* Lusaka.
*Area:* 290,586 sq. mi. (752,614 km²).
*Government:* Republic.
*Largest cities (1980 est.):* Lusaka (641,000)*, Kitwe (341,000)*, and Ndola (323,000)*.
*Population:* 1983 estimate—6,243,000; density—21 persons per sq. mi. (8 per km²).
*Economy:* Based mainly upon the mining industry, with construction and agriculture also important.
*Metropolitan area—includes city and suburbs.

## Zimbabwe

(Zimbabwe)
Zimbabwe is a nation located in southern Africa. It is bordered by Zambia, Mozambique, the Republic of South Africa, and Botswana. Most of the workers are engaged in agriculture.
*Capital:* Salisbury.
*Area:* 150,804 sq. mi. (390,580 km²).
*Government:* Republic.
*Largest cities (1979 est.):* Salisbury (118,500) and Bulawayo (85,700).
*Population:* 1983 estimate—7,926,000; density—49 persons per sq. mi. (19 per km²).
*Economy:* Based almost equally on agriculture, mining, and manufacturing.

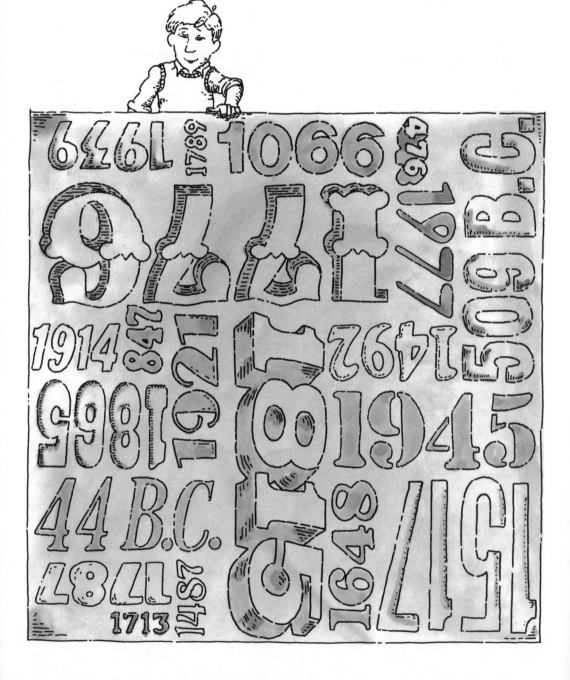

# Important dates in history

Did you know that Julius Caesar was killed in 44 B.C.? Do you know what events were taking place in literature and art at the time of Napoleon's conquest of Europe? Do you know in approximately what year the colonial period ended in the history of the United States?

This unit is a review of important dates and events in history. For convenience, the unit has been divided into sections, one on world history and one on the history of the United States. Those sections are further divided by subject area—arts, sciences, philosophy, and so on—and by time periods.

# 1. World history

The following section outlines some important dates in world history. The section is divided into seven categories: (1) political events, (2) social events, (3) religion, (4) philosophy, (5) literature, (6) the arts, including music, and (7) science and technology. Chronologically, the history is divided into these broad headings: Prehistory and Ancient Times (?-476 A.D.); The Middle Period (477 -1492);

The Early Modern Period (1493-1699); European Ascendancy (1700-1899); Since 1900 (1900-Present). Each heading encompasses an important historical epoch.

You can use this unit to gain overall perspective on the events that make up world history. And you can use this unit to review key points in history or find areas of interest to explore further.

## Prehistory and ancient times

### Political events

**8000 B.C. People are nomads**
During this period, people are organized into small tribes and clans. These tribes and clans follow a nomadic existence, traveling constantly to find sources of food.

**8000 B.C.- Settlements begin**
**3500 B.C.** Agriculture and the domestication of animals begins. A steady food supply permits people to form settlements.

**3500 B.C. Cities in India**
The cities of Mohenjo-daro and Harappa are formed in the Indus Valley.

**3200 B.C. Sumerian city-states**
A system of sophisticated city-states emerges in the southern part of Mesopotamia, called Sumer.

**3100 B.C. Egypt united**
The city-states of Lower and Upper Egypt are united by Menes, also called Na'rmer. Menes' reign marks the beginning of the First Dynasty.

**2330 B.C. Sumer united**
The state of ancient Sumer is created by Sargon of Akkad.

**1830 B.C. Rise of Babylon**
The First Dynasty of Babylon is founded by King Sumuabum.

**1728 B.C.- Hammurabi the Great**
**1686 B.C.** Hammurabi of Babylon completes the conquest of Mesopotamia.

**1600 B.C. First Hittite state**
The Kingdom of the Hittites, a warlike people who later are to control much of the Middle East, is founded by Labarnas.

**1600 B.C. Rise of Crete**
The Minoan culture is solidified on the island of Crete in the Mediterranean Sea. Under a powerful monarchy based in the city of Knossos on Crete, the Minoans expand their influence throughout the Mediterranean area.

**1570 B.C.- The Egyptian Empire**
**1370 B.C.** The power of the Egyptian state is increased and expanded under the rule of a succession of vigorous soldier kings.

**1500 B.C. Shang Dynasty beings**
Kings of the Shang Dynasty establish control over the Yellow River plain in China.

**1450 B.C.- The Hittite Empire**
**1200 B.C.** The Hittite Kingdom expands into Syria, Palestine, and portions of Mesopotamia.

**1290 B.C.- Reign of Ramses II**
**1224 B.C.** Ramses II, helps restore Egyptian power with a series of military campaigns against the Hittites.

**1200 B.C. India invaded**
Aryan tribes from the Iranian Plateau invade and begin the conquest of India.

**1115 B.C.- Middle Assyrian Empire**
**1078 B.C.** King Tiglath-pileser I develops the Assyrian state into a tightly centralized military machine. He helps create an empire that stretches from the Mediterranean Sea to the Persian Gulf.

**1100 B.C. Greece invaded**
The Dorians invade Greece, destroying the Mycenaean civilization, a civilization that was closely related to the Minoan. The Dorian invaders plunge the Greek Peninsula into a "Dark Age" that lasts until about 800 B.C.

**1100 B.C.- Phoenician expansion**
**888 B.C.** Based in the Mediterranean cities of Sidon and Tyre, the Phoenicians begin a policy of political and economic expansion.

**1027 B.C. China centralized**
The Western Chou Dynasty is established in China. The Chou state features a strong king supported by a military aristocracy based on land tenure.

**1020 B.C. Kingdom of Israel**
Saul is anointed the first king of the Israelites.

**1000 B.C. King David of Israel**
Under King David, the city of Jerusalem is captured and made the capital of the Kingdom of Israel.

**900 B.C. Etruscans settle Italy**
The Etruscans, a group of people from Asia Minor, settle the Italian Peninsula.

**800 B.C.- Revival in Greece**
**600 B.C.** The city-states that later will dominate the Greek Peninsula begin to rebuild. These include Athens, Sparta, Corinth, and Thebes.

**760 B.C. Greeks in Italy**
Colonists from the Greek Peninsula establish settlements in southern Italy.

**753 B.C. Rome founded**
The traditional date for the founding of the city of Rome by Romulus.

**605 B.C.- Nebuchadnezzar II**
**562 B.C.** The Neo-Babylonian Empire, led by King Nebuchadnezzar II, the Great, establishes control over much of the Middle East.

**550 B.C. Persian Empire founded**
Cyrus the Great establishes an empire that extends from the Indus River to the Mediterranean Sea.

**517 B.C. Persians invade India**
Under Darius I, a Persian army occupies the city of Gandhara in India.

**509 B.C. The Roman Republic**
Traditional date for the end of the monarchy and the founding of the Roman Republic.

**500 B.C. Kingdom of Kush**
The central African Kingdom of Kush is founded.

**490 B.C.- The Persian Wars**
**479 B.C.** Greek city-states led by Athens and Sparta beat back Persian attempts to conquer the Greek Peninsula.

**477 B.C. Delian League founded**
Several Greek city-states under the leadership of Athens form an alliance to offset the growing power of Sparta.

**460 B.C.- First Peloponnesian War**
**446 B.C.** The Delian League wages war against Sparta.

**431 B.C.- Great Peloponnesian**
**404 B.C. War**
With aid from Persia, Sparta defeats Athens.

**359 B.C.- Rise of Macedonia**
**336 B.C.** The Peloponnesian Wars leave the Greek city-states weak and divided. The unrest is ended by the intervention of King Philip of Macedonia who defeats an allied Greek army at the Battle of Chaeronea in 338 B.C.

**336 B.C. Philip assassinated**
After enforcing the formation of a Hellenic League and declaring war on Persia, Philip II is assassinated. He is succeeded by his son, Alexander III, the Great.

**333 B.C. Battle of Issus**
Alexander the Great defeats the Persians under Darius III, thus laying the foundation for the creation of a great world empire.

**321 B.C.- Maurya Empire grows**
**184 B.C.** The Emperor Chandragupta founds the Maurya Dynasty in India.

**300 B.C. Aksum founded**
The kingdom of Aksum is founded in what is today Ethiopia.

**272 B.C. Asoka's empire**
The Emperor Asoka of India increases the political, economic, and cultural influence of the Indian Empire.

264 B.C.- **First Punic War**
241 B.C.　Carthage and Rome wage war to settle which city-state will control the Mediterranean Sea. The war ends with Carthage and Rome sharing control of Sicily.

221 B.C.　**Unity in China**
The Ch'in Dynasty restores a strong government in China.

218 B.C.- **Second Punic War**
201 B.C.　Led by Hannibal, Carthage renews its war against Rome. After numerous early victories, Hannibal's army is defeated by a Roman army at the Battle of Zama (202 B.C.).

202 B.C.　**Han Dynasty begins**
The Han family, a warrior clan, seizes control of the government of China.

149 B.C.- **Third Punic War**
146 B.C.　The Roman Government becomes alarmed over a revival of Carthaginian power. When Carthage becomes involved in a conflict with a Roman ally, Rome uses the occasion to declare war. The city-state of Carthage is obliterated.

149 B.C.- **Romans in Greece**
148 B.C.　Rome intervenes in the Fourth Macedonian War. Macedonia becomes a Roman province.

146 B.C.　**Greece occupied**
The city-state of Corinth is destroyed by a Roman army. The remaining Greek city-states pay tribute to Rome.

60 B.C.　**First Triumvirate**
Julius Caesar, Crassus, and Pompey join in alliance to divide control of Rome.

58 B.C.- **Caesar in Gaul**
51 B.C.　Julius Caesar conquers Gaul, gaining for himself the reputation of a vigorous hero and skillful general.

51 B.C.　**Triumvirate ends**
The death of Crassus (53 B.C.) and Pompey's fear of Caesar's growing popularity cause an end to the alliance.

48 B.C.　**Pompey assassinated**
After Caesar's victory at the Battle of Pharsalus, Pompey flees to Egypt, where he is executed by the king, Ptolemy XII.

48 B.C.- **Caesar triumphant**
45 B.C.　Campaigns in Egypt, Syria, and Spain leave Caesar the master of the Roman state.

44 B.C.　**Caesar dies**
A conspiracy of nobles assassinates Caesar.

27 B.C.　**Caesar Octavianus**
After a long period of civil war, Gaius Julius Caesar Octavianus, the great-nephew of Julius Caesar, gains control of the Roman state. He takes the titles Imperator and Augustus. Augustus Caesar's rule marks the beginning of the Roman Empire.

Note: All dates given from this point are dates A.D.

64　**Rome burns**
A crisis in government is caused by a great fire that destroys much of the city of Rome. The Emperor Nero deflects criticism by blaming the Christians.

66-70　**Revolt in Judea**
The Jewish people revolt against Roman occupation. The revolt is crushed when the city of Jerusalem is captured and destroyed by Titus.

84　**Romans take Britain**
The Roman General Agricola completes the conquest of Britain.

135　**Jewish Diaspora**
A second Jewish revolt is crushed, and the Jewish people are forced to leave their homeland.

284　**A new order begins**
The Emperor Diocletian divides the Roman Empire into two parts, each part ruled by a separate emperor.

300　**The Mayas in America**
The Maya Indians develop the first of the important civilizations to flourish in America.

306　**Age of Constantine**
Constantine I the Great becomes co-emperor with Galerius of the Roman Empire. In 324, Constantine reunites the empire under his sole rule.

320　**India's Golden Age**
The Gupta Dynasty seizes power in India ending five centuries of disorder and disunity.

330　**A new Roman capital**
Constantine I moves the capital of the empire from Rome to the city of Byzantium on the Bosporus. The city is renamed Constantinople.

360　**Japan enters the scene**
The Korean Peninsula is conquered by a Japanese army.

410　**Sack of Rome**
The Visigoths, led by Alaric, loot and burn the city of Rome.

451　**Attila the Hun**
Led by Attila, a large force of barbarian tribesmen invades the Roman Empire.

**476** **Fall of Rome**
Traditional date for the end of the Roman Empire in the West. Odoacer, a Goth serving as a general in the Roman army, deposes Romulus Augustulus.

### Social events

**3200 B.C.** **Sumerians organize**
Sumerian society is divided into formal classes made up of priests, soldiers, and free citizens.

**2500 B.C.** **Egypt's society frozen**
Egypt's rigid social structure, which lasts with little modification for 2000 years, takes shape.

**1700 B.C.** **Code of laws written**
*The Code of Hammurabi* is the earliest example of a written law code.

**1200 B.C.** **Caste system in India**
The caste system is introduced in India by Aryan invaders.

**1027 B.C.-** **China's Mandate of**
**256 B.C.** **Heaven**
The Chinese develop a belief in a "Mandate of Heaven," one of the first declarations of a people's right to revolt against an unpopular government.

**750 B.C.** **Ancient Greek society**
The poet Homer presents a vivid picture of the social structure of ancient Greece in the epics the *Iliad* and the *Odyssey*.

**594 B.C.** **Solon's reforms**
Solon institutes a reform and codification of the laws and constitution of the city-state of Athens.

**133 B.C.** **Reform in Rome**
Tiberius Gracchus, a nobleman, is elected to public office on a platform of social reform. His aim is to break up large estates

and redistribute land to the poor.

**123 B.C.** **Reformers fail**
Gaius Gracchus fails in his attempts to carry through the land reform program proposed by his brother Tiberius.

Note: All dates given from this point are dates A.D.

**212** **Edict of Caracalla**
Extends Roman citizenship to all free inhabitants of the empire.

### Religion

**5000 B.C.** **Neolithic religion**
Neolithic peoples decorate sacred caves and build stone temples to worship various animal-gods and fertility goddesses.

**3500 B.C.** **New gods emerge**
People of the Near East develop highly formalized religions revolving about deities in human form representing cosmic forces and fertility.

**1370 B.C.** **Akhenaton reigns**
The Egyptian King Akhenaton attempts to introduce monotheism, the worship of one god, into Egypt's religious system.

**1200 B.C.** **Jews claim one God**
The Hebrews, also called Jews, develop and spread their idea of one God.

**600 B.C.** **Zoroaster's religion**
The Persian prophet Zoroaster formulates a religion that interprets the universe as a struggle between good and evil.

**587 B.C.** **Temple destroyed**
The Temple in Jerusalem is destroyed by Babylonians who occupy the kingdom of Judah.

**563 B.C.** **Buddha is born**
Buddha is born in Nepal. He founds Buddhism which becomes one of the major religions of the world.

**516 B.C.** **Second temple built**
The Hebrews complete the Second Temple in Jerusalem.

**270 B.C.** **Hinduism formalized**
The collection of cults and beliefs that become the Hindu religion begins to be organized by the Brahmins.

**8 B.C.** **Jesus is born**
Jesus of Nazareth is born in Judea, a Roman province. He is the founder of Christianity, which becomes the dominant religion of the Western Hemisphere.

Note: All dates given from this point on are dates A.D.

**29** **Christ crucified**
Traditional date for the execution of Christ by the Romans in Jerusalem.

**70** **Second temple razed**
Roman forces capture. Jerusalem and destroy the Jews' Second Temple.

**200** **Jewish laws compiled**
Rabbi Judah Hanasi completes the *Mishnah,* the first compilation of Jewish law and tradition.

**249** **Christians persecuted**
The Roman Emperor Decius orders the first general persecution of Christians.

**300** **Aksum converted**
The Kingdom of Aksum in Africa is converted to Christianity.

305 **Monasticism begins**
Saint Anthony forms the
first Christian monastic
community in the Egyp-
tian desert.

313 **Edict of Milan**
Constantine, by the Edict
of Milan, grants Christians
in the Roman Empire
freedom of religion.

325 **Christians consult**
The first ecumenical
council of the Christian
church meets in the city
of Nicaea.

360 **Buddhism spreads**
Buddhist missionaries
from China begin the con-
version of the people of
Japan.

392 **Christianity recognized**
Under Theodosius I,
Christianity becomes the
official state religion of
the Roman Empire.

405 *Vulgate* **completed**
Saint Jerome completes
the *Vulgate*, a revision of
the Latin Bible which for
centuries is the only version authorized by the
Roman Catholic Church.

Philosophy

2700 B.C. **Imhotep the Sage**
The Egyptian Imhotep
considers the rules of correct conduct for a proper
life.

1100 B.C. **Egypt's pessimism**
The *Tales of Wenamun*
consider the meaning of
life.

600 B.C. **Milesian philosophers**
Traditional date for the
formal beginning of Greek
philosophy by Thales,
Anaximander, and
Anaximenes of the city
of Miletus.

551 B.C. **Confucius born**
Confucius, the most re-
spected and influential
philosopher in Chinese
history, is born. His ideas
stress the need to develop
moral character.

530 B.C. **Pythagoras teaches**
Pythagoras, a Greek
philosopher, teaches that
number is the essence of
all things.

469 B.C. **Birth of Socrates**
The philosopher Socrates
is born in Athens. He be-
comes a martyr to free-
dom of thought.

427 B.C. **Plato born**
Plato is born in Athens. He
writes *The Republic*, a
work which tries to define
justice in a perfect state.

384 B.C. **Birth of Aristotle**
Aristotle, Plato's greatest
pupil, is born. He is the
foremost scholar of the
ancient world.

124 B.C. **Confucius accepted**
The Chinese government
establishes the Imperial
University to educate government officials in Con-
fucian ideals.

106 B.C. **Birth of Cicero**
Cicero becomes the lead-
ing Roman philosopher,
specializing in ethics and
jurisprudence.

Note: All dates given from
this point are dates A.D.

161- **Roman Stoicism**
180 The Roman Emperor
Marcus Aurelius becomes
the leading exponent of
the Stoic philosophy.

354- **St. Augustine**
430 The *City of God* and other
writings by St. Augustine
form the basis of philo-
sophical thought during
the Middle Ages.

Literature

2500 B.C. **Epic poems written**
The *Epic of Gilgamesh* and
the *Epic of Creation*, the
oldest epic poems in
world literature, are written in Mesopotamia.

1800 B.C. **Egyptian literature**
The high point of ancient
Egyptian literature with
such classics as *King
Khufu and the Magicians*
and *The Shipwrecked
Sailor* written.

750 B.C. **Greek epics written**
The Greek Homer com-
poses the *Iliad* and the
*Odyssey,* two famous classical epics.

500 B.C. **Hindu literature**
The classic Hindu religious
epic, the *Mahabharata,*
begins to take form.

500 B.C. **Lyric poetry begins**
Greek poets develop and
use the lyric meter in
poetry.

480 B.C- **Greek drama flourishes**
404 B.C. Greek dramatists Sophocles, Euripides, and Aes-
chylus develop the
tragedy. Aristophanes
writes his most popular
comedies.

450 B.C. **Historical writing**
Herodotus, called the
"Father of History," writes
a history of the Persian
Wars.

400 B.C. **History flourishes**
In the tradition of
Herodotus, the Greek his-
torians Thucydides and
Xenephon continue the
story of Greece's conflict
with Persia.

70 B.C.- **Writings of Cicero**
43 B.C. The writings of Cicero, a
master of Latin prose,
dominate Roman litera-
ture during his lifetime.

**28 B.C. Roman history**
The Roman historian Livy publishes his first work.

**19 B.C. Virgil writes epic**
The Roman poet Virgil writes the *Aeneid,* an epic poem considered the greatest work of Latin literature.

Note: All dates from this point are dates A.D.

**50 Chinese literature**
The Chinese historian Pan Ku begins compiling a history of past Chinese emperors.

**75 Biography begins**
The Greek Plutarch writes a series of biographies of the lives of famous Greeks and Romans.

**80 Tacitus writes**
The most famous Roman historian Tacitus begins writing his famous study of German tribes in Gaul.

**161- The emperor-writer**
**180** The Emperor Marcus Aurelius writes and publishes his *Meditations.*

The arts

**13,000 B.C. Neolithic Spain**
Neolithic hunters paint pictures of animals on rock walls and ceilings of caves near Altamira, Spain.

**7500 B.C. Neolithic Africa**
Neolithic hunters in what is today the Sahara paint pictures on exposed walls of rock of people hunting animals.

**5000 B.C. Prehistoric Italy**
Crudely engraved pottery in Italy is gradually replaced with refined, attractively painted vases.

**4500 B.C. Where Joshua fought**
The walled city of Jericho of Biblical fame is built.

Potters fashion glazed ware and vessels decorated with geometric designs.

**4000 B.C. Grecian idols**
Neolithic Greeks form small sculptures in both clay and stone. Female idols are the favorite subject.

**3000 B.C. Bronze age culture**
Using bronze, craftsmen are able to produce more intricate and sophisticated jewelry and artworks than neolithic craftsmen had been able to make from stone.

**2850 B.C.- Egyptian architecture**
**2052 B.C.** The monumental Sphinx of Giza and Pyramid of Khufu rise in desert sands.

**2000 B.C.- Isle of Crete**
**1700 B.C.** Minoan architects design and build huge, rambling palaces on the Island of Crete.

**1750 B.C. Egyptian jewelry**
Men and women wear collars of stringed beads, silver ear loops, and bracelets. Advances are made in the design of copper jewelry.

**1347 B.C.- Egypt's legacy**
**1335 B.C.** Egyptian craftsmen and artists produce a treasure of jewelry, ornaments, art objects, and decorated weapons and household items for King Tutankhamon.

**1100 B.C. Iron is used**
The use of iron for the production of decorated weapons and jewelry begins.

**438 B.C. The Greeks build**
The Parthenon, a temple to honor the goddess Athena, is built in Athens. The Parthenon marks the

development of the classic Greek style.

**300 B.C. Praxiteles sculpts**
Praxiteles creates a timeless masterpiece in a statue of Hermes, messenger of the gods.

**200 B.C.- Classic Greek sculpture**
**100 B.C.** Aphrodite, a Greek goddess, is forever immortalized in marble. As Venus de Milo, she stands in the Louvre, Paris.

Note: All dates given from this point are dates A.D.

**200- Early frescoes done**
**300** Early Christians decorate their underground graves, or catacombs, with frescoes. The paintings are spiritual and symbolic of life to come.

Science and technology

**8000 B.C. Agriculture begins**
The planting of crops and the domestication of wild animals begins in the Middle East.

**7000 B.C.- Tools improved**
**3600 B.C.** Neolithic and early Bronze Age people develop important tools such as the wheel, plow, and water wheel.

**3000 B.C.- Writing begins**
**2500 B.C.** The earliest known examples of cuneiform writing begin to be used in Sumer.

**2800 B.C.- Pyramids built**
**2100 B.C.** Leaders of the ancient world in engineering and architecture, the Egyptians build huge pyramids along the Nile River.

**2000 B.C. First major canal**
The Egyptians construct a canal connecting the Nile River and the Red Sea.

1750 B.C. **Trade grows**
Egyptian, Babylonian, and
Minoan trade and indus-
try flourish. Mathematics
and astronomy are
studied extensively.

1500 B.C. **Iron used**
The Hittites introduce the
use of iron to western Asia
and Egypt.

1500 B.C.- **Chinese bronze work**
1027 B.C. During the Shang dynasty,
the Chinese become skil-
led at casting bronze.

1400 B.C. **The Phoenician
alphabet**
The Phoenicians develop
an alphabet of 22 charac-
ters. This alphabet is so
successful that it is
adopted by both the
Greeks and Romans.

1000 B.C. **Phoenicians explore**
Great sea going traders,
the Phoenicians are prob-
ably the first Mediterra-
nean people to sail the Atlantic Ocean, perhaps
reaching the British Isles.

600 B.C. **Mayas develop calendar**
The Mayas develop an ac-
curate calendar.

500 B.C. **Medical school founded**
Darius I founds a medical
school in Egypt. It is the
first scientific institution
supported by a govern-
ment.

460 B.C.- **Athens is trade center**
430 B.C. Athens becomes the
center of manufacturing
and trade in the Mediter-
ranean region.

400 B.C. **Medical advances**
The Greek physician
Hippocrates teaches that
diseases have natural, not
supernatural, causes.

330 B.C. **Aristotle and science**
Aristotle's studies in logic
and the classification of
plants and animals con-
tribute to the foundations
of science.

312 B.C. **Appian Way begun**
The Appian Way is begun.
It is the first important
link in an extensive system
of Roman roads.

300 B.C. **Euclidean geometry**
The Greek mathematician
Euclid formulates the
basic concepts of
geometry.

300 B.C. **Numerals developed**
The Hindus develop the
symbols that we still use
today for numerals.

287 B.C. **Archimedes born**
Archimedes, a great Greek
scientist, is born. He discovers the principle of
specific gravity, the law of
floating bodies, and the
theory of the lever.

221 B.C.- **Great Wall of China**
206 B.C. The Great Wall of China is
completed by the Ch'in
kings. The wall protects
the country from invaders.

50 B.C. **Romans build**
Roman engineers continue
construction of sophisti-
cated aqueducts and
bridges. Experiments in
the use of concrete are
begun.

Note: All dates given from
this point are dates A.D.

105 **Paper invented**
The Chinese invent paper,
using the bark of mulberry
trees.

150 **Anatomy studied**
The Greek physician Galen
lays the foundation for the
study of anatomy and
physiology.

150 **Ptolemy's theory**
The Greek astronomer
Ptolemy develops a theory
that the earth is the center
of the universe.

# The middle period

### Political events

486 **Frankish state founded**
Traditional date for the
founding of the Merovin-
gian Dynasty and the
Frankish Kingdom.

497 **Gothic Italy**
Theodoric, King of the Os-
trogoths, is recognized
ruler of Italy by the em-
peror of the Roman Em-
pire in the East.

500 **Huns in India**
Hun raiders weaken the
power of Aryan kingdoms
in India.

527- **Eastern Empire**
565 **solidified**
The Eastern Empire is so-
lidified during the reign
of Emperor Justinian I at
Constantinople.

589 **China revival**
The Sui Dynasty is victorious over an alliance of
petty kings and warlords.

622 **A new power**
Traditional date for the
beginning of the Com-
monwealth of Islam by
Muhammad in the city of
Medina in Arabia.

**635- Islamic expansion**
**738** Under a succession of vigorous generals, Muslim
political and military
power expands from
Arabia.

**645 Japan reorganizes**
The Fujiwara clan seizes
power in Japan, initiating
a period of sweeping political reform.

**661 Muslim Empire**
The Omayyad Caliphate is
founded. Capital of the
first Muslim Empire is established at Damascus in
Syria.

**690 West African Empire**
The Songhai Empire on
the middle Niger domi-
nates West Africa.

**711 Muslims in Spain**
The Muslims begin their
conquest of Spain.

**732 Battle of Tours**
Led by Charles Martel, the
Franks beat back a Muslim
invasion of Europe.

**751 New Frankish Dynasty**
The Merovingian Dynasty
falls and the Carolingian
Dynasty is founded by
Pepin the Short, a descen-
dant of Charles Martel.

**768- Charles the Great**
**814** The son of Pepin the
Short, Charles shares rule
with his brother until 771.
Charles is known in his-
tory as Charlemagne.

**800 New western empire**
Pope Leo III crowns Char-
lemagne emperor of the
Roman Empire in the
West.

**843 Treaty of Verdun**
Charlemagne's empire is
divided into eastern, central, and western
kingdoms.

**862 First Russian Dynasty**
Rurik, a Viking warlord,
captures the Russian city-
state of Novgorod.

**871- Alfred of England**
**899** Alfred the Great, Saxon
King of England, battles
Viking raiders and begins
the rebuilding of England.

**878 Vikings defeated**
Alfred the Great defeats
the Vikings at the Battle of
Edington.

**880 Expansion in Russia**
The Viking Prince Oleg establishes control over the
city-state of Novgorod and
the city-state of Kiev. This
marks the founding of the
Kievan Principality.

**935- Unrest in Japan**
**941** Local warlords and military clans break the power
of the central government.
Japan is divided by dozens
of warring factions.

**960 Sung Dynasty**
A period of weakness and
civil war in China is ended
by the accession of the
Sung Dynasty.

**962 Holy Roman Empire
founded**
Otto I, the Great, a de-
scendant of Charlemagne,
is crowned Emperor. He
changes his title from
Roman Emperor in the
West to Holy Roman Em-
peror.

**969 Fatimids conquer Egypt**
The Fatimid Dynasty gains
control of Egypt and
founds the city of Cairo.

**987 Capetian Dynasty
founded**
Hugh Capet is elected
King of the West Franks.
His state becomes the
basis for the modern state
of France.

**995 Fujiwara revival**
Michinaga, head of the
Fujiwara clan, helps to re-
store the authority of the
central government of
Japan.

**998- Muslim India expands**
**1030** Mahmud of Ghazni leads
raids into Hindu India.

**1000 Kingdom of Ghana**
The Kingdom of Ghana in
West Africa, with its capital
at the city of Kumbi,
reaches its high point.

**1037 Iran conquered**
The Muslim Seljuk Turks
conquer most of the Mus-
lim Arab kingdoms in Iran.

**1066 Normans invade
England**
William the Duke of Nor-
mandy invades England
and defeats the Anglo-
Saxon King Harold at the
Battle of Hastings.

**1071 Battle of Manzikert**
The Seljuk Turks destroy
Byzantine power in Asia
Minor.

**1100 New African states**
The Kingdom of Diara and
the Kingdom of Sosso suc-
ceed Ghana as the leading
powers in West Africa.

**1154- England consolidated**
**1399** The House of Plantagenet
begins the organization of
the state of England.

**1180- France consolidated**
**1223** Philip II Augustus, King of
France, consolidates the
French monarchy and
formalizes the organiza-
tion of the French state.

**1187 Jerusalem recaptured**
A Muslim army led by
Saladin recaptures the city
of Jerusalem from Chris-
tian Europeans.

**1190 Mongols rise**
The war chief Temujin begins the creation of a Mongol Empire in central Asia.

**1192 Shogun rules Japan**
Yoritomo, leader of the Minamoto clan, becomes the first Shogun, or "Great General," to rule Japan. The office of emperor becomes purely ceremonial.

**1200 Growth of Mali**
The Kingdom of Mali politically and militarily dominates West Africa.

**1206 Mongol Empire founded**
Temujin is elected Genghis Khan, or "Emperor within the Seas" of the Mongols.

**1215 Magna Carta**
The English nobility forces King John to accept a charter recognizing the rights under the law of English nobles.

**1237- Mongols in Europe**
**1240** Mongol armies occupy Russia and attack Poland and Hungary.

**1271 Mongols in China**
Kublai Khan leads the Mongols to the final conquest of China. He founds the Yüan Dynasty, which rules China until 1368.

**1273 Rise of the Hapsburgs**
Rudolf of Hapsburg is elected King of Germany. The Hapsburg family plays an important role in European politics until the 20th century.

**1274- Mongols in Japan**
**1281** The Japanese government turns back two attempts by Mongols from China to invade Japan.

**1290 Ottoman State begins**
The Seljuk prince Othman founds a principality called Othmanli. From this base, the Turkish Muslim state that becomes the Ottoman Empire grows.

**1300 Italian revival**
Italian city-states such as Florence, Venice, and Genoa begin achieving political power through domination of Europe's trade and banking.

**1312- Mandingo Empire**
**1337** The Emperor Mansa Musa, a vigorous political and military leader, consolidates a brilliant and powerful state centered in the city of Timbuktu in West Africa.

**1336- Civil war in Japan**
**1392** A long period of unrest occurs, during which various clans battle for control of Japan.

**1337 Hundred Years' War begins**
The war is fought between France and England, over English claims to the throne of France. The war ends in 1453 with England's claims thwarted.

**1346 Battle of Crécy**
During the Hundred Years' War, this battle marks the defeat of French knights by English bowmen.

**1356 Battle of Poitiers**
During the Hundred Years' War, the French forces are decimated by an English army led by the Black Prince.

**1368 Ming Dynasty founded**
The Ming Dynasty begins its 300-year rule of China.

**1369- Mongol unrest**
**1405** Tamerlane, a Mongol Khan, ravages central Asia, Mesopotamia, India, and Turkey.

**1380 Battle of Kulikovo**
A Russian force defeats a Mongol army, marking the beginning of the Mongol withdrawal from Russia.

**1421 New capital for China**
The capital of China is moved to the city of Peking.

**1428 Battle of Orléans**
Joan of Arc leads a French army to victory over the English. The battle is the turning point toward a final French victory in the Hundred Years' War.

**1453 Constantinople falls**
The Ottoman Turks capture the city of Constantinople. This marks the end of the Roman Empire in the East.

**1455 Wars of the Roses begin**
The House of York and the House of Lancaster battle for the throne of England.

**1462- Ivan III, the Great**
**1505** A brilliant political leader, he begins the consolidation of the modern Russian state.

**1485 Wars of the Roses end**
Henry Tudor, member of a branch of the House of Lancaster, defeats Richard III of the House of York at the Battle of Bosworth Field.

**1492 Spain consolidated**
King Ferdinand and Queen Isabella complete the reconquest of Spain. The last Muslims are expelled from Spanish soil.

## Social events

**527- Justinian's Code**
**565 compiled**
The Code of Justinian organizes Roman law. The code becomes the basis for law as it develops in many European and Latin-American countries.

**700- European feudalism**
**1000** Europe's social structure is frozen by feudalism, which organizes society into rigidly defined classes.

**970 University started**
The University of Al-Azhar is founded in Cairo. The Arab Muslims are among the first to establish universities.

**1000- The guild system**
**1200** Merchants and craftsmen form guilds to protect profits and as mutual aid societies.

**1085 Domesday survey**
William the Conqueror orders a census of people and goods in England.

**1100- Universities in Europe**
**1300** Universities develop out of schools at cathedrals and monasteries. The universities organize and formalize the teaching of law, medicine, and theology.

**1100- Rise of towns**
**1400** New social structures begin to emerge as towns, which had decayed since Roman times, begin to reorganize.

**1185- Kamakura period**
**1333** A feudal structure is gradually formalized and consolidated in Japan.

**1300 League formed**
Merchants from cities in northern Germany form the Hanseatic League to protect their commercial interests, and advance their social goals.

**1347- The Black Death**
**1350** The Black Death, a form of bubonic plague, destroys a fourth of the population of Europe. Europe's social structure is completely overturned as a result of the plague.

**1450- Slave trade flourishes**
**1865** Europeans take as many as 10 million people from Africa to work as slaves.

## Religion

**480 Church's influence grows**
After the fall of Rome, the Roman Catholic Church becomes the most powerful political and social influence in Western Europe.

**500 *Talmud* completed**
Jewish scholars in Mesopotamia complete the *Talmud.*

**500 Nubians converted**
The Nubian kingdoms in Africa are converted to Christianity.

**529 Monte Cassino opens**
St. Benedict founds the monastery of Monte Cassino and organizes what becomes the Benedictine order of monks.

**610 Muhammad begins preaching**
Muhammad, founder of Islam, begins preaching in Mecca.

**622 Islamic era begins**
Muhammad travels secretly to Medina. His journey, called the "Hegira," marks the traditional beginning of the religion of Islam.

**652 *Koran* written**
The teachings of Muhammad are collected into a book, called the *Koran*. The *Koran* remains to this day the basic foundation of the religion of Islam.

**756 Donation of Pepin**
Pepin the Short, King of the West Franks, grants the papacy authority over lands in central Italy, thus establishing the Papal States.

**1000- Judaic Golden Age**
**1300** The Jewish community in Spain and North Africa, under tolerant Muslim governments, enjoys a spiritual and cultural golden age.

**1054 Christianity divided**
Rivalries between the church at Rome and the church at Constantinople result in a separation between Eastern Orthodox churches and the Roman Catholic Church.

**1099 First Crusade**
Led by Godfrey of Bouillon, Christian crusaders capture the city of Jerusalem from the Muslims.

**1231 Inquisition begins**
Pope Gregory IX begins the Inquisition, a special court to investigate people suspected of heresy.

**1302 Papal power grows**
Pope Boniface VIII issues a papal document, *Unam Sanctam*. It declares that the kings of nations are subject to the Holy Roman emperor, and the emperor's power is derived from the pope.

**1378- Papacy divided**
**1417** The *Great Schism* results in several Roman Catholic churchmen claiming to be the pope at the same time. The dispute is settled at the Council of Constance.

1380 **English Bible**
The first complete English translation of the Bible is made by John Wycliffe, an English priest.

1492 **Spanish Jews expelled**
Ferdinand and Isabella expel all Jews from Spain.

### Philosophy

524 **Death of Boethius**
Boethius, the last classical philosopher, is executed.

600 **Chinese influence spreads**
The ethical system of Confucius spreads to Japan where it influences Japanese thought.

800 **Carolingian revival**
Philosophy and learning are revived at the court of Charlemagne by such men as Alcuin and Einhard.

1100- **European philosophy**
1200 The height of scholasticism in Europe, featuring such figures as Bernard of Clairvaux, Anselm, and Peter Abélard.

1150 **Classical revival**
The Muslim philosopher Averroës revives interest in Plato and Aristotle.

1225- **St. Thomas Aquinas**
1274 A great theologian and philosopher of the Christian church, St. Thomas Aquinas argues that faith rests on a rational foundation and that philosophy does not conflict with Christianity.

1300- **Rise of humanism**
1500 European philosophy begins to turn from study of the spiritual to study of the material as "people" become the center of the universe.

### Literature

700 **A new epic**
The Anglo-Saxon epic poem, *Beowulf*, is written.

712 **Literature in Japan**
The first known example of Japanese literature, the *Record of Ancient Things*, is published.

780 **Early encyclopedia**
The Chinese historian Tu Yu compiles an encyclopedia, a chronology of world history.

810 **European revival**
After a long period of decay, a revival of literature in Europe begins with publication of Einhard's *Life of Charlemagne*.

935 **Japanese poetry**
The height of Japanese classical poetry is marked by the publication of the *Kokinshū*, an anthology of over a thousand well-known poems.

1000 **Japanese classic**
The noblewoman Lady Murasaki writes *The Tale of Genji*, still considered to be the greatest Japanese novel.

1100 **Frankish epic poetry**
The French epic poem, *Song of Roland*, is written.

1100 **Muslim poetry popular**
A Persian Muslim poet, Omar Khayyam, writes *The Rubaiyat*, a collection of quatrains that gains popularity throughout the Muslim world.

1200 **Age of German epics**
The German epic, *Song of the Nibelungs*, is collected and written down.

1321 **Dante popular**
The Italian author Dante Alighieri writes the *Divine Comedy*, the first serious literary work written in a modern European language.

1348- ***The Decameron***
1353 *The Decameron*, a collection of short stories, is written by Giovanni Boccaccio. His style is copied by writers all over Europe.

1350- **Petrarch writes poems**
1374 A founder of the humanist movement, Petrarch writes more than 400 poems.

1350 **Revival in Japan**
After a period of literary decline, there occurs a revival of literature symbolized in the style of lyric drama called *No*.

1377 **Robin Hood**
The first stories featuring Robin Hood appear in England.

1400 **Chaucer publishes**
The English writer Geoffrey Chaucer publishes his major work, *The Canterbury Tales*.

### The arts

532- **Hagia Sophia built**
537 Byzantine Emperor Justinian builds the Church of the Holy Wisdom in Constantinople. It is better known as the Hagia Sophia.

540- **Early music**
604 The Gregorian chant, a form of singing without musical accompaniment, is developed by churchmen under St. Gregory I, the Great.

700- **Manuscripts illuminated**
800 *The Books of Kells*, an illuminated manuscript, is completed.

**800 Charlemagne and the arts**
Charlemagne builds the cathedral at Aix-la-Chapelle. He encourages a revival of art.

**900 Celtic stonework**
Celtic stone masons in Ireland carve complex, highly decorated crosses to mark graves.

**1000 Jewelers flourish**
Rulers wear crowns of gold and silver studded with precious stones.

**1100 New art style**
A style of architecture, sculpture, and painting called the romanesque reaches its highest development. The style is derived from classical Roman forms.

**1163 Early gothic style**
One hundred and fifty years of work begins on Notre Dame Cathedral in Paris, France. The gothic style replaces romanesque as the prevailing art form in Europe.

**1200 Classic Chinese artist**
Hsia Kuei paints idealized Chinese landscapes on silk scrolls. He paints in ink.

**1200 The Byzantine style**
Byzantine artists develop a distinctive style, concentrating on the outward expression of inner spirituality.

**1305 Painting revival**
The Italian master Giotto paints *The Descent from the Cross*. He introduces realism into paintings.

**1320- Realism reinforced**
**1330** Simone Martini paints the St. Martino chapel below the church of St. Francis of Assisi in Siena, Italy. The pictures are scenes from the life of St. Martin and the style continues the trend toward realism begun by Giotto.

**1359 Viennese Gothic**
Work begins on the nave of St. Stephen's Cathedral in the city of Vienna.

**1415 Donatello masterpiece**
The Italian sculptor Donatello creates *St. George* in marble. A relief below the statue pictures *St. George Killing the Dragon*.

**1434 Flemish symbolism**
Jan van Eyck paints *The Arnolfini Wedding*. Christ is represented by a single lighted candle.

**1450 Monk and artist**
Fra Angelico, a Dominican monk and artist, paints one of his most famous creations. It is titled *The Annunciation*.

**1450- Persian art**
**1537** Persian painter Kamal ad-Din Bihzad excells in painting miniatures. He draws both battle and nature scenes.

**1478 Classical revival**
Sandro Botticelli is inspired by the myth of Venus. His painting, *Birth of Venus*, marks a revival of classicism in art.

**1485 Italian genius**
Leonardo da Vinci paints the *Madonna of the Rocks*. He is one of the greatest of the Italian Renaissance painters.

**Science and technology**

**500 Theories of the earth**
Hindu astronomers and mathematicians develop theories about the rotation of the earth.

**600 Zero developed**
Hindu mathematicians develop the concept of zero and the use of decimal places in mathematics.

**770 Wood-block printing**
The Chinese invent wood-block printing.

**800 Number system adopted**
The Arabs adopt from India the number system that we use today.

**960- Inventions in China**
**1279** During the Sung Dynasty, the Chinese invent the magnetic compass, gunpowder, and movable type for printing.

**1267 Roger Bacon**
Roger Bacon, an English scientist, writes *Opus maius*, a summary of his system of knowledge.

**1346 Gunpowder in Europe**
Gunpowder is used during the Battle of Crécy, probably for the first time in Europe.

**1440 Movable type used**
Johannes Gutenberg, a German printer, is the first European to use movable type.

**1454 First book printed**
Johannes Gutenberg prints the Latin Bible, the first large book printed in Europe using movable type.

# The early modern period

### Political events

**1492 America reached**
Christopher Columbus reaches land in the Western Hemisphere.

**1493 Songhai revival**
Led by Askia Muhammad, the Songhai Empire enjoys a final burst of military expansion.

**1497 Cabot in Canada**
John Cabot explores islands off the coast of what is today Canada.

**1498 Da Gama in India**
Vasco da Gama, a Portuguese navigator, reaches India by sailing around Africa.

**1509 Henry VIII of England**
Henry VIII ascends the throne of England.

**1516 Hapsburg dynasty grows**
Charles Haspburg becomes Charles I, King of Spain, and Charles V, Holy Roman Emperor.

**1517 Songhai defeated**
The Haussa Confederation wins a war against Songhai.

**1517 Luther**
Martin Luther's break with the Church of Rome causes political unrest in Europe.

**1519- Cortés in Mexico**
**1521** The Aztec Empire in what is today Mexico is destroyed by Hernando Cortés.

**1520 Ottomans expand**
Suleiman I, the Magnificent, greatest of the Turkish sultans, ascends the throne.

**1526 The Mogul Empire**
Babar, a descendant of Tamerlane, establishes Muslim control over most of northern India.

**1529 Turks at Vienna**
The forces of Suleiman I penetrate Europe to the city of Vienna where they mount an unsuccessful siege.

**1532 Peru invaded**
A Spanish force led by Francisco Pizarro lands in what is today Peru.

**1533 First czar**
Ivan IV, the Terrible, is the first Russian ruler to use the title czar.

**1537 Italian decline**
The Italian city-states begin to fall under the control of France, Spain, and the Holy Roman Empire.

**1543 Portuguese in Japan**
First Europeans visit Japan, establishing trade relations between Europe and Japan.

**1552 Russian expansion**
Russian forces move eastward, capturing control of the Volga River.

**1555 Peace of Augsburg**
Temporarily halts civil war in the Holy Roman Empire.

**1556 New king in Spain**
The Holy Roman Emperor Charles abdicates. He leaves the Kingdom of Spain to his son, Philip II.

**1558 Elizabeth I, Tudor**
Elizabeth I becomes Queen of England. She reigns until 1603, during a period of expansion.

**1562- Civil war in France**
**1598** Catholics and Protestants (the Huguenots) fight eight wars for control of the French throne.

**1568- Japan active**
**1600** One of the most vigorous periods in Japanese history, marked by the expansion of Japanese influence abroad.

**1571 Empire of Kanem**
The Empire of Kanem in Africa gains control of most of the territory around Lake Chad.

**1571 Battle of Lepanto**
An allied European fleet defeats the Turkish fleet, marking the beginning of the end of Muslim control of the Mediterranean Sea.

**1588 Armada defeated**
The key battle in a major war between Spain and England, the Spanish Armada, or fleet, is completely defeated.

**1589 New French dynasty**
The House of Bourbon, which rules France until 1792, gains the throne.

**1592 Japanese expansion**
A Japanese army of over 200,000 men invades Korea but is defeated.

**1598 Edict of Nantes**
The civil wars in France are ended by the Edict of Nantes.

**1600- Tokugawa Shogunate**
**1867** The capital of Japan is established at the city of Edo (Tokyo). The Tokugawa family gains and retains the title of Shogun. The title of Emperor remains purely honorary as shoguns rule Japan.

**1603 House of Stuart**
King James VI of Scotland becomes James I of England as the Tudor family dies out.

**1608 Quebec Founded**
The French explorer Champlain founds the city of Quebec.

**1613 Romanov rule in Russia**
Michael Romanov becomes Czar of all the Russians, founding the dynasty that rules Russia until 1917.

**1618- The Thirty Years' War**
**1648** What is today Germany is devastated by 4 major wars that are together called the Thirty Years' War.

**1624 Richelieu in France**
Cardinal Richelieu becomes chief minister of France.

**1627 Shah Jahan rules India**
The Mogul emperor Shah Jahan gains the throne of India.

**1642- Civil War in England**
**1648** The Roundheads (Puritan supporters of Parliament) battle the Cavaliers (Anglican supporters of the king) for control of England's government.

**1643- Louis XIV in France**
**1715** The reign of Louis XIV, the most famous of the French monarchs. France pursues a vigorous policy designed to control Europe.

**1644 Manchus conquer China**
The Manchus, a group of people from what is today Manchuria, gain control of China and rule until 1912.

**1648 Treaty of Westphalia**
The treaty ends the Thirty Years' War.

**1649 English monarchy falls**
The parliamentary party, victorious in the Civil War, executes King Charles I.

**1652 Cape Town founded**
Dutch settlers led by Jan van Riebeeck found the city and Cape Colony at the southern tip of Africa.

**1653 Cromwell gains power**
Control of England, which is now a commonwealth (republic), is seized by Oliver Cromwell.

**1656 Ottoman revival begins**
The decline of the Ottoman Empire is temporarily reversed by grand vizier (prime minister) Muhammad Kiuprili.

**1660 English monarchy restored**
Parliament restores the monarchy. Charles II becomes king.

**1660 Mandingo Empire falls**
The Kingdom of Segu and the Kingdom of Kaarta replace the Mandingo Empire as the chief states along the upper Niger in Africa.

**1682- Liberation of Hungary**
**1699** After having occupied Hungary for many years, the Ottoman Turks are driven out by the armies of the Holy Roman Empire.

**1688- The Glorious Revolution**
**1689** King James II, in conflict with Parliament, flees from England. Parliament offers the throne to James's daughter Mary, and her husband William of Orange.

**1689- Peter I of Russia**
**1725** Known as Peter the Great, this czar begins to modernize Russia.

**1697- Charles XII of Sweden**
**1718** For a short period of time, Sweden becomes a first-class power. Charles follows a vigorous political and military policy in East Europe.

**Social events**

**1500- Europe's middle class**
**1700** The feudal structure decays as the traditional nobility is gradually replaced by a rising middle class made up of bankers, merchants, and successful craftsmen.

**1689 English Bill of Rights**
William and Mary, joint rulers of England, accept the Bill of Rights. This document assures the basic civil rights of English citizens.

**Religion**

**1517 Reformation begins**
The Protestant Reformation begins when Martin Luther, a Roman Catholic priest, protests certain practices of the Roman Catholic Church.

**1520- Reformation spreads**
**1536** Swedish and Danish kings make Lutheranism the state religion of Sweden, Finland, Norway, and Denmark.

**1534 English reformation**
An act of Parliament declares that the king, not the pope, is the head of the church in England.

**1536 Calvin prominent**
*The Institutes of the Christian Religion* by John Calvin offers a systematic presentation of Protestant beliefs.

**1545- The Counter**
**1563 Reformation**
At the Council of Trent, the Roman Catholic Church responds to the

Protestant Reformation with internal reforms. Many of the abuses that had caused the Protestant Reformation are corrected.

**1555 Peace of Augsburg**
A compromise, known as the Peace of Augsburg, allows the ruler of each German state to determine whether Catholicism or Lutheranism will be its official religion.

**1560 Scottish Reformation**
Protestantism, introduced by John Knox, becomes the state religion of Scotland.

**1563 *Thirty-nine Articles***
The *Thirty-nine Articles* organize the teachings of Anglicanism, a moderate form of Protestantism, which becomes the state religion of England.

**1598 Edict of Nantes**
The Edict of Nantes gives French Protestants religious freedom and civil rights.

**1611 The King James Bible**
Scholars complete a new version of the Bible in the English language as authorized by King James.

**1647 Quakers founded**
The Society of Friends, also called Quakers, is founded in England.

Philosophy
**1530- The social contract**
**1596** The French philosopher Jean Bodin introduces the idea that the state is the result of a social contract.

**1532 *The Prince* published**
In *The Prince*, Niccolò Machiavelli, an Italian statesman, urges rulers to use any means to achieve their goals.

**1533- Essays by Montaigne**
**1592** In a series of essays, the French writer Montaigne expresses his doubt about the ability of reason to find truth.

**1605 The scientific method**
Francis Bacon, an English philosopher, writes *The Advancement of Learning*. He calls for the development of a logical methodology for the study of natural phenomena.

**1632 Galileo's masterpiece**
Galileo, considered the founder of modern experimental science, writes *A Dialogue on the Two Principal Systems of the World*.

**1637- Age of Descartes**
**1650** The French philosopher René Descartes says that truth can be found through the use of reason alone. He is considered the founder of modern philosophy.

**1651 The *Leviathan***
English political philosopher Thomas Hobbes publishes his major work, *Leviathan*, a work studying man's relationship to the state.

**1663 Spinoza writes**
In his writings, the Dutch philosopher Baruch Spinoza writes that the highest good man can attain is the intellectual love of God.

**1685- Berkeley's "idealism"**
**1753** George Berkeley, an Irish philosopher, argues that nothing exists unless it is perceived by the mind. His philosophy is called "idealism."

**1690 John Locke**
An English philosopher, John Locke, publishes his major work, *An Essay Concerning Human Understanding*. His writing has great influence on political science.

Literature
**1500 Erasmus shakes Europe**
Christian humanist Desiderius Erasmus writes *Praise of Folly*, ridiculing the manners of the day.

**1516 *Utopia* written**
An English scholar, Thomas More, writes *Utopia*, an account of an ideal society.

**1532- Works by Rabelais**
**1534** A Frenchman, François Rabelais, writes *Gargantua and Pantagruel*, a comic satire of French society.

**1599- Height of Shakespeare**
**1608** At the height of his career, William Shakespeare writes several comedies and almost all of the tragedies which have made him the world's most famous playwright.

**1600 Japanese drama**
The classical Japanese dramatic form, the Kabuki, is developed.

**1605 Cervantes publishes**
The Spanish writer Miguel de Cervantes publishes his great work, *Don Quixote*.

**1616 Jonson famous**
Ben Jonson is the first playwright to publish an edition of his own works.

**1635 De Vega dies**
The most noted of the early Spanish writers, Lope de Vega, dies.

**1636 New French drama**
Pierre Corneille, called the founder of French heroic

comedy, stages *The Cid*, a play which sets new standards for drama.

**1662  A Molière masterpiece**
Jean Baptiste Poquelin (Molière), the greatest French writer of comedy, produces *The School for Wives*, his first stage triumph.

**1664  Racine begins**
Jean Racine stages his first tragedy, *La Thébaïde*.

**1667  Milton's masterpiece**
English poet John Milton writes the great epic, *Paradise Lost*.

**1681  Poem by Dryden**
English poet laureate John Dryden writes the poem *Absalom and Achitophel*.

**The arts**

**1498-  The *Pietà* completed**
**1499**  At age 23, Michelangelo creates the *Pietà*. In this sculpture Mary cradles the lifeless body of Christ.

**1503  *Mona Lisa* completed**
Da Vinci completes what has become the world's most famous painting, the *Mona Lisa*.

**1504  Raphael emerges**
Raphael, Italian Renaissance painter, paints the *Marriage of the Virgin*. It is one of his early masterpieces.

**1506  Da Vinci's influence**
Influenced by Da Vinci's *Madonna of the Rocks*, Raphael paints the *Madonna of the Goldfinch*.

**1511  Michelangelo as painter**
Michelangelo, known primarily as a sculptor, is immortalized as a painter by his work in the Sistine Chapel in the Vatican.

**1550  Book of Kings**
Early kings of Persia are illustrated in the *Book of Kings*. It is one of the greatest works of Persian miniaturists.

**1565  Flemish master**
Pieter Bruegel the Elder, a great Flemish master, paints *Return of the Hunters*, a classic of the early Flemish style.

**1575  English church music**
Thomas Tallis, called the "Father of English Church Music," joins William Byrd to publish a set of motets, a kind of church music. The title is *Sacred Songs for Chorus*.

**1581  First ballet**
A royal wedding in Paris plays host to Italian dancers performing the *Ballet Comique de la Reine*.

**1586  A new style**
El Greco of Spain joins the great masters of all times with his painting *The Burial of Count Orgaz*. El Greco's use of slightly distorted forms sets new styles for art.

**1598  Bernini born**
Gian Lorenzo Bernini, baroque artist who designs the plaza of St. Peter's Church in Rome, is born in Italy.

**1611  Peter Paul Rubens**
Rubens, the Flemish master, helps to define the baroque style in his oil, *Elevation of the Cross*.

**1642  Rembrandt prominent**
*The Night Watch*, the most famous of Rembrandt's paintings, is completed. He paints many religious and mythological scenes.

**1653  Taj Mahal built**
The Indian ruler Shah Jahan builds an exquisite tomb, the Taj Mahal.

**1660  Painted sunlight**
*Young Woman with a Water Jug* is painted in oils by Jan Vermeer.

**1685-  Age of Bach**
**1750**  Johann Sebastian Bach, as composer, musician, and choirmaster, sets the format for what is called the baroque style in music.

**Science and Technology**

**1500  Da Vinci's experiments**
Leonardo da Vinci uses observation and experiments to make many discoveries in anatomy, aerodynamics, and architectural engineering.

**1543  Modern astronomy**
The Polish astronomer Nicolaus Copernicus rediscovers the theory that the earth moves around the sun. He lays the foundation for modern astronomy.

**1600  Modern science founded**
The Italian physicist Galileo founds modern experimental science.

**1609  Astronomy expands**
Johannes Kepler establishes astronomy as an exact science.

**1628  Harvey publishes**
William Harvey publishes his theory on the circulation of blood.

**1650  Microscope made**
Anton van Leeuwenhoek produces the first practical microscope.

**1687  The new physics**
Sir Isaac Newton publishes the *Principia*, which summarizes basic laws of mechanics.

# European ascendancy

### Political events

**1700-** **Great Northern War**
**1721** Sweden is thoroughly defeated and replaced by Russia as the leading power in the Baltic.

**1701-** **War of Spanish**
**1714** **Succession**
An alliance of England, Holland, and the Holy Roman Empire goes to war against Louis XIV of France, who has established his grandson as King of Spain. The allies fear union of France and Spain.

**1713** **Treaty of Utrecht**
The treaty marks the official end of the War of Spanish Succession though some fighting continues until 1714.

**1713-** **Rise of Prussia**
**1740** Under the leadership of King Frederick William I, Prussia begins its rise to leadership in Germany.

**1714** **New English dynasty**
The Stuart dynasty dies out without direct heirs, and the House of Hanover is given the throne.

**1717** **The English in India**
The British East India Company begins its penetration of India.

**1740-** **Frederick II, the Great**
**1786** Under the vigorous political and military leadership of Frederick II, Prussia becomes a leading power.

**1740-** **Austrian War**
**1748** Also known as the War of Austrian Succession, the war begins when Maria Theresa inherits the throne of Austria. European monarchs, led by

Frederick II of Prussia, refuse to recognize the right of a woman to inherit this throne.

**1751** **Chinese in Tibet**
A Chinese force invades and occupies Tibet.

**1756-** **Seven Years' War**
**1763** The war begins over boundary disputes between British and French colonies in North America.

**1762-** **Catherine II, the Great**
**1796** Catherine, the most famous Russian czarina (queen), continues the reforms begun by Peter the Great.

**1763** **Treaty of Paris**
The treaty ends the Seven Years' War, leaving England the world's leading power.

**1772** **Poland divided**
The first of three partitions of Poland. The territory of Poland is divided between Austria (the Holy Roman Empire), Prussia, and Russia.

**1775-** **American Revolution**
**1783** Thirteen of Britain's North American colonies revolt.

**1780-** **Austrian reform**
**1790** Joseph II becomes Emperor of Austria, and begins a period of reform designed to modernize the empire.

**1783** **Treaty of Paris**
The United States is recognized as a sovereign nation.

**1789** **French Revolution**
The Estates General meets in France, marking the beginning of the French Revolution.

**1793** **Louis XVI executed**
The French revolutionary government orders the execution of King Louis XVI.

**1793** **Ottoman reform**
The Sultan Selim III issues the *New Regulations* which call for comprehensive reform of the Ottoman Empire.

**1795** **Unrest in Japan**
Beginning of the decline of the authority of the shogunate in Japanese government.

**1796** **Napoleon in Italy**
Napoleon Bonaparte comes into prominence by leading French forces to smashing victories in Italy.

**1796** **Unrest in China**
A period of government weakness and rebellion against the government begins.

**1799** **French dictatorship**
Napoleon is elected First Consul and becomes military dictator of France.

**1804** **Napoleon emperor**
Napoleon Bonaparte is crowned Emperor of the French.

**1812** **Napoleon in Russia**
The beginning of the end for the First French Empire as Napoleon suffers defeat in Russia.

**1814** **Napoleon abdicates**
The Bourbons are restored to the throne of France.

**1815** **Battle of Waterloo**
Napoleon attempts to regain power. He is crushed at Waterloo by a joint British and Prussian army.

**1815 Congress of Vienna**
The nations of Europe gather in Vienna to restore order after the upheavals caused by Napoleon.

**1824 Spain loses colonies**
Spain's colonies in what is now South America declare and gain independence.

**1830- British reform**
**1846** A series of laws reform the political system of England.

**1841- First Opium War**
**1842** The weakness of the Chinese government is demonstrated when the Chinese fail to stop British sale of opium in China.

**1847 Liberian Republic**
Supported by the United States, freed slaves found the first Black African Republic.

**1848 European unrest**
Democratic revolutions against monarchies break out all over Europe.

**1848 A new France**
The French monarchy is overthrown again, and the Second French Republic is declared.

**1852 Second Empire**
Napoleon III, a descendant of Napoleon Bonaparte, overthrows the French Republic, and founds the Second Empire.

**1853 Perry in Japan**
The United States Commodore Matthew C. Perry heads a delegation to Japan, the first outsiders to land in force for many years.

**1853- Crimean War**
**1856** Russian attempts to annex Turkish territory are

blocked by Great Britain and France.

**1857- Sepoy Mutiny**
**1858** British control of India is shaken as Indian troops revolt against English officers.

**1861 Italy unified**
Led by Count Cavour, the Kingdom of Piedmont expels the Austrians and founds the modern Italian state.

**1862 Bismarck prominent**
Otto von Bismarck becomes prominent in the Prussian government and begins his drive to make Prussia pre-eminent in Germany.

**1867 Dominion of Canada**
The British parliament grants Canada dominion status.

**1868 Disraeli ministry**
Benjamin Disraeli, leader of the English Conservative Party, forms his first, but short-lived, ministry.

**1868 Gladstone ministry**
William Gladstone, leader of the English Liberal Party and Disraeli's great adversary, forms his first ministry.

**1868 Meiji Restoration**
The Emperor Mutsuhito eliminates the shogunate and embarks Japan on a program of modernization.

**1870 Franco-Prussian War**
Bismarck tricks Napoleon III into a war that proves disastrous for France.

**1870 Republican France**
The defeat of Napoleon III by Bismarck causes the founding of the Third French Republic.

**1871 Germany unified**
Bismarck uses the prestige gained by Prussia in the war with France to gain support for declaration of the German Empire.

**1875 The British in Suez**
Disraeli secretly purchases control of the Suez Canal from Egypt.

**1877 The British in Africa**
The British government annexes the South African Republic.

**1882 The Triple Alliance**
An anti-French alliance of Germany, Austria-Hungary, and Italy is engineered by Bismarck.

**1885 Indians unite**
The Indian National Congress is founded to work for independence for India.

**1888 Kaiser Wilhelm II**
Wilhelm II, the last German Kaiser (emperor), comes to the throne.

**1890 American unity**
The Pan American Union is founded.

**1894 Czar Nicholas II**
Nicholas II, the last Russian czar, comes to the throne.

**1894- Dreyfus Affair**
**1906** Captain Dreyfus, a Jewish officer in the French Army, is wrongfully convicted of treason. The struggle to acquit Dreyfus, because of the anti-Semitic overtones of the case, rocks France.

**1896- Young Turks**
**1908** A movement led by young Turkish military officers struggles to reform the decaying Ottoman Empire.

**1898  Spanish-American War**
Defeat by the United States marks Spain's end as a great power.

**1899-  Boer War**
**1902**  Dutch settlers in southern Africa (Boers) unsuccessfully attempt to block British expansion.

**1899  Peace conference**
The first International Peace Conference is held at The Hague.

### Social events

**1764  Penal reform started**
Beccaria of Italy publishes *On Crimes and Punishments*. The book provides impetus for penal reform.

**1776  Colonies rebel**
Basing their ideas on many social thinkers, American thinkers produce the *Declaration of Independence*. This document supports the natural right of citizens to rebel against a government that has become unresponsive to the needs of the governed.

**1777  English prison reform**
A study by John Howard leads to prison reform in England.

**1789  French declare rights**
*The Declaration of the Rights of Man and of the Citizen*, written by representatives of all classes of French society, becomes a landmark in the story of human liberty.

**1791  Americans declare rights**
The first 10 amendments to the new United States Constitution explain and protect the fundamental rights and freedoms of every citizen. These first 10 amendments become known as the *Bill of Rights*.

**1802  Child labor limited**
The First Factory Act in Great Britain limits the working hours of children.

**1804  Code Napoleon issued**
Napoleon combines many local French civil laws into one code. The Code Napoleon recognizes many human liberties and civil rights and influences law codes around the world.

**1807  Slave trade abolished**
The British Parliament forbids the slave trade throughout the Empire.

**1832  Britain liberalizes**
The First Reform Act in Britain gives the middle class greater voice in government.

**1841  Mentally-ill cared for**
Dorothea Dix of the United States leads a drive for better treatment of mentally-ill patients.

**1844  Consumer cooperatives**
A group of English weavers opens a cooperative store. This marks the beginning of the modern consumer-cooperative movement.

**1858-  Serfdom abolished**
**1861**  Alexander II abolishes serfdom in Russia with a series of laws culminating in the Emancipation Edict of 1861.

**1863  U.S. slavery abolished**
The Emancipation Proclamation outlaws slavery in the United States.

**1864  Red Cross founded**
The International Red Cross is founded, originally to care for sick and wounded soldiers.

**1870  British education**
Great Britain establishes a national system of education, thereby recognizing the right of every child in Britain to a minimum level of education.

**1878  Salvation Army founded**
William Booth founds the Salvation Army in England. The intent of the organization is to help improve living conditions for poor workers in English cities.

**1881-  French education**
**1886**  Free public education is established in France.

**1891  *Rerum Novarum***
Pope Leo XIII issues an encyclical giving the Roman Catholic Church's position on social affairs and the conditions of the working classes.

### Religion

**1744  Methodism founded**
John Wesley organizes a series of meetings that mark the formal beginning of Methodism.

**1844  YMCA founded**
The Young Men's Christian Association is founded in England.

**1869-  Papal authority set**
**1870**  Vatican Council I declares the pope infallible, that is, incapable of error, when dealing with matters concerning faith and morals.

**1870  Papal states lost**
The government of Italy claims sovereignty over the Papal States. The papacy's political authority is limited to Vatican City.

**1897  Zionism begins**
Theodor Herzl founds the Zionist movement, a movement to re-establish in Palestine the nation of Israel.

## Philosophy

**1700-1800 The Enlightenment**
Building on foundations laid by such men as Descartes, Hobbes, and Locke, European thinkers publicize the ideas of respect for human reason and human rights.

**1739-1740 Hume's epistemology**
In his major work, *A Treatise of Human Nature*, David Hume argues that knowledge is limited to experience and that complete understanding of any event or natural phenomenon is not possible.

**1762 Rousseau's romanticism**
In his book, *The Social Contract*, Jean Jacques Rousseau gives his views on government as the expression of the general will of all the people. His ideas influenced the French Revolution.

**1776 Adam Smith's economics**
A Scottish philosopher, Adam Smith, writes *The Wealth of Nations*. He establishes the importance of world trade and control of sources of raw materials to the economic growth of nations.

**1781 Kant critiques reason**
German philosopher Immanuel Kant writes the *Critique of Pure Reason*. The book explores the nature and limits of the human mind.

**1820 Hegel on history**
In his writings, the German philosopher, Georg Hegel, establishes the philosophy of history as an important field of study.

**1824 Comte and sociology**
Auguste Comte, founder of the philosophy known as "positivism," originates a concept of social science which he calls sociology.

**1843-1845 Existentialism begins**
The Danish philosopher Søren Kierkegaard is considered one of the founders of "existentialism." He writes about the nature of religious faith.

**1843 The utilitarian movement**
John Stuart Mill, leader of the utilitarian movement, writes *System of Logic*, his chief work.

**1859 Evolution explodes**
Charles Darwin, an English biologist, writes *Origin of Species*. He believes that living things evolved from simpler forms with the fittest species surviving and weaklings sacrificed by nature.

**1860 Spencer's evolutionism**
In his writing, British philosopher Herbert Spencer tries to work out a philosophy, based on the scientific discoveries of his day, which can be applied to the interpretation of all reality.

**1863 Idealism attacked**
Ernest Renan, a French philosopher, attacks democracy as an idealist system, calling instead for government by an intellectual elite.

**1867 *Das Kapital* published**
In his major work, *Das Kapital*, the German philosopher Karl Marx describes the flaws of the free enterprise system and develops an evolutionary explanation for the flow of history.

**1870-1900 Darwin extended**
Darwin's notion of biological evolution and survival of the fittest is applied to society in a movement termed "Social Darwinism." It is used to justify the exploitation of the economically weak by the economically strong.

**1872-1888 Nietzsche emerges**
German philosopher Friedrich Nietzsche teaches that the driving force of change through history is the "will to power."

**1888 Romantic revival**
Led by the French philosopher Henri Bergson, European thinkers begin a reaction against materialism, claiming that intuition and not intellect is the best vehicle for interpreting reality.

## Literature

**1714 Pope prominent**
Alexander Pope publishes his most famous poem, *Rape of the Lock*.

**1726 A famous satire**
Jonathan Swift writes *Gulliver's Travels*, a satire of life in 18th century England.

**1754 Fielding dies**
The English novelist Henry Fielding dies. His *The History of Tom Jones, a Foundling* is a landmark in the development of the novel.

**1755 Johnson's dictionary**
Samuel Johnson, the greatest English writer of his day, completes his often humorous *Dictionary of the English Language*.

**1759 *Candide* written**
The French author Voltaire writes the philosophical tale *Candide*.

**1759 Scottish poet is born**
Robert Burns, the national poet of Scotland, is born.

**1780 Motoori writes**
A revival of Japanese interest in Japan's early history is begun by Motoori, who writes the *Exposition of the Record of Ancient Things.*

**1791 Boswell's biography**
James Boswell sets new standards for the art of biography with his *The Life of Samuel Johnson.*

**1796 Birth of Haliburton**
Thomas Chandler Haliburton, called the "father of American humor," is born in Nova Scotia.

**1799 Schiller's masterpiece**
Friedrich Schiller, second only to Goethe as a German author, publishes his greatest drama, *Wallenstein.*

**1799 Balzac born**
The French writer Honoré de Balzac is born. He becomes a leading 19th century novelist.

**1801 Romanticism begins**
François-René de Chateaubriand writes the romantic novel, *Atala.*

**1804 Popular Schiller**
Schiller's play *William Tell* achieves popularity all over Europe.

**1806 Wordsworth prominent**
William Wordsworth writes the poem, "Ode: Intimations of Immortality."

**1810 Medieval revival**
Sir Walter Scott, a Scottish romantic writer, produces *The Lady of the Lake,* a long verse poem that marks a romantic revival of interest in the Middle Ages.

**1812- Grimm brothers publish**
**1815** Two brothers, Jakob and Wilhelm Grimm, publish a book of traditional German fairy tales. This book is considered part of the Medieval revival.

**1816 Latin-American novel**
José Joaquin Fernandez de Lizardi writes *The Itching Parrot,* a novel about the Mexican Revolution and the first novel published in Latin America.

**1817 Keats begins**
John Keats, the English poet, publishes his first volume, titled *Poems.*

**1818 Mary Shelley writes**
Mary Wollstonecraft Shelley publishes her classic novel *Frankenstein, or The Modern Prometheus.*

**1818 Shelley in Italy**
Percy Bysshe Shelley, leading English romantic poet, moves to Italy where he enjoys his most productive period.

**1823 Major work by Byron**
Lord Byron begins his major work, the epic poem *Don Juan.*

**1829 Balzac emerges**
Balzac begins publication of his monumental, many-volumed work, *The Human Comedy.*

**1831 Stendhal publishes**
Marie Henri Beyle (Stendhal), one of the first writers of psychological novels, publishes *The Red and The Black.*

**1831 Romanticism continues**
Victor Hugo, leader of the romantic movement in France, publishes *The Hunchback of Notre Dame.*

**1832 Age of Goethe**
The writer Goethe, called by many Germany's greatest writer, completes his most famous work *Faust,* a verse play.

**1835 Classic fairy tales**
Danish writer Hans Christian Andersen publishes the first of the 168 fairy tales that will make his name a household word.

**1846 Sand prominent**
Amantine Lucile Aurore Dupin (George Sand) publishes her finest novel *The Haunted Pool.*

**1847 Charlotte Brontë writes**
Charlotte Brontë writes *Jane Eyre,* her most famous work.

**1847 Emily Brontë writes**
Emily Brontë, the sister of Charlotte, writes the classic *Wuthering Heights.*

**1847 Anne Brontë prominent**
The third of the Brontë sisters, Anne publishes *Agnes Grey,* her most famous work.

**1848 Thackeray gains fame**
English novelist William Makepeace Thackeray publishes *Vanity Fair,* his famous satire of British society.

**1850 Novel by Dickens**
Charles Dickens writes *David Copperfield,* one of his many novels describing social conditions in 19th-century England.

**1854 Canadian prominent**
French-Canadian poet Octave Crémazie begins writing religious and patriotic poems.

**1857 Flaubert publishes**
French novelist Gustave Flaubert writes *Madame Bovary*, a study of 19th century middle-class morality.

**1860 Birth of Chekhov**
Anton Chekhov, Russia's most famous playwright, is born.

**1860 Quebec poets write**
The School of Quebec poets use French-Canadian patriotism as their dominant theme.

**1861 Nature poet born**
Archibald Lampman, called Canada's finest nature poet, is born.

**1862 Novel by Turgenev**
Russian novelist Ivan Sergeevich Turgenev writes *Fathers and Sons*, the first in a distinguished line of psychological novels by Russian authors.

**1865- Tolstoy's major work**
**1869** Russian novelist Leo Tolstoy writes *War and Peace*.

**1866 Classic Russian novel**
Russian novelist Fyodor Dostoevsky writes *Crime and Punishment*.

**1867 Spanish poet born**
Rubén Darío, one of the most important Spanish-language poets, is born in Nicaragua.

**1867 Novel by Isaacs**
Jorge Isaacs of Colombia writes the classic Latin-American novel *Maria*.

**1870 Strindberg writes**
Swedish writer August Strindberg begins writing. His plays influence the development of naturalism and expressionism in drama.

**1872- Spanish folk tales**
**1902** Ricardo Palma edits a 10-volume collection of folk tales of Latin America.

**1874 Canadian writer born**
Lucy Maud Montgomery, author of *Anne of Green Gables*, is born.

**1879 Social drama**
Norwegian dramatist Henrik Ibsen writes *A Doll's House*. Ibsen is known as the father of modern drama, concentrating on works that explore the social problems of the day.

**1880 *Orion* published**
With the publication of *Orion*, Sir Charles G. D. Roberts lays the foundation for a distinctive Canadian literary form.

**1885 Zola prominent**
French naturalist author Emile Zola writes *Germinal*.

**1892 German revival**
Gerhart Hauptmann publishes *The Weavers*. The play describes the revolt of exploited workers.

**1897 Dracula born**
The British author Bram Stoker publishes the classic horror story *Dracula*.

**1898 Gordon publishes**
Canadian author Charles Gordon, writing under the name Ralph Connor, publishes the classic Canadian novel, *Black Rock*.

### The arts

**1710 After the Fire**
Architect Christopher Wren redesigns St. Paul's Cathedral after the Great Fire of London.

**1717 Orchestral suite**
*Water Music*, an orchestral suite, by George Frideric Handel debuts in England.

**1717 The rococo style**
The rococo style, featuring intricate ornamentation, is typified by the French painter Antoine Watteau. He portrays members of the French nobility off for a holiday on the island of Cythera in *The Embarkation for Cythera*.

**1729 Bach's greatest work**
Johann Sebastian Bach completes what many believe to be his greatest work, *The Passion According to St. Matthew*.

**1732 Haydn born**
Known as the father of the symphony, composer Joseph Haydn is born in Austria.

**1762- Mozart prominent**
**1791** Wolfgang Amadeus Mozart completes over 600 works in a brief 36-year life span. His work marks the transition from baroque to classical music forms.

**1770- Age of Beethoven**
**1827** Ludwig van Beethoven refines the classical symphonic style in his nine symphonies. Beethoven's style affects composers throughout the 19th century.

**1770 Danish sculptor**
The Danish sculptor Bertel Thorvaldsen is born. His most famous work is the *Lion of Lucerne*.

**1784 The classical revival**
Ancient Roman mythology inspires Jacques Louis David of France. He paints *The Oath of the Horatii*.

**1787 Mozart's greatest opera**
Wolfgang Amadeus Mozart's opera, *Don Giovanni*, is performed for the first time in Prague.

**1797 Schubert born**
Franz Schubert, composer of music in many forms, is born in Austria. He begins writing music when he is 13 years old.

**1810- Art in Canada**
**1871** Pioneer Canadian painter Paul Kane records North American Indian life in his vivid paintings.

**1810 Polish genius born**
Frédéric Chopin, a master of piano composition, is born near Warsaw, Poland.

**1833 Brahms born**
Johannes Brahms, a great German composer, is born. His many works will include symphonies and collections of mood-setting songs.

**1836 Schumann's major work**
Robert Schumann of Germany composes *Fantasia in C major*.

**1838 New artistic realism**
Camille Corot paints *A View near Volterra*, in which nature is realistically interpreted.

**1839 Cézanne born**
Paul Cézanne, a founder of cubism and abstract art, is born in France.

**1840 Rodin born**
Auguste Rodin, prominent 19th-century sculptor, is born in France.

**1846 Mendelssohn prominent**
Felix Mendelssohn's oratorio, *Elijah*, is first performed in England.

**1855 Realism expands**
Gustave Courbet paints a masterpiece of realism. He calls it *The Artist's Studio*.

**1859 Wagner prominent**
The German composer Richard Wagner completes his major opera *Tristan and Isolde*.

**1863 New style in art**
French artist Edouard Manet concentrates on presenting beauty as an ideal in his painting *Luncheon on the Grass*.

**1874 The Viennese waltz**
Johann Strauss, Jr., composes *Die Fledermaus*. He is known as the "Waltz King."

**1881 Impressionist landmark**
*The Luncheon of the Boating Party*, an impressionist painting by Pierre Renoir, is completed.

**1888 Van Gogh works**
Vincent Van Gogh captures *The Night Café* on canvas. Another of his best-known paintings is *Sunflowers*, a robust still life.

**1892 Tchaikovsky prominent**
*The Nutcracker Suite*, a major work by Russian composer Peter Tchaikovsky, is completed. Besides operas and ballet music, he composes many concertos for piano and violin.

**1897 Gauguin's romanticism**
Paul Gauguin idealizes the people of the South Sea Islands. Representative of his work is *Where Do We Come From? What Are We? Where Are We Going?*

**Science and technology**

**1700 Seed drill invented**
Jethro Tull invents the seed drill. It helps to revolutionize agriculture.

**1730 Biology classifications**
Carolus Linnaeus develops the method of classifying plants and animals.

**1738 Industry grows**
The roller-spinning machine is patented by John Wyatt. It is the forerunner of sweeping advances in the textile industry.

**1766 Hydrogen discovered**
Sir Henry Cavendish discovers hydrogen, which he calls "inflammable air."

**1769 Steam engine improved**
James Watt of Scotland patents an improved steam engine. It becomes the chief source of power for industry.

**1774 Oxygen discovered**
Joseph Priestley discovers oxygen.

**1777 Modern chemistry begins**
Antoine Lavoisier lays the foundation for modern chemistry when he explains that an object unites with oxygen when it burns.

**about 1796 Fight against smallpox**
Edward Jenner discovers a method of vaccination against smallpox.

**1803 Atomic theory developed**
John Dalton announces the atomic theory.

**1803 New papermaking method**
Henry and Sealy Fourdrinier invent a machine for making cheap paper quickly.

**1826- Photography invented**
**1839** Joseph Niepce and Louis Daguerre invent a method of photography.

**1831  Electricity induced**
Michael Faraday induces an electric current with a moving magnet. This leads to the development of the electric motor as an important source of energy.

**1839  Cell theory proposed**
Matthias Schleiden and Theodor Schwann theorize that all living things are composed of cells.

**1856  Bessemer process**
Henry Bessemer perfects a method for producing steel from pig iron.

**1860  Electromagnetic theory**
James Clerk Maxwell develops the electromagnetic theory.

**1860  New power source**
Jean Joseph Étienne Lenoir builds one of the first practical internal-combustion engines.

**1866  Mendel's Laws**
Gregor Mendel publishes his explanation of the laws of heredity.

**1867  Dynamite invented**
Alfred Bernhard Nobel of Sweden invents dynamite.

**1868  Typewriter perfected**
Three Americans develop the first practical typewriter.

**1869  The Periodic Table**
Dmitri Mendeleev develops the periodic table of elements, classifying them by their atomic weights and properties.

**1869  Railroads span U.S.**
The Union Pacific and Central Pacific Railways jointly complete the first transcontinental railroad across the United States.

**1876  Pasteur's discoveries**
Louis Pasteur finds that microorganisms cause fermentation and disease.

**1879  Psychology grows**
Wilhelm Wundt founds the first laboratory of experimental psychology.

**1882  Great medical advance**
Robert Koch discovers that bacteria cause tuberculosis.

**1884  Linotype invented**
Ottmar Mergenthaler patents the Linotype machine. The machine speeds up the typesetting process and makes printing less costly.

**1884  Rayon invented**
An artificial silk, called rayon, is invented by Hilaire Chardonnet in France.

**1885  Railroad spans Canada**
The Canadian Pacific Railway is built across Canada.

**1889  Photography improved**
George Eastman develops a practical photographic film.

**1895  X-rays discovered**
Wilhelm K. Roentgen discovers X-rays.

**1895  Wireless invented**
Guglielmo Marconi invents the wireless telegraph.

**1898  Radium isolated**
Marie and Pierre Curie isolate the element radium.

# Since 1900

### Political events

**1900  Boxer Rebellion**
The Chinese rebel unsuccessfully against foreign domination of China.

**1904-  Russo-Japanese War**
**1905**  Japan enters world politics as a great power by defeating Russia.

**1911-  Chinese revolution**
**1912**  Sun Yat-sen helps to overthrow the Manchus and establish the Republic of China.

**1914-  World War I**
**1918**  Germany, Austria-Hungary, the Ottoman Empire, and their allies battle Britain, France, Russia, the United States, and their allies.

**1917  U.S. in the war**
The entrance of the United States on the side of Britain and France tips the balance against Germany.

**1917  Russian revolution**
Led by Nikolai Lenin the Bolsheviks (Communists) overthrow a provisional government that had gained power on the abdication of the czar.

**1919  The War ends**
Monarchies in Germany, Austria, and Turkey are overthrown. New nations, such as Poland, Czechoslovakia, and Yugoslavia are created. Germany is blamed and punished for the war as a result of the Versailles conference.

**1920  Nations unite**
The League of Nations is founded.

**1922  Rise of Fascism**
The Fascist Party, led by
Benito Mussolini, seizes
control of Italy.

**1922  U.S.S.R. founded**
Led by Nikolai Lenin, the
Communist Party reor-
ganizes Russia as the
Union of Soviet Socialist
Republics.

**1923  Turkish reform**
The Young Turk Move-
ment, led by Kemal
Atatürk, forms the Repub-
lic of Turkey.

**1929  The Great Depression**
Caused by economic re-
verses in the United States,
a major depression
sweeps the world.

**1931  Canada independent**
The Statute of Westminster
grants Canada independ-
ence within the British
Commonwealth.

**1933  Nazis rise**
Nazi leader Adolf Hitler
becomes dictator of Ger-
many.

**1935-  Ethiopia invaded**
**1936**  Italian troops conquer
Ethiopia.

**1937  Japan expands**
Japan and China, battling
on and off since 1928,
open general hostilities.

**1938  German expansion**
Germany annexes Austria.

**1938  Munich Pact**
To avoid a general war,
British and French leaders
agree to Hitler's seizure of
part of Czechoslovakia.

**1939  Spanish Civil War**
Spanish Fascists, led by
Francisco Franco, com-

plete the overthrow of the
Spanish Republic.

**1939  World War II begins**
Germany invades Poland.
Britain and France declare
war on Germany.

**1941  Hitler invades Russia**
With Britain the only
major European nation
still standing against him,
Adolf Hitler leads Germany
and her allies in a massive
invasion of the U.S.S.R.

**1941  U.S. in the war**
The Japanese bomb
American naval facilities at
Pearl Harbor. The United
States enters the war.

**1945  UN founded**
Representatives of 50 na-
tions meet in San Fran-
cisco to organize the
United Nations.

**1945  German collapse**
After Hitler commits
suicide, German forces
surrender on May 7.

**1945  The atomic bomb**
The first atomic bombs
used in warfare are
dropped by the United
States on the Japanese
cities of Hiroshima and
Nagasaki.

**1945  Japan falls**
Japanese forces surrender
on September 2.

**1946  Philippine independence**
The United States grants
independence to the
Philippines.

**1946  Cold War begins**
The capitalist nations and
the communist nations, allies in the battle against
fascism, turn hostile
toward each other.

**1947  Truman Doctrine**
President Harry S. Truman
declares American sup-
port for any nation that
resists communism.

**1947  India independent**
The British withdraw from
their former colony of India. Two nations are
formed, India and Paki-
stan.

**1948  The Marshall Plan**
The Marshall Plan, spon-
sored by the United States,
provides aid to the war-
torn nations of Europe.

**1949  Communists rule China**
The Chinese Communist
Party ends a long civil war
by driving the Chinese
Nationalist government to
the Island of Taiwan and
establishing the People's
Republic of China.

**1950  War in Korea**
Communist troops from
North Korea invade the
Republic of South Korea.
Led by the United States,
UN troops intervene.

**1956  The Suez crisis**
UN-sponsored forces halt
a British-French-Israeli invasion of Egypt caused by
conflict over control of the
Suez Canal.

**1957  Vietnam War widens**
Conflict in Vietnam, going
on since 1946, expands as
the United States enters
the civil war on the side of
South Vietnam.

**1957  Common Market**
The Common Market, an
economic alliance of
European nations, is
formed.

**1959  Communist Cuba**
Fidel Castro establishes a
communist dictatorship in
Cuba.

1967 **Arab-Israeli War**
An Arab alliance is smashed by Israeli forces.

1970 **Unrest in Canada**
French Canadian separatists begin a terrorist campaign against the government of Canada.

1975 **New African age**
Although some small colonies remain, Portugal grants independence to the last large European colony in Africa.

1975 **Vietnam War ends**
The communist government of North Vietnam defeats the government of South Vietnam.

1979 **Revolution in Iran**
The Shah's government falls; under the leadership of the Ayatollah Ruhollah Khomeini, Iran is declared an Islamic republic.

1979 **Peace in Middle East**
Egypt and Israel sign a treaty in Washington, D.C., ending 30 years of war.

1980 **War in Afghanistan**
Russian troops fight in Afghanistan to support the leftist Afghan government against rebel tribes.

1980 **Unrest in Poland**
Thousands of Polish workers strike, demanding independent labor unions and economic and political reform.

1982 **Falklands war**
Britain defeats Argentina in air, land, and sea battles to retain control of the Falkland Islands in the South Atlantic Ocean.

1982 **Lebanese massacre**
Lebanese Christian militia kill hundreds of Lebanese and Palestinian civilians living in refugee camps in Beirut.

1983 **Korean airliner tragedy**
A Soviet fighter plane shoots down a Korean civilian airliner flying in Soviet airspace, killing all 269 persons on board. The incident sparks worldwide concern and protest.

1983 **Bomb kills U.S. troops**
A terrorist bomb explodes in marine headquarters in Lebanon, killing more than 200 U.S. troops.

1983 **Grenada invaded**
Pan American troops, including 1,900 U.S. military personnel, invade Grenada to overthrow the Marxist government in power there.

**Social events**

1906- **Women gain vote**
1919 Finland grants suffrage to women in 1906, Norway in 1913, and Denmark in 1915. Britain and the U.S. follow suit in 1918 and 1919.

1911 **Chinese upheaval**
China's social structure, which had remained unchanged since acceptance of the thought of Confucius, is completely overturned with the fall of the Manchu dynasty.

1920- **Gandhi prominent**
1948 Mohandas Gandhi uses nonviolent resistance to gain independence from British control for India.

1922 **World Court organized**
The League of Nations forms an International Court of Justice.

1946 **UNESCO established**
The United Nations Education, Scientific and Cultural Organization is established.

1948 **WHO founded**
The World Health Organization is established.

1955 **Concern over the atom**
The first international conference on peaceful uses of atomic energy is held in Geneva, Switzerland.

1955 **Caste attacked**
India passes legislation attacking the caste system which has governed society in India since the Aryan invasions.

1960- **Women's rights**
Present The modern feminist movement influences social and cultural changes around the world.

1970- **Environmental**
Present **movement**
Groups in many nations hold demonstrations and take political action to fight air and water pollution. Others express concern about the potential hazards of nuclear power plants.

1970- **Energy concerns**
Present The costs of oil and other energy sources contribute to worldwide inflation. Many nations around the world promote energy conservation and the development of alternate energy sources.

1981 **Antinuclear protests**
Huge antinuclear demonstrations in West Germany, Britain, and elsewhere in Europe mark the start of a new upsurge in public concern over the possibility of nuclear war.

**Religion**

1920- **Revivalism spreads**
1935 A spirit of Christian revivalism, begun in the United States by such people as Billy Sunday and Aimee Semple

McPherson, spreads throughout the Christian world.

**1942-** **The Holocaust**
**1945** In the most extensive persecution of all time, the Nazis slaughter six million Jews during World War II.

**1947** **Dead Sea scrolls**
The oldest known manuscripts of books of the Bible are discovered in caves near the Dead Sea.

**1948** **W.C.C. formed**
The World Council of Churches is founded in Amsterdam, The Netherlands. The intent of the council is to foster a spirit of Christian ecumenism.

**1948** **Israel founded**
The United Nations establishes the state of Israel, in Palestine. This is the first sovereign Jewish state since Roman times.

**1962-** **Vatican Council II**
**1965** Vatican Council II permits the use of local language in place of Latin in the Roman Catholic liturgy and liberalizes the church's position on relations with non-Catholics.

**1977** **Women in religion**
For the first time, women are ordained as priests in the Anglican Church. Their ordination causes a split in the Church's hierarchy.

**1979** **Islam and government**
Iran and Pakistan form governments ruled by the law of Islam. Movements in Saudi Arabia, Bangladesh, Egypt, Kuwait, and Turkey also work for a return to Islamic rule.

**1982** **Pope in Britain**
Nearly 450 years after England broke away from the Roman Catholic Church, Pope John Paul II travels to Great Britain. He joins the archbishop of Canterbury in a historic religious service symbolizing the goal of Christian unity.

## Philosophy

**1908** **Violence glorified**
Georges Sorel's *Reflections on Violence* expounds violence as the only logical method to cause political change.

**1918-** **Pessimism grows**
**1922** Oswald Spengler publishes his influential *The Decline of the West*, predicting the collapse of Western civilization because of its materialism.

**1920-** **Logical positivism**
**present** Positivist thinkers claim that a statement or experience is meaningful only if it is verifiable by appeal to experience.

**1921** **Wittgenstein**
Ludwig Wittgenstein, an Austrian philosopher living in England, greatly influences the philosophical movement called "positivism."

**1927** **Analyzing our existence**
The writings of Martin Heidegger analyze reality in terms of human existence, the form of being we know best. He is considered an "existentialist."

**1929** **Whitehead writes**
English philosopher Alfred North Whitehead writes *Process and Reality*. His writings attempt to narrow the gap between philosophy and science, between realism and idealism.

**1932** **Jaspers publishes**
Karl Jaspers, a leading German existentialist philosopher, writes *Philosophy*, publicizing the existentialist position in Germany.

**1934-** ***A Study of History***
**1961** Arnold Toynbee revives the idealist philosophy of history through publication of his monumental 12-volume work.

**1935-** **Camus gains fame**
**1960** Albert Camus, winner of the 1957 Nobel prize, writes novels and plays which explore the existentialist problem.

**1937** **Semantics grows**
Led by Rudolf Carnap, a school of philosophical thought grows which attempts to interpret reality in terms of an analysis of the meaning of languages.

**1943** **Sartre's existentialism**
French philosopher Jean-Paul Sartre becomes the leading exponent of the philosophy of existentialism.

**1950** **Nobel prize for Russell**
British philosopher Bertrand Russell receives the Nobel prize for literature "as a defender of humanity and freedom of thought."

**1960-** **Philosophy on hold**
**present** The influence of semanticism and existentialism grows. Eastern philosophies derived from Hinduism and Buddhism begin to penetrate Western thought. Commentaries on earlier thinkers rather than original works become the norm.

**1976** **Heidegger dies**
Martin Heidegger, a leader of the existentialist movement, dies.

1980 **Sartre dies**
French existentialist Jean-Paul Sartre, who influenced two generations of thinkers, dies in April.

### Literature
1902 **Gide publishes**
André Gide publishes the new romanticist novel *The Immoralist.*

1904 **Chekhov famous**
Anton Chekhov publishes his most famous work, *The Cherry Orchard.*

1908 **D'Annunzio's influence**
The writings and political activities of poet Gabriele D'Annunzio strengthen the nationalist movement in Italy.

1910 **Mystical revival**
Such writers as Paul Claudel, Jacques Maritain, and Stefan George exhibit a new mysticism.

1912 **Claudel publishes**
French playwright Paul Claudel writes *Tidings Brought to Mary.*

1912 **A Shaw masterpiece**
George Bernard Shaw, who becomes the leading English language dramatist, writes *Pygmalion.*

1918 **Proust prominent**
Marcel Proust publishes the second volume of *Remembrance of Things Past.*

1921 **Drama by Pirandello**
Luigi Pirandello writes *Six Characters in Search of an Author,* one of many philosophical plays.

1921 **Social themes grow**
In his play, *R.U.R.,* a study of social dehumanization, Czech writer Karel Čapek introduces the word "robot."

1922 **War novels**
The writings of German war hero Ernst Jünger emphasize war and suggest the rebirth of Germany, influencing radical conservative thinking in that country.

1922 **Eliot famous**
T. S. Eliot publishes a long poem, *The Waste Land.* It is an outcry against the spiritual bankruptcy of Western culture.

1922 **Joyce publishes**
James Joyce's novel *Ulysses* is published, setting new forms for the 20th century novel.

1923 **Nobel for Yeats**
William Butler Yeats, leader of the Irish Literary Revival, wins the Nobel prize for literature.

1923- **O'Casey's fame grows**
1926 Irish playwright Sean O'Casey gains fame after three of his plays are successfully staged.

1924 **Europe's despair**
Thomas Mann captures the gradual collapse of European culture in his symbolic novel *The Magic Mountain* which becomes popular in the 1920's.

1925 **Hesse prominent**
The German pessimist novelist Hermann Hesse gains great prominence among Europe's youth.

1926 **Kafka's alienation**
Franz Kafka, the apostle of modern man's alienation from himself, writes his cryptic novel *The Trial.*

1927 **Akutagawa dies**
Ryunosuke Akutagawa, Japan's best known modern novelist, dies.

1928 **Lawrence shocks Europe**
English novelist D. H. Lawrence writes *Lady Chatterley's Lover,* shocking Europe with its realistic portrayal of modern morality.

1929 **Anti-war classic**
Erich Maria Remarque, German novelist, publishes the classic, *All Quiet on the Western Front.*

1934 **Thomas begins**
The Welsh poet Dylan Thomas publishes his first work, *Eighteen Poems.*

1936 **Trilogy completed**
The American author John Dos Passos gains a worldwide reputation with his three-novel study of the disintegration of American culture titled *U.S.A.*

1940 **Canadian epic written**
Canadian poet E. J. Pratt writes *Brébeuf and His Brethren,* the epic poem of early French-Canadian history.

1945 **Nobel for Mistral**
Poet Gabriela Mistral of Chile is the first Latin-American writer to win the Nobel prize for literature.

1946 **Guatemalan masterpiece**
Miguel Angel Asturias of Guatemala publishes what many believe to be his finest novel, *Mr. President.*

1947 **The Frank Diary**
*The Diary of Anne Frank,* written by Anne Frank, a German-Jewish child who was eventually killed by the Nazis, is published.

1951 **Classic Anouilh**
Jean Anouilh, prominent French playwright, publishes his most famous drama, *The Waltz of the Toreadors.*

## 1961 Hemingway dies
Ernest Hemingway, noted
American author, dies. His
work is world famous as
having broken new ground
for the novel form.

## 1963 Sartre's autobiography
Noted French author and
philosopher Jean-Paul
Sartre publishes *Words,*
the first volume of his
long-awaited auto-
biography.

## 1963 Auden's essays
*The Dyer's Hand,* a collection of critical essays by
the distinguished British
author W. H. Auden, is
published.

## 1964 Behan dies
Brendan Behan dies. This
most famous of 20th cen-
tury Irish authors wrote
such works as *Borstal Boy*
and *The Hostage.*

## 1966 Nabokov's memoirs
Noted Russian author
Vladimir Nabokov pub-
lishes *Speak, Memory,* a
remembrance of his life as
an internationally known
author.

## 1969 Nobel for Beckett
Samuel Beckett, an advo-
cate of the "Theater of the
Absurd," wins the Nobel
prize for literature with
such works as *Waiting for
Godot* and *Molloy.*

## 1973 Greene publishes
The noted English author
Graham Greene publishes
*The Honorary Consul,* the
best of his later novels.

## 1973 Neruda dies
Pablo Neruda, Chilean
poet who has achieved
worldwide fame, dies.
Neruda was the recipient
of the 1971 Nobel prize for
literature.

## 1973- Russian classic
## 1976
Russian author Alexander
Solzhenitsyn publishes his
three-volume study of re-
pression in the Soviet
Union, *The Gulag Ar-
chipelago.*

## 1976 Bellow established
Saul Bellow, an American
author, solidifies his
worldwide influence by
winning the Nobel prize
for literature.

## 1978 More from Grass
West German novelist
Günter Grass publishes
*The Flounder,* perhaps his
finest work.

## 1982 Nobel to García Márquez
Colombian novelist Gabriel
José García Márquez wins
the Nobel prize for literature. Many critics rank
him among the most im-
portant authors in the history of Latin American literature.

### The arts

## 1900 Cubism begins
Paul Cézanne leads the
way to a new art form—
cubism and the abstract—
He paints *The Clockmaker.*

## 1905 Fauvism popular
Henri Matisse leads the
fauvist movement and
creates *Landscape at Col-
lioure.* He uses bright colors and flat patterns.

## 1905 Debussy prominent
Claude Debussy writes *La
Mer,* an orchestral com-
position that represents a
revival of romanticism in
music.

## 1906 Early Wright
Frank Lloyd Wright de-
signs Unity Temple in Oak
Park, Ill.

## 1907 Artists' group
Robert Henri forms a
group of eight artists. They

specialize in presenting
realistic scenes from
everyday life, and are
called the "Ashcan School."

## 1910 Der Rosenkavalier
Richard Strauss writes the
music, Hugo von Hofmann-
sthal the libretto, for the
opera *Der Rosenkavalier.*

## 1913 New musical forms
Igor Stravinsky's ballet,
*The Rite of Spring,* is per-
formed for the first time.

## 1913 Expressionism grows
Wassily Kandinsky paints
*Little Pleasures, No. 174,* a
landmark of expressionist
art.

## 1919 Bauhaus founded
The designer Walter Gro-
pius founds the Bauhaus,
school of design, in
Weimar, Germany. The
"Bauhaus Style" of mod-
ern design developed at
this school still influences
architects and designers.

## 1919 Spanish ballet
The Spanish composer
Manuel de Falla produces
his famous ballet the
*Three-Cornered Hat.*

## 1920 Dadaism
The Dadaists attempt to
purge art of its preten-
sions. They describe their
works as "anti-art."

## 1922 German revival
Paul Klee of Germany
completes the *Red Bal-
loon.* His work typifies the
post-World War I revival of
the arts in Germany.

## 1923 Kodály prominent
Hungarian musician Zol-
tán Kodály composes a
choral work, *Psalmus
Hungaricus.*

## 1925 Mondrian a leader
*Lozenge Composition in a
Square,* a painting by Piet

Mondrian, is presented. His style influences architecture and commercial design as well as painting.

**1929 Surrealism grows**
*Accommodations of Desire*, a surrealist painting by Salvador Dali, is completed.

**1931 Mexican artist**
Diego Rivera, noted Mexican muralist, paints *Agrarian Leader Zapata*. It is part of a large mural featuring the history of Mexico.

**1942 Hopper prominent**
Edward Hopper of New York captures loneliness in his painting *Nighthawks*. This quality is exhibited in many of his paintings.

**1943 Bartók composes**
Hungarian composer Béla Bartók writes the *Concerto for Orchestra*.

**1952 New abstractionism**
Willem de Kooning, an abstract painter, completes *Woman, I.*

**1954 Andrew Wyeth**
*Teel's Island*, a painting by Andrew Wyeth, is completed. His rural scenes are reminders of American life during an earlier age.

**1958 Electronic music**
Edgard Varèse, called the father of electronic music, composes *Poème Electronique*.

**1960 African art revival**
Ondongo of Africa paints a watercolor of *Musicians with Three Drums*.

**1960- Music history made**
**1970** The Beatles, an English rock group, changes the form of popular music

through its compositions, arrangements, and methods of presentation.

**1962 War Requiem**
Benjamin Britten's composition, *A War Requiem*, is performed for the first time. It is called by many one of Britten's finest works.

**1964 Chagall triumphs**
Marc Chagall completes his monumental painting for the ceiling of the Paris Opera House.

**1965 Artistic landmark**
English sculptor Henry Moore's *Reclining Figure* goes on display at Lincoln Center in New York City.

**1968 American contemporary**
Artist Robert Bechtle completes a photographic-like oil painting, *60 T-Bird*. The painting symbolizes a new return to realism in the arts.

**1971 Social art**
Black American artist William Walker uses art as social comment in his mural *Wall of Love*.

**1973 Architectural landmark**
The Sears Tower, the world's tallest skyscraper, is completed in Chicago, Ill.

**1973 Picasso dies**
Pablo Picasso, the giant of art in the 20th century, dies.

**1976 Michelangelo revisited**
Several large wall decorations thought to be by Michelangelo are discovered in a basement room in Florence, Italy.

**1983 Balanchine dies**
George Balanchine, considered one of the most

influential choreographers in ballet history, dies in April.

### Science and technology

**1900 The quantum theory**
Max Planck advances the quantum theory to explain certain properties of heat energy.

**1900 Psychoanalysis founded**
Sigmund Freud develops psychoanalysis to treat hysteria.

**1903 Powered flight**
Wilbur and Orville Wright fly the world's first power-driven, heavier-than-air machine at Kitty Hawk, N.C.

**1904 Vacuum tube perfected**
Sir John A. Fleming perfects the diode, a vacuum tube that can detect radio signals.

**1905 Einstein's theory**
Albert Einstein presents his Special Theory of Relativity.

**1909 Bakelite invented**
Leo H. Baekeland, an American chemist, invents the first synthetic resin, Bakelite.

**1910 Chemotherapy used**
Paul Ehrlich originates chemotherapy, the treatment of disease with chemicals.

**1911 The atomic structure**
Ernest Rutherford explains his theory of atomic structure.

**1913 Assembly lines used**
Henry Ford pioneers the use of the assembly line method to produce Model T cars.

**1920 First radio programs**
Station KDKA in Pittsburgh, Pa., schedules the

first regular radio broadcasts.

**1923 Television tried**
Pictures are televised between New York City and Philadelphia.

**1928 Penicillin discovered**
Alexander Fleming discovers penicillin, the first antibiotic.

**1930 First analog computer**
Vannevar Bush invents the analog computer.

**1938 Atomic age begins**
Otto Hahn and Fritz Strassmann find lightweight atoms after bombarding uranium with neutrons.

**1941 First TV shows**
Commercial television is started in the United States.

**1942 First chain reaction**
Enrico Fermi and his associates achieve the first successful nuclear chain reaction.

**1945 First Canadian reactor**
At Chalk River, Ontario, the Canadians build the first nuclear reactor outside the United States.

**1946 Electronic computer**
John W. Mauchly and John P. Eckert, Jr., develop the first electronic computer, called "ENIAC."

**1947 Transistors developed**
American scientists invent the transistor, which replaces the vacuum tube.

**1953 Polio conquered**
Jonas Salk produces the first effective vaccine against polio.

**1954- St. Lawrence Seaway**
**1959** Canada and the United States build the St. Lawrence Seaway. It opens the Great Lakes to seagoing vessels.

**1955 Solar battery used**
A solar battery is used to send telephone messages.

**1957 First satellite**
Russia launches the first artificial satellite.

**1957 DNA produced**
Arthur Kornberg produces artificial DNA, the basic chemical of the gene, in a test tube.

**1960 First laser**
Scientists in the United States construct and operate the first ruby laser.

**1961 First people in space**
Yuri Gagarin of Russia and Alan B. Shepard, Jr., of the United States become the first people to fly in space.

**1962 TV via satellite**
Television programs are relayed between the United States and Europe via the Satellite *Telstar I.*

**1962 New energy source**
The first Canadian nuclear powered electric generating station begins operating at Rolphton, Ontario.

**1962 Laser breakthrough**
The first semiconductor laser is built and demonstrated.

**1965 Tunnel completed**
The world's longest automobile tunnel, the 38,280-foot (11,688-meter) Mont Blanc Tunnel is completed in the Alps.

**1966 Mystery solved**
Scientists discover the secret of the structure of the genetic code, thus adding

greatly to our understanding of heredity.

**1969 People on the Moon**
Two Americans land on the Moon and bring moon rocks and dust back to earth for study.

**1975 New transportation**
A transportation breakthrough is achieved when a British seagoing hovercraft clocks a speed of 75 mph (121 kph).

**1978 "Test-tube" babies**
Two babies, the first to be conceived in a laboratory and implanted in the mother's body, are born in England and India.

**1979 Elementary glue**
An international team of physicists conduct experiments in West Germany that may prove the existence of gluon, a fundamental particle of matter.

**1980 Medical breakthrough**
Scientists in Switzerland and the United States use gene-splicing techniques to create bacteria capable of producing human interferon in the laboratory. Interferon is a natural body substance that fights viruses and may also be effective in treating cancer.

**1981 Space shuttle**
The United States launches the space shuttle *Columbia*, the first reusable spaceship.

**1983 Second solar system**
The Infrared Astronomical Satellite (IRAS), a joint British-Dutch-U.S. project, provides scientists with the strongest evidence ever found for the existence of a second solar system, located around the star Vega.

# 2. American History

The following section outlines some important dates in U.S. history. The section is divided into seven categories: (1) political events, (2) social events, (3) religion, (4) philosophy, (5) literature, (6) the arts, including music, and (7) science and technology. Chronologically, history is divided into these broad headings: America Before Colonial Times (1492-1606); The Colonial Heritage (1607-1753); The Movement for Independence (1754-1783); Forming a New Nation (1784-1819); Expansion (1820-1849); The Irrepressible Conflict (1850-1869); Industrialization and Reform (1870-1916); A New Place in the World (1917-1929); Depression and a World in Conflict (1930-1959); and The Contemporary Period (since 1960).

You can use this unit to help you review significant dates in U.S. history and to gain an overall sense of the development of the United States. Viewed as a whole, the chronology illustrates the highlights of American life.

## America before colonial times

**Political events**

**1492 Columbus sees New World**
Christopher Columbus sails from Spain and discovers the Western Hemisphere.

**1513 Florida explored**
Ponce de León of Spain searches for the Fountain of Youth in the West Indies; he finds instead a place that he names Florida.

**1521 Cortés defeats the Aztecs**
The Spanish conquistador Hernando Cortés defeats the Aztec Indians in Mexico.

**1534 Cartier reaches Canada**
Jacques Cartier of France is the first European to arrive in Canada.

**1540 - American Southwest**
**1542 explored**
Francisco Coronado of Spain explores the American Southwest.

**1565 Oldest U.S. city founded**
Spaniards found St. Augustine, Fla., the oldest city in what is now the U.S.

**1585 Raleigh settlement fails**
Sir Walter Raleigh fails in his attempt to establish a permanent British settlement in what is now the state of North Carolina.

**The arts**

**1600's Folk arts flourish**
Folk arts and household arts flourish in the Colonies. Craftworkers produce furniture, pottery, glassware, silverware, quilts, embroidery, signs, and weather vanes—to name just a few things.

**1600's Colonial architecture**
Many buildings, like the Paul Revere House in Boston, Mass., are built in the Colonies. The various European styles of architecture are blended, and the resulting new style is called colonial architecture.

**1600- Limners ply trade**
**1700** Folk artists called *limners* travel through the Colonies, painting simple portraits of local residents.

**1600- Gravestone carvings**
**1700's** Stonecutters make ornamental carvings, in various decorative motifs, on gravestones.

# The colonial heritage

## Political events

**1607 Jamestown founded**
The first permanent British settlement is founded in Jamestown.

**1619 First blacks arrive**
The first blacks in the English colonies are brought to Jamestown by a Dutch vessel.

**1619 First legislature founded**
Virginia establishes the House of Burgesses.

**1620 Mayflower Compact signed**
English Pilgrims sign the Mayflower Compact, the first agreement for self-government in America.

**1735 Freedom of press affirmed**
New York newspaper publisher Peter Zenger is acquitted of a libel charge that grew out of his criticism of the British government.

## Social events

**1636 First college founded**
Harvard College, the first college in the Colonies, is founded on October 28.

**1647 Public schools started**
The first public school system supported by taxes is set up in Massachusetts.

**1731 Franklin founds library**
Benjamin Franklin founds the first subscription library in the U.S., the Library Company of Philadelphia. Members pay dues, which are pooled to buy books.

## Religion

**1607 Colonists worship**
The Anglican Church begins holding regular services in Jamestown.

**1639 Baptist church set**
The religious leader Roger Williams founds a Baptist church in Providence, in the Rhode Island Colony.

**1649 Religious freedom set**
Maryland passes the first religious tolerance act in North America.

**1654 Jews arrive**
A group of 24 Jews land in New Amsterdam (now New York City) in the New World. The governor does not want them to perform military service but he is overruled by the Dutch West India Company.

**1658 Jews to Rhode Island**
Jews found a second community in the Colonies, this one in Newport, Rhode Island.

**1682 Pennsylvania founded**
Quaker William Penn founds the colony of Pennsylvania as a haven for English Quakers suffering from persecution.

**1689 Mather on witchcraft**
Cotton Mather publishes his *Memorable Providences Relating to Witchcraft and Possessions.* This work is credited with stirring up hatred of "witches" in Salem, Mass.

**1690's Salem witch trials held**
Twenty persons are executed as a result of the Salem witch trials.

**1701 Mather fired**
Increase Mather is removed from his post as president of Harvard College. He and his son Cotton, both conservative Congregationalists, have been outspoken in attacking their liberal colleagues.

**1706 Presbyterians meet**
Presbyterians in the colonies of Maryland, Delaware, and Pennsylvania form an informal presbytery, or church body.

## Philosophy

**1733- Franklin's almanac**
**1758** In this period, Benjamin Franklin publishes his *Poor Richard's Almanac.* The *Almanac* contains a great number of brief proverbs, many of them witty. Taken as a whole, Franklin's proverbs had a strong influence on the political and social philosophy of the Colonies.

## Literature

**1608 Smith on the Colonies**
John Smith's book *A True Relation of such occurrences and accidents...as hath hapned in Virginia* is published in England; it is probably the first personal account of life in the Colonies.

**1640 First book published**
*The Bay Psalm Book,* a collection of psalms in verse, is published. It is the first book published in the Colonies.

**1650 First poetry book**
Anne Dudley Bradstreet publishes the first volume of original poetry written in the Colonies.

**1702 Cotton Mather's famous book**
Cotton Mather, a minister, publishes what may be his greatest work, *Magnalia Christi Americana (Ecclesiastical History of New England).*

## Science and technology

**1621 Blast furnace operates**
The first blast furnace in
the Colonies is placed in
operation at Falling Creek,
Va.

**1646 Ironworks built**
The first successful American ironworks is built
north of Boston, Mass.

**1672 Major cities linked**
The completion of the
Boston Post Road links
Boston and New York City.

**1724 Irrigation employed**
South Carolina rice growers use irrigation systems
to increase the size of
their rice crops.

**1728 First botanical garden**
John Bartram, a famous
botanist, plants the first
botanical garden in
America.

**1739 First glass factory**
The first successful American glass factory is started
in Salem County, N.J.

**1743 Science group formed**
Benjamin Franklin founds
the American Philosophical Society, which becomes the chief center of
colonial science.

**1751 Hospital started**
One of the first public
hospitals in America is
chartered in Philadelphia,
Pa.

**1752 Franklin's famous kite**
Benjamin Franklin flies a
kite during a storm in a
basic experiment. He
proves that lightning is a
form of electricity.

# The movement for independence

## Political events

**1763 Treaty of Paris signed**
France loses most possessions in North America
after defeat by British and
Americans.

**1765 Stamp Act unites Americans**
Colonists protest taxation
without representation
after Parliament passes the
Stamp Act.

**1770 Boston Massacre occurs**
On March 5, British troops
fire on and kill American
civilians.

**1773 Colonists dump tea**
Rebelling against British
laws, colonists disguised
as Indians dump British
tea in the harbor at Boston
on December 16.

**1774 Intolerable Acts passed**
Parliament passes the Intolerable Acts as a
punishment for colonial
rebellion.

**1774 The Colonies organize**
Meeting in Philadelphia,
delegates from 12 colonies
hold the First Continental
Congress.

**1775 Revolutionary War begins**
The Revolutionary War begins on April 19, as British
soldiers attack the patriots
at Lexington and Concord.

**1775 Battle of Bunker Hill**
On June 17, the British
Army defeats the patriots.

**1776 Independence declared**
On July 4, the Declaration
of Independence is
adopted.

**1777 Burgoyne defeated**
Britain's General John
Burgoyne surrenders at
Saratoga on October 17.

**1777 Winter at Valley Forge**
General George
Washington leads his army
to its winter quarters at
Valley Forge, Pa., on December 19.

**1778 France allies with patriots**
The United States and
France sign an alliance
on February 6.

**1779 Patriots win at sea**
Captain John Paul Jones
captures a major British
ship, the *Serapis*, on
September 23.

**1781 British fleet defeated**
The French drive a British
naval force from
Chesapeake Bay on
September 15.

**1781 British Army surrenders**
A British Army surrenders
at Yorktown, Va., on
October 19, officially
ending the war.

**1781 Articles signed**
The first central
government is established
by the Articles of
Confederation.

**1783 Treaty of Paris signed**
The Americans and the
British sign the Treaty of
Paris on September 3; the
Revolutionary War is
officially over.

## The movement for independence

### Religion

**1725- Revivalism grows**
**1775** The sermons of Jonathan
Edwards, a Puritan minis-
ter, inspire a religious revival movement in New Eng-
land called "The Great
Awakening."

**1763 Synagogue dedicated**
The Jewish synagogue at
Newport, R.I., is dedicated.
It is the oldest synagogue
in the U.S. still standing in
contemporary times.

**1769 Missions in California**
Junipero Serra, a Francis-
can missionary from
Spain, establishes the first
Catholic mission in
California—near what is
today San Diego.

### Philosophy

**1754 Edwards publishes**
Jonathan Edwards, a Puri-
tan minister, publishes his
major philosophical work,
*Freedom of Will.*

**1774 Jefferson on rights**
Thomas Jefferson's pam-
phlet *A Summary View of
the Rights of British
America* is printed. In
this pamphlet, Jefferson
sets forth a political
philosophy that will lead
to revolution—namely,
that England has no right
to govern the Colonies
from afar.

**1776 Paine's rallying state-
ment**
Tom Paine's pamphlet
*Common Sense* is pub-
lished. The pamphlet con-
tains a stirring demand for
independence and lists
reasons why independ-
ence is absolutely
necessary.

### Literature

**1770 Wheatley's first poem**
Black poet Phillis Wheatley
publishes her first poem,
"An Elegiac Poem on the
Death of that celebrated
Divine…George
Whitefield."

**1771- Franklin on his life**
**1790** Benjamin Franklin begins
writing his autobiography
in 1771 and works on it,
without finishing it, for the
rest of his life. The book is
still considered a classic
today.

**1782 Crèvecoeur on America**
Jean de Crèvecoeur pub-
lishes his *Letters from an
American Farmer.* The
book presents a vivid de-
scription of life in the new,
young nation.

### The arts

**1766 Copley shows in London**
John Singleton Copley,
perhaps the greatest por-
trait painter in the Col-
onies, exhibits his work in
London.

### Science and technology

**1756 Stagecoach line opens**
A stagecoach line links
New York City and
Philadelphia.

**1757 City lights up**
The first street lights in
the Colonies are installed
in Philadelphia.

**1760 First wagons built**
The first Conestoga wag-
ons are built in Pennsyl-
vania. The pioneers use
these sturdy covered wag-
ons in their move west-
ward.

**1765 First medical school**
The first medical school in
the Colonies is established
in Philadelphia.

**1775 Iron production grows**
Colonial ironworks are
producing one-seventh of
the world's iron.

**1776 Smith on economics**
Adam Smith publishes the
first systematic classification of classical
economics.

---

# Forming a new nation

### Political events

**1787 Constitution adopted**
The Constitution of the
United States is signed on
September 17 in
Philadelphia; it replaces
the Articles of
Confederation.

**1789 Washington elected
President**
In February, George
Washington is elected the
first President of the
United States.

**1790 Political parties formed**
Disputes over government
policies lead to the
formation of political
parties.

**1791 Bill of Rights adopted**
By December 15, 10
amendments to the
Constitution are approved,
guaranteeing freedom of
speech, religion, press,
and peaceful assembly.

**1792 Washington reelected**
George Washington is
reelected President.

**1800 Capital moved**
The federal government is
moved from Philadelphia
to Washington, D.C.

**1803 Judicial review set**
In deciding the case
*Marbury v. Madison*, the
Supreme Court of the U.S.
establishes the principle of
judicial review.

**1803 Louisiana Purchase
made**
The size of the U.S.
doubles when President
Jefferson buys the
Louisiana Territory from
France.

**1804- West is explored**
**1806** The Lewis and Clark
expedition explores the
lands west of the
Mississippi River.

**1812- War of 1812 waged**
**1814** The U.S. goes to war with
Great Britain to protect
freedom of the seas and
the American shipping
trade.

### Social events

**1787 Prison reformers meet**
A group of Philadelphia
Quakers organizes a
prison reform group; it is
later called the Pennsyl-
vania Prison Society.

**1792 First local union set**
Philadelphia, Pa., shoe-
makers organize the first
local union in the U.S.

**1800 Library of Congress set**
The Library of Congress is
established by the U.S.
Congress; the Library is to
serve as the national li-
brary and to provide re-
search assistance to Con-
gress.

### Religion

**1789 Catholic bishop elected**
Roman Catholic priests in
the U.S. elect John Carroll
as the first bishop in
the U.S.

### Philosophy

**1785 Madison on liberty**
James Madison writes his
*Memorial and Remon-
strance on the Religious
Rights of Man*. This was a
statement advocating re-
ligious freedom and defin-
ing civil rights as separate
from religion.

**1787- The Federalist papers**
**1788** Alexander Hamilton,
James Madison, and John
Jay write most of the es-
says that are later pub-
lished as *The Federalist*. In
the Federalist papers, the
authors lay out their political philosophy—
especially, the need for a
strong central government.

### Literature

**1817 "Thanatopsis" published**
William Cullen Bryant
writes "Thanatopsis," a
brilliant poem about
death.

### The arts

**1795 Peale's master work**
Painter Charles Willson
Peale completes his pic-
ture *The Staircase Group*,
a portrait of his family.

**1795- Stuart and Washington**
**1796** President George
Washington sits for three
different portraits by artist
Gilbert Stuart.

**1814 National anthem
composed**
During the War of 1812,
Francis Scott Key writes
"The Star-Spangled
Banner."

### Science and Technology

**1787 First steamboat**
John Fitch demonstrates
the first workable steam-
boat in the U.S.

**1790 Cotton-spinning
machine**
Samuel Slater builds the
country's first successful
water-powered machine
for spinning cotton.

**1791 Banneker and the
Capital**
Benjamin Banneker, a free
black and a mathemati-
cian, helps survey the city
of Washington, D.C. He
later publishes an annual
almanac of weather pre-
dictions and tide calculations.

**1793 Cotton gin invented**
Eli Whitney builds the first
cotton gin. This machine
cleans cotton faster than
50 persons working by
hand.

**1798 Mass production**
Eli Whitney makes mus-
kets, or guns, using the
first mass-production
methods.

**1807 Steamboat perfected**
Robert Fulton dem-
onstrates the first com-
mercially successful
steamboat. It rev-
olutionizes the shipping
industry of the new na-
tion.

**1811 National Road begun**
Work begins on the Na-
tional Road, which will
eventually link the East
and the Midwest.

**1819 Plow improved**
Jethro Wood produced an
improved cast-iron plow,
which features replaceable
pieces at points of greatest
wear.

# Expansion

**1820** **Missouri Compromise set**
The Missouri Compromise is approved by Congress in March; Missouri is admitted as a slave state, Maine is admitted as a free state at the same time, and slavery is forbidden in all other areas of the U.S. north of the 36°30' latitude.

**1823** **Monroe Doctrine issued**
On December 2, President James Monroe announces the Monroe Doctrine, which warns European nations not to interfere with free nations in the Western Hemisphere.

**1838-** **"Trail of Tears" forged**
**1839** Troops drive thousands of Cherokee and Choctaw Indians from their homes, west across the Mississippi River on a "Trail of Tears."

**1845** **"Manifest destiny" rises**
Many Americans come to believe that it is their "destiny" to control all of North America.

**1846-** **Mexican War fought**
**1848** In a dispute over territory, the U.S. goes to war with Mexico. The new land that is gained becomes the southwestern U.S.

**1848** **Gold Rush begins**
The discovery of gold at Sutter's Mill in California on January 24 triggers a frantic gold rush.

Social events

**1836** **First child labor law**
Massachusetts passes the first law limiting child labor in the United States.

**1840's** **Immigration stepped up**
"Great waves" of immigration to the United States begin; Germany, Ireland, Italy, Sweden, Norway, and the Austro-Hungarian empire are some of the countries from which the migrants come.

**1841** **Mental patients aided**
Dorothea Dix begins her drive to provide better care for the mentally ill.

**1842** **Unions ruled legal**
A Massachusetts court legalizes labor unions.

**1846** **Smithsonian founded**
The Smithsonian Institution is founded in Washington, D.C.; the Smithsonian is a national institution devoted to research and learning.

**1848** **Feminists organize**
Meeting in Seneca Falls, N.Y., delegates to the first Women's Rights Convention publicly declare that "all men and women are created equal."

Religion

**1824** **Sunday School movement**
The American Sunday School Union is formed, as the Sunday School movement grows.

**1825** **Unitarian Church founded**
Clergyman William Ellery Channing organizes the American Unitarian Association.

**1830** **Mormon Church founded**
Joseph Smith and his associates start the Church of Jesus Christ of Latter-day Saints, or Mormon Church, on April 6.

**1834** **Convent burned**
Amid an atmosphere of fear and prejudice, the townspeople in Charlestown, Mass., burn down a Roman Catholic convent of the Ursuline order.

**1838** **Mormons to Nauvoo**
Ordered out of Missouri, about 15,000 Mormons migrate to Illinois and found the city of Nauvoo.

**1838** **Missionary to Indians**
Jesuit Pierre De Smet begins his long career of converting Indians to Christianity. Other Catholic orders and other denominations also send missionaries to work among the Indians.

**1840-** **Immigrants arrive**
**1900** Great waves of immigration increase the population of the U.S. and alter the religious composition of the country. The Roman Catholic Church increases in size, as many Catholics arrive from central and eastern Europe. The Lutheran Church also grows, as many Lutherans arrive from the Scandinavian countries.

**1844** **Joseph Smith killed**
A newspaper in Nauvoo that has opposed Mormon leader Joseph Smith is burned down. Smith and his brother are jailed at Carthage for the crime; a mob breaks into the jail and kills Smith and his brother.

**1845** **Southern Baptists meet**
The Southern Baptist Convention is organized in Augusta, Ga. Baptists in the South have been arguing with Baptists in the

North over the slavery issue.

**1847 Mormons settle in Utah**
Brigham Young, the new Mormon leader, starts a Mormon settlement in the Great Salt Lake Valley, in what is now the state of Utah.

**1848 Oneida group formed**
John Humphrey Noyes founds a cooperative religious settlement called the Oneida Community in Putney, Vt. The community is based on personal communication with God and harmonious living with peers.

**1849 Apply for statehood**
The Mormons, who have set up a civil government in the Great Salt Lake Valley, apply for admission to the Union as the *State of Deseret*. Instead of granting statehood, Congress sets up the Territory of Utah the next year.

### Philosophy

**1830 Alcott publishes**
Bronson Alcott publishes his *Observations on the Principles and Methods of Infant Instruction*.

**1834- Alcott runs school**
**1839** Philosopher Bronson Alcott operates the experimental Temple School in Boston, Mass.

**1839- Fuller lectures**
**1844** Margaret Fuller, a transcendentalist philosopher, conducts a series of "conversations" for women in Boston, Mass. The lectures—which cover philosophy, literature, and education—are a successful experiment in adult education.

**1840 Fuller edits magazine**
Margaret Fuller becomes

the editor of the *Dial*, a magazine of transcendentalist philosophy.

**1841 Emerson's first essays**
Ralph Waldo Emerson publishes his brilliant *Essays, First Series*. The famed essay "Self-Reliance" is included in this series.

**1841 Parker gives major talk**
Theodore Parker, a Unitarian clergyman and transcendentalist philosopher, delivers a sermon called "Discourse on the Transient and Permanent in Christianity." Parker's ideas were to prove influential in the areas of religion, philosophy, and social reform.

**1841- Brook Farm set up**
**1847** A group of transcendentalists, led by philosopher George Ripley, operate Brook Farm, an experimental community. Brook Farm is located in West Roxbury, Mass.

**1844 Emerson's second essays**
*Essays, Second Series*, by Ralph Waldo Emerson, is published.

**1845- Emerson lectures**
**1846** Philosopher Ralph Waldo Emerson delivers a lecture series called *Representative Men*.

### Literature

**1820 Short story set**
Washington Irving completes "Rip Van Winkle." With this piece, he creates a new literary form, the short story.

**1823- Cooper on the frontier**
**1841** James Fenimore Cooper writes a series of five novels about the frontier called *The Leatherstocking Tales*. The five in-

clude *The Deerslayer* and *The Last of the Mohicans*.

**1845 "The Raven" by Poe**
Edgar Allan Poe writes "The Raven," a sad poem about a man who feels haunted after the death of his love.

**1846 Poems by Emerson**
The transcendentalist philosopher Ralph Waldo Emerson publishes *Poems*, a volume of his verse.

**1847 Longfellow's poetry**
Henry Wadsworth Longfellow publishes one of his best poems, *Evangeline*.

**1849 Parkman on Indians**
Historian Francis Parkman publishes *The Oregon Trail*, an account of life among the Indians of the Northwest.

### The arts

**1820 Actor's debut**
One of the first great American actors, Edwin Forrest, makes his initial stage appearance.

**1825 Recognition for Cole**
Painter Thomas Cole first receives recognition for his landscapes of the Hudson River Valley in New York state.

**1832 Catlin on Indians**
George Catlin completes his portrait of the Mandan chief *Four Bears*. Catlin paints many Indian chiefs and tribesmen during his career.

**1840 Trinity Church**
Building begins on the Trinity Church in New York City, which was designed by architect Richard Upjohn. The architect has adapted traditional Gothic design to the New World.

1840 **A Greenough sculpture**
Horatio Greenough completes his massive sculpture of George Washington.

1840's **Minstrels entertain**
Minstrel shows become a popular form of musical entertainment. Troupes such as Christy's Minstrels dance and sing, usually in blackface makeup.

1846 **Song hit by Foster**
Composer Stephen Foster writes the song "Oh! Susanna," perhaps the most popular of his 200-plus songs.

### Science and Technology

1825 **Erie Canal completed**
The Erie Canal is opened, providing a water passage between New York and the Great Lakes.

1830 **Passenger train travel**
Peter Cooper builds the "Tom Thumb," the first American-made steam locomotive. It pulls one of the first passenger trains.

1834 **Reaper helps farming**
Cyrus McCormick patents a reaping machine that makes it possible to harvest larger wheat crops.

1834 **Threshing machine**
John and Hiram Pitts patent the first threshing machine, advancing the development of large-scale farming.

1835 **Colt perfects revolver**
Samuel Colt develops the first successful repeating pistol.

1837 **Steel plow developed**
John Deere builds the first steel plow. This plow is especially suitable for the heavy prairie sod.

1837 **First telegraph message**
Samuel F.B. Morse demonstrates the first successful telegraph, which proves to be the fastest communication available to date.

1839 **Rubber industry advanced**
Charles Goodyear makes rubber stronger through a process called vulcanization.

1842 **Ether kills pain**
Crawford Long uses ether as an anesthetic in surgery.

1846 **Sewing machine improved**
Elias Howe patents a practical sewing machine.

# The irrepressible conflict

### Political events

1850 **The Compromise of 1850**
A series of laws are passed to deal with the issue of slavery in the new territory acquired from Mexico. The chief terms are the banning of slavery from California and the enactment of the Fugitive Slave Law to tighten the slavery system.

1854 **Kansas-Nebraska Act**
Congress passes the Kansas-Nebraska Act, which sets up the two territories of Kansas and Nebraska and allows the citizens of those territories to vote on whether they wish to have slavery or not.

1857 **Dred Scott ruling made**
In the Dred Scott decision, the U.S. Supreme Court rules that blacks are not citizens.

1859 **John Brown raids arsenal**
John Brown, a radical abolitionist, captures the arsenal at Harpers Ferry, Virginia, hoping to start a slave revolt.

1860 **Lincoln elected President**
Abraham Lincoln, a Republican from Illinois, is elected 16th President of the United States; he is dedicated to preserving the Union.

1860 **South Carolina secedes**
In December, the state of South Carolina becomes the first to secede from the Union.

1861 **Confederacy is formed**
On February 4, South Carolina and five other states that have seceded from the Union meet in Montgomery, Ala., and declare the formation of a new nation, the Confederate States of America; a total of 11 states eventually join the Confederacy.

1861 **Civil War begins**
On April 12, Southern troops fire on Fort Sumter in Charleston Harbor. The Civil War begins.

1861 **First Battle of Bull Run**
One of the first major battles of the war occurs at

Manassas, Va.; the army of the North is defeated at Bull Run.

**1862 Monitor and Merrimack**
On March 8 the Confederate ironclad ship *Merrimack* sinks two Northern ships, but on March 9 the Union ironclad *Monitor* appears and fights the *Merrimack* to a draw.

**1862 Union wins at Shiloh**
General Ulysses S. Grant wins the Battle of Shiloh at Pittsburg Landing, Tenn., for the Union on April 6 and 7.

**1862 Lands in the West open**
The Homestead Act is passed, offering free land to settlers in the West.

**1862 Bull Run revisited**
The Second Battle of Bull Run takes place August 29 and 30; the South wins again.

**1863 North wins in the West**
General Grant leads the Union Army to victory in the Siege of Vicksburg, Miss., from May 19 to July 4.

**1863 North wins at Gettysburg**
Confederate General Robert E. Lee leads his army in an attack on Gettysburg, Pa., July 1-3; the Northern victory here is a turning point in the war.

**1863 Slaves are freed**
President Lincoln issues the Emancipation Proclamation on January 1; slaves in the Confederate States are declared free.

**1864 Truth visits White House**
Sojourner Truth, a former slave who has traveled widely to speak out against slavery, visits President Lincoln in the White House.

**1864 Grant forges on**
The North under General Grant and the South under General Lee fight an inconclusive battle, the Battle of the Wilderness, in a heavily wooded area of northern Virginia on May 5 and 6; Grant and his army continue moving south.

**1864 Sherman marches**
Union General William Tecumseh Sherman begins his "March through Georgia" by leaving Atlanta in flames on November 15 and moving southeast throughout the state.

**1865 Civil War ends**
On April 9, General Lee surrenders to General Grant at the Appomattox Court House in Virginia.

**1865 Lincoln Assassinated**
On April 14, John Wilkes Booth shoots President Abraham Lincoln at Ford's Theatre in Washington, D.C.

**1865- Reconstruction pro-**
**1877 ceeds**
The South is gradually returned to the Union in the Reconstruction era; amendments to the U.S. Constitution abolish slavery, make blacks citizens, and grant them voting rights.

**1867 Alaska purchased**
The United States buys Alaska from Russia for $7.2 million.

**1868 Andrew Johnson on trial**
The House of Representatives votes impeachment charges against President Andrew Johnson, but the Senate votes not to remove him from office.

**1869 Women seek the vote**
Susan B. Anthony and Elizabeth Cady Stanton found the National Woman Suffrage Association, to help win the vote.

### Social events

**1862 Land-Grant colleges set**
The Morrill, or Land-Grant, Act of 1862 provides land to each state; the land is to be sold to finance a college for agriculture and the mechanical arts in each state.

**1867 Farmers organize**
The National Grange is founded to assist farmers in obtaining fairer prices for their products.

### Religion

**1866 Black Baptists meet**
A state convention of Black Baptists is formed in North Carolina.

### Philosophy

**1854 Major work by Thoreau**
Henry David Thoreau publishes a book of essays; called *Walden,* the book discusses nature and the human spirit.

**1859 Darwin on evolution**
Charles R. Darwin publishes his theory of evolution in *On the Origin of Species by Means of Natural Selection, or the Preservation of Favoured Races in the Struggle for Life.* Though Darwin is a British naturalist, *The Origin of Species* —as it comes to be known—has a profound impact on U.S. philosophy and psychology.

**1860 Lectures published**
Ralph Waldo Emerson's lectures on *The Conduct of Life* are published. The lectures were first given in 1851.

## The irrepressible conflict

### Literature

**1850 Hawthorne on sin**
Nathaniel Hawthorne's
*The Scarlet Letter* is published. It is a novel about
the tragic consequences of sin.

**1851 Melville's masterpiece**
*Moby Dick*, by Herman
Melville, is published.
*Moby* is a novel about
whaling and about the
nature of life.

**1851- Stowe on slavery**
**1852** Harriet Beecher Stowe
writes *Uncle Tom's Cabin*,
a famous antislavery novel.

**1855 Poetry by Walt Whitman**
Walt Whitman publishes a
volume of poetry called
*Leaves of Grass*. This great
volume contains the moving poem "Song of Myself."

**1861 Dickinson begins writing**
Emily Dickinson begins
writing poetry seriously
and in volume. Only a few
of her poems are published during her lifetime,
however.

**1866 Whittier's "Snow-Bound"**
Poet John Greenleaf Whittier publishes what may
be his best work, "Snow-Bound," a long poem
about winter in a Quaker
community.

### The arts

**1862 Popular Civil War song**
Walter Kittredge writes the
rousing Civil War song
"Tenting on the Old Camp
Ground."

**1867 Currier and Ives**
*Home for Thanksgiving*, a
Currier and Ives print, is
first published.

### Science and technology

**1852 Otis improves the
elevator**
Elisha Otis builds an
elevator that uses safety
devices to protect against
falling.

**1859 Petroleum industry**
The first commercially
successful oil well is
drilled near Titusville, Pa.

**1861 Telegraph across nation**
The transcontinental telegraph line, connecting the
eastern U.S. with California, is completed.

**1865 Railway sleeping cars**
George Pullman introduces a new sleeping car
for overnight train travel.

**1866 Cable across Atlantic**
After four unsuccessful attempts, a telegraph cable
is laid across the Atlantic
Ocean by Cyrus Field.

**1867 Typewriter developed**
Christopher Sholes plays a
major role in developing
the typewriter; it is
patented in 1868.

**1868 Air brakes perfected**
Trains are made faster and
safer with the addition of
new air brakes, perfected
by George Westinghouse.

**1869 Transcontinental
railway**
In Promontory, Utah, the
last spike is driven into the
first transcontinental railway line.

# Industrialization and reform

### Political events

**1876 Sitting Bull defeats Custer**
A band of Sioux and
Cheyenne defeats General
George Armstrong Custer
at the Little Bighorn River
in Montana in June.

**1877 Federal troops leave
South**
The Reconstruction period
ends offically as federal
troops are withdrawn.

**1884 Statue of Liberty erected**
The people of France give
a 150-foot statue to the U.S.
as a symbol of friendship.

**1896 Segregation upheld**
The Supreme Court of the
U.S. rules in *Plessy v. Ferguson* that a state may
provide "separate but
equal" facilities for whites
and blacks.

**1898 Hawaii annexed**
The Hawaiian Islands are
annexed by the U.S.

**1898 U.S. battleship sinks**
In February, the battleship
*Maine* explodes in the
harbor at Havana, Cuba;
"yellow journalists" in the
U.S. use this event to agitate for war with Spain.

**1898 War with Spain**
On April 25, war with
Spain is declared by the
U.S.

**1898 War ends**
On December 10, the Paris
Peace Treaty is signed,
ending the Spanish-
American War; the U.S.
gains possession of Guam,
Puerto Rico, and the
Philippines as part of the
settlement.

**1901 McKinley assassinated**
President William McKinley is assassinated in September.

**1904 Canal land leased**
The United States purchases the rights to the land in Central America on which the Panama Canal is scheduled to be built.

**1914 Canal opened**
On August 15, the U.S. opens the Panama Canal.

### Social events

**1870- Population doubles**
**1916** More than 25 million immigrants enter the U.S.; the population more than doubles.

**1876 ALA founded**
The American Library Association (ALA) is founded to help organize and encourage U.S. libraries; in the same year, Melvil Dewey publishes his Dewey Decimal Classification system.

**1879 Willard seeks temperance**
Frances E. Willard, an educator and social reformer, becomes president of the Woman's Christian Temperance Union; she organizes a drive toward national prohibition.

**1881 Red Cross started**
Clara Barton, a nurse known as "the angel of the battlefield" in the Civil War, helps establish the American branch of the Red Cross.

**1881 Tuskegee Institute set**
Booker T. Washington, an influential black leader and educator, starts the Tuskegee Institute in Alabama, a vocational school for blacks.

**1883 Civil service reformed**
Congress passes the Civil Service Reform Act, also called the Pendleton Act; it eventually improves the morale and efficiency of the federal civil service.

**1886 Labor group formed**
The American Federation of Labor (AFL) is founded by Samuel Gompers in Columbus, Ohio.

**1889 Hull House founded**
Jane Addams and Ellen Starr found a Chicago settlement house called Hull House; they use Hull House as a base from which to work with slum dwellers.

**1892 Lynching at peak**
Some 230 persons, mostly blacks, are lynched, or hanged by mobs without trial. This is the peak of lynching, which began about 1882 and which continued to 1968.

**1892 Labor deaths at Homestead**
Ten persons die when guards attack strikers at the steel mills in Homestead, Pa.

**1894 Pullman clash violent**
Federal troops battle strikers at the Pullman plant in Chicago, with heavy loss of life and considerable property damage.

**1896 "A cross of gold"**
Populist leader William Jennings Bryan makes an impassioned speech before the Democratic National Convention in Chicago, asking the delegates not to "crucify mankind upon a cross of gold"; Bryan supports free coinage of silver to benefit "the producing masses."

**1903 University founded**
The University of Puerto Rico is founded in San Juan; a branch campus is later opened in Mayaguez.

**1909 NAACP founded**
The National Association for the Advancement of Colored People (NAACP) is founded to work for the rights of blacks.

**1911 Urban League founded**
The National Urban League is founded to assist blacks in getting jobs and housing.

**1914 Family planning aided**
Margaret Sanger founds the American Birth Control League, to provide birth control information and devices. The group later changes its name to Planned Parenthood-World Population (PPWP).

**1916 Child labor law passed**
Congress passes the first federal law regulating child labor.

### Religion

**1875 Eddy publishes**
Mary Baker Eddy publishes her major work, *Science and Health with Key to the Scriptures.*

**1879 Christian Science set**
Mary Baker Eddy and her husband found the Church of Christ, Scientist—also known as the Christian Science Church.

**1880 Baptists organize**
The National Baptist Convention of America is formed, to bring unity to the Baptists in the U.S.

**1880 Salvation Army arrives**
The Salvation Army, founded two years earlier in England, is introduced into the U.S. The Army provides shelter, food, and other types of aid to the poor within a religious framework.

1886 **Bible school founded**
Dwight L. Moody founds the Moody Bible Institute in Chicago; the Institute is a school for training workers in various fields of Christian service.

1887 **Catholic University founded**
The Catholic University of America is established in Washington, D.C.; it is designated the official Roman Catholic university in the U.S.

1890 **Abandon polygamy**
The Mormons outlaw the practice of polygamy, or having more than one wife at the same time. Congress has blocked statehood for Utah because of strong feelings in the U.S. against polygamy.

1901 **Pentecostal landmark**
A worshipper at an evangelical meeting of the Holiness movement in Topeka, Kan., begins "speaking in tongues"—or speaking unintelligible words in a spirit of religious ecstasy. This incident is the start of the spread of the Pentecostal movement.

1915 **Baptists split**
The Baptist church is split by factions, in a dispute over church property and church publications. The National Baptist Convention, U.S.A., Inc., is formed. It proves to be a larger group than the parent group, the National Baptist Convention of America.

### Philosophy

1870 **Philosophy club formed**
A group of philosophers, including Charles Sanders Peirce, William James, Chauncey Wright, and Oliver Wendell Holmes Jr., meet in Cambridge to discuss philosophy; they call their group "the Metaphysical Club."

1870's **Birth of pragmatism**
The term "pragmatism" is added to the language of philosophy. American philosopher Charles Sanders Peirce coins the term to refer to a particular method of logic.

1877 **Wright publishes**
A collection of the writings of Chauncey Wright is published; the book is called *Philosophical Discussions*.

1879- **Philosophy school**
1888 The Concord Summer School of Philosophy and Literature is operated in this period. The school begins in the home of Bronson Alcott, a leading transcendentalist philosopher. Later the school is moved to a center dedicated to transcendentalism.

1892 **Idealism movement begins**
Josiah Royce, leader of the movement called idealism, publishes *The Spirit of Modern Philosophy*, the first of five famous books.

1896 **Essay on pragmatism**
Philosopher William James publishes the essay "The Will to Believe." The essay is a major work on pragmatism.

1899 **Dewey on education**
In his book *School and Society*, John Dewey sets forth the principles of progressive education.

1901- **James lectures**
1902 William James delivers a series of lectures in Scotland called *The Varieties of Religious Experience*.

1905- **Santayana publishes**
1906 Philosopher George Santayana completes a five-volume work, *The Life of Reason*.

1909 **Pragmatism debated**
William James publishes *The Meaning of Truth*, a collection of writings debating various aspects of pragmatism.

1912 **Empiricism explored**
A series of essays by William James is published posthumously under the title *Essays in Radical Empiricism*.

### Literature

1876 **Twain on the river**
Mark Twain's novel *The Adventures of Tom Sawyer* is published. The book portrays a boy's adventures on the Mississippi River.

1881 **James in flower**
*The Portrait of a Lady*, a novel by Henry James, is published.

1881 **Another Twain classic**
*The Prince and the Pauper*, a novel by Mark Twain, is published.

1884 **Twain's masterpiece**
Mark Twain's novel *The Adventures of Huckleberry Finn* is published. Like *Tom Sawyer, Huck Finn* is set on the Mississippi River.

1885 **Howells on success**
William Dean Howells' novel *The Rise of Silas Lapham* is published. The novel deals with the life of a self-made success.

1889 **Twain on King Arthur**
Mark Twain publishes his take-off on the Arthurian

legends, *A Connecticut Yankee in King Arthur's Court.*

1901 **Realism from Norris**
Frank Norris' novel *The Octopus* is published. The book is a realistic account of the struggles surrounding railroad expansion.

1903 **A classic by London**
Jack London's novel *The Call of the Wild* is published.

1903 **Mature James**
Henry James's novel *The Ambassadors* is published.

1913 **Major poem by Lindsay**
Vachel Lindsay's poem "General William Booth Enters into Heaven" is published. Lindsay's poetry features strong rhythms and vivid images.

1914 **Amy Lowell's poetry**
*Sword Blades and Poppy Seeds*, a volume of imagist poetry, is published by Amy Lowell.

**The arts**

1872 **Whistler's famous work**
James McNeill Whistler paints the portrait known as *Whistler's Mother.*

1876 **Winslow Homer**
Painter Winslow Homer completes one of his most famous paintings of the sea, *Breezing Up.*

1880 **Sousa leads band**
John Phillip Sousa, the "march king," is appointed leader of the U.S. Marine Band.

1880's **Barnum joins Bailey**
Two "greats" in the circus world, P. T. Barnum and James A. Bailey, become partners. Their joint circus is called Barnum & Bailey's "Greatest Show on Earth."

1883 **Met founded**
The Metropolitan Opera House opens in New York City, with *Faust* as its first offering.

1884- **Early skyscraper**
1885 The Home Insurance Building, designed by William LeBaron Jenney, is erected in Chicago. This building is usually considered the first skyscraper.

1885- **Richardson masterwork**
1887 The Marshall Field Wholesale Store in Chicago, designed by architect H. H. Richardson, is completed.

1886- **Adler and Sullivan**
1889 The Auditorium Building, designed by Dankmar Adler and Louis H. Sullivan, is erected in Chicago.

1887 **Residential architecture**
The firm of McKim, Mead, & White designs the W. G. Low house in Bristol, R. I.

1892 **Work by Cassatt**
Mary Cassatt completes her famed painting *The Bath*.

1893 **Famed Stieglitz photo**
*Winter on Fifth Avenue, New York*, a photograph by Alfred Stieglitz, first appears.

1893 **Columbian Exposition**
The World's Columbian Exposition opens in Chicago. Featured is the Great White City of vast buildings designed by famous architects. Also featured are large statues by prominent sculptors like Augustus Saint-Gaudens and Daniel Chester French.

1898 **Work by Eakins**
Realistic painter Thomas Eakins completes *The Clinic of Dr. Agnew.*

1899 **Isadora Duncan**
The modern dancer Isadora Duncan performs in Chicago.

1903 **Remington painting**
Painter Frederic Remington completes his *Fight for the Waterhole.* Remington paints mostly scenes of the American frontier.

1910 **Black orchestra.**
James Reese Europe, leader of a black dance band, starts a black symphony orchestra.

1911 **Ives's third symphony**
Charles Edward Ives completes his *Third Symphony.* It is not until 1947, however, that he receives the Pulitzer prize for music for this work.

1911- **Woolworth Building**
1913 The Woolworth Building is erected in New York City. The building is a Gothic skyscraper designed by Cass Gilbert.

1914 **"St. Louis Blues"**
Black composer W. C. Handy writes "The St. Louis Blues." Handy's work has a major effect on ragtime and jazz music.

1916 **Wright hotel**
The Imperial Hotel in Tokyo, Japan, is begun; the quakeproof hotel was designed by the American architect Frank Lloyd Wright.

**Science and technology**

1876 **Telephone is invented**
Alexander Graham Bell invents the telephone.

1877 **Phonograph invented**
Thomas Edison, the "Wizard of Menlo Park," creates the phonograph, which he calls his favorite invention.

**1879 Electric light invented**
Thomas Edison adds the electric light to his long list of inventions.

**1884 Linotype patented**
Ottmar Mergenthaler patents the linotype, which speeds the printing process. Two years later, the New York City *Tribune* uses the new machine to set type.

**1884 First skyscraper begun**
Work on the world's first skyscraper, the Home Insurance Building, is begun in Chicago.

**1896 Ford builds first car**
Henry Ford completes his first automobile, paving the way for later mass production.

**1897 First U.S. subway built**
The first U.S. subway is built in Boston.

**1903 First airplane**
Wilbur and Orville Wright fly the first power-driven airplane at Kitty Hawk, N.C.

**1909 Peary reaches North Pole**
On April 6, Commander Robert E. Peary of the U.S. Navy is the first person to reach the North Pole.

**1916 Carver receives acclaim**
George Washington Carver is honored by the Royal Society of Arts in London for his agricultural research with peanuts and other products.

# A new place in the world

## Political events

**1917 U.S. enters World War**
Following a period of unlimited submarine warfare by Germany, the U.S. enters World War I on the Allied side.

**1918 Fourteen Points listed**
President Woodrow Wilson announces his Fourteen Points necessary to conclude a peace settlement to World War I.

**1918 Armistice signed**
The armistice ending World War I is signed on November 11 in France.

**1919 Prohibition begins**
The 18th Amendment to the U.S. Constitution is enacted, prohibiting the manufacture and sale of alcoholic beverages.

**1919 Women get vote**
The 19th Amendment to the U.S. Constitution is enacted, granting women the vote.

**1920 Versailles Treaty spurned**
The U.S. Senate votes not to ratify the Treaty of Versailles, drawn up after Germany surrendered in World War I.

**1924 Teapot Dome scandal**
A Senate investigation in February and March uncovers a major scandal, called the Teapot Dome scandal, in the Administration of President Warren G. Harding.

**1924 Indians made citizens**
By Act of Congress, Indians born in the U.S. are declared citizens.

**1927 Sacco and Vanzetti die**
Nicola Sacco and Bartolomeo Vanzetti are executed in August for killing a paymaster and his guard during a robbery in South Braintree, Mass.; many believe they have been condemned for their political ideas.

**1929 Stock market crashes**
On October 24, the stock market crashes, ruining many if not most investors; the crash heralds the beginning of the Great Depression.

## Social events

**1919 First public strike**
Police in Boston, Mass., go on strike; this is the first strike by public workers in the U.S.

## Religion

**1922 McPherson builds temple**
Evangelist Aimee Semple McPherson builds the Angelus Temple in Los Angeles. She is the founder of the International Church of the Four-square Gospel and is well-known for her revival meetings.

## Philosophy

**1919 Adams wins Pulitzer**
Philosopher and historian Henry Brooks Adams wins a Pulitzer prize for his best-known work, *The Education of Henry Adams.*

**1924 Whitehead to Harvard**
English philosopher Alfred North Whitehead joins the faculty of Harvard University in Cambridge, Mass.

**1926 Durant publishes**
Will Durant publishes the major work *The Story of Philosophy*.

**1928 Summary work**
V.L. Parrington's important work *Main Currents in American Thought* is acclaimed. The book surveys the important trends in American philosophy.

**1929 Whitehead's major work**
While on the faculty of Harvard University, English philosopher Alfred North Whitehead publishes the book *Process and Reality*.

### Literature

**1917 O. Henry collected**
The complete works of O. Henry, mainly short stories, are published.

**1918 Sandburg on war**
Carl Sandburg's poem "Grass" is published. The poem deals with the horrors of war.

**1918 Cather on the prairie**
Willa Cather's novel *My Antonia* is published; it deals with the struggles of an immigrant girl on the prairie.

**1919 Anderson's short stories**
Sherwood Anderson published his first collection of short stories, entitled *Winesburg, Ohio*.

**1919 Pulitzer for Tarkington**
Booth Tarkington wins the Pulitzer prize for literature for his novel *The Magnificent Ambersons*.

**1920 Romantic poet**
*A Few Figs from Thistles*, a volume of poetry by Edna St. Vincent Millay, is published.

**1923 Cummings innovates**
*Tulips and Chimneys*, a book of poems by e e cummings, is published. The literary world is startled by cummings' revolutionary approach to titles, punctuation, and line breaks.

**1925 Jay Gatsby appears**
F. Scott Fitzgerald publishes the novel *The Great Gatsby*.

**1925 Dreiser's naturalism**
Theodore Dreiser, a leading writer in the naturalism movement, publishes the novel *An American Tragedy*.

**1926 Hemingway emerges**
Publication of *The Sun Also Rises* signals the emergence of Ernest Hemingway as a major novelist.

**1926 Lewis refuses prize**
Sinclair Lewis is awarded the Pulitzer prize for literature for the novel *Arrowsmith*. He turns down the prize, apparently feeling that he should have received it sooner—for *Main Street* or *Babbitt*.

**1929 Hammett begins**
Dashiell Hammett publishes two detective novels, *Red Harvest* and *The Dain Curse*.

**1929 Wolfe on youth**
Thomas Wolfe's first novel, *Look Homeward, Angel*, is published.

**1929 Thurber and White unite**
*Is Sex Necessary?*, a humorous book by James Thurber and E. B. White, is published.

**1929 A classic by Faulkner**
The novel *The Sound and the Fury*, by William Faulkner, is published. The novel uses the stream-of-consciousness technique in a striking manner.

### The arts

**1917 Ryder dies**
Romantic painter Albert Pinkham Ryder dies. His works are colorful, strange, and imaginative.

**1920's Jazz in flower**
Jazz composers and artists win a wide audience. Popular jazz personalities include Louis Armstrong, Sidney Bechet, Bix Beiderbecke, Edward (Duke) Ellington, Earl (Fatha) Hines, and Joseph (King) Oliver.

**1920-1940 The blues flourish**
Singer Bessie Smith reigns as "empress of the blues." Other prominent blues performers include Billie Holliday, Blind Lemon Jefferson, and Huddie (Leadbelly) Ledbetter.

**1921 Famed Steichen photo**
Photographer Edward Steichen takes his photograph *Three Pears and an Apple*.

**1924 Gershwin's major work**
Composer George Gershwin completes his *Rhapsody in Blue*, on a commission from jazz bandleader Paul Whiteman.

**1924 Varèse experiments**
Edgard Varèse composes *Octandre*, an instrumental piece that utilizes disordered sounds.

**1927 Kern's major hit**
*Show Boat*, perhaps the greatest musical by composer Jerome Kern, is first produced.

1928 **Mickey Mouse**
Cartoonist Walt Disney produces the film *Steamboat Willie*, in which he introduces the character of Mickey Mouse—who proves to be a beloved figure in U.S. popular culture.

**Science and technology**

1920 **Panama Canal opens**
The Panama Canal opens on July 12; work had begun in 1904. Official opening had been in 1914.

1921 **Einstein honored**
Albert Einstein wins the Nobel prize in physics for his study of quanta.

1926 **Rocket launched**
Space pioneer Robert H. Goddard launches the first liquid-fuel rocket.

1927 **Lindbergh's flight**
Charles A. Lindbergh makes the first nonstop solo flight across the Atlantic Ocean.

1927 **Compton honored**
American scientist Arthur Holly Compton is co-winner of the Nobel prize in physics. He is honored for discovering "the Compton effect," or variations in the wavelengths of X rays.

1929- **Plastics industry grows**
1937 Chemists learn to make cellulose acetate, acrylics, and polystyrene.

1932 **Earhart's flight**
Amelia Earhart becomes the first woman to fly solo across the Atlantic Ocean.

# Depression and a world in conflict

**Political events**

1933 **New Deal begins**
President Franklin D. Roosevelt begins the "New Deal" in an effort to end the depression.

1939- **Neutrality weighed**
1940 The U.S. remains officially neutral as Germany invades Poland and World War II begins.

1941 **Lend-Lease begins**
The U.S. decides to expand its aid to the Allies. The Lend-Lease Act gives the President the power to transfer arms and food to the Allies.

1941 **Pearl Harbor attacked**
On December 7, Japan launches a surprise attack on the U.S. military installations at Pearl Harbor on the island of Oahu in Hawaii.

1941 **Europeans declare war**
On December 11, Germany and Italy declare war on the U.S., and the U.S. declares war on Germany and Italy.

1942 **Japan takes Philippines**
From January to May, Japan's troops successfully battle U.S. troops for control of the Philippine Islands.

1942 **Allies land in Africa**
On November 8, American and British troops land in North Africa, in the largest amphibious invasion to date in World War II.

1942 **Solomon Islands won**
United States forces claim victory on November 12 after a three-day naval battle for control of the Solomon Islands.

1943 **Allies land on Sicily**
On July 10, American, British, and Canadian troops land on Sicily, in the second largest amphibious invasion of the war.

1944 **Normandy invaded**
On June 6, D-Day, Allied troops invade the Normandy coast of France.

1944 **Philippines recaptured**
United States troops led by Gen. Douglas MacArthur land on Leyte on October 20, in the first stage of the battle to recapture the Philippine Islands.

1944 **Allies hold the line**
American and British troops hold back the German Army at the Battle of the Bulge in December.

1945 **Iwo Jima captured**
In February and March, U.S. troops battle to capture from the Japanese the island of Iwo Jima in the Pacific.

1945 **Okinawa invaded**
The U.S. invades the island of Okinawa near Japan; the battle lasts for 3 months.

1945 **Victory in Europe**
Following the death of Germany's dictator, Adolf Hitler, on April 30, Germany's military leaders sign surrender terms on May 7 in Reims, France.

**1945 United Nations founded**
The United Nations (UN)
Charter is adopted on
June 26 by the 50 nations
meeting in San Francisco,
Calif.

**1945 Atomic bombs dropped**
Atomic bombs are
dropped on Hiroshima,
Japan, on August 6 and on
Nagasaki, Japan,
on August 9.

**1945 Japan surrenders**
Japan offers to surrender
on August 10. The official
terms of surrender are
signed on September 2.

**1947 Cold war heats up**
President Harry S. Truman
announces his "Truman
Doctrine": the U.S. will give
aid to any nation striving
to resist Communism; the
U.S. and Russia are en-
gaged in the cold war.

**1948 Marshall Plan set**
The European Recovery
Program, or Marshall Plan,
begins supplying massive
amounts of financial aid to
Western European na-
tions.

**1948- Berlin blockade broken**
**1949** The Russians blockade
West Berlin on June 24,
1948, hoping to drive out
the Western allies; the allies use an airlift of gigantic proportions to break
the blockade.

**1949 NATO organized**
The U.S. and 11 European
nations form the North Atlantic Treaty Organization
(NATO).

**1950 "McCarthyism" in flower**
Senator Joseph R. McCar-
thy, Republican from Wis-
consin, accuses the U.S.
Department of State of
harboring Communists.

**1950 Troops to Korea**
On June 30, President
Truman sends troops to
South Korea, which was
invaded by North Korea
on June 25.

**1950 Troops land at Inchon**
United States troops land
at Inchon, Korea, behind
enemy lines in September
and move north to the
Yalu River.

**1950 Allies retreat**
China enters the war on
the side of North Korea on
October 25; the Chinese
attack the Allies, who
begin retreating on
November 26.

**1951 MacArthur fired**
President Truman re-
moves Gen. Douglas
MacArthur as commander
in chief of U.S. forces in
Korea.

**1953 Korean truce set**
A truce ending the Korean
War is signed on July 27.

**1954 Army-McCarthy hear-
ings**
Senator Joseph R. McCar-
thy begins nationally televised hearings in April on
possible Communist influ-
ences in the U.S. Army; he
accuses the Army of
"coddling Communists."

**1954 Court says desegregate**
On May 17, the Supreme
Court rules in *Brown v.
Board of Education of To-
peka* that segregated public schools are a denial of
blacks' civil rights.

**1954 Censure McCarthy**
In December, the U.S. Senate votes to censure
Senator Joseph R. McCar-
thy for "contemptuous"
conduct.

**1955 King begins rights
crusade**
Dr. Martin Luther King, Jr.,
begins organizing a
movement to protest dis-
crimination against blacks.

**1959 Two new states added**
Alaska and Hawaii are
admitted to the Union;
they are the 49th and 50th
states.

Social events

**1932 Injunctions limited**
The Norris-La Guardia Act
limits the use of federal
court injunctions in
strikes and labor disputes.

**1935 NLRB created**
Congress passes the Na-
tional Labor Relations Act,
or Wagner Act, to protect
the rights of labor; the National Labor Relations
Board (NLRB) is created to
settle disputes.

**1942 Japanese interned**
The U.S. government
moves all Japanese on the
West Coast, including
aliens and native born, to
relocation camps in Ar-
kansas, Colorado, Utah,
and other states.

**1946 New suburb started**
Construction begins on
the town of Levittown,
N.Y., a new type of suburb;
a "planned community,"
Levittown features mass-
produced houses that look
alike and a master plan for
streets and highways.

**1947 Taft-Hartley Act set**
The Labor-Management
Relations Act, or Taft-
Hartley Act, is passed by
Congress and passed
again over the veto of Pres-
ident Harry S. Truman; the
Act limits union activities
in a variety of ways.

1953 **HEW founded**
A new department is
added to the U.S. Cabinet,
the Department of Health,
Education, and Welfare
(HEW), which is designed
to coordinate federal
policies in those three
broad areas.

1955 **AFL-CIO created**
The Congress of Industrial
Organizations (CIO), a collection of industrial un-
ions, merges with the
American Federation of
Labor (AFL), a collection of
craft unions, to form one
"umbrella" organization,
the AFL-CIO.

1957 **Crisis at Little Rock**
Arkansas Governor Orval
E. Faubus sends national
guardsmen to block black
students from entering
Central High School in Little Rock, Ark.; the students
are admitted after Presi-
dent Dwight D.
Eisenhower sends federal
troops to the school.

**Religion**

1930 **Black Muslims founded**
Elijah Muhammad and
W.D. Farad found the Na-
tion of Islam, or the Black
Muslim movement.

1933 **Day founds paper**
Dorothy Day founds the
*Catholic Worker*, a
monthly publication. Day
is a leader in the Catholic
Worker movement in the
U.S., and she works to
further social change in
New York City.

1937 **Catholic Unionists meet**
The Association of
Catholic Trade Unionists is
formed, to extend the
church's influence and
ideology to labor matters.

1948 **Brandeis opens**
Brandeis University is
founded; located in
Waltham, Mass., Brandeis
is sponsored by the
American Jewish com-
munity but is a nonsec-
tarian institution.

1949 **Graham begins crusades**
Billy Graham, an evangelist
preacher, begins his
large-scale campaigns for
converts throughout the
world.

1950 **Unity sought**
The National Council of
the Churches of Christ in
the U.S.A. is formed. A
number of Protestant and
Eastern Orthodox de-
nominations form the
Council to promote Chris-
tian unity.

1950 **Graham goes on radio**
Evangelist Billy Graham
starts a radio program,
called "The Hour of
Decision."

1950's **Bishop Sheen to TV**
Roman Catholic Bishop
Fulton J. Sheen is the host
for a television series called
"Life Is Worth Living";
Bishop Sheen becomes a
well-known personality in
America.

**Philosophy**

1931 **Cohen publishes**
Morris R. Cohen, a noted
defender of reason and
scientific thinking, pub-
lishes the book *Reason and
Nature*.

1934- **Mumford published**
1951 Lewis Mumford,
philosopher and social critic, completes *The Renewal
of Life*, a four-volume
philosophy of civilization.

1935 **Peirce's papers
published**
The *Collected Papers of
Charles Sanders Peirce* are

published posthumously.
The *Papers* are edited by
Charles Hartshorne and
Paul Weiss.

1938 **Alcott published**
Selected writings of tran-
scendentalist philosopher
Bronson Alcott (1799-1888)
are published posthu-
mously under the title
*The Journals of Bronson
Alcott.*

1939 **Dewey on culture**
*Freedom and Culture*, a
book by John Dewey, is
published.

1951 **Major article by Quine**
The American philosopher
Willard Van Orman Quine
publishes his article "Two
Dogmas of Empiricism."
This article is one of
Quine's chief contribu-
tions to epistemology, or
the study of knowledge.

1953 **Book by Quine**
Willard Van Orman Quine,
the influential logician and
philosopher, publishes the
book *From a Logical Point
of View.*

1954 **Nagel publishes**
*Sovereign Reason*, a book
by science philosopher
Ernest Nagel, is published.

1958 **Randall on function**
In his book *Nature and
Historical Experience*,
John Herman Randall pre-
sents a traditional concept
of the function of
philosophy.

**Literature**

1930- **Trilogy on U.S. culture**
1936 John Dos Passos writes
the three novels that make
up the trilogy *U.S.A.*

1931 **Buck's best**
Pearl Buck's novel *The
Good Earth* is published.
The story is set in China
and is the first in a series.

**1935 Maxwell Anderson**
*Winterset*, a play by Maxwell Anderson, is published. The play is based on the Sacco-Vanzetti case.

**1938 Play by Thornton Wilder**
*Our Town*, a play by Thornton Wilder, receives the Pulitzer prize for drama.

**1939 Sandburg on Lincoln**
Carl Sandburg's *Abraham Lincoln: The War Years* is published in four volumes.

**1940 Landmark in black fiction**
Richard Wright's first novel, *Native Son*, is published.

**1940 Pulitzer for Steinbeck**
John Steinbeck receives the Pulitzer prize for literature for his novel *The Grapes of Wrath*.

**1941 Hellman on Nazism**
Lillian Hellman's play *Watch on the Rhine* is published. The play centers on a man of integrity pursued by Nazis.

**1943 Saroyan on life**
William Saroyan's novel *The Human Comedy* is published.

**1943 Frost wins Pulitzer**
Robert Frost is awarded the Pulitzer prize for poetry for the fourth time. "Stopping by Woods on a Snowy Evening" is one of his best-known poems.

**1945 Gwendolyn Brooks**
*A Street in Bronzeville*, the first book of poems by Gwendolyn Brooks, is published. *Bronzeville* deals with life in the black ghettos of Chicago.

**1945 Williams to the fore**
*The Glass Menagerie*, a play by Tennessee Williams, is first performed.

**1949 Willy Loman appears**
Arthur Miller's play *Death of a Salesman* is published. The play is a tragedy about the life of salesman Willy Loman.

**1950 Bradbury and fantasy**
*The Martian Chronicles*, a book of stories by Ray Bradbury, is published.

**1951 Salinger's major work**
J. D. Salinger's novel *The Catcher in the Rye* is published.

**1952 Vonnegut's first novel**
*Player Piano*, the first novel by Kurt Vonnegut, Jr., appears.

**1954 Bellow emerging**
Saul Bellow wins the National Book award for fiction for his novel *The Adventures of Augie March*.

**1957 O'Neill's final work**
*A Long Day's Journey into Night*, a play by Eugene O'Neill, is published—four years after the playwright's death.

**1957 Pulitzer for Wilbur**
Richard Wilbur receives the Pulitzer prize for poetry for his volume *Things of This World*.

**1959 Roth to prominence**
*Goodbye, Columbus*, a book of stories by Philip Roth, is published.

**1959 Updike's first novel**
*The Poorhouse Fair*, a novel by John Updike, appears.

### The arts

**1931 Still premiere**
*The Afro-American Symphony*, by black composer William Grant Still, is first performed.

**1936 Balanchine on Broadway**
The ballet *Slaughter on Tenth Avenue*, by choreographer George Balanchine, is produced as part of the musical *On Your Toes*.

**1943 Robeson on stage**
Black actor and singer Paul Robeson stars in the title role of *Othello*, a dramatic play that becomes a long-running hit.

**1944 Rodgers and Hammerstein**
Richard Rodgers and Oscar Hammerstein II win the Pulitzer prize for drama for their musical play *Oklahoma!*

**1949- Television expands**
**1951** The number of television sets in American homes expands from 1,000,000 to 10,000,000 in just two years.

**1951 Cage's music**
Composer John Cage completes *Music of Changes*. In his work, Cage breaks away from many of the old conventions regarding sound.

**1953 Pollock's painting**
Jackson Pollock, the abstract painter, completes his *Ocean Grayness*.

**1954 Landmark jazz festival**
The first large American jazz festival is held in Newport, R. I.

### Science and technology

**1934 Urey honored**
Harold C. Urey wins the Nobel prize in chemistry for the discovery of deuterium, or heavy hydrogen.

**1937 Vitamin C**
Albert Szent-Györgyi wins the Nobel prize in physiology or medicine for

the isolation of Vitamin C, or ascorbic acid.

### 1938 Nobel for Fermi
Enrico Fermi wins the Nobel prize in physics for his discovery of radioactive elements.

### 1938– Blood plasma research
### 1940
Black physician Charles Drew conducts research on blood plasma. Dr. Drew helps set up blood banks, which save many lives.

### 1942 Manhattan Project
The Manhattan Project is organized by the U.S. Army Corps of Engineers to supervise the development of an atomic bomb.

### 1944 Mark I developed
The Mark I digital computer is developed, after years of research.

### 1951 Two share Nobel
Glenn T. Seaborg and Edwin M. McMillan win the Nobel prize in chemistry for the discovery of plutonium and other transuranic elements.

### 1951 UNIVAC computer
The UNIVAC is first of a variety of electronic computers mass-produced during the fifties.

### 1953 Color broadcasts begin
The first television broadcasts in color begin.

### 1954 Solar energy explored
Bell Telephone Laboratories develops the solar battery.

### 1955 Nuclear submarine built
The U.S. builds the *Nautilus*, the first nuclear-powered submarine.

### 1955 Polio vaccine developed
Dr. Jonas Salk develops a vaccine to prevent polio.

### 1957 Nuclear energy
The first full-scale U.S. nuclear power plant opens in Shippingport, Pa.

### 1958 Satellite orbits earth
The first U.S. satellite orbits the earth.

### 1958 Heredity studies
Americans George W. Beadle, Edward L. Tatum, and Joshua Lederberg win the Nobel prize in physiology or medicine. The three are honored for their studies of heredity.

### 1959 Two honored on DNA
Severo Ochoa and Arthur Kornberg win the Nobel prize in physiology or medicine. The two are honored for their synthesis of ribonucleic acid and deoxyribonucleic acid (DNA).

# The contemporary period

### Political events
### 1962 Cuban missile crisis
The U.S. learns that the Soviet Union has missile bases in Cuba; President John F. Kennedy orders a naval blockade of Cuba and forces removal of the missiles.

### 1963 Rights marchers to capital
More than 200,000 persons take part in the civil rights demonstration called the March on Washington on August 28 in Washington, D.C.

### 1963 President Kennedy slain
President John F. Kennedy is shot and killed in Dallas, Tex., on November 22; Lee Harvey Oswald is arrested

for the crime but is then shot and killed himself.

### 1964 Civil rights laws passed
Congress passes the Civil Rights Act of 1964 and other legislation guaranteeing equal protection of the laws to blacks.

### 1964 Gulf of Tonkin incident
North Vietnamese PT boats attack U.S. destroyers in the Gulf of Tonkin.

### 1964 Gulf of Tonkin resolution
Congress passes the Gulf of Tonkin resolution, which authorizes the President to "take all necessary measures to repel any armed attack against the

forces of the United States and to prevent further aggression."

### 1965 Bomb North Vietnam
President Lyndon B. Johnson orders the bombing of military targets in North Vietnam.

### 1965 LBJ sends troops
President Johnson sends U.S. Marines to Da Nang, South Vietnam, in March; they are the first U.S. ground troops, as opposed to advisers, to be sent to Vietnam.

### 1965 Rights confrontation
Police use tear gas and whips to turn back voting rights marchers in Montgomery, Ala.

**1965 Voting Rights Act**
Congress passes the Voting Rights Act of 1965 in August, to equalize standards for voting in the 50 states.

**1965 Urban riots touched off**
Blacks riot in the Watts section of Los Angeles, Calif., in August, calling national attention to conditions in U.S. inner city areas.

**1967 More riots hit cities**
In the "long, hot summer," riots occur in about 75 U.S. cities.

**1968 Dr. King slain**
On April 4, in Memphis, Tenn., civil rights leader Dr. Martin Luther King, Jr., is shot and killed.

**1968 Peace talks begin**
Preliminary peace talks begin between the U.S. and North Vietnam.

**1969 Troops massed**
Some 543,000 U.S. troops are in Vietnam by February, the largest number of the war.

**1969 Antiwar protests escalate**
Peace demonstrators march in major U.S. cities on Moratorium Day, October 15; about 300,000 persons march on Washington, D.C., on November 15 to protest the continuation of the war and the bombing of Cambodia.

**1970 Senate acts on war**
On June 24, the U.S. Senate repeals the Gulf of Tonkin resolution which gave the President broad powers to wage war.

**1972 Watergate burglary foiled**
On June 17, a group of persons are arrested for breaking into the Democratic Party headquarters in the Watergate complex in Washington, D.C.; the men arrested prove to be employees of President Richard M. Nixon's reelection committee.

**1973 War ends officially**
The U.S., North Vietnam, South Vietnam, and the Viet Cong sign a cease-fire agreement in January.

**1973- Watergate facts dis-**
**1974 closed**
Investigators reveal that high officials of the Nixon Administration were involved in covering up the Watergate break-in in 1972.

**1973 Vice-President resigns**
Vice-President Spiro T. Agnew resigns from office on October 10; at the time, he was under investigation on bribery charges in Maryland.

**1973 Ford appointed**
Gerald R. Ford is appointed Vice-President by President Nixon.

**1974 Nixon resigns**
On August 8, President Nixon announces that he is resigning from office effective the following day; he denies any wrongdoing but most observers link his resigning to threats of impeachment.

**1978 Canal treaties ratified**
The Senate ratifies treaties providing for the transfer of the Panama Canal to Panamanian control on December 31, 1999.

**1978 Camp David accords**
Egypt and Israel agree to a framework for peace at a 12-day summit mediated by President Carter at Camp David, Maryland.

**1979 U.S.–China ties**
The United States and China establish full diplomatic relations after a break of nearly 30 years.

**1981 Hostages released**
On January 20, Iranian militants release 53 Americans who had been held hostage in the U.S. Embassy in Teheran since November 4, 1979.

**1983 Reagan urges aid**
President Ronald Reagan urges increased aid for the government of El Salvador in its fight against leftist rebels, and for antileftist forces elsewhere in Central America.

**1983 U.S.-Soviet chill**
U.S.-Soviet relations plummet after a Soviet jet fighter shoots down a civilian Korean airliner, killing all 269 persons on board, including 61 Americans.

**1983 Fighting in Lebanon**
U.S. military forces stationed in Lebanon as part of an international peace-keeping effort become involved in fighting among various factions. A terrorist bomb explodes in marine headquarters in Lebanon, killing more than 200 U.S. troops.

**1983 Grenada invaded**
Pan American troops, including 1,900 U.S. military personnel, invade Grenada to overthrow the Marxist government in power there.

**Social events**

**1961 Peace Corps started**
President John F. Kennedy gets congressional approval to start the Peace Corps, a government agency that sends Ameri-

can citizens to foreign countries to promote peace, health, and welfare.

**1962 Meredith enrolls**
James Meredith becomes the first black to enroll in the University of Mississippi at Oxford. Attorney General Robert F. Kennedy sends U.S. marshals to maintain order when whites riot.

**1962 Chavez organizes**
Cesar Chavez founds the National Farm Workers Union to organize farm laborers in the grape fields. The group organizes strikes and boycotts against California grape growers.

**1962 School prayer banned**
The Supreme Court of the U.S. rules that required prayers and devotional Bible readings in public schools are unconstitutional.

**1963 Right to counsel**
In *Gideon v. Wainwright*, the Supreme Court rules that states must provide free legal counsel to any person accused of a felony who cannot afford to pay for counsel.

**1964 "Freedom summer" set**
A number of civil rights groups, including the Student Nonviolent Coordinating Committee (SNCC), send students to Mississippi to register black voters; three workers are killed by whites.

**1964 War on Poverty set**
President Lyndon B. Johnson initiates the creation of the Office of Economic Opportunity

(OEO), a government agency designed to wage the "War on Poverty."

**1966 "Black power" urged**
Stokely Carmichael urges that blacks be militant in seeking "black power," politically and economically.

**1966 NOW founded**
The National Organization for Women (NOW) is founded by a group of persons including Betty Friedan, author of *The Feminine Mystique*.

**1966 Miranda expands rights**
Ruling in the case *Miranda v. Arizona*, the Supreme Court of the U.S. states that criminal suspects must be fully informed of their rights when they are arrested; otherwise, confessions or statements by the suspect may not be used in court.

**1969 Desegregation ordered**
The Supreme Court of the U.S. rules that desegregation of all public school systems must take place "at once."

**1972 Indians protest**
The American Indian Movement (AIM) and other Indian rights groups hold a sit-in at the headquarters of the U.S. Bureau of Indian Affairs in Washington, D.C., to protest the bureau's policies.

**1973 Seize Wounded Knee**
Members of the American Indian Movement (AIM) seize the village of Wounded Knee, S. Dak.; they demand the return of certain lands taken from Indians in violation of treaty agreements.

**1973 Abortion rights ruling**
The Supreme Court of the U.S. rules that states may not prohibit a woman's right, under certain conditions, to have an abortion during the first six months of pregnancy.

**1976 Death penalty approved**
On July 2 the Supreme Court of the U.S. rules that the death penalty may be used again in the U.S.; the Court says that state laws passed since its 1972 decision against the death penalty are fair and just in their application of capital punishment.

**1978 Taxpayers revolt**
California voters approve Proposition 13, which sharply limits state and local authority to tax. Similar proposals begin in other states, indicating growing resistance to steadily rising taxes.

**1978 Bakke decision**
In the case of *Regents of the University of California v. Allan Bakke*, the Supreme Court rules that rigid quota systems used to achieve racial balance may constitute unfair discrimination against non-minority persons.

**1979 Inflation rate soars**
The inflation rate tops 13%, the highest rate since 1946.

**1982 Unemployment soars**
The U.S. unemployment rate rises to over 10 per cent—the highest level in 40 years.

**1982 ERA defeated**
The Equal Rights Amendment is defeated when only 35 of the necessary 38 states ratify it before the June 30 deadline. The amendment was proposed

as the 27th Amendment to the Constitution to assure equal treatment of men and women under the law.

### Religion

**1960 Pentecostal revival**

Father Dennis Bennett tells his congregation at St. Mark's Episcopal Church in Van Nuys, Calif., that he has experienced the Pentecostal spirit. The Pentecostal movement, which emphasizes faith healing and speaking in tongues, grows in the U.S. for the second time.

**1960's Catholic Church changes**

In the wake of the Second Vatican Council, the Roman Catholic Church in the U.S. undergoes a series of changes. The liturgy of the Mass is changed from mainly Latin to mainly English, special masses utilize folk music and folk dancing, and dress codes for nuns are relaxed.

**1972 "Jesus movement" grows**

The International Student Congress on Evangelism is held in Dallas, Tex., and more than 75,000 young people attend. Evangelist Billy Graham says the event proves the power of "the Jesus revival" among the nation's youth.

**1974 Women ordained**

On July 29, eleven women are ordained priests of the Episcopal Church by three bishops jointly celebrating a service in Philadelphia, Pa.; the ordinations are considered "irregular" because the denomination has not yet approved ordination for women.

**1979 Pope visits U.S.**

Throngs of Americans welcome Pope John Paul II to six U.S. cities.

**1983 Presbyterians reunite**

Representatives of the United Presbyterian Church in the U.S.A., a northern group, and the Presbyterian Church in the United States, a southern group, vote to create a unified body called the Presbyterian Church (U.S.A.). The two groups had split in 1861.

### Philosophy

**1963 Moral responsibility**

The *Journal of Philosophy*, a publication associated with Columbia University in New York City, publishes a "Symposium on Human Action." The symposium discusses moral freedom, moral responsibility, and the relationship of knowledge to action.

**1966 Quine's papers**

Various papers by Willard Van Orman Quine are published in two volumes, *Selected Logic Papers* and *The Ways of Paradox and Other Essays.*

**1971 Essays published**

The U.S. philosopher Horace M. Kallen publishes a volume of essays, *What I Believe and Why—Maybe.*

**1972 Women as philosophers**

The Society for Women in Philosophy holds its first conference in Chicago, Ill.

**1975 Eastern philosophy**

Robert M. Pirsig's book *Zen and the Art of Motorcycle Maintenance: An Inquiry into Values* is published. The novel deals in a popularized form with Oriental and classical

Greek philosophy. The popularity of Pirsig's book is but one indication of a current interest in Eastern philosophy.

**1983 Hoffer dies**

Eric Hoffer, a self-educated longshoreman who became a well-known political and social philosopher, dies in May. His first book, *The True Believer*, was published in 1951.

### Literature

**1961 Surrealism and comedy**

Joseph Heller's novel *Catch-22* is published.

**1963 Baldwin essays**

*The Fire Next Time*, a nonfiction work on race relations by James Baldwin, is published.

**1965 Vintage O'Connor**

*Everything That Rises Must Converge*, a book of short stories by Flannery O'Connor, is published a year after her death.

**1967 Pulitzer for Albee**

Playwright Edward Albee is voted the Pulitzer prize for drama for his play *A Delicate Balance.*

**1971 A new look at history**

Dee Brown's *Bury My Heart at Wounded Knee* is published and becomes a best seller. The book is a nonfiction account of the U.S. actions against the American Indians in the 19th century.

**1976 Searching for roots**

The biographical novel *Roots*, by Alex Haley, is published. *Roots* is a fictional account of Haley's family saga, ranging from Africa to the U.S.

**1977 Robert Lowell dies**

Poet Robert Lowell dies in September. He is generally

considered the leading contemporary American poet.

1980 **Eudora Welty honored**
Eudora Welty wins the National Medal for Literature for the "excellence of her past and continuing contribution to literature."

1982 **Cheever dies**
John Cheever, noted author of novels and short stories, dies in June. Cheever won a Pulitzer prize in 1979 and received the National Medal for Literature shortly before his death.

**The arts**
1961 **A major work by Kahn**
The Richards Medical Research Building at the University of Pennsylvania is completed. The building was designed by architect and planner Louis I. Kahn.

1967 **Geodesic dome**
An innovative and startling structure, the geodesic dome, is erected as the American exhibit at Expo 67 in Montreal, Canada. The dome is designed by R. Buckminster Fuller.

1969 **Mies dies**
Architect Ludwig Mies van der Rohe dies. Mies, who worked by the principle "less is more," is often considered the leading U.S. contemporary architect.

1974 **Graham to Far East**
The U.S. Department of State sponsors a tour of the Far East by modern dancer Martha Graham and her troupe.

1976 **Calder show**
"Calder's Universe," an

exhibition of more than 200 works by the American sculptor Alexander Calder, opens in New York City.

1980 **Copland honored**
Orchestras and dance companies across the U.S. celebrate composer Aaron Copland's 80th birthday by performing his works.

1983 **Award to Pei**
Architect I. M. Pei, a Chinese-born American known for his creative urban designs, receives the Pritzker Architecture Prize.

1983 **Williams dies**
Award-winning playwright Tennessee Williams, whose works include *The Glass Menagerie* and *A Streetcar Named Desire*, dies in February.

**Science and Technology**
1960 **Communications satellite**
The U.S. launches *Echo I*, the first passive communications satellite.

1962 **Glenn in orbit**
Astronaut John Glenn becomes the first American to orbit the earth in space.

1962 **Watson honored**
American Scientist James D. Watson shares the Nobel prize in physiology or medicine with two British colleagues. The three are cited for their research on the molecular structure of DNA.

1964 **Townes and lasers**
American scientist Charles H. Townes shares the Nobel prize in physics with two Russian scientists. The three are honored for their research on lasers and masers.

1966 **Mulliken and molecules**
Robert S. Mulliken wins

the Nobel prize in chemistry for his research on the structure of molecules.

1969 **Man walks on moon**
Astronaut Neil Armstrong becomes the first person to walk on the moon.

1972 **Bardeen wins again**
John Bardeen becomes the first person to win the Nobel prize twice for work in the same field. He wins the physics prize for his work in superconductivity; in 1956 he was honored for inventing the transistor.

1977 **Human-powered flight**
A group of Californians headed by Paul MacCready, Jr., sponsor a successful test flight of the "Gossamer Condor." The "Condor" is a human-powered aircraft.

1979 **Three Mile Island**
A failure in the cooling system of the Three Mile Island nuclear power plant near Harrisburg, Pennsylvania, causes the worst nuclear accident in U.S. history.

1979- **Planetary discoveries**
1981 Unmanned planetary probes discover new moons and rings around Jupiter and Saturn as *Pioneer 11* and 2 *Voyager* spacecraft relay photographs back to Earth.

1980 **Volcano erupts**
On May 18, a massive eruption of Mount St. Helens blows away more than 1,000 feet (300 meters) of the mountaintop and kills at least 34 persons.

1982 **Artificial heart**
The first permanent artificial heart implant is performed in Salt Lake City, Utah.

# Glossary: Unit 7

**abstract expressionism** A school of painting that flourished after World War II until the early 1960's. The artists believed that painting should be a natural act of free expression. Their paintings were studies in color and form often created through means other than brush strokes.

**humanism** *(HYOO muh nihz uhm)* A way of looking at our world that emphasizes the importance of human beings, our nature, and our place in the universe. Although humanism had its roots in the life and thought of ancient Greece and Rome, it actually flourished as a historical movement in Europe from the 1300's to the 1500's. The humanist approach to the study of man formed the intellectual core of the cultural reawakening called the *Renaissance*.

**idealism** A philosophical theory that sees the universe as being made up of mind, or reason. Some idealists recognize that matter exists but believe that mind is far more important. Others insist that consciousness, or reason, forms the basis for all reality. Philosopher George Berkeley took the position that nothing was real except ideas and impressions. He explained the apparent reality of objects by the theory that all objects were ideas in the mind of God.

**pragmatism** *(PRAG muh tihz uhm)* A philosophy developed by William James, Charles Peirce, and John Dewey that stated an idea must be judged by how it works, rather than by how it looks or sounds. Pragmatists consider a proposition true so long as it proves effective in linking the past and future. An idea may be true under certain circumstances, but false under others. Pragmatism has been called a peculiarly American philosophy.

**realism** In the arts, the attempt to portray life as it is. To the realist, the artist's main function is to describe as accurately and honestly as possible what can be observed through the senses. Realism began in the arts in the 1700's and by the mid-1800's was a dominant art form. In part, it was a revolt against classicism and romanticism, styles of art that idealized life.

**romanticism** *(roh MAN tuh sihz uhm)* A style in the arts and literature that emphasizes passion rather than reason, and imagination and inspiration rather than logic. The style favors full expression of the emotions and free, spontaneous action rather than restraint and order. Romanticism contrasts with another style called *classicism*, which stresses reason and order. The term *romantic movement* usually refers to the period from the late 1700's to the mid 1800's.

**social contract** A theory published by Rousseau in 1762, that government should rest on the consent of the governed.

**surrealism** A movement of art and literature, founded in Paris in 1924 by poet André Breton. Surrealism uses art as a weapon against the evils and restrictions that surrealists see in society. Surrealists claim to create forms and images not primarily by reason, but by unthinking impulse and blind feeling—or even by accident. Much of the beauty sought by surrealism is violent and cruel. In this way, surrealists try to shock the viewer or reader and show what they consider the deeper and truer part of human nature to be.

**symbolism** A literary movement started by a group of French poets between 1885 and 1895, led by Stéphane Mallarmé. The movement gave a spiritual atmosphere to the world by attributing to it a sacred, mystical quality. Visible realities became symbols for the invisible world of the spirit.

**transcendentalism** *(TRAN sehn DEHN tuh lihz uhm)* A philosophy that became influential during the late 1700's and 1800's. It was based on the belief that knowledge is not limited to, or solely derived from, experience and observation. Transcendentalism also stated that the solution to human problems lies in the free development of individual emotions. According to this philosophy, reality exists only in the world of the spirit. What a person observes in the physical world are only appearances, or impermanent reflections of the world through their senses and understanding. But they learn about the world of the spirit through another power, called *reason*.

**utilitarianism** *(yoo TIHL uh TAIR ee un nihz uhm)* The doctrine that the goal of life is "the greatest happiness of the greatest number." Whatever brings about this happiness has "utility." Utilitarians hold that the most definite mark of happiness is pleasure. Philosopher Jeremy Bentham first developed this idea in England.

# People who made history

**8**

When did Charlemagne die? Who was Benito Juarez? Your classwork probably often presents you with the names of unfamiliar people. These people may have been heads of government, soldiers, scientists, artists, any people who left a mark on history.

This unit is a quick reference biographical dictionary of historically significant people. While the unit makes no pretense at being all-embracing, effort has been made to include those persons who are most often referred to in the average student's classwork.

# Famous people

**Abraham** (about 1800 B.C.), whose name means "father of nations," was the founder of the ancient kingdom of Israel. A native of Ur, Abraham obeyed God's command to lead the Hebrew people to Palestine, where he established his people as a nation. He is considered a patriarch of the Jewish people.

**Adams, Samuel** (1722-1803), an American patriot and politician during the Revolutionary War period, was a leader of the independence movement. He opposed British tax laws such as the Stamp Act and the Tea Act and helped organize demonstrations against them. Adams was one of the signers of the Declaration of Independence and after the war served as governor of Massachusetts.

**Addams, Jane** (1860-1935), was a social worker and humanitarian. She established Hull House, a neighborhood center in Chicago for immigrants and the poor. Addams worked for numerous reforms, was active in women's movements and peace movements, and wrote several books. In 1931, she shared the Nobel peace prize.

**Aeschylus** (525?-456 B.C.), a tragic dramatist, ranked with Sophocles and Euripides as one of the most important playwrights of ancient Greece. His plays emphasized divine justice and power. Aeschylus wrote about 80 plays in all, of which only 7 survive, including *Seven Against Thebes*, *Prometheus Bound,* and *Agamemnon.*

**Aesop** (620?-560? B.C.), a legendary character, probably a Greek slave and reputedly ugly and deformed, was credited as the author of fables—short stories with moral lessons. His tales about animals such as the slow tortoise and the swift hare, and the frugal ant and the wastrel

grasshopper have been enjoyed for centuries and remain popular today.

**Albertus Magnus, Saint** (1206?-1280), born Count Albert von Bollstadt in Swabia, Germany, joined the Dominican order as a young man. He became a learned scholar in theology, philosophy, and science. He taught for many years in various universities, and his pupils included Thomas Aquinas. Albertus Magnus was canonized by the Roman Catholic Church in 1932.

**Alcott, Louisa May** (1832-1888), an American writer, is best known for her novel *Little Women,* the largely autobiographical story of the girlhood experiences of four sisters. She was a member of the New England literary group that included Henry David Thoreau, Ralph Waldo Emerson, and her father, Bronson Alcott.

**Alexander the Great** (356-323 B.C.), a pupil of the Greek philosopher Aristotle, at the age of 20 succeeded his father, Philip II of Macedon, to the throne. He united the Greek city-states and conquered the Persian Empire, Egypt, and northern India. Alexander ruled over the greatest empire of the time and founded the city of Alexandria in Egypt.

**Alfred the Great** (849-899), a Saxon king in England, defeated the Danes who tried to conquer his kingdom in Wessex. With his kingdom as the center, he paved the way for the unification of England and issued a code of laws for governing the people. A learned man, Alfred promoted education and Christianity and translated books from Latin to Anglo-Saxon.

**Al-Mansur** (712?-775), whose father was descended from a first cousin of Muhammad, the founder of Islam, was the second caliph in the Abbasid dynasty. He built Baghdad, which he made his capital, into a great city. Interested in learning, Al-Mansur had Greek and Latin writings translated into Arabic.

**Ampère, Andrè Marie** (1775-1836), was a French physicist and mathematician who formulated the laws of electromagnetism. He discovered that electric currents moving in the same direction attract but that those moving in opposite directions repel. Ampère also discovered that a coil of electrically charged wire acts as a magnet.

**Amundsen, Roald** (1872-1928), was a Norwegian explorer who determined the exact position of the North Pole and in 1911 became the first person to reach the South Pole. He also navigated the Northwest Passage through North America and crossed the North Pole in a dirigible. Amundsen disappeared on a North Pole rescue attempt.

**Anthony, Susan B.** (1820-1906), was a leader of reform movements in the United States who worked for women's suffrage, temperance, and the abolition of slavery. She edited the magazine *The Revolution*, was arrested for voting in 1872, and was president of a national women's suffrage group for several years.

**Antony, Mark** (82?-30 B.C.), a friend and fellow commander of Julius Caesar, became a consul in the Roman government. After Caesar's assassination, he was a member of the triumvirate that ruled Rome and later commanded the eastern empire. Pursuing Cleopatra of Egypt while trying to widen his control over the empire, he was defeated by Octavian and committed suicide.

**Aquinas, Saint Thomas** (1225?-1274), an Italian theologian who was influenced by the teachings of the Greek philosopher Aristotle, constructed a system of theology that became the basis for many doctrines of the Roman Catholic Church. Among his writings are *Summa contra Gentiles* and *Summa Theologica*, considered the most complete account of his theology.

**Archimedes** (287?-212 B.C.), although he considered himself to be a mathematician, is best remembered for his inventions. His inventions included a screw to raise irrigation water and a catapult for military use. Living in Syracuse on the island of Sicily, he also developed the laws of displacement and buoyancy in water and a more precise figure for pi.

**Aristophanes** (445?-385? B.C.), who wrote during the Golden Age of Athens in ancient Greece, is considered one of the greatest writers of comedy of all time. In his plays, he satirized many contemporary figures and events. His known works include *Clouds, Wasps, Birds, Frogs,* and *Lysistrata.*

**Aristotle** (384-322 B.C.), a student of Plato, was the greatest Greek philosopher after Plato's death. Considered one of the greatest of logicians, he also lectured on government and ethics and laid the foundations for psychology. Aristotle established a school in Athens; earlier, Alexander the Great had become his pupil.

**Armstrong, Neil A.** (1930- ), an American astronaut, was the first person to set foot on the moon. A naval pilot between 1949 and 1952, he made his first space flight in 1966. A part of the crew of *Apollo XI*, Armstrong and another astronaut stepped onto the moon on July 20, 1969, and briefly explored the lunar surface. Armstrong later became a professor of engineering.

**Arnold, Benedict** (1741-1801), although remembered as a traitor, was one of the best Revolutionary War generals. He fought in several important battles. Passed over for promotions and court-martialed by enemies, Arnold arranged for the British to take over West Point. When the plot was discovered, he joined the British.

**Astor, John Jacob** (1763-1848), a German by birth, was the founder of a wealthy American family. He became successful in the fur trade and shipped furs to Europe and to China. He extended his control over the fur trade throughout much of North America and established a post at Astoria, Ore. Astor accumulated real estate in New York City and left a fortune of about $20 million.

**Atahualpa** (1500?-1533), became the emperor of the Inca empire after defeating his brother Huáscar in a civil war. He was the last Inca to rule Peru before Spaniards under the command of Francisco Pizarro invaded the empire and conquered it. Alleging that he might arouse his people against the Spaniards, Pizarro had Atahualpa put to death.

**Atatürk, Kemal** (1881-1938), was the first president of the Turkish Republic, serving from 1923 until his death. He led armies against the British in World War I, and after the war he worked for the independence and unification of Turkey. Atatürk modernized Turkey, abolishing ancient dress, old penal codes, and the practice of polygamy. He achieved many other social, economic, and religious reforms.

**Attila** (406?-453), called the "Scourge of God," was a fierce leader of the Huns. He led his soldiers to conquer much of eastern and central Europe. Turned back in France, he invaded Italy but withdrew when the Pope interceded. The Huns returned to the Danube area, where Attila died while celebrating his wedding.

**Attucks, Crispus** (1723?-1770), often assumed to have been a black man, was a leader of the mob in the Boston Massacre. He was one of three men killed by British soldiers. His background, however, is uncertain. He may have been a mulatto, or he may have been of mixed Negro and Indian blood. Attucks' place of birth and his occupation, like his ancestry, are also unknown.

**Audubon, John James** (1785-1851), a failure in business, found success as a painter of American birds. His first group of 435 paintings, *Birds of America*, was first published in England between 1826 and 1838. Audubon later published numerous editions of his paintings of birds and other animals.

**Augustine, Saint** (354-430), as an intelligent and well-educated Italian youth, led a carefree, worldly life before converting to Christianity at about the age of 30. He became one of the important philosophers of early Christianity and served as the bishop of Hippo in North Africa for more than 30 years. Augustine's writings include *City of God* and his autobiographical *Confessions.*

**Augustus Caesar** (63 B.C.-A.D. 14), known originally as Octavian, became the first Roman emperor in 27 B.C. He expanded the empire to the north and east. During his reign, the Roman Empire reached the peak of its glory in a period of peace and great artistic production, particularly by literary figures such as Virgil, Ovid, and Horace.

**Aurangzeb** (1618-1707), the last effective Mogul emperor of India, took the throne by imprisoning his father and killing two of his brothers. He was a harsh ruler, and his religious persecutions of both Muslims and Hindus led to widespread revolts.

These and other outbreaks brought about the end of the Mogul empire in India.

**Austen, Jane** (1775-1817), an English author, wrote six novels, including *Pride and Prejudice, Sense and Sensibility,* and *Northanger Abbey.* As she herself had experienced them, she portrayed the attitudes, hopes, fears, and superficialities of the English middle class with sympathy and understanding.

**Bach, Johann Sebastian** (1685-1750), a giant among composers, was also a great organist who was attached to many important churches and courts in his native Germany. Among his religious works are the *Mass in B Minor* and *The Passion According to St. Matthew.* His instrumental music includes the *Brandenburg Concertos, The Well-Tempered Clavier,* and *The Art of the Fugue.*

**Bacon, Francis** (1561-1626), an English philosopher, politician, and writer, is best remembered for his practical essays. Particularly interested in learning, he planned but never completed an encyclopedia of all knowledge. In *Novum Organum,* Bacon stressed the inductive scientific method of collecting data and arriving at tentative conclusions.

**Bacon, Roger** (1214?-1292?), a medieval philosopher probably born in England, emphasized experience as a means of knowing. Interested in science, he stressed the superiority of conclusions based on observation over those based on reason. A Franciscan, he was imprisoned for some of his views. His greatest work was *Opus Maius,* a discourse on scientific subjects.

**Balboa, Vasco Núñez de** (1475-1519), was one of the early Spanish explorers of America. He became the governor of Darién in Panama and led expeditions seeking gold. In 1513, he led 200 men on an expedition to discover the Pacific Ocean. Under charges of treason, probably false, Balboa was condemned and executed by beheading.

**Balzac, Honoré de** (1799-1850), a prolific French writer, studied law but turned to literature as a profession. He wrote many novels, including *The Human Comedy,* a group of novels that deal with the lives of more than 2,000 different characters representing all walks of life. Among his best-known books are *Old Goriot* and *Droll Stories.*

**Banneker, Benjamin** (1731-1806), was a black mathematician who published an almanac containing weather predictions and astronomical calculations. Also a surveyor, Banneker came to the attention of Thomas Jefferson, who helped him win appointment to the group that laid out the boundaries of the District of Columbia.

**Barnum, Phineas T.** (1810-1891), perhaps the greatest American showman, created the modern circus. Barnum presented the Swedish singer Jenny Lind, as well as the midget General Tom Thumb and the elephant Jumbo, to American audiences. Because of Barnum, expressions like *white elephant* (fake) and *ballyhoo* (strident publicity) became a part of the English language.

**Barton, Clara** (1821-1912), won acclaim as a battlefield nurse during the Civil War and was appointed superintendent of nurses for one of the Union armies. Serving as a nurse in Europe during the Franco-Prussian War, she became interested in the Red Cross movement. Barton later organized the American National Red Cross and served as its president.

**Becket, Saint Thomas à** (1118?-1170), an English cleric and archbishop of Canterbury, opposed the plans of King Henry II to weaken the authority of the Roman Catholic Church in England. When Henry II indicated that he wanted to be rid of Becket, four knights took this to mean his death and killed Becket at Canterbury. Two years later, the church made him a saint.

**Bede** (673?-735), an English Roman Catholic priest, wrote more than 30 works on history, science, hymns, the lives of saints, grammar, and the Bible. His most famous work is the *Ecclesiastical History of the English Nation*, covering events up to the year 731. For his many achievements, he was given the title "the Venerable Bede" and was canonized.

**Beebe, William** (1877-1962), became famous for designing the bathysphere, in which he made many undersea explorations to observe marine life. Curator of ornithology at the New York Zoological Society, Beebe traveled widely throughout the world, particularly in tropical regions. His popular books include *Beneath Tropic Seas*.

**Beethoven, Ludwig van** (1770-1827), a German-born composer generally credited with beginning the romantic movement in music, expanded musical form and used daring harmonies. His compositions include nine symphonies, an opera, five piano concertos, a violin concerto, more than 30

sonatas, and numerous string quartets and religious works.

**Bell, Alexander Graham** (1847-1922), a painter and a teacher of the deaf, invented the telephone. With the aid of his assistant, Thomas A. Watson, Bell carried out many experiments that in 1876 produced one of the first instruments that successfully transmitted voices over a distance.

**Ben-Gurion, David** (1886-1973), promoted the creation of the state of Israel and became the nation's first prime minister, serving from 1948 to 1953 and again from 1955 to 1963. Born in Poland, he emigrated to Israel and became a Zionist (independence) leader. In 1930 he formed the United Labor, now the Mapai, political party.

**Bentham, Jeremy** (1748-1832), an English jurist and philosopher, taught that the morality of ideas, actions, and institutions should be judged on the basis of how well they promote the greatest good for the greatest number of people. His philosophy, called utilitarianism, brought about some court and other reforms.

**Bessemer, Sir Henry** (1813-1898), an English inventor and engineer, developed a means of removing impurities from iron ore. Called the Bessemer process, it greatly increased the quantity and quality of steel production in the 1800's. He established steelworks at Sheffield, England, to produce parts for guns and steel rails.

**Bethune, Mary McLeod** (1875-1955), a black educator, founded a school for black women in 1904 in Daytona Beach, Fla., that later merged with a men's school to become Bethune-Cookman College. She was the school's president for many years and later held several positions in the federal government. Bethune also established mission schools for blacks.

**Bismarck, Otto von** (1815-1898), became the first chancellor of the German Empire in 1871 after he had unified his country after wars with Austria and France. To solidify and secure Germany's position, he created the Triple Alliance through a series of treaties with Austria-Hungary and Italy that lasted until the outbreak of World War I.

**Blackstone, Sir William** (1723-1780), an English jurist, wrote the influential *Commentaries on the Laws of England.* This extensive treatise was frequently quoted in the 1700's and became the basis for legal education in England. It was also influential in the American Colonies, where it served as a source book on English law.

**Blackwell, Elizabeth** (1821-1910), was the first woman physician in the United States. Born in England, she moved to the United States as a child. She graduated from medical school in 1849 and opened a hospital for women and children in 1853. Elizabeth and her sister, Emily, founded the Women's Medical College of the New York Infirmary for Women and Children in 1857.

**Blake, William** (1757-1827), was an English mystic, poet, engraver, and painter. He illustrated his own books as well as the writings of others. A romantic poet, Blake's works include two volumes, both entitled *Songs of Innocence*, which treat similar subjects from contrasting points of view. His engravings include *Illustrations of the Book of Job*.

**Boccaccio, Giovanni** (1313?-1375), an Italian author, wrote *The Decameron*, a collection of tales supposedly related by a group of men and women isolated in Florence, Italy, during a plague. The stories are humorous and earthy and were retold by many later writers. Boccaccio also served in several diplomatic posts for the Florentine government.

**Bohr, Niels** (1885-1962), a Danish physicist, elaborated on Ernest Rutherford's theory that the atom consists of a positively charged nucleus with negatively charged electrons revolving around it. Bohr's research was a major step toward the practical use of nuclear energy. Bohr won the Nobel prize in physics in 1922.

**Boleyn, Anne** (1507-1536), was the second wife of Henry VIII of England. When Henry divorced his first wife to marry Anne, the act brought about the separation of England from the Roman Catholic Church and the establishment of the Church of England. Anne's daughter became Elizabeth I. Charged with infidelity after Henry tired of her, Anne was beheaded.

**Bolívar, Simón** (1783-1830), born into the middle class, joined the Latin-American independence movement and fought many successful battles against the Spanish. Colombia, Ecuador, Venezuela, and other countries gained their freedom from Spain because of Bolívar's military leadership. For several years, Bolívar was president of Colombia, and unsuccessfully worked for Latin-American unity.

**Boone, Daniel** (1734-1820), an almost legendary frontiersman, participated in the French and Indian Wars and later led an early group of first pioneers into Kentucky. He helped lay out the Wilderness Road and found settlements. In 1799, Boone moved West to become a pioneer in Missouri.

**Booth, John Wilkes** (1838-1865), an actor and member of a prominent theatrical family, assassinated President Abraham Lincoln in Ford's Theatre in Washington, D.C., on April 14, 1865. A Southerner, he considered Lincoln to be a tyrant and an enemy of the South. Fleeing the theater after the shooting, Booth was hunted down in Virginia, where he was shot to death.

**Brahe, Tycho** (1546-1601), a Danish astronomer, made important discoveries through systematic observation of the planets, an innovation at the time. He observed a new star and suggested that comets originate in outer space, not in the earth's atmosphere, as had been thought. Brahe's theories and astronomical tables were of great value to succeeding astronomers.

**Brahms, Johannes** (1833-1897), a German romantic composer, wrote music in all major forms except opera and ballet. His compositions include *Variations on a Theme by Haydn, Academic Festival Overture*, four symphonies, two piano concertos and a violin concerto, Hungarian dances, and many songs. His music is known for its dramatic qualities.

**Braille, Louis** (1809-1852), a Frenchman blinded by an accident at the age of 3, studied music and became an organist. As a teacher at the National Institute for the Blind in Paris, he developed a system of writing using raised points that could be read with the fingertips. His system, called braille, opened a new means of communication for the blind.

**Brooks, Gwendolyn** (1917-    ), a black American poet and writer, published several collections of poetry, including *A Street in Bronzeville*. A Guggenheim scholar, she won the Pulitzer prize in 1950 for her volume of poetry *Annie Allen*. The first black woman to win the prize, Brooks was named poet laureate of Illinois in 1968.

**Brown, John** (1800-1859), an American abolitionist, embodied the hostility between the North and the South in the decade before the Civil War. He helped blacks escape from slavery and fought pro-slavery groups in Kansas. In 1859, Brown and his followers briefly seized the federal arsenal at Harper's Ferry, Va. The arsenal retaken, Brown was convicted of treason and hanged.

**Bryan, William Jennings** (1860-1925), a politician, served from 1891 to 1895 in the House of Representatives. A spokesman for the free-silver movement, he ran unsuccessfully for the presidency as a Democrat in 1896, 1900, and 1908. Bryan served as secretary of state during the administration of President Woodrow Wilson and later attacked the teaching of evolution in schools.

**Buddha** (563?-483? B.C.), developed a philosophy of peace based on enlightenment, on which he founded a religion. Born Prince Siddhartha Gautama in Nepal, he taught his followers to forsake desire, seek goodness, escape from sorrow, and follow an eightfold path to righteousness and enlightenment.

**Burr, Aaron** (1756-1836), an American politician, was Vice-President under Thomas Jefferson from 1801 to 1805. Under the system of that time, Jefferson won the Presidency over Burr on the 36th ballot in the House of Representatives. In a duel in 1804, Burr killed Alexander Hamilton, who was largely responsible for Burr's having lost the Presidency and another office. Later, he was involved in a mysterious plot to establish an independent nation in the Southwest.

**Byrd, Richard** (1888-1957), an American admiral and explorer, greatly furthered knowledge of the Antarctic region. Beginning in 1928, he led numerous expeditions to Antarctica. During the last expedition in 1955 and 1956, he flew over the South Pole for the third time. Byrd became the foremost authority on Antarctica of his time.

**Cabot, John** (1450?-1498?), a navigator and explorer born in Italy, made two voyages for King Henry VII of England. Although he was sailing for Asia, both times he reached islands in the North Atlantic. On the first voyage, he landed on Cape Breton Island or Newfoundland. Setting out again, Cabot and his party were lost; however, his voyages helped England establish claims on the islands.

**Caesar, Julius** (100?-44 B.C.), a Roman general and politician, conquered what is now France and twice invaded England. He later took over the Roman government and fought several wars, one in Egypt. Fearing a dictatorship, Caesar's enemies conspired together and assassinated him.

**Calhoun, John C.** (1782-1850), a powerful politician, was the foremost spokesman for states' rights before the Civil War. He was a representative and a senator from South Carolina and was Vice-President from 1825 to 1832. Calhoun's last speech in the Senate opposed the Compromise of 1850, a measure that was meant to settle the slavery issue (see "Millard Fillmore" in Unit 9, page 343).

**Calvin, John** (1509-1564), a Swiss theologian born in France, developed a stern and forbidding Protestant theology based on faith rather than good works. He believed in predestination and free will. Calvinism was a highly individualistic religion, and vestiges of it can be found today in Presbyterian, Congregational, and other faiths.

**Carnegie, Andrew** (1835-1919), born in Scotland, became an American industrialist and philanthropist. He emigrated to the United States at age 13 and worked his way up to an important position in a railroad company. Carnegie later became a steel manufacturer and eventually accumulated a fortune of some half billion dollars. He gave away much money to philanthropic causes.

**Carroll, Lewis** (1832-1898), was the pen name of Charles L. Dodgson, an English mathematician and writer. For a girl named Alice, he developed imaginative stories that were later published as *Alice's Adventures in Wonderland.* When the book quickly became a children's favorite, he wrote a sequel, *Through the Looking Glass.* A professor, he also published works on mathematics.

**Cartier, Jacques** (1491?-1557), a French sailor, became an explorer of Canada for King Francis I. In 1534, he discovered the Gulf of St. Lawrence and the St. Lawrence River. On other voyages, he journeyed far up the St. Lawrence River and located the future sites of Quebec and Montreal. Cartier's voyages gave France huge land claims in North America.

**Caruso, Enrico** (1873-1921), was perhaps the greatest operatic tenor of his time. Born in Italy, he sang in opera houses in Russia, Italy, England, and in South American countries but had his greatest success with the Metropolitan Opera Company of New York City. Caruso had a large repertoire of more than 40 operas.

**Castro, Fidel** (1926-    ), a Cuban revolutionary leader, became prime minister after he overthrew dictator Fulgencio Batista in 1959. He established a Communist state, nationalized businesses, and began land reforms. Castro reportedly aided guerrilla movements in other Latin-American countries, and he sent Cubans to support Communist movements in Africa.

**Catherine of Aragon** (1485-1536) was the first of the six wives of King Henry VIII of England. The daughter of Ferdinand and Isabella of Spain, she was the mother of Mary I. Henry's insistence on divorcing her led to England's break with the Roman Catholic Church and the establishment of the Church of England. After her divorce, Catherine lived a life of religious devotion in prison (see "Henry VIII" in this unit).

**Catherine II** (1729-1796) was an empress of Russia who became known as "the Great." When her husband Peter was deposed and murdered, Catherine took the throne. Although interested in European liberalism, she ruled autocratically, and the misery of the serfs increased during her reign. Catherine extended Russian borders to include a part of Poland and the Crimea. She also conquered Siberian tribes.

**Cato, Marcus Porcius, the Elder** (234-149 B.C.), a Roman consul and senator, helped bring about the destruction of Carthage in northern Africa in the Third Punic War. He viewed Carthage as Rome's mortal enemy and closed all of his speeches in the senate with a plea for its destruction. Known as Cato the Elder, he tried to revive values that Rome had held in its early days.

**Cavour, Camillo Benso** (1810-1861), an Italian statesman, served as prime minister of Sardinia from 1852 to 1861. Under his leadership, Sardinia joined France to drive Austria from Lombardy. Sardinia then took control of Lombardy and other areas of Italy. Working with Giuseppe Garibaldi and others, Cavour succeeded in making Italy a unified nation.

**Cervantes, Miguel de** (1547-1616), a Spanish author, wrote *Don Quixote*, sometimes called the world's greatest novel. Begun while Cervantes was in prison, the work tells the adventures of the idealistic Don Quixote and his servant Sancho Panza and is a satire on chivalry. Cervantes held several minor military and diplomatic posts and wrote plays, poems, and other works.

**Cézanne, Paul** (1839-1906), a French painter, used forms such as the cone, the cube, and the sphere in his works. Trained in the impressionistic school of art, he established his own style in painting that emphasized solid masses of color. Cézanne influenced the cubist school of painters.

**Champlain, Samuel de** (1567?-1635), was a French explorer of the New World and for several years served as governor of the French colony at Quebec in Canada. He discovered Lake Champlain and explored extensively along the St. Lawrence River, Georgian Bay, and Lake Ontario. Champlain promoted the fur trade and maintained a friendship with the Algonkian Indians.

**Charlemagne** (742-814) was king of the Franks (Germans) and emperor of the Romans. Defeating the Saxons, the Bavarians, the Avars, the Lombards, and others, he created an empire sprawling over much of central and western Europe. A patron of culture, he did much to promote scholarship and education within his realm.

**Chaucer, Geoffrey** (1340?-1400), an English public official, diplomat, and poet, wrote *The Canterbury Tales*. In the poem, a group of pilgrims journeying to Canterbury tell stories for their amusement as they proceed. Chaucer also wrote several other poems, including *The Book of the Duchess*.

**Chavez, Cesar** (1927-    ), was the first labor leader who effectively organized migrant workers. A migrant worker himself, he worked to unionize field laborers in the 1960's in spite of much opposition. Chavez established the National Farm Workers Association and in 1966 signed the first contract with California growers.

**Chekhov, Anton** (1860-1904), a Russian author, wrote many plays and short stories in which he stressed human loneliness and people's failure to understand one another. Among his stories are "Kashtanka," "The Party," "The Darling," and "Ward No. 6." Chekhov's plays include *The Cherry Orchard, Uncle Vanya,* and *The Three Sisters*.

**Chopin, Frédéric** (1810?-1849), a pianist and composer born in Poland, was a child prodigy and wrote lyrical works for the piano, many based on popular dance forms. Settling in Paris with George Sand, a woman writer, Chopin composed two piano concertos and many shorter works — mazurkas, polonaises, preludes, études, nocturnes, ballades, and songs.

**Churchill, Winston** (1874-1965), a British states-man and author, began his career as a soldier and reporter. He later entered Parliament and headed various ministries. In 1940, he became prime minister, leading Great Britain during World War II. He also served as prime minister again from 1951 to 1955. Churchill wrote on English history and also wrote a history of World War II that won him the Nobel prize in literature in 1953.

**Cicero** (106-43 B.C.), a Roman lawyer, statesman, and writer, served as a consul. Exiled for refusing to support the First Triumvirate, he devoted him-self to writing. He later became a leader of the senate and opposed Mark Antony's ambition to rule Rome. Feared because of his ability as an orator, Cicero was condemned to death and was killed while trying to escape.

**Cincinnatus, Lucius Quinctius** (519?-439? B.C.), a Roman patriot, was appointed dictator and led an army that defeated the Aequians in central Italy. After his victory, he resigned. Given absolute power a second time, he once more resigned after slaying a traitor threatening Rome. To later Ro-mans, Cincinnatus became a symbol of old-fashioned virtues.

**Clark, George Rogers** (1752-1818), led troops against the British in the Northwest Territory dur-ing the Revolutionary War. He financed his own campaigns and was never reimbursed for his ex-penses. Clark's successes helped secure the Northwest for the United States under the peace treaty of 1783 that ended the war.

**Clay, Henry** (1777-1852), represented Kentucky for many years in the House of Representatives, where he served several terms as speaker, and in the Senate. He tried unsuccessfully for the presi-dency three times. Clay's greatest renown came from the Missouri Compromise and the Compro-mise of 1850—agreements that he worked out to ease the conflict between the North and South over the slavery issue.

**Cleopatra** (69-30 B.C.), an Egyptian queen who at various times ruled with her two brothers (who were also her husbands), became the mistress of Julius Caesar and bore him a son. She later be-came the lover of Mark Antony and bore him twins. When Antony was defeated in Egypt by Octavian, Cleopatra committed suicide to avoid the humiliation of being taken to Rome for exhibi-tion as a captive.

**Clinton, De Witt** (1769-1828), promoted the Erie Canal, completed in 1825 when he was governor of New York. The canal helped New York City de-velop as the country's most important port. Clin-ton also served as mayor of New York City, as a state senator, and as lieutenant governor. He was an unsuccessful Federalist candidate for the pres-idency in 1812.

**Cochise** ( ?-1874), a chief of the Chiricahua Apache, was captured by white soldiers under a flag of truce and accused of a crime he had not committed. Escaping, the embittered Cochise led his warriors in 10 years of intermittent warfare against whites. A brilliant leader, he finally was forced to accept life on a reservation.

**Columbus, Christopher** (1451-1506), an Italian navigator, made four voyages of exploration of the Americas for Spain in the 1490's and early 1500's. He was searching for a route to Asia and reached what he thought were the Indies. Because of his efforts, Spain made vast land claims in the Ameri-cas, but Columbus died in poverty and obscurity.

**Confucius** (551?-479? B.C.), a Chinese philospher, centered his teachings on human relationships, not gods. He taught moral responsibility, kindness and generosity, filial piety, respect for elders and superiors, and the duty of rulers to govern wisely and well. Confucianism came to be one of the most influential philosophies in Chinese society.

**Conrad, Joseph** (1857-1924), a Polish-born British author, wrote mostly about sailors and the sea, which he knew from firsthand experience. Among his writings are *Lord Jim* and *Heart of Darkness*. Although he did not learn English until he was 20 years old, Conrad became an elegant stylist in the language.

**Constantine** (275?-337), called "the Great," was an emperor of the Roman Empire. He favored Chris-tianity during his rule and moved his capital from Rome to Byzantium, renaming the city Constan-tinople. In 325, Constantine called Christian lead-ers together at the Council of Nicaea to settle disputes over doctrine.

**Cook, James** (1728-1779), a British mariner, made voyages of exploration throughout the world. He mapped portions of the eastern coasts of North America and of New Zealand, Australia, and New Guinea; sailed across the Antarctic Circle; reached New Caledonia; charted much of the western coast of North America; and explored the Bering Strait. Cook was killed in Hawaii.

**Copernicus, Nicolaus** (1473-1543), a Polish astronomer, is considered the founder of modern astronomy. He developed the theory that the earth is a moving planet, and he attacked Ptolemy's theory—then generally accepted—that the earth was fixed in the universe and never moved. Copernicus' major work was *Concerning the Revolutions of the Celestial Spheres* (1543).

**Cortés, Hernando** (1485-1547), a Spanish explorer, conquered the Aztec Indians after bitter fighting and won Mexico for Spain. As the first governor of Mexico (then called New Spain), he spread Spanish control and influence and began the first settlement in Lower California.

**Crick, Francis H. C.** (1916-    ), a British biologist, shared the Nobel prize for physiology or medicine in 1962 for his work with deoxyribonucleic acid (DNA), the substance that transmits genetic information. Crick also helped develop radar during World War II.

**Cromwell, Oliver** (1599-1658), an English Puritan, led parliamentary forces to defeat, depose, and behead King Charles I in 1649. Beginning in 1653, he ruled England as Lord Protector Cromwell, mostly without the aid of Parliament, until his death. After a short rule by Cromwell's son Richard, Charles II, the son of Charles I, came to the throne.

**Curie, Marie** (1867-1934),a Polish-born chemist, made important discoveries in radioactivity with her husband Pierre. Together, the Curies discovered radium and polonium and shared the Nobel prize in physics in 1903 with another scientist. A professor at the Sorbonne in Paris, she won the Nobel prize in chemistry in 1911.

**Curie, Pierre** (1859-1906), a French physicist and chemist, did his first important work on the magnetic properties of metals, and with his wife Marie made important discoveries in radioactivity. The Curies discovered radium and polonium, for which they shared the Nobel prize in physics in 1903. Curie was a professor of physics and chemistry.

**Cyrus the Great** (reigned 559-529 B.C.) established the ancient Persian Empire. He extended his empire by defeating several rulers—including As-

tyages, the king of Media; King Croesus of Lydia; and Nabonidus, the king of Babylon. Cyrus freed the Jews from captivity, allowing them to return to Palestine.

**Da Gama, Vasco** (1469?-1524), a Portuguese navigator, rounded the Cape of Good Hope with an expedition in 1497 and sailed to India. He was the first to establish an all-water route from Europe to the East and was instrumental in opening the spice trade of the Indies to the Portuguese. Da Gama established Portuguese colonies on Mozambique and Sofala.

**Dalton, John** (1766-1844), an English chemist, developed the first clear statements of the atomic theory of matter. He also established the law of multiple proportions, developed formulas of molecular atomic composition, and although it proved to be inaccurate, produced a table of atomic weights. He also made the first detailed description of color blindness (Daltonism).

**Dante Alighieri** (1265-1321), an Italian poet, wrote the *Divine Comedy.* Inspired by his love for a woman named Beatrice, the allegorical work describes the narrator's struggle through hell, purgatory, and heaven. Dante also wrote love poems, as well as prose works.

**Darius I** (558?-486 B.C.), called "the Great," ruled the Persian Empire as its king. In an invasion of Greece, his armies were defeated at the Battle of Marathon. Darius ran his empire efficiently, reorganizing the administration, building roads, and reforming the tax system. He died while preparing for a second invasion of Greece. His son Xerxes succeeded him.

**Darwin, Charles** (1809-1882), a British naturalist, in 1859 published *The Origin of Species,* a theory of evolution. He first began to develop the theory as the result of observations he made on a five-year voyage around the world. Darwin also wrote *The Descent of Man,* which deals with human evolution from lower animals.

**David** (?-973? B.C.), the successor to Saul, was the second king of Israel. He won fame as a boy for killing Goliath, the Philistine giant. A harpist, poet, and composer of psalms, David tried to make his kingdom secure with the defeat of several surrounding tribes, but his reign was troubled by rebellions. David was succeeded by Solomon, his son by Bathsheba.

**Da Vinci, Leonardo** (1452-1519), an Italian genius of the Renaissance, was a scientist, inventor, engineer, sculptor, and painter. Among his many accomplishments, he drew up plans for a flying machine, designed fortifications for Italian rulers, and wrote on astronomy and botany. His paintings include *The Last Supper* and *Mona Lisa*.

**Davis, Jefferson** (1808-1889), became president of the Confederate States of America in 1861. He had earlier served the United States government as a solider, as a representative and senator, and as secretary of war. After the Civil War, he spent two years in prison and then retired to Mississippi, where he wrote a defense of the Confederacy and of his presidency.

**Davy, Sir Humphry** (1778-1829), an English chemist, was the first scientist to isolate a number of elements, including potassium, sodium, strontium, calcium, and magnesium. He invented the Davy lamp, used in coal mining, and also experimented with "laughing gas" (nitrous oxide) as an anesthetic. Davy's interests were wide ranging, and he wrote several books on various subjects in chemistry.

**Debs, Eugene V.** (1855-1926), an American labor leader, formed the American Railway Union in the 1890's and as the result of a strike went to prison for contempt of court. Debs became a Socialist and ran for the presidency five times between 1900 and 1920. He conducted his last campaign while in prison for opposing United States participation in World War I.

**Degas, Edgar** (1834-1917), a French impressionistic painter, developed a style using pastel colors for spectacular effects. Although he painted some still lifes, his favorite subjects were the people of everyday life. He often painted ordinary people, such as women ironing or bathing.

**De Gaulle, Charles** (1890-1970), a French military leader and statesman, was the leader and symbol of the French resistance movement during World War II. As prime minister and later president of the Fifth Republic in the 1960's, he improved France's economy and ended the war with Algeria by granting independence to that colony. Although he was criticized for his dictatorial rule, De Gaulle brought stability to postwar France.

**Demosthenes** (384?-322 B.C.), an Athenian statesman who was regarded as the greatest of the Greek orators, was a lifelong defender of Greek independence. He spoke out frequently against Philip of Macedon's designs on Greece and formed an army to resist Macedonian invasion. When the Greeks met defeat, Demosthenes committed suicide rather than allow himself to be captured.

**Descartes, René** (1596-1650), a French mathematician and philosopher, devoted himself to settling questions about existence and reality. As a starting point, he argued that thought is proof of one's existence. From the existence of the self, he developed proofs of the existence of other realities and of the existence of God. Descartes' writings turned modern philosophy away from the concerns of the Middle Ages.

**De Soto, Hernando** (1500?-1542), a Spanish adventurer, accompanied Francisco Pizarro in the conquest of the Incas of Peru. Although he gained much wealth from the conquest, he later searched for more gold by leading a party to explore the lower Mississippi River Valley, the Ozark Mountains, and portions of the American Southeast, including Florida. De Soto died on the banks of the Mississippi and was buried in the river.

**Dewey, John** (1859-1952), an American philosopher, had a great influence on American educational practices. He taught that experience is fundamental and that the value of an idea lies in its results. In education, he emphasized learning through activity rather than lectures or memorization. Dewey became one of the leaders of the "progressive" movement in education.

**Dias, Bartolomeu** (1457?-1500), a Portuguese navigator, discovered the Cape of Good Hope in 1488, opening the path by sea from Europe to the East. Ten years later, Vasco da Gama duplicated Dias's feat but continued eastward to India, beginning Portuguese domination of the spice trade with the Indies. Dias also traded with Africa and sailed to Brazil.

**Dickens, Charles** (1812-1870), an English novelist, portrayed the lives of the lower classes in the 1800's. He often included social comments on the wretched conditions under which the poor lived and was credited with some social improvements that were made. His novels include *Pickwick Papers, David Copperfield, A Tale of Two Cities, Great Expectations, Bleak House,* and *A Christmas Carol.*

**Dickinson, Emily** (1830-1886), a poet who was unknown to the public in her lifetime, came to be considered among the greatest writers in American literature. Apparently because of her unfulfilled love for a married man, she withdrew from society to write on death, immortality, and love. By her own wish, her poems were not published during her lifetime. The first volume of Dickinson's poems was published in 1890.

**Didérot, Denis** (1713-1784), a French writer, edited an encyclopedia, a task that took him 20 years. A monumental work, the encyclopedia stressed scientific objectivity. Several other important French writers aided Didérot in his project, and it contained contributions from such influential French thinkers as Rousseau and Voltaire.

**Diocletian** (245?-313) was proclaimed Roman emperor at a time of great disunity. Dividing the empire into four separate and self-ruled districts, he tried to bring order after 50 years of civil war. Trying to restore the traditional Roman gods, Diocletian carried on severe persecutions of the Christians during much of his reign.

**Disraeli, Benjamin** (1804-1881), a British politician and statesman, was the only Jewish person to serve as prime minister of England. A novelist early in his life, he was elected to Parliament in 1837, becoming prime minister in 1868 and serving again from 1874 to 1880. During his terms, Disraeli strengthened British imperialism abroad.

**Dostoevsky, Fyodor** (1821-1881), a Russian novelist, often wrote about people who sought salvation through suffering as they struggled with good and evil. Accused of political conspiracy, he spent several years in prison in Siberia and was plagued by poverty and misfortune throughout his life. Among his novels are *The Brothers Karamazov*, *The Idiot*, and *The Possessed*.

**Douglas, Stephen A.** (1813-1861), a powerful representative and senator from Illinois, helped pass the Compromise of 1850. He promoted the idea of popular sovereignty—that the people of a territory should decide on slavery. His Kansas-Nebraska Bill in 1854, which was based on popular sovereignty, led to civil war in Kansas. His debates with Abraham Lincoln over slavery gained national attention for Lincoln, and Douglas was defeated in his bid for the presidency in 1860.

**Douglass, Frederick** (1817-1895), escaped slavery to become a writer and a leader in the antislavery movement. He founded a newspaper, during the Civil War raised black Union regiments, and later held several government posts. In the *Narrative of the Life of Frederick Douglass*, he wrote about his upbringing as a slave in Maryland and his life after escaping.

**Drake, Sir Francis** (1540?-1596), an English navigator and plunderer of Spanish treasure ships, sailed the *Golden Hind* around the world between 1577 and 1580. Returning to England with much Spanish wealth, he was knighted by Queen Elizabeth I. Drake later participated in the successful battles against the Spanish Armada that was sent to invade England.

**Du Bois, W. E. B.** (1868-1963), a black educator, writer, and leader, argued for black-white equality rather than gradual economic improvement for blacks. Du Bois wrote several books, including *The Souls of Black Folk*, about the lives of blacks in the United States. He helped form the National Association for the Advancement of Colored People in 1909.

**Dunbar, Paul Laurence** (1872-1906), a black American poet, became famous for poems written in dialect that expressed blacks' feelings. His poems were often humorous and were published in volumes that include *Majors and Minors, Joggin' Erlong, Lyrics of the Hearthside*, and *Lyrics of Lowly Life*. Dunbar became a model of achievement for blacks, and many schools were named after him.

**Duns Scotus** (1265?-1308), an English theologian, disagreed with his contemporary Thomas Aquinas on several theological and philosophical doctrines and founded a system called Scotism. He studied at Oxford and became a professor of theology there and at Paris and Cologne. Duns Scotus wrote commentaries on the Bible and on the Greek philosopher Aristotle.

**Earhart, Amelia** (1897-1937?), an American aviator, was the first woman passenger to cross the Atlantic Ocean by air and the first woman pilot to fly solo across the Atlantic. She was the first woman pilot to fly from Hawaii to the mainland of the United States and the first to cross the continent solo in both directions. Earhart disappeared in the Pacific Ocean under mysterious circumstances while on a round-the-world flight.

**Edison, Thomas Alva** (1847-1931), perhaps the foremost technological genius of his time, invented the electric light bulb and the phonograph. Edison also made improvements on the typewriter, storage battery, ticker tape machine, electric-powered train, and electric generator. Altogether, he produced more than 1,000 inventions.

**Edward the Confessor** (1002?-1066) codified Anglo-Saxon laws and built a church on the site of Westminster Abbey, where he is buried. Placed on the throne by the powerful Earl Godwin, Edward spent much of his reign quarreling with Godwin over policies involving both the state and religion. The king became interested in religion early in his life and was canonized by the Roman Catholic Church in 1161.

**Einstein, Albert** (1879-1955), a German-born mathematician and physicist, developed the theory of relativity and contributed to the quantum theory and numerous other discoveries in modern physics. A resident of the United States after 1933, he influenced the government to begin work on an atomic bomb. Einstein was awarded the Nobel prize for physics in 1921.

**Eleanor of Aquitaine** (1122?-1204) was the wife of Louis VII of France and later of Henry II of England. She was the mother of two English kings—Richard I, the Lion-Hearted, and John, the signer of the Magna Carta. England fought several wars to hold her lands in France, the beginning of centuries of hostility between the two countries. Eleanor herself was a party to intrigues involving her faithless English husband and her sons (see "Henry II" in this unit).

**Eliot, T. S.** (1888-1965), an American who became a British subject in 1927, was one of the most influential poets and critics of his time. Among his best-known poems are "The Love Song of J. Alfred Prufrock," *The Waste Land*, "Ash Wednesday," "The Hollow Men," and "Gerontion." Many of his poems involve religious themes. Eliot won the Nobel prize for literature in 1948.

**Elizabeth I** (1533-1603) ruled during a time of great expansion of English power and a time of great literary production. William Shakespeare lived during her reign, and English exploration and discovery overseas increased the country's position among European nations. In 1588, Elizabeth's navy defeated the Spanish Armada to make England the greatest sea power of the age.

**Elizabeth II** (1926-    ) is Queen of the United Kingdom of Great Britain and Northern Ireland. She is also head of the Commonwealth of Nations. Elizabeth was 25 years old when she succeeded to the throne of her father, George VI, in 1952. Her reign has been marked by frequent state visits to all parts of the Commonwealth. Elizabeth married Philip Mountbatten in 1947.

**Emerson, Ralph Waldo** (1803-1882), an American poet, philosopher, and essayist, was among the leading writers of his time and an associate of such literary figures as Henry David Thoreau and Walt Whitman. Emerson based his philosophy on individualism and self-reliance. *Concord Hymn* is among his most popular poems.

**Engels, Friedrich** (1820-1895), a German Socialist, collaborated with Karl Marx on *The Communist Manifesto*. Involved in revolutionary activity in Germany, Engels fled to England where he was a manufacturer and a leader of the Socialist movement. He edited and published many of Marx's writings. Engels' own writings include *The Condition of the Working Class in England*.

**Erasmus, Desiderius** (1466?-1536), a Dutch scholar, was a Christian humanist of the Renaissance. He favored internal reform of the Roman Catholic Church, rather than a break with the church. He stressed faith and grace over works. Erasmus lived and studied in several important university centers.

**Ericson, Leif** (about 1000), a Norse sailor and adventurer, has been credited with discovering North America long before Columbus. Sailing west, he came upon a land that he named Vinland because of the grapevines he found there. The land Ericson reached has been identified by different historians as the Labrador Peninsula, Newfoundland Island, or New England.

**Euclid** (about 300 B.C.), a Greek mathematician, was the founder of geometry. His work *The Elements* remained the foundation of geometry until the early 1900's. The text is a model of mathematical and logical thinking. Euclid lived in Alexandria, Egypt, during the reign of Ptolemy I, and founded a school for mathematicians there.

**Faraday, Michael** (1791-1867), an English physicist and chemist, made important discoveries in electromagnetism. He discovered that passing a magnet through a coil of copper wire produces a flow of electric current, a principle on which the electric motor and generator are based. As a chemist, Faraday developed the law of valences.

**Farragut, David G.** (1801-1870), was a Union naval commander in the Civil War. Known as "Old Salamander," he commanded Union forces blockading the South along the lower Mississippi River, and won fame for his victory at Mobile Bay, Ala., in 1864. Farragut also participated in many other military actions, including the Mexican War. He was a native of Virginia.

**Faulkner, William** (1897-1962), a Mississippi writer, portrayed Southern life in a place called Yoknapatawpha County that he created. He regretted the loss of traditional Southern values. Among his novels are *Sartoris*, *The Sound and the Fury*, *Absalom, Absalom!*, *Intruder in the Dust*, and *As I Lay Dying*. Faulkner won the Nobel prize for literature in 1949.

**Fermi, Enrico** (1901-1954), was a physicist whose work led to the development of the atomic bomb. He became professor of theoretical physics at the University of Rome in 1926, but he left Italy for the United States in 1938 after winning the Nobel prize for physics. At the University of Chicago in 1942, Fermi led a team that produced the first atomic chain reaction.

**Fleming, Sir Alexander** (1881-1955), a British bacteriologist, discovered penicillin, probably the most useful of all antibiotics. It proved to be an extremely useful drug during World War II and was credited with saving many lives. For his work in bacteriology, Fleming shared the Nobel prize in medicine in 1945.

**Ford, Henry** (1863-1947), a pioneer American automaker, made the automobile available to the middle class when he introduced the Model T— a plain but sturdy, reliable, and relatively inexpensive automobile. He developed the use of moving assembly lines and interchangeable parts in the manufacture of automobiles. He and his son established the Ford Foundation, a philanthropic organization.

**Francis of Assisi, Saint** (1181?-1226), an Italian cleric, abandoned a life of wealth and ease to embrace poverty. He founded the Franciscan order in 1209. Known as a gentle man, Francis was a missionary in Italy, Spain, and Egypt, and he visited Palestine. He was canonized by the Roman Catholic Church two years after his death.

**Franklin, Benjamin** (1706-1790), was perhaps the best-known person in the American Colonies. A signer of the Declaration of Independence and the Constitution, he was a philosopher, politician, inventor, scientist, diplomat, writer, printer, statesman, and civic leader of Philadelphia. Among his many literary works was *Poor Richard's Almanac*.

**Frederick I** (1121?-1190), known as Barbarossa or Red Beard, was a king of Germany and the Holy Roman Emperor. Often involved in unsuccessful conflicts with the pope, he set out on the Third Crusade, during which he drowned while crossing a river. His reign was marked by the advancement of learning and the development of towns and cities as well as by internal peace in his kingdom.

**Frémont, John C.** (1813-1890), was an explorer of the Western United States who won the nickname "the Pathfinder." He explored the area that is now Oregon, Nevada, and California and organized the seizure of California during the Mexican War. In 1856, Frémont became the first Republican candidate for the presidency. He led Union troops during the Civil War. Later, he served as territorial governor of Arizona.

**Freud, Sigmund** (1856-1939), an Austrian physician, founded psychoanalysis, a method of treating emotional problems through recall of repressed thoughts and feelings. Freud believed that the unconscious is a collection of memories that can govern human behavior. Freud also investigated the importance of infantile experiences, sexuality, and dreams. Among his writings are *The Interpretation of Dreams*, *Three Essays on the Theory of Sexuality*, and *General Introduction to Psychoanalysis*.

**Frobisher, Sir Martin** (1535?-1594), an English navigator during the reign of Elizabeth I, searched unsuccessfully for the Northwest Passage through North America. He reached Frobisher Bay, explored Labrador, and entered the Hudson Strait. He later participated in the sea battles against the Spanish Armada.

**Fulton, Robert** (1765-1815), an American artist, engineer, and inventor, developed the first practical steamboat, the *Clermont*, which in 1807 steamed up the Hudson River from New York City to Albany. He also invented a machine for spinning thread, a machine for weaving rope, a dredge for cutting channels for canals, and a successful submarine.

**Galen** (130?-200?), the foremost physician of the Roman world, made discoveries about human anatomy that became the basis of medicine for centuries. He studied anatomy at Alexandria, Egypt, and in Rome gave lectures, conducted anatomical demonstrations, and served as physician to gladiators. He wrote several books, and, even though his works contained many errors, his authority went unquestioned throughout much of the Middle Ages.

**Galileo** (1564-1642), an Italian astronomer and physicist, made important astronomical observations that confirmed the Copernican theory that the planets revolve around the sun. The Roman Catholic Church rejected his evidence and forced Galileo to recant his view. He built telescopes, discovered the law of the pendulum, and experimented with gravity.

**Gandhi, Mohandas K.** (1869-1948), the father of modern India, led the movement that forced Great Britain to grant India its independence in 1947. Trained as a lawyer, he fought discrimination in South Africa but returned to India to work for independence. Gandhi practiced passive resistance and civil disobedience and was frequently jailed for his actions.

**Garibaldi, Giuseppe** (1807-1882), was a leader of the movement that united Italy and was later a member of the Italian parliament. He led troops that freed Lombardy from Austria and conquered the Kingdom of the Two Sicilies. These areas became part of the Kingdom of Italy and were joined by Rome in 1870 to form the modern nation of Italy.

**Gauguin, Paul** (1848-1903), a French painter, produced brilliant canvases in bright colors with sweeping brushwork. Beginning his career as an impressionist, he was not well accepted. He left France for Tahiti, where he lived for most of the remainder of his life. In Tahiti, Gauguin produced some of his greatest paintings and won acclaim in Europe.

**Gauss, Karl Friedrich** (1777-1855), a German mathematician and astronomer, established the mathematical theory of electromagnetism. A child prodigy, he produced his first important original work at the age of 19. Gauss made numerous contributions to astronomy, geometry, algebra, and number theory. He also invented a form of the telescope.

**Genghis Khan** (1167-1227), a Mongol conqueror, successfully invaded northern China and turned his forces toward the west. He also conquered parts of the Middle East. Though a military genius, he left few permanent influences on the lands he conquered. His grandson, Kublai Khan, founded the Mongol dynasty in China.

**Geronimo** (1829-1909) was a chief of the southern Apache Indians, who resisted control by whites. Rather than go to a reservation, Geronimo moved his people from Arizona to Mexico. From there he led raids on American settlements. After surrendering in 1886, he and his tribe were sent to Oklahoma, where Geronimo spent the rest of his life.

**Giacometti, Alberto** (1901- 1966), a Swiss sculptor, portrayed exaggeratedly long and slender human figures. At first, his work brought him little attention or praise, but he began to receive recognition after World War II. His use of bronze and terra cotta and his unusual sense of space and proportion earned him a secure place among modern sculptors.

**Giotto** (1267?-1337), an Italian painter, architect, and sculptor, was among the first to portray human figures realistically in three instead of two dimensions. *The Descent from the Cross* and *The Madonna Enthroned with Saints* are two of his most famous paintings.

**Gladstone, William Ewart** (1809-1898), a British politician, began his long tenure of more than 60 years in Parliament as a Conservative but switched to the Liberal Party. He worked to expand suffrage, to increase elementary education, and to provide relief for Irish tenant farmers. Between 1868 and 1894, Gladstone served four terms as British prime minister.

**Glenn, John** (1921-     ), in 1962 became the first American astronaut to orbit the earth. In the spacecraft *Friendship 7*, he made three orbits during a flight of nearly five hours. As a naval pilot in 1957, Glenn made the first transcontinental nonstop flight in a supersonic aircraft. Glenn later became active in Democratic politics and was elected a senator from Ohio.

**Goddard, Robert Hutchings** (1882-1945), an American physicist, was a pioneer in the development of rockets. His experiments with solid and liquid rocket fuels, his work in the mathematical foundations of rocketry, and his many other discoveries led to the development of satellites, space exploration, and nuclear missiles.

**Goethe, Johann Wolfgang von** (1749-1832), a German poet and writer, inaugurated the romantic and modern movements in German literature. Among his works are the novel *The Sorrows of Young Werther,* a romantic love story, and the verse play *Egmont.* His play *Faust* is considered one of the most important works in modern Western literature.

**Gompers, Samuel** (1850-1924), an American labor leader born in England, was, except for one year, president of the American Federation of Labor from 1886 to 1924. He worked to improve the position of trade unionists and to abolish the court injunction as means of stopping strikes. Gompers supported free collective bargaining between employees and employers.

**Gorgas, William Crawford** (1854-1920), a United States Army physician, led a successful battle against yellow fever in Havana, Cuba. He became the chief sanitary officer of the Panama Canal Commission and eliminated yellow fever as a threat to workers building the canal. In 1914, Gorgas was made surgeon general of the Army.

**Goya, Francisco** (1746-1828), a Spanish artist, became the court painter, a position that brought him prosperity. His position, however, did not prevent him from painting subjects, including the royal family, as he saw them. Among his works are *The Family of Charles IV* and *The 3rd of May,* which depicts the French invasion of Spain. Goya also painted scenes of torture and of bullfighting.

**Greco, El** (1541?-1614), a painter, was born Domenikos Theotokopoulos in Crete but became famous in Spain, where he produced most of his work, as "the Greek." He painted many mystical religious scenes and landscapes, including *Christ Carrying the Cross* and *View of Toledo.*

**Greeley, Horace** (1811-1872), a newspaper editor and publisher, founded the *New York Tribune* in 1841. Greeley was influential in the antislavery movement and in efforts to ban alcoholic beverages. A Republican, he worked for the election of Abraham Lincoln. In 1872, the Liberal Republicans and Democrats formed a coalition to nominate Greeley for the presidency, but he lost the election to Ulysses S. Grant.

**Gropius, Walter** (1883-1969), a German-born architect, founded the Bauhaus school to coordinate the work of architects, artists, and building craftsmen. He created spare, functional designs that used materials in innovative ways. Beginning in 1937, Gropius taught at Harvard University and designed many buildings in the United States.

**Gutenberg, Johannes** (1395?-1486?), a German printer, invented type molds for casting individual letters. His invention made movable type practical. Gutenberg could produce any quantity of individual letters, arrange them into words, and place the type in a frame. His most famous production was the *Mazarin* (or *Gutenberg*) *Bible.*

**Hadrian** (76-138), a Roman emperor, improved the empire's fortifications, patronized the arts, curbed graft, and built many edifices in Rome. He had Salvius Julianus draw up a legal code that later became the basis for the Justinian Code. Hadrian established the Euphrates River as the empire's eastern boundary and visited Britain, where he supervised the building of Hadrian's Wall.

**Haile Selassie I** (1892-1975), the last emperor of Ethiopia, claimed descent from King Solomon and the Queen of Sheba. He established a constitution in 1931, but lost his throne when Italy conquered Ethiopia in 1936. He returned to power after Italy's defeat in Africa during World War II and ruled until he was deposed in 1974.

**Hamilton, Alexander** (1755?-1804), who helped draft the United States Constitution, was the first secretary of the treasury. As an advocate of a strong federal government, he established a tax system, a mint, and a central bank. An able but controversial politician and diplomat, Hamilton was killed in a duel with Vice-President Aaron Burr.

**Hammurabi** (ruled about 1850-1750 B.C.) ruled the Babylonian empire during its greatest period of growth and prosperity. He enlarged the empire, established price and wage controls, and set up an efficient system of taxation. He established the Code of Hammurabi, a set of laws containing almost 300 definitions of crime and punishment.

**Handel, George Frideric** (1685-1759), a composer born in Germany who became a British subject, wrote both religious and secular music. He wrote several oratorios, including the *Messiah*; more than 40 operas; and many instrumental works.

A favorite of the British royalty and people, he wrote *Water Music* and *Fireworks Music* for royal occasions.

**Hannibal** (247-183 B.C.) began training for the military early in life and became Carthage's greatest general. He fought the Romans in Spain, and led an army through the Alps on Rome in the Second Punic War. Finally defeated in North Africa by Scipio, Hannibal became the civilian leader of Carthage. Faced with Roman captivity, he committed suicide.

**Hardy, Thomas** (1840-1928), a British novelist and poet, studied architecture but devoted most of his life to literature, becoming one of the most popular writers of his time. Among his novels are *Tess of the D'Urbervilles*, *The Return of the Native*, *Far from the Madding Crowd*, *Jude the Obscure*, and *The Mayor of Casterbridge*.

**Harvey, William** (1578-1657), an English physician, demonstrated the route of the circulation of blood in the human body. Many who clung to the theories of the Greek physician Galen attacked Harvey vigorously. However, his conclusions, which were based on sound observations, were eventually accepted. Besides working in anatomy, Harvey also made contributions to embryology.

**Hawthorne, Nathaniel** (1804-1864), an American writer, used symbolism to explore moral issues and human psychology. His novels include *The Scarlet Letter* and *The House of the Seven Gables*. Hawthorne's best-known short stories include "Young Goodman Brown" and "Ethan Brand."

**Haydn, Joseph** (1732-1809), an Austrian composer, mastered the forms of the symphony and string quartet and established standards that influenced later composers. He wrote masses, several operas, oratorios, including *The Creation*, trios, more than 80 string quartets, and more than 100 symphonies. For many years, Haydn was supported by the Esterhazy family in Vienna.

**Hearst, William Randolph** (1863-1951), a powerful newspaper publisher, became famous for sensational news stories called "yellow journalism." He was partly responsible for arousing public opinion against Spain, which led to the Spanish-American War in 1898. Hearst's chain of newspapers made him wealthy, and he established a 240,000-acre estate, San Simeon, in California.

**Hegel, Georg Wilhelm Friedrich** (1770-1831), a German philosopher, was one of the most influential thinkers of the 1800's. He integrated earlier philosophies into a new system that stressed the historical sequence of philosophical ideas. His works include *Logic*, *Encyclopedia of the Philosophical Sciences*, and *Philosophy of Right*.

**Hemingway, Ernest** (1899-1961), one of the most popular American writers, was a master of a simple, terse prose style used to describe adventures that were concerned with moral values. He won the Pulitzer prize for fiction in 1953 and the Nobel prize in literature in 1954. Among his novels are *A Farewell to Arms*, *To Have and Have Not*, *The Sun Also Rises*, and *For Whom the Bell Tolls*.

**Henry, Patrick** (1736-1799), an American patriot known for his oratory, supported the Revolutionary cause in Virginia. A member of the Virginia House of Burgesses, he also served in the First Continental Congress and was on the committee that wrote Virginia's first state constitution. Henry was governor of Virginia during the Revolutionary War.

**Henry II** (1133-1189), through his marriage to Eleanor of Aquitaine, ruled over western France as well as England. When he quarreled with Thomas à Becket, the archbishop of Canterbury, over the power of the Roman Catholic Church, four of his knights murdered Becket. Henry II established the English common law and circuit courts. Late in his reign, his two sons led rebellions against him.

**Henry VIII** (1491-1547), who had six wives, brought about a church-state crisis with the divorce from his first wife. The divorce led to England's break with the Roman Catholic Church and the establishment of the Church of England. Two of his wives, Anne Boleyn and Catherine Howard, were executed. Henry VIII unified power in England and improved the English navy.

**Henson, Matthew** (1867-1955), a black man, gained fame as the only American to accompany American explorer Robert E. Peary to the North Pole in 1909. For more than 20 years, he went on expeditions with Peary and was often honored for his part in the explorations. Henson wrote *A Negro Explorer at the North Pole*.

**Heraclitus** (500's or 400's B.C.), a Greek philosopher, made change the basis of his teachings. He believed that everything constantly changes but that change is guided by logos, or intelligent laws. Heraclitus became known as "the weeping philosopher" because of his gloomy view that there are no lasting things in life.

**Herodotus** (484?-424? B.C.), called the "Father of History," traveled throughout most of the known world of the time and reported and commented on the customs, religion, and behavior of the people he came in contact with. Born in Asia Minor, he wrote a comprehensive history of the Persian empire, describing its beginnings, rise, and unsuccessful invasions of Greece.

**Hertz, Heinrich** (1857-1894), a German physicist, discovered electromagnetic waves and described their important characteristics. He demonstrated that the transmission of ultrahigh-frequency waves would produce oscillations in a distant wire loop. The development of radio, radar, and television was made possible by Hertz's discoveries.

**Heyerdahl, Thor** (1914-    ), a Norwegian ethnologist, in 1947 sailed a balsa-wood raft from Peru to islands in Polynesia to demonstrate that Polynesia could have been settled by ancient Peruvians. He told of his adventures on the trip in *Kon-Tiki*. Later, Heyerdahl and others built a reed boat, called *Ra-2*, in which they sailed from Africa to the West Indies.

**Hidalgo, Miguel** (1753-1811), a revolutionary Mexican priest, was one of the early leaders in the Mexican independence movement. Rallying followers in the village of Dolores, he marched south toward Mexico City. Although Hidalgo won some victories, the Spanish finally defeated his forces and captured him. Hidalgo was put to death, but his campaign began the war for Mexican independence.

**Hillary, Sir Edmund** (1919-    ), a New Zealand mountain climber and author, in 1953 with a companion became the first person to reach the top of Mount Everest in the Himalayas. He later led an expedition to climb Mount Makalu I. His books describing his experiences include *High Adventure* and *High in the Thin Cold Air*.

**Hippocrates** (460?-377? B.C.), a Greek physician called the "Father of Medicine," was the first to show that diseases have natural causes. He prescribed medicines and diets, practiced surgery, and set broken bones. Hippocrates formulated rules of conduct for doctors that became the basis for the Hippocratic oath.

**Hitler, Adolf** (1889-1945), the leader of the Nazi Party, ruled Germany from 1933 to 1945. He rearmed Germany and began World War II with an invasion of Poland in 1939. Hitler planned to conquer Europe and to exterminate all Jews. At first successful, German armies later met defeat by the Allies. Hitler committed suicide in an underground bomb shelter.

**Hobbes, Thomas** (1588-1679), an English philosopher, developed the theory that government arises as a social contract to protect the rights of individuals. He argued that, because humans are selfish, they need the rule of an all-powerful sovereign. Also a writer on physics and psychology, he believed that only matter exists. His most famous work is *Leviathan*, in which he describes his political theory.

**Ho Chi Minh** (1890-1969) led Vietnam to independence from France after World War II and became the founder and president of the Democratic Republic of Vietnam (then North Vietnam). A Socialist and later a Communist, he conducted a long war to unify North and South Vietnam, a campaign that eventually succeeded in 1975, after his death.

**Holmes, Oliver Wendell** (1809-1894), an American physician and medical educator, was better known as an essayist, poet, and novelist. His *The Autocrat of the Breakfast-Table* is a collection of essays, many humorous. Holmes's most popular poems include "Old Ironsides," "The Last Leaf," and "The Wonderful One-Hoss Shay."

**Holmes, Oliver Wendell, Jr.** (1841-1935), an American jurist, served for nearly 30 years on the Supreme Court of the United States, after having been a law professor at Harvard University and a justice on the Massachusetts Supreme Judicial Court. He believed in judicial restraint and in social experimentation. Holmes won attention for his dissenting opinions on many Supreme Court cases.

**Homer** (about 800? B.C.) was the reputed author of the Greek epic poems *The Iliad* and *The Odyssey*, which tell the story of the Trojan War and of Odysseus' long journey from Troy back to Greece. There has been a long controversy among scholars over whether the epics were the work of several authors or of only one. Other poems once attributed to Homer are now thought to be the work of other poets.

**Homer, Winslow** (1836-1910), was a painter who portrayed objects realistically but with drama and vitality. A war correspondent with Union troops during the Civil War, he painted such popular war pictures as *Prisoners from the Front.* Homer painted many seascapes of the Atlantic Coast.

**Hooke, Robert** (1635-1703), an English scientist, described the law of elasticity and the kinetic theory of gases. He made important astronomical observations and discoveries about the earth's and the moon's gravity. He also developed a reflecting telescope, a marine barometer, and a spring to regulate watches. Hooke is also credited with having discovered plant cells.

**Houston, Samuel** (1793-1863), born a Virginian, represented Tennessee in Congress and was governor of the state. He moved to Texas and worked for independence from Mexico and for admission of Texas to the Union. Houston became president of the Republic of Texas and, later, governor of the state and a senator from Texas.

**Howe, Elias** (1819-1867), an American inventor, in 1846 became the first person to patent a workable sewing machine. He found little interest for his invention in the United States and scarcely more in England, where he sold manufacturing rights. When other people in the United States began to manufacture sewing machines, Howe began a long and successful lawsuit to protect his patent.

**Hudson, Henry** (?-1611), an English navigator and explorer, made discoveries in the New World for Holland and England, giving each country some claims to land. He explored the Hudson River, Hudson Strait, and Hudson Bay. On his fourth voyage, his crew mutinied and cast him and eight others adrift in a small boat that apparently was lost.

**Hughes, Langston** (1902-1967), was a black American poet and writer. Many of his poems were set to music, and they were translated into several languages. His works include *Not Without Laughter, Shakespeare in Harlem, I Wonder As I Wander, The Weary Blues*, and *The Ways of White Folks.*

**Huygens, Christian** (1629-1695), was a Danish astronomer, mathematician, and physicist. The first to use a pendulum to regulate a clock, he also developed the wave theory of light, improved methods of grinding lenses, constructed telescopes, and discovered a satellite and a ring of Saturn. Huygens also invented the measuring device known as the micrometer.

**Ibn Khaldun** (1332-1406), considered the greatest Arab historian, wrote a history of the known world. Born in Tunis in North Africa, he saw history as a series of civilizations, each growing and expanding through cooperation and then declining because of corruption and selfishness. Ibn Khaldun held government posts in Egypt for several years and also wrote an *Autobiography.*

**Ibsen, Henrik** (1828-1906), a Norwegian playwright, is often called the father of modern drama. His works are realistic—that is, they deal with real-life social problems in a direct manner. Some of Ibsen's best-known plays are *A Doll's House, An Enemy of the People*, and *Hedda Gabler.* Ibsen worked in the theater in Norway, as a stage manager, and later received a grant to travel and write.

**Ikhnaton** (1300's B.C.), an Egyptian pharaoh also known as Akhenaton, was married to Nefertiti and was the first Egyptian ruler to promote the worship of one deity. He tried to abolish belief in many gods among the Egyptians and to make Aton, the sun god, the only deity. The movement did not survive his death. Ikhnaton was the father-in-law of Tutankhamon.

**Innocent III** (1160?-1216) exercised perhaps the greatest power of any Roman Catholic Pope. Using his power to excommunicate and to mete out spiritual punishment, he dealt harshly with European monarchs such as Otto IV of Swabia and John of England. He promoted the Fourth Crusade, which resulted in the capture of Constantinople. Innocent III convened Lateran IV, a council that dealt extensively with Church doctrine.

**Ivan IV** (1530-1584) was the first czar of Russia. He conquered the area along the Volga River, expanded Russia into Siberia, made Moscow the capital, and reduced the power of the nobility. He acquired the name "the Terrible" because of his cunning and cruelty and because he killed his own son.

**Jackson, Thomas J.** (1824-1863), a Confederate general of the Civil War, earned the nickname "Stonewall" for his stand against Union forces at the first battle at Bull Run, Va., in 1861. A religious man much loved by his troops, Jackson was considered one of the Confederacy's finest generals. He was accidentally killed by his own men during a battle at Chancellorsville, Va.

**James, Henry** (1843-1916), an American novelist and short-story writer, often wrote from the point of view of one of his characters and emphasized human relationships and the individual in relation to society. Among his novels are *The American*, *The Portrait of a Lady*, *Daisy Miller*, *Washington Square* and *The Bostonians*. James spent much of his life in Europe.

**Jay, John** (1745-1829), was the first chief justice of the United States. A diplomat and lawyer, he served in the Continental Congress, conducted foreign affairs, worked for the ratification of the Constitution, and negotiated a treaty with England. Jay served on the Supreme Court from 1790 to 1795. He was elected governor of New York and resigned from the Supreme Court in 1795.

**Jenner, Edward** (1749-1823), a British physician, discovered vaccination. He developed a smallpox vaccine that used cowpox virus to immunize against the disease. By 1800, Jenner's vaccine was widely accepted. He received many honors, including a grant from Parliament and an honorary degree in medicine from Oxford University.

**Jesus Christ** (dates uncertain, but about 8 B.C. to A.D. 29) proclaimed the moral and theological teachings that became the foundation of the Christian religion. Accompanied by twelve disciples, He was a critic and teacher who was credited with healing and other miracles. Although many accepted Jesus as the Messiah, Jewish religious leaders condemned Him. He was executed by crucifixion but, according to the Gospels, arose in three days and, after many days teaching His disciples, ascended into heaven.

**Joan of Arc, Saint** (1412-1431), a French peasant girl, believed that she heard voices directing her to aid her country. She led a French army to victory over the English at Orleans in 1429 and defeated the English in other battles. Later imprisoned by the English, she was tried as a witch and heretic by the French and burned at the stake. The Roman Catholic Church canonized her in 1920.

**Jones, John Paul** (1747-1792), was an American naval commander during the Revolutionary War. He won several engagements against the British, the greatest as commander of the *Bonhomme Richard*, which defeated the British ship *Serapis*. After the war Jones wrote on naval tactics and, at the invitation of the Empress Catherine, served for a time in the Russian navy.

**Joyce, James** (1882-1941), an Irish writer, created some of the most complex and difficult masterpieces of modern literature in the English language. His major works include the novels *A Portrait of the Artist as a Young Man* and *Finnegan's Wake* and the short-story collection *Dubliners*. Though Joyce lived away from Ireland after 1904, he set all of his work in Ireland and continued to explore the character of the Irish people.

**Juárez, Benito** (1806-1872), worked to establish constitutional government in Mexico and to end foreign interference in the government. An Indian, he was elected president of Mexico in 1861. When the French invaded Mexico, Juárez led a successful war against them and captured Maximilian, who had been offered the throne by Mexican nobles under French influence. Juárez was elected to two additional terms as president; he is regarded as a great hero of Mexican independence.

**Jung, Carl** (1875-1961), a Swiss psychologist and psychiatrist, was influenced by Sigmund Freud but also developed his own theories, called analytical psychology. Like Freud, Jung stressed the importance of the unconscious, but he also emphasized the importance of "racial memory" and the will to live. In treating patients, he focused on present problems rather than childhood trauma. Jung originated the distinction between introverts and extroverts.

**Justinian I** (482-565), called "the Great," was an emperor of the eastern Roman Empire. In wars against Vandals, Huns, and Franks, he won back much of the original empire that had been lost. He was responsible for the Corpus Juris Civilis, known as the Justinian Code, a body of civil law he had drawn up to govern his realm. The code became the basis for most European law.

**Kant, Immanuel** (1724-1804), a German philosopher, examined the nature and limits of human knowledge in the *Critique of Pure Reason*. For Kant, knowledge comes from the mind's involvement with the objects it experiences, and so the nature of human knowledge depends partly on the nature of the mind. He also wrote *Critique of Practical Reason*, a work on ethics that argued for absolute moral standards.

**Keats, John** (1795-1821), was an English romantic poet who expressed experiences of the senses, as well as ideas, in his works. Among Keats's best known poems are "Endymion," "Hyperion," "The Eve of St. Agnes," "On a Grecian Urn," and "La Belle Dame sans Merci." Plagued by poor health, he contracted tuberculosis and died in Italy, a young man.

**Keller, Helen** (1880-1968), became a famous American lecturer and writer even though she had lost her sight and hearing before she was 2 years old. Taught to speak and to read and write in braille, she graduated from high school and college. She devoted her life to working on behalf of the blind and published several books about her experiences.

**Kelvin, William Thomson, Lord** (1824-1907), a British mathematician and physicist, invented the mirror galvanometer and the siphon recorder and was an electrical engineer in charge of laying the Atlantic cable. He established a thermodynamic scale with -273.15 C as absolute zero. Lord Kelvin also contributed inventions and discoveries in numerous other fields.

**Kenyatta, Jomo** (1890?-1978), a leader for African independence, fought for the freedom of Kenya from British rule after World War II. He spent some time in jail for anti-British activities. When Kenya became free in 1963 after years of strife, Kenyatta became president of the new nation and became one of the important spokesmen for Africa in the 1970's.

**Kepler, Johannes** (1571-1630), a German astronomer and mathematician, discovered three important laws of planetary motion. One of these laws states that planets have elliptical, or oval, orbits—rather than circular orbits. Kepler was the first astronomer to support Copernicus' findings openly. When his friend and colleague Tycho Brahe died, Kepler was appointed imperial mathematician by Rudolph II, the Holy Roman Emperor.

**Key, Francis Scott** (1779-1843), an American lawyer, wrote the poem that was used as the lyrics of "The Star-Spangled Banner." From an American warship, he witnessed the bombardment of Fort McHenry in the harbor of Baltimore during the War of 1812. The successful American defense of the fort inspired Key to write the poem which Congress made the national anthem in 1931.

**Keynes, John Maynard** (1883-1946), an English economist who was an adviser to the British government, achieved worldwide attention with his book *The Economic Consequences of the Peace.* He argued that governments should stimulate the economy with spending during times of slowdown to prevent unemployment and depression. His writings on government and economics became very influential.

**King, Martin Luther, Jr.** (1929-1968), was the foremost black leader of the civil rights movement in the 1950's and 1960's. A Baptist minister who believed in passive resistance and nonviolent civil disobedience, Dr. King led many demonstrations against racial discrimination in the United States and spent time in jail. One of his most important public rallies was a "March on Washington" that brought thousands to the capital. Dr. King received the Nobel peace prize in 1964. He was assassinated in Memphis, Tenn.

**Kipling, Rudyard** (1865-1936), an English writer, was born in India and lived there for several years. India was the setting for many of his stories, novels, and poems. Among Kipling's popular works are *The Jungle Book, The Light That Failed, Just So Stories,* and *Barrack-Room Ballads,* which includes the poems "Gunga Din" and "On the Road to Mandalay." He was awarded the Nobel prize in literature in 1907.

**Klee, Paul** (1879-1940), a Swiss artist, developed an original style used to express the subconscious mind and fantasy. Living much of his life in Germany, he founded a movement called Blue Four in collaboration with German abstract artists. Klee taught for a time at the Bauhaus, a German school of design founded by the architect Walter Gropius.

**Knox, John** (1515?-1572), a Scottish Protestant theologian, statesman, and writer, successfully worked to develop the Presbyterian denomination in Scotland to establish Presbyterianism as the official religion. Knox preached a stern and righteous doctrine and was a bitter enemy of Mary, Queen of Scots, a Roman Catholic who was queen of Scotland.

**Koch, Robert** (1843-1910), a German physician and bacteriologist, developed a method of growing and observing bacteria and found a vaccine for preventing anthrax in cattle. He also isolated the germ that causes tuberculosis and conducted research on bubonic plague in India and on other diseases. Koch won the 1905 Nobel prize in physiology or medicine.

**Kosciusko, Thaddeus** (1746-1817), a Polish patriot, arrived in America in 1776 to take part in the Revolutionary War. He participated in the Battle of Saratoga and built fortifications on the Hudson River. Returning to Poland, Kosciusko fought unsuccessfully to prevent the partition of his country among Prussia, Russia, and Austria.

**Kublai Khan** (1216-1294), established the Yüan, or Mongol, dynasty of China after expanding the conquests of his grandfather, Genghis Khan. He completed the conquest of China and made Peking his capital. Kublai Khan attempted unsuccessfully to conquer Java and Japan. He treated the people he conquered humanely and was a patron of arts and letters.

**La Salle, Robert Cavelier, Sieur de** (1643-1687), a French explorer in the New World, explored the Mississippi River Valley and claimed to have first reached the Ohio River. He named Louisiana and claimed the Mississippi Valley for France. Named viceroy of North America by Louis XIV, La Salle attempted unsuccessfully to establish a colony at the mouth of the Mississippi.

**Lavoisier, Antoine Laurent** (1743-1794), a French chemist, wrote the first chemical equation. He also gave the first scientific analysis of fire. Lavoisier was the author of *Elements of Chemistry*, the first modern chemistry textbook. Because he was a member of a financial company associated with the government, Lavoisier was put to death as an aristocrat during the French Revolution.

**Lee, Robert E.** (1807-1870), a Confederate general, commanded troops in the East in the Civil War. For a time, he successfully fought off Northern invasion of the South. When he tried to carry the war to the North, he met disastrous defeat at Gettysburg. His army was worn down by General Ulysses S. Grant, and in 1865 Lee surrendered at Appomattox Court House in Virginia.

**Lewis, Meriwether** (1774-1809), an American explorer, led an expedition with William Clark to explore the Louisiana Purchase. The party moved up the Missouri River from a point near St. Louis, crossed the Great Divide, and traveled down the Columbia River to the Pacific Ocean. The expedition returned with much valuable information on the new territory.

**Liliuokalani** (1838-1917), the last queen of Hawaii, had only a two-year reign. Wealthy American settlers on the islands led a revolt against her and established a republic in 1893. She tried in vain to reclaim her throne. After some hesitation because of the circumstances under which the queen had been deposed, the United States Congress in 1898 voted to annex Hawaii as a territory.

**Lindbergh, Charles A.** (1902-1974), became in 1927 the first person to fly solo nonstop across the Atlantic Ocean. Taking off from Long Island, N.Y., he landed in Paris 33½ hours later. A rich and famous man, he promoted commercial and military aviation. The kidnapping and murder of his son was the most sensational crime of the 1930's. Lindbergh's biography, *The Spirit of St. Louis*, won a Pulitzer prize in 1954.

**Linnaeus, Carolus** (1707-1778), a Swedish botanist and naturalist, developed a system for classifying plants and animals according to genus and species. Also a physician, a teacher, and a writer of several books on plants, Linnaeus is considered the founder of the modern system of botanical names.

**Lister, Sir Joseph** (1827-1912), an English surgeon, founded antiseptic (germ-free) surgery. Realizing the role played by bacteria in infections, Lister used carbolic acid to kill bacteria in operating rooms and on instruments. Because of his work, mortality rates after surgery, formerly very high, were reduced to a small percentage of those operated on.

**Livingstone, David** (1813-1873), a Scottish missionary and explorer in Africa, reached Lake Ngami, explored the Zambezi River, and reached Victoria Falls. Disappearing for a time, he was found and rescued by Henry M. Stanley, a newspaperman. Livingstone continued exploration and missionary work in Africa until his death there.

**Livy** (59 B.C.-A.D. 17), a Roman historian during the reign of Augustus, wrote *History from the Founding of the City*, a history in 142 volumes. Written over a period of 40 years, only 35 of the books have survived. Although Livy included legends and myths in his work, it is considered a principal source on the history of Rome.

**Locke, John** (1632-1704), an English philosopher, also wrote on education, psychology, and political theory. Locke believed that a government exists to promote the welfare of the people, and that if it does not do so, the people have a right to change it. His ideas were used to justify the American Revolution.

**London, Jack** (1876-1916), an American writer, became famous for novels and short stories about dogs, such as *The Call of the Wild* and *White Fang*, and his tales of the sea. An adventurer in Alaska and at sea, in his writings London reflected his interest in primitive violence as well as his socialistic political opinions.

**Longfellow, Henry Wadsworth** (1807-1882), was a poet and a teacher of languages and literature. He was the most popular American literary figure of his time. Longfellow spent 18 years as a professor at Harvard University. Among his best known poems are *The Courtship of Miles Standish*, an account of life among the Pilgrims, and *The Song of Hiawatha*, which he based on an Indian legend.

**Louis XIV** (1638-1715), the Sun King, became the ruler of France at the age of 4. Presiding over a glittering court, he encouraged the arts, and the writers of his time contributed much to French literature. Louis XIV also led France into four major wars. Although a great monarch in many respects, his wars left France in debt with declining influence in Europe.

**Louis XVI** (1745-1793), suffered the consequences of misrule by the French monarchy when the French Revolution began. He was forced to call a meeting of the national assembly, which had not met for 175 years. Captured while trying to flee France, Louis XVI and his queen, Marie Antoinette, were executed by guillotine.

**Luther, Martin** (1483-1546), originally a German priest in the Roman Catholic Church, criticized corruption and broke with the church in 1517 to establish the Protestant Reformation. He believed that faith, rather than works, is the basis of salvation. Luther's teachings became the foundation for the Lutheran and other Protestant denominations that were formed in Europe.

**MacArthur, Douglas** (1880-1964), commanded United States forces in the Pacific area during World War II. His "island-hopping" strategy pushed Japan toward defeat. He later headed the occupation government in Japan. MacArthur commanded United Nations forces in the Korean War until 1951 when, following disputes with

President Harry S. Truman, he was relieved of his command.

**Machiavelli, Niccoló** (1469-1527), an Italian Renaissance literary figure and statesman, wrote *The Prince*, a book on practical politics. He was a member of the Florentine government from 1498 to 1512. Machiavelli's political writings emphasized that the first consideration of a ruler must be success, not morality.

**Magellan, Ferdinand** (1480?-1521), a Portuguese navigator, led the first expedition to sail around the world. Leaving Spain in 1519, the fleet rounded Cape Horn on South America and proceeded across the Pacific Ocean. Although Magellan was killed in the Philippine Islands, one ship survived the remainder of the journey and reached Spain in 1522.

**Malthus, Thomas Robert** (1766-1834), an English clergyman and economist, wrote *Essay on the Principle of Population*, in which he argued that population growth tends to outrun food supplies and that excessive population growth encourages war and disease epidemics. He was pessimistic about the possibility of human survival unless population growth were checked. Malthus was also a history professor.

**Manet, Édouard** (1832-1883), a French painter, was a forerunner of the impressionists. Influenced by painters such as Goya, Velázquez, and Rembrandt, Manet produced flatly silhouetted forms that became popular. Among his works are *Le Bon Bock, Luncheon on the Grass, The Absinthe Drinkers, Argenteuil*, and *Boating*.

**Mann, Horace** (1796-1859), was a politician and educational reformer who did much to promote free public schools in the United States. He founded the first state normal school in the nation, in Lexington, Mass., and improved public control and financial support for schools in the state. He later served as president of Antioch College in Ohio.

**Mann, Thomas** (1875-1955), had a long literary career in which he became perhaps the foremost German novelist of the 1900's. He left Germany in 1933 when the Nazis came to power. Among his many complex and difficult works are *Buddenbrooks, Joseph and His Brothers, Doctor Faustus, Mario and the Magician, Death in Venice, Tonio Kröger*, and *The Magic Mountain*.

**Mao Tse-tung** (1893-1976), the leader of the Chinese Communist revolution, based his movement on the peasants. In the 1930's, he led his followers to northern China, established a government, and fought Japanese invaders. After the Communist victory over Nationalist Chinese forces in 1949, Mao became both chairman of the party and head of state.

**Marconi, Guglielmo** (1874-1937), an Italian engineer and inventor, developed wireless telegraphy. He produced the first practical wireless telegraph in 1895 and sent the first transatlantic signal in 1901. His other inventions included a magnetic detector and a directional aerial. In 1909, Marconi shared the Nobel prize in physics.

**Marcus Aurelius** (121-180), a Roman emperor, was also a learned Stoic philosopher. Although he is considered one of the few "good emperors" of Rome, his reign was marked by barbarian invasions, wars, epidemics, severe economic difficulties, and persecution of Christians.

**Maria Theresa** (1717-1780), was the Holy Roman empress, the archduchess of Austria, and the queen of Hungary and Bohemia. The War of the Austrian Succession and the Seven Years' War shrank her empire, but she remained an influential monarch during her long reign of nearly 40 years.

**Marie Antoinette** (1755-1793), the daughter of Maria Theresa, was the wife of King Louis XVI of France. She was blamed for being extravagant, frivolous, and insensitive, particularly to the poor. During the French Revolution, she and the king attempted to flee the country. They were captured, tried, and executed by guillotine.

**Marquette, Jacques** (1637-1675), a French Jesuit missionary and explorer, made an expedition with the fur trader Louis Joliet that followed the Mississippi River as far south as the Arkansas River. For a number of years, he did missionary work among American Indians. One of the most important French explorers of America, Marquette kept a journal of his Mississippi voyage, which was published posthumously.

**Marshall, John** (1755-1835), was one of the most influential justices of the United States. During his 34-year term, he made the Supreme Court of the United States an important branch of the government. By affirming the power to declare laws un-constitutional, many of his decisions strengthened the power of the Court. He also increased the power of the federal government over the states.

**Marx, Karl** (1818-1883), a German philosopher, collaborated with Friedrich Engels on *The Communist Manifesto*. A Socialist who was forced to leave Germany for England, he wrote *Das Kapital*, an analysis of capitalism that became the basis for the Communist movement. Marx believed that economic conditions govern human behavior.

**Mary, Queen of Scots** (1542-1587), the daughter of King James V of Scotland and the mother of James I of England, was one of the last Roman Catholic rulers of Scotland. When revolt forced her to flee Scotland in 1568, she found refuge in England with her cousin, Queen Elizabeth I. Found guilty of aiding a plot to overthrow Elizabeth, Mary was beheaded.

**Mather, Cotton** (1663-1728), was an influential Puritan clergyman. The son of a minister, Increase Mather, Cotton Mather was considered a prime mover behind the witchcraft trials in Massachusetts in the 1690's. He wrote on many subjects, including the history of New England. Deeply interested in science and education, Mather became one of the founders of Yale College.

**Mazzini, Giuseppe** (1805-1872), an Italian patriot, spent many years in exile for his efforts to unify Italy. An advocate of a republic, he was displeased when Italy, except for Rome, was unified in 1861 under a king. He tried to organize a republican revolt in Sicily but failed. Mazzini died before his dream of a united republican Italy was fulfilled.

**Mead, Margaret** (1901-1978), an anthropologist, made firsthand studies of island societies in the South Pacific. She was also a commentator on the problems of contemporary American society. She was curator of technology at the American Museum of Natural History in New York City. Among her writings are *Coming of Age in Samoa*, *Growing Up in New Guinea*, and *Male and Female*.

**Medici, Lorenzo** (1449-1492), known as "the Magnificent," was a member of the Medici family that ruled Florence, Italy, during the Renaissance. Although an immoral and tyrannical ruler, he encouraged the building of libraries and other public structures, making Florence one of the world's most beautiful cities. He himself was a learned man and an accomplished writer and poet.

**Meir, Golda** (1898-1978), born in Russia and a long-time resident of Milwaukee, emigrated to Palestine, became active in the Zionist movement, and served as prime minister of Israel from 1969 to 1974. She was also a minister to the Soviet Union, minister of labor, and minister for foreign affairs. Meir was secretary-general of the Mapai (Labor) Party from 1966 to 1969.

**Melville, Herman** (1819-1891), an American writer, based several of his books on his experiences as a seaman in the South Pacific. His most famous novel, *Moby Dick*, recounts the destructive efforts of Captain Ahab to capture a whale. Melville's other works, most of which are about the struggle between good and evil, include *Redburn, Billy Budd,* and *The Confidence-Man.*

**Mendel, Gregor Johann** (1822-1884), an Austrian monk and botanist, established that certain characteristics of animals and plants are inherited. He also determined that certain characteristics are dominant and others recessive. His conclusions were based on extensive work in breeding garden peas. Mendel laid the foundations for the modern study of heredity and genetics.

**Mendeleev, Dmitri** (1834-1907), a Russian chemist, developed the periodic table of the elements, which gave a system to the properties of elements. On the basis of the table, he predicted the existence of elements that were then unknown but were later discovered. Mendeleev also made contributions to meteorology as well as to petroleum chemistry.

**Metternich, Prince von** (1773-1859), an Austrian statesman and minister of foreign affairs, guided the establishment of the Holy Alliance in 1815 following the Napoleonic Wars. He created a European balance of power that lasted until 1914. Antidemocratic in his politics, Metternich helped suppress nationalistic and democratic revolts in Europe in the 1840's.

**Michelangelo** (1475-1564) was an Italian painter, architect, sculptor, and poet of the Renaissance. He painted the frescoes on the ceiling of the Sistine Chapel in Rome and *The Last Judgment* on one wall. Michelangelo designed a chapel and tombs for the Medici family. Among his sculptures are the *Pietà* and a colossal figure of David.

**Mies van der Rohe, Ludwig** (1886-1969), a German-born architect, used glass, steel, and brick to create buildings with simple, even austere, lines. His work includes the Seagram Building in New York City; several buildings on the campus of the Illinois Institute of Technology in Chicago, where he taught after 1938; and apartment buildings in Chicago.

**Mill, John Stuart** (1806-1873), an English economist and philosopher, favored women's rights, higher pay for workers, and cooperative agriculture, among other progressive causes. Among Mill's works are *System of Logic, On Liberty,* and *Principles of Political Economy.* His book *Utilitarianism* explains his philosophy that pleasure, in its widest sense, is the basis for human action.

**Milton, John** (1608-1674), an English poet, wrote his greatest works, *Paradise Lost, Paradise Regained,* and *Samson Agonistes,* after he had become totally blind. A Puritan, he wrote on politics and on religion in such works as *The Tenure of Kings and Magistrates* and *Of Reformation in England.* Milton also wrote *Areopagitica,* a defense of freedom of the press.

**Monet, Claude** (1840-1926), a French painter, was a leader of impressionism, a name that derived from his painting *Impression: Sunrise.* His technique was to place separate spots of color side by side in such a way that the eye would blend them from a distance. Among his other paintings are *The Haystacks* and *The Thames.*

**Montesquieu** (1689-1755), was a French philosopher and writer who satirized contemporary French society and wrote a history of Rome. His *The Spirit of the Laws* deals with different forms of government. Montesquieu believed that governmental checks and balances among the executive, judicial, and legislative branches are necessary. His ideas formed the basis for the separation of powers in the United States Constitution.

**More, Saint Thomas** (1477?-1535), an English statesman, served King Henry VIII as lord chancellor. He opposed Henry's plan to divorce his first wife. After Henry VIII established the Church of England, More continued his opposition and was tried for treason and beheaded. He wrote *Utopia,* a futuristic work describing practices such as communal ownership, universal education, and religious toleration.

**Morgan, John Pierpont** (1837-1913), was one of the most powerful financiers in American history.

His banking house in New York City financed many new industries across the country and marketed government bonds. He helped organize the United States Steel Corporation. Although he gave much money for education and philanthropy, Morgan was criticized for the considerable financial power that he wielded.

**Morse, Samuel F. B.** (1791-1872), best known for his invention of the telegraph, was also a painter and a sculptor. He spent many years developing a device that would transmit sound by means of electric wires, and with associates carried out a successful test of the telegraph in 1844. His success won Morse fame and wealth.

**Moses** (1200? B.C.), a great leader of the Israelites, was born in Egypt. To escape Egyptian persecution, Moses led his people across the Red Sea to the Promised Land of Palestine. On the journey, he received the Ten Commandments from God on Mount Sinai. Although he saw Palestine from a distance, Moses did not live to enter the Promised Land.

**Mozart, Wolfgang Amadeus** (1756-1791), an Austrian composer, wrote operas, chamber music, concertos, symphonies, and church music. He was a child prodigy. Among his most popular works are the operas *Don Giovanni* and *The Magic Flute*. Mozart wrote 41 symphonies, including the *Jupiter* (Number 41).

**Muhammad** (570?-632), the Prophet, founded the religion of Islam, whose followers are called Muslims. A trader in Mecca in Arabia, at about age 40 he experienced visions that led him to become a prophet and teacher. He became a civic as well as a religious leader in Medina and attracted many converts. Many of his teachings were collected in the Koran.

**Muñoz Marín, Luis** (1898-1980), formerly a journalist, in 1949 became the first elected governor of Puerto Rico. Under his leadership, Puerto Rico became a commonwealth of the United States. Muñoz Marín worked to attract industry that would provide jobs, in order to raise the people's economic level and to improve living conditions on the island.

**Mussolini, Benito** (1883-1945), founded the Fascist Party and in the 1920's became the dictator of Italy. Under his rule, Italy conquered Ethiopia and attacked Albania and Greece. Italy fought in support of Germany in World War II but was defeated by Allied armies in 1943. Mussolini was captured and executed by partisans.

**Napoleon I** (1769-1829), emperor of France, seized control of the government in 1799 and began to conquer Europe. A brilliant military leader, he created a vast empire but met a disastrous defeat in Russia in 1813. Exiled, Napoleon returned to France in 1815 but was defeated by English and Prussian forces at Waterloo. He died in exile.

**Nasser, Gamal Abdel** (1918-1970), an Egyptian army officer, led a revolt against King Farouk in 1952 and later became president of Egypt. He took control of the Suez Canal in 1956 and adopted a more militant policy toward Israel and the West. Nasser did not succeed in uniting Arab nations under Egyptian leadership, but he did bring about economic reforms in Egypt.

**Nebuchadnezzar II** (died 562 B.C.), a Babylonian king, built Babylon into one of the most beautiful cities of the ancient world. He may have been responsible for building the Hanging Gardens. He destroyed Jerusalem and placed the Israelites in captivity. According to the Bible, Nebuchadnezzar suffered periodically from debilitating delusions.

**Nehru, Jawaharlal** (1889-1964), was a leader in the independence movement in India and became the country's first prime minister in 1947. He supported state-controlled economy and favored neutrality in the Cold War between the Communist powers and the United States. Nehru retained control of the Ruling Congress Party and was prime minister until his death.

**Nero** (37-68), an emperor of Rome, led a dissipated private life that included acts such as the murder of his mother. The creature of his advisers, he ruled well during the first part of his reign when he had competent aides. Under later advisers, his reign was marked by misrule and persecution of Christians. Nero was deposed as emperor, and he committed suicide.

**Newton, Sir Isaac** (1642-1727), an English scientist and mathematician, made revolutionary contributions in mathematics, astronomy, and physics that became the foundations of modern physical science. He developed the law of gravity, discovered that sunlight is a mixture of colors, established laws of motion, invented calculus, and constructed a reflecting telescope. His writings include *Mathematical Principles of Natural Philosophy* and *Optiks.*

**Nietzsche, Friedrich** (1844-1900), a German philosopher and writer, was a critic of Christianity who searched for a morality outside religion. He valued the "superman," a person who uses power creatively. As a psychologist, Nietzsche valued the power more than morality or feelings. *The Antichrist* and *Thus Spake Zarathustra* are among his writings.

**Nightingale, Florence** (1820-1910), an English nurse, hospital reformer, and philanthropist, introduced sanitary practices into hospitals and thereby reduced the incidence of infectious diseases. Born into wealth, she became a nurse and directed nursing operations in the Crimean War. Known as "The lady with the lamp," she later founded the Nightingale Home for Nurses in London and was an adviser for many countries concerning military hospitals.

**Nkrumah, Kwame** (1909-1972), led the African nation of Ghana to independence from Great Britain in 1957 and became the nation's president in 1960. He promoted education, health and welfare, and industrialization, but he tended to rule dictatorially. When the country had economic difficulties, the army ousted him in 1966. Nkrumah lived in exile in Guinea.

**Nobel, Alfred Bernhard** (1833-1896), a Swedish chemist, became a wealthy man through his invention of dynamite. The use of his invention in warfare troubled him, and he set up the Nobel Fund, with an initial sum of more than $9 million, to award annual prizes for those who make contributions to international peace and other fields. The Nobel prize has become the world's most important award.

**Nyerere, Julius Kambarage** (1922-    ), was a leader in the African independence movement. After Tanganyika became free from British rule in 1961, he became prime minister and then president of the country. As head of the government, Nyerere developed socialistic programs for his country, though he promoted democracy. Tanganyika later joined Zanzibar to become Tanzania.

**O'Higgins, Bernardo** (1778-1842), was the leader of the movement to free Chile from Spain. With José de San Martín of Argentina, he led an army across the Andes Mountains to defeat the Spanish

at Chacabuco and won final victory in 1818. O'Higgins became the ruler of Chile but was deposed in 1823.

**O'Keeffe, Georgia** (1887-    ), an American artist, created lyrical paintings of flowers and scenes of the Southwest that often included animal skulls. She painted in both abstract and realistic styles. O'Keeffe's paintings include *Lake George, Black Iris, Canada, Farmhouse Window and Door,* and *A Cross by the Sea.*

**Paine, Thomas** (1737-1809), born in England, became the foremost pamphleteer of the American Colonies. His most famous pamphlet, *Common Sense,* succinctly stated the patriot cause and inspired popular support for it. Later works included *Rights of Man* and *The Age of Reason.*

**Pasteur, Louis** (1822-1895), a French chemist and bacteriologist, developed pasteurization, a process that destroyed bacteria in wine and milk. He also investigated plant diseases, advanced the knowledge of immunity from disease, and developed a successful vaccine against rabies. The Pasteur Institute in Paris was founded in his honor. He is buried in a magnificent tomb in the building that houses the Institute.

**Peary, Robert E.** (1856-1920), an American naval officer and explorer, led numerous Arctic expeditions. In 1909, with Matthew Henson and four Eskimos, he reached the North Pole. Controversy over prior discovery arose, however, between him and Frederick A. Cook, who claimed to have reached the pole on an earlier expedition. A congressional investigation awarded the honor to Peary.

**Penn, William** (1644-1718), an English Quaker, founded the colony of Pennsylvania in 1681, primarily as a refuge for those suffering religious persecution. Although he owned Pennsylvania, he visited America only twice. Penn did not achieve wealth from the colony, but he frequently had to fight off efforts to take it from him.

**Pepin the Short** (714?-768) was the king of the Franks who founded the Carolingian dynasty. He helped Pope Stephen II expel the Lombards from Ravenna in northern Italy and expanded his own kingdom to include Aquitaine in France. Pepin carried out educational and religious reforms and left his kingdom to his sons Carloman and Charlemagne.

**Pericles** (490?-429 B.C.), an Athenian statesman, encouraged art, literature, and architecture during his rule, known as the "Age of Pericles." He expanded democracy in the city and Athenian influence throughout the Mediterranean world. Pericles also prepared Athens for war with Sparta; he led Athenians in the Peloponnesian War against Sparta from 431 B.C. to 429 B.C., when he died of the plague.

**Peter I** (1672-1725), called "the Great," was a czar of Russia who expanded Russian power in wars with Turkey, Persia, and Sweden. He improved his army and built a navy. Peter modernized Russia, introducing Western civilization and making the country an important European power. He founded the city of St. Petersburg (now Leningrad) and made it his capital.

**Philip II** (1527-1598), king of Spain, was a defender of the Roman Catholic faith who promoted the Inquisition and Counter Reformation. Trying to invade and conquer Protestant England, he launched the Great Armada, a Spanish naval force that the English defeated in 1588. The defeat of the Armada marked the beginning of a decline in Spanish power.

**Philip II** (382-336 B.C.), king of Macedonia, was a military genius who conquered the Greek city-states. He organized the Greek cities into the League of Corinth, which later helped them mount their attack against Persia. Philip was assassinated and was succeeded by his son Alexander the Great, who carried on his father's conquests.

**Picasso, Pablo** (1881-1973), a Spanish-born artist, painted in nearly every modern art form, including cubism. He did most of his work in France and produced a prodigious number of paintings and drawings. Among his paintings are *The Three Musicians, Guernica,* and *Les Demoiselles d'Avignon.* Picasso also produced many works of sculpture.

**Piccard, Jacques** (1922-     ), a member of a distinguished family of scientists, became an oceanographer and designer of equipment for undersea exploration. He descended 35,800 feet (10,910 meters) into the Pacific Ocean in a bathyscaph and studied ocean currents while submerged in the Gulf Stream. Piccard became a spokesman against pollution of the oceans and the environment as a whole.

**Pitt, William** (1708-1778), an English statesman, was an influential member of Parliament, who as secretary of state helped organize the British victory over France in the Seven Years' War. At times out of favor with the king, he later entered the House of Lords as Earl of Chatham and frequently spoke in favor of American colonial rights.

**Pitt, William, The Younger** (1759-1806), an English statesman, entered Parliament at the age of 21 and became prime minister almost three years later, serving until 1801 and again from 1804 to 1806. He is considered one of the greatest prime ministers of Britain, surpassing even the excellent reputation of his father. Pitt's most important foreign achievements were in dealing with the effects of the French Revolution, the early years of Napoleonic rule, and French expansion.

**Plato** (427?-347? B.C.), a Greek philosopher who was a pupil of Socrates, opened an academy in Athens and made it the intellectual center of Greece. In his dialogues, Plato taught that ideas are more real than the physical world, and in *The Republic* described an ideal state ruled by philosopher kings. Aristotle, who succeeded Plato as the intellectual leader of Greece, was his pupil.

**Pliny the Elder** (23-79), a Roman writer, admiral, and lawyer, produced many works on history, science, rhetoric, and military tactics. Only one work survives, his monumental *Natural History,* an encyclopedia of science. Pliny was killed by the eruption of Mount Vesuvius that destroyed the city of Pompeii.

**Pliny the Younger** (61?-113?), a Roman writer who was a nephew of Pliny the Elder, served for a time as the Roman governor of Bithynia and Pontica in the Near East. His description of the treatment of early Christians was one of the first historical accounts of the new religion. In his *Letters,* Pliny described the scholarly and gentlemanly life he led.

**Pocahontas** (1595?-1617) was the daughter of the chief of the Powhatan tribe in Virginia. As a young girl, she reportedly saved the life of Captain John Smith. Colonists took her hostage during a conflict with her father and his warriors. She met John Rolfe, whom she married and accompanied to England. About to return to Virginia, Pocahontas died of smallpox.

**Poe, Edgar Allan** (1809-1849), an American writer, created poems and short stories of mystery and horror that focused on human madness. His tales of mystery include "The Murders in the Rue Morgue," "The Purloined Letter," and "The Masque of the Red Death." Among his well-known poems are "Ulalume," "The Raven," and "Annabel Lee."

**Polo, Marco** (1254?-1324?), a member of a Venetian merchant family, made a journey to China with his father and uncle. During the visit, Marco entered the diplomatic service of the Chinese ruler, Kublai Khan. Leaving China, the Polos returned to Venice in 1295 after a 24-year absence. Marco wrote *Description of the World.*

**Pompey** (106-48 B.C.), a Roman statesman and general known as "the Great," gained prominence in the Roman civil wars and was elected consul. With Caesar and Marcus Crassus he ruled Rome as a part of the First Triumvirate. After disagreements with Caesar, he was defeated in battle, and fled to Egypt, where he was killed by Ptolemy.

**Ponce de León, Juan** (1474-1521), a Spanish explorer, accompanied Christopher Columbus on his second voyage and later became governor of Puerto Rico. Searching for Bimini, reputed to be the site of the mythical Fountain of Youth, he explored part of Florida. Trying to found a colony in Florida, he was wounded in a battle with Indians and died.

**Ptolemy I** (367?-283 B.C.), a general under Alexander the Great, became king of Egypt after Alexander's death. Making Alexandria his capital, he expanded his rule to include Cyrene, Crete, and Cyprus. He encouraged education and was responsible for establishing the great library and museum at Alexandria.

**Pulaski, Casimir** (1748-1779), was a Polish patriot who, after an unsuccessful revolt against Russian rule, came to America to join in the Revolutionary War. After service under George Washington, he was made a brigadier general and was in charge of the cavalry corps. Pulaski died from wounds suffered during the American siege of Savannah, Ga.

**Pythagoras** (500's B.C.), a Greek mathematician and philosopher, developed the Pythagorean Theorem in geometry. As a philosopher, he taught that numbers are central to all things and believed in the transmigration of souls. Pythagoras apparently was the first philosopher to believe that the earth is a sphere and that the sun, moon, and planets move.

**Raleigh, Sir Walter** (1552?-1618), an English courtier, navigator, historian, and poet, attempted unsuccessfully to found a colony in America. He was at times a favorite of the English court and at other times was in disfavor. Charged with treason and imprisoned by King James I, he wrote *History of the World.* Released to conduct an expedition for gold in South America, he disobeyed the restrictions that had been placed on him, for which he was beheaded.

**Rembrandt** (1606-1669), a Dutch artist, used sharp contrasts of light and dark in his paintings. In his many portraits, he often painted himself and members of his family. Rembrandt produced many drawings and etchings. Among his works are *The Night Watch, Aristotle Contemplating the Bust of Homer,* and *The Prodigal Son.*

**Renoir, Pierre Auguste** (1841-1919), a French painter who was a leader of the impressionists, produced many landscapes, paintings of flowers, and works featuring children and young girls. He frequently used his children and his wife as models. Among his works are *The Luncheon of the Boating Party, The Bathers,* and *Mme. Charpentier and Her Children.*

**Revere, Paul** (1735-1818), was a colonial silversmith and patriot who participated in the Boston Tea Party. In 1775, he was one of those who rode from Boston with a warning of the British advance on Lexington, Mass. He fought in the Revolutionary War and also cast bronze cannons for the army. After the war Revere returned to his trade in Boston.

**Richard I** (1157-1199), the English king known as the Lion-Hearted, joined a crusade that captured some territories from the Muslims. On his return he was taken prisoner in Austria and freed only after ransom was paid. Leaving his government in his advisors' hands, Richard embarked on a war against France, during which he was killed.

**Richardson, Henry Hobson** (1838-1886), an American architect, first attracted attention with his design for Boston's Trinity Church, which he based on the Romanesque style of the Middle Ages. He eventually developed an innovative style in designs for commercial buildings, public buildings, and houses. Richardson strongly influenced architects such as Louis Sullivan. Only a few of his buildings remained standing in the 1970's; these included Glessner House in Chicago.

**Richelieu, Cardinal** (1585-1642), was a French cleric and statesman who virtually ran the government of King Louis XIII. He rescinded political privileges of the Huguenots, curbed the nobility's power, conducted war against Spain, and furthered French interests during the Thirty Years' War. Richelieu encouraged the arts and the founding of the French Academy.

**Rivera, Diego** (1886-1957), a Mexican artist, painted murals in which labor and revolution were the major themes. He was a Communist, and many of his paintings embodied his view of the oppression of workers. He has been credited with influencing social changes in Mexico that have improved the lives of the lower classes. Rivera helped persuade the Mexican government to allow artists to decorate the interiors of public buildings.

**Robespierre** (1758-1794), was a leader in the French Revolution. As a radical Jacobin, he successfully urged the execution of King Louis XVI. A member of the ruling group, he was partially responsible for the Reign of Terror, which executed thousands of people. When his fortunes turned, Robespierre himself was executed by guillotine.

**Rockefeller, John D.** (1839-1937), founded the Standard Oil Company and became wealthy from the oil business. He was strongly criticized for building monopolies and for such business practices as demanding rebates on freight rates from railroad companies. He established the Rockefeller Foundation for philanthropic endeavors.

**Rodin, Auguste** (1840-1917), was an influential French sculptor. He developed a realistic and perfectionist style in early works like the *Age of Bronze* that many people found startling. Rodin's other statues and busts include *The Gate of Hell*, *Saint John the Baptist*, *The Bather*, *Adam and Eve*, and *The Thinker*.

**Roentgen, Wilhelm** (1845-1923), a German physicist, through investigations of the mysterious fogging that appeared on photographic plates placed near glass tubes charged with electricity, discovered X rays. He found that X rays would pass through flesh but not bone, a discovery that revolutionized medicine. Roentgen won the first Nobel prize in physics, in 1901, for his discovery.

**Rousseau, Jean Jacques** (1712-1778), a French philosopher and writer, believed that human be-

ings are naturally good but are corrupted by social and political institutions. He championed the "natural" man and natural rights. Rousseau emphasized feelings over reason and impulsiveness over restraint, particularly in education. His writings include *Emile* and *The Social Contract*.

**Rubens, Peter Paul** (1577-1640), a Flemish painter, was also a diplomat and a scholar. A master of several languages, he undertook diplomatic missions to Spain and England. He is remembered chiefly as a painter, however. His landscapes, portraits, and religious and historical paintings include *Elevation of the Cross*, *The Descent from the Cross*, and *The Battle of the Amazons*.

**Russell, Bertrand** (1872-1970), an English philosopher and mathematician, wrote *Principles of Mathematics* and, with Alfred North Whitehead, *Principia Mathematica*, works that established the foundations for modern mathematics and logic. He frequently espoused such unpopular causes as pacifism, which sometimes got him dismissed from teaching positions and arrested. A writer on many subjects, Russell won the 1950 Nobel prize in literature.

**Salk, Jonas** (1914-    ), an American scientist, developed a vaccine against poliomyelitis that was tested on nearly two million children. Found safe, it became the first effective means of reducing frequent epidemics of polio. Salk made other important contributions in the field of immunization.

**San Martín, José de** (1778-1850), an Argentine soldier and statesman, helped free South America from Spanish rule. He joined Bernardo O'Higgins to defeat Spanish forces in Chile and later fought for the independence of Peru. He became disenchanted with political quarreling in South America and withdrew from politics. San Martín's achievements, however, allowed other statesmen to complete the battle for independence.

**Schiller, Johann Christoph Friedrich von** (1759-1805), a German playwright and poet, is generally considered to be the greatest dramatist ever to write in the German language. Political freedom is a frequent theme in his plays, which include *Wallenstein*, *Don Carlos*, *The Robbers*, *Maria Stuart*, and *William Tell*.

**Schweitzer, Albert** (1875-1965), a German clergyman, philosopher, physician, and musician, served for many years as a medical missionary in Africa. He established a hospital in Lambaréné, in what is now Gabon, and treated thousands of patients. When he won the Nobel peace prize in 1952, Schweitzer used the money to establish a leper colony. An organist, he was an authority on Bach.

**Scipio, Publius Cornelius** (236?-184? B.C.), a Roman general known as Scipio the Elder, defeated the Carthaginians in Spain and invaded Africa from Sicily. He defeated the great Carthaginian general Hannibal in battle at Zama. His victory ended the Second Punic War between Rome and Carthage and earned Scipio the title "Africanus Major."

**Shakespeare, William** (1564-1616), generally considered the greatest dramatist and poet in any language, prospered as an actor and playwright at the Globe Theatre in Elizabethan London. His comedies include *The Comedy of Errors*, *A Midsummer Night's Dream*, and *Taming of the Shrew*. Among his tragedies are *Romeo and Juliet*, *Hamlet*, and *Macbeth*.

**Shelley, Percy Bysshe** (1792-1822), an English poet, wrote romantic lyric poems. A revolutionary, he lived much of his life outside England. Many of his works reflect his hatred of tyranny and his belief in human perfectability. Among his poems are "Ode to the West Wind," "To a Skylark," and "Adonais."

**Sherman, William Tecumseh** (1820-1891), was a Union general in the Civil War. He captured and burned Atlanta in a destructive "march to the sea" through Georgia that ended at Savannah. After the war, he became commanding general of the Army. Sherman wrote an account of his military experiences in his *Memoirs*.

**Siqueiros, David Alfaro** (1898-1974), a Mexican artist, painted frescoes and murals upholding revolutionary ideals. A radical, he joined revolutionary forces when he was 15 years old and was later imprisoned in Mexico and expelled from the United States. His murals can be seen in buildings in Mexico City.

**Sitting Bull** (1834?-1890), a Sioux leader and medicine man, helped prepare Sioux warriors for battle against the whites led by General George A. Custer at Little Bighorn. Retreating to Canada after the battle, Sitting Bull returned in 1881 and was imprisoned for two years. He was later killed by an Indian policeman, allegedly while resisting arrest.

**Smith, Adam** (1723-1790), a Scottish economist, wrote *The Wealth of Nations*, arguing that labor is the basic source of wealth. He urged that markets and trade be free from government control. Smith believed that unfettered economic self-interest produces the greatest good for the greatest number of people.

**Smith, Joseph** (1805-1844), was the founder of the Church of Jesus Christ of Latter-day Saints, or the Mormon Church. His converts met persecution in several Midwestern states, sometimes because of their practice of polygamy. When a mob killed Smith and his brother Hyrum in Illinois, many Mormons migrated to the Great Salt Lake Valley in Utah.

**Socrates** (369?-399 B.C.), a Greek philosopher, taught mainly by asking questions, a technique called the "Socratic method." He tried to develop principles for good conduct but was accused of corrupting youth by destroying their faith in the gods. Put on trial, he was found guilty and carried out his sentence by drinking poison hemlock. Socrates left no writings but is a character in most of the dialogues of his student Plato.

**Solomon** (around 973-around 933 B.C.) succeeded his father David as king of Israel. Under Solomon, the kingdom reached its peak in prosperity and influence. His greatest accomplishment was the building of the Temple of Jehovah in Jerusalem. Known for his wisdom, Solomon was the reputed author of books of the Bible, including Proverbs and Ecclesiastes.

**Solon** (639?-559? B.C.) was a Greek poet and lawgiver. Elected a ruler of Athens, he carried out many economic and political reforms. Solon's greatest achievement was a constitution that provided for rule by a council of 400 and for a system of public courts, a milestone in Athenian democracy.

**Sophocles** (496?-406? B.C.), a Greek tragedian, wrote 100 plays, of which only 7 have survived. His central characters are people who choose courses of action that can lead only to suffering or death, a fate they face heroically. Among Sophocles' works are *Electra*, *Antigone*, and *Oedipus Rex*.

**Stalin, Joseph** (1879-1953), dictator of the Soviet Union from 1929 until his death, eliminated his political enemies and ruled his country through secret police terrorism. He formed agricultural collectives and developed industry. Stalin led the Soviet Union during World War II and later expanded Soviet influence in Eastern Europe.

**Stevenson, Robert Louis** (1850-1894), a Scottish author, wrote many popular novels, essays, and poems. He traveled widely and lived the last few years of his life in Samoa in the South Pacific Ocean. His works include *Treasure Island, Kidnapped, The Strange Case of Doctor Jekyll and Mr. Hyde,* and *A Child's Garden of Verses.*

**Stowe, Harriet Beecher** (1811-1896), an American writer and the daughter of a noted Congregational minister, wrote the antislavery novel *Uncle Tom's Cabin.* The novel was very popular, but aroused much antipathy in the South. It was credited with making the question of slavery a moral issue and helping to bring on the Civil War.

**Sullivan, Louis** (1856-1924), an American architect, changed American design from historical imitation to the development of a distinctly American style. He adapted traditional principles to modern requirements in his designs for skyscrapers. His buildings included the Wainwright Building in St. Louis and the Stock Exchange Building in Chicago. Sullivan wrote *Autobiography of an Idea.*

**Sun Yat-sen** (1866-1925), a Chinese revolutionary, helped bring about the downfall of the Ch'ing dynasty. When the revolution succeeded in 1911, the Chinese Republic was established. Sun failed to unify China, however, and carried on several years of struggle with rival political leaders. It was only after his death that unity was achieved.

**Swift, Jonathan** (1667-1745), an English writer and Anglican clergyman who was born and lived much of his life in Ireland, satirized many of the cruelties and excesses of his time. His most famous work, *Gulliver's Travels,* satirized political institutions. He wrote about poverty in Ireland in *A Modest Proposal* and about religious corruption in *A Tale of a Tub.* Swift was a friend of many of the important English writers of the time.

**Tacitus** (about 55-about 120), a Roman politician, orator, and historian, wrote several works on the history of the Roman Empire. Biased in favor of the republican form of government, he criticized the emperors and the imperial system. Among his works are *Histories, Annals, Germania, Life of Agricola,* and *Dialogue on Orators.*

**Tchaikovsky, Peter Ilich** (1840-1893), a Russian composer, wrote melodic and emotional romantic music. He composed the opera *Eugène Onégin,* the ballets *Swan Lake* and *Nutcracker,* and the symphonic poem *Romeo and Juliet.* Tchaikovsky's symphonies include *Symphony No. 5* and *Symphony No. 6,* the "Pathétique."

**Tereshkova, Valentina** (1937-      ), a Soviet cosmonaut, was the first woman in space. Untrained as a pilot, she made parachuting a hobby and later joined the Soviet space program. Her historic space flight occurred in June 1963. During the flight, she spent more than 70 hours in orbit and made 48 orbits around the earth.

**Thomson, Sir Joseph John** (1856-1940), an English physicist, discovered the electron. Experimenting with cathode tubes, he established that the rays they emitted were not light waves but were composed of particles of matter. Thomson also discovered the first isotopes of elements and in 1906 won the Nobel prize in physics.

**Thoreau, Henry David** (1817-1862), was an American writer and philosopher. Along with his friend and colleague Ralph Waldo Emerson, Thoreau elaborated the transcendentalist philosophy of individualism and mysticism. His works include *Walden, A Week on the Concord and Merrimack Rivers,* and the essay "Civil Disobedience."

**Tocqueville, Alexis de** (1805-1859), a French writer and politician, wrote *Democracy in America,* after a visit to the United States in 1831 to study prisons. In the book, he skillfully analyzed the American character and American politics. He also wrote *The Old Regime and the French Revolution.* De Tocqueville held several positions in the French government.

**Tolstoy, Leo** (1828-1910), a Russian novelist, believed in social reform and nonviolence. Born an aristocrat, he later gave up worldly pleasures, adopted a fundamentalist form of Christianity, and lived a simple, pious life. Tolstoy's novels include *War and Peace, Anna Karenina,* and *Resurrection.*

**Toulouse-Lautrec, Henri de** (1864-1901), a French artist, often painted dance hall scenes, circus performers, and cabaret scenes. An accident early in life left him deformed, and dissipated living brought about his early death. A designer of posters and an illustrator and lithographer, his works include *The Ringmaster* and *In the Circus Fernando.*

**Trotsky, Leon** (1897-1940), a Russian revolutionary, led the army against forces opposed to the revolution of 1917. After Lenin's death, he lost the struggle for leadership to Stalin. Banished from the country, Trotsky was murdered in Mexico. He wrote several books, including *My Life.*

**Tubman, Harriet** (1820?-1913), born a slave, escaped to the North in 1849 and began a campaign against slavery. She worked with the Underground Railroad and helped more than 300 blacks escape from slavery. After the Civil War began, she offered her services to the Union Army and worked as a nurse, cook, and spy.

**Turgenev, Ivan Sergeevich** (1818-1883), a Russian novelist, usually portrayed liberals as ineffectual, even though he was a liberal. His most famous novel is *Fathers and Sons,* in which he popularized the term *nihilist.* Turgenev also wrote the short story "First Love" and the novels *Rudin, A Nest of Gentlefolk,* and *On the Eve.*

**Tutankhamon** (reigned about 1347-1335 B.C.), an Egyptian pharaoh, ruled for only a few years. After changes by his predecessor, he restored the traditional religion and moved the capital back to Thebes. When his tomb in the Valley of the Kings near Luxor was discovered in the 1920's, it was largely untouched by grave robbers. Thousands of objects, many of them solid gold, were removed from the tomb and placed in the Cairo Museum in Egypt. King Tut's treasures toured the United States in the 1970's.

**Twain, Mark** (1835-1910), whose real name was Samuel Langhorne Clemens, was an American writer whose novels and stories appealed to children but also made perceptive comments on American society. His boyhood experiences serve as background for *The Adventures of Tom Sawyer,* and *The Adventures of Huckleberry Finn.* He also wrote about his experiences in the West. Twain's many other writings include *A Connecticut Yankee in King Arthur's Court* and *The Mysterious Stranger.*

**Tweed, William Marcy** (1823-1878), whose name became synonymous with graft, was the political boss of New York City for many years. He and his associates in the Tweed Ring cost the city millions of dollars through fraudulent supply and building

contracts. Tweed was arrested in 1871, convicted, and jailed.

**Van Gogh, Vincent** (1853-1890), a Dutch painter, used thick brushstrokes to produce works of brilliant color. Many of his paintings seem to reflect the mental illnesses that he experienced for much of his life. Mental disturbances finally drove him to suicide. Among Van Gogh's works are *Self Portrait, The Starry Night,* and *Le Pont d' Arles.*

**Vercingetorix** (?-46 B.C.) led the Gauls and Arverni in a revolt against the Romans that slowed Julius Caesar's conquest of Gaul. Using guerrilla tactics, he raided Roman supply lines and fought only under favorable conditions. After defeating Vercingetorix, the Romans took him as a captive in chains to Rome, where he was executed.

**Verdi, Giuseppe** (1813-1901), an Italian composer, wrote operas with dramatic plots and beautiful melodies. Among his best known operas are *Il Trovatore, Rigoletto, La Traviata,* and *Aida.* Verdi also wrote the *Requiem Mass.* His operas are considered to be among the finest written and are often performed today.

**Verne, Jules** (1828-1905), a French author, wrote science fiction that accurately forecast many technological developments some years before they actually appeared. Among his novels are *A Journey to the Center of the Earth, Twenty Thousand Leagues Under the Sea, Around the World in Eighty Days, The Mysterious Island,* and *From the Earth to the Moon.*

**Victoria** (1819-1901), in 63 years as queen of Great Britain and Empress of India, had the longest reign of any English monarch. During her rule, the British Empire was at the peak of its size and power, and the queen commanded domestic and foreign affairs during the latter half of the 1800's. With Victoria as the symbol, the era became known as the Victorian Age.

**Virgil** (70-19 B.C.), a Roman poet, modeled his greatest work, the *Aeneid,* partly on Homer's *Iliad* and *Odyssey.* Virgil's epic poem, a tribute to Rome, deals with the founding of the city, the growth of its power, and the civilizing effects of the Roman empire. Virgil's other works include the *Eclogues* and the *Georgics.*

**Voltaire** (1694-1778) was the pen name of the French writer François Marie Arouet. Perhaps the most influential thinker of his time, he advocated religious toleration in his poem *La Henriade* and satirized social wrongs in *Candide*. Voltaire also wrote histories, encyclopedia articles, and dramas.

**Von Braun, Wernher** (1912-1977), a rocket engineer, was in charge of Germany's efforts to build rockets during World War II. He developed the V-2 rocket used against England in the latter days of the war. After the war, he worked for the United States contributing to the development of the powerful rockets used in space flights.

**Wagner, Richard** (1813-1883), a German composer, wrote operas that he called music dramas. His operas are long and costly to stage but are often performed today. His works *The Rhine Gold, The Valkyrie, Siegfried,* and *The Twilight of the Gods* comprise a group called *The Ring of the Nibelung,* based on heroic themes and myths from the ancient German past. Wagner's other operas include *Tristan and Isolde* and *Parsifal.*

**Washington, Booker T.** (1856-1915), the best-known black leader of his time, organized Tuskegee Institute, a school for blacks in Alabama, and served as its president. Washington accepted separation of the races and believed that education and skills would eventually elevate blacks economically. He wrote *Up from Slavery.*

**Watson, James D.** (1928-      ), an American biologist and chemist, worked on the development of a model of deoxyribonucleic acid (DNA), the substance that acts as a code in conveying genetic information from one generation to the next. He shared a Nobel prize in 1962. Watson's writings include *The Double Helix.*

**Watt, James** (1736-1819), A Scottish engineer and inventor, improved the steam engine. He invented the condensing steam engine and made numerous other improvements on existing engines. The patent on the Watt steam engine made him wealthy. The watt, a unit of electric power, is named for him. Watt also did work in metallurgy and chemistry.

**Webster, Daniel** (1782-1852), a lawyer and politician, served many years as a United States senator from Massachusetts, beginning in 1827. He was an eloquent spokesman for the Union during the states' rights controversy before the Civil War. Webster was also secretary of state under Presidents William Henry Harrison and John Tyler.

**Wellington, Arthur Wellesley, Duke of** (1769-1852), a British general and statesman, won decisive victories in the Peninsular War against Napoleon. His later victory at Toulouse in 1814 forced Napoleon to abdicate his throne. When Napoleon returned from exile, Wellington defeated him with the aid of Prussian troops at Waterloo in 1815.

**Wesley, John** (1703-1791), an English Anglican minister, founded the Methodist Church. The church grew out of societies that Wesley organized and before which he preached. Methodism spread rapidly in England and in America. Between 1735 and 1738, Wesley served as a chaplain and missionary to Indians in Georgia.

**Wheatley, Phillis** (1753?-1784), considered the first black woman poet in America, was brought to America as a slave in 1761. Purchased by John Wheatley, a Boston tailor, she became his wife's personal servant. A child prodigy, she published her first poem in 1770. She moved to England for a year and was very popular there. She published many religious poems.

**Whitman, Walt** (1819-1892), an American poet, wrote poems praising America and democracy. He was a newspaperman and editor, was active in the antislavery movement, worked as a nurse during the Civil War, and later held minor government jobs. Whitman is considered to be one of the first poets to write in a distinctively American style. His volume *Leaves of Grass* is considered a literary classic.

**Whitney, Eli** (1765-1825), an American inventor, developed the cotton gin that separated cotton fibers from the seeds. The invention vastly increased the amount of cotton that could be grown and harvested. Later he used interchangeable parts to mass-produce guns for the government. Whitney's arms factory made him wealthy.

**Willard, Emma Hart** (1787-1870), made important contributions to education for women in the United States. She founded a girls' boarding school in Vermont and later a girls' seminary in New York that became famous as the Emma Willard School. Her school emphasized teacher training and educated hundreds of young women. She also wrote history textbooks and poetry.

**William I** (1027?-1087), an English king known as "the Conqueror," led an invasion and conquest of England from Normandy in 1066. To centralize his power, he forced all landholders, including the nobility, to swear allegiance directly to him. During his reign, he took an extensive census and survey of the English land, which was compiled in the Domesday Book.

**Wolfe, Thomas** (1900-1938), wrote long and lyrical autobiographical novels. Born and raised in North Carolina, Wolfe taught at New York University from 1924 to 1930 before turning to writing full time. Among his works are *Look Homeward, Angel; Of Time and the River; You Can't Go Home Again;* and *The Web and the Rock.*

**Wordsworth, William** (1770-1850), an English poet, was a romantic writer of poems about nature. In collaboration with Samuel Taylor Coleridge, he wrote *Lyrical Ballads,* poems that denounce artificiality and glorify the senses. Among his poems are "I Wandered Lonely as a Cloud," "She Was a Phantom of Delight," "Lines Composed a Few Miles above Tintern Abbey," "The Prelude," and "Ode: Intimations of Immortality."

**Wren, Sir Christopher** (1632-1723), an English architect, designed plans for the rebuilding of some 50 churches, including St. Paul's Cathedral, after the London fire of 1666. He also designed a master plan for the city of London, but it was not adopted. Wren's other works include the library of Trinity College at Oxford and additions to Hampton Court Palace.

**Wright, Frank Lloyd** (1867-1959), an American architect, designed hundreds of houses and other buildings. He developed a horizontal "prairie style" for houses and other buildings, and he established architectural schools in Wisconsin and in Arizona. Wright also designed the Imperial Hotel in Tokyo and the Guggenheim Museum in New York City.

**Wright, Wilbur and Orville** (1867-1912 and 1871-1948), after experimenting with kites and gliders, constructed and flew the first powered airplane on December 17, 1903. They contracted with the United States government for military planes and established factories in France and in Germany. Throughout their lives, the Wright brothers worked for progress in aviation.

**Xerxes I** (519?-465 B.C.), a Persian king descended from Cyrus the Great and Darius I, invaded Greece with nearly 200,000 men in 480 B.C. The Persians won at Thermopylae but were later defeated at

Salamis and Plataea. Xerxes' invasion was the last Persian attempt to conquer the Greeks. He spent the last years of his life in dissolute living and was murdered by a soldier.

**Yamato Clan** (about 200-646), was a ruling group of Japan that took its name from the Yamato Plain, near the city of Nara. During the period of the Yamato rule, Chinese and Buddhist influences were great in Japan, and the Shinto religion flourished. The period ended with the Taika Reform and the establishment of a strong central government in Japan.

**Young, Brigham** (1801-1877), was a convert to the Mormon faith who became a leader in the church. Three years after the Mormon leader, Joseph Smith, was killed in Illinois in 1844, Young led the Mormons west to Great Salt Lake Valley where they established settlements. He was the first governor of the Territory of Utah. Partly because he practiced polygamy, the United States government removed him as governor. He was put on trial but was not convicted.

**Zapata, Emiliano** (1880?-1919), a Mexican revolutionary, joined the revolt against President Porfirio Díaz in 1910. An Indian who remained independent of other revolutionary movements, he was committed to land redistribution and refused to recognize the new Mexican government. Zapata continued his opposition, frequently with armed resistance, until his assassination.

**Zenger, John Peter** (1697-1746), born in Germany, emigrated to New York and became a printer. When his newspaper criticized the British governor, Zenger was arrested for seditious libel. Represented by the lawyer Andrew Hamilton, who argued truth as a defense for libel, Zenger was acquitted. The case helped establish the principle of freedom of the press in America.

**Zwingli, Huldreich** (1484-1531), a Swiss clergyman, was among the first clericals to demand reforms in the Roman Catholic Church and to support the Protestant Reformation. Although they had some religious differences, Zwingli supported Martin Luther. Zwingli was killed in fighting between Zurich and the Catholic provinces of Switzerland.

# Presidents and Prime Ministers

**9**

How much do you really know about the people who have filled the office of President of the United States? While most students are able to name many of the Presidents, few students know very much about the backgrounds and terms in office of these persons. Reading about the important events in each Presidency is a convenient way of reviewing important events in American history.

This unit presents a biography of each of the 38 persons who has served as President of the United States. And the unit is completed by a handy reference table of Canada's Prime Ministers.

# 1. Presidents of the United States

The following table lists the Presidents of the United States by terms in chronological order, the order in which they served. Use of the table will enable you to relate the order of presidential succession to the chronological flow of the history of the United States.

A biography of each President follows the table. Presidential biographies have been arranged in alphabetical order for easy reference.

## Table of Presidents of the United States

| Name | Served |
|---|---|
| 1. George Washington | 1789-1797 |
| 2. John Adams | 1797-1801 |
| 3. Thomas Jefferson | 1801-1809 |
| 4. James Madison | 1809-1817 |
| 5. James Monroe | 1817-1825 |
| 6. John Quincy Adams | 1825-1829 |
| 7. Andrew Jackson | 1829-1837 |
| 8. Martin Van Buren | 1837-1841 |
| 9. William Henry Harrison | 1841 |
| 10. John Tyler | 1841-1845 |
| 11. James K. Polk | 1845-1849 |
| 12. Zachary Taylor | 1849-1850 |
| 13. Millard Fillmore | 1850-1853 |
| 14. Franklin Pierce | 1853-1857 |
| 15. James Buchanan | 1857-1861 |
| 16. Abraham Lincoln | 1861-1865 |
| 17. Andrew Johnson | 1865-1869 |
| 18. Ulysses S. Grant | 1869-1877 |
| 19. Rutherford B. Hayes | 1877-1881 |
| 20. James A. Garfield | 1881 |
| 21. Chester A. Arthur | 1881-1885 |
| 22. Grover Cleveland | 1885-1889 |
| 23. Benjamin Harrison | 1889-1893 |
| 24. Grover Cleveland | 1893-1897 |
| 25. William McKinley | 1897-1901 |
| 26. Theodore Roosevelt | 1901-1909 |
| 27. William Howard Taft | 1909-1913 |
| 28. Woodrow Wilson | 1913-1921 |
| 29. Warren Gamaliel Harding | 1921-1923 |
| 30. Calvin Coolidge | 1923-1929 |
| 31. Herbert C. Hoover | 1929-1933 |
| 32. Franklin Delano Roosevelt | 1933-1945 |
| 33. Harry S. Truman | 1945-1953 |
| 34. Dwight David Eisenhower | 1953-1961 |
| 35. John Fitzgerald Kennedy | 1961-1963 |
| 36. Lyndon Baines Johnson | 1963-1969 |
| 37. Richard M. Nixon | 1969-1974 |
| 38. Gerald R. Ford | 1974-1977 |
| 39. James Earl Carter, Jr. | 1977-1981 |
| 40. Ronald Wilson Reagan | 1981- |

# John Adams

Born: Oct. 30, 1735
Died: July 4, 1826
Place of Birth: Braintree, Mass.
Political Party: Federalist
Term: 1797-1801
Electoral Vote: 71
Vice-President: Thomas Jefferson

Adams, John (1735-1826), was the second President of the United States. The son of a farmer, John Adams rose to become a prominent lawyer, a key figure in the movement for independence from Great Britain, and a leader among those who shaped the new republic.

Born in Braintree (now Quincy), Mass., on Oct. 30, 1735, Adams received a degree from Harvard College in 1755. He then studied law, eventually opening an office in Boston. In 1764, he married Abigail Smith, daughter of a minister.

Early in his career, John Adams became involved in opposing British tax and trade policies for the colonies. He was one of the leaders of the successful attack against the Stamp Act of 1765, which placed a tax on legal papers and other documents.

A delegate to the First Continental Congress, Adams spoke out strongly against the Intolerable Acts. These British laws aimed to punish Massachusetts and Boston for the Boston Tea Party of December, 1773. Serving in the Second Continental Congress, Adams spoke out strongly for an end to ties with Britain. He helped draft, and was one of the signers of, the Declaration of Independence.

During the Revolutionary War, Adams spent much of his time abroad as a diplomat in France and in Holland. In Holland, he obtained a $1,400,000 loan to help America carry on the war. In 1782, Adams joined Benjamin Franklin and John Jay to negotiate the Treaty of Paris, which ended the Revolutionary War. Three years later, he became the first United States minister to Britain, serving until 1788.

By the time Adams sailed for home, a new Constitution had been written and a new government was about to be established. He was chosen the first Vice-President under George Washington, and he remained in that office during Washington's second term.

Two political parties formed during Washington's presidency. One, the Federalist Party, supported Washington's policies and a strong central government. The other, the Demo-cratic-Republican Party, under the leadership of Thomas Jefferson and James Madison, stressed states' rights. Adams ran against Jefferson for the presidency in 1796. Adams won more electoral votes, and, under the provisions of the Constitution at that time, he became President. Jefferson, as runner-up, became Vice-President.

John Adams' single term as President was a troubled one. There had been war between France and England since the beginning of the French Revolution in 1789. Both England and France had seized American ships. Adams wanted the United States to remain neutral. But other Federalists, led by Alexander Hamilton, who had opposed the French Revolution, wanted war with France. Pursuing his neutralist course, President Adams sent delegates to France to work out an agreement. But the French diplomats offered to negotiate only in return for a bribe and other payments. The situation became known as the XYZ Affair, after the unnamed French officials involved. It produced great controversy in the United States and increased the demands for war. Adams supported the building of more warships, and he made Washington commander of the Army. But Adams refused to abandon his policy of neutrality, and he finally got a treaty with France in 1800.

To curb criticism of their party and policies by Republicans and by Frenchmen in the United States, the Federalists pushed harsh laws through Congress. Under the Alien and Sedition Acts, the President was authorized to deport aliens by a simple order.

Shortly before the election of 1800, John and Abigail Adams moved into the still unfinished White House, living in just a few rooms. By this time, Adams' political fortunes had declined drastically. He had few friends, and many members of his own party would not support him. Still, in 1800, he received 65 electoral votes to Thomas Jefferson's 73.

Leaving the presidency, Adams retired from all political activity. He died on his country's birthday, July 4, 1826, at age 90.

# John Quincy Adams

Born: July 11, 1767
Died: Feb. 23, 1848
Place of Birth: Braintree, Mass.
Political Party: Democratic-Republican
Term: 1825-1829
Electoral Vote: 84
Vice-President: John C. Calhoun

Adams, John Quincy (1767-1848), was the sixth President of the United States. Short, stout, bald, aloof, and one of the great intellectuals of his time, John Quincy Adams enjoyed a brilliant governmental career until he achieved the presidency. Then he suffered troubles similar to those that his father, John, had experienced.

The sixth President of the United States was born in the same house as his father in Braintree (now Quincy), Mass., on July 11, 1767. When he was nearly 11, he accompanied his father on a diplomatic mission to France. At age 14, he became secretary to Francis Dana, the first United States diplomat in Russia. Returning home in the 1780's, he graduated from Harvard College and became a lawyer.

During his father's Administration, Adams served as minister to Prussia. In 1797, he married Louisa Catherine Johnson, the daughter of the United States consul general in London.

Adams, a member of the Federalist Party, won election to the Massachusetts senate in 1802 and to the United States Senate the following year. England and France were at war, and to ensure American neutrality, President Thomas Jefferson in 1807 imposed an embargo on trade with either country. This hurt New England commercial interests, and when Adams supported Jefferson, he was forced to resign from the Senate. But in 1809, Madison appointed him minister to Russia, where he served for five years. Then, in 1814, Adams served in the American delegation that negotiated the Treaty of Ghent, which ended the War of 1812 with England. Adams was minister to Great Britain from 1815 to 1817.

Following the election of Republican James Monroe to the presidency in 1816, Adams became secretary of state. He favored the country's expansion and was especially influential in the development of the Monroe Doctrine in 1823.

Both James Madison and James Monroe had been secretary of state before assuming the presidency. It was expected that Adams would succeed Monroe as President. The presidential campaign of 1824, however, was a four-man race. Adams, Andrew Jackson, Henry Clay, and William Crawford all received electoral votes. Jackson received the highest number of votes, 99, but not a majority. Clay had the least number of votes, putting him out of the race. The House of Representatives decided the winner, and with Speaker of the House Clay supporting him, Adams became President. When Adams made Clay secretary of state, Jackson's followers declared that Adams and Clay had struck a corrupt bargain. They bitterly opposed Adams throughout his Administration.

Even poorer at public relations than his father, John Quincy Adams spent four unhappy years in the White House. He refused to pass out political jobs to those who had supported him. This won him no friends. He favored federal spending on roads and canals. This made him unpopular with supporters of states' rights. He tried to persuade Britain to allow more American trade with the British West Indian colonies, but instead lost trade there altogether. His attempts to curb speculation in public lands annoyed Westerners. He refused to force Cherokee Indians to move out of Georgia, which aroused Southern anger. When Andrew Jackson won the presidency in 1828, Adams left the office with relief.

Unlike his father, Adams did not retire from politics after serving as President. He was elected to the House of Representatives in 1830, an accomplishment which pleased him more than gaining the presidency. He remained in the House until 1848, serving with great distinction, as independent and grumpy as ever, but earning the title "Old Man Eloquent" for his speeches. Adams' effort to lead the fight against "gag rules" in the House was his most memorable act as a congressman.

Adams suffered a stroke in 1846 but recovered partially. Then he suffered a second stroke on the floor of the House in February 1848. He died two days later.

# Chester A. Arthur

Born: Oct. 5, 1829
Died: Nov. 18, 1886
Place of Birth: Fairfield, Vt.
Political Party: Republican
Term: 1881-1885
Electoral Vote: None
Vice-President: None

Arthur, Chester A. (1829-1886), was the 21st President of the United States. He succeeded to the presidency following the assassination of James A. Garfield in 1881. Arthur is remembered as a machine politician who believed firmly in the patronage system of rewarding supporters with government jobs. Yet, during his Administration, the first national civil service reform legislation was enacted.

A New Englander, Chester A. Arthur was born in Fairfield, Vt., on Oct. 5, 1829. His father was a Baptist minister. After graduating in 1848 from Union College in Schenectady, N. Y., Arthur taught school and studied law. He joined a New York City law firm in 1854. As a lawyer, he became known for his defense of civil rights for free blacks. His courtroom successes included winning a case that led to the desegregation of city streetcars in New York City. In 1859, Arthur married Ellen Lewis Herndon, a naval officer's daughter. He also became active in politics as a member of the Republican Party, which had been founded in 1854.

Arthur served as a delegate to the New York Republican state convention in 1860. As a result of his work on behalf of Governor Edwin D. Morgan, who won reelection, Arthur was eventually appointed quartermaster general of New York. In this position, he was responsible for awarding contracts to provide supplies for Union troops in the Civil War.

After the war, Arthur became a member of the faction of the Republican Party known as "Stalwarts," led by Senator Roscoe Conkling of New York. During the Grant Administration (1869-1877), Arthur served as collector of the Port of New York.

The Stalwarts and their rivals, the "Half-Breeds," led by Maine Senator James G. Blaine, clashed at the 1880 Republican presidential convention. The Stalwarts supported former President Ulysses S. Grant for the nomination, and the Half-Breeds backed Ohio Senator James A. Garfield. Garfield became the candidate, and, in an attempt to gain Stalwart support, the convention named Arthur as his running mate. Garfield and Arthur won.

But Garfield's Administration was short-lived. Only a few months after his inauguration, Garfield was assassinated by Charles J. Guiteau, a disappointed office seeker who claimed to be a Stalwart (see Garfield, James A.). Arthur became President in September, 1881.

The assassination led to a public outcry against the "spoils system" of distributing government jobs on the basis of political preference (see Jackson, Andrew). Arthur resisted the calls for reform as long as he could, but yielded after many Republican members of Congress were defeated in the elections of 1882. The result was the Pendleton Civil Service Act of 1883. This legislation established a Civil Service Commission, classified government jobs, and set up a system for advancement. At first, relatively few jobs were placed on the civil service list and freed from political influence. The Pendleton Act, however, was an important piece of legislation that set the stage for later civil service reform.

In 1882, President Arthur signed the first law prohibiting Chinese immigration. He also supported the Anti-Polygamy Act of 1882, which was aimed at Mormons and which made it illegal for a man to have more than one wife.

New York Republicans lost the 1882 governor's race to the reform candidate, Grover Cleveland, a Democrat who later became President. Because they did not think Arthur had given the party sufficient support, Republican leaders blamed him for the defeat. Partly as a result of the 1882 loss, the Republicans in 1884 refused to nominate Arthur for the presidency. Instead, they selected James G. Blaine, leader of the so-called Half-Breed faction.

Soon after his retirement from the presidency, heart trouble and Bright's disease forced Arthur to quit his law practice. He died in 1886.

# James Buchanan

Born: April 23, 1791
Died: June 1, 1868
Place of Birth: near Mercersburg, Pa.
Political Party: Democrat
Term: 1857-1861
Electoral Vote: 174
Vice-President: John C. Breckinridge

Buchanan, James (1791-1868), was the 15th President of the United States. With a solid diplomatic and congressional career behind him, Buchanan became President at a time when tension over slavery was building rapidly in the United States. During his Administration, the first of the Southern States withdrew from the Union.

The son of a country store owner, James Buchanan was born near Mercersburg, Pa., on April 23, 1791. He was the second of 11 children. As a boy, he worked in his father's store and later graduated from Dickinson College in Carlisle, Pa. He then studied law and began practice in Lancaster, Pa., in 1812.

Buchanan entered politics in 1814, winning election to the Pennsylvania legislature. He served two terms. He then resumed his law practice for a brief period, returning to politics following the death of his fiancée in 1819. Buchanan never married.

Beginning in 1821, James Buchanan served 10 years in the United States House of Representatives. A Democrat, he strongly supported President Andrew Jackson. In 1831, Jackson made Buchanan minister to Russia. Buchanan was a senator from Pennsylvania from 1834 to 1845, and secretary of state under President James K. Polk from 1845 until 1849. During Buchanan's time as secretary of state, the United States settled the Oregon boundary dispute with Britain and won a war with Mexico. The United States gained a large amount of territory in the Southwest as a result of the war.

The Democrats lost the 1848 election, and Buchanan retired from politics. When his party regained power under President Franklin Pierce in 1853, Buchanan became minister to Great Britain.

Running against the first Republican presidential candidate, John R. Frémont, Buchanan was elected President in 1856. He presided over a nation sharply divided over the slavery issue and threatening to disintegrate. Buchanan considered slavery to be immoral, but constitutional. He believed the federal government should not become involved in the issue.

Buchanan avoided taking a strong stand on slavery. He preferred middle-of-the-road positions and compromise. At a time when extremists on both sides demanded action, Buchanan's moderation contributed to his unpopularity.

The slavery issue was most bitterly contested in Kansas, which was about to become a state. Pro- and antislavery factions fought for control of the Kansas government. A state constitution permitting slavery came up for a vote in Kansas in 1857. The antislavery group boycotted the election, and slavery was approved. President Buchanan favored congressional acceptance of the constitution, since both sides had had a chance to express their views. This angered Senator Stephen A. Douglas of Illinois, who wanted Kansas to be a free state. Douglas persuaded Congress to return the constitution to the Kansas voters.

The controversy over "bleeding Kansas" split the Democratic Party into Northern and Southern factions. And in 1860, neither group favored Buchanan as a presidential candidate. The split helped elect Republican Abraham Lincoln to the presidency. Between the time of Lincoln's victory and his inauguration, seven Southern states seceded from the Union.

Early in 1861, Buchanan agreed to send a supply ship to Fort Sumter, in the Charleston, S.C., harbor to relieve the federal garrison there. Firing on the ship, Southerners forced it to withdraw. Because no blood had been shed, Buchanan took no action against the South.

Northerners sharply criticized Buchanan for his lack of action. But his cautious course did postpone the beginning of the Civil War and left open the possibility of a peaceful solution under Lincoln's administration. However, in April, 1861, Southerners captured Fort Sumter. Lincoln declared the South in a state of rebellion and called for volunteers to the Army. Buchanan approved this action and urged fellow Democrats to support the new President.

James Buchanan spent the years during and after the war on his estate near Lancaster, Pa. He died there in 1868.

# James Earl Carter, Jr.

Born: Oct. 1, 1924
Place of Birth: Plains, Ga.
Political Party: Democrat
Term: 1977-1981
Electoral Vote: 297
Vice-President: Walter F. Mondale

Carter, James Earl, Jr. (1924-    ), was elected the 39th President of the United States in 1976. A Georgian, Jimmy Carter became the first person from the deep South to win the presidency.

James Earl Carter, Jr., was born in Plains, Ga., on Oct. 1, 1924. He graduated from high school there, then attended Georgia Southwestern College at Americus and the Georgia Institute of Technology at Atlanta. He won admission to the United States Naval Academy at Annapolis in 1943, graduating with a commission in 1946. That year, he married Rosalynn Smith, whom he had known since childhood. Carter spent the next seven years in the Navy, serving part of that time in the nuclear submarine program.

The death of his father in 1953 caused Carter to resign from the Navy to take over the family business, which included a peanut warehouse and about 2,500 acres of farmland. He proved a highly successful manager, and, at the same time, became active in local civic affairs and statewide organizations.

From 1962 to 1966, Carter served in the Georgia senate, where he posted a liberal record and spent much of his time on educational matters. In Plains, Carter in 1965 spoke out strongly for the admission of blacks to the Plains Baptist Church, where he was a deacon.

Carter was elected governor of Georgia in 1970. Beginning his governorship in 1971, Carter called for an end to racial discrimination. His most notable achievement as governor was to reduce the number of state agencies from 300 to 22. He also claimed credit for a $166 million surplus in the state treasury upon leaving office.

After leaving the governorship in 1975, Carter began organizing and campaigning for the 1976 Democratic presidential nomination. His efforts paid off. He won a number of 1976 primary elections, presenting himself as a stranger to Washington, not bound by old ways of doing things. At the Democratic National Convention in New York City, he easily won the nomination on the first ballot. Carter chose Senator Walter F. Mondale of Minnesota as his running mate. Carter and Mondale defeated their Republican opponents, President Gerald R. Ford and Kansas Senator Robert J. Dole. Carter won 297 electoral votes, against Ford's 241.

The U.S. economy was Carter's major domestic concern. With Carter's support, Congress passed laws to create jobs, lower the federal income tax, and deregulate much of the nation's transportation system. Carter opposed several costly government projects. His 1980 program to fight inflation called for cutting federal spending, restricting credit, and voluntary wage and price restraints. Despite these actions, severe inflation and unemployment continued.

In 1977, Carter created a new Department of Energy. During his term, Congress approved most of his energy program, which was designed to decrease consumption, end dependence on foreign oil, and find new energy sources.

In foreign affairs, Carter came out in favor of human rights around the world. In 1979, the SALT II treaty, limiting the use of nuclear weapons, was negotiated with the Soviet Union. But the Soviet invasion of Afghanistan in late 1979 and 1980 put a strain on U.S.–Soviet relations. In response, Carter called for curtailing trade with the Soviet Union, boycotting the 1980 Olympic games in Moscow, and delaying Senate ratification of SALT II.

Carter achieved several other major foreign policy goals. In 1978, the Senate approved the Panama Canal treaties, gradually returning control of the canal to Panama. Carter was praised for helping to establish full diplomatic relations with China and for helping to bring about the peace treaty between Egypt and Israel.

But he was plagued during the last year of his term with his attempts to gain the release of U.S. hostages being held by militants in Iran. He applied economic and diplomatic pressures and carried on extensive negotiations. A failed military rescue attempt in April, 1980, drew sharp criticism. The hostages were not released until the day that Carter left office.

In 1980, Carter was defeated in his bid for a second term by his Republican opponent, former Governor Ronald W. Reagan of California.

# Grover Cleveland

Born: March 18, 1837
Died: June 24, 1908
Place of Birth: Caldwell, N.J.
Political Party: Democrat
Terms: 1885-1889; 1893-1897
Electoral Vote: 219; 277
Vice-Presidents: Thomas A. Hendricks;
              Adlai E. Stevenson

Cleveland, Grover (1837-1908), was the 22nd and 24th President of the United States. He was the only President to serve two nonconsecutive terms in office. As President, Cleveland stood by the principles of conscientiousness, self-control, and government impartiality. However, his beliefs led to some difficulties in his administration during a time of social change.

The son of a poor Presbyterian minister, Grover Cleveland was born on March 18, 1837, in Caldwell, N.J. He went to work at an early age in a general store. At 17, Cleveland left home for Buffalo, N.Y., where he studied law. He worked for the Democratic Party, served as assistant district attorney for Erie County, and then was elected sheriff.

Graft and corruption characterized city governments in the late 1800's. Cleveland won election as mayor of Buffalo in 1881 on a reform ticket. He conducted an honest and impartial administration, believing that government should grant favors to no one group. From 1883 to 1885, he served as governor of New York.

Promoting honest government gave Cleveland a national reputation. There had been corruption in the federal government, and voters were ready for national reform. As a result, Cleveland won the Democratic presidential nomination in 1884 and was elected, though by only 23,000 votes.

President Cleveland opposed veterans' pension bills. He favored lower tariffs. He sought repeal of a law that allowed people to use silver to pay obligations contracted in gold, a practice that was draining the nation's gold reserves. He supported the Interstate Commerce Act of 1887, which permitted the federal government to regulate railroads.

Cleveland became the first President to marry in the White House. He married 21-year-old Frances Folsom, daughter of a former law partner, in 1886.

Cleveland's honesty, impartiality, and willingness to stand on principle made him a popular President. However, his policies on pensions, cheap money, and tariffs gained him enemies among veterans, industrialists, and farmers. In 1888, although Cleveland won the popular vote by 90,000 votes, he lost to Republican candidate Benjamin Harrison in the Electoral College, 233 to 168.

Frances Cleveland predicted that she and her husband would return to the White House in 1893. She was right. President Harrison did many things Cleveland had refused to do. He supported high tariffs, greater coinage of silver, and veterans' pensions. By 1892, American voters were ready for Cleveland again. He easily defeated Harrison.

Cleveland's second term was troublesome. He failed to win a reduction in tariffs. A severe economic depression began in 1893. The drain on gold reserves forced Cleveland to borrow money from New York lenders. Labor unrest was widespread. "Coxey's Army," a group of unemployed workers, marched on Washington, D.C., to demand government relief. In Illinois, workers at the Pullman railroad car plant went on strike. The American Railway Union supported them and refused to handle Pullman cars. Declaring that the strike interfered with mail delivery, Cleveland sent federal troops to bring it to an end.

In 1892, the Populist Party, a splinter group of farmers and some labor representatives, had opposed the two major parties. The Populist candidate for President received a million votes. By 1896, the Populists, who supported the free coinage of silver, had gained control of the Democratic Party. Democrats that year turned to William Jennings Bryan, a free silver advocate, as their presidential candidate.

Cleveland spent the remaining years of his life in Princeton, N.J., serving as a university lecturer and trustee and writing magazine articles. He died there in 1908.

# Calvin Coolidge

Born: July 4, 1872
Died: Jan. 5, 1933
Place of Birth: Plymouth Notch, Vt.
Political Party: Republican
Terms: 1923-1929
Electoral Vote: 382
Vice-President: Charles G. Dawes

Coolidge, Calvin (1872-1933), was the 30th President of the United States. A shy, closemouthed New Englander known as "Silent Cal," Coolidge held public office throughout most of his adult life.

Coolidge was born in the village of Plymouth Notch, Vt., on July 4, 1872. His father was a farmer and storekeeper. After completing secondary school, Coolidge entered Amherst College in Massachusetts in 1891, graduating with honors four years later. In 1897, he became a lawyer in Northampton, Mass.

Politics attracted Coolidge soon after his graduation from college, and in 1899, he won election to the Northampton city council. Later, he served two terms as city solicitor. He married Grace Anna Goodhue, a school teacher, in 1905.

In 1906, Coolidge was elected a Republican member of the Massachusetts house of representatives. Then, in 1909, he became mayor of Northampton. Continuing his political climb, he served in the state senate from 1911 to 1915, and became lieutenant governor in 1916. He became governor of Massachusetts three years later.

His action during a strike by Boston policemen in 1919 earned Coolidge a nationwide reputation. Although it was contrary to police department rules, a group of policemen had organized a labor union. As a result, the Boston police commissioner suspended 19 of them. This led to a strike by policemen and a great deal of turmoil in the city. Governor Coolidge acted. Declaring that "there is no right to strike against the public safety by anybody, anywhere, any time," he called out the National Guard. The strike was ended.

In 1920, Calvin Coolidge became the Republican nominee for the vice-presidency, joining presidential candidate Warren G. Harding. The slender, retiring Coolidge stood in sharp contrast to the friendly, outgoing Harding. But they were the team Americans wanted, and they won a resounding victory.

President Harding died early in August, 1923, just as news of wrongdoing among Cabinet and other officials became public (see Harding, Warren G.). Coolidge then became President.

Republicans believed that the government should help business by supporting low taxes and high tariffs. Aside from that, they felt the government should interfere as little as possible in the economy or in people's lives. Coolidge thoroughly agreed. "The business of America is business," he said. Under his administration, high tariff rates continued, taxes—especially on high incomes and inheritances—were reduced, and there was no government aid for farmers suffering from low prices for their products.

In foreign affairs, Coolidge opposed United States participation in the League of Nations. His administration worked out a plan by which Germany could pay the huge damage payments the victorious Allies demanded after World War I. Following the Mexican Revolution in 1917, relations between Mexico and the United States became strained over the question of foreign-owned oil properties. Various disputes with Mexico were settled, and relations improved during Coolidge's presidency.

Referring to the fact that Coolidge's face rarely wrinkled with a smile or a laugh, an observer concluded that he had been "weaned on a pickle." Coolidge treasured silence, saying that "the things I don't say never get me into trouble."

But Americans generally were satisfied with Coolidge and his policies. They overwhelmingly elected him President in 1924.

The Coolidge era was a time of prosperity for millions of people. Industrial wages and farm incomes, however, remained relatively low. Speculation on the stock market went unchecked. Some observers warned that the economy was on a dangerous course, and that disaster would result. But neither Coolidge nor anyone else took action to change things. The stock market crash came in the fall of 1929, the year Coolidge left office.

Calvin Coolidge spent the remaining years of his life on his estate near Northampton. He died in 1933.

# Dwight David Eisenhower

Born: Oct. 14, 1890
Died: March 28, 1969
Place of Birth: Denison, Tex.
Political Party: Republican
Terms: 1953-1961
Electoral Vote: 442; 457
Vice-President: Richard M. Nixon

Eisenhower, Dwight David (1890-1969), was the 34th President of the United States. He won acclaim as commander of the Allied forces in Europe during World War II. Like military heroes George Washington and Ulysses S. Grant before him, Eisenhower was twice elected President.

Eisenhower was born in Denison, Tex., on Oct. 14, 1890. The Eisenhower family moved to Abilene, Kans., when he was 2 years old. After high school graduation in 1909, Eisenhower went to work. But the following year, he won appointment to the U.S. Military Academy at West Point. He graduated as a second lieutenant in 1915, and in the summer of 1916, he married Mamie Geneva Doud, a wealthy meat packer's daughter.

During World War I, Eisenhower served as a tank-training officer. After the war, like other military officers in peacetime, his progress through the ranks was slow. He became a colonel in 1941. His record, however, attracted the attention of General George C. Marshall, Army chief of staff. After the United States entered World War II in December, 1941, Marshall appointed Eisenhower to the War Plans Division. Soon thereafter, Marshall had Eisenhower promoted to major general and placed him in command of U.S. forces that were to invade North Africa, Sicily, and Italy. His performance earned him further promotion and appointment as commander of Allied forces preparing for the invasion of France. The invasion on June 6, 1944, was successful, and in less than a year, the war in Europe ended. In November, 1945, Eisenhower succeeded Marshall as Army chief of staff.

With Eisenhower's support, all of the U.S. armed forces were unified under a single secretary of defense in 1947. In 1948, Eisenhower resigned to become president of Columbia University. Two years later, he was appointed commander of the North Atlantic Treaty Organization troops.

In 1948, both Republicans and Democrats sought Eisenhower as their presidential candidate, but he refused to enter politics. Four years later, however, he agreed to stand for the Republi-

can nomination, and he won it easily. With California Senator Richard M. Nixon as his running mate, Eisenhower defeated Democrat Adlai Stevenson by more than 6 million popular votes. He was elected to a second term in 1956, again defeating Adlai Stevenson.

Americans looked upon Eisenhower as a father figure, whom they referred to by his nickname, "Ike." His warm and ready smile generated confidence. As President, Eisenhower tended to stress the power and responsibilities of the states, rather than the federal government. Even so, he resisted conservative efforts to diminish or dismantle such federal social programs as Social Security and welfare aid. He also approved the establishment of the Department of Health, Education, and Welfare. He supported a multimillion dollar federal interstate highway program. In 1954, the Supreme Court handed down a decision declaring that school segregation on the basis of race was unconstitutional. Eisenhower did not wholeheartedly approve of the decision, but when the state of Arkansas defied it in 1957, he sent U.S. troops to Little Rock to enforce it.

In foreign affairs, Eisenhower brought the Korean War to a close in 1953 (see Truman, Harry S.). He insisted on reducing the size of the armed forces and on keeping the U.S. stockpile of nuclear weapons at a fixed level. The Cold War, however, continued (see Truman, Harry S.). The Eisenhower Administration extended aid to France, which was fighting a rebellion by nationalist and Communist forces in Indochina, its colony in Southeast Asia. Eisenhower also sent U.S. military advisers into Indochina. The President in 1957 announced the Eisenhower Doctrine, which committed U.S. forces to the Middle East if they were necessary to halt what might be perceived as Communist aggression. Under the doctrine, he ordered troops into Lebanon to help defend that nation's government against left-wing forces. In 1960, the Soviets shot down a U.S. spy plane over Russia. Eisenhower took responsibility for the spying. He refused, however, to apologize for it. As a result, the Russians canceled a summit meeting scheduled for that year.

The 22nd Amendment, adopted in 1951, prevented Eisenhower from running for a third term, which he might have won. Leaving the presidency in 1961, he retired to his farm near Gettysburg, Pa., where he wrote his memoirs. Eisenhower died in March 1969.

# Millard Fillmore

Born: Jan. 7, 1800
Died: March 8, 1874
Place of Birth: Locke Township, N.Y.
Political Party: Whig
Term: 1850-1853
Electoral Vote: None
Vice-President: None

Fillmore, Millard (1800-1874), was the 13th President of the United States. He became the second Vice-President to succeed to the presidency, but that was not his only claim to recognition. During the bitter sectional controversy over slavery in the early 1850's, Fillmore kept the nation on a compromise course.

Fillmore was born into a farm family in Locke Township, N.Y., on Jan. 7, 1800. He received little formal schooling, and at age 15 became apprenticed to a clothmaker. After buying his freedom from his master, Fillmore taught school and studied law. He began practicing law in 1823 in East Aurora, N.Y. Three years later, he married Abigail Powers, a Baptist minister's daughter.

A seat in the New York assembly, to which he was elected in 1828, marked Fillmore's first political experience. In 1832, he won election to the U.S. House of Representatives, where he served two terms.

Fillmore joined the Whig Party when it was formed in the 1830's. In Congress, he generally supported Whig policies of high tariffs and federal aid for domestic improvements. After serving in Congress, he ran for the governorship of New York in 1844, but lost.

Fillmore remained prominent enough to gain the Whig nomination for the vice-presidency in 1848. War hero General Zachary Taylor was the presidential nominee. Democrats split that year, many of them voting for the Free Soil Party, a group that opposed the extension of slavery. Taylor and Fillmore won the election.

Taylor died 16 months after his inauguration, and Millard Fillmore became President. The United States had won a war with Mexico in 1848, and had acquired vast new territories in the West, including California (see Polk, James K.). A gold rush in California rapidly increased the population there, and by 1849, the territory was ready for admission to the Union. The issue of California statehood brought the slavery issue to the surface again. With the admission to statehood of Iowa and Wisconsin, the number of slave and free states stood at 15 each. California's admission would upset the balance, giving antislavery forces more representation in Congress. President Taylor had opposed compromise on the California question. But in Congress, such men as Daniel Webster, Henry Clay, and Stephen A. Douglas proceeded with compromise measures anyway.

President Fillmore proved as willing to bend on the issues as Taylor had been opposed. Fillmore signed the bills that made up the Compromise of 1850. One of the bills admitted California as a free state. Another organized New Mexico and Utah as territories, allowing the people there to settle the slavery question when the territories were admitted as states. Another bill forbade the slave trade in the District of Columbia. Finally, to appease the South, a fourth bill provided for a stronger fugitive slave act.

Millard Fillmore wholeheartedly supported compromise, and he urged the nation to accept it. But historians disagree on whether the Compromise of 1850 was really a compromise, or only a truce between the North and the South. The Fugitive Slave Law, which increased the use of federal power to return runaway slaves to their masters, upset those who wanted slavery abolished. Agitation against the law in Wisconsin eventually caused the supreme court there to declare the Fugitive Slave Law null and void within the state. Similar action occurred in Pennsylvania. Fillmore, however, insisted on rigid enforcement of the Fugitive Slave Law, and this cost him support in the North. In 1852, the Whigs passed him over to nominate an antislavery candidate, General Winfield Scott, for president.

A month after he left office in 1853, Fillmore's wife died. He remarried in 1858. He resumed his law practice in New York, but he was not finished with politics. The Know-Nothings, an anti-Catholic, anti-immigrant group, nominated him

for the presidency in 1856. The Whigs that year also turned to Fillmore as their nominee. He ran third, however, behind the candidate of the newly formed Republican Party and the Democratic winner, James Buchanan. Although he opposed many of Abraham Lincoln's policies, Fillmore was relatively inactive during the Civil War. He died in 1874.

# Gerald R. Ford

Born: July 14, 1913
Place of Birth: Omaha, Nebr.
Political Party: Republican
Term: 1974-1977
Electoral Vote: None
Vice-President: Nelson A. Rockefeller

Ford, Gerald R. (1913-    ), was the 38th President of the United States. In 1973, Gerald R. Ford became the first appointed Vice-President. A year later, he became the first person to take office as President following a chief executive's resignation.

Ford was born in Omaha, Nebr., on July 14, 1913. Following his parents' divorce in 1915, he lived with his mother in Grand Rapids, Mich. Educated there, Ford went on to the University of Michigan, graduating in 1935. He later attended Yale Law School, earning his degree in 1941.

After serving as a naval officer during World War II, Ford returned to Grand Rapids to practice law. He was elected to the U.S. House of Representatives as a Republican in 1948. That same year he married Elizabeth (Betty) Bloomer, a dancer and fashion model.

In Congress, Ford established a record as a conservative, hard-working, and loyal party member. He served for a time as chairman of the Republican Conference and was a member of the Warren Commission, which investigated the assassination of President John F. Kennedy. He also served as House minority leader, beginning in 1965.

In 1973, Vice-President Spiro Agnew was charged with taking bribes and evading income tax payments. He resigned his office. President Richard M. Nixon then appointed Ford Vice-President, with congressional approval. During the Watergate investigation, Ford made numerous speeches defending the President and proclaiming his belief in Nixon's innocence. Under threat of impeachment, Nixon resigned the presidency on Aug. 9, 1974, and Ford became President (see Nixon, Richard M.). Ford then appointed Nelson

Rockefeller Vice-President. For the first time in U.S. history, the two highest offices in the land were filled by persons who had not been elected to them.

Because of the Watergate scandal, public confidence in government was low when Ford took office. Ford's popularity suffered when he granted Nixon a pardon for any crimes he might have committed while President. Ford was also criticized by liberals for his program of limited amnesty to Vietnam draft evaders. The program required up to two years of public service work to avoid prosecution.

Inflation and recession were two of Ford's most difficult domestic problems. The annual rate of inflation topped 10 per cent, and the rate of unemployment went beyond 9 per cent. Ford established the Council on Wage and Price Stability, and approved legislation to lower taxes and to create some federal service jobs. Inflation slowed somewhat, and unemployment dropped only very slowly as the nation moved toward economic recovery in 1975 and 1976.

In foreign affairs, Ford continued Nixon's policy of improving relations with China and the Soviet Union. Ford met with Soviet leaders in Vladivostok and journeyed to China to confer with leaders there. United States aid to South Vietnam continued until early in 1975, when Congress refused the additional funds Ford requested. In April of that year, the Vietnam War ended in a victory for North Vietnam.

Ford's bid for the 1976 Republican presidential nomination was hotly contested by Ronald Reagan, former governor of California. Both men entered numerous primaries and arrived at the Republican convention with an almost equal number of committed votes. Ford won the nomination, however, on the first ballot. He selected Kansas Senator Robert J. Dole as his running mate.

Ford and Dole lost the election to Democrats Jimmy Carter and Walter F. Mondale. After leaving the presidency, Ford remained active in Republican affairs. He left open the possibility that he might run again in 1980.

---

# James A. Garfield

Born: Nov. 19, 1831
Died: Sept. 19, 1881
Place of Birth: Orange, Ohio
Political Party: Republican
Term: 1881
Electoral Vote: 214
Vice-President: Chester A. Arthur

Garfield, James A. (1831-1881), was the 20th President of the United States. He was the fourth chief executive to die in office and the second to be assassinated. His death stimulated the enactment of important governmental reform.

Born in Orange, Ohio, on Nov. 19, 1831, Garfield received his early education in the local schools. At age 20, he entered what is now Hiram College in Ohio, and after three years there, continued at Williams College, in Massachusetts. After graduating from Williams in 1856, Garfield became a professor of literature and ancient languages at Hiram. At age 26, he was named president of the college. In 1858, he married Lucretia Rudolph, an Ohio farmer's daughter. Garfield served in the Union Army during the Civil War. He rose from lieutenant colonel to major general.

James Garfield's political career had begun in 1856, when he campaigned for Republican presidential candidate John C. Frémont. In 1859, Garfield was elected to the Ohio senate. While still in the army, he won election to the U.S. House of Representatives. After the war, he was reelected to eight additional terms.

The Ohio legislature elected Garfield to the U.S. Senate in 1880, and he became a member of the delegation to the Republican presidential convention. The delegates were deadlocked between former President Ulysses S. Grant and Senator James G. Blaine of Maine. On the 36th ballot, Garfield was chosen as the compromise candidate. Chester A. Arthur was named his running mate. In the election, Garfield and Arthur defeated the Democratic candidates by only about 40,000 votes, but they won in the electoral college, 214 to 155.

The Republican infighting displayed at the convention continued into Garfield's Administration. In his appointments, Garfield favored the faction known as the "Half-Breeds," headed by Blaine. Their rivals were the "Stalwarts," led by Senator Roscoe Conkling of New York. Blaine had been instrumental in swinging the nomination to Garfield, and the President rewarded Blaine by making him secretary of state. Garfield infuriated Conkling and his faction by appointing a Half-Breed as collector of the Port of New York City.

Since the Grant Administration in the late 1860's and 1870's, politics had been characterized by widespread corruption. Garfield himself had been accused of accepting bribes while in the House, though the charges were never proved. He admitted taking $5,000 from a construction company in return for his aid in obtaining a paving contract in Washington, D.C., but he claimed the act was not improper. Political machines controlled state and city governments. At each election, machine workers rounded up the vote, herding recently arrived immigrants to the polls in large cities. Ballots and political favors were bought and sold. Many persons were encouraged to vote "early and often," for a fee, moving from one polling place to another. The "spoils system" of filling jobs continued to be practiced (see Jackson, Andrew).

Garfield's assassination in 1881 stimulated an effort to change the system and reduce the corruption in American politics. In the summer of that year, President Garfield planned to attend a class reunion at Williams College. As he stood at the crowded Washington railroad station on July 2, waiting to board his train, a man stepped from the throng. Firing two pistol shots at the President, the man shouted: "I am a Stalwart, and Arthur is President now!" Garfield fell to the floor, alive, but badly wounded. Police immediately arrested the attacker,

Charles J. Guiteau, who turned out to be a disappointed office-seeker.

One bullet had wounded Garfield's arm slightly. The other had lodged in his back, and doctors were unable to locate it. For 80 days, Garfield clung to life, while an uncontrollable infection set in. Gradually, his strength gave way. On Sept. 19, 1881, in a house in New Jersey where he had been moved, the President died.

# Ulysses S. Grant

Born: April 27, 1822
Died: July 23, 1885
Place of Birth: Point Pleasant, Ohio
Political Party: Republican
Terms: 1869-1877
Electoral Vote: 214; 286
Vice-Presidents: Schuyler Colfax; Henry Wilson

Grant, Ulysses S. (1822-1885), was the 18th President of the United States. As commander of the Union forces during the Civil War, Ulysses S. Grant became a national hero, and his war record gained him the presidency. But Grant proved incapable as President. Most historians consider his administration one of the poorest on record, because of scandals that involved some of his chief appointees.

Grant was born on April 27, 1822, in Point Pleasant, Ohio. His father was a tanner and farmer. After completing elementary and one year of secondary school, Grant won appointment to the United States Military Academy at West Point. He graduated as a second lieutenant in 1843. He fought at Monterrey and Veracruz during the Mexican War. In 1848, he married Julia Dent, a West Point classmate's sister.

Tired of the loneliness of army life, Grant resigned his commission in 1854. During the next few years, he unsuccessfully tried farming, dealing in real estate, and storekeeping. The outbreak of the Civil War in 1861 brought him an opportunity for success.

Grant began his Civil War service as a colonel in a regiment of Illinois volunteers. He soon rose to the rank of brigadier general. Early in 1862, he led troops against Fort Henry on the Tennessee River. The Union forces captured the fort easily. Later, he fought a Confederate army to a standstill at Shiloh. Grant then captured Vicksburg, Miss., giving Union forces control of the Mississippi River. His next victory came at Chattanooga, Tenn.

Grant's success in the west attracted President Abraham Lincoln's attention. In 1864, Lincoln brought Grant east, and placed him in command of all Union forces. Grant's major strategy was to attack repeatedly. Although his army suffered heavy losses, Grant gradually wore down the Confederate forces under General Robert E. Lee. On April 9, 1865, Lee surrendered to Grant at Appomattox Court House, Va.

Ulysses S. Grant's wartime popularity brought him the Republican nomination for President in 1868. He won election by a huge majority. Grant won a second term in 1872 by easily defeating New York newspaper publisher Horace Greeley, the candidate of both the Democrats and of a splinter Republican group. Although Grant himself was not involved, his administration is best remembered for political corruption.

The first transcontinental railway system from the Midwest to California was completed in 1869. Railroad promoters had formed a separate construction company, Credit Mobilier, to build one of the roads. The company profited handsomely by charging as much as $50,000 a mile for track that actually cost about half that much to lay. To conceal their scheme, company officials bribed some government officials, and several members of Congress. In St. Louis, members of the "Whiskey Ring" sealed their bottles of liquor with counterfeit revenue stamps. As a result, the Treasury lost millions of dollars in taxes, and members of the St. Louis group gained about $2.5 million. Evidence indicated that government officials sold trading post rights on Indian reservations for their own profit. There were other scandals, too.

The Grant administration did succeed in reducing the national debt. It also reached a settlement with Great Britain over the issue of payments for Civil War damages caused by ships built in Britain for the Confederacy. But Grant ran into trouble when he tried to purchase the Dominican Republic for the United States. His action angered those who supported black independence and political rights. And during Grant's second term, his administration had to weather an economic depression that began in 1873.

Grant left the White House in 1877 with about

$100,000 in savings. He invested it in a banking firm, and lost it all. To pay his debts, Grant wrote his memoirs, which earned his family half a million dollars. Author Mark Twain was his publisher. He died of cancer in 1885, shortly after completing the work.

# Warren Gamaliel Harding

Born: Nov. 2, 1865
Died: Aug. 2, 1923
Place of Birth: near Blooming Grove, Ohio
Political Party: Republican
Term: 1921-1923
Electoral Vote: 404
Vice-President: Calvin Coolidge

Harding, Warren Gamaliel (1865-1923), was the 29th President of the United States. Harding was an able politician. But he is most commonly remembered for the scandals that occurred during his administration.

The son of a farmer, Harding was born on Nov. 2, 1865, near what is now Blooming Grove, Ohio. Following his graduation from secondary school, he taught school, studied law, and sold insurance. In 1884, Harding and two partners bought the *Marion Star*, a failing Ohio newspaper. The paper prospered under Harding's guidance. In 1891, Harding married Florence Kling DeWolfe.

Harding entered politics in 1898, when he won election to the Ohio senate as a Republican. In 1903, he became lieutenant governor of Ohio. He lost the race for the governorship in 1910, but four years later, he won election to the United States Senate. As a senator, he usually supported the Republican leadership.

Urged on by his wife and by Ohio political friend Harry M. Daugherty, Harding made himself available as a compromise candidate at the Republican presidential convention in 1920. He had numerous assets. He was conservative, and the public was ready for conservatism. He was a fine orator. And, people said, the tall, white-haired Harding "looked like a President." He won nomination on the tenth ballot. In November 1920, he was elected by about 60 per cent of the popular vote over Democrat James M. Cox. The election was the first in which women throughout the nation voted.

Harding offered no program. He would, he had said, return the country to "normalcy," a word he

made popular, and which meant different things to different people. To Americans weary of war and the affairs of a troubled world, normalcy, whatever its meaning, seemed ideal.

Harding did not believe in a strong presidency. He felt the country's leadership should come mainly from Congress. Congress kept the United States out of the League of Nations. It raised tariff rates to new heights. It imposed immigration quotas for the first time. And it reduced taxes, especially on high incomes.

President Harding made both wise and poor choices in selecting his advisors. Secretary of Commerce Herbert Hoover and Secretary of State Charles Evans Hughes were widely respected. But Harding appointed incompetent friends to several important positions, including Albert B. Fall as secretary of the interior, Daugherty as attorney general, and Charles R. Forbes as head of the Veterans' Bureau. These men, and others, became involved in scandal.

In exchange for bribes, Fall arranged for oil companies to lease government-owned petroleum reserves in California and Wyoming. This affair became known as the Teapot Dome scandal, because one of the oil reserve areas was located in Teapot Dome, Wyo. Forbes took bribes for awarding building contracts for veterans' hospitals to certain construction firms. Daugherty was accused of mismanagement and bribery. Fall went to prison for one year, Forbes was jailed for two years, and Daugherty was eventually freed of charges. Harding was not personally involved in any of the wrongdoing. He was, however, responsible for the men he had placed in office.

The United States suffered a brief economic depression in 1921, and farm prices did not recover rapidly afterward. Partly because of this, Republicans lost a number of congressional seats in 1922. The following summer, to bolster his administration's image, Harding set off on a cross-country speaking tour that took him into Canada and to Alaska. While on the trip, Harding received the first news of the Teapot Dome scandal. Arriving at Seattle on the return journey, the President became ill. He insisted on continuing, but became ill again in San Francisco. He died there on August 2. The precise cause of his death was never made clear. Some evidence of food poisoning seemed to exist, but other evidence indicated a heart attack.

# Benjamin Harrison

Born: Aug. 20, 1833
Died: March 13, 1901
Place of Birth: North Bend, Ohio
Political Party: Republican
Term: 1889-1893
Electoral Vote: 233
Vice-President: Levi P. Morton

Harrison, Benjamin (1833-1901), was the 23rd President of the United States. He was the only grandson of a President also to become President. His grandfather was William Henry Harrison.

Benjamin Harrison was born on his grandfather's estate in North Bend, Ohio, on Aug. 20, 1833. He was named after his great-grandfather, a signer of the Declaration of Independence. After spending his early years on the farm, Harrison attended a small college near Cincinnati. In 1852, he graduated from Miami University of Ohio. The following year, he married Caroline Lavinia Scott, daughter of a woman's college president.

Harrison became a lawyer in 1854 and moved to Indianapolis. He won election there as city attorney in 1857. Beginning in 1860, he served three terms as reporter for the Indiana Supreme Court.

In 1862, Harrison recruited the 70th Regiment of Indiana Volunteers. Although only 5 feet 6 inches tall, he proved an able and fearless commander, leading his unit in numerous battles. He ended the war as a brigadier general.

Following the war, Harrison resumed his law practice. He failed in his attempt to win the Indiana governorship in 1876. But in 1881, he gained a seat in the Senate, as a Republican. Seven years later, Harrison became the Republican nominee for the presidency. His war record and his popularity with Civil War veterans were great assets. And his relationship to William Henry Harrison, the hero of the Battle of Tippecanoe in 1811, helped, too. Harrison did not, however, win the popular vote. He lost by 90,000 votes to Democratic President Grover Cleveland. But Harrison won the electoral vote, 233 to 168, and thus became President of the United States.

Harrison's Administration is best remembered for four pieces of legislation: the Dependent Pension Act, which benefited veterans; the McKinley Tariff Act; the Sherman Silver Purchase Act; and the Sherman Antitrust Act.

As a senator, Harrison had supported a veterans' pension bill, which President Cleveland vetoed. The measure, passed under Harrison's Administration in 1890, raised the federal pension outlay to $159 million from $88 million.

Tariffs were an important issue during the late 1800's. Industrialists wanted high tariffs, or taxes, on imported manufactured goods. Farmers and working people supported low tariffs. The McKinley Tariff Act set rates at the highest they had ever been, increasing the cost of living for everyone.

Low prices for farm products caused farmers to demand an inflationary increase in the money supply. In particular, they wanted an increase in the amount of silver coins in circulation. Owners of silver mines supported the idea. The Sherman Silver Purchase Act allowed the government to buy silver with notes that could be redeemed in silver or gold. Most note holders preferred gold. As a result, the nation's gold supply dwindled. This helped to create a financial crisis in 1893 and eventually a depression.

After the Civil War, some large businesses and industries formed trusts, which gave control of production and markets to a few firms and destroyed competition. Such practices tended to increase prices, to the disadvantage of farmers and other working people and also threatened the well-being of small-business men. The Sherman

Antitrust Act of 1890 outlawed trusts that could be shown to hinder trade.

By the 1890's, the industrial growth of the United States had made it one of the world's great powers. In keeping with the spirit of the time, President Harrison approved a program to create a two-ocean navy. His administration also negotiated trade treaties with Latin American countries, and hosted the first Pan-American Conference in Washington in 1889. In far-off Hawaii, American sugar and pineapple planters led a successful revolt against the queen, Liliuokalani, in 1893. The new Hawaiian government wanted Hawaii to be annexed to the United States, and requested territorial status. In the meantime, Harrison had lost the 1892 election to Grover Cleveland. Despite his election loss, Harrison presented the Hawaii annexation bill to the Senate. Before the Senate could act, however, the Cleveland Administration took power and rejected Hawaii's request for annexation.

After leaving the presidency, Harrison returned to his law practice. He died in Indianapolis in 1901.

---

# William Henry Harrison

Born: Feb. 9, 1773
Died: April 4, 1841
Place of Birth: Charles City County, Va.
Political Party: Whig
Term: 1841
Electoral Vote: 234
Vice-President: John Tyler

Harrison, William Henry (1773-1841), was the ninth President of the United States. As President, he is remembered for four things. At age 68, he was the oldest man elected to the office. He served the shortest term: about 30 days. He was the first president to die in office. And, most important, after Harrison, presidential campaigns were never the same again.

The youngest son of seven children, Harrison was born in Virginia in 1773. His father, Benjamin, was a signer of the Declaration of Independence.

For most of his adult life, Harrison was either in the army or in government. He joined the army after attending Hampden-Sydney College in Virginia and became an officer. While in the army, Harrison married Anna Symmes, daughter of a wealthy landowner.

In 1798, President John Adams appointed Harrison secretary of the Northwest Territory, an area later divided into the states of Ohio, Indiana, Illinois, Michigan, Minnesota, and Wisconsin. Between 1801 and 1812, Harrison served as appointed governor of the Indiana Territory.

In 1811, Indians of the Northwest became resentful over attempts to settle on Indian land. Led by Tecumseh, the Indians tried to drive out the settlers. Governor Harrison led U.S. forces to victory over the Indians at Tippecanoe Creek, near present-day Lafayette, Ind. During the War of 1812, Harrison commanded U.S. troops against Indian and British forces at the battle of the Thames, in Canada.

Harrison's military record helped him politically. Following the war, between 1816 and 1828 he served the state of Ohio as a state senator and a U.S. congressman and senator. In 1828, he became minister to Colombia, a position that he held for one year.

Returning from Colombia, Harrison became a member of the new Whig Party, led by such giants in Congress as Daniel Webster and Henry Clay. Because the party was young and made up of opposing interests, Whig leaders in 1836 sought a candidate for President who had taken no strong stand on such issues as high tariffs and internal improvements. In the end, in order to satisfy all interests, the Whigs nominated four regional candidates. Harrison was one of the four, and he was presented as a military hero. Although Harrison made a good showing, he and the other Whigs lost to the sole Democratic candidate, Martin Van Buren, who had been Andrew Jackson's Vice-President.

The Whigs turned to Harrison again four years later, this time as their one candidate. They chose John Tyler of Virginia as their vice-presidential candidate. The Democrats stayed with Van Buren. And the 1840 campaign proved an exciting one, much different from any past presidential campaign.

For the first time, a presidential candidate "stumped" the country, taking his campaign to the people. Harrison gave more than 20 speeches, appearing before as many as 100,000 persons at a time. Besides "stump" speeches, politicans organized barbecues, torchlight parades, and campfire rallies. Campaign slogans and songs found their place in American politics. "Tippecanoe and Tyler Too" became the principal Whig Slogan. Others were "To Guide the Ship, We'll Try Old Tip," and "Farewell, Dear Van,

Your're Not Our Man." One song ran, in part:
Tippecanoe and Tyler too,
Oh, with them we'll best little Van, Van,
Van is a used-up man.

The energetic campaign paid off. In 1836, slightly more than 1,500,000 votes had been cast. In 1840, the total was 2,402,405. Harrison received 53 per cent of the popular vote, defeating Martin Van Buren.

On Inauguration Day, President Harrison caught a cold. He died of pneumonia a month later.

---

# Rutherford B. Hayes

Born: Oct. 4, 1822
Died: Jan. 17, 1893
Place of Birth: Delaware, Ohio
Political Party: Republican
Term: 1877-1881
Electoral Vote: 185
Vice-President: William A. Wheeler

Hayes, Rutherford B. (1822-1893), was the 19th President of the United States. He won the first disputed presidential election in the history of the United States, the election of 1876.

The son of a store owner, Hayes was born in Delaware, Ohio, on Oct. 4, 1822. His father died before Rutherford was born. Hayes graduated from Kenyon College in Ohio in 1842, then attended Harvard Law School, and was admitted to the bar in 1845.

After a slow start, Hayes established a successful law practice in Cincinnati, Ohio. In 1852, he married Lucy Ware Webb, a physician's daughter. Appointed city attorney in 1858, he remained in that position until the outbreak of the Civil War. Hayes served as a major of a regiment of Ohio volunteers during the war, and he proved to be an able commander. He rose to the rank of major general.

Hayes was elected to Congress while still in the army. He took his seat in the House as a Republican in December 1865. He served until 1867, when he won the first of three terms as governor of Ohio.

Fraud and corruption in government had marred the Republican Administration of war hero Ulysses S. Grant (see Grant, Ulysses S.). Democrats saw a chance for victory in 1876 as the Republicans split over the corruption issue and could not agree on a candidate. The Republicans eventually chose Hayes as a compromise candidate, but he lost to the Democratic nominee, Samuel J. Tilden,

by about 200,000 votes. Returns from four states—Louisiana, South Carolina, Florida, and Oregon—were disputed, and both sides claimed victory. Congress created an electoral commission to decide which electoral votes should go to whom. The issue was not decided until 1877, a few days before the inauguration.

To solve the problem, Southern Democrats agreed not to oppose the Hayes election. In return, the Republicans agreed to the removal of federal troops that had been stationed in the South since the Civil War. The final electoral vote was 185 to 184 in Hayes's favor. He pulled the troops out a month later.

The removal of the troops allowed Southern Democrats to regain political control of the South gradually. Northern Democrats felt that the bargain between the Southerners and the Republicans was corrupt, and many historians agree. But others have concluded that the wounds of war needed healing, and the troops would have soon been withdrawn in any case.

Hayes had won a reputation as an able and honest administrator as governor of Ohio, and he believed that government appointments should be based on merit rather than political connections. He announced that he would not seek a second presidential term so that he could push for a federal merit system, an effort that would gain him enemies. He advocated reform, but Congress refused to accept his proposals. Although he failed,

Hayes opened the way to later civil service reform.

True to his word, Rutherford B. Hayes did not seek a second term as President. In 1881, following the inauguration of James A. Garfield, he retired to his home in Fremont, Ohio, and withdrew from politics. Hayes devoted the years following his presidency to religion, prison reform, and philanthropy. He died at his home in 1893.

# Herbert Clark Hoover

Born: Aug. 10, 1874
Died: Oct. 20, 1964
Place of Birth: West Branch, Iowa
Political Party: Republican
Term: 1929-1933
Electoral Vote: 444
Vice-President: Charles Curtis

Hoover, Herbert Clark (1874-1964), was the 31st President of the United States. He enjoyed a reputation as a brilliant engineer, public servant, and government official. Then, blamed for the severe economic depression that began during his presidency, Hoover found his reputation badly tarnished.

West Branch, Iowa, was Hoover's birthplace. He was born on Aug. 10, 1874, and orphaned at age 9. He then lived with relatives in Iowa and later in Oregon. Hoover completed secondary school in Oregon and went on to Stanford University to study mining engineering. At age 23, he got a job managing gold mines in Australia. Returning to the United States, he married Lou Henry, a banker's daughter, in 1899. He and his bride then left for China, where he continued his mining career. Later, Hoover became a partner in an engineering firm in London. In 1908, he opened his own firm, which, by 1914, made him a millionaire.

Hoover won international fame for his direction of relief work in Belgium during World War I. He then became head of the United States Food Administration, which directed food distribution in the United States during the war. After the war, Hoover administered the distribution of food to millions of people in Europe. His achievements made Hoover a popular figure. He refused to be nominated as the Republican presidential candidate in 1920, but he accepted the position of secretary of commerce under President Warren G. Harding. Hoover remained in that office until he was nominated for the presidency in 1928.

For many people the 1920's were prosperous years. And in 1928, the Republicans had no trouble persuading voters that the Republican Party was responsible for prosperity. The Republicans promised that good times would continue under Hoover. Hoover won an overwhelming victory over Democrat Al Smith, the first Catholic ever nominated for the presidency by a major party.

A shy, retiring man, with a round face and ruddy complexion, Hoover displayed little warmth in public. But he was an excellent administrator.

During his Administration, the London Naval Treaty, limiting the size of navies, was signed. Some friendly overtures were made toward Latin American nations. Hoover brought home U.S. troops that had been stationed in Nicaragua since 1912 and agreed to withdraw U.S. forces from Haiti, where they had been since 1915. With Hoover's approval, Congress established the Federal Farm Board, which purchased surplus crops and encouraged the formation of cooperatives to raise farm income.

On the other hand, he signed the Hawley-Smoot Tariff Bill, which raised import duties enormously. Because the new tariffs increased the price of manufactured goods and discouraged trade, they contributed to the depression that began in 1929.

Seven months after Hoover's inauguration, the stock market collapsed, causing losses estimated at $40 billion. The market did not recover, and the United States slid into a terrible depression. By 1932, about 12 million persons were out of work.

Hoover favored government aid to business. When the depression continued longer than he had expected it to, he supported the establishment of the Reconstruction Finance Corporation, which offered loans to depression-hit businesses. He opposed direct federal aid to the unemployed. But, when the relief load became unbearable for state and local governments, he approved federal loans to states to help them out. Hoover also supported such federal projects as dam construction to put people to work.

The unemployed and homeless lived in colonies of tar-paper shacks called "Hoovervilles" and slept on park benches under old newspapers called "Hoover blankets." After being persuaded that prosperity would last forever, Americans now blamed Hoover for the depression hardships.

Hoover left office in 1933 an unpopular man, overwhelmed by the Democratic victor, Franklin D. Roosevelt. Hoover spent the rest of his life in public service. He served on numerous commissions, and also wrote his memoirs. He died in 1964, at age 90.

---

# Andrew Jackson

Born: March 15, 1767
Died: June 8, 1845
Place of Birth: Waxhaw settlement, S.C.?
Political Party: Democrat
Terms: 1829-1837
Electoral Vote: 178; 219
Vice-Presidents: John C. Calhoun; Martin Van Buren

Jackson, Andrew (1767-1845), was the seventh President of the United States. Unlike earlier Presidents, Andrew Jackson came from a poor frontier family. But he gained a military reputation that greatly aided him in politics. He became the first Westerner and the first "man of the people" to be elected President.

Jackson was born in a log cabin on the border between North and South Carolina on March 15, 1767. His father died a few days before Andrew's birth, and his mother died of cholera when he was 14.

At age 17, Jackson began to study law in Salisbury, N.C. and was eventually admitted to the bar. But he became better known for his brawling and dueling than for his legal talent. Moving west in the late 1780's, Jackson settled in Nashville, Tenn. There he met Rachel Donelson Robards, a divorcée and daughter of a widowed boarding-house keeper. He married her in 1791. At the time of their marriage, however, Jackson and his wife did not realize that her divorce from her first husband had not yet become final. When they learned this, they went through another marriage ceremony after the divorce was completed. In addition to practicing law, Jackson made money by buying and selling land. By the late 1790's, he owned two plantations. One, the Hermitage, near Nashville, became his lifelong home.

Jackson's political career began when he helped write the Tennessee constitution. After that state's admission to the Union in 1796, he won election to the U.S. House of Representatives. Jackson later served a brief term in the Senate, and served as a Tennessee supreme court justice for six years.

In 1814, as a major general in the Tennessee militia, Jackson led a band of volunteers against the Creek Indians. The Creek had destroyed a fort and massacred more than 200 people in Alabama. Jackson defeated the Creek and forced them to give up millions of acres of land in Alabama and Georgia. Later that year, President James Madison ordered Jackson to New Orleans. There, Jackson organized the city's defenses in preparation for what would be the final battle of the War of 1812 against the British. The attack came in January 1815, and resulted in a stunning American victory over the British forces. Although a peace treaty had been signed in Europe the month before, Jackson gained a national reputation as the "hero of New Orleans." Following the war, he led an expedition against the Seminole Indians in Florida and then retired to the Hermitage.

Jackson did not remain in retirement long, however. Tennessee politicians were soon talking of him as a presidential nominee. And in 1824, as one of four candidates, Jackson received the highest number of electoral votes, 99. But this fell short of a majority, and the House of Representatives had to choose the winner. Henry Clay, speaker of the House, had received the lowest number of votes in the election and thus was out of the running. He threw his support behind John Quincy Adams, whom the House then selected as President. After taking office, Adams appointed Clay as secretary of state. This infuriated Jackson and his followers. They charged that Adams had made a corrupt bargain with Clay for the presidency. Jackson's followers spent the next four years preparing for the election of 1828.

During the early 1800's, the West was a land of opportunity. And as more Western states joined the Union, that region grew in political influence. In more and more states, property qualifications for voting were set aside. The frontier, where a person had to depend on his own ability to make a living in the wilderness, was an equalizer. Accomplishment, rather than wealth and social position, was the measure of a person's worth. A broadly based political democracy was developing and a period of history described as the "age of the common man" was about to begin. It was under these circumstances that Andrew Jackson, a "self-made man," helped found and became the leader of the new Democratic Party.

The controversy over Adams' election four years earlier was only one of many issues raised in the 1828 campaign, which became the bitterest of any in American history. Because the Jacksons had been married before her divorce was final, Mrs. Jackson was called an adulteress. Jackson never shook his belief that the vicious accusations against him and his wife contributed to her death from a heart attack in December 1828. With strong support from farmers and working men, Jackson won the election with 56 per cent of the popular vote, and a 95-vote margin in the electoral college.

As a "people's President," Jackson opened the White House to huge crowds on Inauguration Day. They caused considerable damage, arousing criticism of the President among some more dignified observers.

Andrew Jackson believed that loyalty, not just competence, qualified a person for a government job. He also believed that "to the victor belong the spoils" of political office. Jackson is credited with introducing the "spoils system" to presidential politics, though the practice of giving jobs to party loyalists had been followed by previous Presidents.

Numerous other controversies marked the Jackson presidency. In 1828, Congress passed a bill setting high tariff rates on imported manufactured goods. This displeased the South, where many such goods were marketed. In 1832, Congress lowered the rates, but only a little. John C. Calhoun of South Carolina, Jackson's Vice-President, argued that under the Constitution, a state had the right to nullify—declare null and void—any federal law that harmed its interest. South Carolina then voted to nullify both tariff laws. Nullification threatened the Union, and Jackson and Congress responded with legislation that authorized the President to use armed force, if necessary, to collect tariffs. South Carolina withdrew its nullification of the tariff laws, but then nullified the armed force bill. In the meantime, a compromise tariff was worked out.

The Bank of the United States, established during George Washington's presidency, possessed great power over the nation's money system and loan policies. Jackson opposed the bank as a monopoly. He also favored gold and silver over paper currency. In 1832, Nicholas Biddle, the bank president, applied for renewal of the institution's charter. Congress consented, but Jackson vetoed the bill. He later withdrew federal deposits from the bank. In spite of severe criticism from business interests, the President had destroyed the bank. That same year, 1832, he easily won election to a second term.

Jackson's Indian policy also met with criticism. Whites in Georgia wanted the Cherokee Indians removed from the state. Jackson supported the Georgians. The Supreme Court of the United States, however, decided that, by treaty, the Cherokee were an independent nation, outside the limits of state control. Jackson refused to enforce the decision, and the Cherokee finally were forced to move.

During Jackson's second term, land speculation and the issuance of paper money by state banks threatened to cause wild inflation. Jackson, therefore, issued the *Specie Circular* in 1836. It required government officials to accept only gold and silver in the sale of public lands. Jackson succeeded in stopping speculation, but he lost support among Westerners. Overexpansion in business and public works projects continued, however, and led to a panic that caused a depression soon after Jackson left office in 1837.

In foreign affairs, Jackson won a British agreement to open all ports in the West Indies to American shipping. The ports had been closed to the United States since the end of the Revolutionary War. In exchange, all U.S. ports were opened to the British.

During Jackson's Administration, various reform groups intensified their demands that slavery be abolished. Slavery became an issue when Texas, which had won independence from Mexico in 1836, applied for admission to the Union as a slave state. Abolitionists opposed admission. Southerners favored it. Although Jackson himself was a slaveholder, he refused to act on the statehood question. He seemed to understand that the Texas issue, and the related problem of slavery, endangered the Union.

Jackson's second Vice-President, Martin Van Buren, succeeded him as President in 1837. Jackson returned to the Hermitage, where he died in 1845.

# Thomas Jefferson

Born: April 13, 1743
Died: July 4, 1826
Place of Birth: Albemarle County, Va.
Political Party: Democratic-Republican
Terms: 1801-1809
Electoral Vote: 73; 162
Vice-Presidents: Aaron Burr; George Clinton

Jefferson, Thomas (1743-1826), was the third President of the United States. One of the most talented men ever to occupy the White House, Jefferson was a political philosopher, a writer, an inventor, an educational reformer, an architect, a scientist, and a statesman. He himself wished to be remembered chiefly as the author of the Declaration of Independence and the founder of the University of Virginia.

Jefferson was born on the family plantation in Albemarle County, Virginia, on April 13, 1743. Jefferson inherited the estate of more than 2,000 acres and more than a dozen slaves at age 14, when his father died. Beginning at age 16, he spent two years at the College of William and Mary, and in 1767, became a lawyer. Five years later, Jefferson married Martha Wayles Skelton, a widow and a lawyer's daughter.

Jefferson's first political experience came in 1769, when he was elected to the Virginia House of Burgesses. His colleagues in the House of Burgesses included such figures as Patrick Henry and Richard Henry Lee. The Virginia legislators opposed British tax and trade policies for the colonies. And in 1775, as relations with England moved toward the breaking point, Jefferson became a member of the Second Continental Congress. Previously, Jefferson had declared that the British Parliament had no authority over the colonies, but that the colonists owed allegiance only to the king. In Congress, he drafted a "Declaration of the Causes and Necessity of Taking up Arms," but the other delegates considered its language of resistance too strong. In the summer of 1776, however, Jefferson was named to a committee to draft a declaration of independence. The other committee members chose Jefferson to prepare the document. The Declaration of Independence, which the Congress adopted that July, is Jefferson's best known work.

At the outbreak of the Revolution, Jefferson, who did not wish to serve in the military, returned to the Virginia legislature. Jefferson was interested in curbing aristocratic power, and he successfully worked for the abolition of *primogeniture* and *entail*. Primogeniture required a property owner to will all his land to his eldest son. Under entail, a person could not dispose of land as he wished, but had to will it to a particular individual. The end of primogeniture and entail meant that numerous large estates in Virginia were broken up. At the time, a person needed to own property to vote. Because more land was available for purchase, more people could now vote. Jefferson's efforts also led to the removal of state support from the Anglican Church in Virginia. As an institution established by law, the church had been supported by public tax money. Jefferson served as governor of Virginia for two one-year terms, in 1779, and again in 1780.

Jefferson's wife died in 1782. He accepted election to Congress the following year in the hope that political activity would divert him from his grief. As a congressman, Jefferson became best known for drafting a law that formed the basis for the political organization of western lands. Later, he served as United States minister to France. There, he sympathized with the French Revolution, which began in 1789, viewing it as a democratic movement similar to the one he had supported in the United States.

The Constitution went into effect while Jefferson was abroad. George Washington was elected President. After Jefferson's return from France, Washington appointed him secretary of state.

Jefferson left the Cabinet in 1795, and planned to retire to his estate, Monticello. But he accepted the Democratic-Republican nomination for the presidency in 1796. His opponent was Federalist John Adams. Adams won the Electoral College vote and became President. Under the provisions of the Constitution at the time, Jefferson, as runner-up, became Vice-President.

Although he was a member of the Adams Federalist Administration, Jefferson continued as leader of the opposition. He particularly opposed the Alien and Sedition Acts of 1798, which were aimed at curbing Democratic-Republican criticism of the Adams government (see Adams, John).

In 1800, Jefferson defeated Adams and won the presidency. Jefferson put his political philosophies into practice by reducing taxes and government expenditures and the size of the Army and the Navy. His presidency, however, is best remembered for three things: the Supreme Court case *Marbury v. Madison*, the expansion of the United States, and growing troubles with Great Britain.

Before leaving the presidency, John Adams had appointed about 200 Federalist judges under the Judiciary Act of 1801. Jefferson's secretary of state, James Madison, refused to issue commissions to the appointees. One of the judges, William Marbury, asked the Supreme Court to order Madison to grant his commission. The Judiciary Act had given the Supreme Court the power to issue such orders. But the Court refused to do so. According to Chief Justice John Marshall, the power given to the Supreme Court under the Judiciary Act was unconstitutional. By his decision in the case of *Marbury v. Madison*, Marshall thus established the principle under which the Court could review laws and determine their constitutionality. Part of this decision pleased Jefferson, but he was skeptical about judicial review. He feared that this gave the Court supreme power over the other two branches of government. To curb judicial power, Jefferson tried to remove several judges from office, including Supreme Court Justice Samuel Chase, an ardent Federalist. He succeeded in removing only one district judge in New Hampshire.

One of President Jefferson's greatest accomplishments was the Louisiana Purchase. At the time, Louisiana was a vast expanse of land beyond the Mississippi River. It had belonged to Spain, which had given it up to France in 1800. The Spaniards had allowed Americans to use the port of New Orleans, which gave western farmers a gateway through which they could move crops down river to the sea and world market. Napoleon Bonaparte, who controlled the territory, closed the port. Jefferson in 1803 instructed James Monroe to help Robert R. Livingston, the minister to France, negotiate with Napoleon for the purchase of New Orleans. To the Americans' surprise, Napoleon offered to sell the entire Louisiana Territory to the United States. Jefferson set aside personal doubts about the constitutionality of federal land acquisition and agreed to the purchase. As a result, at a total cost of about $15 million, or a few pennies an acre, Jefferson doubled the size of the United States.

Jefferson easily won reelection in 1804. He defeated the Federalist candidate, Charles C. Pinckney, by an electoral vote of 162 to 14.

Foreign affairs caused problems during much of Jefferson's second term. Great Britain and France were at war in 1803. Both countries tried to destroy each other's ocean commerce. This benefited U.S. commercial interests, because it opened much of the West Indies-Europe trade to United States shipping. Increased trade, however, made it difficult for President Jefferson to maintain American neutrality in the war and at the same time uphold freedom of the seas. Both Britain and France interfered with U.S. vessels. British sailors began deserting to join American merchantmen. British warships stopped American ships to remove the deserters, but they frequently took American sailors, also. The United States was not prepared for war, and Jefferson thought he could end the British and French conflict by denying both nations goods made in America or transported in American ships. The result was the Embargo Act of 1807. It forbade any American trade with the warring countries.

The embargo did not help the situation. Britain and France survived without American trade. Merchants in New England and elsewhere lost money. Shipbuilders were out of work. Warehouses overflowed with goods. Some shippers evaded the law by smuggling. In 1809, just as Jefferson left the presidency, Congress repealed the Embargo Act.

Jefferson was 65 when he retired to Monticello. He devoted much of the remainder of his life to writing, studying, and corresponding with political leaders. His major achievement in retirement was the creation of the University of Virginia, which opened in 1825. At the end of a long life, Jefferson died on July 4, 1826, 50 years after the adoption of the Declaration of Independence.

# Andrew Johnson

Born: Dec. 29, 1808
Died: July 31, 1875
Place of Birth: Raleigh, N.C.
Political Party: Democrat (National Union)
Term: 1865-1869
Electoral Vote: None
Vice-President: None

Johnson, Andrew (1808-1875), was the 17th President of the United States. A Tennessee Democrat, Johnson became Abraham Lincoln's Vice-President in 1865 and succeeded to the presidency following Lincoln's assassination. Johnson was the only President ever to be tried on impeachment charges.

Andrew Johnson was born on Dec. 29, 1808 in Raleigh, N.C. He was apprenticed to a tailor at age 14, and two years later he ran away to South Carolina. There, Johnson set up a tailor shop. Later, he then moved to Tennessee. In 1827, at age 18, he married 16-year-old Eliza McCardle, a shoemaker's daughter.

Johnson became a Democratic follower of Andrew Jackson, who was first elected President in 1828. Johnson's own political career began that same year, when he was elected an alderman in Greenville, Tenn. He later served as the city's mayor. In 1835, he was elected to the Tennessee House of Representatives, and he later held a seat in the state senate. Johnson became a U.S. congressman in 1843. He was known chiefly as a supporter of cheaper western land for settlers.

Johnson lost his seat in the House in 1853, but won election as governor of Tennessee. Four years later, he returned to Washington as a member of the Senate. A slaveholder himself, Johnson generally upheld slavery interests. He was, however, a staunch Union man. When the Civil War began, he supported the war measures of Republican President Abraham Lincoln. When Tennessee voted to secede, Johnson refused to go along.

Johnson's loyalty earned him the post of military governor of Tennessee after federal armies gained control of the western part of the state in 1862. He prepared Tennessee for reentry into the Union (which was accomplished in 1866). In 1864, the Democratic Party split. One group supported the Democratic peace candidate, General George McClellan, for the presidency. Democrats who supported the war then joined with other Republicans to nominate Lincoln for a second term. Since he was considered an outstanding War

Democrat, Andrew Johnson received the vice-presidential nomination.

Abraham Lincoln was assassinated six weeks after his second inauguration. Johnson became President. And he soon became embroiled in bitter conflicts with Congress.

The end of the war brought numerous problems for the Johnson Administration. Foremost among these problems were the rebuilding of the South, the reentry of the seceded states to the Union, and provisions for blacks freed from slavery. Lincoln's plan for Reconstruction had been to mend the Union as quickly as possible, and in general, Johnson followed Lincoln's lead. Congress was not in session when Johnson became President. He offered amnesty and a pardon to all Southerners, except leaders of the Confederacy, who were willing to swear loyalty to the Constitution of the United States. He also appointed governors for the former Confederate states, and those states soon sent representatives to Congress.

Southern whites ignored blacks' newly won civil rights. Johnson's plan was too mild for so-called Radical Republicans, who wanted to punish the South and to protect freed blacks. Over Johnson's consistent opposition, the Radicals refused to seat Southern members of Congress. Congress then passed the 14th Amendment, which gave civil rights to blacks. Congress also divided the South into five military districts. Most Southern whites were not allowed to vote, and numerous blacks were elected to public office in the South.

Relations between Johnson and Congress grew steadily worse, and to curb his power, Congress in 1867 passed the Tenure of Office Act. It forbade the President to remove any official whom he had appointed with the consent of the Senate without also obtaining senatorial approval for the removal. Johnson ignored the act and fired Secretary of War Edwin M. Stanton, an enemy. As a result, the House of Representatives began impeachment proceedings against Johnson, and he was tried in the Senate. The effort to remove Johnson from office failed by only one vote.

Johnson was not nominated for the presidency in 1868, and he returned to Tennessee. He then ran unsuccessfully for Congress and, in 1874, finally won a seat in the Senate. Back in Tennessee, he suffered a stroke and died in the summer of 1875.

# Lyndon Baines Johnson

Born: Aug. 27, 1908
Died: Jan. 22, 1973
Place of Birth: near Stonewall, Tex.
Political Party: Democrat
Terms: 1963-1969
Electoral Vote: 486
Vice-President: Hubert H. Humphrey

Johnson, Lyndon Baines (1908-1973), was the 36th President of the United States. Johnson took office after the assassination of President John F. Kennedy in 1963. He oversaw the enactment of much social legislation and presided over a nation increasingly divided on the issue of the Vietnam War.

Johnson was born on Aug. 27, 1908, near Stonewall, Tex. He entered Southwest Texas State Teachers College in 1927, but later dropped out because of a lack of funds. After working for a time, he returned and was graduated in 1930. Following a brief career as a teacher, Johnson went to Washington as secretary to Texas Representative Richard M. Kleberg. In 1934, he married Claudia Alta (Lady Bird) Taylor, the daughter of a wealthy family.

During the mid-1930's, Johnson served in the National Youth Administration, which employed young people and enabled them to finish high school or college. Johnson won a seat in the House of Representatives in a special election in 1937. During World War II, while still in Congress, he became a naval lieutenant commander. In 1942, he was reelected to the House. He moved on to the Senate in 1948.

Johnson became Senate minority leader in 1953 and majority leader in 1955. He thoroughly mastered the mechanics of the legislative process and the art of compromise, and he could be counted on to deliver votes. In 1960, Johnson became a candidate for the Democratic presidential nomination. He lost the nomination to John F. Kennedy, who then chose Johnson as his running mate. Kennedy was assassinated in November, 1963, and Johnson took the oath of office as President.

The following year, Johnson was elected President in his own right by a huge majority. During his administration, he pushed for legislation to launch what he called the "Great Society." Congress passed 226 out of the 252 bills that the President submitted. Various pieces of civil rights legislation curbed discrimination against blacks. Congress established the Office of Economic Opportunity to pour money into job training and other programs to aid the poor. Lyndon Johnson rode a crest of popularity higher than most Presidents before him. Then, the continuing war in Southeast Asia led to his downfall.

Vietnam had been a French colony since the late 1800's, as part of French Indochina. The Japanese took it during World War II. After the war, the Vietnamese resisted French efforts to return as colonial masters. Many of the Vietnamese rebels were Communists. The United States aided France in its fight against the Vietnamese, but by the mid-1950's, the rebels had won. Vietnam then was split into two nations. The North was Communist-controlled. The government in the South was called a republic, and it received United States support. Communists and other rebels in the South tried to overthrow the South Vietnamese government, and eventually they were aided by Communist North Vietnam. The Eisenhower Administration sent military advisers to the South. Along with military supplies, the Kennedy Administration began sending troops to South Vietnam in the early 1960's. Troop commitments continued under Johnson, until the total number of U.S. forces exceeded half a million.

Even with massive United States aid, the South Vietnamese government seemed unable to win the war. The government became increasingly corrupt and dictatorial. More and more Americans opposed continued involvement in what appeared to be an unwinnable war, and continued support for an oppressive regime. The conflict was costing thousands of American lives. Johnson resisted the criticism and continued to step up the war effort, declaring that, "I'm not going down in history as the first American President to lose a war." Opposition to the war mounted as thousands of Americans took to the streets to protest. The nation was becoming more and more divided.

Despite his growing unpopularity, nearly everyone expected Johnson to be the Democratic nominee for President in 1968. But in March of that year, he made a surprise announcement. At the conclusion of a televised speech, he declared that he would not be a candidate for reelection. Early in 1969, after nearly 40 years in the nation's capital, Lyndon B. Johnson left Washington, D.C., for the final time. He retired to his Texas ranch and died there in 1973.

# John Fitzgerald Kennedy

Born: May 29, 1917
Died: Nov. 22, 1963
Place of Birth: Brookline, Mass.
Political Party: Democrat
Term: 1961-1963
Electoral Vote: 303
Vice-President: Lyndon B. Johnson

Kennedy, John Fitzgerald (1917-1963), was the 35th President of the United States. Young, witty, and sophisticated, John F. Kennedy promised to lead the nation from the conservative 1950's to a "New Frontier" of bold experimentation and social change. Kennedy was the first Catholic to be elected to the presidency, and he was the fourth President to be assassinated.

Kennedy was born into a wealthy family in Brookline, Mass., on May 29, 1917. He attended elementary schools there and in Riverdale. After a prep school secondary education, he entered Harvard University, graduating in 1940. During World War II, Kennedy saw action as a naval lieutenant in the Pacific. His political career began in 1946, when he was elected to the House of Representatives as a Democrat. He was reelected twice, then won a Senate seat in 1952. The following year, Kennedy married Jacqueline Lee Bouvier, the daughter of a Wall Street broker.

In 1956, Kennedy unsuccessfully sought the Democratic vice-presidential nomination. He won reelection to the Senate in 1958, and soon began to prepare for the presidential nomination two years later. In 1960, after a hard-driving, tireless campaign that brought him numerous primary victories, Kennedy gained the nomination on the first ballot. His campaign for the presidency was equally energetic and carefully planned. But he defeated Republican candidate Richard M. Nixon by only a narrow popular majority. In the Electoral College, Kennedy won by a vote of 303 to 219.

President Kennedy unleashed a flood of legislative proposals on such matters as unemployment, health care, civil rights, aid to Appalachia and other depressed areas, trade expansion, and an increased minimum wage. Congress, though Democratic, proved to be more conservative than Kennedy. It raised the minimum wage to $1.25 an hour, granted aid to depressed areas, and passed tariff-cutting legislation. But it did not establish a Department of Urban Affairs, as Kennedy requested, nor did it provide health care for the aged. Civil rights legislation made little progress under Kennedy. However, he did use federal troops to integrate the Universities of Alabama and Mississippi when blacks were denied admission to those institutions. In 1961, Kennedy issued an executive order that established the Peace Corps, which some consider his greatest achievement. Under the Peace Corps, thousands of Americans went to underdeveloped countries to teach and to provide other services.

The Kennedy Administration waged the Cold War vigorously (see Truman, Harry S. and Eisenhower, Dwight David). The U.S. stockpile of nuclear weapons grew. Kennedy continued Eisenhower's policy of sending aid to South Vietnam to combat a rebellion that involved Communists and that was supported by Communist North Vietnam. Closer to home, Kennedy approved a plan to use American-trained Cuban exiles as an invasion force to bring down Cuba's Communist government. The invasion in 1961 at the Bay of Pigs failed miserably, and Kennedy was sharply criticized for the incident. In 1962, Russia constructed nuclear missile sites in Cuba. Kennedy publicly forced the Soviets to back down and dismantle the sites. In 1963, Russia and the United States agreed to limit nuclear testing.

On Nov. 22, 1963, as he rode in a motorcade in Dallas, Tex., Kennedy was assassinated by Lee Harvey Oswald. While in police custody, Oswald himself was shot and killed by nightclub owner Jack Ruby. Some persons questioned whether Kennedy's assassination resulted from a conspiracy, or was simply the act of a single individual. Although a government commission later concluded that Oswald acted alone, the issue has never been cleared up to everyone's satisfaction.

# Abraham Lincoln

Born: Feb. 12, 1809
Died: April 15, 1865
Place of Birth: Hardin County, Ky.
Political Party: Republican
Terms: 1861–1865
Electoral Vote: 180; 212
Vice-Presidents: Hannibal Hamlin;
　　　　　　　　Andrew Johnson

Lincoln, Abraham (1809-1865), was the 16th President of the United States. He governed a nation torn apart by the Civil War, and his major task was to end the conflict and restore the Union. He did not have the opportunity, however, to "bind up the nation's wounds." Shortly after the war ended in 1865, Lincoln was assassinated.

Abraham Lincoln was descended from pioneers who had moved farther and farther west with each generation. He was born in Hardin County, Ky., on Feb. 12, 1809. When he was 7, his family crossed the Ohio River and settled in Indiana. In 1830, when Lincoln was 21, the family moved again, this time to Illinois.

Settling on his own in New Salem, Lincoln failed in a business venture, served briefly in the Black Hawk War of 1832, and became village postmaster. In 1834, as a member of the Whig Party, he was elected to the Illinois legislature. He served four terms and at the same time studied law. He became a lawyer in 1837 and moved to the state capital, Springfield.

Lincoln remained a Whig, but his ambition for national political office was unfulfilled until 1847, when he won election to the U.S. House of Representatives. In Congress, he became best known for his opposition to the Mexican War (see Polk, James K.). This stand cost him reelection. He returned to his law practice in Illinois. There, in 1842, he married Mary Todd, a Kentuckian.

The extension of slavery into new territories and states was an issue that stirred the nation in the 1850's. Lincoln believed that the Constitution did not prohibit slavery, but he opposed its extension. He expressed his position in his campaign for the Senate in 1854, during which he debated Senator Stephen A. Douglas of Illinois. Douglas refused to take a stand against slavery. Lincoln lost the election. He unsuccessfully ran for Douglas' own seat in 1858, and once more debated the senator on the slavery issue. Newspaper coverage of the 1858 debates brought Lincoln nationwide attention.

By 1860, Lincoln had become a member of the new Republican Party, which was dedicated, among other things, to opposing the extension of slavery. That year, Lincoln became a candidate for the presidential nomination. Because he had spent relatively little time in public life, Lincoln had few enemies. This, plus his moderate views on slavery, appealed to many delegates at the 1860 Republican convention in Chicago. Lincoln won the nomination on the third ballot.

The Democrats split over the slavery issue. Southern party members split among themselves to form two parties, both with presidential candidates. Northern Democrats chose Stephen A. Douglas as their candidate. Lincoln won in the Electoral College, though he failed to gain a majority of the popular vote.

Southerners feared the Republican victory doomed slavery. In December 1860, South Carolina seceded from the Union. In January, Mississippi, Florida, Alabama, Louisiana, and Georgia followed. Later, Virginia, Texas, Arkansas, Tennessee, and North Carolina left the Union to join the Confederate States of America.

As President, Lincoln's immediate task was to hold such border states as Kentucky and Maryland in the Union. He held the border states, but he had to decide what to do about Fort Sumter, a federal fort in the Charleston, S.C. harbor. To withdraw troops from Sumter would arouse Northern criticism. To send supplies and additional troops there would generate Southern hostility. Lincoln chose to send supplies only. But before a ship could arrive, Confederate troops fired on Fort Sumter and forced it to surrender. Lincoln declared the South to be in a state of rebellion and called for volunteers to the Union Army. The Civil War had begun.

Lincoln's major problems lay in the East, where he had difficulty finding a suitable commander for the Army of the Potomac. General George B. McClellan lost the Peninsular Campaign, which was aimed at Richmond, Va., to Confederate General Robert E. Lee in 1862. As a result, Lincoln removed McClellan. The next appointee, John Pope, met defeat at the second Battle of Bull Run in August of that year. Lincoln turned once again to McClellan, who held back Lee at Antietam, but failed to pursue the Confederates. Lincoln then appointed General Ambrose E. Burnside commander. Burnside failed to win at Fredericksburg, and his successor, General Joseph Hooker, lost at Chancellorsville early in May 1863. Lee then invaded the North, moving into southern Pennsylvania. There, at Gettysburg in July, 1863 General George Meade defeated the Confederate forces, and Lee retreated into Virginia.

The Union enjoyed more success in the West. In 1862, General Ulysses S. Grant took the Confederate Fort Henry on the Tennessee River. Next, he fought Southern armies to a standstill at Shiloh, in Tennessee. Then he captured Vicksburg, which put the Mississippi River in Union hands, and later went on to victory at Chattanooga, Tenn. Lincoln made Grant a lieutenant general and brought him east to command all Union forces.

In addition to conducting the war, Lincoln had to keep the loyal states united. This proved difficult. Union failures on the battlefield aroused much discontent. Republicans criticized Lincoln for not pursuing the war more vigorously. "Copperhead" Democrats, who were sympathetic toward the South, wanted to make peace. In addition, various groups demanded the abolition of slavery. Lincoln hesitated to move on the slavery issue, for fear of offending the border states of Kentucky, Missouri, Maryland, and Delaware, where slavery was permitted. After the Battle of Antietam in 1862, which could be called a Union victory, Lincoln issued the Emancipation Proclamation. The document, which was issued in final form on Jan. 1, 1863, freed slaves in all the states then in rebellion. It could be enforced, however,

only where Union troops were in control. Still, the Proclamation cheered abolitionists. It also made the abolition of slavery a war aim, in addition to the preservation of the Union.

As the war dragged on, however, Lincoln lost popularity. He faced strong opposition in his bid for reelection in 1864. Democrats nominated General McClellan as their candidate. The Republicans chose John C. Frémont, a radical Republican who was a general and a famed explorer. Frémont later withdrew, and Lincoln defeated McClellan by 212 to 21 electoral votes. By the time of Lincoln's second inauguration in March 1865, the end of the war was near.

In 1864, General William T. Sherman besieged and captured Atlanta, Ga. He then moved to cut a 60-mile-wide path of destruction from Atlanta to the sea at Savannah, Ga. Much of the South lay in ruins.

In Virginia, troops under Ulysses S. Grant suffered heavy losses as they fought to a series of standoffs with Lee's Army of Northern Virginia. Lee held off Grant in the two-day Battle of the Wilderness in May 1864, but Grant pushed forward to clash again with Lee at the Spotsylvania Court House that same month. Grant proceeded toward Richmond, the capital of the Confederacy, and once more met fierce resistance, at Cold Harbor, in June. Finally, he lay siege to the Southern army at Petersburg. In the meantime, the Northern cavalry under General Philip Sheridan defeated Confederate forces in the Shenandoah Valley of Virginia. The Union destruction of the valley eliminated it as a source of Confederate food. Hemmed in at Petersburg and Richmond, Lee finally asked for terms. He surrendered to Grant at Appomattox Court House in Virginia, on April 9, 1865. The Civil War was over.

In his second inaugural address, Lincoln had called for "malice toward none" and "charity for all," and for an effort "to bind up the nation's wounds" and "achieve and cherish a just and lasting peace." But he himself was not to take part in the nation's reconstruction.

On the night of April 14, 1865, less than a week after the war had ended, Lincoln and his wife attended Ford's Theatre in Washington, D.C. There, in the presidential box, at about 10 o'clock, John Wilkes Booth shot Lincoln in the head. Booth was a well-known actor, a Marylander, and a Confederate sympathizer. Carried to a nearby house, Lincoln died at about 7:30 the following morning.

# James Madison

Born: March 16, 1751
Died: June 28, 1836
Place of Birth: Port Conway, Va.
Political Party: Democratic-Republican
Terms: 1809-1817
Electoral Vote: 122; 128
Vice-Presidents: George Clinton; Elbridge Gerry

Madison, James (1751-1836), was the fourth President of the United States. Madison was responsible for the system of checks and balances that is built into the American government, and he is known principally as the "Father of the Constitution."

Born on March 16, 1751, in Port Conway, Va., Madison was the son of the owner of a plantation called Montpelier. He received most of his early education at home. At age 18, he entered what is now Princeton University in New Jersey.

In 1774, Madison was elected to the Committee of Safety in Orange County, Virginia. Two years later, after he helped draft a constitution for the state, he was elected to the Virginia legislature. In 1779, he won election to the Continental Congress. He returned to the Virginia assembly in 1783.

Madison served as one of Virginia's representatives at the Constitutional Convention in 1787. His suggestions made him a leader in the process of writing the document. His ideas for a two-house legislature and a sharing of power among the legislative, judicial, and executive branches won acceptance. After the convention, he worked to win ratification of the Constitution by the states.

In 1789, Virginians sent Madison to the U.S. House of Representatives. In Virginia, in 1794, he married Dolley Payne Todd, a young widow. Madison became a leading opponent of the Federalist Party, which favored business and commercial interests and a strong central government. He and Thomas Jefferson formed the Democratic-Republican Party, which favored states' rights. Jefferson was elected to the presidency in 1800, and he made Madison secretary of state. During his term as secretary, the United States purchased Louisiana from France. There were also problems because of a war between Great Britain and France. Both nations interfered with American shipping. In 1807, Congress passed the Embargo Act, which halted trade with both nations. This did more harm than good, however. It hurt American commercial interests, and the Congress repealed the act in 1809.

Madison was elected President in 1808. Problems with France and Britain continued, and Congress passed the Macon Act. The law provided that if either France or Britain would stop interfering with American shipping, the United States would stop trade with the other nation. France declared, falsely, that it would cease harassment. Trade with Britain was halted. When France's trickery was discovered, there were angry outcries in the United States against the French.

Feelings against Britain were aroused when the British in Canada encouraged Indians to attack American frontier settlements. The British also continued to harass American shipping. Americans began to talk of war. Westerners favored war with Britain to stop the Indian attacks. They also hoped to annex Canada. Other factions approved of fighting Britain to restore freedom of the seas. Finally, in 1812, Congress declared war on Great Britain.

Madison was easily reelected President a few months after the war began. But the conflict went badly for Madison and his Administration. The British blockaded the Atlantic Coast. United States shipping declined. In 1814, the British landed troops in Maryland. Shortly thereafter they occupied Washington, D.C., and burned the Capitol and some other public buildings. James and Dolley Madison fled. Only fierce American resistance at Fort McHenry in the Baltimore harbor prevented the British from taking the capital of the United States.

American forces fought the British to a draw in battles in southern Ontario, and U.S. naval forces won a battle on Lake Erie. In 1815, Andrew Jackson defeated the British in the Battle of New Orleans, shortly before a peace treaty was ratified.

Following the war, the United States entered a period of prosperity and expansion. Road and canal building helped the Westward movement and brought the country's various regions together. Protective tariffs helped the birth and growth of American industries. The downfall of the Federalists gave the Democratic-Republicans dominance over the government.

James Madison retired from the presidency to Montpelier in 1817. He continued his life-long study of government and history and later became president of the University of Virginia. He died in 1836.

---

# William McKinley

Born: Jan. 29, 1843
Died: Sept. 14, 1901
Place of Birth: Niles, Ohio
Political Party: Republican
Terms: 1897-1901
Electoral Vote: 271; 292
Vice-Presidents: Garret A. Hobart;
                Theodore Roosevelt

McKinley, William (1843-1901), was the 25th President of the United States. William McKinley was chief executive at a time of great industrial and territorial expansion. In 1901, six months into his second term, McKinley was assassinated.

Born in Niles, Ohio, on Jan. 29, 1843, McKinley received his early education in public and private schools. After serving in the Union army during the Civil War, he studied law. In 1867, he opened an office in Canton, Ohio. Two years later, as a Republican, he was elected prosecuting attorney of Stark County. In 1871, he married Ida Saxton, granddaughter of a Canton newspaper publisher.

In 1876, McKinley was elected to the U.S. House of Representatives. In Congress, he supported protective tariffs, and the tariff law bearing his name set rates at new high levels. He also favored the unlimited coinage of silver, an inflationary measure. After being defeated for reelection to the House in 1890, he was elected to two terms as governor of Ohio.

McKinley became a close friend of Mark Hanna, a wealthy industrialist who used his influence and financial resources to promote McKinley for the presidency. McKinley easily won nomination at the Republican convention in 1896, and went on to defeat Democratic candidate William Jennings Bryan by more than 600,000 votes.

Industrialization had proceeded rapidly since the end of the Civil War, and by the turn of the century, there was no doubt that the United States was a world power. During the 1890's, the government began a construction program to achieve a two-ocean navy. In 1898, the United States expanded its territory by annexing Hawaii.

The Caribbean colony of Cuba revolted against Spain in 1895. Many American newspapers, particularly those which practiced sensational "yellow journalism," agitated for U.S. involvement. These newspapers printed many stories that emphasized Spanish harshness and oppression. A clamor arose in the United States for intervention in Cuba, but McKinley resisted the demand.

The President did dispatch the battleship Maine to Havana harbor, for the stated purpose of protecting American lives and property on the island. On Feb. 15, 1898, the Maine blew up. Although the cause of the explosion has never been determined, Spain was blamed. War fever reached a high pitch, and "remember the Maine" became a common slogan. McKinley finally bowed to the demand for war with Spain.

Less than four months later, the conflict ended. United States naval forces defeated Spanish fleets off the Philippines and in the Caribbean. The United States invaded Cuba and was victorious over Spanish forces there. When the war with Spain ended, the United States gained possession of Cuba, Puerto Rico, the Philippines, and the island of Guam in the Pacific.

The United States gave Cuba self-governing powers in 1901 but reserved the right to intervene there whenever necessary. It kept Puerto Rico as a colony. The status of the Philippines became a controversial issue. Traditionally, the United States had opposed colonialism. Further, Filipinos wished to be independent. Business groups in the United States tended to favor annexation. So did those who believed it was the United States' mission to educate Filipinos and to convert them to Christianity, though many Filipinos had already become Catholics under Spanish rule. President McKinley finally decided on annexation. His decision touched off a revolt by Filipino nationalists that cost the United States numerous casualties before peace was restored.

During McKinley's first administration, the nation had enjoyed prosperity. Running for reelection in 1900, he promised four more prosperous years. He won easily. In September 1901, McKinley attended the Pan-American Exposition in Buffalo, N.Y. At a reception in Buffalo on September 6, an anarchist named Leon F. Czolgosz shot the President. Czolgosz said he wanted "to kill a great ruler." McKinley died a week later, and Theodore Roosevelt became President.

# James Monroe

Born: April 28, 1758
Died: July 4, 1831
Place of Birth: Westmoreland County, Va.
Political Party: Democratic-Republican
Terms: 1817-1825
Electoral Vote: 183; 231
Vice-President: Daniel D. Tompkins

Monroe, James (1758-1831), was the fifth President of the United States. He was the last of the "Virginia dynasty" of Presidents, which included George Washington, Thomas Jefferson, and James Madison. Monroe is best remembered for the Monroe Doctrine, which he proclaimed in 1823. The doctrine warned European nations against interfering in the affairs of independent countries in the Western Hemisphere.

James Monroe was born on April 28, 1758, in Westmoreland County, Virginia. He entered the College of William and Mary at age 16, but did not finish. He left school to fight in the Revolutionary War.

Monroe's political service began in 1782, when he was elected to the Virginia Assembly. The next year, he was elected to the national Congress, where he spent three years. After marrying Elizabeth Kortright, a New York merchant's daughter, he returned to the Virginia legislature. In 1788, he was a member of the state convention that ratified the U.S. Constitution. He was elected to the United States Senate in 1790, and helped organize the Democratic-Republican Party (see Jefferson, Thomas).

From 1794 to 1796, Monroe served as minister to France. Then in 1799, he won the governorship of Virginia. In 1803, he was a member of the delegation that negotiated the Louisiana Purchase from France. Afterward, Monroe served as minister to Great Britain. In 1810, he once again was elected to the Virginia legislature. Then, after a brief period as governor, he became President James Madison's secretary of state. In 1816, Monroe won the presidency.

The Federalist Party, concentrated in New England, had opposed the War of 1812, mainly because the conflict damaged that region's trade. As a result, Federalists were accused of a lack of patriotism, and the party dissolved after 1816. The Democratic-Republican Party was the only one in existence in the United States during Monroe's Administration. The absence of interparty battling caused the period to be known as the "era of good feeling."

It was also an era of growing nationalism, prosperity, and expansion. To promote nationalism, Speaker of the House Henry Clay advanced his American System. One part of this plan called for federally supported road and canal construction. It also included a high tariff to protect young American industries from foreign competition. High tariff laws were enacted in 1816, in 1818, and again in 1824. Monroe added territory to the nation in 1819 by buying Florida from Spain.

Slavery and sectionalism became issues in 1820. Missouri had applied for statehood as a slave state in 1819. Its admission would upset the balance between slave and free states that then existed. Southerners favored Missouri's admission to the Union; Northerners opposed it. After months of debate, Henry Clay worked out a compromise. Missouri would come in as a slave state, Maine as a free state, and slavery would be prohibited in the rest of the Louisiana Territory north of Missouri's southern border. Monroe approved the Missouri Compromise, and in that same year, 1820, he was reelected President.

By the early 1820's, most Latin American colonies had won independence from Spain and Portugal. There was some evidence, however, that certain European nations might band together to return the new nations to colonial status. Britain wanted to issue a joint declaration with the United States opposing such a move. But Monroe's secretary of state, John Quincy Adams, advised him that the United States should issue a declaration on its own. Adams assumed that the United States could depend on British seapower to enforce any declaration. The result was the Monroe Doctrine, proclaimed in 1823. It protected the Western Hemisphere from any further European colonization.

The era of good feeling ended in 1825. Four candidates vied for the presidency in 1824 (see Adams, John Quincy, and Jackson, Andrew). None won a majority of the electoral votes, and the House of Representatives decided the election in favor of John Quincy Adams. The result was political bitterness that lasted throughout the 1820's.

After Monroe left the presidency, he retired to his estate, Oak Hill, in northern Virginia. Mounting debts forced him to sell his plantation and move to New York to live with one of his daughters in 1830. He died there the following year.

---

# Richard M. Nixon

Born: Jan. 9, 1913
Place of Birth: Yorba Linda, Calif.
Political Party: Republican
Terms: 1969-1974
Electoral Vote: 301; 520
Vice-Presidents: Spiro T. Agnew; Gerald R. Ford

Nixon, Richard M. (1913-     ), was the 37th President of the United States. From the start to the finish of his political career, Richard M. Nixon remained a controversial figure. In 1974, he became the first person to resign the presidency.

Nixon was born in Yorba Linda, Calif., on Jan. 9, 1913. He attended elementary and high schools in Yorba Linda, Whittier, and Fullerton. He graduated from Whittier College in 1934 and then attended Duke University School of Law, where he received his degree in 1937. He married Thelma Catharine Ryan, known by the nickname Pat, in 1940. Nixon practiced law until 1942, when he went to Washington, D.C., to work for the Office of Price Administration, an agency in charge of price controls and rationing during World War II. Later in 1942, he became a naval lieutenant j. g. and served in the Pacific.

Following the war, Nixon in 1946 ran as a Republican for the seat in the House of Representatives held by Californian Jerry Voorhis, who had served five terms. At the time, there was a rising fear of Communist influence in the United States (see Truman, Harry S.). Nixon was criticized for taking advantage of this fear by implying that Voorhis, a liberal, was a Communist sympathizer. Nixon won the election.

As a member of the House Un-American Activities Committee, Nixon made a name for himself by conducting a lengthy investigation into the background of former State Department official Alger Hiss, who was accused of having spied for Russia during the 1930's. Hiss was later convicted of perjury. In 1950, Nixon ran for the Senate from California against Representative Helen Gahagan Douglas. He won the election but again was criticized for using campaign tactics similar to those he had employed against Voorhis.

By 1952, Nixon was a well-known public figure, and he was chosen by the Republicans to run for the vice-presidency that year. He and presidential candidate Dwight D. Eisenhower were elected, and re-elected four years later.

As Vice-President, Nixon was more active than most of his predecessors in the office had been. He attended Cabinet and various commission and council meetings, made a tour of Latin America, and journeyed to the Soviet Union.

Nixon was nominated in 1960 by the Republicans to succeed Eisenhower, but he lost the election to Democrat John F. Kennedy in a close race. Two years later, he failed in an attempt to win election as California's governor. He then moved to New York to join a law firm.

In 1968, Nixon returned to politics and again secured the Republican nomination for the presidency. This time he won, defeating Democrat Hubert H. Humphrey by 301 to 191 electoral votes.

Foreign affairs, especially the war in Vietnam, attracted much attention during the Nixon years. Nixon's policy called for the gradual withdrawal of American ground forces and the strengthening of South Vietnam's ability to carry on the war against North Vietnam alone. Troop withdrawal pleased most Americans, but it did not proceed rapidly enough to suit longtime opponents of the war.

Then, in April, 1970, Nixon ordered an invasion of Cambodia for the stated purpose of wiping out Communist supply bases. To many people, it appeared that Nixon was widening the war instead of ending it. There were demonstrations against the Cambodian invasion. At Kent State College in Ohio, national guardsmen killed four demonstrating students. Police in Jackson, Miss., killed two students there. United States involvement in Vietnam finally ended in January 1973.

Nixon had been known for his strong stand against Communism and such Communist nations as China and Russia. Yet, in 1972, he took an important step toward improving U.S.-Chinese relations by journeying to China to confer with that nation's leaders. That same year, he flew to Moscow to meet with Soviet officials.

In November 1972, Nixon easily won reelection over Democrat George McGovern. The electoral vote was 520 to 17.

Inflation and recession were problems during Nixon's second term. Both became especially troublesome after the fall of 1973, when oil-producing nations increased petroleum prices.

President Nixon also had problems within his Administration. Vice-President Spiro Agnew was accused of having accepted bribes while serving as a government official in Maryland. Agnew was also charged with income tax evasion. Agnew steadfastly denied his guilt, but in October 1973, he finally pleaded no contest to the income tax charge. He was fined and resigned from the vice-presidency. Nixon appointed Michigan Congressman Gerald R. Ford to the office.

The President's gravest domestic problem, however, stemmed from a burglary. On June 17, 1972, Washington police arrested five men who had broken into the Democratic national headquarters in the Watergate office and apartment building. The men were carrying electronic surveillance equipment. One of the men, James W. McCord, Jr., was a former Central Intelligence Agency (CIA) employee who was connected with the Republican Committee to Re-elect the President. Two additional men were arrested later. They were E. Howard Hunt, a former CIA agent who also worked for the election committee, and G. Gordon Liddy, a former FBI agent. Liddy and McCord pleaded not guilty to burglary and conspiracy charges. All seven were tried and found guilty of burglary.

In 1973, the grand jury that investigated the Watergate break-in uncovered evidence of political spying through electronic means, other politically inspired break-ins and burglaries, illegal Republican campaign contributions, and other improper activities. A Senate committee began its own investigation. It appeared that numerous presidential aides had been involved in the Watergate scandal and related matters. Nixon denied any such involvement by his aides.

Testifying before the Senate committee, however, former White House counsel John W. Dean III insisted that numerous men around the President had been involved, and that Nixon himself, as early as September 1972, had tried to keep his officials from being indicted for participation in the Watergate affair. Dean also revealed an "enemies list" of about 250 persons who the Administration intended to harass by such means as tax audits. He further said that the CIA had been used to block an FBI investigation of Watergate. Nixon continued to deny any cover-up of the Watergate affair by anyone then in the government. He did have the Justice Department appoint a special prosecutor to investigate Watergate.

The Senate committee also learned that Nixon had regularly tape-recorded his conversations in his White House office. A long controversy then began over whether Nixon would give up certain tapes the committee requested for its investigation. But when the prosecutor, Archibald Cox, insisted on obtaining crucial tapes, Nixon had him fired.

Under a new special prosecutor, Leon Jaworski, the Watergate investigation continued into 1974. Nixon at last offered to provide edited versions of certain tapes. These showed that he and his aides had discussed such things as "hush money," clemency for the Watergate burglars, and how to restrain the Watergate investigation. Public confidence in Nixon's integrity eroded.

Many persons began to talk of impeaching Nixon on charges of obstruction of justice. In the meantime, at Jaworski's request, the Supreme Court ordered Nixon to turn over all the tapes the investigators wanted. Nixon complied. These tapes revealed new evidence concerning a cover-up. One tape in particular indicated that, contrary to his repeated denials of involvement, Nixon had known of the cover-up plan less than a week after the Watergate break-in. The House Judiciary Committee now voted to recommend articles of impeachment against Nixon. Nixon resigned from office on Aug. 9, 1974, and left immediately for California. Vice-President Ford was sworn in as President. One of Ford's first acts was to pardon Nixon for any crimes that he might have committed while in office.

The number of people indicted in connection

with Watergate for obstruction of justice, burglary, conspiracy, perjury, and other crimes finally totaled more than 50. The leading figures among those sent to prison were such presidential aides as H.R. Haldeman and John D. Ehrlichman, and former Attorney General John Mitchell.

# Franklin Pierce

Born: Nov. 23, 1804
Died: Oct. 8, 1869
Place of Birth: Hillsboro, N.H.
Political Party: Democrat
Term: 1853-1857
Electoral Vote: 254
Vice-President: William R. King

Pierce, Franklin (1804-1869), was the 14th President of the United States. A Democrat, Pierce presided over a nation that was being torn apart by the slavery issue, as the possibility of compromise became more and more remote.

Franklin Pierce was born on Nov. 23, 1804, in Hillsboro, N.H. His father had fought in the Revolutionary War and later became governor of New Hampshire. Pierce was educated in private academies and at Bowdoin College, where he graduated in 1824. He then studied law and opened a practice in Concord, N.H. in 1827.

A follower of Andrew Jackson, Pierce was elected to the New Hampshire House of Representatives in 1828. He served a total of three terms. In 1833, he moved on to a seat in the House of Representatives in Washington, D.C., then to the Senate. In 1834, he married Jane Means Appleton, a college president's daughter. Pierce served as an army officer during the Mexican War, and participated in the capture of Mexico City in 1847.

In 1852, the Democratic convention deadlocked over the selection of a presidential candidate. Pierce had supported the Compromise of 1850 and strict enforcement of the Fugitive Slave Law (see Fillmore, Millard). This won him support among Southern Democrats. He gained the nomination on the 49th ballot and was elected President with 254 electoral votes.

President Pierce favored United States expansion. Under his Administration, the country made the Gadsden Purchase, which gave it additional land from Mexico. A railroad was proposed to run over the newly acquired land to California. He also supported the idea that the United States had the right to seize Cuba from Spain. But public opposition to the annexation of Cuba, where slavery existed, forced him to back down.

The extension of slavery was the most impor-

tant domestic issue during the Pierce years. The Compromise of 1850 had quieted concern over the problem only slightly. Senator Stephen A. Douglas of Illinois wished to organize the Kansas and Nebraska territories, for he had an interest in a company that planned to build a transcontinental railroad through the area. The bill he proposed upheld "popular sovereignty"—the right of the people of a territory to decide for themselves whether to permit slavery. This violated the Missouri Compromise of 1820, however, which prohibited slavery in the Louisiana Territory, north of Missouri's southern boundary. Kansas and Nebraska were to be formed from part of that region. Even though passage of the Kansas-Nebraska bill would destroy the compromise between the North and South, and inflame public opinion, Pierce supported it. After many disagreements, the bill became law. Northerners and Southerners flocked to Kansas, the first of the two territories to be organized, in an effort to load the population for or against slavery. Violence followed as pro- and anti-slavery forces struggled for control of the Kansas government (see Buchanan, James).

Douglas' bill, and the "bleeding Kansas" aftermath, led to turmoil among the nation's political parties. In 1854, a new organization, the Republican Party, was formed. Among other things, the Republican Party came out strongly against the extension of slavery. Democrats, especially those in the South, defended the institution. The Whig Party completely disappeared, as many of its Northern members joined the Republicans.

Pierce found little support for renomination in 1856. His support of the Kansas-Nebraska bill led people to believe he was a Northerner with Southern principles. The Democratic nomination in 1856 went to James Buchanan. Pierce died in 1869.

# James K. Polk

Born: Nov. 2, 1795
Died: June 15, 1849
Place of Birth: near Pineville, N.C.
Political Party: Democrat
Term: 1845-1849
Electoral Vote: 170
Vice-President: George M. Dallas

Polk, James K. (1795-1849), was the 11th President of the United States. Polk was a supporter of expansion, and he presided over a nation that was growing rapidly.

The eldest of ten children, James Polk was born on Nov. 2, 1795, into a farming family near Pineville, N.C. When he was 11, the family moved to central Tennessee. Polk graduated from the University of North Carolina in 1818, studied law, and was admitted to the Tennessee bar in 1820.

Early in his political career, Polk became a close friend of Andrew Jackson. Polk was first elected to public office in 1823, when he won a seat in the Tennessee House of Representatives. A year later, he married Sarah Childress, a country merchant's daughter.

In 1825, Polk won election to the United States House of Representatives, where he served seven terms. He was speaker of the House from 1835 to 1838. Jackson supported Polk for governor of Tennessee in 1839, and Polk won. But he lost two tries for reelection.

Polk became a candidate for the presidency in 1844. The principal issues of the time concerned Texas and Oregon. Texas had won independence from Mexico in 1836 and wished to become a state. The boundary of Oregon was the subject of a dispute with Great Britain. Polk claimed that the territories had always belonged to the United States, and so he came out for the "reannexation" of Texas and the "reoccupation" of Oregon.

This position pleased those who believed that the United States was destined to dominate the continent. It especially earned Polk support in the South and West. And when the Democrats at the 1844 convention could not agree on another candidate, Polk received the nomination. During the campaign, he returned to the expansionist theme, and "54-40 or Fight" became the principal Democratic slogan. It referred to the proposed northern boundary of Oregon at 54°40' latitude. Polk gained the presidency by about 40,000 popular votes over the Whig candidate, Henry Clay.

During the 1840's, thousands of Americans made the long trek to Oregon. Many of them settled north of the Columbia River on territory that Great Britain claimed. Since 1818, the United States and Britain had occupied the area jointly. But Polk and his supporters were determined to gain sole U.S. possession of the territory as far north as the latitude of 54°40'. Polk eventually settled for a compromise with the British, however, and agreed that the 49th parallel should mark the boundary between Oregon and Canada.

Although Texas had been independent since 1836, its entry into the Union had been blocked by the slavery issue. Northerners opposed the addition of another slave state. Southerners supported it. But with expansionist sentiment in the air, outgoing President John Tyler had persuaded Congress to annex Texas by simple resolution in 1845.

Mexico had not recognized Texas' independence. In addition, the government claimed that the Nueces River, not the more southerly Rio Grande, was the true boundary between Mexico and Texas. In January 1846, President Polk ordered General Zachary Taylor to lead troops into the disputed area. Mexican forces responded to what they considered to be an invasion of their country, and fired on Taylor's men. The Mexican War had begun.

General Taylor quickly defeated the Mexicans in two battles in northern Mexico. Then he took the city of Monterrey. Next he won a smashing victory at the Battle of Buena Vista. General Winfield Scott led another invasion of Mexico, aimed at the capital city, which he took in September 1847.

The following year, Mexico and the United States signed the Treaty of Guadalupe Hidalgo. Under its terms, Mexico gave up claims to Texas, and ceded land forming all or part of Arizona, New Mexico, California, Colorado, Nevada, Utah, and Wyoming. The United States gave Mexico $15 million. President Polk had gained his second foreign policy objective, and much more besides.

Polk had promised not to seek reelection, and he did not. He retired to Nashville, Tenn., where he died of cholera after a short illness in 1849.

# Ronald Wilson Reagan

Born: Feb. 6, 1911
Place of Birth: Tampico, Ill.
Political Party: Republican
Term: 1981–
Electoral Vote: 489
Vice-President: George Herbert Walker Bush

Reagan, Ronald Wilson (1911–    ), was elected the 40th President of the United States in 1980. A Republican, he defeated President Jimmy Carter, the Democrat, and Representative John B. Anderson of Illinois, who ran as an independent.

Reagan was born on Feb. 6, 1911, in Tampico, Ill. In search of work, his father, a shoe salesman, moved the family to several Illinois towns. When Reagan was 9, the family settled in Dixon, Ill., where he attended elementary and high school.

The year 1928 found him at Eureka College in Illinois, where he paid his college expenses with a partial scholarship, savings from his summer lifeguard job, and money earned washing dishes at a fraternity house. While majoring in economics and sociology, he played football, joined the track team, and served as captain of the swimming team. He had leading roles in many college plays and became president of the student body.

After graduation in 1932, Reagan became a sports announcer in Iowa. While in California in 1937 reporting on the spring training of the Chicago Cubs baseball team, he made a screen test and signed a contract to act in films. He made more than 50 feature films between 1937 and 1964.

Reagan entered the U.S. Army Air Force in 1942 during World War II. He spent most of the war helping to make training films. He had married actress Jane Wyman in 1940. The couple had a daughter and adopted a son. They were divorced in 1948. In 1952, Reagan married actress Nancy Davis. They have two children.

During his movie career, Reagan was active in the Screen Actors Guild. He served five terms as its president (1947–52), and during the period of strong anti-Communist feeling in the United States, he worked to remove suspected Communists from the movie industry. In 1960, he served a sixth term as president and led the successful strike for payments to actors for sales of their films to television.

Reagan first gained nationwide political attention in 1964 when he made a stirring TV speech on behalf of the Republican candidate for President, Barry M. Goldwater. Reagan attacked high taxes, wasteful government spending, the growth of government agencies, the rising crime rate, and soaring welfare costs. These became themes in his political life.

Reagan's first public office was the governorship of California from 1967 to 1975. In 1980 Reagan gained the Republican nomination for President. He won the presidency by a large plurality.

Reagan's first major domestic programs were economic. In February 1981, Reagan proposed a plan that included tax cuts with wide reductions in welfare and other social programs, plus a large increase in defense spending. He also worked to curb federal agencies' roles in regulating business and industry. His policies became known as Reaganomics.

In mid-1981, a recession struck. Inflation slowed, but unemployment soared, contributing to a sharp loss of tax revenue and record-high federal deficits. The economy began to improve in 1983, as economic production rose and unemployment declined.

In foreign affairs, Reagan won approval in 1981 for a controversial proposal to sell advanced radar-equipped military airplanes to Saudi Arabia. He also won a struggle with Congress over his defense program. Military build-ups and worsening relations with the Soviet Union deepened public concern about nuclear war. In 1983, U.S.-Soviet relations reached a new low after a Soviet jet fighter shot down a Korean civilian airliner flying in Soviet airspace. All 269 persons on board— including 61 Americans—were killed.

Conflicts in Central America, Lebanon, and the Caribbean added to international tensions. Reagan urged increased aid for the government of El Salvador in its fight against leftist rebels. In Lebanon, the administration helped arrange a cease-fire in 1982. But new fighting broke out in 1983, and U.S. Marines serving as a peace-keeping force became involved. More than 200 U.S. troops were killed when a terrorist bomb exploded in their headquarters. In the Caribbean, Pan American forces, including U.S. Marines, invaded the island nation of Grenada in an attempt to overthrow the Marxist regime in power there.

# Franklin Delano Roosevelt

Born: Jan. 30, 1882
Died: April 12, 1945
Place of Birth: Hyde Park, N.Y.
Political Party: Democrat
Terms: 1933-1945
Electoral Votes: 472; 523; 449; 432
Vice-Presidents: John Nance Garner; Henry A. Wallace; Harry S. Truman

Roosevelt, Franklin Delano (1882-1945), was the 32nd President of the United States. Breaking the precedent that had been set by George Washington, Franklin D. Roosevelt ran for and won a third term in office in 1940, and then gained a fourth term in 1944. He presided over a nation struggling to overcome the deepest economic depression in its history, and went on to lead the United States during World War II.

The son of a wealthy New York family, Roosevelt was born on Jan. 30, 1882, on his family's estate in Hyde Park. He was a distant cousin to Theodore Roosevelt, the country's 26th President. Educated by tutors until he was 14, Roosevelt attended Groton preparatory school in Massachusetts, from which he graduated in 1900. He then went on to graduate from Harvard University in 1903, and he later studied law at Columbia University. He married a distant cousin, Eleanor Roosevelt, in 1905.

Politics interested Roosevelt much more than the law. In 1910, as a Democrat, he was elected to the New York senate. Then, as a result of working for Woodrow Wilson in the 1912 presidential campaign, he was appointed Assistant Secretary of the Navy. Roosevelt held this position during World War I.

By 1920, Roosevelt was well known in Democratic circles, and he received the vice-presidential nomination that year. Although the Democrats lost to Republican Warren G. Harding, Roosevelt's participation in the campaign made him known nationally.

About a year after the election, disease threatened to end Franklin D. Roosevelt's political career. He was stricken by polio at the family summer home on Campobello, an island off New Brunswick, in August 1921, and was left partially paralyzed. Roosevelt followed a strict schedule of exercise to overcome the paralysis of his hands and back. But for the remainder of his life, he wore braces on his legs and had to use canes or other assistance in order to walk.

Roosevelt appeared at the Democratic National Convention in 1924 to nominate New York's Governor Al Smith for the presidency. Smith did not receive the nomination that year, but he won it four years later, and Roosevelt once again supported him. Although Smith lost in 1928, that year, Roosevelt was elected to the New York governorship. He was reelected by a huge majority two years later. His success as governor placed Roosevelt in line as a possible presidential nominee in 1932.

The year 1932 appeared to be as good a year for Democrats as 1920 had been for Republicans. Following a decade of prosperity, the stock market had crashed late in 1929 (see Hoover, Herbert C.). The following year, the deepest economic depression in the country's history set in. Republicans, especially President Herbert Hoover, were blamed for the disaster. By the summer of 1932, more than 12 million people were unemployed.

At their convention in Chicago in 1932, Democrats nominated Roosevelt on the fourth ballot. Roosevelt then flew to Chicago and became the first presidential nominee to make an acceptance speech at a national convention. In his speech, he avoided specifics, but he promised a "new deal" to lift the country out of the depression. Roosevelt won election with a large majority of the popular vote and with 472 electoral votes to Hoover's 59.

After the election, the depression grew worse. There was widespread suffering. Shortly before Roosevelt's inauguration in March 1933, depositors began to take their money out of banks in an effort to protect their savings. As a result of the mass withdrawals, many banks collapsed. Once in office, Roosevelt immediately declared a "bank holiday." All banks were closed until each could be evaluated. The soundest banks then reopened.

Roosevelt next called Congress into a special session that became known as the "Hundred Days." The heavily Democratic Congress, which was actually in session for 99 days, enacted legislation designed to counteract the depression. Among other things, Congress appropriated a half billion dollars for state and city relief programs. It established the Works Progress Administration

(WPA), to put people to work on such public projects as road building and school construction. It set up the Civilian Conservation Corps (CCC), which was designed to employ young men on conservation projects. As a further conservation measure, Congress authorized the construction of dams under the Tennessee Valley Authority (TVA). And, in an effort to raise farm incomes, it passed the Agricultural Adjustment Act (AAA).

The New Deal marked an increasing government role in the economy which continued even after Roosevelt's presidency ended. Many New Deal items aroused conservative opposition on the grounds that they were socialistic. The New Deal did not pull the country completely out of the depression, but that fact did not diminish Roosevelt's popularity. He easily won reelection in 1936.

After 1936, Roosevelt's concern shifted more and more to foreign affairs. He initiated the Good Neighbor Policy toward Latin America. But events farther from home attracted more attention. The number of right-wing dictatorships in the world had increased. In Italy, Fascist dictator Benito Mussolini held power. Adolf Hitler and his Nazi Party controlled Germany. In Japan, an aggressive militaristic group governed. Japan occupied Manchuria in 1931, and six years later invaded China. Italy conquered Ethiopia in 1936. In 1938, Germany annexed Austria, and the following year, Czechoslovakia. These actions alarmed Roosevelt. He wished to use United States influence and aid as a counterweight against aggression. He feared that Germany might eventually dominate all of Europe and pose a severe threat to the United States. But the nation favored neutrality, and neutrality laws passed during the 1930's prevented Roosevelt from acting.

In September 1939, World War II erupted in Europe as Hitler conquered Poland, and England and France declared war on Germany. By the spring of 1940, Germany had conquered Belgium, The Netherlands, Denmark, Norway, and finally France. American attitudes toward neutrality began to change. U.S. aid flowed to Britain in ever-increasing amounts as the British stood alone against Germany. Congress enacted a draft law. America began to rearm. Declaring that the nation needed continuous leadership in such times, Roosevelt ran for and won a third term in 1940.

The Roosevelt Administration had opposed Japanese expansion. The opposition grew stronger after the fall of The Netherlands and France, when Japan moved to occupy French and Dutch colonies in Asia. To remove the threat of American power in the Pacific, the Japanese attacked the United States naval base at Pearl Harbor, Hawaii, on Dec. 7, 1941. The American Pacific fleet was badly crippled, but not destroyed, and the United States was now in World War II. Earlier in 1941, Germany had invaded Russia. Now Germany and its ally Italy declared war on the United States.

Under Roosevelt's command, United States military leaders conducted a global strategy. In the Pacific, U.S. forces took island after island, and gradually pushed the Japanese back. American troops participated in the invasions of North Africa, Sicily, and Italy in 1942-1943. On June 6, 1944, Allied armies crossed the English Channel and invaded France. The German armies fought fiercely, but finally retreated, while the Russians moved toward Germany from the east.

The strain on Roosevelt of three terms in office was obvious as 1944 began. But the voters elected him to a fourth term in November of that year. Then, on April 12, 1945, Roosevelt suffered a cerebral hemorrhage and died. Vice-President Harry S. Truman became President.

# Theodore Roosevelt

Born: Oct. 27, 1858
Died: Jan. 6, 1919
Place of Birth: New York, N.Y.
Political Party: Republican
Terms: 1901-1909
Electoral Vote: 336
Vice-President: Charles W. Fairbanks

Roosevelt, Theodore (1858–1919), was the 26th President of the United States. A flamboyant, decisive man of boundless energy, Roosevelt was a strong and immensely popular President.

Theodore Roosevelt was born into a well-to-do family in New York City on Oct. 27, 1858. Early in his life, Roosevelt displayed great curiosity and determination. He suffered from asthma, but by following a vigorous schedule of exercise, he overcame his affliction and gained great physical strength. Roosevelt was educated by tutors, then entered Harvard University at age 18. He graduated from there in 1880. Shortly thereafter, he married Alice Hathaway Lee, a Bostonian and daughter of a wealthy investment banker. She died in childbirth in 1884.

After briefly attending Columbia University Law School, Roosevelt decided to enter politics. In 1881, at age 23, he was elected to the New York assembly as a Republican. He won reelection twice. Beginning in 1884, he spent two years working on cattle ranches he owned in the West. He also wrote several books. He returned to politics in 1886, when he lost a bid to become mayor of New York. Near the end of that year, he married Edith Kermit Carow.

In 1895, Roosevelt became president of the Board of Police Commissioners for the City of New York. While serving on the police commission, he fought dishonesty in the department. As a result, Roosevelt earned a reputation as a reformer. He took part in the successful presidential campaign of Republican William McKinley in 1896. After McKinley took office, Roosevelt was rewarded with the post of Assistant Secretary of the Navy.

At the time, the United States was becoming more and more prominent as a world power. Roosevelt forcefully supported the expansion of U.S. economic, political, and military influence. In 1895, Cubans began a revolt against their Spanish colonial government. Roosevelt urged that the United States intervene to free Cuba from Spanish rule. The United States finally did declare war on Spain in 1898, and Roosevelt left the government to head a volunteer force known as the Rough Riders, which fought in Cuba.

Roosevelt's military record helped him win election as governor of New York shortly after he returned from Cuba in 1898. As governor, he pursued a course independent from regular party leaders and established a record of reform. In 1900, the Republicans chose him as their vice-presidential nominee to run with President McKinley, who sought a second term. McKinley and Roosevelt won. Roosevelt did not think the vice-presidency would further his career. But then, in 1901, McKinley was assassinated, and Roosevelt became President.

No one was sure of Roosevelt's positions. He was known as a reformer. But progressive Republicans, who favored close government regulation of business and industry, pro-labor legislation, and conservation programs, did not entirely trust him. Conservatives also tended to distrust him.

In practice, Roosevelt managed to steer a middle course. He successfully moved against such business monopolies, called *trusts*, as Standard Oil, American Tobacco, and the Northern Securities Company. As a result, Roosevelt became known as a "trust buster."

In 1904, Roosevelt won election to the presidency by a margin of more than 2½ million popular votes, the largest majority to that time. He continued to uphold reform legislation, including the Hepburn Railroad Rate Act, the Food and Drugs Act, and the Meat Inspection Act.

A French company had tried and failed to dig a canal through Panama. When American officials wanted to take the project over, Roosevelt approved. Panama was then a part of Colombia. Colombia refused the sum offered by the Americans for rights to build the canal. With the aid of some Americans, and with Roosevelt's tacit approval, Panamanians then staged a rebellion against Colombia. Roosevelt sent a United States warship to prevent Colombian forces from reaching Panama. Panama became independent, and its representatives signed a treaty that gave the United States the authority to build a canal and to control land alongside it. The Panama Canal opened in 1914. In 1905, Roosevelt negotiated a treaty ending the Russo-Japanese War. Two years later, to "show the flag," he sent a fleet of U.S. warships on a goodwill tour around the world.

William Howard Taft succeeded Roosevelt in the presidency in 1909. Roosevelt went off to Africa to hunt big game. After his return to the United States, he became increasingly critical of Taft's performance (see Taft, William Howard). In 1912, Roosevelt decided to try to regain the presidency. Progressive Republicans nominated him as their candidate on the "Bull Moose" ticket, and conservative Republicans remained with Taft. The Republican split helped Democratic candidate Woodrow Wilson win the election.

Roosevelt strongly supported United States preparedness when World War I broke out in Europe in 1914. He constantly criticized President Wilson's efforts to keep the United States neutral.

After the war, Roosevelt opposed United States membership in the League of Nations (see Wilson, Woodrow). He feared such membership would hinder America's freedom in foreign affairs. There was talk of a Roosevelt nomination for the 1920 presidential campaign, but early in 1919, he died suddenly of a blood clot in the heart.

# William Howard Taft

Born: Sept. 15, 1857
Died: March 8, 1930
Place of Birth: Cincinnati, Ohio
Political Party: Republican
Term: 1909-1913
Electoral Vote: 321
Vice-President: James S. Sherman

Taft, William Howard (1857-1930), was the 27th President of the United States. Taft's first love was the law, and he was reluctant to run for the presidency in 1908. In 1921, eight years after leaving office, he achieved his highest goal, appointment as Chief Justice of the United States.

A lawyer's son, William Howard Taft was born in Cincinnati, Ohio, on Sept. 15, 1857. He was a large child, and as President, he stood 6 feet tall and weighed 300 pounds. Taft attended Yale University. He was graduated from Yale in 1878 and from Cincinnati Law College two years later.

Taft's first political job was as an assistant county attorney in Ohio. In 1882, President Chester A. Arthur appointed Taft a district collector of internal revenue. Four years later, he married Helen Herron, the daughter of one of President Rutherford B. Hayes' law partners. In 1901, Taft was made civil governor of the Philippines, which had become a U.S. possession as a result of the United States victory in the Spanish-American War. Taft performed ably in that position, and he became so devoted to his work in the Philippines that he turned down an appointment to the Supreme Court in 1902. In 1904, however, Taft accepted when President Theodore Roosevelt offered him appointment as secretary of war.

As an administrator, Taft won popular acclaim, and he became Roosevelt's choice for the Republican presidential nomination in 1908. Taft won an easy victory in the election that year.

Taft was uncomfortable in the presidency. He found it difficult to follow the flamboyant Roosevelt, who had been a public favorite. Moreover, Taft presided over a Republican Party that was divided into conservative and liberal factions. The conservatives unabashedly favored big business. The liberals wanted to curb the huge business monopolies, called trusts. They also wanted to increase government regulation of the economy in general, and secure gains for labor. Taft was a conservative but tried to steer a middle course. He eventually lost control of his party.

Taft supported several policies that pleased the liberals. He took more action under the 1890 Sherman Antitrust Act than had Roosevelt. He also set up the Tariff Board to make detailed studies of tariff rates. During his administration, Congress established the Children's Bureau, set up the postal savings and parcel post systems, passed a law that required the public disclosure of political campaign expenses, and placed the regulation of telegraph, telephone, and cable systems under the Interstate Commerce Commission.

On the other hand, Taft offended the liberals on numerous occasions. He refused to support their efforts to reduce the vast political power wielded by Speaker of the House Joseph Cannon of Illinois. Cannon personally decided which legislation would pass and which would fail. The liberals won the fight against Cannon in spite of Taft's position.

In foreign affairs, Taft followed the policies of his immediate predecessors and extended American economic and political influence. He supported the granting of loans by U.S. banks and businesses to other countries, especially in Latin America. This led to an extension of American economic and political control in the indebted nations. Taft's policy became known as "dollar diplomacy."

As Taft's Administration continued, former President Theodore Roosevelt became more and more critical of Taft. Roosevelt denied any renewed interest in the presidency, but in 1912, he reversed himself and accepted nomination by the liberal wing of the Republican Party. Conservatives chose to stay with Taft. With the Republicans split, Democrat Woodrow Wilson won the presidency.

In 1913, Taft became a professor of constitutional law at Yale. President Warren G. Harding appointed him Chief Justice of the United States in 1921. On the Supreme Court he established a conservative record. Taft died in Washington, D.C., in 1930.

# Zachary Taylor

Born: Nov. 24, 1784
Died: July 9, 1850
Place of Birth: near Barboursville, Va.
Political Party: Whig
Term: 1849-1850
Electoral Vote: 163
Vice-President: Millard Fillmore

Taylor, Zachary (1784-1850), was the 12th President of the United States. Zachary Taylor's popularity as a war hero after 40 years of military service propelled him into the White House. But his term was one of the shortest in presidential history, for he died after only 16 months in office.

A Southerner, Taylor was born on Nov. 24, 1784, near Barboursville, Va. Taylor's father was rewarded with 6,000 acres of land in Kentucky for his Revolutionary War service, and he settled the family there in 1785. Taylor gained his interest in the military from hearing about his father's army experience and from the Indian wars that were being fought in Kentucky during his boyhood. In 1808, he became a lieutenant in the United States Army. Two years later, he married Margaret Mackall Smith, the daughter of a Maryland planter.

Taylor fought against Indians in Indiana during the War of 1812. He later served in Wisconsin during the Blackhawk War in 1832. In 1837, he led a successful expedition against the Seminole Indians of Florida.

Texas won its independence from Mexico in 1836 and wished to become a state. The dispute over the extension of slavery delayed its admission, however, for Texas would be a slave state, and Northerners opposed its entry into the Union. But in 1845, public opinion favored territorial expansion, and the United States annexed Texas. Mexico, which had never recognized Texan independence, threatened war. In addition, Mexico insisted that the southern boundary of Texas lay along the Nueces River, not the more southerly Rio Grande. Early in 1846, President James K. Polk ordered Zachary Taylor to lead U.S. troops into the disputed area. Mexican forces fired on the Americans and war began.

Taylor, known as "Old Rough and Ready," defeated Mexican troops in two battles. He then took the city of Monterrey. Because of his success, Taylor seemed the logical choice to command the U.S. drive toward Mexico City. But President James K. Polk, a Democrat, thought otherwise. Polk feared that Taylor, who leaned towards the Whigs,

might become a political hero. So Polk chose General Winfield Scott to lead the invasion. Taylor, in the meantime, went on to achieve his greatest fame in the Battle of Buena Vista in 1847; he won a two-day battle in which his forces were outnumbered four to one.

The Whigs now had a military hero in their midst, and they capitalized on their opportunity. In 1848, they nominated Taylor for the presidency and selected Millard Fillmore of New York for the vice-presidency. Neither Whigs nor Democrats raised the slavery issue during the campaign. But a third party, the Free Soil Party, entered the contest with a pledge to halt the extension of slavery. Former President Martin Van Buren was the Free Soil candidate. Van Buren drew enough votes away from Democrat Lewis Cass to ensure Taylor's election.

Gold had been discovered in California in 1848, and Americans flocked west. California's population grew rapidly, and the territory was soon ready for statehood. But at the time, the number of free and slave states was equal. California's admission would tip the balance in favor of the free states. Compromise or conflict seemed inevitable.

Taylor supported California's admission, and he opposed a compromise on the issue. Since he himself was a slaveholder, this position seemed to go against his interests and his Southern heritage, and it dismayed Southerners. Taylor, however, was first and foremost a nationalist. Further, the time he had spent in the Northwest as a soldier had made him as much a Westerner as a Southerner. Basically, he believed in retaining slavery where it already existed, but he was opposed to its extension.

As Congress debated a compromise, Taylor died in the summer of 1850. Millard Fillmore became President and a compromise was enacted.

# Harry S. Truman

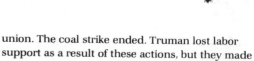

Born: May 8, 1884
Died: Dec. 26, 1972
Place of Birth: Lamar, Mo.
Political Party: Democrat
Terms: 1945-1953
Electoral Vote: 303
Vice-President: Alben W. Barkley

Truman, Harry S. (1884-1972), was the 33rd President of the United States. The peppery and outspoken Truman was elevated to the presidency upon the death of Franklin D. Roosevelt in 1945.

Lamar, Mo., was the place of Truman's birth on May 8, 1884. He attended elementary and high school in Independence, Mo. After graduation, he worked for a railroad, in a newspaper mailing room, and as a bank clerk. Then he turned to farming. During World War I, Truman served as a captain of artillery.

After the war, Truman opened a men's clothing store in Kansas City. The business failed. He then entered politics. With the support of the Pendergast political machine in Kansas City, he was elected a county judge in 1922. In 1934, again with machine help, Truman won election to the United States Senate. He became known in the Senate for his work as head of a committee investigating fraud in war contracts during World War II. And in 1944, Truman became the Democratic compromise candidate for the vice-presidency, as Roosevelt sought a fourth term. Roosevelt's death in April 1945 made Truman President.

The war in Europe ended in May 1945. Truman's most momentous decision as President concerned the war in the Pacific. He ordered an atomic bomb dropped on Hiroshima and Nagasaki, Japan.

After the Japanese surrender in August 1945, Truman faced many difficult domestic problems. Among them were labor unrest and the question of price controls. There were many strikes during 1945 and 1946, as organized labor sought pay increases to compensate for growing inflation. In some cases, Truman took harsh action. When railroad unions threatened to walk out, tying up the nation's transportation system, the President asked Congress for authority to draft strikers into the Army. The railroad unions backed down. When union leader John L. Lewis refused to send his striking coal miners back to work, Truman had a court injunction served on him. The court levied heavy fines against Lewis and the mineworkers'

union. The coal strike ended. Truman lost labor support as a result of these actions, but they made him popular among millions of other Americans.

Foreign affairs attracted much attention during Truman's Administration. Russia and the United States had been allies against Germany in World War II. But soon after the war ended, differences began to divide them. Russia refused to support free elections in Poland, which it had liberated from German control. With Russian aid, Poland became a Communist nation. The Truman government perceived Russia as an aggressor. President Truman concluded that Russia had plans to control Western Europe and probably intended to dominate the world. Truman established the policy of "containment," which endorsed resistance to the advance of Communism anywhere in the world. The period known as the Cold War began.

The foreign policy position against Communism had domestic effects. The discovery of a Soviet spy ring in Canada in 1946 aroused fears that Communist agents might be operating in the United States as well. Truman tended to downplay the fear of domestic Communists, though he set up a loyalty review board to check on government employees. Some employees resigned, and some others were dismissed, but no Communists or evidence of spying were discovered.

Despite this action, Truman was labeled "soft on Communism," and he was criticized by many people for his handling of the strikes and price controls. By 1948, he was an unpopular President. It appeared that for the first time since 1933, Republicans would control the White House. They nominated New York Governor Thomas E. Dewey as their presidential candidate. Democrats had no choice but to go along with Truman. Then, following the party's adoption of a strong civil rights plank, Southern delegates walked out of the 1948 Democratic convention. They formed their own party, known as the Dixiecrats. Many liberal Democrats threw their support behind yet another candidate, Henry Wallace, who headed the Progressive Party. With the Democrats badly split, Republican chances looked better than ever.

But Truman conducted a strong, scrappy, and tireless campaign. He blamed the Republican-controlled Congress for the nation's troubles. And to the surprise of almost everyone, he won the election.

The Allied victory in World War II had freed Korea from Japanese control. Russia occupied North Korea, and the United States occupied the South. Both nations withdrew their troops later. Russia left a totalitarian government in the North. South Korea, supported by the United States, formed a republic. In June 1950, North Korea invaded the South. President Truman immediately dispatched U.S. troops to aid South Korea and persuaded the United Nations to send troops also. The invasion was eventually repelled, and the Korean War ended in 1953 with the country divided as before.

Meanwhile, fear of Communists continued in the United States. A group accused of giving atomic secrets to Russia was uncovered. The members of the group were convicted. Some were imprisoned. Two others, Julius and Ethel Rosenberg, were executed. Alger Hiss, a former state de-

partment official, was accused of having spied for Russia in the 1930's. Convicted of perjury, Hiss was sentenced to five years in prison.

These cases, plus the Communist victory in China and the Korean War, offered some politicians a chance to play upon American fears. Foremost among these politicians was Senator Joseph R. McCarthy of Wisconsin. Beginning in 1950, he kept the country in an uproar for four years with charges that Communists had infiltrated the U.S. government. McCarthy employed highly unethical methods in his investigations, and he proved no cases. Yet for a time, millions of people supported him. Government leaders feared to act against him.

In 1950, Congress passed the McCarran Internal Security Act. One portion of the act required members of the Communist Party in the United States to register with the government. Truman vetoed the bill, calling it unconstitutional. But Congress overrode his veto.

Truman retired from the presidency in 1953 and returned to Independence, Mo. There he oversaw the construction of the Truman Library and wrote his memoirs. He died in Independence in 1972.

---

# John Tyler

Born: March 29, 1790
Died: Jan. 18, 1862
Place of Birth: Greenway, Va.
Political Party: Whig
Term: 1841-1845
Electoral Vote: None
Vice-President: None

Tyler, John (1790-1862), was the 10th President of the United States. He became the first Vice-President to succeed to the presidency upon the death of a President. He took office after the death of President William Henry Harrison in 1841. Tyler spent his presidential years in conflict with Congress.

John Tyler was born in Greenway, Va., on March 29, 1790. He graduated from William and Mary College in Williamsburg, Va., at age 17. He then studied law and became a lawyer in 1809.

Turning to politics, Tyler won election to Virginia's House of Delegates at age 21. He took time out from the legislature to serve briefly in the War of 1812, and in March 1813, he married Letitia Christian, the daughter of a well-to-do Virginia planter. Three years later, Tyler ran for and won a

seat in the United States House of Representatives. He remained there until he ran for the Senate and lost in 1821. After serving briefly as chancellor of William and Mary College and two years as governor of Virginia, Tyler finally was elected to the Senate in 1827.

Tyler opposed the second Bank of the United States, which had been chartered in 1816, and federal support for internal improvements. He based his opposition on the belief that such measures led only to a bigger and more powerful federal government. In 1828, Congress passed a tariff law that placed high taxes on imported manufactured goods. Southerners opposed the measure. Andrew Jackson's first Vice-President, John C. Calhoun of South Carolina, later argued that a state had the constitutional right to nullify—

declare null and void—any federal law it opposed. South Carolina nullified the high tariff laws of 1828 and 1832. Congress, with Jackson's support, then passed a bill authorizing the President to use force if necessary to collect tariffs. South Carolina backed down. As a senator, Tyler opposed both nullification and Jackson's handling of the matter. Told by the Virginia legislature to support the President, Tyler resigned from the Senate instead. He also withdrew from the Democratic Party.

In 1840, the Whig Party named Tyler as running mate to presidential candidate William Henry Harrison. Whigs had formed their party in the 1830's out of a loose coalition of interests, some of which actually opposed one another. Farmers, manufacturers, and Southerners, for example, could not agree on the tariff question even though all three groups supported the Whig Party. Tyler won the Whig nomination because he had been an anti-Jackson man, and he was a Southerner. Because Harrison was an Ohioan, Tyler gave geographical balance to the ticket. But Harrison died unexpectedly a month after his inauguration, and Tyler became President. His troubles began soon afterward.

Whigs in Congress pushed through bills for internal improvements, high tariffs, and a new Bank of the United States. A Jackson veto in 1832 had abolished the second Bank. Tyler stuck to his principles and responded with vetoes. An armed mob then attacked the White House, shouting insults and pelting windows with rocks. But Tyler stood firm. Congress passed another bank bill, and Tyler again vetoed it. This resulted in another mob scene, and the mob burned Tyler in effigy. The President had kept the Cabinet chosen by Harrison, and now all but Secretary of State Daniel Webster resigned. Tyler next vetoed a Whig measure that gave income from federal land sales to the states. This caused the sponsor of the bill, Henry Clay, to resign from the Senate.

Whigs began to disown Tyler and referred to him as "His Accidency." In January 1843, Whigs in Congress moved to impeach Tyler, but they failed. The fact was that Tyler had never been a Whig in the first place, and he was an accidental President.

Texas won independence from Mexico in 1836. It wished to join the Union. Northerners opposed this, because Texas would be an additional slave state. Southerners, Tyler included, supported annexation. In 1844, Democrat James K. Polk, who favored admitting Texas, was elected President. Before leaving office in 1845, Tyler approved a joint congressional resolution making Texas a state.

Tyler supported Virginia's secession from the Union in 1861, and he served in the Confederate congress. He died in Richmond, Va., in 1862.

---

# Martin Van Buren

Born: Dec. 5, 1782
Died: July 24, 1862
Place of Birth: Kinderhook, N.Y.
Political Party: Democrat
Term: 1837-1841
Electoral Vote: 170
Vice-President: Richard M. Johnson

Van Buren, Martin (1782-1862), was the eighth President of the United States. He was recognized as a highly skilled political organizer. But he became President shortly before the nation slid into its first severe economic depression. His steadfast refusal to provide government relief proved him to be a man of principle, but it cost him his political popularity.

Martin Van Buren was born in Kinderhook, N.Y., on Dec. 5, 1782, into a Dutch family of long standing in the community. At age 14, he began to study law, and he made his first courtroom appearance as a lawyer when only 15. Van Buren opened a law practice in Kinderhook in 1803, and four years later he married Hannah Hoes, a distant cousin. He entered politics as a member of the Democratic-Republican Party and a follower of Thomas Jefferson, who became President in 1800. Van Buren was elected to the New York senate in 1812, and four years later became that state's attorney general. In 1821, the New York legislature sent him to the United States Senate.

After winning reelection to the Senate in 1827, Van Buren resigned the following year, when he was elected governor of New York. Then, as a reward for his aid in managing the 1828 presidential campaign, President Andrew Jackson made Van Buren his secretary of state.

In 1831, Jackson nominated Van Buren as minister to Great Britain, but the Senate refused confirmation. Jackson then made Van Buren his vice-presidential running mate in 1832, placing him firmly in line for the presidency. Jackson and Van Buren won the 1832 election. And in 1836, Van Buren was the Democratic presidential candidate. He defeated the leading Whig candidate, William Henry Harrison, by 97 electoral votes.

Martin Van Buren became President at an unfortunate time. During the Jackson presidency, land speculation had run wild. States made unsound investments in canal and road building. Joining in the speculative frenzy, banks extended many insecure loans for land purchases and business expansion. President Andrew Jackson attempted to cool the situation with the *Specie Circular*, issued in 1836. It required that land be purchased only with gold or silver. This halted land speculation, but it did not save the country from a severe depression that began soon after Van Buren took office in 1837. Many banks failed, and the financial crash became known as the Panic of 1837.

The depression threw thousands of people out of work, but President Van Buren turned down all ideas for government action to alleviate the hardship. He clung to the belief that government intervention would do the economy more harm than good. Van Buren concerned himself chiefly with federal government finances. Jackson had destroyed the

Bank of the United States, and had placed federal deposits in private and state banks (see Jackson, Andrew). Van Buren feared that those banks might fail, and he wanted to set up an independent treasury to hold federal government funds. Congress finally approved an independent treasury bill in 1840, but it abolished the treasury a year later, after Van Buren had left office.

Van Buren's failure to act against the depression earned him criticism. In addition, abolitionists criticized him for spending federal money to subdue and remove the Seminole Indians in Florida. They believed Florida would become another slave state. Proslavery groups attacked him for refusing to agree to demands that Texas be annexed. Texas had won independence from Mexico in 1836 and would have entered the Union as a slave state. And Van Buren received little credit for peacefully settling a boundary dispute between Maine and New Brunswick, a Canadian province.

Although Van Buren's Administration had been an unhappy one, he was willing to try for another term, and the Democrats renominated him in 1840. The Whigs again turned to war hero William Henry Harrison. Van Buren lost by an electoral vote of 234 to 60. But he managed to gain more than a million of the 2,400,000 popular votes cast. The election had brought out the greatest turnout of voters up to that point in American history.

Martin Van Buren remained a staunch Democrat and active in politics for the remainder of his life. He died in 1862.

---

# George Washington

Born: Feb. 22, 1732
Died: Dec. 14, 1799
Place of Birth: Westmoreland County, Va.
Political Party: None
Terms: 1789-1797
Electoral Vote: 69; 132
Vice-President: John Adams

Washington, George (1732-1799), was the first President of the United States. Unlike any other American President, Washington has been honored with an unblemished reputation and consistent national acclaim. His unique role in the history of the United States has made him revered as the "Father of His Country."

Washington was born in Westmoreland County, Va., on Feb. 22, 1732. Although he had some formal schooling, most of his education came through his

daily experiences living and working on the family plantation.

While in his teens, George Washington became a surveyor, and his work took him on numerous trips to the back country of Virginia. At age 20, he became a major in the Virginia militia. In the fall of 1753, he led a small party into western Pennsylvania to deliver a message from Virginia's Governor Robert Dinwiddie to the French commander of Fort Le Boeuf, near present-day Erie, Pa. Dinwiddie warned the French to evacuate the region but the commander refused. Later, Dinwiddie sent Washington to secure a fort that Virginians had built at the juncture of the Allegheny and Monongahela rivers in Pennsylvania. The French captured the fort, however, before Washington and his force arrived, and named it Fort Duquesne. Washington's men built another fort, named Fort Necessity, south of Fort Duquesne. Washington not only failed to attack Fort Duquesne, but he was unable—even with British help—to hold Fort Necessity.

The British and Virginians were not finished with Fort Duquesne. In the spring of 1755, Washington and a group of militiamen accompanied a force under British General Edward Braddock on a march against the stronghold. The French and their Indian allies attacked the column and defeated it. Braddock was mortally wounded in the action.

Washington saw little additional action during the French and Indian War. His exploits, though, had made him known throughout the American Colonies. For the next 15 years, Washington devoted himself to managing his plantation, Mount Vernon, on the Potomac River in northern Virginia. In 1759, he married Martha Custis, a wealthy widow. During the years before the Revolutionary War, Washington also served in the Virginia legislature, the House of Burgesses.

George Washington became one of the first persons to express opposition to the British tax and trade policies that led to the Revolution. He was a member of both the First and Second Continental Congresses. After the early battles, in the Spring of 1775, the Congress chose Washington as commander in chief of the Continental Army.

Standing 6 feet, 2 inches tall, with an erect posture, Washington was an impressive military figure. But he presided over more defeats than most successful commanders. Desertion and the almost constant lack of adequate supplies caused Washington to be frequently discouraged. His major contribution to the war effort, through determination and sheer force of personality, was to keep an army in the field and to inspire it to continue fighting. With the aid of a French army and navy, Washington won the most important battle of the Revolutionary War, at Yorktown, Va., in 1781. The fighting ended soon afterwards.

Washington returned to his beloved Mount Vernon after the Revolution, and stayed there for five years. He was then called upon to participate in the construction of a new government.

In 1781, Congress had adopted the Articles of Confederation, which provided for a national government and listed the powers to be held by it and by the states. Most of the power rested with the states. The national government could not, for example, levy taxes or regulate trade. A number of prominent Americans, including Washington, concluded that the Articles had to be amended to strengthen the central government. And for that purpose, 55 men gathered in Philadelphia in the summer of 1787. Washington was chosen president of the convention. The delegates proceeded to throw away the Articles of Confederation and write a new Constitution. After the Constitution had been ratified by the states, Washington became, as everyone expected, the first President of the new nation. He was the only person to be elected to the office unanimously, not only once, but twice.

Washington was inaugurated on April 30, 1789. Because he was the first President, heading a new government, everything he did would set a precedent. How should the President be addressed? As "Mr. President." What about relations with Congress? At first, distant. What should be the President's role in legislation? Advise little, but exercise the veto when necessary. Washington first used his veto power in 1792, when he acted against a bill that would have increased the number of U.S. representatives from 67 to 120. What about advisers? With the cooperation of Congress, Washington established the first Cabinet. It consisted of Alexander Hamilton as secretary of the treasury, Thomas Jefferson as head of the state department, Henry Knox as secretary of war, and Edmund Randolph as attorney general.

During Washington's Administration, the federal government assumed the Revolutionary War debts of the states. It established the First Bank of the United States. It sent an army to put down a threatened rebellion among western Pennsylvanians who refused to pay a tax on whiskey. Following the French Revolution in 1789, Europe was at war. Washington steered a narrow path of neutrality, even though he was beset with demands that the United States side with Britain on the one hand, or France on the other.

As a war measure, both England and France sought to cut off one another's trade with neutral nations. Britain halted U.S. ships on the high seas. The British frequently removed sailors they claimed were deserters from British vessels, some of whom actually were Americans. The British seizure of American sailors added fuel to the demands for war with Britain. Washington, however, stood firm for neutrality, and he dispatched John Jay, chief justice of the United States, to England to work out a treaty. The British consented to trade agreements, and they agreed to give up forts they still held in the northwestern part of the United States. But the Jay Treaty contained no mention of the issue of British harassment of American ships. George Washington realized that he had a highly emotional issue on his hands, and for a time, he did not make the treaty public. There was a public uproar when the news got out, and the Senate split sharply on the issue, though it finally ratified the treaty. After considerable further thought, Washington signed it.

Washington hated factionalism, but he nonetheless presided over the development of political parties in the United States. Originally, those who favored the ratification of the Constitution were known as Federalists. Those opposed were called Anti-Federalists. In the government, those who favored strong central power, business and commercial interests, and Washington's policies in general, were called Federalists. Alexander Hamilton, secretary of the treasury, was the chief Federalist leader. Those who stressed states' rights and the interests of farmers and small-businessmen became known as Democratic-Republicans. They were led by Thomas Jefferson

and James Madison. Jefferson and Hamilton disagreed on such issues as the Bank of the United States, the government's assumption of states' war debts, and on whether the United States should favor Britain or France in the European war. Criticism of the Jay Treaty came chiefly from Democratic-Republican newspapers. This and other criticism disturbed Washington, who believed in discussion of public issues, but not in what he considered unjustified complaint.

Weary of argument, factionalism, and of public service in general, Washington refused nomination for a third term. He thus set a precedent that went unbroken until 1940, when Franklin D. Roosevelt campaigned for and won a third term. In 1797, Washington handed over the reigns of government to John Adams, who had served during both terms as his Vice-President. Washington then retired to Mount Vernon. While he managed his plantation, he kept in touch with government leaders, and from time to time he visited the capital, then located in Philadelphia.

Early in December 1799, while riding in a cold rain, Washington caught a chill. Laryngitis developed. Following the standard medical procedure of the time, Washington's physician drained blood from his veins. This only weakened him. And on December 14, Washington died.

---

# Woodrow Wilson

Born: Dec. 29, 1856
Died: Feb. 3, 1924
Place of Birth: Staunton, Va.
Political Party: Democrat
Terms: 1913-1921
Electoral Vote: 435; 277
Vice-President: Thomas R. Marshall

Wilson, Woodrow (1856-1924), was the 28th President of the United States. Woodrow Wilson achieved national acclaim as a university president and as New Jersey's governor before going on to the presidency. As President, he encouraged the enactment of much reform legislation and guided United States participation in World War I.

A native of Virginia, Wilson was born in the small town of Staunton on Dec. 29, 1856. He was the son of a Presbyterian minister. He graduated from Princeton University in 1879. Wilson practiced law for a year and then entered Johns Hopkins University for graduate work in government and history, completing a Ph.D. in 1886. A year ear-

lier, he had married Ellen Louise Axson, whose father was also a Presbyterian minister. She died in August, 1914, and about a year later, Wilson married Edith Bolling Galt, a widow.

Wilson taught at Bryn Mawr College, Wesleyan University, and Princeton University. He became president of Princeton in 1902. In 1910, with the New Jersey Democratic Party suffering from the effects of widespread corruption, party leaders needed an outsider with integrity. They approached Wilson, who accepted their nomination for the governorship and won election by a large majority.

As governor, Wilson separated himself from regular party leaders and pushed for reform. He obtained such reforms as a corrupt practices law, a primary election law, and employers' liability legislation. His record as governor brought him national attention, and in 1912, he won the Democratic nomination for the presidency.

Republicans that year were split. One faction followed President William Howard Taft, the other favored former President Theodore Roosevelt. Wilson easily won election with about 6,300,000 popular and 435 electoral votes.

In the presidency, Wilson continued as a reformer. He achieved lower tariff rates, the establishment of the Federal Reserve Board to regulate banks and the nation's currency, the inauguration of the Federal Trade Commission to oversee trade practices within the country, and the Adamson Act, which granted railroad workers an eight-hour day. Beginning in 1914, however, foreign affairs occupied much of the President's attention.

Mexico was in the midst of turmoil, as various factions struggled for control of the government. At the time of Wilson's election, power rested in the hands of Victoriano Huerta, who established himself as dictator. The Wilson administration wanted to unseat Huerta, and so it sold arms to rival factions. In 1914, at Tampico, Mexican soldiers arrested some American sailors on shore leave. Upon a protest by the United States, Huerta offered apologies, but he refused to salute the American flag. Wilson then sent troops to occupy Vera Cruz. Brazil, Argentina, and Chile finally mediated the dispute. Later, a group led by Francisco Villa raided U.S. communities across the Texas border. Wilson dispatched troops, who unsuccessfully pursued Villa into Mexico. Finally, in 1917, Mexico achieved a stable government and a new constitution. Wilson extended United States recognition to Mexico.

World War I began in Europe in August 1914. With the majority of Americans supporting him, Wilson declared the United States neutral in the conflict and attempted to hold to that policy. But he also insisted on American freedom of the seas. That put United States ships and Americans traveling to Europe in danger of attack by German submarines, which were trying to cut Great Britain and France off from outside contact. The torpedoing of the British liner *Lusitania* in 1915, for example, cost 128 American lives. Wilson finally obtained German agreement to curb unrestricted submarine warfare.

In 1916, the Democrats used the slogan, "He kept us out of war," and Wilson won election to a second term. But after Germany renewed unrestricted submarine activity early in 1917, neutrality once again became difficult to maintain. War came increasingly near as German submarines sank a number of American ships. Finally, early in April 1917, Wilson asked for and obtained a declaration of war by Congress.

United States troops arriving in France helped turn back a German offensive in 1918 and achieve Allied victory. Wilson hoped to restrain European nationalism, which had been responsible for many wars, and to establish a firm basis for lasting peace. With those goals in mind, he offered Fourteen Points as a basis for settlement, and he promoted them at the peace conference held at Versailles, France, in 1919. Among the points were a ban on secret treaties and agreements, armament reduction, freedom of the seas, and an association to settle international disputes and keep the peace. The association became known as the League of Nations.

Wilson won some of his points and lost others. The victorious European allies redrew the map of Europe in their own interests and burdened Germany with a huge bill of compensation for war damages. They agreed on what Wilson considered the most important point, however, the League of Nations.

Returning home temporarily, Wilson found a Republican-controlled Senate unwilling to accept United States membership in the League without amendments providing the U.S. with greater freedom of action as a League member. Wilson returned to the peace conference and won agreement to some changes, but not enough to satisfy the critics in the Senate. Back in the United States once more, Wilson decided to take his plea for American membership in the League to the people. He embarked in the fall of 1919 on a wide-ranging speaking tour. But on September 25, while traveling between Pueblo, Colo., and Wichita, Kans., Wilson fell ill. Early in October, he suffered a stroke. For the remainder of his term, Wilson remained an invalid. His wife helped him carry out necessary presidential duties. The Senate voted twice to refuse to accept the Treaty of Versailles without reservations concerning U.S. participation in the League of Nations.

Crippled, Wilson retired from the presidency in 1921 to a life of relative inactivity. He died in 1924.

# 2. Prime Ministers of Canada

## Canada's Prime Ministers

| Name | Dates served | Party | Birthplace | Birth and death dates |
|------|--------------|-------|------------|-----------------------|
| Sir John A. Macdonald | 1867-1873 | Conservative | Glasgow, Scotland | 1815-1891 |
| Alexander Mackenzie | 1873-1878 | Liberal | Logierait, Scotland | 1822-1892 |
| Sir John A. Macdonald | 1878-1891 | Conservative | Glasgow, Scotland | 1815-1891 |
| Sir John J. C. Abbott | 1891-1892 | Conservative | St. Andrews, Lower Canada (now Quebec) | 1821-1893 |
| Sir John S. D. Thompson | 1892-1894 | Conservative | Halifax, N.S. | 1844-1894 |
| Sir Mackenzie Bowell | 1894-1896 | Conservative | Rickinghall, England | 1823-1917 |
| Sir Charles Tupper | 1896 | Conservative | Amherst, N.S. | 1821-1915 |
| Sir Wilfrid Laurier | 1896-1911 | Liberal | St. Lin (now Laurentides), Quebec | 1841-1919 |
| Sir Robert L. Borden | 1911-1917 | Conservative | Grand Pré, N.S. | 1854-1937 |
| Sir Robert L. Borden | 1917-1920 | Unionist | Grand Pré, N.S. | 1854-1937 |
| Arthur Meighen | 1920-1921 | Unionist | St. Mary's, Ont. | 1874-1960 |
| W. L. Mackenzie King | 1921-1926 | Liberal | Berlin (now Kitchener), Ont. | 1874-1950 |
| Arthur Meighen | 1926 | Conservative | St. Mary's, Ont. | 1874-1960 |
| W. L. Mackenzie King | 1926-1930 | Liberal | Berlin (now Kitchener), Ont. | 1874-1950 |
| Richard B. Bennett | 1930-1935 | Conservative | Hopewell Cape, N.B. | 1870-1947 |
| W. L. Mackenzie King | 1935-1948 | Liberal | Berlin (now Kitchener), Ont. | 1874-1950 |
| Louis S. St. Laurent | 1948-1957 | Liberal | Compton, Que. | 1882-1973 |
| John G. Diefenbaker | 1957-1963 | Progressive Conservative | Neustadt, Ont. | 1895-1979 |
| Lester B. Pearson | 1963-1968 | Liberal | Toronto, Ont. | 1897-1972 |
| Pierre E. Trudeau | 1968-1979 | Liberal | Montreal, Que. | 1919- |
| Charles Joseph Clark | 1979-1980 | Progressive Conservative | High River, Alta. | 1939- |
| Pierre E. Trudeau | 1980- | Liberal | Montreal, Que. | 1919- |

Silent Spring
The Adventures of
kleberry Finn
KING ARTHUR
MACBE
Nat Turner
BLACK BEAUTY
The Grapes of Wrath
Portrait of a Lady
Hamlet
David Copperfield
Madame Curie
OOTS
Catcher in the Rye

# Highlights of literature

**10**

Do you sometimes have trouble following the plot of a piece of literature that has been assigned to you to read? Do you sometimes forget the name of a leading character? If so, this unit can help you.

This unit consists of synopses of both fictional and nonfictional works of literature that you might be likely to encounter in classwork. While space does not permit that every possible title be included, research indicates that the titles covered in this unit are among those assigned to a significant number of students across the country.

# 1. Works of literature

This section contains a brief summary of more than 300 works of literature that you might encounter in the course of your schoolwork. The list of books has been arranged alphabetically by the title of the book. The name of the author follows the title. For your convenience, the type of book ("novel," "biography," and so on) is indicated in parentheses. Section 2 is an index by author.

The editors present this list as an aid to you in selecting books of interest. The list includes a representative sample of books actually being read or recommended in junior high and senior high schools. Though the list is not exhaustive, it does represent a sampling of school recommendations and does include a variety of material.

**Abraham Lincoln's World,** by Genevieve Foster (biography)

The author tells Lincoln's life story against the background of his times. Lincoln's years span a period of territorial expansion in which railroads replace canals as the major link between the Midwest, East, and South. They are also years of the growing agrarian-industrial conflict in Congress, the struggle over slavery, and the Civil War.

**Act One,** by Moss Hart (autobiography)

The life story of a prominent American playwright, *Act One* relates Hart's early years as well as the events leading to his success on Broadway. Born in poverty in the Bronx, Hart is encouraged by an aunt to become interested in the theater. The book is a candid first-person history, is often amusing, and tells much about the inner workings of the New York theater.

**Adam Bede,** by George Eliot (novel)

Adam Bede, a village carpenter, loves Hetty Sor-rel, a pretty but selfish girl. She, however, dreams of marriage with Arthur Donnithorne, a young squire. Arthur seduces her, but then breaks off the relationship. After she consents to marry Adam, Hetty discovers that she is pregnant. She allows the child to die and is sentenced to prison. Adam is drawn to Dinah Morris, a young preacher, whom he marries.

**Adam of the Road,** by Elizabeth J. Gray (novel)

In the 1300's, a young man named Adam wanders throughout southeastern England to search for his minstrel father and to recover his lost dog. His travel brings him many adventures. He goes to St. Alban's Abbey, to London, to Winchester, and then back to London, where the three are reunited.

**The Adventures of Huckleberry Finn,** by Mark Twain (novel)

After his worthless father shows up to demand a fortune Huck has found, Huck escapes to Jackson's Island in the Mississippi River. From there, he and Jim, a runaway slave, float down the river on a raft. They experience several adventures and are joined by the Duke of Bridgewater and the Dauphin, both frauds. The Dauphin sells Jim to Tom Sawyer's Aunt Sally, but Huck and Tom contrive to free him. Jim is recaptured, but he has been granted freedom in his former owner's will. Huck learns that his father is dead and his fortune safe. Huck decides to leave Aunt Sally, who might adopt and "sivilize" him, a fate that Huck believes would be his ruin.

**The Adventures of Tom Sawyer,** by Mark Twain (novel)

Punished for playing hookey by having to whitewash a fence, Tom cleverly gets his friends to do the work. After quarreling with his sweetheart,

Becky Thatcher, Tom goes off with Huck Finn. They witness Injun Joe's murder of the town doctor, a crime that Joe attempts to pin on Muff Potter. With Huck, Tom hides on Jackson's Island. Everyone believes them drowned, and a memorial service is held. The two are discovered in the church gallery witnessing the ceremony. At Potter's trial, Tom testifies against Injun Joe. Tom and Becky are reconciled, but they get lost for several days in a cave where Tom sees the escaped Injun Joe. When Joe later is found dead, Tom and Huck divide his fortune. The Widow Douglas adopts Huck, and he surrenders his freedom.

**After the Fall,** by Arthur Miller (play)

Quentin reviews his life before an invisible psychiatrist. He agonizes over guilt, existence, and responsibility. Quentin notes his failures with various women, particularly his second wife, Maggie, a singer and sex symbol. Other important people in his life include his brother, his mother, a young divorcée, his first wife, and a girl he is thinking of marrying. Seeking love again, Quentin takes a new bride.

**Agamemnon,** by Aeschylus (play)

His ship becalmed on the way to Troy, Agamemnon sacrifices his daughter Iphigenia to the gods in exchange for a strong wind. While he fights the Trojan War, his wife Clytemnestra—who never forgives him for the sacrifice—becomes the lover of Aegisthus. When the war ends, Agamemnon returns to Greece with Cassandra—a beautiful captive who predicts misfortune for him. Cassandra proves right, for Clytemnestra and Aegisthus slay Agamemnon.

**The Alchemist,** by Ben Jonson (play)

During a plague, Lovewit leaves his London house in charge of Face, his servant. With Subtle, an alchemist, and Doll Common, Face makes the house a center for fleecing gullible people. Sir Epicure Mammon, Tribulation Wholesome, Dapper, and Able Drugger are among those rooked. When Lovewit suddenly returns, Subtle and Doll Common flee. Face then works himself back into his master's good graces by arranging for him to marry Dame Pliant.

**Alice's Adventures in Wonderland,** by Lewis Carroll (novel)

Alice falls asleep and dreams that she follows a rabbit down into his hole, only to find herself in a wonderland. There everything seems fantastic and illogical, yet everything appears real. She nearly drowns in her own tears and then encounters such unusual creatures as the grinning Cheshire Cat, the Mock Turtle, and the March Hare. Alice also has strange experiences with such peculiar people as the Mad Hatter, the Queen of Hearts, and the Duchess. Eventually Alice awakens.

**All My Sons,** by Arthur Miller (play)

To be certain of an income for his family, Joe Keller betrays his business partner, and, to save his business, he sells defective aircraft parts. His son Chris finds out about Joe's actions and reminds him of his ethical responsibilities. Joe, however, insists that family loyalty comes first and that the profit motive is honorable. When he learns what his father has done, another son in the military commits suicide. Then Joe shoots himself.

**America's Own Mark Twain,** by Jeanette Eaton (biography)

The details in this book about Mark Twain's life are factual, even though numerous fictional devices are used. The book follows Twain through his childhood, his life as a Mississippi River pilot, and his experiences as a writer. Included are accounts of his life in the West and his later years as a lecturer in Europe and in the United States.

**America's Paul Revere,** by Esther Forbes (biography)

The author, an authority on Paul Revere, describes in detail the social, economic, and political world in which Revere lived and gives an account of his life. The biography presents numerous little-known facts about the silversmith, probably known to most people only through inaccurate sources.

**America's Robert E. Lee,** by Henry Steele Commager (biography)

This book follows the leader of the Confederate forces in the Civil War from birth through his education and military career to his surrender to General Ulysses S. Grant at Appomattox Court House. The biography focuses on Lee's role in the war in the East, but also describes action in other battles in various parts of the country.

**...And Now Miguel,** by Joseph Krumgold (novel)

The boy Miguel Chavez and his family live in New Mexico. For generations, members of his family have herded sheep. Each year, the men take the flocks to the Sangre de Cristo Mountains for summer grazing. For the first time, 12-year-old Miguel wants to go along. Eventually, Miguel gets his wish.

**Animal Farm,** by George Orwell (novel)

Animals overthrow their drunken master and take over the farm themselves, intending to better their lives. The pigs, being the most clever, become the leaders and eventually establish a dictatorship under which all are equal, but some—the pigs—are more equal than others. Conflicts develop between the new masters and the other animals. The story is an allegory about political dictatorships.

**Anna Karenina,** by Leo Tolstoy (novel)

Trapped in a cold and unsatisfying marriage, Anna falls in love with Aleksei Vronsky, a dashing cavalry officer. Her determination to fulfill her love leads her to abandon her husband and family to live with Vronsky in Italy. When he grows bored and feels trapped, he welcomes the chance to go to war. The bereft Anna commits suicide by throwing herself in front of a train.

**Antigone,** by Sophocles (play)

Creon forbids the burial of the rebel Polynices' body, threatening death to anyone who defies his command. Following the Greek belief that the spirit of an unburied body is tortured, Polynices' sister Antigone defies Creon's order. He then has her sealed alive in a cave. Creon's son Haemon, who is in love with Antigone, finds that she has hanged herself in the cave. Creon relents too late. Haemon kills himself, and Creon's wife, Eurydice, also commits suicide.

**April Morning,** by Howard Fast (novel)

Fifteen-year-old Adam Cooper joins the Lexington, Mass., militia on April 19, 1775, as the first shots of the American Revolution are fired. The boy relates his feelings and experiences during a 24-hour period. He finds how confusing and horrible war can be, but the heat and stress of battle help the youth become a man.

**The Ark,** by Margot Benary-Isbert (novel)

Four children—Matthias, Joey, Margaret, and Andrea—live in post-World War II Germany, a country defeated and divided. After the Soviets take over their home in East Germany, they make their way with their mother to West Germany. The family members experience many problems in making a new life for themselves.

**Around the World in Eighty Days,** by Jules Verne (novel)

An English gentleman named Phileas Fogg ends a discussion in his London club about world travel by betting that he can circle the earth in 80 days. Taking his French servant Passepartout with him, and using steamships, railroads, and other means of transportation, Fogg wins the bet. He and his servant experience many difficulties and adventures along the way.

**Arrowsmith,** by Sinclair Lewis (novel)

After practice as a doctor and as a public health officer hampered by politics, Martin Arrowsmith joins a research center in New York City. He develops a serum and sets up a test for it on a West Indian island during an epidemic. After his wife and a fellow scientist die of the plague, Arrowsmith abandons the experiment. Later he marries a rich widow, but his social life interferes with his work. Arrowsmith finally leaves his wife and New York City for work in a Vermont laboratory, free of social and political pressures.

**As You Like It,** by William Shakespeare (play)

Frederick has taken over the lands of his brother the duke. Celia, Frederick's daughter, and Rosalind, the duke's daughter, live at Frederick's court. Rosalind falls in love with Orlando, the son of Sir Rowland de Boys, the Duke's friend. Learning of this, Frederick banishes Rosalind from the court, and Celia accompanies her. Rosalind assumes male dress, and Celia travels as Aliena, his/her sister. They go to the forest of Arden where they meet Orlando, who does not recognize them. Oliver, Orlando's elder brother, falls in love with Celia. A wedding is planned, but just before the ceremony Rosalind and Celia throw off their disguises. Frederick has a change of heart and wishes to restore the duke's lands to him. All ends happily.

**The Autobiography of an Ex-Colored Man,** by James Weldon Johnson (novel)

A light-skinned black man "passes" as a white man. He lives in both the North and the South and in Europe and becomes a successful member of white society. Various experiences, including a love affair and a marriage to a white woman, make him question the worth of denying his race. His observations of blacks lead him to admire their struggles.

**The Autobiography of Benjamin Franklin,** by Benjamin Franklin (autobiography)

The colonial leader recounts his growing up, his printer's apprenticeship, the establishment of his own paper, and life in colonial Philadelphia. With his scientific and numerous other interests,

Franklin shows himself to be a man truly imbued with the spirit of the Enlightenment of the 1700's. Because Franklin never completed the work, it ends fairly abruptly.

### The Autobiography of Malcolm X, by Malcolm X (autobiography)

A black man whose early ambitions are thwarted tells of his life as a thief, pimp, and drug runner. Arrested on a theft charge, he is sentenced to prison. While there, he converts to the Black Muslim faith and takes the name Malcolm X. Upon his release he becomes a Black Muslim and rises in the organization. After breaking with the Black Muslim leader, Malcolm X forms his own mosque, makes the pilgrimage to Mecca, and becomes a more orthodox Muslim.

### Banners in the Sky, by James Ullman (novel)

The boy Rudi Matt joins a party led by Captain Winter, an Englishman, to climb the Citadel Mountain. This is a feat that has never been accomplished. The men survive avalanches and other hazards. Rudi makes it to the top first, and thereafter the peak is called Rudisberg, or Rudi's Mountain.

### Barabbas, by Pär Lagerkvist (novel)

Little is known about the real-life person Barabbas beyond the bare fact that, upon the mob's insistence, he instead of Jesus was saved from execution and released. This book, translated from Swedish, displays a great deal of imagination in telling how Barabbas' life changed after the Crucifixion. He is converted to Christianity, works as a missionary in the Mediterranean world, and finally dies in Rome as a martyr of the early Christian church.

### Barchester Towers, by Anthony Trollope (novel)

Mrs. Proudie, the wife of the new bishop of Barchester, and Mr. Slope compete for control of the diocese. They disagree over filling the wardenship of Hiram's Hospital with Mr. Harding, the former warden, or Mr. Quiverful, Mrs. Proudie's candidate. Mrs. Proudie is successful. Although Harding loses, he does win the post of dean of the parish, a position that Slope had hoped to obtain himself. Mr. Slope wants to marry the widowed Mrs. Bold, although he is also attracted to Signora Vesey-Neroni, the daughter of Canon Stanhope. Both women reject him.

### Ben and Me, By Robert Lawson (biography)

A mouse that resides in Benjamin Franklin's fur cap tells of his life with the colonial leader. The mouse is not particularly modest. He claims to inspire and aid Franklin at various times with inventions and diplomatic affairs. The book thus uses a humorous framework to relate the biography of a famous figure of American colonial times.

### Beowulf, by unknown author (poem)

Beowulf and his men come to rid Heorot, Hrothgar's great hall, of the monster Grendel, who for years has haunted the hall and killed Hrothgar's men. Grendel invades the hall and devours one of Beowulf's men. Unarmed, Beowulf wrestles the monster and tears off one of its arms. Mortally wounded, Grendel leaves. Grendel's mother comes to the hall and avenges her son's defeat by killing a man and stealing Grendel's arm. Beowulf pursues her to an underwater cave where he cuts off both her and Grendel's heads. Beowulf becomes king and reigns for 50 years.

### Beyond Sing the Woods, by Trygve Gulbranssen (novel)

A Norwegian family begins its climb to success with Dag Bjornal. He marries a girl from fertile valley lands and begins to develop wealth that he can pass on to his descendants. The one remaining son of Old Dag eventually becomes engaged to a beautiful girl. Their marriage will ensure the continuation of the family line.

### Big Red, by Jim Kjelgaard (novel)

Big Red, a champion Irish setter, is a poor candidate for life in the wild, but that is where he finds himself. He becomes friends with the boy Danny, who knows a great deal more about wild animals and mongrel dogs than he does about purebreds. Danny and Big Red experience numerous adventures, including fighting off Old Majesty, a legendary killer bear.

### Black Arrow, by Robert Louis Stevenson (novel)

Richard Shelton's guardian, Sir Daniel Brackley, has fought on both sides in the War of the Roses in the 1400's. He has added to his fortune by becoming the guardian of orphaned children and by acquiring land. Shelton's task is to thwart Sir Daniel's plots against him, in the course of which he saves the life of Richard, the Duke of Gloucester and future king of England. He also rescues the pretty Johanna Sedley and marries her.

### Black Beauty, by Anna Sewall (novel)

A thoroughbred horse is badly injured by a drunken groom and then sold to the keeper of a livery stable. Black Beauty becomes a cab horse and later a cart horse and is overworked and badly treated. Eventually he is bought by a farmer who takes good care of him and nurses him back to health. The farmer sells the horse to some ladies, ensuring that Black Beauty will end his days peacefully.

**Black Boy,** by Richard Wright (autobiography)

Born in 1909, Richard Wright spends the first 19 years of his life in the South. He gives an account of growing up as a black man in a segregated society. Of a rebellious nature, Wright has numerous harrowing experiences at the hands of whites, as do other blacks he knows. The account ends as he leaves for Chicago to make a new life.

**The Black Stallion,** by Walter Farley (novel)

The only survivors of a shipwreck, a 17-year-old boy and a wild black stallion, manage to live on an uninhabited island until they are rescued. With the aid of a retired jockey, the boy tames the stallion and decides to race him. After long and careful training, the stallion is entered in a race, which he wins dramatically.

**Black Thunder,** by Arna Bontemps (novel)

In Virginia in 1800, a black slave named Gabriel Prosser leads a rebellion against his master, Thomas Prosser, and other whites. Gabriel manages to organize more than a thousand slaves and plans to march on Richmond, seize an arsenal, and capture the town. A severe rainstorm and betrayal by two of his followers prove Gabriel's undoing, however, and the rebellion fails.

**Bleak House,** by Charles Dickens (novel)

Lady Dedlock nurses a potentially ruinous secret—before her marriage she bore an illegitimate daughter to a man named Captain Hawdon. She believes that her daughter is dead, but the girl actually lives as Esther Summerson, a ward of Mr. Jarndyce at Bleak House. When Lady Dedlock becomes curious about her former lover, her inquiries arouse the interest of her lawyer, Tulkinghorn. He discovers her secret and threatens to expose it. The lady's maid murders him, but Lord Dedlock learns his wife's secret anyway. She finds out that Hawdon is dead, and then she herself is found dead near his grave. Esther, who is devoted to Jarndyce, agrees to marry him. He later releases her from the promise, however, so that she can marry her true love, Woodcourt, a doctor.

**Blues for Mister Charlie,** by James Baldwin (play)

In a small Southern town, 21-year-old Richard Henry, after having lived for some time in the North and having become a drug addict, has returned home, only to be killed. Both blacks and whites examine the racial forces that make it necessary for Richard to die. At a trial, the white man accused of the murder is found not guilty.

**The Boy Who Could Make Himself Disappear,** by Kim Platt (novel)

Roger Baxter is a seventh-grader who suffered a childhood accident that has left him with a speech impediment. He also develops emotional problems because of his parents' divorce and their indifference toward him. Roger gradually loses touch with reality and enters a schizophrenic world.

**Brave New World,** by Aldous Huxley (novel)

In a future civilization, people have become increasingly dependent on science, which is used to control their lives. Henry Ford and the Model T (the original Ford car) are the gods, society is homogenized, babies are produced in test tubes, the family no longer exists, and people are tranquilized much of the time. Most are content with their lot, but the few remaining people capable of human emotions find it difficult either to live in or to escape from this society.

**The Bridge of San Luis Rey,** by Thornton Wilder (novel)

In the 1700's in Peru, a bridge spanning a canyon collapses, dropping five people to their deaths. A friar, Brother Juniper, witnesses the tragedy and decides to investigate the lives of the five to try to discover why they died at that particular moment. He finds that the lives of all touched at some point, and he makes other discoveries that get him into trouble with his religious superiors.

**Buddenbrooks,** by Thomas Mann (novel)

A German family slowly declines through four generations. The founder, Johann Buddenbrooks, Sr., is a prosperous merchant, and his son Johann is a prominent diplomat. The third generation, Thomas and Christian, are less devoted and successful. The family business is finally sold. In the fourth generation Hanno, a weak and dreamy artistic boy, dies before marriage, and the family line ends.

**Bury My Heart at Wounded Knee,** by Dee Brown (nonfiction)

This book examines the winning of the West

from an Indian point of view. Whites are presented as aggressors destroying the region's original inhabitants and its natural resources as well. According to the author, Indian attacks on white settlements are not so much acts of aggression as they are retaliations for white people's acts against the Indians.

**Caddie Woodlawn,** by Carol Brink (novel)

Eleven-year-old Caddie Woodlawn lives on the Wisconsin frontier in 1864. Although she is slight in size, her parents allow her to become a tomboy. She has many adventures during the annual cycle on a pioneer farm—planting, caring for crops, and harvesting.

**Call It Courage,** by Armstrong Sperry (novel)

"Boy Who Is Afraid," a Polynesian, has from infancy been taught to fear the sea. With his dog, in an outrigger canoe, he leaves his people, most of whom worship courage. Facing a wild and unsympathetic nature alone, the boy and his dog are cast by a furious storm onto an uninhabited island. "Boy Who Is Afraid" demonstrates his courage as he uses his wits to survive by providing food and shelter for himself.

**The Call of the Wild,** by Jack London (novel)

Buck, the offspring of a St. Bernard and a Scotch shepherd, is stolen from a California ranch and taken to the Klondike. Acquired by John Thornton, Buck is well trained as a sledge dog. Giving his entire allegiance to his new master, Buck drags a thousand-pound load on a sledge in order to win a bet for Thornton. When Indians murder Thornton, Buck reverts to a wild animal, leaving civilization to lead a wolf pack.

**The Canterbury Tales,** by Geoffrey Chaucer (poem)

A number of English religious pilgrims of the 1300's leave an inn on their way to a shrine at Canterbury. On the way to Canterbury and on the way back, each pilgrim is to tell four stories for the group's entertainment. The teller of the best tales will have a free dinner at the inn on their return. In the end, there are 24 tales, ranging from the Knight's Tale to the Wife of Bath's Tale, the Franklin's Tale, and the final story, the Parson's Tale. All are entertaining; some are serious, but others are bawdy.

**Captains Courageous,** by Rudyard Kipling (novel)

Harvey Cheyne, the spoiled son of an American millionaire, falls overboard from an Atlantic ocean liner. He is picked up by fishermen and taken to a schooner commanded by Disko Troop. The captain refuses to return the boy to New York City until the fishing season is over and in the meantime puts him to work on the ship. Although he protests vigorously, Harvey has no choice, and his experiences help him mature.

**Catch-22,** by Joseph Heller (novel)

On the small island of Pianosa in the Mediterranean Sea during World War II, a group of air force men suffer the brutal frustrations of military life. Captain Yossarian, Major Major Major, Milo Minderbinder, and others are members of a bombing squadron. Colonel Cathcart, their commander, keeps increasing the number of missions each man must serve before relief. This policy gradually kills most of Yossarian's friends. Seeing no alternative, he deserts.

**Catcher in the Rye,** by J. D. Salinger (novel)

Aware that he is about to be expelled from a private school, 16-year-old Holden Caulfield leaves the institution a few days before the start of the Christmas vacation. He spends two days and nights on his own in New York City before returning home. What Holden sees and does and experiences during this time brings out his attitudes toward the corruption of adult society and his relationship with his sister Phoebe.

**Cat's Cradle,** by Kurt Vonnegut (novel)

Felix Hoenikker, a nuclear scientist, invents ice-nine, a substance that turns all liquid in the world into ice. Bokonon is a religious prophet who teaches his own unique doctrines that include ideas such as "karass" (personal relationships) and "granfalloon" (organizations or groups).

**The Cherry Orchard,** by Anton Chekhov (play)

As privileged members of the Russian upper class, the Ranevskis have ignored practical matters and, through neglect, are on the brink of bankruptcy. Lopakhin, the son of a serf but now a wealthy merchant, encourages the Ranevskis to sell the cherry orchard for a housing development. This idea horrifies the family, and the Ranevskis agonize over their fate. When the cherry orchard is eventually auctioned off, the jubilant Lopakhin buys it. As the sad and helpless family departs its beloved estate, they hear the sound of axes chopping down cherry trees.

**The Clouds,** by Aristophanes (play)

Strepsiades enrolls in Socrates' Thinking School

to learn false logic. He is not an apt pupil, however, and his son, Pheidippides, enrolls in his place. Having learned well, Pheidippides helps his father confuse his creditors, but then uses an unjust argument to justify beating his father. Strepsiades rallies other Athenians to burn down Socrates' school.

## The Comedy of Errors, by William Shakespeare (play)

Aegeon and his wife Aemilia—who has become an abbess—have identical twin boys, both named Antipholus. The two boys have male slaves, both named Dromio, who are identical twins. A shipwreck has separated one Antipholus and his Dromio from the other two. One Antipholus sets out in search of his brother. Their father sets out in search of one son. Numerous cases of mistaken identity occur, resulting in arrests and much confusion. Finally, the entire family, including the mother, is reunited.

## The Confessions of Nat Turner, by William Styron (novel)

After leading an unsuccessful slave uprising in Virginia in 1831, Nat Turner has dictated a confession. Recalling his childhood and youth, he relates his feelings about being sold a number of times, as well as his intense religious life. He plans and carries out his rebellion but is captured, tried, and executed.

## A Connecticut Yankee in King Arthur's Court, by Mark Twain (novel)

Knocked unconscious in a fight, an American of the late 1800's awakens in England at Camelot in the 500's. Because he knows about eclipses, electricity, and gunpowder, the Knights of the Round Table believe that the Yankee is a magician, and he becomes influential at court. After a period in France, the Connecticut Yankee returns to find England in civil war, King Arthur dead, and the kingdom destroyed. When the Yankee is wounded in battle, the magician Merlin puts him into a sleep that lasts until the 1800's.

## The Count of Monte Cristo, by Alexandre Dumas (novel)

Edmund Dantès is falsely accused of crime and imprisoned. He eventually escapes, carrying with him knowledge that he received from a fellow prisoner of a treasure hidden on the island of Monte Cristo. He finds the treasure and becomes the Count of Monte Cristo. Dantès then devotes himself to vengeance on his enemies.

## Cress Delahanty, by Jessamyn West (novel)

A 12-year-old girl grows into a 16-year-old young woman. In growing up, Cress has many problems, especially with boys and her parents. In turn, her parents have problems with her. Cress gets into many humorous situations as she moves into adolescence and tries to find her place in the world.

## Crime and Punishment, by Fyodor Dostoevsky (novel)

Raskolnikov, a poverty-stricken student, broods over his situation and that of his helpless mother and young sister. He carefully plans and carries out the robbery and murder of an old woman pawnbroker. He is surprised in the act and must also murder the pawnbroker's sister. Raskolnikov tries to justify his act by his desperate need for money. He comes to think of himself as a superman who will improve society. His conscience is too strong for such rationalization, however. He confesses to Sonya, a young girl forced into prostitution, with whom he falls in love. She convinces Raskolnikov to confess the crime. Tried and convicted, Raskolnikov is exiled and finally repents. The faithful Sonya follows him.

## The Crock of Gold, by James Stephens (novel)

Leprechauns, little people who at night go about secretly clipping humans' coins, bit by bit develop their own crock of gold. The gold is necessary as a ransom fund should a leprechaun be captured. With the aid of the Philosopher of Coilla Doraca, Meehawl MacMurrachu steals the crock. The theft gets everyone into trouble with the leprechauns. Not until the Thin Woman of Inis Magrath enlists the help of Angus Og are things set right again.

## The Crucible, by Arthur Miller (play)

Rumors of witchcraft spread through Salem, Mass., in the late 1600's. When Abigail Williams is accused of wrongdoing, she claims that her soul has been bewitched. She and her friends make charges against other people—including Elizabeth Proctor, whose husband Abigail had once seduced. When John Proctor is later himself accused of witchcraft, he dies rather than save his life by a false confession.

## Cry, the Beloved Country, by Alan Paton (novel)

Stephen Kumalo, a humble Zulu parson, goes from the countryside of South Africa to the city of Johannesburg to look for a sick sister. He finds her, but discovers that she has become a prostitute.

His brother, he learns, has lost his religion, and his son is a murderer. Through his family's lives, Kumalo witnesses the tragedies of racial segregation in South Africa.

**Cyrano de Bergerac,** by Edmond Rostand (play)

An ugly man with an unusually large nose, Cyrano is in love with Roxanne, his cousin. She, however, favors Christian, a dull but handsome man. Cyrano selflessly helps Christian, even writing love letters for him. When Christian is killed in battle, Roxanne retires to a convent. For 15 years, Cyrano visits her weekly but one day has an accident. Before he dies, Roxanne learns of his love and his past sacrifices on her behalf.

**Dandelion Wine,** by Ray Bradbury (novel)

In Green Town, Ill., in the summer of 1928, a 12-year-old boy named Douglas Spaulding lives in an extraordinary world. He encounters not only a happiness machine, but also a pair of sneakers with magical powers. As Douglas grows older, he grows more comfortable with his views on the mysteries of life.

**Darkness at Noon,** by Arthur Koestler (novel)

Nicholas Rubashov, formerly a powerful political leader, is arrested, accused of numerous crimes, and tortured. His memories and his contacts with other prisoners also produce confusion and suffering within Rubashov. He finally confesses as his captors want him to and is executed. At the same time, a young girl in whose house Rubashov once lived wonders if she should denounce his father to the authorities, so that she and her fiancé can obtain his apartment.

**David Copperfield,** by Charles Dickens (novel)

After his mother's death, his cruel stepfather sends David to London to work. He lives with the optimistic Mr. Macawber but runs away to his great aunt. After his schooling, he works for Mr. Wickfield, a lawyer, and becomes a friend of his daughter Agnes. Unaware of Agnes' love for him, David marries Dora Spenlow, who dies soon after. Neither marriage nor success as a writer has brought him happiness. David and Macawber become involved in helping Agnes extricate her father from debts to Uriah Heep. David realizes that he has always loved Agnes, marries her, and finds happiness.

**Death at an Early Age,** by Jonathan Kozol (nonfiction)

The author, who spent a year as a fourth grade teacher of mostly black pupils, in Boston, Mass., writes of his experiences. He contends that the Boston schools—and those in other cities—tend to be brutal, neglectful of pupils' needs, and prejudiced against blacks. In his angry book, Kozol accuses school systems of psychological and spiritual murder, particularly of black pupils.

**Death Be Not Proud,** by John Gunther (nonfiction)

The author pays tribute to his son's courage and gallantry after a 15-month struggle against a brain tumor. The book is also a testament to the parents' loving care for their son. Without being morbid or sentimental, the father gives a straightforward description of the young man's final months and days.

**Death Comes for the Archbishop,** by Willa Cather (novel)

Two missionary priests, Jean Latour and Joseph Vaillant, establish a diocese in the territory of New Mexico in the mid-1800's. Latour is aristocratic and scholarly; Vaillant, a peasant type. Both are courageous and determined, and they overcome all adversaries to build a cathedral in the wilderness. Latour becomes archbishop of Santa Fe, a position he holds for nearly 40 years.

**A Death in the Family,** by James Agee (novel)

Jay and Mary Follet and their children, Rufus and Catherine, have loving and kind relationships with each other and with their relatives. When Jay is killed in an automobile accident, his death has repercussions within the family and among the relatives. The young boy Rufus has his first experience of death, and the story is told primarily from his point of view.

**Death of a Salesman,** by Arthur Miller (play)

At age 63, Willy Loman faces the fact that dreams and reality for him and his son Biff, a former football hero, are widely different. Willy retreats into imagined successes of the past, where his only happiness seems to lie. Biff remains jobless and without ambition. Willy concludes that he is much to blame for his son's situation and decides on suicide so that Biff can have his insurance money. Only the family and a few friends, but no business acquaintances, attend the funeral.

**A Delicate Balance,** by Edward Albee (play)

A family is disrupted by the sudden and unwelcome appearance of two friends, who say they are running from what they call the "terror." The visit prompts the family members to analyze themselves. The parents, Tobias and Agnes, suffer guilt pangs over the death of a son. Their daughter, a divorcée, also suffers from guilt, as does Agnes' sister Claire, who is an alcoholic. The love that binds them together helps them maintain a "delicate balance" in their lives.

## The Diary of a Young Girl, by Anne Frank (nonfiction)

A young German-Jewish girl—hiding with her parents in a warehouse in Holland from Nazi Germans during World War II—writes about her experiences. In the diary, kept from 1942 to 1944, she records events as well as her thoughts and emotions. She tells about parties that the family held, in spite of being in hiding, and about her first love. (The Germans eventually found the hiding place and shipped the Franks off to concentration camps. Anne died at Bergen-Belsen in 1945.)

## The Diary of Samuel Pepys, by Samuel Pepys (nonfiction)

Beginning his diary on January 1, 1660, Pepys continues it until failing eyesight forces him to stop on May 31, 1669. At first, he is very poor but later is appointed to a salaried government post. The diary records gossip and intrigue within the court of King Charles II of England. Also included are anecdotes about the music of the time, the London fire of 1665, and much candid personal information.

## Doctor Zhivago, by Boris Pasternak (novel)

Orphaned at age 10, Yuri Zhivago is brought up among the Moscow intelligentsia and becomes a member of the Russian upper class. After attending a university, he becomes a doctor. At the same time, he is well educated in the arts and literature. He writes poetry and opposes Communism. Getting caught up in the revolution of 1917 and in the civil war that follows, Zhivago loses everything.

## A Doll's House, by Henrik Ibsen (play)

Nora Helmer has committed forgery in order to get money to save her husband's life. When he discovers her act, he becomes furious. He thinks only of his own reputation, even though she has repaid the money. Nora then realizes that her husband has always treated her as a doll, an adorable pet, but never as a real person. She leaves her husband and family in order to fulfill herself.

## Don Quixote, by Miguel de Cervantes (novel)

Don Quixote, a country gentleman, has read so many books on chivalry that he has come to fancy himself a knight. He sets out with Sancho Panza, his practical and realistic squire, to right the world's wrongs. Don Quixote has become so idealistic that he mistakes flocks of sheep for armies and windmills for giants. After numerous failures, however, Don Quixote becomes completely disillusioned.

## Drums Along the Mohawk, by Walter Edmonds (novel)

Gilbert Martin and his young bride, Lana, live in the Mohawk River Valley of northern New York during the Revolutionary War. With other settlers, they suffer from raids by the British and by Iroquois Indians. One of the most severe is the battle of Oriskany in 1777.

## An Enemy of the People, by Henrik Ibsen (play)

Dr. Stockman discovers that the popular health baths in a small Norwegian town are contaminated. He wants to publicize the fact to protect people from typhoid fever. Those who control the town and the baths protest because the news would affect their profits from the baths. They denounce Stockman as an enemy of the people. Arrayed against politicians and the establishment, Stockman is defeated.

## Erewhon, by Samuel Butler (novel)

A man comes upon the land of Erewhon where, like the name, everything is backward. Disease is considered a crime, and such misdeeds as embezzlement evoke sympathy. In relating his adventures, the man satirizes religious institutions, parental cruelty, and the development of machinery that must be abolished before it overcomes the inhabitants. Accompanied by a woman with whom he has fallen in love, the man finally escapes Erewhon in a balloon.

## Ethan Frome, by Edith Wharton (novel)

Zeena Frome, a complaining hypochondriac, spends much of the small income of her husband, Ethan, on medicines and quack cures. Her cousin, Mattie Silver, comes to the farm to live with them, and she and Ethan are attracted to one another. Because Zeena is jealous, she contrives to oust Mattie and hire a girl in her place. Ethan and Mattie set out for the railroad station, but realize that they cannot part. Later, as they coast in a sled, Ethan steers it into a large tree. They are crippled, not killed, and are doomed to remain as invalids on the farm. Zeena becomes the faithful nurse; Mattie, a complaining person.

**Exodus,** by Leon Uris (novel)

The British hold Palestine as a mandate and try to stop European Jews from migrating to the area. The Zionist movement keeps the idea of a Jewish homeland alive, however, and the state of Israel is finally established after World War II. Ari Ben Canaan, a member of an immigration organization, and Kitty Fremont, an American nurse, become involved in creating the new country.

**The Faerie Queene,** by Edmund Spenser (poem)

King Arthur, the perfect knight, has a vision of the Faerie Queene (Elizabeth I of England) and sets out in search of her kingdom. Other knights undertake quests that involve moral virtues. Their adventures illustrate qualities such as temperance, friendship, justice, and courtesy.

**Fahrenheit 451,** by Ray Bradbury (novel)

Montag is a fireman in a society where firemen burn books. One night, an old lady refuses to leave her house when the firemen torch her books, and Montag watches her die. Also, he falls in love with her niece Clarisse, who loves books and honors the past. After struggling with the moral and political questions involved, Montag becomes a fugitive and joins "the book people." He is hunted by the Mechanical Hound.

**Far from the Madding Crowd,** by Thomas Hardy (novel)

Sergeant Troy, an attractive soldier, deserts Fanny Robin and allows her to die in childbirth in a workhouse. He then marries Bathsheba Everdone but mistreats her. Troy disappears and is presumed dead. Boldwood, a farmer attracted to Bathsheba, murders Troy when he returns. When Boldwood goes bad, Bathsheba marries a farmer, Gabriel Oak, who has served her faithfully for many years.

**The Fire Next Time,** by James Baldwin (nonfiction)

In the form of a letter to his nephew, the author gives his view of black history and life in the United States during the century following the Emancipation Proclamation. In another essay on the Black Muslims, Baldwin shows his sympathy toward the organization, though he does not believe that the goal of complete black separation can be realized in the United States.

**For Whom the Bell Tolls,** by Ernest Hemingway (novel)

Fighting for the Loyalist side in the Spanish Civil War, the American Robert Jordan joins a guerrilla band to help blow up a bridge. During three days with the group, he falls in love with Maria, observes the growing dissension among the members, and becomes convinced that the attack will fail. Jordan blows up the bridge anyway, is wounded, and remains behind as a doomed rearguard awaiting enemy forces.

**The Forsyte Saga,** by John Galsworthy (novel)

During the 1800's, members of the Forsyte family, particularly Soames Forsyte, are obsessed with acquiring material possessions. By the 1920's, in an English society shattered by World War I, the Forsyte family has changed drastically. There is a feeling among members of the family that the only goal in life is to enjoy the present because there may well be no future.

**Forty Days of Musa Dagh,** by Franz Werfel (novel)

Gabriel Bagradian, an Armenian who has spent 23 years in Paris, returns to his homeland in 1915. He becomes involved in the Armenian struggle to escape extermination by the Turks. In the 40-day Turkish siege of Musa Dagh, the villagers hold out under Bagradian's leadership until a French force relieves them.

**The Frogs,** by Aristophanes (play)

The great Greek playwrights have died, and no capable writer of tragedies remains. When Dionysus goes to Hades to bring back such a writer, Aeschylus and Euripides are holding a contest for the throne of tragedy. Dionysus is asked to be the judge. He chooses the poetry of Aeschylus because it weighs more. A chorus of frogs irreverently comments on the action.

**Gandhi, Fighter Without a Sword,** by Jeanette Eaton (biography)

Concentrating first on Mohandas Gandhi's years in southern Africa, the biography shows his involvement in the struggle for human rights and the development of his ideas on passive resistance. Included is an account of his principal activity in Africa—leading protests against laws and customs that discriminated against Indians. The biography describes Gandhi's return to India to head the movement against the British that resulted in Indian independence in 1947, the year before his assassination.

**Giant,** by Edna Ferber (novel)

Bick Benedict manages the family ranch of 2-1/2

million acres in Texas. Visiting the Lynnton family in Virginia, Bick is forced to defend himself as a newly rich Texan. He marries Leslie Lynnton and returns to Texas. At first, Leslie does not care for the emptiness of Texas or for the emphasis on cattle, oil, and materialism. She adjusts, however, and helps Bick mature.

**Giants in the Earth,** by O. E. Rolvaag (novel)
Four Norwegian pioneer families set out from Minnesota in 1873 to establish a settlement in the Dakota Territory. Living at first in sod huts, they plant crops and gradually improve their lot. A few additional families arrive. For the most part, however, life remains bleak. The settlers suffer plagues of locusts, hailstorms, drought in summers, and severe winter cold and blizzards. But the parents hope that life will be easier for their children in the future.

**The Glass Menagerie,** by Tennessee Williams (play)
Life for withdrawn, crippled Laura Wingfield centers on a collection of glass animals. Her father has long since fled the family, her brother Tom dreams of leaving his factory job and home, and her mother Amanda imagines the young man whom Laura might eventually meet. One night Tom brings home Jim O'Connor, Laura's high school idol. Jim is kind to her but finally confesses that he is engaged. After an argument with Amanda, Tom leaves home, and Laura retreats into herself and her figurines.

**The Golden Notebook,** by Doris Lessing (novel)
Anna, a novelist, keeps four notebooks. One covers experiences she had in Africa beginning at age 5. Another spans her years as a member of the Communist Party in England. In the third, Anna is writing an autobiographical novel, and in the last notebook, she keeps a diary. In love with a writer and fearing insanity, Anna tries to bring the four facets of her life and personality together in one golden notebook, an extremely difficult task.

**Gone with the Wind,** by Margaret Mitchell (novel)
Impoverished by the Civil War and Reconstruction, Scarlett O'Hara tries to keep the family plantation. To obtain tax money, she marries her sister's fiancé. After he is killed, Scarlett marries Rhett Butler, a war profiteer, but she clings to a girlhood love for the aristocratic Ashley Wilkes. Her selfishness and the death of their child drive Butler away. Alone, Scarlett realizes that Butler was her one true love.

**The Good Earth,** by Pearl Buck (novel)
Aided by his wife O-lan, Wang Lung endures periodic floods, famine, and disease to build up his estate. Although he becomes a rich peasant, Wang never loses his attachment to the soil. He takes a second wife, but O-lan remains the faithful household manager until her death. Two sons they produce superintend their father's affairs, and the third becomes a revolutionary leader. The sons lack Wang's reverence for the soil, and after his death they sell the land to live in the city.

**Goodbye, Columbus,** by Philip Roth (novella)
Neil Klugman, an impoverished young man who works in the public library, falls in love with Brenda Patimkin, a wealthy young woman from the suburbs. Her parents oppose the relationship, mainly for social reasons. For a time, it appears that love might triumph, but Brenda finally cannot oppose her parents and she breaks off the romance.

**Goodbye, Mr. Chips,** by James Hilton (novel)
Mr. Chipping, known to three generations of English schoolboys at Brookfield as Mr. Chips, holds an affectionate place in the lives of those who have known him. Chips' long career at the school touches and influences numerous young lives throughout the years. At the end of a long life, Chips dies peacefully in his sleep.

**Goodbye, My Lady,** by James Street (novel)
Skeeter convinces his Uncle Jesse that there is a strange creature lurking in the swamp. They discover that the creature is a dog, though it licks itself like a cat and makes sounds like a laughing child. Skeeter captures the animal and tames and trains it. The two become closely attached to each other. A representative of the dog's owner arrives, however, and Skeeter must give up the animal. He does, however, receive a $100 reward.

**Go Tell It on the Mountain,** by James Baldwin (novel)
John Grimes struggles with his religious feelings, as well as with his harsh father. He has a growing awareness of his sexuality and of racism. In three generations of his family, religion has often caused suffering and fostered a sense of unworthiness. John finally has a religious conversion, but it is partly an act of defiance against his father and partly a sexual experience.

**The Grapes of Wrath,** by John Steinbeck (novel)
The Joad family, along with a former preacher

named Casy, migrates from Oklahoma to California in the 1930's. Migrant jobs at low pay are the only work available. Casy, who becomes a labor organizer, is killed. Tom, the eldest Joad son, kills Casy's murderer. To escape the police, Tom leaves the family to become an organizer himself. Jobless, facing starvation, the Joads still persist for, as Ma says at the novel's end, "We ain' gonna die out."

**Great Expectations,** by Charles Dickens (novel)

Pip, brought up by his sister, the wife of blacksmith Joe Gargery, becomes acquainted with Miss Havisham, whose lover deserted her. Pip falls in love with her ward, Estella. Mysteriously, Pip receives money, and he goes to London. Misfortunes befall him, and Pip learns that the source of the money is Estella's father, an escaped convict for whom he once did a favor. He finds himself penniless and learns that Estella has married. Pip begins his life anew and is finally united with Estella.

**The Great Gatsby,** by F. Scott Fitzgerald (novel)

Jay Gatsby renews his acquaintance with Daisy, a cousin of his neighbor Nick Carraway. Daisy, married to Tom Buchanan, begins an affair with Gatsby. Tom takes Myrtle Wilson as his lover, but Wilson locks up his wife. She escapes, but in fleeing is killed by Gatsby's car, driven by Daisy. Tom allows Wilson to believe that Gatsby was the driver. After killing Gatsby, Wilson commits suicide.

**Greek Gods and Heroes,** by Robert Graves (nonfiction)

The author retells many well-known tales of gods, goddesses, and heroes of ancient Greece. Included are the stories of Theseus and the Minotaur, King Midas and his golden touch, the ten labors of Hercules, Orpheus, and Demeter's lost daughter Persephone, whose misfortune created the seasons. The book includes the important figures of Greek myth and their stories.

**The Greek Way,** by Edith Hamilton (nonfiction)

The author interprets various aspects of ancient Athens and its culture and applies Greek ideas to modern times. She discusses the Athenian mind and spirit, art, the philosopher Plato, the playwright Aristophanes and Greek comedy, and the tragedians Aeschylus, Euripides, and Sophocles. In addition, the author points out moral and ethical values that Westerners have inherited from the Greeks.

**The Green Grass of Wyoming,** by Mary O'Hara (novel)

Thunderhead, a white stallion, comes out of his mountain valley to round up mares from various ranches. Thunderhead handles his harem skillfully. He protects the mares and finds grass and water for them. Ken captures Thunderhead and trains him. Finally, Ken enters the stallion in a race that Thunderhead wins.

**Green Mansions,** by William Henry Hudson (novel)

Following an unsuccessful rebellion in Venezuela, Abel Guevez de Argensola flees to the jungle. After suffering many hardships, he hears the birdlike singing of the beautiful Rima, with whom he falls in love. She agrees to return with Abel to the world he has left, but she is captured by Indians and burned to death. Abel returns to the coast with her ashes, but he can never forget the "bird-girl" he knew.

**The Growth of the Soil,** by Knut Hamsun (novel)

Isak draws elemental strength and simplicity from the soil itself. He is the epitome of the pioneer, one who chooses a place to settle, erects a hut, and plants crops. He marries, produces a family, and after hard work builds up an estate to pass onto his heirs.

**Gulliver's Travels,** by Jonathan Swift (novel)

Lemuel Gulliver, a ship's physician, keeps a journal of his voyages to several places. On one journey, he visits Lilliput, a land inhabited by people only six inches tall. On another, he visits the land of Brobdingnag where the people are giants and Gulliver is a Lilliputian. Gulliver also travels to Laputa where "wise" men live, and later to Houyhnhnmland where horses run the government. His experiences convince him that humanity has corrupted reason.

**The Hairy Ape,** By Eugene O'Neill (play)

Yank, a stoker on a transatlantic steamer, personifies the brutalizing effect of machines on humans. He is unaware of other worlds besides the stoking room, however, until Mildred Douglas, daughter of the ship's owner, visits one day. The atmosphere, and especially Yank, shock her. Yank broods and finally, at a zoo, finds that a gorilla is the only creature to which he can relate. Yank frees the animal, but together they are very destructive. Then, crushed in the animal's arms, Yank meets death.

**Hamlet,** by William Shakespeare (play)

Hamlet, prince of Denmark, learns from the ghost of his dead father that his uncle Claudius, now king and married to his mother, murdered his father. Hamlet swears vengeance. Testing the ghost's story, Hamlet stages the events in a play before the royal couple, and the new king betrays himself. After upbraiding his mother, Hamlet by accident kills Polonius, the father of his sweetheart Ophelia. Returning from a mission to England, Hamlet finds Ophelia dead and her brother Laertes bent on vengeance for their father's death. Hamlet and Laertes duel. Laertes kills Hamlet with a poisoned sword, but not before Hamlet has dealt him a fatal wound and has also killed the king. The queen drinks poison intended for her son and dies.

**Hawaii,** by James Michener (novel)

Hawaii is formed out of volcanic activity, and plant and animal life begins. South Seas Islanders become the first human inhabitants. American missionaries and Chinese and Japanese settlers later emigrate to Hawaii. Conflicts develop and old patterns of life break down. Out of the various settlers in Hawaii, a unique civilization develops.

**Heart of Darkness,** by Joseph Conrad (novella)

Marlow tells companions about his experiences and observations as captain of a river steamer in Africa. In his account of colonial exploitation, he tells of a trader named Kurtz, who reportedly wielded great power over the native population. Marlow recounts his search for the sinister Kurtz, who had discovered destructive forces in the jungle and in the human soul.

**Hedda Gabler,** by Henrik Ibsen (play)

Neurotic and ruthless, Hedda holds her meek and scholarly husband in contempt, but she is concerned that he may lose out on an appointment at the university. She learns that her onetime lover, Lövberg, has reformed through the influence of another woman. The success of his book makes him a rival to her husband. Hedda leads Lövberg to believe that the manuscript of his other book has been lost. As he despairs, she hands him a pistol, urging him to kill himself. When Judge Bruck uses Hedda's taunt against her, Hedda kills herself.

**Henry IV, Part I,** by William Shakespeare (play)

While Prince Hal leads a frivolous life with the comical Falstaff, Henry Percy (Hotspur) threatens a rebellion against Hal's father, the king. With the aid of Hal, who kills Hotspur, Henry defeats the rebel forces. After the battle, Falstaff comes upon the body of Hotspur and claims to have killed him.

**Henry IV, Part II,** by William Shakespeare (play)

Unsuccessful rebellions continue against King Henry. Falstaff and Prince Hal—along with such characters as Point, Pistol, Mistress Quickly, and Doll Tearsheet—continue their riotous behavior. Upon the death of King Henry, Falstaff expects to enjoy great power under Hal, the new monarch. As Henry V, however, the new king renounces his former ways and acquaintances. He banishes Falstaff from the court and imprisons him.

**Here Is Alaska,** by Evelyn Stefansson (nonfiction)

The wife of a famous Arctic explorer, Vilhjamur Stefansson, the author gives detailed information about Alaska. She discusses the Eskimo people, giving anthropological information about them as well as discussing their modern situation. The book also discusses the white residents of Alaska, the development of the area as a territory and as a state, its natural resources such as oil, and its politics and economy.

**Hiroshima,** by John Hersey (nonfiction)

The author examines the effect of the first atomic bomb in the year after it had been dropped on Hiroshima, Japan, on August 6, 1945. Hersey concentrates on a widow with three children, two doctors, a missionary priest, the pastor of a Japanese Methodist Church, and a former clerk in a factory. The author shows in great detail how the bomb and its aftermath affected these people.

**Homer Price,** by Robert McCloskey (novel)

Homer's father owns a tourist camp just outside the town of Centerberg. Homer's hobby is building radios. Among his adventures is taming a skunk. The scent upsets a lot of people, but the skunk helps catch some robbers. Next, Homer meets Super-Duper, a comic book hero. He also has adventures with doughnuts, a huge ball of yarn, an old man with a beard, and prefabricated houses.

**House Made of Dawn,** by N. Scott Momaday (novel)

Abel, an American Indian, is drafted into the United States Army in 1945. In the Army, and later on a reservation, Abel experiences great difficulty in dealing with the dominant white civilization. The author uses Abel's life to show how the white culture prevents Indians from finding themselves.

**The House of the Seven Gables,** by Nathaniel Hawthorne (novel)

The old mansion in which the spinster Hepzibah Pyncheon resides has long suffered from the curse of Matthew Maule, the dispossessed former owner. The impoverished Hepzibah forsakes her family pride and opens a shop. Clifford, her bachelor brother, returns home from years in prison for a crime he did not commit but for which he was convicted through actions of a cousin, Judge Pyncheon. The judge dies, Clifford is rehabilitated, and he and Hepzibah find some happiness in their declining years. The curse is broken when a descendant of Maule marries a Pyncheon.

**How Green Was My Valley,** by Richard Llewellyn (novel)

Welsh people in a coal mining valley during the late 1800's persevere in a difficult life. Huw Morgan remembers the valley when it was green but has lived to see it turn black under slag heaps, other waste, and pollution. Life in the valley is in many respects bleak, but the stalwart Morgan family displays nobility in the face of adversity.

**The Human Comedy,** by William Saroyan (novel)

The Macauley family lives in Ithaca, Calif. Mr. Macauley has died, survived by his widow and four children. Bess is 18 years old; Marcus is about to enter the Army. Homer is a messenger boy for Western Union, and the baby is four-year-old Ulysses. The book has little or no plot, but Saroyan develops the idea that love and goodness are all that is necessary to conquer the family's many problems.

**The Hunchback of Notre Dame,** by Victor Hugo (novel)

Frollo, an archdeacon of Notre Dame cathedral in medieval Paris, desires Esmeralda, a gypsy dancer in love with another man. He denounces her as a witch, but Quasimodo, the Hunchback bell ringer of the cathedral, saves her temporarily by taking her to the cathedral belfry. Esmeralda is finally executed as a witch, after which Quasimodo throws Frollo from the cathedral tower.

**I, Claudius,** by Robert Graves (novel)

Born in 10 B.C., Claudius becomes emperor of Rome in A.D. 41. He grows up to become a powerful Roman during the reign of Augustus, the first emperor, and the reigns of Tiberius and Caligula. This historical novel is embellished with many colorful details about the personal life of Claudius.

**I, Juan de Pareja,** by Elizabeth Borton de Treviño (novel)

Juan de Pareja is a young black slave in Spain in the 1600's who serves the famous artist Velásquez. Because laws forbid slaves from learning the arts, Juan de Pareja must learn to paint in secret to fulfill his ambition. With Velásquez at his side, he shows a painting to King Philip IV and is granted his freedom. Juan and Velásquez remain friends and companions for life.

**I Know Why the Caged Bird Sings,** by Maya Angelou (autobiography)

The author relates her childhood and adolescent experiences as a black girl in rural Arkansas and in St. Louis and San Francisco. She grows up during the 1930's, a period of economic depression when blacks, especially in the South and in large cities, live rigidly segregated lives. Maya and her family suffer many hardships, but like many blacks of the time, they endure with dignity and courage.

**I Never Promised You a Rose Garden,** by Hannah Green (novel)

Deborah Blau had an operation for a brain tumor at age five. She later suffered indignities in a camp where she was the only Jew. Deborah gradually retreats further into her own world, the Kingdom of Yr. At 16, she is undergoing psychiatric treatment in which the doctor struggles to bring her back from the Kingdom of Yr to the real world. The psychiatrist, however, does not promise her that reality is pleasant.

**I Remember Mama,** by John Van Druten (play)

An American-Norwegian family lives in San Francisco around 1900. The oldest daughter in the family has written a history of the family. Her reading from her manuscript evokes memories of Mama and a number of both comical and tragic episodes in the family's life. Mama is remembered as the wise and resourceful one, the backbone of the family.

**I Wonder as I Wander,** by Langston Hughes (nonfiction)

The black poet tells about periods of his life and his impressions of people and places. He writes about his journeys to Havana, St. Marc, and Haiti and records his impressions of the South. He also tells about his trips to Russia, Samarkand, Australia, Japan, and China, as well as to European cities such as Barcelona, Madrid, and Paris. The author includes an essay on the black educator Mary McLeod Bethune.

**The Idylls of the King,** by Alfred, Lord Tennyson (poem)

After the noble and idealistic King Arthur forms the Round Table, the perfect kingdom is marred by an illicit relationship between Lancelot and Queen Guinevere. There is growing disillusionment, followed by warfare. After the last great battle, only Arthur, Bedivere, and the evil Modred remain alive. Arthur slays Modred, but receives a mortal wound. Bedivere, the last surviving knight, relates the final scenes of the king's life.

**The Iliad,** by Homer (poem)

During the Trojan War, Agamemnon and Achilles quarrel after Agamemnon's seizure of Achilles' female slave. When Achilles sulks in his tent, refusing to take further part in the war, the Greek cause suffers. Hector then kills Patroclus, Achilles' friend, an act that brings Achilles into the fight again. He kills Hector in personal combat. Life deteriorates within Troy, and the Greeks are victorious.

**I'm Really Dragged But Nothing Gets Me Down,** by Nat Hentoff (novel)

In the 1960's, several people experience the social turmoil of the time. In the midst of the Vietnam war, some resist the draft. Others try to deal with marijuana, the drug scene as a whole, racism, civil rights, and the generation gap. There is little plot to speak of, but the numerous characters are vividly and dramatically drawn.

**The Incredible Journey,** by Sheila Burnford (novel)

A golden Labrador retriever, an old bull terrier, and a Siamese cat make a 250-mile journey through the wilderness of Canada. Although domesticated animals, the three manage to survive numerous hardships and dangers by working cooperatively. They share the food they catch and defend and encourage one another. The animals eventually arrive at their journey's end.

**The Inspector General,** by Nikolai Gogol (play)

Khlestakov, a minor Russian civil servant, is stranded in a small town. Expecting a visit from an important government inspector, the town's corrupt officials believe that Khlestakov is that inspector. Khlestakov takes advantage of the situation to gain numerous favors. He is found out when the postmaster reads a letter detailing the hoax that he has mailed to a friend. By then, however, Khlestakov has left town, and the real inspector general has arrived.

**Invincible Louisa,** by Cornelia Meigs (biography)

This life of Louisa May Alcott describes her upbringing and her unflagging unselfishness and loyalty toward her family. The book also covers her literary activities, particularly her associations with such New England writers as Ralph Waldo Emerson and Henry David Thoreau.

**The Invisible Man,** by Ralph Ellison (novel)

A young black man has faith in himself and in mankind. He is dismissed from a black college, however, for pointing out to the founder how blacks actually live in the South. In New York City, he becomes a tool of Communists. When he observes a riot in Harlem, the man realizes that he is without identity as a human being and that he will have to contend with both blacks and whites to affirm his identity.

**Island of the Blue Dolphins,** by Scott O'Dell (novel)

The Lost Woman of San Nicolas, a young Indian girl, is accidentally abandoned on a remote island off the California coast, when tragedy strikes her tribe and its members leave. She has no companions, no weapons, not even pots to cook in. The girl manages to survive, however, and to construct a tolerable and even comfortable environment for herself.

**Ivanhoe,** by Sir Walter Scott (novel)

The knight Ivanhoe loves Rowena, his father's ward. His father wants her to marry another man, and he banishes Ivanhoe, who goes on a crusade. With King Richard I, Ivanhoe returns to England to battle the forces of John, the king's brother, who is trying to usurp the throne. Richard and his knights defeat John's forces. Ivanhoe is wounded, captured, and taken to a castle. Richard and his knights, aided by Robin Hood and his men, take the castle. When Rebecca, who had nursed Ivanhoe back to health, is accused of witchcraft, Ivanhoe becomes her champion by defeating Bois-Guilbert, her accuser. Ivanhoe and Rowena are reunited.

**Jane Eyre,** by Charlotte Brontë (novel)

An orphan, Jane Eyre becomes a teacher. As the tutor to the daughter of Edward Rochester, Jane falls in love with him. They cannot marry because his demented wife is living. Jane leaves Rochester and is taken in by St. John Rivers, a minister, who wants to marry her. When she receives a telepathic message from Rochester, Jane returns to him. She finds his house burned, Rochester blind, and his wife dead. Marrying Rochester, Jane restores him to happiness.

## Jazz Country, by Nat Hentoff (novel)

Tom Curtis, a senior in high school, must decide between college and trying to become a professional jazz trumpeter. When he tries to play jazz in New York City, blacks tell him that his life has been too easy. They say that, being white, he has no conception of what it is like to be black and, therefore, has no chance to be successful in jazz. As Tom struggles to learn and be accepted, he begins to realize more about himself and finally goes to college.

## J.B., by Archibald MacLeish (play)

J.B. (Job); Zuss, the circus balloon seller (God); and Nickles, the popcorn seller (Satan) enact a play. J.B. has prospered and believes that God has been good to him. A son is then killed in war, a daughter is raped and murdered, and a son and a daughter die in an automobile accident. An air raid destroys J.B.'s bank. Even after an atomic attack, J.B. clings to his faith, although his wife Sarah curses God. J.B. persuades Sarah to accept their lot and begin again.

## Johnny Got His Gun, by Dalton Trumbo (novel)

A World War I soldier lies seriously wounded in a hospital. His face has been shot away, and he has lost both arms and both legs. He has memories of his childhood and youth. He also recognizes his present state and wonders how he can communicate with those about him and what the future holds.

## Johnny Tremain, by Esther Forbes (novel)

An orphan at age 14, Johnny Tremain becomes an apprentice to a silversmith in 1773. He does well, until he breaks a crucible of molten metal and severely burns his hand. He later becomes a dispatch carrier and meets patriots such as John Hancock, Paul Revere, and John Adams. As the Revolutionary War begins, Johnny takes part in the Battle of Lexington. Later, his injured hand healed, he returns to his trade.

## A Journal of the Plague Year, by Daniel Defoe (nonfiction)

H.F., a resident of London during the year of the bubonic plague, 1664-1665, describes life in the stricken city in minute and vivid detail. The man relates how the plague began and how it spread. He describes the measures taken to control the disease—including the closing of infected houses—and the collection and burial of the dead. He also relates how thousands fled their families and homes to escape the disease.

## A Journey to the Center of the Earth, by Jules Verne (novel)

Professor Hardwigg learns from an old manuscript about the possibility of descending to the center of the earth. With his nephew Henry and with Hans, he enters a silent volcanic crater in Iceland to begin the descent. Deep within the earth, they find prehistoric monsters, huge forests, other gigantic vegetation, and seas. They experience numerous hazards and adventures before finding a way to ascend to the earth's surface. They come out in India.

## Jubilee, by Margaret Walker (novel)

Vyry, a black slave, lives in the South during the Civil War. As a worker in the Big House, Vyry dreams of a home of her own and an education for her children. Freed with her children after the war, Vyry undergoes many hardships and indignities, but she perseveres and eventually realizes her dreams.

## Julius Caesar, by William Shakespeare (play)

Cassius and Casca, suspicious of Caesar's ambition, plot to assassinate him. They win Brutus to their cause, and he strikes the first dagger blow. Antony arouses the citizens with a speech at Caesar's funeral. With Octavius, Caesar's nephew, and Lepidus, Antony forms a triumvirate to oppose the forces of Brutus and Cassius. When the armies meet at the battle of Philippi, Brutus and Cassius are defeated, and they kill themselves.

## Kidnapped, by Robert Louis Stevenson (novel)

David Balfour's uncle, Ebenezer, unlawfully holds David's inheritance. The uncle has the youth kidnapped and put on a ship for America. During the voyage, Alan Breck—a Scots patriot—is picked up from a sinking boat. Following a shipwreck, he and David make their way back to Britain. They witness the murder of Colin Campbell and are suspected of the deed. Traveling across the Highlands, they escape, and David finally recovers his rights of inheritance.

## Kim, by Rudyard Kipling (novel)

Kimball O'Hara is the orphaned son of a former Irish sergeant stationed in India. Kim spends his childhood wandering in Lahore and meets a lama from Tibet whom he accompanies on his travels. Kim comes upon his father's old regiment, which adopts him. Later he shows ability for secret service details and goes to work with Hurree Babu, a native agent. Kim distinguishes himself by capturing the papers of Russian spies in the Himalaya Mountains.

**King Lear,** by William Shakespeare (play)

The king decides to divide his kingdom among his three daughters, according to their affection for him. Both Goneril and Regan flatter Lear, and each receives a third. Although devoted to her father, Cordelia says that she loves him only as a daughter should. Lear disinherits Cordelia, and she marries the king of France. Regan and Goneril fail to support Lear. When they turn him out of their homes, Kent looks after the old king, who becomes mad. Cordelia lands with a French army to restore her father's rights. The English, commanded by Edmund, defeat the French. Cordelia and Lear are taken prisoner. Cordelia is hanged, and Lear dies of grief. Edgar kills his brother Edmund. Goneril, jealous of her sister's love for Edmund, poisons Regan and stabs herself to death.

**Kon-Tiki,** by Thor Heyerdahl (nonfiction)

The author theorizes that ancient people from Peru colonized Polynesia by riding rafts made of balsa logs across 4,000 miles of Pacific Ocean. To test the theory, he and five other men construct a balsa raft in Peru and set out across the Pacific. Weeks later, they come ashore on an island near Tahiti. Heyerdahl proves that such a journey was possible.

**Kristen Lavransdatter,** by Sigrid Undset (novels)

The young girl Kristen grows up in Norway in the 1300's. At the age of 15 she is betrothed to Simon, but she eventually marries Erlend and has several children. Because of an act of treason, Erlend loses most of his land. Kristen becomes manager of his remaining estate. When the Black Death appears, Kristen dies of the plague.

**A Lantern in Her Hand,** by Bess Aldrich (novel)

As a young bride, Abbie Deal moves from Iowa to Nebraska. She helps her husband build their rude hut, and they begin their new life together. They suffer the usual hardships of the plains frontier—drought, grasshoppers, and blizzards. After a long pioneer life, Abbie Deal dies peacefully, surrounded by children and grandchildren.

**Lassie Come-Home,** by Eric Knight (novel)

The prize collie Lassie belongs to an English family and is particularly attached to young Joe.

The family falls on hard times and, in order to raise money, is forced to sell Lassie. The dog is purchased by a wealthy Scotsman and taken to his estate. Lassie escapes from a kennel and begins a successful 400-mile journey home.

**The Last of the Mohicans,** by James Fenimore Cooper (novel)

As the French and Indians besiege Fort William Henry, Alice and Cora Munro, daughters of the English commander, journey toward the fort with two companions. The treacherous Magua plans to betray the party to hostile Indians. The scout Hawkeye (Natty Bumppo) and two Mohicans, Chingachgook and his son Uncas (the last of the Mohicans), foil his plot, however. After the English surrender, the sisters are captured. Alice is rescued, but Cora remains in Magua's hands. When Uncas attempts to free her, both die, and Hawkeye kills Magua.

**Le Morte D'Arthur,** by Sir Thomas Malory (fiction)

King Arthur, the embodiment of chivalry, and his group of knights establish a perfect kingdom and the Round Table. Eventually, the kingdom dissolves and the Round Table comes to an end. Because of Lancelot's sin, Arthur's quest for the Holy Grail fails, but the virtuous Galahad succeeds.

**Les Misérables,** by Victor Hugo (novel)

Jean Valjean, a poor man, steals a loaf of bread for his sister's starving children. He is caught and sentenced to prison and is given additional years for attempting to escape. Released, Valjean is befriended by a bishop and starts anew, becoming a successful industrialist and the mayor of a French town. Valjean has further brushes with the law and is returned to prison. After escaping, he befriends a young girl, Fantine, and her child Cosette. When Fantine dies, Valjean provides for Cosette's future.

**A Light in the Forest,** by Conrad Richter (novel)

John Butler, a boy living in colonial America, is captured by Delaware Indians at the age of four. Cuyloga, a tribal leader, adopts him. As True Son, John grows up knowing nothing but Indian life in the forest. At age 15, he is forcibly returned to his parents. Having rejected white civilization, John is more Indian than white, and he longs to return to his adoptive father. He finds, however, that he has no choice but to remain with whites.

**The Light That Failed,** by Rudyard Kipling (novel)

Dick Helder, a young artist who does sketches of

British soldiers in the Sudan in the 1890's, becomes well known for his work. He falls in love with the shallow Maisie but discovers that a sword wound he received on the head in the Sudan will result in his blindness. When Maisie fails to stand by him, Helder returns to the army, and exposes himself to enemy gunfire, and is killed.

**The Little House on the Prairie,** by Laura Ingalls Wilder (novel)

After having lived in Wisconsin for a number of years, the Ingalls move to Oklahoma. The family finds life on the prairie much different. They are fascinated by the Indians they meet and by the Longhorn steers and other animals they observe. The Ingalls experience a prairie fire. Like numerous pioneers, they remain on the move and finally head for the Dakota Territory.

**The Little Prince,** by Antoine de Saint-Exupéry (novel)

A pilot is forced to crash-land his plane in a desert in North Africa. There he meets a little boy who is a prince on his own planet, Asteroid B612. The Little Prince tells about life on his planet, about his flowers, and about things that he has encountered on earth, such as an echo, a snake, roses, and a fox. When the boy returns home, the pilot parts with him sadly.

**Little Women,** by Louisa May Alcott (novel)

The March sisters—Jo, Beth, Amy, and Meg— live in a small New England town. They have domestic problems, as they attempt to increase the family income and cope with adolescent love. Beth, a delicate child with a flair for music, dies young. Jo, a tomboy who wants to be a writer, marries a German professor. Meg marries a teacher, and Amy weds Laurie, a grandson of the neighboring Laurence family.

**The Little World of Don Camillo,** by Giovanni Guareschi (novel)

Don Camillo, a militant priest in an Italian village, opposes the mayor, Peppone, who is a Communist. Although friends, the two frequently are on opposite sides on issues that arise in the village. Their disagreements often lead to humorous situations. When in doubt or confused, Don Camillo retires to his altar to discuss the situation with his truest friend—God.

**Long Day's Journey into Night,** by Eugene O'Neill (play)

Mary Tyrone is a drug addict, the victim of a quack doctor who fed her morphine during an illness after her son Edmund's birth. The sickly Edmund fears that his actor-father will send him to a cheap sanitarium to die. James, the other son, drinks to avoid reality and blames Edmund for his mother's addiction. James, the father, curses his family. The family members have little to look forward to except their own destruction.

**Look Homeward, Angel,** by Thomas Wolfe (novel)

Eugene Gant is the youngest of six children of a stonecutter, Oliver, and his crafty wife Eliza. With his brothers and sisters, he grows up in a small town. Solitary and searching, Eugene finishes a private high school and enters a university, where he continues to be alone and "different." Upon graduation, he breaks with his family to seek his own path through life.

**Looking Backward,** by Edward Bellamy (novel)

Young Julian West begins an hypnotic sleep in 1887. When he awakens, it is 113 years later. The boy learns that by the year 2000 injustice and inequality in the United States have been eradicated. Democratic state capitalism has replaced private enterprise, and there is no crime, poverty, or war. Everyone is considerate and leads an ethical life.

**Lord Jim,** by Joseph Conrad (novel)

When his ship appears to be sinking, Jim, an officer, abandons the ship and passengers. The ship does not sink, and Jim becomes a disgraced outcast living with natives on the island of Patusan. A group of Jim's white friends murder a Patusan, his best friend and the son of the chief. According to Patusan justice, Jim must die. He wins back his lost honor by triumphing in death.

**Lord of the Flies,** by William Golding (novel)

A group of English schoolboys are marooned by a plane crash on a deserted island. They must provide for themselves and establish a government. The boys elect a leader, agree on rules, and the leader appoints subordinates. Everything seems quite civilized. Savagery asserts itself, however, and the situation disintegrates. The boys eventually retrogress to a state of near anarchy and then dictatorship.

**Lost Horizon,** by James Hilton (novel)

Four people are kidnapped and taken to a lamasery known as Shangri-La in a remote area of Tibet. It is a pleasant, peaceful spot where the pace of life is relaxed and slow. People grow old but do not show their age. Eastern ways of life prevail.

**Macbeth,** by William Shakespeare (play)

Three witches hail Macbeth as king of Scotland but predict that sons of Banquo will occupy the throne. Urged on by his ambitious wife, Macbeth murders King Duncan. Macbeth is crowned king but, worried about Banquo and his son, plots their deaths. Banquo is slain, but the son escapes. When Macbeth consults the witches, they tell him to beware of Macduff. The witches say that no man born of woman can harm him, but that he must fear the coming of Birnam Wood to his castle. Macbeth has Macduff's family slain. Macduff returns from exile with an army, shielded by branches from Birnam Wood, that advances on Macbeth's castle. When Macbeth and Macduff meet, Macduff informs him that he was not born in a normal childbirth. In the battle, Macbeth is killed.

**Madame Curie,** by Ève Curie (biography)

A daughter of the scientist tells her mother's life. Born Marie Sklodowski in Poland in 1867, she goes to Paris to study physics and chemistry. There she meets and marries Pierre Curie. After long experimentation, the Curies discover radium, for which they share the Nobel prize for physics in 1903. After Pierre's death in 1906, Marie is appointed to succeed him as a professor at the Sorbonne. In 1911 she wins the Nobel prize in chemistry.

**Main Street,** by Sinclair Lewis (novel)

Carol Milford marries Dr. Will Kennicott, who lives in Gopher Prairie. Carol finds the town dull and intolerant. Few people support her efforts to beautify the community or to start a drama club. She falls in love with Erick Valborg, with whom she runs off, but her husband later brings her back home. Carol feels respect, not love, for him, but since she can make nothing of her own life, she resigns herself to Gopher Prairie.

**A Man for All Seasons,** by Robert Bolt (play)

Despite urgings from Henry VIII, Sir Thomas More refuses to sanction his divorce, which had led to a break with the Pope and to the establishment of a new church in England. More's stand as a Roman Catholic and his refusal to acknowledge Henry as head of the English church leads him to be convicted of treason and executed.

**Manchild in the Promised Land,** by Claude Brown (autobiography)

The author recounts his childhood and young manhood in the Harlem area of New York City. He paints a vivid picture of street life in the black ghetto and of his own experiences in a gang. Vandalism, mugging, stealing, maiming, even murder, and drugs are part of his life. Of his street friends, only three avoid death or prison. Brown emerges from the confines of the ghetto to become a writer.

**The Mayor of Casterbridge,** by Thomas Hardy (novel)

While drunk, Michael Henchard sells his wife and child to Newson, a sailor. After he is sober, he pledges not to drink for 20 years. Eighteen years later Henchard is the rich and respected mayor of Casterbridge. His wife returns with a child that is Newson's but that Henchard thinks is his. Henchard quarrels with his business partner, his wife dies, and he discovers that the child is not his. Newson, thought dead, returns to claim his daughter. She marries Henchard's rival, who becomes the new mayor.

**A Member of the Wedding,** by Carson McCullers (novel)

Twelve-year-old Frankie wants to belong. When her brother Jarvis and his fiancée ask her to be a member of their wedding party, she mistakenly assumes that she will afterward leave on their honeymoon with them. Painfully corrected of her notion, Frankie runs away, determined to find exciting experiences. When she returns home, she has further unhappiness but finds friendship with Mary Littlejohn, with whom she plans a trip around the world.

**The Merry Adventures of Robin Hood,** by Howard Pyle (novel)

An outlaw hero of medieval England, Robin Hood leads a band of men, including Little John and Friar Tuck, who fight mainly with long bows. The band, along with Maid Marian, live in Sherwood Forest in Nottinghamshire. Robin and his group favor the downtrodden, taking from the rich to give to the poor. They are also protectors of women and children.

**Microbe Hunters,** by Paul de Kruif (biography)

This book of short biographies of bacteriologists begins with Anton Van Leeuwenhoek, a Dutch lens grinder who discovered bacteria in the 1700's. Among the other scientists included are Louis Pasteur, Robert Koch, Elie Metchnikoff, Walter Reed, and Paul Ehrlich—all of whom contributed to progress in safeguarding human health.

**A Midsummer Night's Dream,** by William Shakespeare (play)

Hermia loves Lysander, and Helena loves Demetrius, who has been promised to Hermia. The four spend a night in a wood near Athens. Oberon and Titania, the fairy king and queen, have quarreled. Oberon has Puck place a magic love potion in the eyes of the sleeping queen so that, upon awakening, she will fall in love with the first person she sees. This proves to be Bottom, the weaver, upon whose head Puck has placed an ass's head. Oberon also has Puck place the potion in Demetrius' eyes so that he will love Helena. Puck manages to place it both in Demetrius' and Lysander's eyes, so that both love Helena. Hermia is left out. The fairies eventually straighten out everything, and the two couples attend the wedding feast of the Duke of Athens.

**The Mill on the Floss,** by George Eliot (novel)

Maggie and Tom Tulliver are children of the man who owns the mill on the Floss. Maggie falls in love with Philip Wakem, a lawyer's son, but because the family hates Philip's father, Maggie obeys Tom and refuses to see Philip any longer. She innocently gets herself into an improper situation with Stephen Guest, and her brother and society ostracize her. When a flood strands Tom at the mill, Maggie rescues him. Brother and sister are reconciled before their boat overturns and both are drowned.

**The Miracle Worker,** by William Gibson (play)

Anne Sullivan becomes the teacher of Helen Keller, deaf and blind since the age of two. The teacher's work is made more difficult by the family, which often spoils Helen out of pity for her. Anne undergoes a long struggle as she tries to discipline Helen Keller and teach her. After a great deal of difficulty and frustration, Helen Keller realizes the connection between language and objects and speaks her first word.

**Moby Dick,** by Herman Melville (novel)

Ishmael ships on the whaler *Pequod*, captained by Ahab. The captain is determined to destroy the white whale, Moby Dick, which had once torn off his leg. After the crew captures several whales, they sight the monster. During the first chase, Moby Dick smashes a whaleboat, and then swamps another boat. The white whale is finally harpooned, but Ahab is caught in the line and carried to sea as Moby Dick smashes the ship. The ship sinks, leaving Ishmael the only survivor.

**Moll Flanders,** by Daniel Defoe (novel)

A woman has been punished for theft by being transported from England to the Virginia Colony. Brought up by the family of the mayor of Colchester, her daughter Moll eventually marries several times and has numerous affairs. She journeys to Virginia, finds her mother, and unwittingly marries her brother. Moll returns to England and becomes a criminal. She in turn is transported to Virginia with one of her former husbands; there they acquire wealth as plantation owners.

**The Moonstone,** by Wilkie Collins (novel)

In 1799, the British capture the city of Seringapatam in India. John Herncastle, an officer, takes the moonstone, a huge diamond, from the forehead of an idol. An Indian priest curses him, predicting misfortune for him and his descendants. Given to Miss Verinder, Herncastle's niece, the stone disappears. Misfortune does befall those connected with the diamond until the mystery of its disappearance is solved and the stone is returned to the idol's head.

**Mr. and Mrs. Bo Jo Jones,** by Ann Head (novel)

While they are seniors at Trilby High, July and Bo Jo secretly marry when she is 16 and he 17. Neither set of parents approves. The two experience the difficulties of a young couple and separate. Eventually they are reunited and after high school go to college. July expresses happiness and relief that the first years of their marriage are over.

**Murder in the Cathedral,** by T. S. Eliot (play)

Thomas à Becket is Archbishop of Canterbury and chancellor to King Henry II of England. Henry attempts to reduce church authority, but Becket resists. Becket meets tempters who remind him of his influence with the king and of his political authority, but Becket rejects the temptations. Four knights accuse Becket of disloyalty, kill him, and then justify their deed.

**My Antonia,** by Willa Cather (novel)

As children, Ántonia Shimerda from Bohemia and Jim Burden from Virginia arrive to live in pioneer Nebraska. Jim lives with his grandparents on a prosperous farm. Ántonia's father, who is inexperienced in farming, fails to succeed on undeveloped land. In despair, he commits suicide. The Burdens employ Ántonia and her brother Ambrosch. Later she works as a maid for other families. Ántonia has a child, and they are deserted by a railroad conductor with whom she had eloped. She returns to work on her brother's farm. The quiet and industrious Antonia later marries Anton Cuzak, by whom she has many children. The two friends, Antonia and Jim, meet again years later.

## My Friend Flicka, by Mary O'Hara (novel)

Ten-year-old Ken is growing up on a ranch in the West. His father, an ex-army officer, raises thoroughbred horses and gives Ken a filly named Flicka. She proves extremely difficult because of an independent and wild streak. Trying to escape to be on her own, the horse nearly kills herself. Ken nurses Flicka to health and eventually tames her.

## The Mysterious Island, by Jules Verne (novel)

In 1865, a balloon carrying five Americans falls into the sea near a deserted island. Once ashore, the men set about providing for themselves. They find minerals from which they fashion tools and weapons, and they make bricks with which they construct an oven to make pottery. The men domesticate an orang-utan. They build a telegraph system and successfully ward off an attack by pirates. Eventually, they are rescued and taken to America, where they live on land that they buy in Iowa.

## National Velvet, by Enid Bagnold (novel)

Velvet, the 14-year-old daughter of a butcher, wins a raffle—the prize being a piebald horse best known for fence jumping. Velvet becomes firmly attached to the animal and later enters him in the Grand National, England's most famous annual steeplechase. After great suspense, Velvet rides the horse to victory in the race.

## Nicholas Nickleby, by Charles Dickens (novel)

Upon the death of the father, Nicholas and Kate Nickleby and their mother are penniless. An uncle, Ralph Nickleby, sends Nicholas to work at an urchins' home, under the direction of the cruel Wackford Squeers. When Squeers mistreats a boy named Smike, Nicholas befriends the boy, thrashes Squeers, and escapes with Smike. Nicholas supports the two as an actor. Nicholas rescues Kate, apprenticed to a dressmaker, by whom she is mistreated. He later falls in love with Madeline Bray, but his uncle wishes to marry her to the old usurer, Gride. However, the uncle's plot fails. After Smike dies, it is discovered that he was the uncle's son, and Ralph Nickleby commits suicide. Nicholas marries Madeline, and Kate marries into a family that had befriended her and Nicholas.

## Nigger, by Dick Gregory (nonfiction)

The author, a comedian, nightclub entertainer, and participant in the civil rights movement of the 1960's, describes what it was like to grow up black in a world of segregation, discrimination, and prejudice. He also discusses the difficulties that members of the civil rights movement faced as they tried to overcome racial barriers in the United States, especially in the South.

## 1984, by George Orwell (novel)

In a totalitarian society characterized by continuous war, hypnotic mass communications, and oppressive government, truth is falsehood and falsehood truth. Seldom is anyone outside the range of a television camera, and the government has total control over people's thoughts and actions. A man and a woman try unsuccessfully to rebel against the sterile and restricted life.

## Nobody Knows My Name, by James Baldwin (nonfiction)

In a series of essays, the author dicusses a variety of topics. He concentrates on black-white relationships and on the problems of being a writer. Among his topics are a conference of black artists and writers in Paris; observations about writers such as Richard Wright, Norman Mailer, and William Faulkner; segregation in the South; and some problems associated with writing a novel.

## Northanger Abbey, by Jane Austen (novel)

Catherine Morland, a minister's daughter, meets Henry Tilney and falls in love with him. They receive his father's approval for marriage. Catherine is rejected by the father, however, after he is led to believe that her parents are poor. He insists that Henry break off the relationship. They obtain his father's consent to marry after he learns the truth about her family background.

## Northwest Passage, by Kenneth Roberts (novel)

Major Robert Rogers is an American ranger at the time of the French and Indian War. Rogers leads an expedition against the Indian town of St. Francis. He then goes to England to try to raise money to conduct a search for a northwest passage to the Pacific Ocean. Rogers later becomes governor of Michilimackinac, a settlement at the head of Lake Michigan. When he gets into trouble with his superiors, he is court-martialed.

## Notes of a Native Son, by James Baldwin (nonfiction)

In a group of essays, the writer considers what

it is like to be black in America. Other subjects include Richard Wright, particularly his novel *Native Son*, the famous novel *Uncle Tom's Cabin*, and the movie version of *Carmen Jones*. Baldwin also writes about a trip to Atlanta, about his father and his childhood, and about his impressions of Paris.

### The Odyssey, by Homer (poem)

After 10 years, Odysseus remains the only living Greek chieftain not yet returned home from the Trojan War. Odysseus encounters numerous adventures on his return, and in the meantime his wife Penelope has put off various suitors. Odysseus finally returns to learn that Penelope's suitors have wasted much of his wealth. He comes to his house in disguise and, with the aid of his son Telemachus, destroys the suitors. Odysseus is finally reunited with Penelope.

### Oedipus Rex, by Sophocles (play)

Warned by Apollo that his son will kill him, Laius, king of Thebes, has Oedipus left to die on a mountain. A shepherd finds the baby and takes him to the king and queen of Corinth, who raise him. Oedipus later learns from an oracle that he will kill his father and marry his mother, and leaves Corinth for Thebes. On the way, he meets Laius but of course does not know him. When they quarrel, Odeipus slays Laius. At Thebes, Oedipus solves the riddle of the Sphinx, which has been threatening the city. He is awarded with the throne and with Jocasta, his own mother, in marriage. They have two sons and two daughters. Eventually, Oedipus and Jocasta discover the truth. The queen hangs herself. Oedipus blinds himself and sets out on a life of wandering.

### Of Courage Undaunted: Across the Continent with Lewis and Clark, by James Daugherty (nonfiction)

In 1803, the United States purchases Louisiana, a vast land of some 15 million acres in the West, from France. President Thomas Jefferson sends Meriwether Lewis and William Clark to lead an expedition to explore the land. Leaving St. Louis, the band journeys up the Missouri River, explores the Yellowstone country, and eventually reaches the Columbia River and the Pacific Ocean. The party returns the following year, bringing back much information about Indians, geography, flora and fauna, and other facts about the area.

### Of Human Bondage, by W. Somerset Maugham (novel)

Philip Carey, a clubfooted orphan, is brought up by an uncle and aunt and studies art. He becomes attached to Mildred, a waitress and occasional prostitute, who uses him to her own advantage and frequently disdains him. Philip eventually forsakes art to become a doctor. He marries and goes to a rural area to practice.

### The Old Man and the Sea, by Ernest Hemingway (novel)

Santiago, an old fisherman, tries once more to overcome his bad luck. He takes his skiff far out into the Gulf of Mexico. He catches a large marlin but must spend hours fighting the fish before he subdues it. Santiago heads for port, only to have sharks attack his catch. He arrives home with nothing but a skeleton. By fighting as well as he could, however, Santiago has prevailed against defeat.

### The Old Wives' Tale, by Arnold Bennett (novel)

Two sisters, Sophia and Constance Baines, have lives that diverge and then come together again. Constance marries Samuel Povey, an assistant in a drapery shop, and spends her entire life in Bursley, the town of her birth. Sophia elopes with Gerald Scales, a salesman and an unpleasant character. He marries her against his will and deserts her in Paris. There she ekes out a living as the keeper of a rooming house. The two sisters are later reunited and live the remainder of their lives in Bursley.

### Old Yeller, by Frederick B. Gipson (novel)

In the Texas hill country in the 1860's, the father of 14-year-old Travis departs on a cattle drive to Abilene. He leaves the boy in charge of his mother, younger brother, and the ranch. The dog Old Yeller appears one day and becomes a member of the family. Many adventures occur to the boy and Old Yeller, including problems with wild hogs and a bear and a fight between two bulls. Old Yeller gets rabies and has to be destroyed.

### Oliver Twist, by Charles Dickens (novel)

Oliver Twist, whose parents are unknown, is brought up in a workhouse presided over by Mr. Bumble. The boy runs away to London, falling in with a group of thieves, including Fagin, Bill Sikes, and Nancy. Oliver later is taken in by Mrs. Maylie and Rose. Nancy reveals to Rose that a mysterious man named Monks had urged that the thieves make Oliver one of them, that Monks knows of Oliver's parentage, and that some relationship exists between Oliver and Rose. Because of her revelations, Sikes murders Nancy. Trying to escape the authorities, he accidentally hangs himself. Monks confesses that he is Oliver's half brother, seeking to get the boy's inheritance for himself. Rose turns out to be Oliver's aunt. Mr. Brownlow adopts Oliver, and Monks dies in prison.

## On Death and Dying, by Elizabeth Kübler-Ross (nonfiction)

After research on dying patients, the author concludes that the dying need to settle unfinished business before they die. From her extensive interviews with the dying, Dr. Kübler-Ross believes that there are five stages associated with dying: denial, anger, bargaining, depression, and acceptance. It is crucial, she says, to understand the feeling of isolation experienced by the dying.

## On the Beach, by Nevil Shute (novel)

Nuclear warfare has wiped out the Northern Hemisphere. In Australia, the people await the arrival of the deadly radioactive cloud drifting slowly southward. A submarine sets out for the West Coast of the United States to check on possible survivors. None are found, but one crew member remains onshore. Members of an Australian community stage an auto race as one last desperate and futile effort to ignore their fate, but the radioactive cloud eventually appears.

## One Flew Over the Cuckoo's Nest, by Ken Kesey (novel)

An Indian inmate of a mental ward tells the story of MacMurphy, a new arrival. MacMurphy becomes the enemy of "Big Nurse" as the two struggle for power. Overcoming the docility of his fellow inmates, MacMurphy incites them to rebellion. "Big Nurse" finally has a frontal lobotomy performed on MacMurphy. A defeated man, he becomes docile like his fellow inmates.

## The Oregon Trail, by Francis Parkman (autobiography)

With his cousin, Parkman makes a journey along part of the Oregon Trail in the 1840's. At Fort Laramie, they visit a Sioux Indian encampment and learn of a plan for a war party to move against the Snake tribe, the Sioux enemy. Directed by a guide, Parkman finds the war party and lives with it for several weeks. He sees no hostile activity, but he does participate in numerous ceremonies and buffalo hunts, all the while learning a great deal about Great Plains Indian life.

## Othello, by William Shakespeare (play)

Othello, the Moorish commander of Venetian forces, makes Cassio instead of Iago his chief lieutenant. The act prompts Iago to seek vengeance. Iago contrives to have Cassio dismissed from his position. He also plants seeds of doubt concerning the faithfulness of Othello's bride, Desdemona, leading Othello to conclude that she loves Cassio. Through Iago's trick, a handkerchief that Othello had given Desdemona is found on Cassio. Othello orders Iago to have Cassio killed, and after accusing Desdemona of infidelity, he strangles her in a jealous fury. Later Othello learns the truth from Iago's wife, after which Iago stabs her. Othello tries to kill Iago but only wounds him, and Othello kills himself.

## Our Town, by Thornton Wilder (play)

In Grover's Corners, N.H., in the early 1900's the various citizens pursue their occupations as they go about their daily lives. George Gibbs courts Emily Webb, and they are married. Emily, however, dies in childbirth, and her friends and neighbors attend her funeral. Despite their loss, the Gibbs and Webb families reaffirm their faith in life.

## The Outsiders, by S. E. Hinton (novel)

Two teenage gangs are rivals in an Oklahoma town. Ponyboy Curtis, a 14-year-old member of the Greasers, has lived with two older brothers since his parents died. A rival gang, the Socs, ambushes Ponyboy and his friend Johnny, who kills one of the Socs. The two boys hide out. About to give themselves up, they come upon a burning building in which children are trapped. They rescue the children, but Johnny later dies from the burns he received.

## A Passage to India, by E. M. Forster (novel)

In the British colony of India, friendship and relations between colonials and their masters are difficult. An English girl, Adela Quested, goes to India to visit her fiance, Ronny Heaslop. On a visit to ancient caves arranged by the Indian Dr. Aziz, Adela hallucinates that Aziz insults her. When he is placed on trial, Adela admits that she was mistaken. As a consequence, she is ostracized by the English community, and Ronny breaks the engagement.

## Penguin Island, by Anatole France (novel)

A missionary mistakes penguins on an island for humans and baptizes them. An assembly in heaven awards them human souls. The penguins acquire clothes and, as a result of violence, develop the ideas of law and private property. The strongest penguin becomes king. The burden of taxation falls on the poor, superstition permeates religion, and the penguins engage in religious wars, persecution, and global wars. The monk tows the island back to the shore.

**Le Père Goriot,** by Honoré de Balzac (novel)

A retired manufacturer, Père Goriot, sees his daughters well married. He arranges for them to take over the fortune he has accumulated. Once they have the fortune, however, they refuse to have anything to do with him and fail to support him as they had promised. Even when he is on his deathbed, they will not come to him because they are attending a ball. When their father dies, they send empty coaches to the funeral.

**The Picture of Dorian Gray,** by Oscar Wilde (novel)

The handsome Dorian Gray has his portrait painted by Basil Hallward. The painter introduces Dorian to Lord Henry Wotton, who in turn introduces him to a life of vice. Dorian's moral deterioration is transferred to a physical deterioration of the portrait's features. The face steadily grows uglier. Dorian eventually stabs Lord Wotton and then the portrait. When Dorian is found dead, his own features reflect his corruption, but the features in the portrait are restored.

**The Pilgrim's Progress,** by John Bunyan (novel)

Christian learns that the city in which he lives will be destroyed. He flees from the City of Destruction and passes through the Slough of Despond, the Valley of Humiliation, the Valley of the Shadow of Death, and other places. He meets characters such as Mr. Worldly Wiseman, Faithful, Hopeful, and the monster, Giant Despair. Christian's wife also makes the pilgrimage and is saved from Giant Despair and other monsters through the aid of Great-Heart and Mercy.

**The Plague,** by Albert Camus (novel)

An epidemic of bubonic plague breaks out in the Algerian port of Oran. The resources of modern medicine can barely control the epidemic. Influenced by the presence of the plague and the reality of death, the people of the city reveal their characters. Dr. Bernard Rieux insists that one must do what one can to further human life without concern for reward.

**The Playboy of the Western World,** by John Millington Synge (play)

Christie Mahon, a peasant boy, leaves home because he mistakenly believes that he has murdered his cruel father. In the village to which he flees, his tales of persecution and defense make him a hero. He becomes a reciter of poetry and a lover. His father then appears, and the people think Christie a liar. He tries, but fails, to kill his father and then goes off with him.

**Portrait of a Lady,** by Henry James (novel)

Isabel Archer, an American girl, inherits an English fortune. Through Madame Merle, she meets Gilbert Osmond, an egocentric dilettante living with his daughter Pansy in Italy, and Isabel marries him. She later discovers that Madame Merle is Osmond's mistress and Pansy's mother and that Madame Merle brought her and Osmond together because of Isabel's fortune. Although disillusioned, Isabel remains married and later takes the young girl Pansy under her protection.

**A Portrait of the Artist as a Young Man,** by James Joyce (novel)

Throughout childhood, adolescence, and early manhood the life of Stephen Dedalus is affected by the narrow world of Dublin. A sensitive youth who wants to be a writer, he begins to resist the things in his society that he finds confining. Dedalus eventually decides to go to Paris to live.

**Pride and Prejudice,** by Jane Austen (novel)

Mrs. Bennet tries to make good matches for each of her five daughters, an endeavor that her husband ridicules. Darcy, an arrogant young man, interferes with his friend Bingley's courtship of Jane because he believes that she is not sincere. Darcy falls in love with Elizabeth, Jane's sister, and proposes, but she rejects him. When Darcy later helps Bingley and Jane as well as a younger sister, Elizabeth changes her mind and agrees to marry him.

**The Prince and the Pauper,** by Mark Twain (novel)

The future Edward VI discovers Tom Canty, a pauper and his twin in appearance. They exchange places, and the real prince is driven from the court. He tours the realm, learning of the cruelties of unjust laws and their administration and of religious prejudice. In the meantime, Tom Canty learns to behave like a prince. Before his coronation, the real Edward proves his identity, and during his brief reign, he tries to rule justly and humanely.

**Principato,** by Tom McHale (novel)

Some 35 years ago, Principato stalked out of his

church because the priest humiliated two young children. He has never returned, although he telephones in his confession every Friday. Principato's stand is known as the Defiance, a term he cherishes. His son Angelo, a mild young man, marries an Irish girl from a Philadelphia family in the undertaking business. Shortly before his death, Principato passes on the Defiance to Angelo.

**Prometheus Bound,** by Aeschylus (play)

Prometheus has stolen fire from the gods and given it to men. As punishment, Zeus has Prometheus bound to a rock in the wilderness of Scythia. Each day an eagle comes to devour his liver, which overnight is restored. Despite his agony, Prometheus refuses to repent of his opposition to Zeus. When Prometheus continues to be unyielding, he is hurled into the underworld.

**Pygmalion,** by George Bernard Shaw (play)

Professor Henry Higgins, a phonetics teacher, trains the voice and manners of Eliza Doolittle, a Cockney flower girl. He transforms Eliza from a poor, rough creature into a well-spoken, middle-class lady. In the process, she falls in love with Higgins. He does not want to marry her, or anyone, but after she has become a lady she cannot return to her former life and ways.

**A Raisin in the Sun,** by Lorraine Hansberry (play)

Mama Younger wants to use her late husband's insurance money to buy a house. Her son, Walter Lee, wants to buy a liquor store, which he thinks will bring wealth. Mama makes a payment on a house and gives Walter Lee the remaining money, but he loses everything. Their house is in a white neighborhood, and they are offered a profit to sell rather than move into it. Walter Lee wants to sell, but the family rejects the offer and prepares to move.

**Rascal,** by Sterling North (nonfiction)

The writer tells how at the age of 12 he adopted a baby raccoon. Named Rascal, the raccoon grows up in the boy's home, sleeping each night in his bed. The two take walks in the woods, go fishing, and enjoy a camping trip. When Rascal becomes a nuisance by raiding neighboring cornfields, he must be kept penned up. Finally, the boy must release the animal to his place in the wild, and Rascal returns to his natural habitat.

**Rebecca,** by Daphne du Maurier (novel)

A young woman has a brief courtship with Maxim de Winter, an English aristocrat, widower, and large landowner, and becomes his second wife. Although the couple seem to be in love, the servants and the neighbors cannot shed their memory of Rebecca, the first wife. They compare the rather shy and sometimes inept new wife unfavorably with her. When a mystery surrounding Rebecca's life and death is eventually revealed, the new wife is accepted.

**The Red Badge of Courage,** by Stephen Crane (novel)

Henry Fleming, a young Union recruit in the Civil War, anticipates his first battle, certain that he will display great bravery. In the face of shelling and gunfire, however, he runs away and fakes a wound. Shame finally overcomes Henry, and he returns to battle. In another encounter, he seizes the colors and leads a charge that carries the day.

**The Republic,** by Plato (nonfiction)

Socrates and other philosophers describe the ideal state. Their aim is to describe a just state, one in which citizens could lead just lives. Such a state, they decide, would include three classes: workers, soldiers, and guardians. The guardians would be philosopher-kings. They would rule wisely, not tyrannically, but they would not abide by the whims of a democratic majority.

**The Return of the Native,** by Thomas Hardy (novel)

To spite the selfish and capricious Eustacia Vye, Damon Wildeve marries the generous Thomasin Yeobright. Thomasin's cousin, Clym Yeobright, arrives in Egden Heath from Paris and marries Eustacia. Her relationship with Wildeve does not end, however, and Clym holds her responsible for his mother's death. Eustacia and Wildeve are accidentally drowned. Clym becomes a wandering preacher, and Thomasin later marries a former suitor.

**Richard III,** by William Shakespeare (play)

Deformed and villainous, Richard plots to inherit the throne from his ailing brother, Edward IV. He has his other brother, George, drowned. Richard marries Lady Anne, but later has her killed. After the king's death, he imprisons Edward's two sons and later has them murdered. Richard's ally, the Duke of Buckingham, turns against him and joins Henry, Earl of Richmond. The forces of the House of Lancaster, led by Henry, meet those of the House of York, headed by Richard, at Bosworth Field. Following a fierce battle, the Lancasters are victorious. Henry kills Richard and becomes Henry VII.

**Riders to the Sea,** by John Millington Synge (play)

Maurya has lost her husband and four sons to the sea, and another son is missing. Two daughters and the sixth son are at home. The remaining son wants to ride to market, but Maurya fears he too will be lost. Before the son leaves, the daughters find a bundle of clothing that proves to belong to the missing son, who has drowned. As she mourns over the bundle, Maurya hears a cry from the sea, and men carry in the body of the lost son.

**Rifles for Watie,** by Harold Keith (novel)

Jeff is a young Union soldier in the Civil War. His commander, General Watie tries to get repeating rifles for his men. Jeff is involved in encounters with Confederate guerrillas, in the battles of Wilson's Creek and Prairie Grove, and in other incidents involving Union and Confederate forces. After the war, Jeff settles in Kansas.

**Robinson Crusoe,** by Daniel Defoe (novel)

The sole survivor of a shipwreck, Crusoe leads a solitary existence but makes a comfortable life for himself on a desert island. He later takes Man Friday, whom he rescues from cannibals, as his companion. Robinson Crusoe and Friday experience many adventures before they capture an English ship and sail to England.

**The Roman Way,** by Edith Hamilton (nonfiction)

The author sketches Roman history and describes the Roman way of life. She concentrates on accounts of the Romans given by great classical writers such as Terence, Virgil, and Juvenal. She makes it clear that the Romans, in contrast to the Greeks, were primarily world conquerors, builders, lawyers, and statesmen.

**Romeo and Juliet,** by William Shakespeare (play)

The Capulet and Montague families are enemies. Romeo, the Montague heir, attends a ball in disguise and meets Juliet, the Capulet heiress. They fall in love and secretly marry. In a brawl, Tybalt, a cousin of Juliet, kills Romeo's friend Mercutio. When Romeo kills Tybalt, he is banished. Unaware of the marriage, Juliet's father wants her to marry Paris. Friar Laurence, who married Romeo and Juliet, gives her a potion that makes her appear dead and places her in a tomb. Before the friar can inform Romeo of the plot, Romeo finds Juliet. Thinking that she is dead, he kills himself. Awakening, Juliet finds his body and kills herself. The Capulets and the Montagues are reconciled too late.

**Roots,** by Alex Haley (nonfiction)

A saga of several generations of American blacks begins in Gambia in West Africa. The author establishes that his family began with Kunta Kinte, an African who was taken as a slave to America in the late 1700's. After dealing with Kunta Kinte's life, the author describes the experiences of Kunta's children and their descendants in the United States, to the time of Haley's own birth. The account is based on fact and constitutes a unique presentation of a portion of black history.

**Saint Joan,** by George Bernard Shaw (play)

Joan of Arc, one of the first French nationalists, puts her conscience above the judgment of the Catholic Church. Nationalism and individualism are dangerous political and religious views for her time. Consequently, Joan of Arc is burned at the stake. When she learns of her later canonization as a saint, she offers to return to earth, but her offer is rejected.

**The Scarlet Letter,** by Nathaniel Hawthorne (novel)

Hester Prynne leaves her aging husband in England to journey to colonial Boston to make a new home for them. When he arrives two years later, he finds her an adulteress, the mother of an illegitimate child. She refuses to name the father. Her husband, assuming the name Roger Chillingworth, seeks to discover the man's identity. He eventually learns that the father is Arthur Dimmesdale, a minister, who has for years been consumed by guilt for his deed. Hester wants to flee to England with Dimmesdale, but he refuses. Instead, Dimmesdale relieves his conscience by publicly confessing his guilt. A broken man, he dies in Hester's arms.

**The School for Scandal,** by Richard B. Sheridan (play)

Charles Surface is in love with Maria, the ward of Sir Peter Teazle, while his brother Joseph attempts to woo Lady Teazle, Sir Peter's young wife. Lady Teazle's flirtations with Joseph arouse her husband's ire. The brothers' rich uncle, Sir Oliver Surface, returns from India in disguise, to test the brothers. Charles pleases Oliver by offering to sell the family pictures, except the one of Sir Oliver himself. Sir Oliver asks Joseph for help but is refused. Joseph is exposed as a scoundrel. Charles is united with Maria, and Lady Teazle and Sir Peter are reconciled.

**The Sea Wolf,** by Jack London (novel)

When a ferryboat sinks, all passengers except Humphrey Van Weyden, a member of the intelligentsia, are lost. A ship captained by the ruthless Wolf Larsen rescues Van Weyden. As Van Weyden is forced to perform menial tasks, a struggle between the primitive Larsen and the civilized Van Weyden begins. The conflict later includes Maude Brewster, a poet whom Larsen also rescues. A storm drives Larsen's vessel to an island. Larsen dies, but Van Weyden and Brewster return to civilization.

**The Secret Sharer,** by Joseph Conrad (short story)

A sea captain recalls his first command. On watch one night, he finds a naked man named Leggart clinging to a ladder on the ship's side. The man has murdered a seaman and is fleeing. As they talk, the captain develops a strong psychological attachment to Leggart. He concludes that, regardless of risk, he must help Leggart escape. He brings his ship dangerously close to shore so that Leggart can swim to safety.

**Sense and Sensibility,** by Jane Austen (novel)

Two sisters, Elinor and Marianne Dashwood, are deserted by their fiances. The sensible Elinor learns that Edward Ferrars has left her because he is secretly engaged to Lucy Steele and feels bound to honor the commitment. His mother, however, disinherits him in favor of his brother. When Lucy becomes interested in the brother, Edward returns to Elinor. The impetuous Marianne follows her ex-lover to London, but becomes disillusioned with him. She marries a former admirer, Colonel Brandon, a more moderate man.

**A Separate Peace,** by John Knowles (novel)

Gene Forester recalls his friendship with Finny, an outstanding athlete, at a boy's boarding school in the 1940's. Finny leads the group in various games, and Gene feels a growing sense of competition with him. Finny has an accident for which Gene is responsible. Gene's guilt about the incident is quieted only after a mock trial is held at the scene of the accident. Finally, Gene leaves school to go to war.

**Seventeenth Summer,** by Maureen Daly (novel)

Angie Morrow and Jack Duluth have their first date in June, and they continue to see each other throughout the summer. Their dates are routine for a small Wisconsin city in the 1940's—soft drinks at the drug store, rides in a jalopy, movies, the Fourth of July parade, dancing to juke box music. By summer's end, Angie and Jack experience their first love, but they must part. She leaves for college; he, for a new home in Oklahoma.

**Shane,** by Jack Schaefer (novel)

A mysterious man in black on horseback approaches a Wyoming farm in the late 1800's and asks for water. The man, named Shane, stays on as a hired hand. He becomes involved in the traditional farmer-rancher quarrel and is beaten up by cowboys. Shane is a reformed gunslinger, however, and he is compelled to kill two cowboys who harass him and the family. He then rides off as mysteriously as he came.

**She Stoops to Conquer,** by Oliver Goldsmith (play)

Because his father has proposed that he marry Miss Hardcastle, Marlow and his friend Hastings pay the Hardcastles a visit. On their way, they become lost. The mischievous Tony Lumpkin directs them to what they believe is an inn, which is in reality the Hardcastle house. Having treated Hardcastle as an innkeeper, Marlow finally exonerates himself for rudeness after his father arrives at the house.

**Siddhartha,** by Hermann Hesse (novel)

A man in search of peace, Siddhartha undergoes widely different experiences. He is first a wanderer, begging for a living. Later he becomes the companion of a courtesan and of a wealthy businessman. Finally, he becomes a simple ferryman, drawing peace, contentment, pleasure, and wisdom from the river and from his mystical view of life.

**Silas Marner,** by George Eliot (novel)

An outcast because of a false accusation of theft, Silas Marner takes refuge in the village of Raveloe. The friendless weaver gradually accumulates a horde of gold, only to have it stolen. On the same day a young child appears at Marner's cottage. Taking her in, Silas shelters and raises the girl Eppie, who brings him much happiness. Years later, Silas' gold is found with the skeleton of Dunstan Cass. Dunstan's brother Godfrey acknowledges Eppie as his daughter from a secret marriage. By then, Eppie has become so attached to Silas that she refuses to leave him.

**Silent Spring,** by Rachel Carson (nonfiction)

The author warns against the indiscriminate use of chemical insecticides. Citing considerable evidence, she argues that such means of insect control dangerously upset the balance of nature. She contends that insecticides are particularly harmful to bird populations.

**Sir Gawain and the Green Knight,** by unknown author (poem)

The mysterious Green Knight allows Sir Gawain to cut off his head on condition that a year later he may return the blow. In a year, Sir Gawain goes to the castle of Lord Bercilak, who has a beautiful wife. During three days, she tempts Sir Gawain. Twice he reports the lady's behavior to Bercilak, but on the third day she gives Gawain a green scarf that he does not mention. Gawain then meets the Green Knight, who is really Bercilak. The knight's first two blows fail. Because of the scarf, the third blow nicks Gawain's neck. Gawain swears to wear the green scarf as a reminder of his temporary moral lapse.

**The Skin of Our Teeth,** by Thornton Wilder (play)

The Antrobus family is like the family of Adam and Eve and, in effect, like all humanity. Living in New Jersey, they experience the invention of the wheel and the alphabet, and they learn that the tomato is edible. They go through an ice age, the Biblical flood, and a horrible war. Despite calamities, the Antrobuses remain together, and they are ready to begin anew.

**The Snow Goose,** by Paul Gallico (novel)

Philip Rhayader, a hunchback, buys an abandoned lighthouse and the marshland around it. Geese visit the area regularly. One day a small girl brings a wounded Canadian goose to Rhayader, and they nurse it back to health. The goose returns each year. During the Dunkirk evacuation in 1940, the Snow Goose leads Rhayader in his boat to trapped British soldiers whom he rescues. On the third trip, German gunfire kills Rhayader.

**So Big,** by Edna Ferber (novel)

When Selina becomes a teacher in a country school near Chicago, the beauty of growing things in the fields intrigues her. She marries Pervus De Jong, an illiterate farmer. When he dies, Selina keeps the farm going, selling produce on the Chicago market. She puts her son Dirk— nicknamed "So Big"—through architectural school. He leaves school to be a bond salesman, but later concludes that he was mistaken to exchange a love of beauty for the acquisition of money.

**The Soul Brothers and Sister Lou,** by Kristin Hunter (novel)

Fourteen-year-old Loretta (Sister Lou) and her friend Fess are members of a black neighborhood club. When a white policeman kills an innocent member of the club, Sister Lou at first feels hatred for whites. She later adopts the nonviolent attitude she has been taught as part of her religion. Fess continues to want revenge, but Sister Lou convinces her that nonviolence is better.

**Soul on Ice,** by Eldridge Cleaver (nonfiction)

Black activist Eldridge Cleaver, a former leader of the Black Panther party, writes of his convictions as he serves a prison term in the 1960's. Cleaver's central theme is the discovery of his blackness. Among other topics, he discusses his days in prison, the assassination of Malcolm X, the white race and its heroes, his relations with his woman lawyer, Vietnam and American blacks and black women.

**The Souls of Black Folk,** by W. E. B. Du Bois (nonfiction)

Black leader Booker T. Washington believed in separatism, cooperation with whites, and gradual progress. Harvard-educated Du Bois, more militant, is certain that the world is not for white folks only, and that blacks should have a place in the American mainstream—as he advocates in this book. He would abolish segregation and racial discrimination. This book is a passionate statement of his credo and of the pain felt by blacks.

**The Sound and the Fury,** by William Faulkner (novel)

The sons of the Compton family—Benjy, Quentin, and Jason—are descendants of southern patricians but now lead degenerate lives on their run-down plantation. Two black servants, Dilsey and her son Luster, help the family, Luster cares for Benjy, a grown man but an idiot. Quentin commits suicide because of guilt and shame. The men's thoughts reveal facts about their useless mother, drunken father, weak uncle, and sister who has run away but has sent back an illegitimate daughter. The daughter eventually runs away after stealing money from Jason, a cynical, conniving man. The blacks endure as the white family distintegrates.

**Sounder,** by William Armstrong (novel)

A coon dog, Sounder lives with a black family in the South. The father steals food for his family and is arrested. As deputies take him away, Sounder lopes after the truck and is shot. He crawls into the woods, and the son searches for him in vain. After a time, the crippled and sick father returns from prison. Sounder soon returns, too. The father dies, and, in deep sorrow, so does Sounder.

**The Story of King Arthur and His Knights,** by Howard Pyle (novel)

In establishing his kingdom, Arthur helps Sir Kay at a tournament and discovers his lineage as he draws the sword from the anvil. Arthur obtains his sword Excaliber and wins his queen Guenevere. Merlin, Sir Pellias, and Sir Gawain also become important people in Arthur's court.

**The Story of My Life,** by Helen Keller (autobiography)

At age 23, the author tells of the serious illness that left her blind and deaf at the age of 2. At age 7, she comes under the tutelage of Anne Sullivan. After great struggle and frustration, Anne disciplines Helen, teaches her braille, and makes progress toward teaching her to talk. At age 10, Helen enters a school for the deaf and learns to speak well. She later goes to high school.

**The Strange Case of Dr. Jekyll and Mr. Hyde,** by Robert Louis Stevenson (novel)

Dr. Jekyll, a dedicated and kindly physician, is fascinated with the forces of good and evil in humans. He develops a drug that can transform him into the diabolic Mr. Hyde, the essence of evil who roams the streets of London by night, engaging in various cruel and vicious pranks. Jekyll has also developed a drug to restore his own identity. The Hyde personality grows stronger, however, until he commits a murder. He finally kills himself when he realizes that he is about to be discovered.

**The Stranger,** by Albert Camus (novel)

Meursault believes that life is absurd and that conventions are phony and unnecessary. He refuses to tell social "white lies" or to believe in religion or in love. He does not grieve for his dead mother and does not take his affair with Marie seriously. Without emotion, he kills an Arab in Algeria. While in prison awaiting trial for the crime, Meursault realizes that life itself is valuable.

**Stride Toward Freedom,** by Martin Luther King, Jr. (nonfiction)

The civil rights leader of the 1950's and 1960's relates the story of the Montgomery, Ala., bus boycott beginning in 1955. When told to move, Rosa Parks insists on remaining in the white section of a city bus. Her arrest leads King and other black leaders to organize a black boycott of the buses. The boycott lasts a full year, helping bring about the much sought after desegregation in public transportation.

**Swiftwater,** by Paul Annixter (novel)

Cam and Bucky Calloway, father and son, live in a northern Maine village. They are the only two remaining trappers in the vicinity. Loving the woods and wildlife, Bucky wants to erect a bird sanctuary, but he meets with various tribulations. After his father's death, Bucky finally succeeds.

**The Swiss Family Robinson,** by Johann Wyss (novel)

The Robinson family is shipwrecked and must construct a life from the beginning on a deserted island. The family's most remarkable achievement is a house in a huge tree, the rooms accessible by a staircase in the tree's trunk, where they remain safe from animal attacks. A ship arrives after several years. Although they can return home, the Robinsons decide to stay.

**A Tale of Two Cities,** by Charles Dickens (novel)

During the French Revolution, Dr. Manette, a physician, is released from prison and taken to London. Charles Darnay, an aristocrat, has fled France and also comes to London. Sydney Carton later saves Darnay from false accusations, and they become friends. Both love Lucie, Manette's daughter, and Darnay marries her. When Darnay later returns to Paris to try to rescue a servant, he is imprisoned. Carton saves him by taking his place. Darnay and Lucie are reunited.

**Tales from Shakespeare,** by Charles and Mary Lamb (nonfiction)

The authors, a brother and sister, rewrite the Shakespearean plays in story form. Mary Lamb retells the comedies; and Charles Lamb, the tragedies. Written in simple language, the work is a faithful account of the stories that Shakespeare used as the plots for his plays.

**The Taming of the Shrew,** by William Shakespeare (play)

Petruchio wants to marry the notoriously shrewish Katharina, the daughter of Baptista. Although Katharina insults and berates him, he pretends to find her gentle and kind. She finally consents, and Petruchio turns the tables. He humiliates and distresses Katharina until she is completely tamed. Meanwhile, her younger sister Bianca has married Lucentio, and Hortensio, who had been Bianca's suitor, has married a widow. The three bridegrooms bet on which wife will prove the most docile, a bet that Petruchio wins, but not without difficulty.

**Tender Is the Night,** by F. Scott Fitzgerald (novel)

Nicole, a wealthy mental patient, falls in love with her psychiatrist, Dick Diver. They marry, and she gradually achieves mental stability. He, however, loses his stability, and Nicole eventually leaves him for a lover. Dick becomes an alcoholic, and disintegrates to an early but inevitable death.

**Tess of the D'Urbervilles,** by Thomas Hardy (novel)

Tess Durbeyfield is seduced by Alec D'Urberville and gives birth to a child who dies in infancy. Working as a dairymaid on a farm, she becomes engaged to Angel Clare, a minister's son. On their wedding night, she confesses her past experience with Alec, and Clare abandons her. Clare later convinces Tess to return to him. One day Clare finds Alec in Tess's company. To free herself from Alec's influence, Tess murders Alec, is tried, found guilty, and hanged.

**Thirty-Nine Steps,** by John Buchan (novel)

Hannay, a young Englishman, returns from the Colonies to England and falls in love with an American girl. She tells him stories of international intrigue, including some secrets of great importance to the British government. The girl is murdered. Hannay tries to get the secrets to the government. Wanted for the girl's murder and pursued by foreign agents, Hannay eventually outwits both sets of pursuers.

**Thirty-Six Children,** by Herbert Kohl (nonfiction)

The author relates his experiences as a sixth grade teacher in a black elementary school in Harlem in New York City. He discusses concepts such as the "disadvantaged" child and "culturally deprived" child—popular ideas in the 1960's. Kohl explains how a teacher goes about his work, dealing with children to change them and awaken them to learning. Generally, the author finds the New York city school system inadequate to its task.

**Thomas Jefferson, Champion of the People,** by Clara Ingram Judson (biography)

This life story begins with Jefferson's boyhood in the 1750's and includes his early education, graduation from William and Mary, and law studies and practice. The biography touches on his writing of the Declaration of Independence, his governorship of Virginia, his service as minister to France, and his presidency. The book also includes his founding of the University of Virginia, Jefferson's favorite achievement.

**The Three Musketeers,** by Alexandre Dumas (novel)

D'Artagnan journeys from Gascony to Paris, hoping to become one of King Louis XIII's Musketeers, an elite group of guards. To prove his swordsmanship, D'Artagnan duels three members of the group—Athos, Porthos, and Aramis—the Three Musketeers. He wins, and becomes their friend. The four experience many adventures in the service of the king.

**The Time Machine,** by H. G. Wells (novel)

An inventor develops a time machine that enables him to travel into the future. The man witnesses a time of gradual degeneration as apelike Morlocks take over, as giant crabs become the only living creatures on earth besides him, and as the sun burns out. The earth itself finally dies.

**To Kill a Mockingbird,** by Harper Lee (novel)

Scout and her brother Jem are children of Atticus Finch, a lawyer, in a small Southern town. The children become involved with Boo Radley, who never leaves his house, with Mrs. Dubose, who has a terrible temper, and with other residents of the town. The children attend a dramatic trial at which Atticus defends a black man.

**Tom Jones,** by Henry Fielding (novel)

A foundling, Tom Jones, is taken in and educated by Mr. Allworthy. After love affairs with Molly Seagrim and Sophia and after various difficulties, Tom is dismissed by Allworthy. He sets out on adventures and in London has an affair with Lady Bellaston. Sophia remains in love with Tom, however, and seeks escape from a forced marriage to Blifil. Tom is eventually discovered to be the son of Allworthy's sister, and he and Sophia are united.

**The Tragical History of Doctor Faustus,** by Christopher Marlowe (play)

Finding no comfort in knowledge, Faustus turns to magic. He summons Mephistopheles, the devil, who agrees to be his slave for 24 years in exchange for Faustus' soul, a promise written in blood. Faustus has a splendid time, traveling and meeting many people of the past and present. He becomes reluctant to keep his bargain with the devil and tries to pray to God and Christ for help. Faustus has surrendered the right to pray, however, and Mephistopheles comes to take possession of his soul.

**Treasure Island,** by Robert Louis Stevenson (novel)

Young Jim Hawkins, the son of an innkeeper,

learns the location of buried treasure. He tells Dr. Livesey and Squire Trelawney, who outfit a ship to seek the treasure. One of those on board is Long John Silver, who leads a group of pirates in an unsuccessful mutiny to take over the ship. Jim Hawkins and his friends eventually retrieve the buried hoard.

**The Trojan Women,** by Euripides (play)

When Troy falls, the male rulers have all been slaughtered. The royal women of Troy are parceled out as slaves to the victorious Spartans. The Spartans also order Asytanax, the son of Hector, put to death. Helen of Troy, who is married to the Spartan ruler Menelaus, and whose kidnapping began the war in the first place, is reunited with Menelaus. She convinces him not to put her to death, even though the Trojans attacked to rescue her. Helen's triumph is a great blow to the surviving Trojan women. The women watch as the city goes up in flames and the walls collapse.

**Tuned Out,** by Maia Wojciechowska (novel)

In New York City in the summer of 1967, 16-year-old Jim discovers that Kevin, his older brother, is using LSD and marijuana. Jim becomes determined to stop his brother from doing so. Relationships between the two become complex as Jim tries to prevent his parents from finding out about Kevin. The parents remain unaware until Kevin is taken to a hospital because of a bad LSD trip.

**Twelfth Night,** by William Shakespeare (play)

The twins Sebastian and Viola are separated by shipwreck. Disguised as Cesario, Viola becomes a page for Duke Orsino, with whom she falls in love. Orsino loves Olivia, and has Cesario speak to her for him. Olivia falls in love with Cesario (Viola). Sebastian and Antonio, a ship captain who rescued him, appear. Olivia mistakes Sebastian for Cesario and marries him. Before Orsino, Antonio claims that Cesario is the person he rescued from the sea; Olivia insists that Cesario is her husband. Sebastian arrives to clear up the confusion, and Orsino marries Viola.

**Twenty Thousand Leagues Under the Sea,** by Jules Verne (novel)

Captain Nemo, a mad reformer, has abandoned civilization to live in the *Nautilus*, a self-sustaining submarine. A ship is sent to seek out the *Nautilus* and destroy it, but the ship is attacked by the submarine. Three passengers are rescued by Nemo and held captive for 10 months. They are treated well, however, and they observe many underwater spectacles. The three admire Nemo but decide to escape after watching him destroy a ship and its passengers.

**Up a Road Slowly,** by Irene Hunt (novel)

Julie's mother dies when Julie is 7. She goes to live with Cordelia, a spinster aunt, whose alcoholic brother lives nearby. By the time Julie is 17, she has experienced her first love with a boy unworthy of her; has grown to love her rather forbidding aunt; has found a new love; and has had a story that she wrote published in a college literary magazine.

**Up the Down Staircase,** by Bel Kaufman (novel)

An English teacher in a New York City high school describes the humorous but frustrating life of teachers and students in schools run by a heavy-handed bureaucracy. She tells about assemblies, faculty meetings, and examination periods. The teacher includes typical student writing and bureaucratic memos and describes students' attitudes toward literature.

**Utopia,** by Sir Thomas More (fiction)

A Portuguese sailor, Raphael Hythlodaye, makes three voyages to America. One of his voyages is to the island of Utopia, which has a communal society. All men are equal. Everyone is educated, prosperous, and wise. Utopia is an ideal society in which everyone shares in the necessities of life.

**Vanity Fair,** by William Makepeace Thackeray (novel)

Becky Sharp and Amelia Sedley are students in a boarding school. Becky is clever, scheming and unscrupulous; Amelia, gentle though unintelligent. Becky marries Rawdon Crawley and rises in society while engaging in extramarital affairs. Amelia marries George Osbourne, an army officer, after disdaining the attentions of Captain William Dobbin. Osbourne is killed in the Battle of Waterloo, but Amelia clings fondly to his memory until Becky reveals his infidelity. Amelia then accepts the faithful Dobbin when he returns from India.

**The Victim,** by Saul Bellow (novel)

Asa Leventhal holds an apparently secure position on a trade journal in New York City. One hot summer his wife is absent from home for a few weeks. During this time, Allbee, a gentile friend, constantly hectors Asa, accusing Asa of having ruined him. The absence of his wife, Allbee's persistence, and memories of an insane mother combine to make Asa feel he is going crazy.

### The Virginian, by Owen Wister (novel)

In the society of Wyoming cowpunchers in the late 1800's, the Virginian becomes well known for his chivalry and daring. The Virginian successfully woos Molly Wood, a pretty schoolteacher originally from Vermont. When his enemy Trampas accuses him of cheating at cards, the Virginian kills him.

### Waiting for Godot, by Samuel Beckett (play)

Vladimir and Estragon are two tramps waiting for Godot, who each day sends word that he will arrive the next day. They quarrel, consider separation, and even contemplate suicide while they wait. Pozzo is a rich man; Lucky, a servant whom he grossly mistreats. Pozzo and Lucky are very dependent on one another, just as are the two tramps. Lucky leads Pozzo about; Vladimir and Estragon wait for Godot.

### Walden, by Henry David Thoreau (nonfiction)

The author recounts his two years in solitude in a cabin he constructed at Walden Pond and explains his philosophy. Thoreau discusses living with the bare essentials of life and gathering and growing what food he needed. He explains his creed that personal experience must be the standard of value and that reading and nature are important in coming to terms with one's life.

### War and Peace, by Leo Tolstoy (novel)

In the years before Napoleon's Russian invasion and its aftermath, Russian people of all classes live their lives against a background of war. Natasha, a vivacious and romantic girl, is in love with the gallant Prince Andrei, a proud ascetic caught in a web of self-doubt. When he dies, she finds contentment as the wife of Pierre Bezukhov, an alienated intellectual trying to find meaning in life. Pierre finds peace by accepting life as it is. The story of these characters' lives is described in alternate chapters; the other chapters detail epic events in the war.

### Washington Square, by Henry James (novel)

Morris Townsend wants to marry Catherine Sloper, who is heir to a fortune. Her father refuses his consent, and the relationship is eventually broken off. After her father's death, Townsend reappears, but Catherine refuses to resume the courtship. Having freed herself from her father and suitor, she intends to remain independent for the remainder of her life.

### Watch for the Tall White Sail, by Margaret Bell (novel)

In 1887, 16-year-old Florence Monroe leaves Victoria, British Columbia, with her family to journey to Wrangall Island in Alaska. She spends the summer cooking for her brothers who work in a fish saltery. Florence experiences many adventures in pioneer Alaska.

### The Way West, by A. B. Guthrie (novel)

One hundred persons prepare to leave Independence, Mo., to head West along the Oregon Trail in a wagon train. Each person or family has a different reason for going West—to establish a better home, to escape creditors, to look for new political opportunities. The party has many problems—hostility from Indians, difficulties fording streams, and wagon breakdowns. After negotiating difficult mountain passes, the train arrives safely in Oregon.

### When Knights Were Bold, by Eva Tappan (nonfiction)

The author describes life in medieval times when knights were a major factor in warfare. She describes a knight's training, beginning as a page, with lessons in riding and sword play that finally lead to the right to be called a knight. The book also deals with the religious organization of the time, town life, and medieval trade.

### When the Legends Die, by Hal Borland (novel)

Thomas Black Bull, an American Indian, is born on a reservation in Colorado around 1900. When his father kills another Indian, the family flees to live in the wild. Thomas' parents die, and he finds refuge and companionship with a friendly bear. A former cowboy finds him and cares for him while the two travel the rodeo circuit. Thomas Black Bull finally returns to his original home.

### White Fang, by Jack London (novel)

The offspring of an Indian dog and a wolf, White Fang is sold to Beauty Smith. He torments the dog to make him even more ferocious so that he can compete in dogfights. A mining engineer, Weedon Scott, rescues the dog. By treating him kindly, the man changes the dog's behavior. He becomes completely domesticated and dies protecting the man's family.

### Why We Can't Wait, by Martin Luther King, Jr. (nonfiction)

In this account, the noted civil rights leader relates the progress of the civil rights movement during the early 1960's. He recounts marches, bombings, and police brutality in Birmingham, Ala. Dr. King includes various other events in the movement leading to the march on Washington, D.C., in 1963, where, before thousands, he delivers his famous speech, "I Have a Dream."

**Wind in the Willows,** by Kenneth Grahame (novel)

The kindhearted Mole, the poetic Water Rat, and the boastful, wealthy, and extravagant Toad—the latter lives in a mansion and likes automobiles—live and talk in a world that is remarkably like human society. They and other animals enjoy adventures and conversation in their lives in the English countryside.

**Winesburg, Ohio,** by Sherwood Anderson (fiction)

George Willard, a young newspaper reporter, feels the confinement of life in a small Midwestern town. In his own experiences and in the frustrated lives of his neighbors, Willard senses the difficulty that people have in realizing their needs without being thought of as "grotesque." He finally decides to leave the town.

**Winter Thunder,** by Mari Sandoz (novel)

A school bus full of children is suddenly caught in a blinding blizzard. The only food is the lunches that the children have packed. They, the driver, and the teacher remain marooned in heavy snow for several days, during which time the bus burns. Finally, nearing despair, they attract an aircraft overhead and are rescued.

**Winterset,** by Maxwell Anderson (play)

Mio is the son of an Italian radical who was framed on a murder charge and executed. Convinced of his father's innocence, Mio tracks down the criminal. In doing so, he falls in love with Miriamne, a sister of one of the gangsters. Although Mio loses the desire for revenge, both he and Miriamne are killed when their knowledge becomes a threat.

**The Witch of Blackbird Pond,** by Elizabeth Speare (novel)

In the late 1600's, 16-year-old Kit Tyler arrives from the island of Barbados to live with her mother's sister and family in colonial Connecticut. Kit dresses fashionably, which annoys the staid Puritan residents of the village. She becomes friends with an outcast Quaker named Hannah, known as the Witch of Blackbird Pond. Kit becomes involved in a witchcraft trial herself, but she is saved by Nat Eaton, the son of a sea captain.

**A Wrinkle in the Sky,** by Madeleine L'Engle (novel)

Meg Wallace's father, a physicist, has not been heard from for some time. Mrs. Whatsit, Mrs. Which, and Mrs. Who whisk Meg and her friends off to a fantasy world, where they find her father. They rescue him and return to earth. Whatsit, Which, and Who suddenly disappear in a gust of wind.

**Wuthering Heights,** by Emily Brontë (novel)

Of unknown parentage, Heathcliff is brought up by Mr. Earnshaw and bullied by Hindley, Earnshaw's son. Heathcliff falls in love with Catherine, Earnshaw's daughter. She will not marry him, however, and he leaves. Heathcliff later returns to the family, a wealthy man bent on vengeance. Catherine has married Edgar Linton but dies giving birth to her daughter Cathy. Heathcliff marries Linton's sister, mistreats her, and brutalizes Hindley's son Hareton. He later forces Cathy to marry his own son, who is sickly and soon dies. After Heathcliff dies, Cathy and Hareton are left to make their lives together.

**The Yearling,** by Marjorie Kinnan Rawlings (novel)

In the backwoods country of northern Florida, young Jody adopts and raises an orphaned fawn, which gives him the companionship and love he craves. After a time, the fawn becomes a yearling and is less tame. It is discovered eating the corn the family depends on. Jody's father orders his son to shoot the animal.

# 2. Index to works of literature

This is an index by author to the literature summaries found in Section 1 of this unit. You can use this list to find the title or titles of works by an author whom you might like to read. For example, if you are interested in Henry James, you would look up his name in this index, locate the titles of two works, and then look up those works in Section 1.

You will note that the summaries in Section 1 are arranged alphabetically by title. The brief summary for each work will give you an idea of the content of that piece of literature.

Chekov, Anton
  *The Cherry Orchard*
Cleaver, Eldridge
  *Soul on Ice*
Collins, Wilkie
  *The Moonstone*
Conrad, Joseph
  *Heart of Darkness*
  *Lord Jim*
  *The Secret Sharer*
Cooper, James Fenimore
  *The Last of the Mohicans*
Crane, Stephen
  *The Red Badge of Courage*
Curie, Éve
  *Madame Curie*

Daly, Maureen
  *Seventeenth Summer*
Daugherty, James
  *Of Courage Undaunted:*
    *Across the Continent*
    *with Lewis and Clark*
Defoe, Daniel
  *A Journal of the Plague Year*
  *Moll Flanders*
  *Robinson Crusoe*
De Kruif, Paul
  *Microbe Hunters*
Dickens, Charles
  *Bleak House*
  *David Copperfield*
  *Great Expectations*
  *Nicholas Nickleby*
  *Oliver Twist*
  *A Tale of Two Cities*
Dostoevsky, Fyodor
  *Crime and Punishment*
Du Bois, W. E. B.
  *The Souls of Black Folk*
Dumas, Alexandre
  *The Count of Monte Cristo*
  *The Three Musketeers*
Du Maurier, Daphne
  *Rebecca*

Eaton, Jeanette
  *America's Own Mark Twain*
  *Gandhi, Fighter Without*
    *a Sword*
Edmonds, Walter
  *Drums Along the Mohawk*
Eliot, George
  *Adam Bede*
  *The Mill on the Floss*

  *Silas Marner*
Eliot, T. S.
  *Murder in the Cathedral*
Ellison, Ralph
  *The Invisible Man*
Euripides
  *The Trojan Women*

Farley, Walter
  *The Black Stallion*
Fast, Howard
  *April Morning*
Faulkner, William
  *The Sound and the Fury*
Ferber, Edna
  *Giant*
  *So Big*
Fielding, Henry
  *Tom Jones*
Fitzgerald, F. Scott
  *The Great Gatsby*
  *Tender Is the Night*
Forbes, Esther
  *America's Paul Revere*
  *Johnny Tremain*
Forster, E. M.
  *A Passage to India*
Foster, Genevieve
  *Abraham Lincoln's World*
France, Anatole
  *Penguin Island*
Frank, Anne
  *The Diary of a Young Girl*
Franklin, Benjamin
  *The Autobiography of*
    *Benjamin Franklin*

Gallico, Paul
  *The Snow Goose*
Galsworthy, John
  *The Forsyte Saga*
Gibson, William
  *The Miracle Worker*
Gipson, Frederick B.
  *Old Yeller*
Golding, William
  *The Lord of the Flies*
Gogol, Nikolai
  *The Inspector General*
Goldsmith, Oliver
  *She Stoops to Conquer*
Grahame, Kenneth
  *Wind in the Willows*
Graves, Robert
  *Greek Gods and Heroes*

  *I, Claudius*
Gray, Elizabeth J.
  *Adam of the Road*
Green, Hannah
  *I Never Promised You a*
    *Rose Garden*
Gregory, Dick
  *Nigger*
Guareschi, Giovanni
  *The Little World of*
    *Don Camillo*
Gulbranssen, Trygve
  *Beyond Sing the Woods*
Gunther, John
  *Death Be Not Proud*
Guthrie, A. B.
  *The Way West*

Haley, Alex
  *Roots*
Hamilton, Edith
  *The Greek Way*
  *The Roman Way*
Hamsun, Knut
  *The Growth of the Soil*
Hansberry, Lorraine
  *A Raisin in the Sun*
Hardy, Thomas
  *Far from the Madding Crowd*
  *The Mayor of Casterbridge*
  *The Return of the Native*
  *Tess of the D'Urbervilles*
Hart, Moss
  *Act One*
Hawthorne, Nathaniel
  *The House of the*
    *Seven Gables*
  *The Scarlet Letter*
Head, Ann
  *Mr. and Mrs. Bo Jo Jones*
Heller, Joseph
  *Catch 22*
Hemingway, Ernest
  *For Whom the Bell Tolls*
  *The Old Man and the Sea*
Hentoff, Nat
  *I'm Really Dragged But*
    *Nothing Gets Me Down*
  *Jazz Country*
Hersey, John
  *Hiroshima*
Hesse, Herman
  *Siddhartha*
Heyerdahl, Thor
  *Kon Tiki*

Pyle, Howard
  *The Merry Adventures of*
    *Robin Hood*
  *The Story of King Arthur*
    *and His Knights*

Rawlings, Marjorie Kinnan
  *The Yearling*
Richter, Conrad
  *A Light in the Forest*
Roberts, Kenneth
  *Northwest Passage*
Rolvaag, O.E.
  *Giants in the Earth*
Rostand, Edmond
  *Cyrano de Bergerac*
Roth, Phillip
  *Goodbye, Columbus*

Saint-Exupéry, Antoine de
  *The Little Prince*
Salinger, J.D.
  *Catcher in the Rye*
Sandoz, Mari
  *Winter Thunder*
Saroyan, William
  *The Human Comedy*
Schaefer, Jack
  *Shane*
Scott, Sir Walter
  *Ivanhoe*
Sewall, Anna
  *Black Beauty*
Shakespeare, William
  *As You Like It*
  *The Comedy of Errors*
  *Hamlet*
  *Henry IV, Part I*
  *Henry IV, Part II*
  *Julius Caesar*
  *King Lear*
  *Macbeth*
  *A Midsummer Night's Dream*
  *Othello*
  *Richard III*
  *Romeo and Juliet*
  *The Taming of the Shrew*
  *Twelfth Night*
Shaw, George Bernard
  *Pygmalion*
  *Saint Joan*
Sheridan, Richard B.
  *The School for Scandal*
Shute, Nevil
  *On the Beach*

Sophocles
  *Antigone*
  *Oedipus Rex*
Speare, Elizabeth
  *The Witch of Blackbird Pond*
Spenser, Edmund
  *The Faerie Queene*
Sperry, Armstrong
  *Call It Courage*
Steele, Henry
  *America's Robert E. Lee*
Stefansson, Evelyn
  *Here Is Alaska*
Steinbeck, John
  *The Grapes of Wrath*
Stephens, James
  *The Crock of Gold*
Street, James
  *Goodbye, My Lady*
Stevenson, Robert Louis
  *Black Arrow*
  *Kidnapped*
  *The Strange Case of Dr. Jekyll*
    *and Mr. Hyde*
  *Treasure Island*
Styron, William
  *The Confessions of Nat Turner*
Swift, Jonathan
  *Gulliver's Travels*
Synge, John Millington
  *The Playboy of the*
    *Western World*
  *Riders to the Sea*

Tappan, Eva
  *When Knights Were Bold*
Tennyson, Lord Alfred
  *The Idylls of the King*
Thackeray, William Makepeace
  *Vanity Fair*
Thoreau, Henry David
  *Walden*
Tolstoy, Leo
  *Anna Karenina*
  *War and Peace*
Treviño, Elizabeth Borton de
  *I, Juan de Pareja*
Trollope, Anthony
  *Barchester Towers*
Trumbo, Dalton
  *Johnny Got His Gun*
Twain, Mark
  *The Adventures of*
    *Huckleberry Finn*
  *The Adventures of Tom Sawyer*

  *A Connecticut Yankee in*
    *King Arthur's Court*
  *The Prince and the Pauper*

Unknown
  *Beowulf*
  *Sir Gawain and the Green Knight*
Ullman, James
  *Banners in the Sky*
Undset, Sigrid
  *Kristen Lavransdatter*
Uris, Leon
  *Exodus*

Van Druten, John
  *I Remember Mama*
Verne, Jules
  *Around the World in 80 Days*
  *A Journey to the*
    *Center of the Earth*
  *The Mysterious Island*
  *Twenty Thousand Leagues*
    *Under the Sea*
Vonnegut, Kurt, Jr.
  *Cat's Cradle*

Walker, Margaret
  *Jubilee*
Wells, H.G.
  *The Time Machine*
Werfel, Franz
  *Forty Days of Musa Dagh*
West, Jessamyn
  *Cress Delahanty*
Wharton, Edith
  *Ethan Frome*
Wilde, Oscar
  *The Picture of Dorian Gray*
Wilder, Laura Ingalls
  *The House on the Prairie*
Wilder, Thornton
  *The Bridge of San Luis Rey*
  *Our Town*
  *The Skin of Our Teeth*
Williams, Tennessee
  *The Glass Menagerie*
Wister, Owen
  *The Virginian*
Wojciechowska, Maia
  *Tuned Out*
Wolfe, Thomas
  *Look Homeward, Angel*
Wright, Richard
  *Black Boy*
Wyss, Johann
  *The Swiss Family Robinson*

# Index

# Respelling table

The *World Book Student Handbook: Student Information Finder* provides pronunciations for many unusual or unfamiliar words. The pronunciation, when it is used, is placed in parentheses immediately following the word in question. In the pronunciation, the word is divided into syllables and respelled according to the way each syllable actually sounds. For example, here is a word used in the glossary for Unit 7, Important dates in history:

**transcendentalism** (TRAN *sehn DEHN tuh lihz uhm)*

The system of respelling used in the *Student Information Finder* is the system used in THE WORLD BOOK ENCYCLOPEDIA. In that system, the syllable that bears the greatest emphasis when the word is spoken appears in capital letters *(DEHN).* If the word is long enough to have a syllable that receives secondary emphasis, that syllable appears in small capital letters *(TRAN).* More than one pronunciation may be included for words that have several accepted pronunciations in English, for words that have distinctive pronunciations in other languages, and for names that have distinctive local pronunciations.

See the list below for examples of respelled syllables and respelled words. Note the variety of examples for the syllable "uh."

In addition to the respellings, *The World Book Student Handbook: Student Information Finder* uses a number of diacritical marks and special characters to indicate the correct spellings for many words and names in languages other than English. These marks have various meanings, according to the languages in which they are used. For example, an acute accent mark (′) over an *é* in a French word indicates that the *é* is pronounced *ay.* An acute accent mark over an *é* in a Spanish word indicates that the syllable containing the *é* bears the main emphasis in the word. These are probably the two most common accent marks that you will encounter in this volume.

| Respelling | Example | |
|---|---|---|
| a | **alphabet** | *AL fuh beht* |
| ay | **Asia** | *AY zhuh* |
| ai | **bareback** | *BAIR bak* |
| ah | **armistice** | *AHR muh stihs* |
| ch | **China** | *CHY nuh* |
| eh | **essay** | *EHS ay* |
| ee | **leaf** | *leef* |
| | **marine** | *muh REEN* |
| ur | **pearl** | *purl* |
| ih | **system** | *SIHS tuhm* |
| y | **Ohio** | *oh HY oh* |
| eye | **iris** | *EYE rihs* |
| k | **corn** | *kawrn* |
| ah | **Ottawa** | *AHT uh wuh* |
| oh | **rainbow** | *RAYN boh* |
| | **tableau** | *TAB loh* |
| aw | **orchid** | *AWR kihd* |
| | **allspice** | *AWL spys* |
| oy | **coinage** | *KOY nihj* |
| | **poison** | *POY zuhn* |
| ow | **fountain** | *FOWN tuhn* |
| s | **spice** | *spys* |
| sh | **motion** | *MOH shuhn* |
| uh | **study** | *STUHD ee* |
| | **blood** | *bluhd* |
| u | **fulbright** | *FUL bryt* |
| | **wool** | *wul* |
| oo | **zulu** | *ZOO loo* |
| zh | **Asia** | *AY zhuh* |
| uh | **Burma** | *BUR muh* |
| uh | **fiddle** | *FIHD uhl* |
| uh | **citizen** | *SIHT uh zuhn* |
| uh | **lion** | *LY uhn* |
| uh | **cyprus** | *SY pruhs* |
| uh | **physique** | *fuh ZEEK* |
| uh | **mountain** | *MOWN tuhn* |
| uh | **Georgia** | *JAWR juh* |
| uh | **legion** | *LEE juhn* |
| uh | **anonymous** | *uh NAHN uh muhs* |

World Book Encyclopedia, Inc., offers a selection of fine porcelain collectible products including *For A Mother's Love Figurine* series. For subscription information write WORLD BOOK ENCYCLOPEDIA, INC., P.O. Box 3405, Chicago, IL 60654.